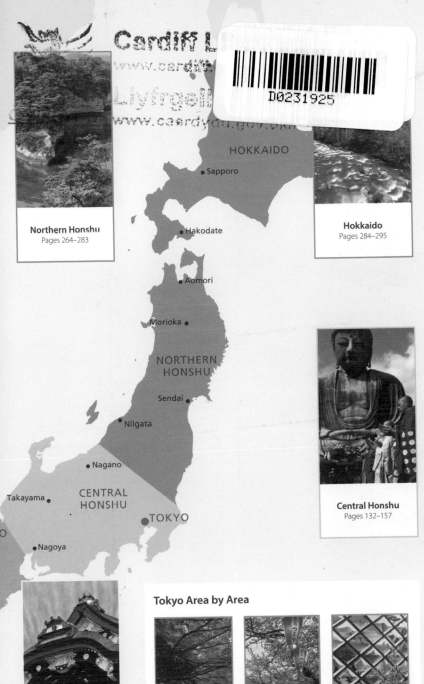

HOKKAIDO

• Sapporo

Northern Honshu
Pages 264–283

Hokkaido
Pages 284–295

• Hakodate

• Aomori

Morioka •

NORTHERN
HONSHU

Sendai •

• Niigata

Central Honshu
Pages 132–157

• Nagano

Takayama •

CENTRAL
HONSHU

TOKYO

O

• Nagoya

Kyoto City
Pages 158–189

Tokyo Area by Area

Central Tokyo
Pages 68–79

Northern Tokyo
Pages 80–91

Western Tokyo
Pages 92–103

EYEWITNESS TRAVEL

JAPAN

ACC. No: 03245138

EYEWITNESS TRAVEL

JAPAN

DK

LONDON, NEW YORK,
MELBOURNE, MUNICH AND DELHI
www.dk.com

Produced by Blue Island Publishing Limited, London, England

Editorial Director Rosalyn Thiro

Art Director Stephen Bere

Senior Editor Jane Simmonds

US Editor Mary Sutherland

Art Editors Tessa Bindloss, Ian Midson

Picture Researcher Ellen Root
Dorling Kindersley Limited

Map Co-ordinator Dave Pugh

DTP Designer Lee Redmond

Contributors John Hart Benson Jr., Mark Brazil, Jon Burbank, Angela Jeffs, Emi Kazuko,
Stephen Mansfield, Bill Marsh, Catherine Rubinstein, Jacqueline Ruyak

Researcher Mayumi Hayashi

Maps Era-Maptech Ltd

Photographers
Demetrio Carrasco, Clive Streeter, Linda Whitwam, Peter Wilson

Illustrators
Richard Bonson, Gary Cross, Richard Draper, Paul Guest, Claire
Littlejohn, Maltings Partnership, Mel Pickering, John Woodcock

Printed in Malaysia

First published in the UK in 2000 by Dorling Kindersley Limited
80 Strand, London WC2R 0RL, UK

14 15 16 17 10 9 8 7 6 5 4 3 2 1

Reprinted with revisions 2002, 2003, 2005, 2007, 2009, 2011, 2013, 2015

Copyright 2000, 2015 © Dorling Kindersley Limited, London
A Penguin Random House Company

MIX
Paper from
responsible sources
FSC™ C018179
www.fsc.org

Front cover main image: View of Mount Fuji from Chureito Pagoda, Central Honshu

◀ Nachi-no-taki waterfall and pagoda, Honshu

Contents

Ukiyo-e wood-block prints,
Tokyo National Museum

The fabulous pavilion at Kinkaku-ji, its gold-leaf outer layer shining in the sun

Crowds in front of Studio Alta,
East Shinjuku, Tokyo

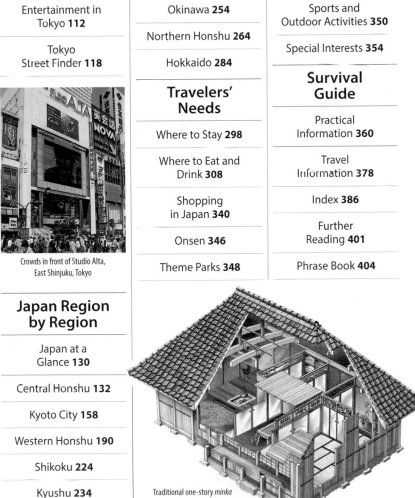

Traditional one-story *minka*
(traditional house)

HOW TO USE THIS GUIDE

This guide helps you to get the most from your visit to Japan. It provides detailed practical information and expert recommendations. *Introducing Japan* maps the country and sets it in its historical and cultural context. Tokyo and the eight regional sections describe important sights, using maps, photographs, and illustrations. Restaurant and hotel recommendations can be found in *Travelers' Needs*, together with general advice about accommodations and Japanese food. The *Survival Guide* has tips on everything from transportation to etiquette.

Tokyo

This city is divided into areas, each with its own chapter. The *Farther Afield* section covers peripheral sights. All sights are numbered and plotted on the chapter's area map. The information for each sight follows the map's numerical order, making sights easy to locate within the chapter.

Sights at a Glance lists the chapter's sights by category, such as Notable Districts, Historic Buildings, Modern Architecture, Parks and Gardens, and Markets.

All pages relating to Tokyo have red thumb tabs.

A locator map shows where you are in relation to other areas of the city.

1 Area Map
For easy reference, sights are numbered and located on a map. City center sights are also marked on the Street Finder on pages 118–27.

2 Street-by-Street Map
This gives a bird's-eye view of the key areas in each chapter.

3 Detailed Information
The top sights in Tokyo are described individually. Telephone numbers and public transportation links are given, along with other practical information. The key to the symbols is on the back flap of the book.

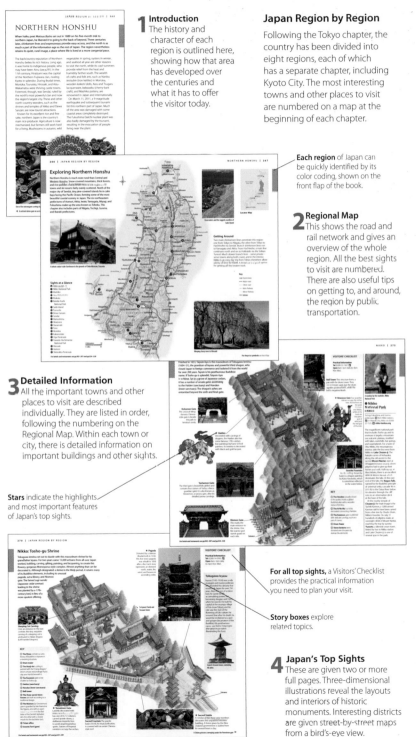

1 Introduction
The history and character of each region is outlined here, showing how that area has developed over the centuries and what it has to offer the visitor today.

Japan Region by Region

Following the Tokyo chapter, the country has been divided into eight regions, each of which has a separate chapter, including Kyoto City. The most interesting towns and other places to visit are numbered on a map at the beginning of each chapter.

Each region of Japan can be quickly identified by its color coding, shown on the front flap of the book.

2 Regional Map
This shows the road and rail network and gives an overview of the whole region. All the best sights to visit are numbered. There are also useful tips on getting to, and around, the region by public transportation.

3 Detailed Information
All the important towns and other places to visit are described individually. They are listed in order, following the numbering on the Regional Map. Within each town or city, there is detailed information on important buildings and other sights.

Stars indicate the highlights and most important features of Japan's top sights.

For all top sights, a Visitors' Checklist provides the practical information you need to plan your visit.

Story boxes explore related topics.

4 Japan's Top Sights
These are given two or more full pages. Three-dimensional illustrations reveal the layouts and interiors of historic monuments. Interesting districts are given street-by-street maps from a bird's-eye view.

INTRODUCING JAPAN

DISCOVERING JAPAN

The following tours have been designed to take in as many of Japan's highlights as possible, while keeping long-distance travel to a minimum. First are two-day tours of the country's most illustrious cities, Tokyo and Kyoto, along with suggestions for day trips to nearby historic towns such as Nikko, Kamakura, and Nara. These itineraries can be combined to form a week-long tour. Next there are seven-day tours, covering Kansai, Western Japan, and Shikoku; Hokkaido and the northern part of Honshu; Central Honshu, including the Japan Alps; and the main southern island of Kyushu. Combined, they map out an unforgettable month-long trip around the Japanese archipelago.

A Week in Kansai & Western Japan

- Visit **Osaka**'s aquarium and hunt down the city's best eats and nightlife in Namba and Dotonbori.
- Survey **Himeji** from the splendid six-story keep of Himeji Castle.
- Stroll around Koraku-en Garden in **Okayama**, and the charming Bikan Historical Area of **Kurashiki**.
- Climb the 785 steps to the top of the venerable Kompira-san shrine in **Kotohira**.
- Bathe at the magnificent public bathhouse of Dogo Onsen in **Matsuyama**.
- Contemplate the horrors of war at the peace park and memorial museum in **Hiroshima**.
- Offer a prayer to the guardian spirits of Itsukushima Shrine on the island of **Miyajima**.

Torii gateway
This breathtaking "floating" entrance to the Itsukushima Shinto Shrine on Miyajima dates from 1875.

A Tour of Kyushu

- Slurp ramen noodles at a *yatai* (outdoor food stall) in buzzing **Fukuoka**.
- Ride on trams around **Nagasaki**, taking in the Atomic Bomb Museum and the view from Glover Garden.
- Discover traditional crafts, a lovely garden, and a fairy-tale castle in **Kumamoto**.
- Take the cable car up to an active volcanic crater on **Mount Aso**.
- Be buried in hot sand at **Beppu**, then soak in the hot springs of **Yufuin**.
- Sail through the mountain gorge at **Takachiho**.
- Gasp at Sakurajima volcano smoking ominously across the bay from **Kagoshima**.

Key

— A Week in Kansai & Western Japan
— A Tour of Kyushu
— A Week in Hokkaido & Tohoku
— A Gourmet Tour of Central Japan

Autumn Leaves on the Tsutaya River, by Katsushika Hokusai (color woodblock print, 1830)

HOKKAIDO

Sapporo

Lake Shikotsu
Lake Toya
Shikotsu-Toya National Park

Noboribetsu

Hakodate

Hirosaki

Kakunodate

Hiraizumi

Dewa Sanzan Shrine

Matsushima Bay
Sendai

Sado Island

Niigata

HONSHU

Wajima
Noto Peninsula

Obuse

Kanazawa
Nagano

Ogimachi

ayama
Matsumoto

Kiso Valley
Tsumago

Tokyo

Nagoya

Fuji Five Lakes
Mount Fuji

0 kilometers   200
0 miles   200

A Week in Hokkaido & Tohoku

- Sip the local beer and tuck into a lamb barbecue in **Sapporo**, Hokkaido's modern capital.

- Get a close-up view of an active volcano and bathe in hot springs in the **Shikotsu-Toya National Park**.

- Survey **Hakodate** from the top of Mount Hakodate, and admire the port's late 19th-century buildings.

- Admire the massive lanterns created for the Neputa festival in the castle town of **Hirosaki**.

- Explore the samurai and merchant quarters of **Kakunodate**, including thatched homes and lovely gardens.

- Be dazzled by the Golden Hall of the temple complex of Chuson-ji, in **Hiraizumi**.

- Count the pine-clad rocky islands of **Matsushima Bay** and admire the beautifully decorated Zuigan-ji Temple.

A Gourmet Tour of Central Japan

- Known as the gateway to the Alps, explore **Nagano** and its famed Zenko-ji Temple, and sample soba noodles.

- Meander through the verdant Kenroku-en Garden and the cutting-edge contemporary art museum in **Kanazawa**.

- Drive around the scenic **Noto Peninsula**, pausing for the daily food market and for lacquerware shopping in **Wajima**.

- Marvel at the World Heritage architecture of A-frame thatched houses in the **Showkawa Valley**.

- Sip sake and sample mountain vegetable dishes and succulent Hida beef in the appealing mountain town of **Takayama**.

- Hike along part of the ancient stone-paved post road connecting Tsumago and Magome, in the **Kiso Valley**.

- Climb the keep of the handsome castle that is at the heart of **Matsumoto**.

Naka Bridge, Takayama
Floats crossing the Miya river as part of the beautiful Takayama cherry blossom festival.

2 Days in Tokyo

Unmissable sights in the Japanese capital include Senso-ji Temple in Asakusa and the grounds of the Imperial Palace. Save some time for casual exploring, since Tokyo's neon dazzle and buzzing energy are attractions in themselves.

- **Arriving** Narita, 60 km (37 miles) northeast of the center, and Haneda, 20 km (12 miles) south, are Tokyo's two international airports, both connected to the city by speedy train lines.

- **Moving on** The journey from Tokyo to Kyoto takes 2 hours and 15 minutes by the fastest Nozomi trains.

Day 1

Morning If you're going to see the best of Tokyo in just two days, you'll need to make an early start, and where better than at **Tsukiji Fish Market** (p72). Spend a couple of hours exploring this famous market and enjoy a sushi breakfast before riding the subway 15 minutes north to reach **Tokyo National Museum** (pp84–7), next to Ueno Park. The museum hosts the world's largest collection of Japanese art, supplemented by other Asian antiquities. Afterward, stroll around **Ueno Park** (pp82–3),

home to a zoo, pagoda, Tosho-gu Shrine, Shinobazu Pond, and the **Shitamachi Museum** (p88), which gives a glimpse of Tokyo's past. Also check out the bustling **Ameyoko Market** (p88), stretching beside and under the raised train tracks between Ueno and Okachimachi stations.

Afternoon You can have lunch in either Ueno or Asakusa, just three subway stops east. This atmospheric area is home to **Senso-ji** (pp90–91), Tokyo's most venerable Buddhist temple, which is best approached via the Nakamise-dori arcade of traditional craft and souvenir shops. Detour across the Sumida River for the bird's-eye view from **Tokyo SkyTree** (p88). Return to Asakusa to join the **Sumida River Trip** (p73) to **Hama Detached Palace Garden** (pp72–3). It's a short walk from here to the **Kabuki-za Theater** (p72) with its dramatic gabled facade.

Day 2

Morning Sign up for a free guided tour of the grounds of the **Imperial Palace** (p75); you'll need to register in advance but worth it for a close-up view of a fragment of this vast compound that has been home to the emperor and his family for nearly 150 years and, before that, was the location of Edo Castle. Explore the excellent collection at the **National**

Tokyo SkyTree, the tallest building in Japan, topped by a broadcasting mast

Museum of Modern Art (p76), housed in a building across the moat that used to surround the castle.

Afternoon Hop on the subway to reach **Harajuku District** (p99), a good spot for lunch. From here, you can crunch down the gravel pathway to **Meiji Shrine** (p98), the city's main Shinto shrine. Check out teen fashions and trends on the shopping street **Takeshita-dori** (p99), followed by more window shopping along tree-lined **Omotesando** (p99), where you'll find the Oriental Bazaar, perfect for souvenirs. The **Nezu Art Museum** (p102) is a lovely introduction to the arts of the region, and it also has a serene garden with a teahouse. Finish the day enjoying the bright lights and electric vibe of either **Shibuya** (pp100–01) or **Shinjuku** (pp94–7), both easily accessed by subway or train.

> ### To extend your trip...
> Among the many day trips you can make are ones to **Nikko** (pp268–9), the mountainous home to the grand **Tosho-gu Shrine** (pp270–71); and **Kamakura** (pp138–40), Japan's ancient seaside capital, dotted with serene temples and shrines.

Sophisticated Omotesando, in Tokyo, with its range of fashion design stores

2 Days in Kyoto

The former imperial capital offers Japan's best collection of temples, palaces, shrines, and gardens. Kyoto is a city steeped in history and tradition, where you can spy geisha on the streets and eat exquisitely presented meals.

- **Arriving** Kansai International Airport is 100 km (63 miles) southwest of Kyoto, connected to the city by a train that takes just over one hour. Kyoto Station is linked by Shinkansen lines to Tokyo and Nagoya to the east, and to Osaka, Fukuoka, and Hiroshima to the west.

The rock and raked-gravel garden at Daitoku-ji Temple, Kyoto

Day 1

Morning Make your way to **Higashiyama** district (pp170–71), on the eastern side of the city, and the hillside perch of **Kiyomizu-dera Temple** (p172), where the wooden terraces provide sweeping views across Kyoto. Wander down cobbled Sannen-zaka and Ninenzaka toward **Maruyama Park** (p166), a famous cherry-blossom viewing location. Pass through the vermilion gate of Yasaka Shrine into **Gion** (p166), Kyoto's geisha quarter, where there are plenty of places for lunch.

Afternoon Admire the wooden buildings lining Hanamikoji-dori on your way to the subway station of Sanjo

Keihan. From here, ride the two stops on the subway to Keage. Admire the beautiful gardens at **Konchi-in** (p175), then explore the precincts of neighboring **Nanzen-ji Temple** (p175). Just north of this quintessential Zen temple is the start of the 2-km- (1-mile-) long **Philosopher's Walk** (p174). Should you need to rest, there are plenty of teahouses along the way. The route ends at **Ginkaku-ji** (p175), the Temple of the Silver Pavilion, where the refined gardens are the star attraction.

Day 2

Morning Having booked a tour with the Imperial Household Agency, enter the **Imperial Park** (p176) to admire its impressive stroll garden, with a delightful pond and arched bridge. Hop on the subway from Imadegawa to Kita-Oji, the closest stop for **Daitoku-ji Temple** (pp176–7),

a walled complex where you can contemplate the artful arrangement of a Zen garden from the teahouse of the sub-temple **Daisen-in** (p177).

Afternoon Take the 15-minute walk from Daitoku-ji to the wooded hills of Kitayama, where you'll find **Kinkaku-ji** (p178), famous for its Golden Pavilion surrounded by gardens and reflected in an ornamental pond. If you've time and energy for one more temple, make it **Ryoan-ji** (p178), the location of Japan's most famous and abstract Zen rock garden. The contrast with the dazzling opulence of **Nijo Castle** (pp164–65), a short taxi ride back toward the center of Kyoto, couldn't be more acute. Having admired the castle's gorgeously decorated interiors, end your day with a meal and nightcap in **Pontocho Alley** (p166), an area where you're sure to spot geisha going about their business.

> **To extend your trip…**
> **Arashiyama** (p180) is a beautiful wooded, riverside district where the imperial court retreated for relaxation. **Nara** (pp194–7), which pre-dates Kyoto as imperial capital, has a spectacular park that is home to wooden temples and a monumental bronze Buddha. The Grand Shrine at **Ise** (p202) is one of Japan's most sacred places.

Geisha in traditional costume in Potoncho Alley, Kyoto

A Week in Kansai & Western Japan

- **Airports** Arrive at Kansai International Airport and depart from Hiroshima International Airport.

- **Transport** The trip from Osaka to Okayama by Shinkansen takes about one hour, as does the journey from Osaka to Takamatsu. Takamatsu to Matsuyama is 2.5 hours. From Matsuyama to Hiroshima Port by hydrofoil takes one hour. A 20-minute ferry trip links Hiroshima Port to Miyajima, or there's a 10-minute ferry ride to the island from Miyajima-guchi, a 55-minute tram journey west of the center of Hiroshima.

Day 1
What **Osaka** (pp204–7) lacks in looks, it makes up for in dynamism and friendliness. The main central sights include the reconstructed **Osaka Castle** (pp204–5) and grounds, the **National Museum of Art** (p205), the **Museum of Oriental Ceramics** (p205), and the **Floating Garden Observatory** (p206). Beside Osaka Bay is the impressive **Osaka Aquarium** (p207), one of the best in Japan. The lively downtown areas of **Namba** and **Dotonbori** (p204) are best for eats and nightlife.

Day 2
Kobe (pp208–9), 15 minutes train journey west of Osaka, has a colorful **Chinatown** (p208) and elegant Meiji-period homes in the hillside **Kitano-cho** (p208) district; both areas deserve at least a quick visit. The star attraction of Himeji, 20 minutes farther down the line, is the spectacular feudal **Himeji Castle** (pp210–13). The main keep looks fantastic after its restoration. Finish your day in **Okayama** (p214) another short hop by Shinkansen bullet train.

Day 3
Rise early to visit Okayama's **Koraku-en Garden** (p214), one of Japan's top-three gardens, which "borrows" the scenery of the black-walled Okayama Castle, across the Asahi River. Take a 15-minute train ride to **Kurashiki** (pp214–15) to stroll around the charming Bikan Historical Area of old merchant houses turned into boutiques, cafés, and guesthouses, and to visit the Ohara Museum of Art, which includes works by the likes of Gauguin and Picasso.

Day 4
From Okayama, take the mammoth Seto-Ohashi Bridge, which leapfrogs the islands of the Inland Sea, to reach **Takamatsu** (p228), the first major urban center on Shikoku. The beautiful Ritsurin Garden is this city's main landmark. A one-hour train journey from here takes you to **Kotohira** (pp228–9), home to the important Shinto shrine Konpira-san, which can be reached by climbing 785 steps up a wooded hillside. The town has lovely traditional inns to stay in and many places to eat.

Day 5
Two hours from Kotohira is **Matsuyama** (p230), Shikoku's largest city. Graced by a splendid hilltop castle, it also boasts the magnificent public bathhouse of Dogo Onsen, where visitors can experience Japanese bathing culture.

Day 6
The Peace Memorial Park of **Hiroshima** (pp218–19) is the obvious draw of this city rebuilt after the destruction of World

The neon lights of Dotonbori, one of Osaka's liveliest quarters

War II. The centerpiece is the Peace Memorial Museum, which presents a balanced view of the why the atomic bomb was dropped here in 1945. While in town, try the local specialty *okonomiyaki*, a savory pancake.

Day 7
The vermilion gate of **Itsukushima Shrine** (p220), rising out of the sea off the coast of **Miyajima** (pp220–21), is one of Japan's most famous sights. Behind the covered walkways and halls of this seaside shrine rises **Mount Misen** (p221), the summit of which provides panoramic views across the Inland Sea.

> **To extend your trip…**
> **Matsue** (pp216–17) has an original castle, samurai houses, and a lovely setting between a lake and the Japan Sea. The pine tree-lined **Amanohashidate Sand Bar** (p216) is also one of Japan's most scenic locations.

Amanohashidate Sand Bar, separating Miyatsu Bay from Asoumi lagoon

A Week in Hokkaido & Tohoku

- **Airports** Arrive at New Chitose Airport, 40 km (25 miles) south of Sapporo, and depart from Sendai Airport in Natori, 2 hours south of Matsushima by train.

- **Transport** The train trip from Sapporo to Noboribetsu takes 1.5 hours; from Noboribetsu to Hakodate, 2 hours; from Hakodate to Hirosaki, 3.5 hours; from Hirosaki to Kakunodate, 3.5 hours; from Kakunodate to Hiraizumi, just shy of 3 hours; from Hiraizumi to Sendai, 1.5 hours; and from Sendai to Matsushima, one hour.

The Golden Hall, one of only two original buildings in Chuson-ji temple, Hiraizumi

Day 1
Learn about the Ainu, the original inhabitants of Japan's main northern island, in the Exhibition Room of Northern Peoples in the Botanical Gardens of **Sapporo** *(p289)*. Hokkaido's dynamic modern capital is perhaps best known for its local brand of beer. Drop by the Sapporo Beer Garden and Museum to taste some and to eat the grilled mutton dish known as "Genghis Khan." Enjoy the nightlife of Susukino, a short walk south of central Odori Park.

Day 2
The volcano-punctuated area of **Shikotsu-Toya National Park** *(pp288–9)* includes a couple of caldera lakes: Lake Shikotsu to the northeast and Lake Toya to the southwest. The latter is close to the highly active volcano Mount Usu, the crater of which can be reached by cable car. Spend the night in the popular hot-spring resort of Noboribetsu.

Day 3
One of the first ports in Japan to open up foreign trade in the late 19th century, **Hakodate** *(p288)* has a wealth of historic Western-style buildings in its Motomachi district, including

a Russian Orthodox Church. The view from the top of Mount Hakodate is spectacular. Tuck into super-fresh seafood at the stalls in the Asa-ichi Market.

Day 4
The 54-km- (33-mile-) long Seikan Tunnel links Hokkaido with the Tohoku region, which covers the north of Honshu. Head for the feudal-era town of **Hirosaki** *(p283)*, where you'll find the remains of a 17th-century castle in a picturesque park renowned for its cherry-blossom festival. Nearby, **Tsugaruhan Neputa Mura** displays the elaborate floats used during the August Neputa Festival.

Day 5
Another town that has preserved its samurai and merchant quarters is

The metal structure of the television tower in Sapporo's Odori Park

Kakunodate *(p282)*. Among the samurai houses open to the public is the large, thatched Aoyagi-ke, where you can eat the local noodle dish udon, and the impressive Ishiguro-ke, with its lovely garden.

Day 6
The cedar-clad hills around **Hiraizumi** *(p280)* harbor a couple of the most important sights in Tohoku: the temple complex of Chuson-ji, which includes the Golden Hall, a temple smothered in gold leaf and mother-of-pearl, and the gorgeous gardens of Motsu-ji, arranged around a large lake. Accommodation is limited around Hiraizumi, so spend the night in the major city of **Sendai** *(p278)*.

Day 7
The bay of **Matsushima** *(p280)*, dotted with some 269 islands, is one of Japan's top scenic views. It's a touristy location but worth visiting for the elegant temple Zuigan-ji, which is a national treasure.

To extend your trip...
Join the pilgrims climbing the 2,446 stone steps to the thatch-roofed **Dewa Sanzan Shrine** *(p278)* on Mount Haguro. Once a place of political exile, **Sado Island** *(p277)* is now a pleasant escape and home to the internationally famous Kodo drummers.

A Gourmet Tour of Central Japan

- **Airports** Arrive and depart from Narita or Haneda airports, both serving Tokyo. An alternative international access point is Central Japan International Airport (Centrair), 30 km (19 miles) south of Nagoya.

- **Transport** Trains are generally the best way to get around the mountainous region, with Nagano connected to Tokyo by a Shinkansen line that will soon extend to Kanazawa. Hire a car in Kanazawa to travel around the Noto Peninsula. Bus (or hired car) is the best way to travel between Kanazawa, and Takayama. From there on, use the train to access the charming post towns of the Kiso Valley and connect up with either Matsumoto or Nagoya.

The alpine regions of Central Honshu and the Japan Sea coast are the ideal places to sample a wide range of Japanese cuisines – from simple noodles to elegantly prepared banquets.

Day 1
The venerable temple of Zenko-ji is the prime attraction of **Nagano** *(p155)*, the gateway to the Japan Alps. From Nagano, you can also make a half-day trip to **Jigokudani Onsen** *(p155)*, the hot pools famous for attracting snow monkeys. Soba noodles made with buckwheat are a specialty here. If you pause in quaint **Obuse** *(p155)* on the way back from Jigokudani Onsen, you could also sample chestnut confectionery and good sake.

Day 2
Kanazawa *(pp152–3)*, by the Japan Sea, has an illustrious heritage. Visit the impressive castle, the Nagamachi Samurai Quarter, and the Higashi (Eastern) Pleasure District of traditional teahouses. Other highlights include Kenroku-en Garden, one of Japan's "great three"

gardens, and the striking architecture and art on display at the 21st Century Museum of Contemporary Art. Sample succulent sushi at Omomicho Ichiba market, or seek out a restaurant serving the refined cuisine known as *kaga ryori*.

Day 3
Freshly caught seafood is a must-try on a trip around the scenic **Noto Peninsula** *(p154)*. Continue to **Wajima** *(p154)*, a port at the northern end of the peninsula that hosts a daily market and is renowned for its high-quality lacquerware. On the way back to Kanazawa, take in the strange rock formations around Sosogi.

Day 4
Three picturesque villages in the **Shokawa Valley** *(p150)* make up a UNESCO World Heritage Site. Aim for **Ogimachi** *(p150)*, where there's an architectural park that displays the distinctive thatched A-frame houses and other traditional buildings from the region. Guesthouses and restaurants here will serve *sansai ryori* (mountain vegetable dishes). Continue to Takayama for your overnight stop.

Day 5
Takayama *(pp148–50)* is one of the most characterful towns in the Japan Alps. The Sannomachi Quarter is packed with wooden buildings housing cafés, shops, and sake breweries. Drop by the **Takayama Festival Floats Exhibition Hall** *(p150)* to see

The bucolic landscape of Kenroku-en Garden, in Kanazawa

Tsumago, in the Kiso Valley, where time seems to have stopped

some of the elaborate floats used in the town's twice-yearly festivals. Takayama is the place to sample *mitarashi-dango* – rice balls dipped in soy sauce and roasted on skewers.

Day 6
Of the 11 Edo-era post towns staged along the **Kiso Valley** *(p146)*, the most picturesque is Tsumago, where it feels like you've stepped back in time. Consider hiking part of the Nakasendo, the Edo-period stone-pathed post road that runs between Tsumago and Magome. Spend the night in one of the Kiso Valley's traditional *minshukus* (B&B).

Day 7
Matsumoto *(p155)* has a splendid 16th-century castle, the Japan Ukiyo-e Museum, with its collection of woodblock prints, and the Matsumoto City Museum of Art, displaying works by local artist Yayoi Kusama. *Sasamushi* (eel steamed inside rice wrapped in bamboo leaves) is one of the town's delicacies.

To extend your trip...
The lively metropolis of **Nagoya** *(p147)* offers a castle, the Tokugawa Art Museum, and several fascinating sights linked to its industrial heritage. The **Fuji Five Lakes** area *(pp144–5)* has several lovely lakeside resorts; if the weather is favorable, you'll be able to see and, depending on the season, climb Mount Fuji.

A Tour of Kyushu

- **Airports** Arrive at Fukuoka Airport and depart from Kagoshima Airport.
- **Transport** It's about 2 hours by train from Fukuoka to Nagasaki. Traveling from Nagasaki to Kumamoto takes 2 hours and 40 minutes, and it's 2 hours and 20 minutes from there to Aso. Beppu is 2.5 hours from Aso. The best way of visiting Takachiho is to hire a car in either Kumamoto or Aso. Going from Kumamoto to Kagoshima by Shinkansen takes 1 hour and 40 minutes. If you are not flying out of Kagoshima, the return trip to Fukuoka by Shinkansen takes 2 hours and 15 minutes.

Fountains and palm trees at Nagasaki Peace Park

Day 1

Fukuoka (pp240–41), Kyushu's biggest city, is a fine introduction to the charms of Japan's largest southern island. Meet friendly locals by pulling up a chair at one of the city's many famous *yatai* (outdoor food stalls) and ordering a bowl of ramen noodles. Fukuoka's eye-catching modern architecture is best viewed at the Canal City and Hawks Town waterside developments. The Hakata Machiya Folk Museum showcases arts and crafts associated with local festivals and culture.

Dining at a *yatai* (street food stall) in the center of Fukuoka

Day 2

Picturesque **Nagasaki** (pp244–7) has a cosmopolitan vibe thanks to centuries of international trade. There's plenty to see here, including Chinese temples and Catholic churches; a mansion that served as the setting for Puccini's opera *Madame Butterfly* in **Glover Garden** (p246); **Hollander Slope** (p246), the old hilltop concession where the foreign community lived in the 19th century; plus the **Atomic Bomb Museum** and **Peace Park** (p247).

Day 3

Its center dominated by Japan's third-largest castle, **Kumamoto** (p248) is the ideal base from which to tour central Kyushu. Visit Suizen-ji Garden early in the morning to avoid the crowds; it's a small stroll garden, taking only 30 minutes to walk around, leaving you plenty of time to tour the traditional crafts center.

Day 4

The town of Aso is the base for sightseeing around the world's biggest caldera, **Mount Aso** (pp248–9). Of the five volcanic cones within the 130-km (80-mile) circumference crater, Mount Nakadake is active; ride the cable car (ropeway) to its forbiddingly steaming summit.

Day 5

In the touristy *onsen* resort of **Beppu** (pp238–9) drop by the Boiling Hells (*Jigoku*) to see bubbling pools of mud and mineral-colored waters. On the beach, experience being buried up to your neck in hot sand. Then head 25 km (16 miles) inland to stay at the smaller, more refined *onsen* town of **Yufuin** (p239), set next to serene Lake Kinrin.

Day 6

Takachiho (p249) is at the heart of a mountainous area rich in local mythology and natural attractions, including caves associated with Shinto deities and the spectacular Takachiho Gorge, which you can see from river level in a rowboat.

Day 7

With the smoking bulk of **Sakurajima Volcano** (p253) brooding across the bay, **Kagoshima** (p252) has an unforgettable setting. Take a boat out to the volcanic island for a closer look and for a dip in one of its *onsen*. Kagoshima has several pleasant gardens, including Iso and Sengan-en, a well-designed aquarium, and a decent art museum.

> **To extend your trip…**
> The **Saga Pottery Towns Tour** (p243), around Karatsu Bay, will appeal to ceramics enthusiasts. For a taste of tropical Japan, fly to **Naha City** (p258), the capital of the southern archipelago of **Okinawa** (pp254–63).

Putting Japan on the Map

Japan is made up of four main islands – Honshu, Hokkaido, Kyushu, and Shikoku – and several thousand smaller ones, lying to the east of mainland Asia, in the northwest of the Pacific Ocean. The archipelago curves across 3,000 km (1,900 miles) between Russia's Sakhalin Island and Taiwan.

Spassk-Dal'niy
Dal'neg
Arsen'yev
RUSSIA
Vladivostok
Nakhodka

Okinawa Archipelago

Naze
Amami Island
Ryukyu Islands
Tokuno Island
East China Sea
Kume Island
Naha
Okinawa Island
Philippine Sea
Yaeyama Islands
Miyako Islands
Iriomote Island
Ishigaki Island

0 kilometers 100
0 miles 50

Yongju
Taejon
Taegu
SOUTH KOREA
15
1
Sunch'on
10
Pusan

Sea of Japan (East Sea)

Matsue
Tottori
Maizuru
Tsu
Fuk
9
27
Hiroshima
Kurashiki
Himeji
Kobe
Kyoto
Okayama
Osaka
Yamaguchi
Takamatsu
Shimonoseki
Tokuyama
Tokushima
Wakayar
Fukuoka
Matsuyama
Kochi
Tanabe
33
55
42
Kurume
Oita
Shikoku
3
56
Shanghai, Qingdao
Nagasaki
Kumamoto
Yatsushiro
Nobeoka
10
East China Sea
Sendai
Kyushu
269
Miyazaki
Kagoshima
Shibushi

Okinawa
Okinawa

A PORTRAIT OF JAPAN

Few people in the modern world are not affected in some way by the ideas, culture, and economy of Japan, yet this country remains for many an enigma, an unsolved riddle. Westernized, but different from any Western country, part of Asia, but clearly unlike any other Asian society, Japan is a uniquely adaptable place where tradition and modernity are part of one continuum.

With over 3,000 islands lying along the Pacific Ring of Fire, the Japanese archipelago is prone to frequent earthquakes and has over 100 active volcanoes. Much of the country is mountainous, while cities consume flat lands and coastal plains. The Tokyo–Yokohama area is the largest urban concentration in the world, and 70 percent of Japan's 127 million people live along the stretch of the Pacific coast between Tokyo and Kyushu.

The remaining slivers of cultivable land are farmed to yield maximum crops. Generous amounts of rainfall, melting snowcaps, and deep lakes enable rice to be cultivated in near-perfect conditions.

Each spring, the Japanese are reminded of their country's geographical diversity as the media enthusiastically tracks the progress of the *sakura zensen*, the "cherry-blossom front," as it advances from the subtropical islands of Okinawa to the northernmost island of Hokkaido.

The Japanese regard themselves as a racially integrated tribe, though different dialects and physical features distinguish the people of one region from another. Moreover, there are many minorities in Japan, from the indigenous Ainu to Okinawans, and an admixture of Koreans, Chinese, Southeast Asians, and Westerners who have made Japan their home.

Buddhist monks gathered for a ceremony in the ancient capital of Nara

Planting rice in flooded paddy fields, Fushimi

A Land of Contradictions

Appearances are often deceptive in Japan, obliging foreign visitors to keep adjusting their perceptions of the country. An exit at a large train station, for example, might deliver you to street level or just as likely funnel you through a modern, high-rise department store. Here, among familiar shops, you might discover a whole floor of restaurants, some with rustic, tatami-mat floors and open charcoal braziers, others with displays of plastic food in the window. Closer inspection might reveal a fortune-teller's stall set up outside a software store, a moxibustion clinic next to a fast-food outlet, or a rooftop shrine to the fox-god Inari by the store's Astroturf mini-golf course.

Priest at Senso-ji, Tokyo

In this country of cherry blossoms and capsule hotels, of Buddhist monks and tattooed gangsters, the visitor finds that rock music, avant-garde theater, and abstract painting are as popular as flower arranging, Noh drama, or the tea ceremony. The Grand Shrine at Ise, torn down and rebuilt every 20 years in identical design and materials, exists not to replace tradition but to preserve and renew it – the ultimate illustration of the Japanese belief in the transience of the material world. Nature, too, retains its key role in the national consciousness, in cities and rural areas alike, often ritualized in the annual cycle of *matsuri* (festivals).

Wherever one looks, a stimulating fusion of East and West reveals itself: Zen priests on Hondas; the *salaryman* bowing deeply to a client on his cell phone; neon signs written in Japanese ideograms; ice-cream flavors that include red-bean paste and green tea. In one of the world's most energetic and industrialized nations, there are moments of carefully arranged beauty too, even tranquillity, with people who still find the time to contemplate the crack or glaze of a tea bowl, and burn incense for the dead.

Society, Values, and Beliefs

Although modern Japanese society developed from a feudal system, Japan today is astonishingly egalitarian. Hereditary titles were abolished along with the aristocracy after World War II, and members of the imperial family, the world's longest unbroken line of monarchs, now marry commoners. Class is defined by education and job status. The people employed by the top government ministries, large corporations, and other prestigious companies are Japan's true elite today.

The Japanese have a practical, syncretic, and polytheistic approach to religion. It is an instrument for petitioning the

Woman on a scooter passing a monk with his begging bowl, Kyoto

Burning incense and praying, Nagano

increasing appeal. Young couples now prefer to live apart from their parents, and men are gradually reducing after-hours socializing, in order to spend more time with their family. The steady increase in the divorce rate and the larger number of women who remain unmarried are other indications of changes taking place. The latter is often a decision on the part of Japanese women who cannot find partners with the right credentials. Thus, what might appear to be a contemporary Western-driven tendency, or an expression of feminist awareness, is a reflection, to some degree, of orthodoxy.

gods to grant such requests as success in business or a school entrance exam, recovery from illness, or an uncomplicated birth. Japanese homes have both Buddhist and Shinto altars. Confucianism is sometimes called Japan's unofficial, third religion after Buddhism and Shinto. More moral code and tool for social organization than religion proper, it has had a profound influence on Japanese thought since its introduction in the 6th century.

Japan's declining birthrate, now fewer than 1.5 births per family, is not enough to sustain current population levels, and the specter of an aging, more state-dependent population, looms. This is not just a result of women choosing not to marry. Cramped living conditions and the need for parents to provide offspring with a first-rate, costly education are among other factors. However, many companies are now making efforts to build women's support systems within the workplace, as well as further reducing long working hours with an aim to improve quality of life for employees.

Lion mask to ward off evil spirits, Takayama

These beliefs, alongside family values and devotion to hard work, combined with a submission to the consensus of the group rather than the individual, have long been major binding elements in Japanese society. Traditionally, most women regarded child-rearing as their main objective. Men aimed to climb the corporate ladder, seeing their work as integral to their identity, and many would socialize exclusively with their work colleagues.

Faultlines, however, have appeared in this monolithic structure, as younger voices question the benefits and value of self-sacrifice. A life outside the group, or in smaller, more intimate, groups, has

Visitors dwarfed by the Great Buddha statue at Kamakura

The landmark Studio Alta screen and neon-lit streets of East Shinjuku, Tokyo

Politics and the Economy

Through much of Japan's history, parallel with the institutions and prevailing ideologies of the day, there has been a distinction between power and office. The emperor had little power from the 12th century onward, being essentially a puppet under first the regents, then the shoguns, and, later, the military government before and during World War II. This distinction persists today in the relationship between bureaucrats, who are given enormous power to oversee the economy, and politicians, who merely co-opt, accommodate, or head off the opposition groups.

The existence of widespread political corruption was revealed in 1983 with the exposure of a scandal in which a former Prime Minister, Kakuei Tanaka, was implicated. Pressure then mounted on Japan's conservative regime. Contentious economic stimulus packages, an unpopular consumption tax, and more scandals connected to corruption, fund raising, and graft, further tarnished the party's image for consistency and reliability. The Liberal Democratic Party (LDP) eventually lost its 38-year-long grip on power in 1993, ending almost four decades of political hegemony. The government was forced into potentially unstable coalition arrangements. In the 1980s the yen soared against the dollar, and Japanese companies made the headlines by buying up

American film studios and over-priced works of art. Japanese tourists, long used to sightseeing in their own country, began to travel abroad in unprecedented numbers. Land prices in Japan, foreigners were confidently told, would continue to rise because "Japan was different from other countries." However, friction over a massive trade surplus with America, growing criticism of Japan's "checkbook diplomacy," and the recession that struck in 1992, bursting its "bubble" economy, have been sobering. Despite the hardships suffered by the unemployed and those forced into early retirement, and the increase in homeless people evident in big cities like Tokyo and Osaka, the 1990s recession brought back a degree of sanity that was missing during the decades of uninterrupted growth. It also prompted the Japanese government to make moves toward long overdue economic reform and a greater opening of its markets to international trade. One of the more

Door attendants at Gucci emporium, Tokyo

recent reforms, enacted in 2014, was to raise consumption tax for the first time in 17 years. Elevated from 5 to 8 percent, this bill was aimed to cover rising social welfare costs linked to Japan's ageing population.

Leisure and the Art of Living

The Japanese take their sports and leisure activities almost as seriously as their work. Traditional sports, in particular, often embody some underlying cultural, spiritual, or aesthetic principle, so that there is not only the method but "the way." This applies especially to ancient disciplines like kyudo (archery), kendo, karate, and aikido. Sumo, the national sport of Japan, originated as an oracular

Baseball, a popular sport in Japan

ritual linked to prayers for a bountiful harvest. Having a similar appeal to sports audiences as Kabuki dramas do to theatergoers, sumo ranks many non-Japanese among its fans. Japan gained many soccer fans after the creation of the J-League in 1993 and its selection, along with Korea, as co-host for the 2002 World Cup. Interest in the sport continues to grow on the back of such successes as Nadesiko Japan, Japan's women's team, becoming the first Asian team to win the FIFA Women's World Cup in 2011. Professional baseball attracts an even larger and more devoted following.

Sumo wrestler preparing for a bout

Traditional leisure activities, such as the pleasures of summer fireworks, and seasonal maple, moon, and snow viewing, are much celebrated in literature and art, in the poetry, diaries, and early novels of the Heian period, and in the screen painting and ukiyo-e woodblock prints of the Edo era.

Visits by geisha and their patrons to discreet hot springs in the alps are the material for some atmospheric novels by writers such as the Nobel laureate Kawabata Yasunari (1899–1972).

Nature and aesthetics fuse in the national appreciation for cherry blossoms, a passion that both charms and perplexes the visitor. *Hanami* (cherry blossom) parties are held throughout the country. Because competition for the best viewing sites can be fierce, company bosses often send their younger scions ahead to claim a good patch under the trees. The cherry, as the Japanese see it, is a felicitous symbol but also a poignant reminder of the evanescent beauty of this floating world. Few nations have extracted so much refined pleasure and sadness from the contemplation of a flower.

The Japanese hunger for innovation and advancement has not devoured their spiritual heritage or the natural grace extended toward visitors. Most travelers return home with the impression, in fact, of an unfailingly generous and hospitable people, for whom politeness and consideration toward a guest are second nature.

Kabuki performance, a traditional entertainment

The Landscape of Japan

Japan lies on the intersection of four plates and is the world's most geologically active zone. The islands themselves were pushed up from the ocean floor by earth movements. Evidence of this activity can be seen in the sharply defined mountain ranges rising from the plains, in smoking volcanoes, and in hot mineral waters that well up from the ground. The Japanese take earthquakes, volcanoes, tsunamis, and typhoons in their stride, building and rebuilding their towns wherever they can find flat land. Modern cityscapes *(see pp28–9)* contrast greatly with the seasonal beauty of the relatively undeveloped mountainous interior, and the national parks, the largest of which are in Hokkaido.

Plate movements, as shown, force the sea-bed to be pushed underneath the lighter rocks of the Japanese archipelago. This causes nearly a thousand obvious earthquakes each year in Japan.

The thickly forested hillsides are relatively un-developed, though some remote peaks are used as the isolated setting for hill shrines and temples.

Maple, birch, cypress, and cedar trees are among the most common woodland mixes on the hillsides, creating stunning fiery colors in the fall.

Typical View of the Land

This idealized representation shows the typical landscape features of central Japan. The plains next to the sea are densely populated, while farther inland thickly forested hillsides rise up steeply to snow-covered mountain peaks and the craters of both dormant and active volcanoes.

Freshwater lakes such as Lake Biwa in Western Honshu *(see p216)* are utilized for industry, irrigation, and recreation.

Faultlines run beneath the sea and land, showing up in some places as a rift in the landscape.

Bamboo groves are found in the tropical and temperate zones of Japan. The fast-growing plant is both a foodstuff and building material.

Paddy fields may not be associated with Japan as much as they are with other parts of Asia; none-theless rice-growing occupies a major part of the cultivable landscape. In suburban areas, small rice plots often take the place of gardens.

Japan's 60 or so active volcanoes are scattered along a line through the main islands. Many of these, such as Sakurajima *(see p253)*, smoke and steam constantly. Explosive eruptions of lava and pyroclastic rock-flows take place every few years.

Sulfur vents are found in volcanic regions, staining the rocks yellow in such places as Hokkaido's Akan National Park *(see p291)* and releasing noxious fumes at Mount Aso *(see pp248–9)* and other craters.

Dormant crater

Fruit and vegetable farming takes up what slivers of cultivable land are left after rice farming, but Japan is forced to import about half its food.

The high, snow-covered mountain areas, such as the Japan Alps near Matsumoto *(see p155)* and parts of Northern Honshu and Hokkaido, have been developed as ski resorts.

Rising from the plain is the near-perfect cone of a dormant volcano, the supreme example of which is Mount Fuji *(see pp144–5)*.

Dissolved particles of iron oxide are responsible for the bright color of this natural steaming lake, one of the so-called "Boiling Hells" of Beppu *(see pp238–9)*.

Heavily built-up and industrialized plains

Most of the major Japanese cities, such as Tokyo, Osaka, and Kobe, are working ports. Land suitable for building is at such a premium that artificial peninsulas and islands have been constructed.

Natural Hot Springs

Geothermal activity at thousands of sites in Japan has created natural hot springs either at ground level or just below the surface. The mineral content of the waters varies; some are declared to have therapeutic benefits for humans, especially for diseases of the nervous system and intestines. The Japanese have bathed in the springs for centuries and have also used them for purification rituals. Many have been developed as spas, or *onsen (see pp346–7)*; the Dogo Onsen in Matsuyama is over a thousand years old *(see p230)*. The water of some springs must be cooled before it is suitable for bathing.

Monkeys bathing in the geothermal waters of Jigokudani *(see p155)*

Modern Japan

Perhaps nowhere else does the modern world of high technology and constant change show itself more poignantly than in Japan. For some people, modern Japan is an anathema, a kitsch distillation of the Western world that destroys traditional culture. Others embrace the nation's fascination with invention and image, and praise it for often leading the West. Few urban buildings are more than 25 years old, and consumer trends may change in a matter of weeks in this economic powerhouse. In some ways, though, the liking for change is a manifestation of ancient religious concepts *(see pp30–33)* that emphasize the importance of impermanence and renewal.

The Japanese automobile industry manufactures about ten million vehicles each year. In a land where space is at a premium, the small car is king.

Tange Kenzo's earthquake-proof Metropolitan Offices *(see p96)* are praised by some and villified by others.

A forest of neon characterizes the shopping and entertainment districts of cities that strive to be modern, such as Tokyo, Fukuoka, and here in Osaka. Vast television screens and public announcements over loudspeakers add to the audio-visual tumult.

The Sony Corporation has grown from 20 employees in 1946 to an electronics empire with assets of $124 billion. The Sony Showroom *(see p70)* displays the latest inventions before they reach the shops.

The Yamanote train line connects Tokyo's main districts in a loop.

Department stores are accessed directly from the world's busiest train station.

High-Tech Toys and Games

Japan has a proud tradition of video games and toys, beginning in the late 1970s with arcade classics like *Space Invaders* and *Pac-Man*. Today the industry continues to flourish, and companies like Nintendo, Sega, and Sony have developed generations of powerful home entertainment systems with sophisticated graphics and audio. Technological phenomena include robotic pets (such as *Tamagotchi*) and motion sensitive devices, with more innovations never far behind.

Tamagotchis for sale in Harajuku

Robot *(robotto)* technology was exported to Japan from the US in 1967. Today, about half of the world's robots are found in Japan, used widely in industry. Some are delightfully zoomorphic.

The oxygen bar, in which customers inhale pure or scented oxygen for health and relaxation instead of imbibing alcohol, originated in Japan and is becoming popular in other countries.

Mount Fuji   The Greater Tokyo conurbation

Modern Cityscapes

Shinjuku district in Tokyo, shown here (see also pp94–7), epitomizes the modern Japanese urban labyrinth. Buildings are constructed wherever land becomes available, using such materials as aluminum, steel, and concrete. Increasingly, flexible-frame technologies are used to withstand earthquakes.

Manga ("comic pictures") are immensely popular in Japan, especially the genre of narrative comics called *gekiga*, which emerged in the 1960s. The content is diverse – politics, baseball, romance, martial arts, and pornography are all popular.

Modern Architecture

An eclectic mix of contemporary building styles can be seen in Japan. Kenzo Tange (1913–2005), who built the Olympic Stadiums in 1964 *(see pp98–9)*, still casts a shadow over younger designers. Foreign practitioners, too, have been influential.

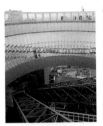

Osaka's Umeda Sky Building (completed 1993) was inspired by the 1960s' dream of a "city in the air." Hara Hiroshi's twin towers are linked by the Floating Garden Observatory, which hovers above the city *(see p206)*.

An amusing, almost cartoonlike building, the Super Dry Hall was built in 1989 by French designer Philippe Starck for the Asahi beer company, near

the Sumida River in the Asakusa district of Tokyo. International architects have designed some of their most ambitious projects in Tokyo.

A modern house, designed by Ando Tadao (1941–), allows light to seep through in unusual ways, such as through glass slots between ceiling and walls. One of the foremost contemporary Japanese architects, Ando's works include the Himeji City Museum of Literature *(see p213)*.

The Tokyo International Forum *(see p75)* is a shiplike structure built by the South American architect Rafael Viñoly in 1996. Its glass-walled atrium, supported by elegant columns and bars, is widely considered to be a masterpiece of engineering.

Shinto: the Native Religion

Shinto is Japan's oldest religion, the "way of the gods." Its core concept is that deities, *kami*, preside over all things in nature, be they living, dead, or inanimate. There are lesser and greater *kami*, worshiped at thousands of shrines (*jinja*) erected on hills and along waysides. From ancient times the emperor's rule was sanctioned by the authority of the greatest gods, said to be his ancestors. Shinto was the state religion from the 1870s to 1940s. Today, few Japanese are purely Shintoists, but most will observe Shinto rituals alongside Buddhist practices. Many Japanese habits, such as an emphasis on purification and an austere aesthetic, are derived at least in part from Shinto.

The *torii* is the most recognizable icon of Shinto. These gateways mark the entrance to the sacred precincts of a shrine. Many are made of vermilion-painted wood; some are constructed in stone, even concrete. All have two rails at the top.

The *shimenawa* is a rope made of twisted rice straw. It is hung over entrances within shrine precincts to separate sacred and secular places. It is also set above doors of houses to ward off evil and sickness. Izumo Taisha *(see p217)* has many examples of *shimenawa*, some of them immense.

Miscanthus grass thatch

The treasures, to the west and east of the main structure, house ceremonial regalia, silks, and paper.

Inari shrines, identifiable by the bibbed stone foxes standing guard within them, are dedicated to the *kami* of cereal crops. The head Inari shrine is at Fushimi *(see p183)*, just south of Kyoto, and 30,000 others are scattered throughout the country.

Ise Inner Grand Shrine

The home of the spirits of all past emperors, the Grand Shrine at Ise (see p202) is the most venerated Shinto site. The inner shrine shown here is dedicated to Amaterasu, the sun goddess, and is said to house her mirror, an imperial sacred treasure. It is not open to the public. The complex is completely rebuilt every 20 years, most recently in 2013, following a tradition begun in AD 690.

The *Shinto priesthood* (kannushi) tended to be transmitted through families, and important families *(shake)* are still connected with some shrines. The *kannushi*, who usually wear white and orange robes, perform purification ceremonies and other rituals.

In the main sanctuary (honden) of a shrine is an object (shintai) believed to be the abode of the kami to whom the shrine is dedicated. Usually only the head priests enter the honden; the hall for worship (haiden) is often separate.

Worshipers stand in front of the haiden hall, pull on a bell rope, toss money into a box, clap three times to summon the resident kami, then stand in silent prayer for a few moments.

Metallic caps cover the exposed grain of the timber.

Forked finials, chigi, are used in traditional Japanese joinery to secure timber frames.

Straight roofline

Ise Shrine has its own style of architecture, called yuitsu shimmei-zukuri, which has been imitated at just a handful of other shrines.

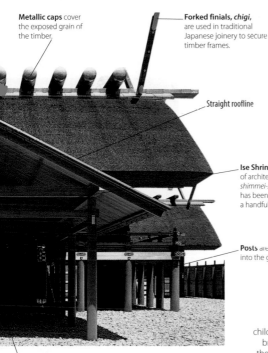

Posts are set directly into the ground.

Fertility is a major concern of Shinto. Some shrines have statues depicting phalluses, lovemaking, childbirth, or milk-engorged breasts. Couples will ask the spirits for conception and good health for mother and child.

About 13,000 cypresses are used to rebuild the shrine every 20 years on alternating, adjacent sites.

Charms and Votive Tablets

Good-luck charms, called omamori, are sold at shrines across Japan. Common themes relate to fertility, luck in examinations, general health, or safety while driving. The charm itself might be written on a piece of paper or thin wooden board and tucked into a cloth bag, which can be worn next to the body or placed somewhere relevant. (Do not open the bag to read the charm or it will not work.) Prayers or wishes can also be written on ema boards and hung at the shrine.

Ema boards wishing for success in examinations

Charms for conception, safe child-birth, and safety while driving

Buddhism in Japan

Buddhism, founded in India, arrived in Japan via China and Korea in the 6th century AD. Different sects *(see p279)* evolved and were adopted over the centuries. The new religion sometimes had an uneasy relationship with Shinto, despite incorporating parts of the native belief system. Buddhism lost official support in 1868 but has flowered again since World War II. The complex cosmological beliefs and morality of Buddhism permeate modern Japanese life, especially in the emphasis on mental control found in Zen Buddhism.

Prince Shotoku (573–621) promoted Buddhism in its early days in Japan *(see p200)*.

Senso-ji temple *(see pp90–91)* is the site of some of Tokyo's main festivals *(see pp46–51)*. Buddhist festivals honor events in the Buddha's life and the return of dead spirits to Earth *(bon)*. They often incorporate Shinto elements.

Memorial stones are erected in cemeteries attached to temples. Called *gorin-to*, many are made up of five different-shaped stones. Plain, box-shaped ones are called *sotoba*.

Worshipers remove their shoes and kneel before the altar in silent contemplation and prayer.

Pagodas, found in some temple complexes, house relics of the Buddha, such as fragments of bone. The relic is usually placed at the base of the central pillar, hidden from view. Three- or five-story *(see p200)* pagodas are common, but access to the upper stories is rarely permitted.

Jizo Statues

Red-bibbed statues of Jizo are found at thousands of temples and along waysides in Japan. Jizo is the guardian *bosatsu* of those who suffer, especially sickly children and pregnant women. Children who have died young, including babies who have been miscarried or aborted, are helped into the next world by Jizo. He is often shown holding a staff in one hand and a jewel talisman in the other. The red bibs are placed on the statues by bereaved mothers and other sufferers.

Jizo, Toji Temple, Kyoto

Jizo and babies, Uwajima, Shikoku

Pilgrimages to Buddhist sites are very popular. Pilgrims, typically dressed in white, walk from site to site, sometimes making epic journeys of many weeks' duration, such as for Shikoku's 88-Temple Pilgrimage (see pp232–3).

The semi-enclosed area at the front of the platform has a burner for incense offerings. Beyond is a type of tabernacle containing a sacred object (honzon), hidden from view.

The Asuka Plain of Western Honshu was the site of the earliest Buddhist worship in Japan (see p201). This bronze image of the Buddha dates from 609.

Tatami mats line the floor of the hondo. The Zen temple hondo is characterized by its relative starkness and lack of ornamentation.

The Buddhist Temple in Japan

Buddhist sites, identifiable by the suffixes -ji and -dera, are usually translated as "temples" (whereas Shinto sites are "shrines"). The temple complex includes a main hall (hondo), shown here, maybe a pagoda, cemetery, buildings used by monks, and often a small Shinto shrine too. The layout of a typical Zen Buddhist temple is shown on page 141.

Meditation is a cornerstone of Buddhism: clearing the mind of cluttered thoughts is the road to Enlightenment. In *zazen* sitting meditation, photographed here in about 1950, a nun uses a *keisaku* stick to slap meditators who seem to be losing their alertness.

Glossary

Amida The Buddha of Infinite Light, as venerated by the Pure Land sect.

Bosatsu Japanese word for bodhisattva, a figure that has attained Enlightenment and helps others.

Amida

Buddha Usually means the historical Buddha, who was born in India in 563 BC.

Butsudan Altar in house.

Enlightenment An expansion of mind as achieved by *bosatsu*.

Hondo Main hall of temple.

Honzon Principal object of worship in main hall.

Jizo A popular *bosatsu*.

Juzu Buddhist rosary.

Kaimyo Buddhist name awarded posthumously.

Kannon The goddess of mercy. Sometimes has 1,000 arms (Senju Kannon).

Karesansui A rock and sand garden inspired by Zen Buddhism and Chinese landscape painting.

Keisaku Stick used to slap shoulders during meditation.

Kannon

Mahayana Major branch of Buddhism, emphasizing the importance of *bosatsu*. Practiced in Tibet, China, Korea, and Japan.

Myoo Deified king of light.

Nio Temple gate guardians (Brahma and Indra in India).

Nirvana Release from the cycle of rebirth and suffering.

Nyorai Epithet for the Buddha.

Pure Land Western Paradise of the Amida Buddha.

Sanmon Free-standing gateway to a temple complex.

Satori Sudden Enlightenment in Zen Buddhism.

Shingon Very popular Buddhist sect (see p279).

Takuhatsu The monks' practice of begging.

Tembu Type of heavenly being.

Tendai Major Buddhist sect (see p279).

Zazen Sitting meditation, popular in Zen.

Zen Major school of Buddhism (see p279).

Tembu

Japanese Gardens

Originating around early Shinto shrines, Japanese gardens have been influenced by the Shinto love of nature and the Buddhist ideal of paradise. Although classic Japanese gardens can be roughly divided into four types – paradise gardens, dry-landscape gardens, stroll gardens, and tea gardens – they share many components and principles, and have continued evolving through the centuries. The common aim was to create a microcosm: stones, water, bridges, and other elements were combined to form an idealized and symbolic miniature landscape. Paradise and dry-landscape gardens were designed to be viewed from a single point or side, while stroll gardens and tea gardens were made to be walked through.

Modern gardens in Japan have altered as architectural styles have changed, but many still use traditional components, such as water, stones, and gravel, in a less sinuous, more geometric way than in the past.

Paradise Garden

Motsu-ji garden in Hiraizumi *(see p280)* is a beautifully preserved example of a paradise garden, designed to evoke the Pure Land, or Buddhist paradise. Use is made of "borrowed landscape" – trees or mountains outside the garden that appear to be part of it. Stones are arranged to create islands and rocky shores.

Dry-Landscape Garden

Attached to Zen Buddhist temples, these gardens of carefully chosen stones grouped amid an expanse of raked gravel provide an object for meditation. A classic dry-landscape garden is at Ryoan-ji Temple, Kyoto *(see p178)*, where the plain, earthen walls enhance the abstract arrangement of the stones.

This waterfall, at Iso Tei-en garden, Kagoshima, exemplifies the art of creating artificial features that look entirely natural.

This sand mound, like a flattened Mount Fuji, is at Ginkaku-ji temple in Kyoto. The raked sand around it resembles a silver sea by moonlight.

The Phoenix Hall at Byodo-in near Kyoto houses an Amida Buddha *(see p33)*. The building is reflected in the pond in front, which represents the Western Ocean.

The "Treasure Ship" stone at Daisen-in, Kyoto *(see p177)*, is one of Japan's most famous stones. Individual stones are not intended as symbols, but this is said to suggest a junk traveling through waves.

Seasons in a Japanese Garden

The Japanese awareness of the seasons is an integral part of their garden design. A careful balance of shrubs and trees is one of the essential ingredients for a harmonious garden. Evergreen trees and bamboos are often planted for year-round greenery; deciduous trees are chosen for their shape when bare as well as when clothed with foliage to ensure year-round interest. In tea gardens, where every detail is symbolic, fallen blossoms or leaves may be arranged by the path to suggest the season. Some gardens are planned for a spectacular effect in one season; many are best visited in spring or fall.

Winter in a Kyoto temple garden

Contrasting maple leaves in fall at Tenryu-ji, Kyoto

Stroll Garden

The views in a stroll garden change with virtually every step, with vistas concealed and revealed. These gardens were popular in the Edo period when they were made by *daimyo* (feudal lords). Kenroku-en in Kanazawa (*see p152*) includes four ponds and uses "borrowed landscape" skillfully.

Murin-an garden in Kyoto is a small stroll garden, designed to look highly naturalistic. A meandering stream, pond, and overhanging trees create a quiet and secluded enviroment through which to walk.

Pruning is prized as an art, bringing out the inherent qualities of a tree. A beautifully pruned tree often forms a focal point in a stroll garden.

Tea Garden

Dating from the Momoyama period (1568–1600), a tea garden consists of a short path, with trimmed plants on either side, leading to a teahouse. The path links the real world to the world of the tea ceremony (*see p173*). In keeping with the simple ceremony, this Kyoto garden has rustic posts and a bamboo fence.

Stone basins were at first purely functional, for washing hands and mouth, but then came to symbolize purification before the ceremony.

Slightly raised and spaced apart, the stones in the path are sprinkled with water before the ceremony to welcome guests; the Japanese thus call the tea garden *rojo* (dewy path).

Traditional Japanese Houses

Known as *minka* or "commoners' houses," traditional dwellings vary widely in their layout and appearance from region to region, often in response to local weather conditions. Made largely of wood and paper, they were designed to be adaptable in their use of the interior space. Although *minka* in their original form are rarely occupied today, partly due to a move toward Western domestic architecture, partly through destruction (often by fire), they can still be seen around Japan and are sometimes open as museums. The way of organizing the living space is, however, still widely used, even in modern, Western-style houses.

Town houses such as these in the Gion area of Kyoto are known as *machiya* and are the urban equivalent of *minka*. The layout differs as the width of the frontage is limited.

The *irori* (hearth) forms the heart of the house, often kept burning as the main source of heat. It is also sometimes used for cooking. In *minka* the hearth is usually sunk into a wooden floor; a *tatami* surrounding indicates a wealthy household.

The *doma* (area with a packed-earth floor) lies just behind the entrance. Here people take off their shoes before stepping up to the wooden surface.

The *engawa* is a space outside, like a veranda, covered with a sloping roof. It may be enclosed by heavy wooden doors, or opened to allow air to circulate. This entrance is mainly used by visitors, who will stand on the stone step to remove their shoes.

The main entrance to the *minka* is through sliding doors.

Types of Roof

Traditionally a *minka* roof is thatched, often with miscanthus reed, though the material varies according to what is available locally. Tiled roofs are also widespread as they are simpler to construct and fire-resistant; the ends of tiles may be decorated with an image, such as a devil, to protect the house. Shingles are also used, sometimes weighted down by stones. Roof shapes vary widely in design and complexity.

An intricate, gabled roof with decorated tile ends

A semi-gabled thatched roof of a *kabuto-zukuri* house

A thatcher at work replacing worn thatch

A Buddhist family altar (*butsudan*) is found in many homes, usually along with a much simpler Shinto altar.

Bedding of futon mattresses and quilts is rolled and stored in a cupboard in the day and unrolled on the floor at night.

Wooden ceilings above the more formal rooms double up as storage space.

Ramma – open and sometimes carved wooden lintels above the *fusuma* – separate the rooms.

The *tokonoma* is a wooden-floored alcove in a formal room, used for displaying a scroll and flowers or ceramics. The scroll is often changed to reflect the season.

Fusuma sliding doors of wood and heavy paper are opened or closed to alter the size of a room.

Tatami mats cover the floor of the formal room or rooms. These straw-and-rush mats are a standard size within each region, and room size is often measured in *tatami* mats. Typically formal rooms are six to eight mats in size, and are used to receive guests.

Vertical beams rest upon foundation stones, which help to minimize dampness inside the house.

Shoji sliding doors open onto the *engawa*. A door consists of a wooden frame and Japanese paper, which allows light to filter through.

A One-Story Minka

This illustration shows features of the layout of a minka. The toilet and washing facilities were usually located outside the main house. The main variations on this basic design include the gassho-zukuri *house (see p151), the* L-shaped magariya, *used to house horses as well as people (found mainly in Iwate prefecture, Northern Honshu), and the* kabuto-zukuri *house, designed to allow in more light and air (found in Yamagata prefecture, Northern Honshu).*

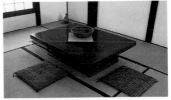

A *kotatsu* is a heater combined with a low table. The heater (traditionally charcoal, now electric) may be situated under the frame, or inside a pit sunk into the floor. A futon is draped under the tabletop for extra warmth in winter. Individuals kneel on cushions or rest their feet in the pit.

Sumo and the Martial Arts

Now more of a professional sport than a martial art, sumo can trace its origins back 2,000 years to Shinto harvest rites, and strong links with Shinto remain in many sumo rituals. There are six sumo tournaments in Japan every year *(see p350)*, broadcast live on TV and followed enthusiastically. Training is a way of life *(see p106)* for sumo wrestlers, and if a tournament is not on, it may be possible to watch practice sessions *(see p115)*. Martial arts are known as *budo*, or the "martial way." They aim to cultivate balance, control, speed, and accuracy in a spiritual, mental, and physical sense. Kendo and kyudo, the least changed since the days of the samurai, are seen as the purest of the martial arts.

Sumo wrestlers were a highly popular subject for Edo-period woodblock prints.

Throwing salt to purify the ring and the fight to come is part of a complex pre-match ritual that the wrestlers undertake. They also stamp, clap, and raise their hands before crouching down in front of their opponent ready to start.

The *gyoji* (referee) wears traditional court costume and uses a fan to signal when to begin.

Grand champions *(yokozuna)* perform pre-match rituals wearing a richly decorated ceremonial apron and a white hemp-rope belt hung with folded paper (as seen at Shinto shrines). This champion is performing *shiko*, lifting his leg and stamping his foot to banish evil spirits and intimidate his opponents.

Sumo Wrestling

Despite their size – there are no weight restrictions – sumo wrestlers (rikishi) *move quickly and with agility, and so matches are often short (10 seconds or so). The loser is the first to touch the ground with any part of his body, except the soles of his feet, or to step out of, or be pushed from, the ring. The referee* (gyoji) *declares the winner.*

A referee pours an offering of sake onto the ring as part of the dedication ceremony before a tournament. The ring is a platform of clay edged by a square of sunken rice-straw bales, with an inner ring (where the match is fought) also marked by sunken bales.

Banners announce a sumo tournament – here at the National Sumo Stadium in Tokyo (see p106). Each tournament lasts 15 days. The lower-ranking wrestlers fight early in the day, while higher-ranking ones appear from mid-afternoon onward.

The wrestlers' hair is oiled and fastened into a topknot (mage).

Only 48 winning techniques are commonly used, but many more have been identified.

Martial Arts

Originally developed as arts of war by the samurai, the martial arts have evolved into forms of austere discipline (shugyo) aimed at spiritual improvement; some are also competitive sports. The modern forms of kendo and kyudo trace their origins to methods practiced in Japanese antiquity.

Kendo means the "way of the sword." Originating from samurai fencing, kendo now uses bamboo swords. Contestants wear extensive padding and protection. In a match, points are gained for hitting the head, torso, forearm, or throat.

Kyudo, or the "way of the bow," has close associations with Zen Buddhism. Although accuracy in hitting a target is important, the emphasis is also on concentration of mind and body.

A loincloth (mawashi) is worn for bouts, along with a thin belt (sagari) hung with threads similar to those seen at Shinto shrines.

Judo developed from jujitsu. A system of self-defense, it is well established as a sport in which throwing and grappling techniques are used to subdue an opponent.

Karate ("empty hand") reached Japan in 1922 from Okinawa. A form of self-defense as well as spiritual and physical training, it has become a sport, consisting of explosive yet controlled kicks, punches, or strikes, and blocking moves.

The ring stands under a suspended roof resembling that of a Shinto shrine. A different-colored tassel hangs from each corner of the roof, representing the four seasons.

Aikido – the "way of harmonious spirit" – uses an opponent's strength and speed against them. Training unites spiritual awareness and physical flexibility.

Japanese Traditional Theater

Four major types of traditional theater are still performed regularly in Japan: Noh, Kyogen, Kabuki, and Bunraku *(see p112 and p188)*. Originating in Shinto rites, Noh was first performed by Kan'ami Kiyotsugu (1333–84) and developed by his son Zeami. Adopted by the *daimyo* (feudal lords), Noh became more ritualistic and ceremonial. Gradually its farcical elements were confined to a separate form, Kyogen. By the 17th century, people wanted a more comprehensible and entertaining form of drama, and Kabuki evolved from Noh, starting in Kyoto. A form of puppet theater, Bunraku, like Kabuki, was aimed at the general populace.

A Noh play is being performed for the imperial household in this 1863 woodblock print by Taiso Yoshitoshi.

The backdrop is a single pine tree, epitomizing the simplicity of Noh staging.

Noh actors may be men or women but the majority are men.

Noh

An austere, restrained, and powerful theatrical form, Noh is performed on a bare, three-sided cypress-wood stage roofed like a shrine, with an entrance ramp to one side. One or two masked characters appear at a time. Their slow, choreographed actions (kata) are performed to music.

Musicians playing traditional drums and flutes sit at the back of the stage and accompany the actors.

A chorus of six to eight people sit to one side and comment on the action.

Kyogen evolved from comic interludes devised as relief from the demanding nature of Noh. A down-to-earth, colloquial form, its characters highlight human foibles and frailties. Masks are rarely used, and costumes are plain. The actors wear distinctive yellow *tabi* socks.

Noh masks are worn by the leading characters; the greatest masks are classified as National Treasures. The mask on the right represents a samurai, and on the far right, a demon.

Noh costumes are usually richly decorated and heavy. Many layers are worn to make the actors seem larger and more imposing.

Kabuki actors were popular subjects for Edo-era woodblock prints. The tradition can still be seen in this modern poster advertising a Kabuki play.

Bunraku

Bunraku puppets are about 1.2 m (4 ft) tall with carved wooden heads, movable hands, and elaborate costumes. The main puppeteer wears traditional formal dress; his two assistants, one on each side, are clothed in black. *Shamisen* music accompanies the action, and a narrator both tells the story and speaks all the parts. Many Kabuki plays were originally written for puppets; Bunraku has in turn borrowed a number of Kabuki dramas.

Bunraku puppet with his puppeteer

Stage right is where less important characters are usually located.

Costumes and wigs are highly elaborate, indicating the status and personality of each character.

The pine trees on Kabuki stage backdrops are a reference to its evolution from Noh.

Kabuki

Kabuki is flamboyant and colorful with a large stage and cast. The major actors are stars, often from famous acting dynasties. Elaborate make-up replaced Noh masks, and a curtain allowed set changes. The musicians and chorus sit behind screens on either side or on stage.

Stage sets often incorporate special effects including trapdoors, revolving sections, and overhead cables for flying.

Stage left is usually occupied by characters of high rank or importance.

The *hanamichi* (flower path) is a raised walkway running from stage right through the audience and is used for dramatic entrances and exits.

Aragoto, or "rough-style" acting, is used in certain plays by male characters who move in exaggerated, choreographed ways and wear stylized makeup. Eye and facial movements are crucial to an actor's success.

Although Kabuki was founded by a woman, Izumo no Okuni, female actors were soon banned as immoral. All actors are now male, and female roles are played by highly skilled *onnagata*.

Traditional Arts and Crafts

In Japan there is no rigid distinction between arts and crafts; both have a long, distinguished history and are equally prized. Many techniques came to Japan from the Asian continent, especially China and Korea, and have since evolved and been refined. Early arts and crafts were dominated by Buddhist influences, but from medieval times onward they became increasingly secular and decorative. Traditional arts and crafts still thrive, with thousands of practitioners making a living from their work. Artisans can be seen at work in many areas.

Metalwork includes items such as samurai swords, temple bells, and tea kettles. This tea kettle is from Morioka (*see p281*).

Calligraphy

Known as *shodo*, the way of writing, the art of calligraphy was intro-duced to Japan along with the Chinese writing system in the 5th century and came to be considered as an essential accomplishment for the cultured person. Traditional writing implements consist of a

brush, ink, an inkstone, and a water vessel. Buddhist monks have often led the development of styles through the centuries. Modern calligraphy has been influenced by Western Minimalist and Abstract art.

A 17th-century example of calligraphy

Calligraphy today, still using traditional methods

Painting

Early paintings include religious mandalas, and scrolls illustrating works such as the *Tale of Genji* (*see p56*). Ink painting thrived in the 14th century; its most famous practitioner was the Zen monk Sesshu (1420–1506). The Kano School (*see p165*) was most noted for its screens. *Ukiyo-e* wood-block prints (*see p89*) predominated in the Edo period. Modern painting in Japan is inspired by Western and traditional sources.

Screen by Shibata Zeshin (1807–91) depicting the four elegant pastimes of painting, music, the game of Go, and calligraphy

Ceramics

Ceramics up to 12,000 years old have been found in Japan. Myriad styles have developed in different areas, fueled by the central role of ceramics in the tea ceremony and cuisine. Kyushu is renowned for its porcelain and stoneware (*see p243*); Hagi (*see pp222–3*) and Inbe (*see p214*) produce stoneware for the tea ceremony; Mashiko (*see p276*) is known for its folk pottery and as the birthplace of 20th-century potter Shoji Hamada.

Bowl from Naha, Okinawa

Potter at work in Kanazawa, Central Honshu

19th-century vase from Kyushu

Textiles

Sophisticated methods of dyeing, weaving, and hand decoration have developed in Japan, resulting in an astonishing range of textiles. Relatively isolated islands and areas evolved their own techniques; for example, the Okinawans use the *kasuri* method to tie-dye threads before weaving. *Yuzen*-dyeing in Kanazawa *(see p152)* uses a paste for resist-dyeing to create complex and colorful designs, often using natural vegetable dyes. Indigo *(ai)* was the most popular dye, though it has largely been replaced by synthetic alternatives. Modern designers such as Issey Miyake continue to experiment boldly with fabrics.

Dyeing *bashofu* fabric in Kijoka village, Okinawa *(see p261)*

Complex design of *samurai* (military nobility) woven into silk

Hand-painting dyes onto fabric, part of the resist-dyeing process

Woodcraft, Bamboo, and Lacquerware

The Japanese admire the grain and color of wood as much as the artifacts that are created from it. Traditional buildings have been made from wood for centuries; some are still in existence as a testament to their makers' craftsmanship. On a smaller scale there are exquisite wooden statues, along with wooden vessels and utensils, and traditional dolls *(see p281)*. To produce lacquerware, for which Japan is famed worldwide, the wood is coated with many layers of lacquer (derived from tree sap) and burnished to a smooth, lustrous finish. Bamboo, being strong and flexible, is used for umbrellas, toys, and baskets.

An 18th-century wooden carving of Amida Buddha

Laquerware box from Aizu-Wakamatsu

Bamboo craftsman at work

Ikebana and Bonsai

Demonstrating the art of *ikebana*, or flower arranging

Ikebana is also known as *kado*, or the "way of flowers," and originated from early Buddhist flower offerings. The tea ceremony required simple arrangements of flowers, while more avant-garde creations have been popular since the late 19th century. Today there are about 3,000 *ikebana* schools in Japan. Bonsai came from China and involves growing and training trees in miniature form; prize specimens are valuable heirlooms. Both *ikebana* arrangements and bonsai may be displayed in the *tokonoma (see p37)* of a traditional home.

An evergreen bonsai tree

Japanese Traditional Dress

Although most Japanese now wear Western-style clothes (*yofuku*), it is not unusual to glimpse a kimono-clad woman in the street or a man relaxing in a lightweight summer kimono (*yukata*). Kimonos are wraparound garments worn by men and women, usually on formal occasions and at festivals. Some people change into a cotton kimono to relax in the evenings. A good kimono can last for years, even generations – it is made to a standard pattern, rather than to fit the wearer; the fitting is done when dressing. The left side of the garment is always wrapped over the right; the opposite is done only when dressing the dead.

Kimono style for women and men has changed little since the Edo period.

A new, formal kimono can cost tens of thousands of yen, but these garments become family heirlooms. Before cleaning, they are taken apart along the seams; for storage they are folded and wrapped in paper.

The haneri is a replaceable neckband, just visible under the kimono.

A length of silk known as the *obiage* holds the *obi* in place.

The obi is a sash up to 4 m (13 ft) long.

The obijime decorative cord further secures the *obi*.

The *obi* sash is usually made of silk and tied tightly at the back. The quality of material and the knot used vary according to the season and formality of the occasion.

A tuck, or *oha-shiori*, at the waist adjusts the length of a kimono.

Yukata are unlined cotton kimonos worn by men and women, often at summer festivals or hot-spring resorts.

The sumptuous fabric used for women's kimonos is often hand-painted, woven, or dyed using one of the many traditional Japanese techniques to produce a complex design.

Tabi socks have a split between the big and second toes.

Zori sandals usually have wedge soles.

Woman's Kimono

This woman is wearing a furisode, a formal kimono with long, flowing sleeves. These are traditionally worn by young, unmarried women on special occasions, such as Coming-of-Age Day in January, and are often made of brightly colored and extravagantly patterned materials.

Women's hairstyles grew increasingly elaborate in the Edo period, reflecting a woman's age and social and marital status. Today, women wear traditional styles only on formal occasions.

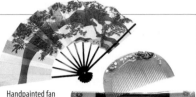

Handpainted fan

Comb and hair pin

Fans, usually bamboo covered with hand-painted paper, are traditional accessories carried by women and men. Combs and hairpins may be tortoiseshell, lacquer, or ivory, and are often exquisitely decorated.

The family crest is known as the *mon*.

The *montsuki* is a formal kimono (which can be worn by men or women) bearing a crest.

The *haori* is an outer coat worn over the kimono.

A pair of braided cords, known as *himo*, are used to tie the kimono.

Hakama are loose trousers, similar to culottes, which are worn over the kimono.

Men's sandals are known as *setta* and have a surface similar to *tatami* mats. The soles are made of leather.

At a traditional wedding, or *tomesode*, the man wears a formal kimono, while the woman wears a white kimono, known as *shiromuku*, and a special headdress.

Children wear miniature versions – often rented – of the adult kimonos on formal occasions, and especially at the Shichi-go-san (Seven-Five-Three) Festival in November (see p51).

Man's Kimono

Formal clothing for a man consists of a black silk kimono; a man's kimono is shorter than a woman's, allowing greater freedom of movement. Over the top go ankle-length hakama *and a long, loose jacket or* haori, *plain apart from the family crest embroidered in white.*

Traditional Shoes

Since the Nara and Heian periods (from the 8th century on), the Japanese have worn variations on thonged rush or leather sandals (*zori*) and wooden clogs (*geta*). Both

Geta wooden clogs

are highly practical for slipping on and off when entering and leaving houses. *Zori* are still worn with formal kimonos, and *geta* with *yukata*. *Geta* often tended to be raised off the ground to prevent the wearer's feet from becoming muddy; in the late 17th century the fashion for courtesans was for 30-cm (12-in) high soles, almost impossible to walk in. *Tabi* split socks are worn with both types of shoes.

Making wooden clogs

Japan's Festivals: Matsuri

Matsuri means both festival and worship, indicating the Shinto origins of Japanese festivals. Some are nationwide, others are local to individual temples and shrines. Matsuri are a link between the human and the divine, often marking stages in the rice-growing cycle (mainly planting and harvest) or historical events. The aim of the matsuri is to preserve the goodwill of the deities *(kami)*. All matsuri follow a basic form: purification (often by water or fire); then offerings; then a procession in which the *kami* is invoked at the shrine and escorted in a portable shrine *(mikoshi)* to a temporary dwelling where there is entertainment such as dancing or archery. The *kami* is then taken back to the shrine.

The basic form of matsuri has changed little over the centuries. This print shows an 18th-century religious festival with men carrying a *mikoshi*.

Omizu-tori has been celebrated at Todai-ji temple, Nara *(see pp196–7)*, since the 8th century to signal the advent of spring. Water is drawn from a sacred well and purified with fire from huge torches.

The *mikoshi* is a colorful, ornate portable shrine in which the *kami* rides en route from and to the shrine.

Takayama Matsuri takes place in spring and fall. Spectacular floats are escorted from the Hie Shrine through the town by people dressed in Edo-period costumes. The aim is to placate the *kami* of plague.

Rice festivals all over Japan were central to the matsuri cycle, but have declined as agricultural techniques have changed. Women plant the rice in spring, symbolically passing their fertility to the crop. Fall festivals give thanks for the harvest.

Aoi Matsuri, or the Hollyhock Festival, in Kyoto, originated in the 6th century. Participants in Heian-period costume parade from the Imperial Palace to Shimogamo and Kamigamo shrines, re-creating the journey of imperial messengers who were sent to placate the gods.

Nebuta Matsuri, held in Aomori in August, is one of Japan's most spectacular festivals, featuring huge paper lanterns. At the end they are carried off to sea as a symbol of casting away anything that might interfere with the harvest.

Obon, the Buddhist Festival of the Dead, takes place in mid-July or mid-August. Ancestors are welcomed back to the world of the living and then bid farewell again. Bon Odori, hypnotic outdoor dancing, takes place.

The bearers of the *mikoshi* tend to take it on a boisterous ride as the gods are said to enjoy revelry.

Participants are dressed in short kimonos known as *happi*, and headbands, or *hachimaki*.

Tanabata Matsuri in July is known as the Weaver, or Star, Festival. Based on a Chinese legend, it is said to be the only day when the two stars Vega (the weaver) and Altair (the herdsman) can meet as lovers across the Milky Way. People write down wishes and poems and hang them on bamboo poles.

Kanda Matsuri, Tokyo

Held in May in alternate years, this festival is one of Tokyo's largest. Numerous floats and portable shrines are paraded through the streets of Tokyo to placate the gods of Kanda Myojin Shrine (see p77). In addition to communicating with the gods, the festival encourages a sense of community.

Equestrian archery is a traditional test of martial skills at matsuri. Archery contests take place at Hachiman shrines as offerings to the god of war; the best known is at Kamakura's Hachiman-gu Shrine *(see p138).*

Jidai Matsuri, or the Festival of the Ages, is a relatively new matsuri. It was initiated in 1895 to commemorate Kyoto's long history. Dressed in historical costumes dating from the 8th century onward, people parade from the Imperial Palace to the Heian Shrine.

JAPAN THROUGH THE YEAR

The year in Japan moves through five seasons: spring, rainy season, summer, fall, and winter. Though less reliable than in the past, perhaps due to global warming, the seasons are still clearly discernible and dictate many of the traditional, agricultural-based matsuri, or festivals. The country follows two calendars: the contemporary Gregorian, and to a lesser degree the ancient Chinese lunar system. Because Japan also has two main religions, Shinto and Buddhism, there are double the number of festivals found in most countries. In fact, the days, weeks, and months are marked by so many festive occasions and national holidays that the year speeds past in a colorful procession of official observations, historic commemorations, sacred rites, and wild celebration.

Cherry blossom along the Philosopher's Walk, Kyoto

Spring

Although spring does not officially begin until the cherry trees bloom in early to mid-April, this is the time the elements begin to warm and thaw. Cherry-blossom parties take place throughout the country. In Golden Week (April 29–May 5) and adjacent weekends many Japanese take the time off to travel.

March

Omizu-tori (*Water-Drawing Festival, Mar 1–14*), Nara. At Todai-ji Temple, water is ritually drawn to the sound of ancient sacred music at 2am on the 13th day (*see p46*).
Hina Matsuri (*Doll Festival, Mar 3*). Throughout Japan, dolls in Heian-period imperial costumes are displayed in homes with young daughters.
Kasuga Shrine Festival (*Mar 13*), Nara. Shrine maidens perform a 1,100-year-old dance.

April

Hana Matsuri (*Buddha's Birthday, Apr 8*). Celebrated at temples nationwide. Sweet tea is poured over a small image of the Buddha to signify devotion.
Takayama Matsuri (*Apr 14–15*), Gifu prefecture. A festival at Takayama's Hie Shrine, famed for its procession of richly decorated floats (*see p46*).
Yayoi Matsuri (*Apr 16–17*), Nikko, Tochigi prefecture. A festival at Futara-san Shrine including colorful floats.

May

Hakata Dontaku Matsuri (*May 3–4*), Fukuoka. Costumed citizens escort legendary gods on horseback.
Hamamatsu Matsuri (*Kite-Flying Festival, May 3–5*), Hamamatsu, Shizuoka prefecture. Amazing kites are flown.
Kanda Matsuri (*Sat & Sun closest to May 15, alternate, odd-numbered years*), Tokyo. Portable shrines are paraded in the neighborhood around Kanda Myojin Shrine; there is also a gala tea ceremony (*see pp46–7*).
Aoi Matsuri (*Hollyhock Festival, May 15*), Kyoto. Magnificent pageantry at the Shimogamo and Kamigamo shrines, reproducing past imperial processions (*see p46*).
Cormorant Fishing (*May 11–Oct 15*), Nagara River, Gifu city. Start of the season of night-time torchlit fishing with trained birds.
Tosho-gu Grand Festival (*May 17–18*), Nikko, Tochigi prefecture. As the highlight, 1,000 men in samurai armor escort three *mikoshi* (portable shrines) through the local streets.

Seasonal vegetables on sale in Naha, Okinawa

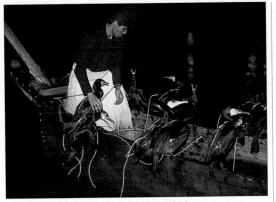

Cormorant fishing in Nagara River, Gifu, between May and October

Sanja Matsuri (3rd Fri–Sun in May), Tokyo. Locals parade *mikoshi* through the streets near the temple of Senso-ji, accompanied by music. Can be quite wild.

Mifune Matsuri (3rd Sun in May), Kyoto. An ancient boat festival charmingly re-enacted on the Oi River.

Rainy Season

From the pleasant climate of late spring, skies cloud and there are torrential downpours which are often the cause of landslides and flooding. A blanket of humidity envelops the landscape. Only Hokkaido, being so far north, manages to steer clear of such discomfort. The rest of Japan finds beauty in viewing hydrangeas and other flowers through the mists of mid-June to mid-July.

June

Sanno Matsuri (Jun 10–16), Tokyo. Portable shrines are carried around Hie Shrine in the Akasaka area.

Rice-Planting Festival (Jun 14), southern Osaka. Girls wearing traditional farmers' costumes ceremonially plant rice in the Sumiyoshi Shrine's fields, praying for a good harvest (see p46).

Chagu-chagu Umakko (Horse Festival, 2nd Sat in Jun), Morioka, Iwate prefecture. Decorated horses parade to Hachiman Shrine.

Summer

Technically summer begins in mid-July, as soon as the last clouds of the rainy season have left the sky. The heat and humidity continue to rise, mountains "open" for the season, and in mid-July, as soon as schools break for the vacations, the sea also "opens" for swimming. The air vibrates with the sound of insects; the rice grows fast; and people do what they can to keep cool. Even as the overheated landscape begins to sigh with exhaustion, frenzied summer celebrations break out, including spectacular firework displays that light up the night skies.

July

Yamakasa Matsuri (Jul 1–15), Fukuoka. Climaxes with a race of giant floats over 5 km (3 miles).

Tanabata Matsuri (Star Festival, Jul 7). Celebrated nationwide to mark a Chinese legend (see p47). Stems of bamboo are decorated with paper streamers inscribed with poems. The week-long Hiratsuka Tanabata in Kanagawa prefecture features Disney-style mechanical exhibits in competition.

Obon (Jul 13–16; held in Aug in most areas). See under August, page 50.

Nachi no Hi-Matsuri (Fire Festival, Jul 14), Nachi-Katsura, Wakayama prefecture. At Nachi Shrine, 12 massive torches are carried by priests in white robes.

Gion Matsuri (Jul 1–29, esp 17 and 24), Kyoto. The city's biggest festival, dating from the 9th century, when the people were seeking the protection of the gods from a deadly pestilence that was ravaging the local population. The streets are especially crowded for the parade of fabulous ancient floats on the 17th.

Kangensai Music Festival (late Jul–early Aug), Miyajima, Hiroshima prefecture. Classical court music and dance performed on beautifully decorated boats at Itsukushima Shrine.

Tenjin Matsuri (Jul 24–25), Osaka. Celebrated at Tenman-gu Shrine. A flotilla of boats carries portable shrines down the Dojima River accompanied by the sound of drumbeats.

Sumidagawa Hanabi Taikai (last Sat in Jul), Tokyo. Spectacular fireworks on the Sumida River near Asakusa; a revival of Edo-era celebrations.

Carrying torches at Nachi no Hi-Matsuri

Fall colors at Sounkyo Gorge in central Hokkaido

August

Neputa Matsuri *(Aug 1–7)*, Hirosaki, and **Nebuta Matsuri** *(Aug 2–7)*, Aomori. These festivals are so spectacular they are televised. Massive illuminated and painted papier mâché figures are paraded on floats *(see p47)*.

Kanto Matsuri *(Aug 3–6)*, Akita. Men compete in balancing huge poles hung with lanterns on their shoulders, foreheads, chins, and hips.

Sendai Tanabata *(Aug 6–8)*, Sendai, Miyagi prefecture. In Sendai's traditional version of the festival celebrated in July elsewhere, streets are decorated with colored paper streamers and hanging banners.

Awa-Odori *(Aug 12–15)*, Tokushima, Shikoku. The whole city sings and dances for four days and nights; the festival originally commemorated the building of the castle here in 1587.

Girls holding bamboo decorated with paper strips, Sendai Tanabata

Obon *(Festival of the Dead, Aug 13–16)*. Religious rites in connection with the Buddhist belief that spirits return to this world to visit loved ones in summer. A big family occasion, with everyone visiting, cleaning, and decorating tombs. Communal Bon Odori dance parties are held most evenings *(see p47)*.

Daimonji Bonfire *(Aug 16)*, Kyoto. Five large bonfires on the hills surrounding the city burn to mark the end of Obon, followed by dancing.

September

Hachiman-gu Festival *(Sep 14–16)*, Kamakura. A procession of floats and horseback archery at the Hachiman-gu Shrine draw a big crowd *(see p47)*.

Fall

Although the children are back at school and the sea is once again "closed," the heat goes on. Now is the time to start thinking about harvesting the rice. Apples flood the shops, leaves start to fall, and snow will soon begin in the north.

October

Kunchi Matsuri *(Oct 7–9)*, Nagasaki. A dragon dance of Chinese origin winds between floats with umbrella-shaped decorations at Suwa Shrine.

Takayama Matsuri *(Oct 9–10)*, Gifu prefecture. Held at Takayama's Hachiman-gu Shrine, this harvest festival is most memorable for a procession with ornate floats.

Kenka Matsuri *(Oct 11–13)*, Himeji, Hyogo prefecture. At Matsubara Shrine, nearly naked youths carrying *mikoshi* challenge each others' skills in balancing.

Doburoku Matsuri *(Oct 14–19)*, Shirakawa-go, Gifu prefecture. A harvest festival with dancing and drinking.

Nagoya Festival *(Fri–Sun in mid-Oct)*. Long procession in Nagoya with impersonations of historical characters.

Tosho-gu Fall Festival *(Oct 17)*, Nikko, Tochigi prefecture. Armor-clad samurai escort a portable shrine.

Jidai Matsuri *(Festival of the Ages, Oct 22)*, Kyoto. One of the city's big three festivals. Citizens in colorful costumes re-create 1,200 years of the city's history at Heian Shrine *(see p47)*.

Kurama Matsuri *(Fire Festival, Oct 22)*, Kyoto. Torches lining the route to Yuki Shrine, Kurama, are set alight, and children march through them holding more torches.

November

Karatsu Kunshi *(Nov 2–4)*, Kyushu. Celebrated at Karatsu Shrine and known for its colorful parade of floats.

Daimyo Gyoretsu *(Nov 3)*, Hakone. A re-enactment of a feudal lord's procession along the old Tokaido road between Edo and Kyoto.

Tori-no-ichi *(Rake Fair, mid-Nov)*, Tokyo. Stalls at the Otori Shrine near Asakusa sell ornately decorated rakes *(kumade)* for raking in money next year.

Shichi-go-san *(Seven-Five-Three Children's Festival, Nov 15)*. Parents take children of these ages to shrines in appreciation of their health and to pray for further blessings. There are wonderful photo opportunities of kimono-clad kids.

Winter

The cold season begins in Hokkaido, Northern Honshu, and to the west of the Japan Alps in late fall, with the first snows. By contrast, the east coast – including Tokyo – rarely experiences more than a few days of snow a year. Southern Kyushu remains quite dry and warm through the winter; Okinawa even more so. The period around New Year is one of the year's peak travel times.

December
On Matsuri *(Dec 15–18)*, Nara. Celebrated at Kasuga Shrine. A procession of courtiers, retainers, and wrestlers of ancient times.
Hagoita-Ichi *(Battledore Fair, Dec 17–19)*, Tokyo. Ornately decorated battledores are sold in the precincts of Senso-ji Temple.
Namahage *(Dec 31)*, Oga, Akita prefecture. Grotesquely masked men visit households with children, scaring them into being good.
Okera Mairi Ceremony *(Dec 31)*, Kyoto. A sacred fire is lit at Yasaka Shrine; people each take some embers home to start their own fires of the new year.

January
New Year's Day *(Jan 1)*. Japan's most important religious festival. Most people eat *soba* noodles the night before to bring long life. Witnessing the first sunrise is considered very lucky. The first few days are family-oriented, with visits to temples and shrines to buy lucky talismans for the year ahead.

Tokyo fireman at the Dezomeshiki, or New Year's Parade

Dezomeshiki *(New Year's Parade, Jan 6)*, Tokyo. Dazzling display by Tokyo firemen in traditional uniforms, performing acrobatic tricks on top of bamboo ladders.
Usokae *(Bullfinch Exchange, Jan 7)*, Dazaifu, Fukuoka prefecture. Festival of Dazaifu Tenman-gu Shrine.
Toka Ebisu Festival *(Jan 9–11)*, Osaka. Celebrated at Imamiya Shrine. Ebisu is worshiped by those who pray for good commercial fortune in the year ahead.

Yamayaki *(Grass Fire Festival, 2nd Sun in Jan)*, Nara. Old grass is burned on Mount Wakakusayama to initiate new growth.

February
Setsubun *(Bean-throwing Festival, Feb 3)*. Nationwide. Celebrities at major temples throw dried soy beans into crowds of onlookers, symbolizing the casting out of bad spirits.
Lantern Festival *(Feb 3 or 4)*, Nara. Some 3,000 candlelit lanterns attract huge crowds to the Kasuga Shrine.
Yuki Matsuri *(Snow Festival, for 7 days starting 2nd week in Feb)*, Sapporo, Hokkaido. Vast sculptures carved from snow and ice fill Odori Park.
Saidai-ji Eyo Matsuri *(Naked Festival, 3rd Sat in Feb)*, Saidai-ji, Okayama prefecture. Celebrated at Saida-ji Temple. Young male devotees wearing *fundoshi* (loin cloths) jostle for a pair of sacred wands thrown into the darkness by priests.

Public Holidays

If a public holiday falls on a Sunday, the following Monday is also a public holiday.
New Year's Day (Jan 1)
Coming-of-Age Day (2nd Mon in Jan)
National Foundation Day (Feb 11)
Vernal Equinox Day (around Mar 20)
Showa Day (Apr 29)
Constitution Memorial Day (May 3)
Greenery Day (May 4)
Children's Day (May 5)
Marine Day (3rd Mon in Jul)
Respect-for-the-Aged Day (3rd Mon in Sep)
Fall Equinox Day (around Sep 23)
Health-Sports Day (2nd Mon in Oct)
Culture Day (Nov 3)
Labor Thanksgiving Day (Nov 23)
Emperor's Birthday (Dec 23)

One of the snow carvings at Yuki Matsuri, Sapporo

The Climate of Japan

Japan's climate varies primarily with latitude, from cool, temperate Hokkaido to subtropical Okinawa. Most of the country is warm, temperate, and rainy; temperatures are cooler year-round in the mountains. The other key distinction is between the Pacific and Japan Sea coasts. Both have a lot of rain in June and July. The Pacific coast also has heavy rainfall and typhoons in August and September but is sunny in winter, while the Japan Sea coast has long spells of rain and snow in winter.

Subtropical Iriomote Island, south of Okinawa Island

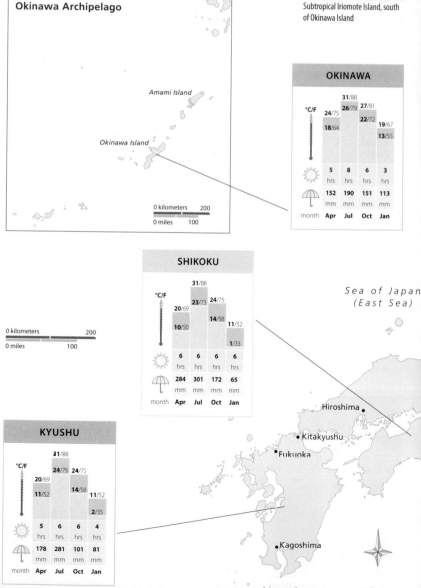

Okinawa Archipelago

Amami Island

Okinawa Island

0 kilometers 200
0 miles 100

OKINAWA

°C/F			
	31/88		
24/75	26/79	27/81	
18/64		22/72	19/67
			13/55

☼	5 hrs	8 hrs	6 hrs	3 hrs

☂	152 mm	190 mm	151 mm	113 mm

| month | Apr | Jul | Oct | Jan |

SHIKOKU

°C/F			
	31/88		
20/69	23/73	24/75	
10/50		14/58	11/52
			1/33

☼	6 hrs	6 hrs	6 hrs	6 hrs

☂	284 mm	301 mm	172 mm	65 mm

| month | Apr | Jul | Oct | Jan |

Sea of Japan (East Sea)

0 kilometers 200
0 miles 100

Hiroshima

Kitakyushu

Fukuoka

KYUSHU

°C/F			
	31/88		
20/69	24/75	24/75	
11/52		14/58	11/52
			2/35

☼	5 hrs	6 hrs	6 hrs	4 hrs

☂	178 mm	281 mm	101 mm	81 mm

| month | Apr | Jul | Oct | Jan |

Kagoshima

HOKKAIDO

Average monthly maximum temperature
Average monthly minimum temperature
Freezing point
Average daily hours of sunshine
Average monthly precipitation

°C/F	Apr	Jul	Oct	Jan
max	11/52	25/77	15/61	-2/28
min	1/33	16/61	5/40	-11/12
sunshine	6 hrs	6 hrs	5 hrs	3 hrs
precipitation	60 mm	78 mm	114 mm	102 mm

NORTHERN HONSHU

°C/F	Apr	Jul	Oct	Jan
max	16/61	28/82	20/69	5/41
min	6/43	21/70	12/54	-1/30
sunshine	6 hrs	6 hrs	5 hrs	2 hrs
precipitation	101 mm	181 mm	159 mm	194 mm

Snow melting in Daisetsu-zan National Park, Hokkaido

Climate Zones

Hokkaido: cool, temperate, rainy conditions, with long, cold winters and short, warm summers; year-round precipitation, though notably drier than the rest of Japan.

Honshu, Shikoku, Kyushu: warm, temperate, rainy conditions. Temperatures vary with latitude: winters from cold to mild, summers from warm to hot; year-round precipitation, heaviest in summer/fall on Pacific coast, in summer/winter on Japan Sea coast.

Okinawa: subtropical. Hot, humid summers and warm winters; heavy rainfall year-round peaking in summer.

Pacific Ocean

CENTRAL AND WESTERN HONSHU

°C/F	Apr	Jul	Oct	Jan
max	19/67	30/86	22/72	9/48
min	9/48	22/72	13/55	0/32
sunshine	6 hrs	5 hrs	5 hrs	6 hrs
precipitation	138 mm	171 mm	129 mm	44 mm

Cherry blossoms in Central Honshu

THE HISTORY OF JAPAN

From the origins of the Japanese race to its military behavior in World War II, Japan's history is still subject to conjecture. What is indisputable is that the people of this archipelago were able to avail themselves of the fruits of continental civilization even as their isolation protected them from attack. As a result, Japan has one of the most distinct of all the many Chinese-influenced cultures in Asia.

During glacial epochs when the sea level was low, Japan's first inhabitants may have reached the archipelago overland from Sakhalin and Siberia, China and Korea, or the Okinawa islands. Crude stone tools found at sites in Aichi and Tochigi prefectures may date back 40,000 years.

Past discoveries posit the emergence of the hunting and gathering society known as Jomon around 14,500 BC. Jomon pottery is among the world's oldest and includes vessels and figurines, particularly of women. Mounds of shells and other evidence indicate that the diet included fish, shellfish, deer, wild pigs, and wild plants and seeds. In the Kanto Plain (near Tokyo), the Jomon culture in its later stages included village-like groupings.

Rice agriculture and bronze, iron, and other crafts are believed to have reached Kyushu island via Korea during the Yayoi period. The Yayoi people spread from Kyushu to Honshu and Shikoku over time, pushing the earlier inhabitants north. Chinese histories record a visit by an envoy of Himiko, queen of Yamatai, to the Chinese kingdom of Wei in 239,

but Yamatai's location is still open to debate. Aristocratic orders emerged, including that of the emperor (a line unbroken to the present day), said to be descended from the sun goddess Amaterasu. Figures of high rank were buried in *kofun* (tumuli), along with clay sculptures, armor, mirrors, and jewelry.

By the late 6th century, tribes that had migrated to the fertile lands of Yamato *(see p191)* were engaged in a power struggle over the introduction of Buddhism. Prince Shotoku, appointed regent by Empress Suiko in 593, helped seal victory for the pro-Buddhist camp. The temple Horyu-ji *(see p200)* was completed in 607.

In 701, the Taiho code, a penal and administrative system based on the Chinese model, was in place. The temples of Nara *(see pp194–9)*, which became the capital in 710, epitomize this Chinese influence and are some of the best intact examples of their kind. With the completion of the *Man'yoshu*, the earliest known Japanese poetry, in 759, the culture began to establish a clear voice of its own.

Periods at a Glance

Jomon	14,500–300 BC
Yayoi	300 BC–AD 300
Kofun /Asuka	300–710
Hakuho	645–710
Nara	710–794
Heian	794–1185
Kamakura	1185–1333
Muromachi	1333–1568
Momoyama	1568–1600
Tokugawa (Edo)	1600–1868
Meiji	1868–1912
Taisho	1912–1926
Showa	1926–1989
Heisei	1989–present

300 BC–AD 300 Continental methods of farming, metalworking, pottery, and other skills reach southwestern Japan via Korea, and spread through islands

710 Heijo-kyo (Nara) made capital

701 Taiho code put in place, the basis of the first Japanese legal system

AD 1	200	400	600

Yayoi earthenware

239 Himiko, queen of Yamatai, sends envoy to kingdom of Wei in China

587 Power struggle over introduction of Buddhism from China

712 *Kojiki* completed, Japan's oldest historical account

Detail from a 16th-century screen painting, showing festivals and seasonal customs month-by-month in the Momoyama period

Court Life and The Tale of Genji

Tale of Genji scroll

Court life in Kyoto focused on romance, aesthetic pursuits, and fastidious observation of precedent and ritual, as documented in the *Pillow Book* of court lady Sei Shonagon in the late 10th century. The *Tale of Genji*, written in the early 11th century by Sei Shonagon's rival, Murasaki Shikibu, a court lady of the Fujiwara clan, is possibly the world's oldest novel. It depicts the loves and sorrows of a fictitious prince, Genji, and, after he dies, the amorous pursuits of a man whom Genji mistakenly thought was his son. The story has been illustrated in countless scrolls and other media.

Heian Period

The powerful Fujiwara family and Emperor Kammu built a new capital, Heian-kyo, now Kyoto *(see pp158–83)*, in 794. The new system, also based on Chinese models, held that the land and people were ultimately the property of the emperor. Tax-exempt status was granted to Buddhist institutions, large landholders, and settlers who would expand the state's frontiers. Meanwhile, the Fujiwara clan gained influence by acting as regents, and intermarriage with the imperial family. A pattern emerged in which emperors would abdicate, name a younger successor, enter a monastery, then exercise power from behind the scenes.

Buddhism's influence continued as proponents such as Saicho adapted it, launching the Tendai, Shingon, and Pure-Land schools *(see p279)*. Powerful temples like Enryaku-ji

(see pp182–3) grew militant in faceoffs with other temples and the government, creating armies of warrior-monks.

Ironically, Buddhism's abhorrence of killing fed the nobility's contempt for the farmer-warriors – the early samurai *(see pp58–9)* – on the frontier, who battled the indigenous Ainu people *(see p291)* and each other. After 1100, the court could no longer control infighting, and tensions rose between two clans of farmer-warriors from the northeast: the Taira and the Minamoto. By 1160, ruthless Taira no Kiyomori was the most powerful man in Japan. But the Minamoto, led by the brothers Yoshitsune and Yoritomo, fought back to defeat the Taira and establish the first military shogunate at Kamakura *(see pp138–41)* in 1185.

Kamakura Shogunate

Deliberately basing his government far from the imperial court in the village of Kamakura, Minamoto no Yoritomo carefully crafted a system that benefited his *bushi* (warrior) peers and brought 150 years of relative peace and stability. Yoritomo's direct heirs were shoguns only in name, however, as they were dominated by hereditary regents from the military Hojo family of Kamakura. The Hojo assumed the prerogatives of power while granting the imperial institution and nobility the privilege of signing off on policy.

Wooden statue of Minamoto no Yoritomo

The *Tale of the Heike*, a chronicle of the war between the Taira and Minamoto clans, was first recited to *biwa* (lute) accompaniment at this time.

Toji temple

794 Heian-kyo (Kyoto) becomes capital, which it remains until 1868

823 Kukai, leading proponent of Shingon Buddhism, appointed head of Toji temple

985 Genshin writes tract promoting Pure-Land Buddhism

1087 Emperor Shirakawa abdicates and becomes first cloistered emperor

| 800 | 900 | 1000 | 1100 |

801 Warriors sent to Northern Honshu to battle Ezo tribes

866 First Fujiwara regent assumes post

940 First uprising by a warrior member of the Taira clan

c.1000 *Tale of Genji* written by court lady Murasaki Shikibu

The Portuguese in Kyushu – the "Southern Barbarians" who introduced firearms and Christianity to Japan

Temples and works of art were created in Kamakura, reflecting Yoritomo's warrior ideals of stoicism, self discipline, frugality, and loyalty. Zen Buddhism, as imported from China, was popular with the samurai, while the Pure-Land, True-Pure-Land, and Nichiren Buddhist sects promoted salvation for the common people.

Mongol invasions were repelled twice in the 13th century, but weakened the resources and command of Kamakura. The end came in 1333, when the Ashikaga clan, led by Takauji, toppled the Kamakura shogunate. However, the power systems instigated by Yoritomo and the Hojo influenced Japanese life for five more centuries.

Muromachi-period sword guard

Muromachi Shogunate

With military power back with the imperial court in Kyoto, arts such as Noh drama and the tea ceremony flowered under the patronage of Shogun Ashikaga Yoshimasa. However, a succession dispute split the court into southern and northern factions.

With leaders engaged in power struggles, chaos and famine were common. The nadir was reached during the Onin War (1467–77), when arson and looting destroyed much of Kyoto.

The Muromachi period, named for the Kyoto district where the Ashikagas built their palace, was a time of craven ambition that unleashed every class in society to vie for advantage. Warfare, once the exclusive business of samurai, now involved armies of footsoldiers (ashigaru) recruited from the peasantry, who could hope for promotion based on success in the battlefields.

In 1542 a trio of Portuguese from a shipwrecked junk emerged in Tanegashima, an island off Kyushu, and introduced firearms to Japan. Francis Xavier, a founding member of the Society of Jesus, established a Jesuit mission at Kagoshima in 1549. The contact with Europeans further destabilized the political situation and set the stage for the first of the great unifiers, Oda Nobunaga, who entered Kyoto in 1568.

1180–85 Minamoto clan defeats the Taira and establishes Kamakura shogunate

Great Buddha statue at Kamakura

c. 1400 Zeami performing Noh dramas and writing

1467 Devastating Onin War begins. Vast sections of Kyoto are burned over the next decade

| 1200 | 1300 | 1400 | 1500 |

1160 Ascendant Taira clan under Taira no Kiyomori suppresses its rivals, the Minamoto, and dominates court life

1281 Second Mongol invasion

1274 First Mongol invasion

1242 Emperor Shijo dies without naming heir, setting off succession dispute

1560–80 Oda Nobunaga victorious in battles for hegemony of Japan

1428 Peasant uprising in Kyoto

1401 Formal relations with China reestablished

The Samurai

The samurai, also known as *bushi*, emerged in the 9th century when the emperor's court in Kyoto, disdaining warfare, delegated the overseeing and defense of far-flung holdings to constables and local farmer-warriors. Affiliated to *daimyo* (lords of noble descent), the samurai formed their own hereditary clans over time and became more powerful than the emperor; from their ranks emerged the shogunates (military dictatorships) of the 12th–19th centuries. Strict codes of loyalty and behavior, called *bushido* ("way of the warrior"), were inspired in part by Zen Buddhism and included ritualized acts of suicide (*seppuku*) to prove honor.

Castle towns were built in strategic positions by powerful samurai. The most distinctive castles, such as at Himeji (*see pp210–13*) and Osaka, date from the 16th century.

Seppuku, also known less formally as *harakiri*, was the honorable method of suicide, whereby the samurai would disembowel himself in front of witnesses.

On the wet and windy night of October 20, the armies massed in the hills around Sekigahara. At 8am the following morning, 100,000 samurai went to war.

Most military archers were mounted on horseback.

Oda Nobunaga (1534–82) was the first of the "Three Heroes" of samurai history, who between them unified most of Japan. The other two were Toyotomi Hideyoshi (1537–98) and Tokugawa Ieyasu (1543–1616).

Battle of Sekigahara

After Toyotomi Hideyoshi died, daimyo *from eastern and western Japan fell into dispute and sent their samurai, led by Tokugawa Ieyasu and Ishida Mitsunari, to battle. Ieyasu won the battle, in a valley in Central Honshu on October 21, 1600, and subsequently founded the Tokugawa shogunate.*

Saigo Takamori (1827–77) was one of the last samurai. After helping to overthrow the Tokugawa shogunate and leading the Satsuma Rebellion, he committed suicide.

The *daimyo* were the hereditary, landholding lords of the feudal era, to whom most samurai swore their allegience. Under the Tokugawa shogunate the *daimyo* were forced to journey to Edo every two years with all their attendants.

Steel swords were first forged in Japan in the 8th century. The samurai wore pairs of swords, long and short, from 1600. They were banned after the Meiji Restoration of 1868.

Every warrior took a musket, spear, or bow into battle, as well as a sword.

Samurai Battledress

The samurai developed remarkably ornate and colorful armor from the 9th century on. The earliest style, *oyoroi*, was designed for archers on horseback. In the Muromachi period it was superseded by lighter armor, *domaru*, worn by foot soldiers, and later a style called *tosei gusoku*, shown here, which helped protect against firearms.

Kabuto (helmet)

Mempo (face defense)

Sode (shoulder defense)

Do (cuirass)

Kote (arm defense)

Kusazuri (upper thigh defense)

Haidate (lower thigh defense)

Suneate (shin guard)

Ronin ("floating men") were samurai without allegiance to particular masters. In the 47 Ronin Incident of 1703, portrayed in the Kabuki play *Chushingura*, a group of *ronin* avenged the killing of their lord, then were ordered to commit suicide by the shogunate (see p107).

Long vertical banners (nobori) were hung on poles to identify different military families and groups of warriors.

Heads were collected in the thousands and set by roadsides.

Screen depicting the Battle of Nagashino in 1575, won by Oda Nobunaga's 3,000 musketeers

Momoyama Period

After Japan had been racked by over a century of debilitating, inconclusive warfare, Oda Nobunaga, who rose through military ranks in the provinces, set out to unify the nation under his rule. From 1568–76 Nobunaga defeated rival warlord Asai Nagamasa; burned down Enryaku-ji, where militant monks had long challenged the court and their Buddhist rivals; drove Ashikaga Yoshiaki into exile; and deployed 3,000 musketeers to massacre the Takeda forces at the Battle of Nagashino. In 1580, in his last great military exploit, Nobunaga obtained the surrender of Ishiyama Hongan-ji, a nearly

Momoyama-period detail at Nishi Hongan-ji, Kyoto

impregnable temple fortress in what is now central Osaka. Surrounded by moats and walls, the temple had been the power base of the Buddhist True-Pure-Land sect.

By 1582, when he was forced to commit suicide by a treasonous vassal, Nobunaga was in control of 30 of Japan's 68 provinces. Nobunaga's deputy, a warrior of humble birth named Toyotomi Hideyoshi, promptly avenged his lord and continued the work of unification, launching epic campaigns that brought Shikoku (1585), Kyushu (1587), the Kanto region (1590), and Northern Honshu (1591) under his control. He followed up by destroying many of the castles and forts belonging to potential rivals, confiscating weapons belonging to peasants, and devising a system in which peasants held their own small plots and paid a fixed tax directly to the central government.

In his later years, Hideyoshi ordered two unsuccessful invasions of Korea and persecuted the Portuguese missionaries and their Japanese converts (see p238). Like Oda Nobunaga, however, Hideyoshi never actually claimed the title of shogun but became obsessed with ensuring the perpetuation of his line after his death. Two years after his death in 1598, however, dissension among his retainers led to the Battle of Sekigahara (see pp58–9), in which Tokugawa Ieyasu emerged victorious.

The Tokugawa Shogunate

Named shogun by the emperor in 1603, Ieyasu split the population into rigidly

1615 Siege of Osaka Castle

Osaka Castle

1635 All foreign commerce confined to artificial island of Dejima in Nagasaki Bay. From 1641, only Dutch and Chinese allowed access

1689 Haiku poet Basho departs on his journey to the north

1707 Last eruption of Mount Fuji

| 1600 | 1625 | 1650 | 1675 | 1700 |

1590 Hideyoshi controls all Japan

1597 Violent persecution of Christians in Nagasaki

1614 Christianity banned

1600 Tokugawa Ieyasu wins battle of Sekigahara, achieves hegemony over Japan

1657 Meireki fire in Edo kills over 100,000

Basho

1703 Suicide of the 47 Ronin (see p59)

defined hereditary classes. To end turf wars, samurai were forbidden to own land and could reside only within certain quarters of castle towns. Farmers were allotted small plots, which they were obliged to cultivate. Artisans formed the next class, merchants the bottom. Movement between regions was strictly regulated, and families or whole villages could be punished for crimes by their kin or neighbors.

Fireman official's garment in Edo

The *daimyo* or lords who governed regions were subject to Tokugawa authority and shuffled to different regions if their service was not approved. After 1635, the *daimyo* and their samurai retinue were forced to reside every other year in the city of Edo (Tokyo), the new seat of the shogunate.

Isolation and The Rise of Edo

William Adams, an Englishman who reached Japan on a Dutch ship in 1600, served Ieyasu in various capacities over the next two decades (as portrayed in James Clavell's 1976 book *Shogun*). During this time, the English, Dutch, Portuguese, Spanish, and New World governments made overtures to the shogunate on trade. However, the increasingly xenophobic Tokugawa regime restricted all foreign shipping to Nagasaki from 1635; only Chinese and Dutch traders were allowed from 1641. This heralded 200 years of isolation from the rest of the world. Persecution of Christians intensified.

While Kyoto remained the official capital through the Tokugawa period, Edo eclipsed it in size and was probably the largest city in the world by around 1700. Edo also hosted an explosion of arts such as Kabuki and Bunraku theater *(see pp40–41)* and the *ukiyo-e* works *(see p89)* of Utamaro, Sharaku, Hokusai, and Hiroshige. Patrons included the merchant class and samurai.

In 1853 Commodore Matthew Perry steamed into Edo Bay with four US vessels to challenge Japan's refusal to enter into international relations. Weakened by unrest from within its own and other ranks, the shogunate could only accede to Perry's demands. Samurai from the Satsuma, Choshu, and Tosa domains in Kyushu, Western Honshu, and Shikoku became the driving force behind a successful restoration of imperial power and a reorganization of the government carried out in 1868.

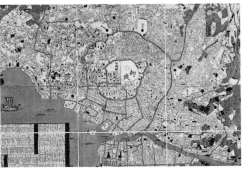

Early map of Edo, which outgrew Kyoto under the Tokugawa shogunate

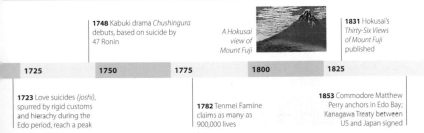

1748 Kabuki drama *Chushingura* debuts, based on suicide by 47 Ronin

A Hokusai view of Mount Fuji

1831 Hokusai's *Thirty-Six Views of Mount Fuji* published

1725	1750	1775	1800	1825

1723 Love suicides *(joshi)*, spurred by rigid customs and hierachy during the Edo period, reach a peak

1782 Tenmei Famine claims as many as 900,000 lives

1853 Commodore Matthew Perry anchors in Edo Bay; Kanagawa Treaty between US and Japan signed

Wood-block print of Sino-Japanese War of 1894–5

Meiji Restoration

Emperor Meiji (1852–1912) was 16 when the restoration of imperial rule was declared on January 3, 1868. Tokyo was swiftly made the new capital.

A new centralized system pressed for changes that would render Japan capable of competing with the West. Military conscription and the elimination of the hereditary samurai class were undertaken to create a modern fighting force, provoking furious resistance from samurai in 1874–6. *Daimyo* domains were gradually transformed into prefectures, although daimyo and court nobles lingered in the form of a new class called *kazoku*. Universal literacy became a goal. By 1884, tax and banking reforms, and an industrial strategy aimed at exports were underway. The Meiji Constitution of 1889, promulgated by the emperor, allowed the military direct access to the throne while creating a house of peers and a lower house.

Following disputes over control of the Korean peninsula, the Sino-Japanese War of 1894–5 ended with Japan's victory over China, but showed that greater military strength would be needed for the nation to contend as an imperial power equal with the West.

By the turn of the century, the transformation to an industrial economy, with textiles the chief export, was well underway. A second imperialist conflict, the Russo-Japanese war of 1904–5, ended with Japan aggrandizing its claims to Korea, which was annexed in 1910, and southern Manchuria.

During the final decade of Meiji's reign, the home ministry stressed reverence for the emperor, the family, the Shinto religion, and military and national heroes. Suppression of groups seen as enemies of the state became the government's prerogative.

War with China and World War II

The attempt to transform Japan from a feudal to a modern industrial state caused severe dislocation. By 1929, when the stock market collapsed, resentment against those who had prospered from exports intensified. Young officers, chafing to restore national pride, began assassinating rich moderates, while militarists and oligarchs in the government believed that seizing land from China and Russia would secure raw materials and improve national security. At the same time, a pan-Asianist movement, which saw Japan on a mission to lead Asia out of servility, construed the Chinese resistance to Japanese domination as an insult. By 1937, the country was embroiled in an unwinnable war with China that further estranged it from the rest of the world.

Women in traditional Japanese and 1920s Western dress

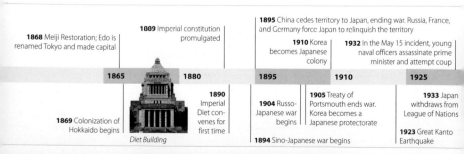

1868 Meiji Restoration; Edo is renamed Tokyo and made capital

1889 Imperial constitution promulgated

1895 China cedes territory to Japan, ending war. Russia, France, and Germany force Japan to relinquish the territory

1910 Korea becomes Japanese colony

1932 In the May 15 incident, young naval officers assassinate prime minister and attempt coup

1865 — **1880** — **1895** — **1910** — **1925**

1869 Colonization of Hokkaido begins

1890 Imperial Diet convenes for first time

Diet Building

1904 Russo-Japanese war begins

1905 Treaty of Portsmouth ends war. Korea becomes a Japanese protectorate

1894 Sino-Japanese war begins

1933 Japan withdraws from League of Nations

1923 Great Kanto Earthquake

Aftermath of the bombing of Tokyo in 1945

When the US cut off Japanese access to oil, Tokyo made the desperate decision to seize Pacific territory in a sneak attack on Pearl Harbor, Hawaii, in December 1941. A few months later, Japan took Southeast Asia.

By 1944, American bombers were decimating Japanese cities, but the Japanese army was determined not to surrender unconditionally, opting instead for a suicidal defensive strategy. In August 1945, the US dropped atomic bombs on Hiroshima and Nagasaki, and the Soviet Union entered the war in the Pacific. Emperor Hirohito ordered the cabinet to sue for peace.

Akihito, who was made emperor in 1989

Japan Since 1945

Although World War II ended in disaster, the experience mobilized the Japanese people toward self-discipline and cooperation. The Allied Occupation force began arriving as millions of homeless Japanese returned to bombed-out cities. The emperor renounced his divine status and land reform was implemented. Against the backdrop of escalating Cold War tensions, the reformist ardor of the occupation leadership soon cooled; a general strike was canceled and communists were purged from government jobs.

By 1952, when the occupation ended, the war in Korea had turned into a boon for the Japanese economy. Industrial production surged as the average household set its sights on obtaining electrical appliances.

In 1960, massive protests against the ratification of the US-Japan Security Treaty rocked Japan, leading to the cancellation of a visit by President Eisenhower. The prime minister resigned.

Prosperity based on exports like automobiles and technological products made Japan one of the world's richest nations and helped keep the Liberal Democratic Party the dominant force in politics since its creation in 1955. In the 2009 general election, they were finally defeated by the Democratic Party of Japan. In March 2011, Tohuku, in northeast Japan, was hit by the largest recorded earthquake in Japan's history. The subsequent tsunami caused massive destruction along the northeast shoreline, and considerable damage to the Fukushima Daiichi nuclear power plant. Despite suffering major damage and loss of life, Japan is recovering.

High-tech games in Roppongi, Tokyo

1937 Sino-Japanese war of 1937–45 begins; 140,000 Chinese massacred in Nanjing

1945 Atomic bombs dropped on Hiroshima and Nagasaki; Japan surrenders

1997 Economic recession in Southeast Asia, spreading to Japan

1995 Great Hanshin Earthquake in Kobe; fanatical cult releases sarin gas on Tokyo Subway

2001 Baby girl born to Crown Prince Naruhito

2014 Consumption tax rises from 5 to 8 percent

| 1940 | 1955 | 1970 | 1985 | 2000 | 2015 |

Prayers of a soldier

1964 Tokyo Olympics; first "bullet train"; government begins to promote computer industry

1989 Emperor Hirohito (Showa) dies; Akihito is new emperor

1941 Japan enters World War II

2011 Major earthquake and tsunami causes destruction to Northern Honshu

Shinkansen ("bullet train")

TOKYO
AREA BY AREA

Tokyo at a Glance

Japan's capital is situated on the banks of the Sumida River, by Tokyo Bay. As the fishing village of Edo it became the shogunate's center of power in 1590. The Shitamachi (low city) of merchants and artisans served the political and intellectual elite in the Yamanote (high city) on the hills to the west. Renamed Tokyo and made capital in 1868, the city was devastated by the Great Kanto Earthquake of 1923, followed by World War II bombing. It has since reinvented itself as one of the world's most modern, exciting, and energizing cities. Transportation is efficient: the easy-to-use Yamanote JR line circles the city, subway lines crisscross the center (see Back End Paper), and *shinkansen* lines link it with the rest of the country. It can be difficult to find individual buildings by their addresses (see pp377 and 383). The Tokyo Street Finder (see pp118–27) locates all the sights, restaurants, and hotels mentioned in this guide.

TOKYO ●

Locator Map

West Shinjuku (see pp96–7) is an area of soaring skyscrapers, providing a visible manifestation of the corporate wealth of Tokyo. The most impressive buildings are the Tokyo Metropolitan Government Offices, designed by Kenzo Tange.

SHINJUKU-DORI

EXPRESSWAY NO. 4

WESTERN TOKYO
(See pp92–103)

AOYAMA-DORI

EXPRESSWAY

Shibuya (see pp100–01) is a mixture of large department stores and smaller shops, all catering to young consumers. Adjacent to Shibuya are the equally fashion-oriented areas of Harajuku and Minami-Aoyama.

East Shinjuku (see pp94–5) comes alive when West Shinjuku shuts down. It encompasses a red-light area, countless bars, and various forms of entertainment from movies to *pachinko* parlors.

◄ Aerial view of Shibuya's famous pedestrian crossing

Ueno Park *(see pp82–3)* is one of Tokyo's most extensive green spaces, always crowded with locals. Spectacular in cherry-blossom season, it also merits an unhurried visit at other times of the year for its boating ponds and many temples, shrines, and museums.

VISITORS' CHECKLIST

Practical Information
🗼 12,810,000. 🛈 Tokyo Kotsu Kaikan: (03) 3201-3331; Narita airport: (0476) 34-8000.
🎎 Kanda Matsuri (Sat & Sun before May 15, alternate years), Sanja Matsuri (3rd Fri–Sun in May), Sanno Matsuri (Jun 16).

Transport
✈ Narita 60 km (37 miles) NE, Haneda 20 km (12 miles) S.

Tokyo National Museum *(see pp84–7)* consists of four main buildings, which exhibit a stunning array of Japanese art and archaeological artifacts – the largest such collection in the world – as well as some fascinating items from elsewhere in Asia.

NORTHERN TOKYO
(See pp80–91)

EXPRESSWAY NO. 1

EXPRESSWAY NO. 3

CENTRAL TOKYO
(See pp68–79)

SAKURADA DORI

EXPRESSWAY NO. 1

Senso-ji Temple *(see pp90–91)* offers an insight into the traditional side of Tokyo. Still attracting thousands of worshipers daily, it also has many craft shops lining its main approach.

| 0 kilometers | 2 |
| 0 mile | 1 |

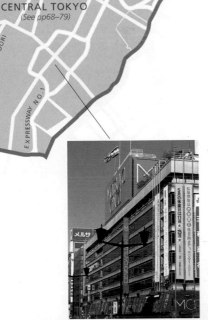

Ginza *(see pp70–71)* provides the archetypal Tokyo shopping experience, with its venerable department stores and small, exclusive shops, which have been joined by various international designer boutiques. Some excellent restaurants are also located here.

CENTRAL TOKYO

Situated to the north and west of the Sumida River, this area has been at the heart of Tokyo since the first shogun, Ieyasu, built his castle and capital where the Imperial Palace still stands today. Destroyed by a series of disasters, including the Great Kanto Earthquake of 1923 and the Allied bombing in World War II, the area has reinvented itself several times over. Ginza and Nihonbashi were commercial centers and are still thriving and prosperous, offering a mix of huge department stores and affluent side-street boutiques. For more down-to-earth shopping, there's the Jinbocho area for books, Akihabara for discount electronics and software, and the early-morning Tsukiji Fish Market. Central Tokyo's continuing political importance is evident in the Hibiya and Marunouchi districts, and the area is also home to two very different shrines: Kanda and Yasukuni. A selection of green spaces provides a respite from the frenetic bustle elsewhere.

Sights at a Glance

Notable Districts
1. Ginza see pp70–71
7. Nihonbashi District
8. Marunouchi District
9. Hibiya District
14. Jinbocho Booksellers' District
17. Akihabara Electronics District

Historic Buildings
2. Kabuki-za Theater
10. Diet Building
11. Imperial Palace

Shrines
13. Yasukuni Shrine
16. Kanda Myojin Shrine

Modern Architecture
6. Tokyo Tower
9. Tokyo International Forum

Parks and Gardens
4. Hama Detached Palace Garden
6. Shiba Park
12. Kitanomaru Park
15. Koishikawa Korakuen Garden

Market
3. Tsukiji Fish Market

River Trip
5. Sumida River Trip

See also Street Finder maps 3, 4, 5 & 6

Koishikawa Korakuen Garden in autumn

For keys to symbols see back flap

❶ Street-by-Street: Ginza
銀座

When Ieyasu moved his military capital to Edo in 1590, Ginza was all swamp and marshland. Once filled in, the area attracted tradesmen and merchants. The silver mint that provided Ginza's name, "silver place," was built in 1612. In 1872 fire destroyed everything and, with the Meiji Restoration in full swing, the government ordered English architect Thomas Waters to rebuild the area in red brick. From then on it was the focus for Western influences and all things modern, and is still one of Tokyo's great centers. Tiny shops selling traditional crafts mix with galleries, landmark department stores, and the ultra-modern Sony showroom for an unrivaled shopping experience.

Shoppers at the Ginza Yon-chome crossing

Mullion Building, housing Hankyu and Seibu department stores

Hankyu and Seibu
department stores focus on fashions, with a mix of Japanese and international labels.

Gallery Center Building
On the second floor of this modern building are a number of exclusive galleries showcasing Japanese and Western art. On the fifth is an auction house, and the sixth has the Youkyo Art Hall, with exhibits by artists working in different media.

Ginza Noh Theater

The Asahi Building
contains a traditional kimono shop, silversmiths, and several boutiques.

Namiki-Dori and Chuo-Dori
are now called "Brand Street" with boutiques such as Gucci, Dior, Louis Vuitton, and Cartier.

HARUMI-DORI

SOTOBORI-DORI

NAMIKI-DORI

MIYUKI-DORI

SUZU

Sony Showroom
Sony's latest technology and gadgets are on display on several floors here, and many can be tried out.

For hotels and restaurants see pp305–307 and pp324–329

Key

— Suggested walk route

▪▪▪ Train line

Printemps is a branch of the French department store. Parisian influence came to Ginza in the 1930s and can also be seen in the nearby French cafés and boutiques.

Wako Department Store
Opposite the San'ai Building, this enduring landmark was originally built in 1894. Its clocktower is a popular symbol of Ginza, and the window displays are always entertaining.

Locator Map
See Tokyo Street Finder map 5

Matsuya department store is another huge store stocking everything from food to bonsai. Restaurant City offers a wide range of cuisines.

Nihonbashi

Mikimoto
Visit the glittering interior of this shop, the original producer of cultured pearls.

Mitsukoshi Department Store
This classic Tokyo store retains an aura of glamour – some people still dress up to shop here. Don't miss the particularly sumptuous kimono department.

Kabuki-za Theater
(see p72)

Ginza Yon-chome crossing, one of the busiest in the world, is Ginza's main intersection.

San'ai Building
Made of glass, this building is at its best at dusk when the lights and neon signs inside shine through the glass, creating a magical effect.

0 meters 100
0 yards 100

❷ Kabuki-za Theater

歌舞伎座

4-12-15 Ginza. **Map** 5 C3. **Tel** (03) 3541-3131. Ⓢ Higashi-Ginza stn, Toei Asakusa & Hibiya lines. 📱 🔲 shochiku.co.jp/play/kabukiza/theater

Tokyo's principal theater for Kabuki *(see p41)* opened in 1889 during the reign of Emperor Meiji – a part of Kabuki's shift from daytime entertainment for the Shitamachi masses in Asakusa to a more high-brow art form.

The building is one of the oldest surviving examples of the use of Western building materials and techniques in traditional Japanese styles. Almost destroyed by the Allied bombing of 1945, the theater was rebuilt in 1951. Demolished again in 2010, the building was then reconstructed; it reopened in March 2013. Performances take place most days *(see p112)*..

A box of fish from Tsukiji market

❸ Tsukiji Fish Market

築地中央卸売市場

Map 5 C4. Ⓢ Tsukijishijo stn, Toei Oedo line. **Open** 5am–1pm daily. 🔲 tsukiji.or.jp/english/accessmap.html

A visit to this bustling fish market, officially Tokyo Central Wholesale Market, is an experience unique to Tokyo. It moved to this location from Nihonbashi after the 1923 earthquake, and its subsequent fires, destroyed the old one.

Every morning except Sunday, auctions are held from about 5:30am to 10am (the busiest time is 5am to 8am). During this time 15,000 restaurateurs and food sellers from all over the city buy 450 types of sea produce from about 1,700 stalls. The market itself is a huge hangar

Nakajima teahouse in Hama Detached Palace Garden

filled with tiny stalls, each crammed with fish still dripping sea water. In spite of the frantic pace most people are quite friendly and tolerant of casual visitors, although tourists can only watch proceedings from within a designated area.

A small bridge marks the entrance to the market. The river wharf where boats unload is over the bridge to the left. Just before the bridge is **Namiyoke Inari Jinja** (Wave-repelling Fox shrine), where fishermen and traders come to pray for safety and prosperity. Opposite is a street lined with shops selling everything from dried tuna to porcelain dishes. In the alleys to the right are more shops and stalls where excellent and cheap sushi, tempura, even curry, are sold.

The market may be moving to the Toyosu district in 2020,

however, a new fresh fish market is planned for this location if the Tsukiji Fish Market vacates it.

❹ Hama Detached Palace Garden

浜離宮庭園

Map 5 B4. **Tel** (03) 3541-0200. Ⓢ Shiodome stn, Oedo line. 🚉 Shinbashi stn, Yamanote line. 🚢 see Sumida River Trip. **Open** 9am–4pm. (Last adm 30 mins before closing.) 📱

Situated where the Sumida River empties into Tokyo Bay, this 25-hectare (62-acre) garden was built in 1654 as a retreat for the shogun's family, who also hunted duck here. America's former president, Ulysses S. Grant stayed in a villa in the gardens during his visit in 1879 and sipped green tea in Nakajima teahouse.

Tuna Fish Supplies

Tsukiji market specializes in *maguro* (tuna) from as far away as New Zealand and the North Atlantic. Japan consumes about 30 percent of the annual global 1.7 million ton tuna catch, and eats 80 percent of its tuna raw, as sashimi, which requires the best cuts of fish. Suppliers

Rows of frozen tuna at Tsukiji fish market

can demand prices of up to 10–20 times that of the lower-grade tuna. The Pacific Ocean's South Blue Fin tuna, a favorite for sashimi, is endangered. In spite of efforts to manage tuna numbers, the Blue Fin tuna population has been declining steadily. The Japanese fishing industry has come under a great deal of scrutiny, with other governments exerting pressure on Japan to keep a closer eye on its activities.

The garden grounds surrounding the duck ponds are still a pleasant, uncrowded place to stroll and sit. All of the original teahouses and villas, trees, and vegetation burned down after a bombing raid on November 29, 1944. **Nakajima teahouse** has been faithfully rebuilt, appearing to float over the large pond. Green tea and Japanese sweets are available here.

❺ Sumida River Trip

隅田川の屋形船

Map 5 C4, 4 F3. 🚢 every 25–35 mins; from Hama Detached Palace Garden 10:35am–4:15pm; from Asakusa 9:50am–6pm. **Tel** (0129) 977-311. 🖥 ☑ suijobus.co.jp/price/index.html

During the Edo period almost all commerce came to Tokyo via its waterways. As wheeled transport, particularly the railways, grew, the rivers and canals declined.

The city's main river, the Sumida, has been cleaned up to an extent, and river traffic is on the increase again. A little-seen view of Tokyo is available on the river trip from Hama Detached Palace Garden to Asakusa in Northern Tokyo. The boat squeezes through a gate in the sea wall into the open water where the Sumida river meets Tokyo Bay.

Hinode Pier is the first stop – it is also possible to start from here, and to take a number of other trips around Tokyo Bay. From Hinode the boat starts back up the river, passing first between Tsukiji and **Tsukuda island**, which escaped the worst of the World War II bombing and remains a center of old Edo culture. During the trip the boat passes under 12 bridges, each painted a different color. It is still possible to glimpse people in the narrow parks that line most of the banks beyond the sea walls. Near Asakusa there are long, low boats that take out groups for lantern-lit evening cruises.

❻ Shiba Park and Tokyo Tower

芝公園と東京タワー

Map 5 A4, 2 F5. 🚇 Shibakoen stn, Toei Mita line. Tokyo Tower: 🚇 Aka-banebashi stn, Oedo line. **Tel** (03) 3433-5111. **Open** 9am–10pm daily. 📷 (extra for higher viewpoint). ☑ tokyotower.co.jp

Shiba Park is a rather fragmented green space. A large part of it is a golf driving range, but a portion in the east is pleasantly landscaped with woods and a water course. The park used to be the Tokugawa family's graveyard. At its center is **Zojo-ji**, the family temple of the Tokugawas. It was founded in 1393 and Ieyasu moved it here in 1598 to protect his new capital spiritually from a southeasterly direction. The

The soaring Tokyo Tower, offering spectacular views of the city

present-day building dates from 1974; nearby are the rebuilt Daimon (big gate) and the Sanmon (great gate, 1622).

To the west of the park is **Tokyo Tower**. Completed in 1958, at 333 m (1,093 ft) tall, it is higher than the Eiffel Tower in Paris, on which it is based. The ground floor has an aquarium and elevators to the observation deck. Other floors house amusements. You can visit two viewpoints – the main one at 150 m (492 ft) and a higher one at 250 m (820 ft), with more spectacular views. Be sure to go on a clear day. As a lofty symbol of the city, Tokyo Tower has been usurped by the 634 m (2,080 ft) Tokyo Sky Tree completed in 2012.

Tokyo's skyline from the vantage point of the Sumida River

View of Mitsukoshi's central hall in Nihonbashi

❼ Nihonbashi District

日本橋地区

Map 5 C1–2, 6 D1. **S** Tokyo stn, Marunouchi line; Nihonbashi stn, Ginza, Tozai & Toei Asakusa lines; Mitsukoshimae stn, Ginza & Hanzomon lines. **R** Tokyo stn, many lines. Tokyo Stock Exchange: **Tel** (050) 3377-7254. **Open** 9–4pm Mon–Fri. Bridgestone Museum of Art: **Tel** (03) 3563-0241. **Open** 10am–6pm Tue–Sun (to 8pm Fri).

Nihonbashi was the mercantile and entrepreneurial center of Edo and Meiji Tokyo. Its name means "Japan's bridge" after the bridge over the Nihonbashi River that marked the start of the five major highways of the Edo period. After the destruction of the 1923 earthquake, shops, businesses, and banks started relocating to Marunouchi and Ginza; even the fish market moved to Tsukiji.

Although the area never regained its original importance, it is still a thriving commercial center, with dozens of bank headquarters as well as huge department stores and smaller traditional shops. **Mitsukoshi** has its main store here, on Mitsukoshimae. It started as a kimono shop in 1673. Head for the basement food market with its free samples, and the sixth-floor bargain counters where you can jostle with Tokyo's thrifty elite. To the west of

A robot trader exhibit, Tokyo Stock Exchange

Mitsukoshi, the **Bank of Japan**, built in 1896 and modeled on the Neo-Classical Berlin National Bank, was the first Western-style building designed by a Japanese architect, Kingo Tatsuno.

On the north bank of Nihonbashi River, just before **Nihonbashi bridge**, is the bronze marker from which distances to and from Tokyo are still measured. The bridge here today dates from 1911.

On the south bank of the river, east of the bridge, is the **Tokyo Stock Exchange**, which lists over 2,000 companies and is one of the world's top five. During the "bubble" economy of 1980s, it was possible to watch the frenetic hand signals of the traders. In 1999 trading was completely computerized, but this is still a great place to see how important commerce remains in Tokyo. The visitors' observation deck overlooks the trading floor and has some interesting exhibits comparing stock markets worldwide, with English and French explanations.

To the south of Nihonbashi bridge, the **Bridgestone Museum of Art** holds one of Japan's best collections of Western art, including works by Manet, Picasso, Rouault, and Brancusi. To its north, the **Pokemon Center** is a shop devoted to the famous animation characters.

❽ Marunouchi District

丸の内地区

Map 5 B1–2. **S** Tokyo stn, Marunouchi line. **R** Tokyo stn, many lines. Tokyo City-i (info center): **Open** 8am–8pm daily. **W** en.tokyocity-i.jp

This district lies to the south and west of Tokyo Station. During the Edo era, it earned the name "Gambler's Meadow" as its isolation made it an ideal place to gamble secretly. In the Meiji period the army used it, selling it in 1890 to Mitsubishi. The arrival of the railway increased the desirability of this barren wasteland as a business site, and after the 1923 earthquake, many other firms moved here.

Tokyo Station, designed by Kingo Tatsuno and completed in 1914, is based on the design of Amsterdam station. Its dome was damaged in the 1945 air raids and subsequently replaced by the polyhedron there today. The original reliefs adorning the domes above the north and south exits are worth a look, as is the Tokyo Station Hotel. Opposite the station's south gate is the shopping mall KITTE.

A short walk west of the station up Miyuki-dori and over the moat via the Wadakura bridge leads to the **Wadakura Fountain Park**, which contains some interesting water features. Returning over the Wadakura bridge, cross Hibiya-dori and turn right. After about 500 m (550 yds) is the **Meiji Seimeikan Building** (1934), with its huge Corinthian columns. Hiroshige, the woodblock print artist, was born on this site in 1797. Beyond, the **Imperial Theater** shows Broadway musicals and popular Japanese dramas.

Tokyo Station's Western-style facade

❾ Tokyo International Forum

東京国際フォーラム

Map 5 B2. **Tel** (03) 5221-9000.
🄢 Yurakucho stn, Yurakucho line;
Tokyo stn, Marunouchi line. 🚇 Tokyo
and Yurakucho stns, many lines.
Open 7am–11:30pm daily.
🆆 t-i-forum.co.jp/en

Designed by the American-based
Rafael Viñoly, and completed in
1996, the Forum is one of down
town Tokyo's most distinctive
and enjoyable buildings *(see
p29)*. A cultural center, it is made
up of two buildings: a curved,
glass atrium soaring 60 m
(200 ft), and a cube-like, white
structure housing four halls
(the largest seating 5,012). A
tree-shaded courtyard separates
the two, while glass walkways
provide an overhead link.

The interior of the huge
atrium is filled with light and
has a ceiling resembling a ship's
hull. There are shops, cafés, and
restaurants, all supported by
state-of-the-art facilities
including high-speed Internet
access available in the lobby.

The imposing granite exterior of the
Diet Building

❿ Hibiya District and the Diet Building

日比谷地区と国会議事堂

Map 2 F3, 5 A2, 5 B2. 🄢 Kokkai-
Gijidomae stn, Chiyoda & Marunouchi
lines; Hibiya stn, Toei Mita, Chiyoda &
Hibiya lines. Hibiya Park: **Open** 24
hours daily. Diet Building: **Tel** (03)
5521-7445. **Open** 8am–5pm Mon–Fri.
📷 (compulsory, by reservation).
🆆 sangiin.go.jp/eng/index.htm

Central Tokyo's only large,
Western-style park, Hibiya Park
is the focus of Hibiya district. Its
location, east of the
political centers of
Kasumigaseki and
the Diet Building,
makes it a favorite
place for protests,
especially on May
Day. The large band-
stand is occasionally
used for concerts.
Completed in 1936,
the **Diet Building**
houses the
legislature of the
Japanese govern-
ment, originally
established as the
Imperial Diet in the
Meiji era. Tours (in
Japanese only) cover
the well-worn inside,
including the Diet
chamber, where
you can see the
deliberations of
Diet members, and
the extravagantly
decorated rooms
used by the emperor
for official functions.

⓫ Imperial Palace

皇居

Map 3 A5, 3 B5, 5 A1, 5 B1. 🄢
Nijubashi stn, Chiyoda line. 🚇 Tokyo
stn, many lines. Imperial Palace:
Open Jan 2, Dec 23. East Garden of
the Imperial Palace: **Tel** (03) 3213-
1111. **Open** 9am–4:30pm Tue–Thu,
Sat, Sun (Mar–Oct: to 5pm; Nov–Feb:
to 4pm). 🆆 kunaicho.go.jp

Ieyasu, the first Tokugawa
shogun, started building his
castle here in 1590. In the Edo
period his successors made
this into the world's largest
castle; now only the inner
circle remains. The emperor
and his family still live in the
western part of the grounds
in the **Imperial Palace**, rebuilt
after the previous one was
bombed in World War II. Public
access is allowed twice a year: at
New Year and on the emperor's
birthday. The rest of the
grounds, bounded by the moat,
is divided into public parks.

The most famous landmark is
the **Nijubashi**, a double-arched
stone bridge, east of the palace.
Completed in 1888, it was the
palace's main entrance. The
huge **Otemon** (Big Hand Gate),
rebuilt in 1967, was the main
gate before Nijubashi was built.
Now it is the entrance to the
**East Garden of the Imperial
Palace**. Just inside is
Sannomaru Shozokan, a
collection of art and artifacts of
the Showa Emperor. Beyond is
the Edo-era **Hyakunin Basho**,
where 100 samurai lived while
standing guard in shifts. Behind
is the **Honmaru**, the castle's
main keep, now just massive
stone walls with good views
from the top. To the east of
the Honmaru is the restful
Ninomaru garden, landscaped
by shogun Iemitsu in 1630.

A glimpse of the Imperial Palace
over Nijubashi

The airy glass-and-metal interior of the Tokyo
International Forum

Tokyo-ites enjoying a summer picnic in Kitanomaru Park

⑫ Kitanomaru Park
北の丸公園

Map 3 A5. **S** Kudanshita stn,
Hanzomon, Toei Shinjuku & Tozai
lines; Takebashi stn, Tozai line.
National Museum of Modern Art:
Tel (03) 5777-8600. **Open** 10am–5pm
Tue–Sun. 🌐 **W momat.go.jp/
english** Crafts Gallery: **Tel** (03) 5777-
8600. **Open** 10am–5pm Tue–Sun. 🌐
Science Museum: **Tel** (03) 3212-8544.
Open 9:30am–4:50pm daily. 🌐
W jsf.or.jp/eng

Lying to the north of the
Imperial Palace, Kitanomaru Park
is reached through the massive
Tayasumon (gate). A former
ground for the Imperial Palace
Guard, the area became a park
in 1969. Before entering, walk
past with Tayasumon on the
left to reach **Chidorigafuchi**
(the west moat), one of Tokyo's
most beautiful cherry-blossom
viewing spots. Row boats can
be rented here.

Within Kitanomaru's pleasant
grounds are a number of
buildings. Near Tayasumon is
the **Nippon Budokan** (see p353).
Built for the 1964 Olympics
martial arts competition, it is
now used mostly for rock
concerts. A short walk farther on
is the **Science Museum**. Some
of the interactive exhibits are
fun, including virtual bike rides
and electricity demonstrations
(explanations are in Japanese).

Five minutes
beyond, over a
main road and left
down the hill, is the
**National Museum
of Modern Art**. The
permanent collec-
tion comprises
Japanese works
from the 1868 Meiji
Restoration to the
present day; visiting
exhibits are often
excellent. Nearby
is the National
Museum of Modern
Art's **Crafts Gallery**.
Inside this 1910
Neo-Gothic brick
building is an
exquisite collection
of modern workings
of traditional
Japanese crafts –
pottery, lacquerware, and
damascene (etched metal artifacts). Some pieces are for sale.

⑬ Yasukuni Shrine
靖国神社

Map 2 F1. **Tel** (03) 3261-8326.
S Kudanshita stn, Hanzomon, Tozai
& Toei Shinjuku lines. **Open** 24 hours
daily. Yushukan: **Open** 9am–5pm
daily. 🌐 **W yasukini.or.jp/english**

The 2.5 million Japanese,
soldiers and civilians, who
have died in war since the
Meiji Restoration are enshrined
at Yasukuni Jinja (Shrine of
Peace for the Nation), which
was dedicated in
1879. Its history
makes it a sobering
place to visit.

Until the end of
World War II Shinto
was the official state
religion, and the
ashes of all who
died in war were
brought here
regardless of the
families' wishes.
Unsettling for some
of Japan's neighbors,
the planners and
leaders of World War II
and the colonization
of China and Korea are also
enshrined here, including
wartime prime minister

Browsing in one of
Jinbocho's bookshops

Tojo Hideki and eight other
Class-A war criminals. Visits
by cabinet ministers, even
in a private capacity, are
controversial.

Beside the shrine is the
Yushukan, a museum
dedicated to the war dead.
Many exhibits put a human
face on Japan at war: under
a photo of a smiling young
officer is a copy of his last letter
home, and there are mementos
of a nurse who died from
overwork. Still, romanticized
paintings of Japanese soldiers
in Manchuria and displays of
guns, planes, and even a
locomotive from the Thai-
Burma Railway may be
troubling to some.

⑭ Jinbocho Booksellers' District
神保町古本屋街

Map 3 B4–5. **S** Jinbocho stn, Toei
Mita, Hanzomon & Toei Shinjuku lines.

Three of Japan's great universities, Meiji, Chuo, and
Nihon, started out in this area
in the 1870s and 1880s, and
soon booksellers sprang up
selling both new and used
books. At one time 50 percent
of Japan's publishers were
based here. Although only
Meiji University is still here,
dozens of bookshops, several
selling ukiyo-e prints, remain, all
clustered around the junction
of Yasukuni-dori
and Hakusan-dori.
For English books
on Oriental subjects
try **Kitazawa Books**
or **Issei-do**; for
ukiyo-e prints, visit
Oya Shobo – all are
on the south side
of Yasukuni-dori,
walking away from
Hakusan-dori.

The change in
the economic status
(and priorities) of
students is evident
here. Shops selling
surf- or snowboards are everywhere. Music shops selling
electric guitars seem as
numerous as the bookshops.

For hotels and restaurants see pp292–307 and pp324–339

Tsutenkyo bridge in Koishikawa Korakuen Garden

⓯ Koishikawa Korakuen Garden

小石川後楽園

Map 3 A3–4. **Tel** (03) 3811-3015. 🚇 Korakuen stn, Marunouchi & Namboku lines. **Open** 9am–5pm daily. 📷

Korakuen, meaning "garden of pleasure last," is one of Tokyo's best traditional stroll gardens, a delightful place to spend a few restful hours. The name Korakuen comes from the Chinese poem *Yueyang Castle* by Fan Zhongyan: "Be the first to take the world's trouble to heart, be the last to enjoy the world's pleasure."

Construction of the garden started in 1629 and finished 30 years later. Once four times its present size of almost 8 hectares (20 acres), it belonged to the Mito branch of the Tokugawa family. An exiled Chinese Scholar, Zhu Shun Shui, helped design the garden including the **Engetsukyo** (full-moon) **bridge**, a stone arch with a reflection resembling a full moon. **Tsukenkyo bridge**, a copy of a bridge in Kyoto, is striking for the contrast between the vermilion of the bridge with the surrounding deep green forest.

The garden represents larger landscapes in miniature. Rozan, a famous Chinese sightseeing mountain, and Japan's Kiso River are two famous geographic features recreated here. In the middle of the large pond is **Horai island**, a beautiful composition of stone and pine trees.

⓰ Kanda Myojin Shrine

神田明神

Map 3 C4. **Tel** (03) 3254-0753. 🚇 Ochanomizu stn, Marunouchi line. 🚇 Ochanomizu stn, Chuo & Sobu lines. **Open** 24 hours daily. Museum: **Open** 10am–4pm Sat, Sun & public hols. 📷 📷 Kanda Matsuri (weekend closest to May 15 in alternate, odd-numbered years).

Myojin is more than 1,200 years old, although the present structure is a reproduction built after the 1923 earthquake. The gate's guardian figures are tight-lipped archers: Udaijin on the right and Sadaijin on the left. Just inside the compound on the left is a big stone statue of Daikoku, one of the *shichi-fuku-jin* (seven lucky gods). Here, as always, he is sitting on top of two huge rice bales.

The vermilion shrine itself and its beautiful interior, all lacquer and gold, are very impressive. Early morning is the best time to glimpse the Shinto priests performing rituals. The Kanda Matsuri (*see pp46–7*) is one of the greatest and grandest of Tokyo's festivals – come early and be prepared for crowds.

Behind the main shrine is a **museum** containing relics from the long history of Myojin. There are also several small shrines, hemmed in by the surrounding office blocks.

Lions on the gate to Kanda Myojin Shrine

⓱ Akihabara Electronics District

秋葉原電気店街

Map 3 C4. 🚇 Akihabara stn, Hibiya line. 🚇 Akihabara stn, Yamanote, Chuo & Sobu lines.

Akihabara electronics district surrounds Akihabara station. Directly under the station is a bazaar of tiny shops along narrow aisles selling any electronic device, simple or complex, from Christmas-tree lights to the latest chip. The market grew out of the ruins of World War II, when the Japanese army had surplus equipment it wanted to dispose of. Students from the nearby universities, who desperately needed money, bought the surplus army parts and made radios – status symbols and much in demand – to sell on roadsides or in tiny shops here. Akihabara and electronics have been synonymous ever since. Later as the economy improved, the focus changed to televisions, washing machines, and refrigerators. You can still see these, dozens at a time, on display, but increasingly the emphasis is on computers, cell phones, and video games.

Brand-name goods are available at a three to ten percent discount – sometimes more. On Chuo-dori, **Laox** (*see p111*) is a famous source of tax-free goods for tourists.

Colorful shop fronts and billboards in Akihabara district

The Imperial Palace, with the Nijubashi in the foreground ▶

NORTHERN TOKYO

The northern districts of Ueno and Asakusa contain what remains of Tokyo's old Shitamachi (low city). Once the heart and soul of culture in Edo *(see p61)*, Shitamachi became the subject of countless ukiyo-e woodblock prints *(see p89)*. Merchants and artisans thrived here, as did Kabuki theater *(see p41)* and the Yoshiwara pleasure district near Asakusa. One of the last great battles in Japan took place in Ueno in 1868 when the Emperor Meiji's forces defeated the Tokugawa shogunate. Ueno and Asakusa are the best parts of Tokyo for just strolling and observing. Life in Asakusa still revolves around the bustling Senso-ji Temple, its main approach packed with shops. Ueno is dominated by its huge park containing the National and Shitamachi Museums, among others. It is still possible to find pockets of narrow streets lined with tightly packed homes, especially in the Yanaka area, which escaped destruction by war and earthquake. Shopping is a pleasure in Northern Tokyo: as well as the traditional arts and crafts shops near Senso-ji Temple, there are specialists in plastic food in Kappabashi-dori, religious goods in neighboring Inaricho, and electronic items at Ameyoko Market.

Sights at a Glance

Temples
8 *Senso-ji Temple pp90–91*

Parks and Gardens
1 *Ueno Park pp82–3*

Notable Districts
6 Inaricho District and Kappabashi-dori
4 Yanaka District

Museums
3 Shitamachi Museum
2 *Tokyo National Museum pp84–7*

Markets
5 Ameyoko Market

Other Sites
7 Tokyo SkyTree

See also Street Finder maps 3 & 4

❶ Ueno Park
上野公園

Ieyasu, the first Tokugawa shogun, built the Kanei-ji Temple and subtemples here in the 1600s to negate evil spirits from the northeast. Judging by how long the Tokugawas lasted, it was a wise move. In 1873, five years after the Battle of Ueno, when the last supporters of the shogun were crushed by imperial forces, the government designated Ueno a public park. Always a popular spot, it has figured in many wood-block prints and short stories. Shinobazu Pond (actually three ponds) is an annual stop for thousands of migrating birds. Several museums and temples are here, as is Japan's oldest zoo.

★ **Tosho-gu Shrine**
This ornate complex of halls is one of Tokyo's few remaining Edo-era structures. Ieyasu was enshrined here and later reburied at Nikko *(see pp268–75)*.

KEY

① **Shitamachi Museum** *(see p88)*

② **Shinobazu Pond**

③ **Benten Hall**

④ **Gojo Shrine** is reached through a series of red torii (gates). Inside, red-bibbed Inari fox statues stand in an atmospheric grotto.

⑤ **The Great Buddhist Pagoda** was built in 1967. A Buddha statue formerly stood on the site; only its head remains.

⑥ **The Pagoda** is a five-story landmark dating from the 17th century and is a survivor from the original Kanei-ji temple complex. Today it stands in the grounds of Ueno Zoo, a popular destination for Japanese schoolchildren, among others, thanks to its giant pandas.

⑦ **Ueno Zoo**

⑧ **The Tokyo Metropolitan Museum,** in a modern red-brick building, has a large collection of contemporary Japanese art, plus special exhibitions.

⑨ **Tokyo National Museum** *(see pp84–7)*

⑩ **Rinno-ji Temple Imperial Cemetery**

⑪ **Tokyo Metropolitan Festival Hall**

⑫ **Japan Art Academy**

⑬ **Ueno Royal Museum**

⑭ **The Tomb of the Shogi Tai** is a small, leafy area containing two tombstones to the many samurai who died in the 1868 Battle of Ueno.

⑮ **Baseball ground**

⑯ **The main walkway** is lined with hundreds of cherry trees. Boisterous hanami (blossom-viewing) parties are held here each spring.

0 meters 100
0 yards 100

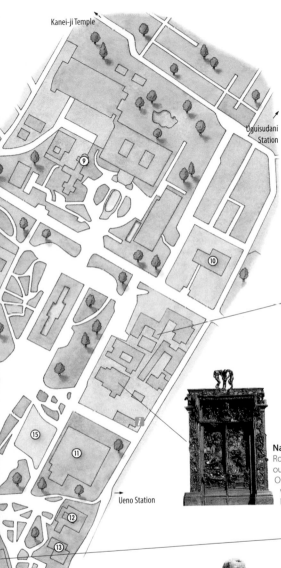

Kanei-ji Temple

Uguisudani Station

Ueno Station

**National Museum of Nature
and Science**
A steam engine and life-sized
blue whale model mark this
museum's entrance. Inside are
exhibits on natural history,
science, and technology.

National Museum of Western Art
Rodin's massive *Gate of Hell* stands
outside this building by Le Corbusier.
On display are various Impressionist
works, plus paintings by Rubens,
Pollock, and others.

Kiyomizu Hall
Part of the original Kanei-ji
Temple, this dates from
1631 and is dedicated to
Senju (1,000-armed)
Kannon. Kosodate Kannon,
the *bosatsu* of conception,
is also here, surrounded by
numerous offerings of dolls.

Saigo Takamori Statue
The leader of the victorious Meiji
forces, Saigo subsequently
instigated the Satsuma rebellion
against the emperor in 1877,
but killed himself when it failed.
He was posthumously
pardoned, and this statue
was erected in 1899.

❷ Tokyo National Museum

東京国立博物館

The group of buildings that makes up the Tokyo National Museum is in a compound in the northeast corner of Ueno Park; tickets to all buildings are available at the entrance gate. The Honkan is the main building. To its east is the Toyokan (see p86). The 1908 Beaux-Arts Hyokeikan is mainly used for special exhibitions. Behind it is the Gallery of Horyu-ji Treasures, containing stunning objects from Horyu-ji Temple, near Nara, and the Heiseikan (see p87). More than 110,000 items make up the collection – the best assembly of Japanese art in the world – and the displays change frequently.

Museum Complex Locator Map

Noh and Kabuki
One of the exquisite kimonos that form part of the textile and mask collection: it dates from the 16th century, when it was used in a Noh play (see p40). The kimono depicts lilies and court vehicles.

Heiseikan

First floor

The museum shop in the basement can be reached via twin staircases outside and a central one inside.

This building dates from 1938 and combines Japanese and Western features.

Gallery of Horyu-Ji Treasures

When the estates of Horyu-ji Temple (see p200) near Nara were damaged during the Meiji reforms, the impoverished temple gave a number of its treasures to the imperial family in exchange for money to finance its repairs. Over 300 of those priceless treasures, including rare and early Buddhist statues, masks used for Gigaku dances, and beautifully painted screens, are housed in this modern gallery, designed by Yoshio Taniguchi.

7th-century gilt-bronze Kannon statue

Rikishi mask, used for Gigaku dances, 8th century

Entrance

Steps down to museum shop

★ Ukiyo-e and Costumes
Popular from the mid-17th through the 19th century, these wood-block prints depicted everything from Kabuki stars to famous landscapes, scenes of market life to scenes from the pleasure quarters, like this 18th-century print of "Two Beauties".

Courtly Art
This collection includes scrolls, wood-block prints, and screens. This 16th-century gold screen is illustrated with a procession of noblemen, a scene from the *Tale of Genji (see p56)*.

Second floor

★ Sculpture
This serene, wooden 12th-century sculpture of the Juichimen Kannon Bosatsu (11-faced goddess of mercy) is about 3 m (10 ft) high. Mainly Buddhist, the pieces in the sculpture collection range from miniature to monumental.

★ National Treasures
The themed exhibition in the National Treasures room changes about every five weeks. Exhibits may be of calligraphy, Buddhist statues, tea utensils, or even armor, like this 16th-century Muromachi period *domaru* armor.

Key to Floor Plan

- ⬜ Donations Gallery
- ⬜ Thematic Exhibition
- ⬛ Sculpture
- ⬜ Lacquerware and ceramics
- ⬜ Swords and metalwork
- ⬜ Folk Culture and Historic Materials
- ⬜ Modern Art
- ⬜ Japanese and Buddhist Art
- ⬜ National Treasures
- ⬜ Courtly Art and Tea Ceremony
- ⬛ Military Attire
- ⬜ Interior Furnishings and Painting
- ⬜ Ukiyo-e, costumes, Noh & Kabuki

Gallery Guide: Honkan
The collection is on two floors. The second floor is a counterclockwise, chronological arrangement of Japanese art as it developed from Jomon-era (from 10,000 BC) clay figures to 19th-century ukiyo-e wood-block prints. In between is everything from calligraphy and tea utensils to armor, as well as textiles used in Noh and Kabuki. The first floor also works best when viewed counterclockwise. Its rooms are themed, with stunning exhibits of sculpture, lacquerware, swords, and Western-influenced modern art.

Tokyo National Museum: Toyokan

Opened in 1968, the Toyokan (Asian Gallery) displays an excellent and eclectic collection of non-Japanese Eastern art that ranges from textiles to sculpture and ceramics. Many of the exhibits are from China and Korea – a consequence of these countries' historic ties with Japan. The layout of the three floors is in a rough spiral, and a well-marked route guides visitors through the collection.

★ Korean Art
Dating from the Bronze Age (100 BC–AD 300), this dagger is one of the older pieces on display in the Korean collection.

★ Chinese Ceramics
Ceramics, such as this 8th-century Tang-dynasty camel, feature in the Chinese art section, along with bronzes, scrolls, jade, textiles, and glassware.

Chinese Buddha
One of a number of beautiful Buddhist statues on the first floor, this 11-faced Avalokitesvara from Xian in China dates from the 11th century.

Third floor

Second floor

Entrance

First floor

Vietnamese Ceramic Bowl
This delicately decorated 15th- to 16th-century bowl is part of the collection of Asian art on the first floor, which also includes fabrics and statuary.

Key to Floor Plan
- ☐ Chinese and Indian sculptures
- ☐ Egyptian and West, Southeast, and South Asian art
- ☐ Chinese art and antiquities
- ☐ Korean and Central Asian art and antiquities

Indian Sculpture
This 2nd-century figure, from the borders of modern Afghanistan and Pakistan, is grouped with the Indian sculptures on the first floor.

Tokyo National Museum: Heiseikan

The Heiseikan opened in 1999 and was purpose-built to house major temporary exhibitions and a superb collection of Japanese archaeological artifacts. Its modern facilities do full justice to the fascinating displays. The first floor houses the Japanese archaeology gallery, with items from 10,000–7,000 BC onward. The temporary exhibitions on the second floor are of mainly – but not only – Japanese art. Captions are in English and Japanese.

★ Haniwa Horse
Haniwa literally means "clay ring," and is used to describe earthenware sculptures that were made for 4th- to 7th-century tombs and were thought to protect the dead. Many forms have been found, including horses and other animals.

First floor

★ Haniwa Male Figure
This *haniwa* is dressed as a warrior. Other human figures that have survived include singers, dancers, and farmers.

Second floor

Entrance

Key to Floor Plan

▢ Archaeological exhibits

▢ Temporary exhibitions

Honkan

Fukabachi Bowl
This large cooking pot is a fine example of Jomon pottery, which is among the oldest in the world. The curved, deep sides allowed the fire to be built up around it, while the flattened base ensured it could be balanced when in the hearth.

★ Jomon Figures
The prehistoric Jomon period (14,500–300BC) produced Japan's first pottery, including *dogu*. This figurine is one of several female figures characterized by bulging eyes.

❸ Shitamachi Museum
下町風俗資料館

2-1 Ueno-koen, Taito-ku. **Map** 3 C3. **Tel** (03) 3823-7451. 🅂 Ueno stn, Hibiya & Ginza lines. 🅁 Keisei-Ueno stn, Keisei line; Ueno stn, many lines. **Open** 9:30am–4:30pm Tue–Sun. 🈳

This museum is dedicated to preserving the spirit and artifacts of Shitamachi *(see p81)*. The 50,000 exhibits include recreations of Edo-era shops, traditional toys, tools, and photographs, all donated by Shitamachi residents.

❹ Yanaka District
谷中地区

Map 3 C1. 🅁 Nippori stn, many lines. Asakura Museum of Sculpture: **Tel** (03) 3821-4549. **Open** 9:30am–4:30pm Tue–Thu, Sat–Sun. 🈳 Daimyo Clock Museum: **Tel** (03) 3821-6913. **Open** Jan 15–Jun 30, Oct 1–Dec 24: 10am–4pm Tue–Sun. 🈳

This quiet area is rewarding to wander through because it survived the 1923 earthquake and bombing of World War II. It preserves something of the feel of old Shitamachi with tightly packed houses in narrow alleys, and traditional food stalls selling rice crackers and old-fashioned candy.

The large **Yanaka Cemetery** is a must-see in cherry-blossom season. Inside is **Tenno-ji**, a temple with a large bronze Buddha dating from 1690. Nearby are tea shops and florists. To the west of Tenno-ji

is the **Asakura Museum of Sculpture**, home of sculptor Fumio Asakura (1883–1964). On the second floor is a delightful room full of his small statues of one of his favorite subjects – cats – but the garden is the real highlight with a traditional composition of water and stone. Sansaki-dori, the area's main street, has some traditional shops. The understated **Daimyo Clock Museum** has 100 Edo-era clocks lovingly presented.

❺ Ameyoko Market
アメ横

Map 3 C3. 🅂 Ueno stn, Hibiya & Ginza lines; Ueno-Okachimachi stn, Oedo line. 🅁 Okachimachi stn, Yamanote line; Ueno stn, many lines.

One of the great bazaars in Asia, Ameyoko is a place where almost anything is available, almost always at a discount. In Edo times, this was the place to come and buy *ame* (candy). After World War II black-market goods, such as liquor, cigarettes, chocolates, and nylons started appearing here, and *ame* acquired its second meaning as an abbreviation for American (*yoko* means "alley"). An area of tiny shops packed under the elevated train tracks, Ameyoko is no longer a black market, but it is still the place for bargain foreign brands, including Chanel and Rolex. Clothes and accessories are concentrated under the tracks, while foods, including a huge range of seafood, line the street that follows the tracks.

Shopping for a bargain at Ameyoko Market

❻ Inaricho District and Kappabashi-dori
稲荷町地区とかっぱ橋通り

Map 4 D3, 4 E2–3. 🅂 Inaricho & Tawaramachi stns, Ginza line.

Inaricho is the Tokyo head-quarters for wholesale religious goods. Small wooden boxes to hold Buddhas and family photos, paper lanterns, bouquets of brass flowers (*jouka*), Shinto household shrines, and even prayer beads can be found here.

Kappabashi-dori, named after the mythical water impss (*kappa*) who supposedly helped built a bridge (*bashi*) here, is Tokyo's center for kitchenware and the source of the plastic food displayed in almost every restaurant window. Although the "food" is for sale, prices are much higher than for the real thing.

❼ Tokyo SkyTree
東京スカイツリー

1-1-2 Oshiage, Sumida. **Map** off 4 F3. **Tel** (03) 5302-3470. 🅂 🅁 Tokyo SkyTree stn & Oshiage stn, Tobu line. **Open** 8am 10pm. 🈳

At 634 m (2,080 ft), this is the tallest building in Japan. While its main function is broadcasting, it also hosts a large mall, restaurant, aquarium, and planetarium. The Tembo Deck, at 350 m (1,150 ft) above ground level, offers 360-degree views across Tokyo, and another viewing deck, Tembo Galleria, is at 450 m (1,475 ft).

Some of the surviving old houses in the Yanaka district

The Floating World of Ukiyo-e

In the Edo period, wood-block prints, called ukiyo-e, or pictures of the pleasure-seeking "floating world," became the most popular pictorial art of Japan. They had a profound influence on artists such as Matisse and Van Gogh. Although today they are credited to individual artists, they were in fact a cooperative effort between the publisher, responsible for financing and distributing the work; the artist, who produced a fine line drawing; the carver, who pasted the drawings onto blocks of wood and carved away what was not to appear on the print, making one block for each color; and the printer, who inked the wooden blocks and pressed them onto the paper – one for each color, starting with the lightest. Editions were limited to 100–200 copies. The first artist known by name was Moronobu, who died in 1694. The golden age of ukiyo-e lasted from about 1790 to the 1850s. Beautiful women, Kabuki actors, scenes from Japan, including Shitamachi, and the supernatural were recurring themes.

A full-color calendar of women published by Suzuki Harunobu in 1765 marked a transition from the earlier black-and-white techniques. Highly popular (and a moneymaker), the calendar was a success, and attracted both financiers and artists to the medium.

After Harunobu's calendar, depictions of women were individualized and eroticized by artists such as Kitagawa Utamaro and Torii Kiyonaga. This print is by Utamaro.

Landscape prints were dominated by Hokusai (1760–1849) and his younger rival Hiroshige (1797–1858). This print is from the latter's *Fifty-Three Stations of the Tokaido*.

This 1825 print by Hokusai shows the carving and printing stages of wood-block print making. Printers relied on vegetable dyes, some of which were very expensive. The red dye *beni*, derived from safflowers, could be worth more than its weight in gold. Some prints required up to a dozen colors.

Ghosts and goblins were a favorite theme, especially in summer (to be scared was thought to be cooling). Utagawa Kuniyoshi (whose print is shown here), Taiso Yoshitoshi, and Kobayashi Kiyochika were masters of the genre, which marked the end of ukiyo-e's golden age.

❽ Senso-ji Temple

浅草寺

Popularly known as Asakusa Kannon, this is Tokyo's most sacred and spectacular temple. In AD 628, two fishermen fished a small gold statue of Kannon, the Buddhist goddess of mercy, from the Sumida River. Their master built a shrine to Kannon, then in 645, the holy man Shokai built a temple to her. Its fame, wealth, and size grew until Tokugawa Ieyasu bestowed upon it a large stipend of land. The Yoshiwara pleasure quarter moved nearby in 1657 only increasing its popularity. The temple survived the 1923 earthquake but not World War II bombing. Its main buildings are therefore relatively new, but follow the Edo-era layout. Although the buildings are impressive, it is the people following their daily rituals that make this place so special.

Five-Story Pagoda
This replica of the original was constructed in 1973.

Nade Botokesan Buddha
This delicate statue has been polished smooth by the hands of those hoping for good luck and help with ailments.

★ **Nakamise-dori**
This alley is a treasure trove of traditional wares, including specialists in obi sashes, haircombs, fans, dolls, and kimonos.

Kaminarimon Gate
"Thunder Gate" burned down in 1865 and was not rebuilt until 1960. The guardian statues of Fujin *(right)* and Raijin *(left)* have old heads and new bodies.

For more details about individual shops here, see pages 110–11

To Asakusa stations and tourist information office

★ Main Hall
Inside the hall (1958) the gold-plated main shrine houses the original Kannon image. Worshipers come to pay their respects by throwing coins and lighting candles.

VISITORS' CHECKLIST

Practical Information
Map 4 E2, 4 F2–3. by station (03) 3842-0181. Asakusa stn, Ginza & Toei-Asakusa lines. Temple: **Open** 6am–5pm daily (Oct–Mar: from 6:30am). Nakamise-dori: **Open** 9.30am–7pm daily. Sanja Matsuri (3rd Fri–Sun in May), Hagoita-Ichi (Battledore Fair, Dec 17–19).
w senso-ji.jp

Transport
Tobu-Asakusa stn, Tobu-Isesaki line.

★ Main Hall
Several large paintings hang inside the main hall. The painting of angels with lotus flowers is a 20th-century work by Insho Domoto.

KEY

① **The Garden**, of Dembo-in (abbot's residence) is a tranquil stroll garden used as a training center for monks. It is a masterly arrangement of trees, bamboo groves, lawns, and water.

② **Awashima Hall**, is dedicated to a deity who looks after women.

③ **This hexagonal temple**, is a rare survivor from the 15th or 16th century.

④ **Yogodo Hall**, houses eight recent Buddha statues.

⑤ **Asakusa Jinja**, built in 1649, is a shrine dedicated to the fishermen who found the Kannon statue.

⑥ **Niten-mon gate** was built in 1618 as the entrance to the original Tosho-gu Shrine.

⑦ **Benten-yama Shoro** belfry stands amid a group of temple buildings. The bell used to ring on the hour in Edo.

⑧ **Statues** donated by a wealthy Edo merchant.

Incense Burner
One of the temple's focal points, this incense burner (jokoro) is constantly surrounded by people wafting the smoke over them to keep them healthy.

Hozo-mon Gate
Built in 1964 of reinforced concrete, this two-story gate has a treasure house upstairs holding a number of 14th-century Chinese sutras.

WESTERN TOKYO

Shinjuku and Shibuya, the dual centers of Western Tokyo, three stops apart on the Yamanote line, started to boom only after the 1923 earthquake. This part of the city is new Tokyo – all vitality and energy, fast-paced, constantly changing, and challenging the more traditional pleasures of Central and Northern Tokyo. Modern architectural landmarks are dotted around, from the Olympic Stadiums of Yoyogi Park to the magnificent twin-towered home for the city government in West Shinjuku. Shibuya, along with neighboring Harajuku and Minami-Aoyama, is the epicenter of both young and haute-couture Japanese fashion. Nightlife is also in plentiful supply with Roppongi's cosmopolitan clubs, bars, and music venues, and the neon lights and *pachinko* parlors of East Shinjuku. In these overwhelmingly modern surroundings, historical sights are few and far between but include the popular Meiji Shrine and the nearby Sword Museum.

Sights at a Glance

Notable Districts
- ① East Shinjuku pp94–95
- ② West Shinjuku pp96–7
- ⑦ Harajuku District
- ⑧ Shibuya pp100–01
- ⑨ Minami-Aoyama District
- ⑩ Roppongi District
- ⑪ Akasaka District

Shrines
- ⑤ Meiji Shrine

Museum
- ④ Sword Museum

Stations
- ③ Shinjuku Station

Parks
- ⑥ Yoyogi Park

See also Street Finder maps 1 & 2

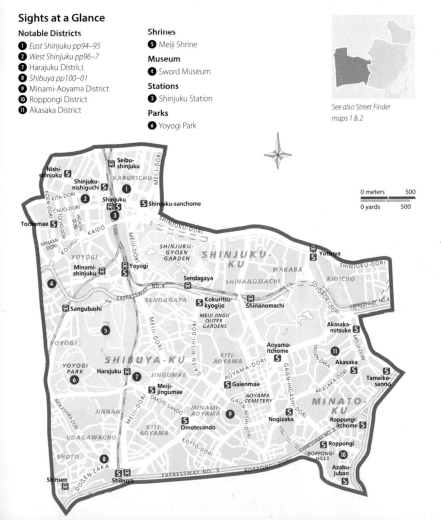

❶ Street-by-Street: East Shinjuku
東新宿

East Shinjuku is where Tokyo plays. The area has been a
nightlife center from Edo times on, when it was the first
night stop on the old Tokaido road to Kyoto. Since Shinjuku
station opened in the 1880s, entertainments have been
targeted at commuters (mainly men) en route back to the
suburbs. Amusements are focused in the tiny bars of Golden
Gai, and in the red-light district of Kabukicho. Daytime
attractions include several art galleries, a tranquil shrine, and
some of Tokyo's best department stores. A late-afternoon
stroll as the neon starts to light up will take in both sides
of this fascinating, bustling area.

Seibu-
Shinjuku
station

SAKURA-

YASUKUNI–DORI

Movie Houses
This corner of Kabukicho is
dominated by cinemas, many
showing the latest blockbusters.

West Shinjuku
(see pp96–97)

Kabukicho
Here hostess bars and
pachinko parlors *(see p101)*
flourish alongside cafés and
restaurants. In this area of
contrasts, prices range from
¥500 for a bowl of noodles
to ¥10,000 for a drink.

Studio Alta
Instantly recognizable by its
huge TV screen, Studio Alta
stands opposite the crossing
from Shinjuku station and is
a favorite place for meeting
up or just hanging out.

Shinjuku
station
(see p97)

↓ Yoyogi

Kinokuniya bookstore
has one of Tokyo's best
selections of foreign books.

Key

— Suggested walk route

▭▭ Train line

Golden Gai
Viewed in the daytime these scruffy alleys look anything but golden. Most of the bars here are just wide enough for a bar, a counter, and a row of stools. Each has a set of regulars – from writers to bikers – and quite a few welcome strangers inside.

Locator Map
See Tokyo Street Finder Map 1

Hanazono Shrine
This Shintō shrine, founded in the mid-17th century, is a calm and surprising oasis among the concrete towers. In the tree-filled compound are a reconstructed traditional vermilion-and-white building and several Inari fox statues.

Imperial Palace

0 meters 100
0 yards 100

Isetan Department Store
One of the most influential department stores in Japan, the stylish Shinjuku Isetan is often the first to showcase upcoming trends and products. Top Japanese and Western designer boutiques make this store a favorite with Tokyo's affluent young. The food hall in the basement is also worth a visit.

Flags café is a convenient coffee stop opposite Mistsukoshi department store.

❷ West Shinjuku
西新宿

Most of Tokyo's skyscraper office blocks (and some of its most expensive land) are clustered just to the west of Shinjuku station. About 250,000 people work here each day. Many of the hotels and some office blocks have top-floor restaurants with views of the city. In 1960 the government designated Shinjuku a *fukutoshin* ("secondary heart of the city"); in 1991, when the city government moved into architect Kenzo Tange's massive 48-story Metropolitan Government Offices, many started calling it *shin toshin* (the new capital). Tange's building was dubbed "tax tower" by those outraged at its US$1 billion cost.

West Shinjuku seen from Tokyo Metropolitan Government Offices

Island Tower

Mitsui Building

Hilton Tokyo

KITA-DORI

GIJIDO-DORI

CHUO-DORI

Sumitomo Building
Inside this block are a shopping center and, at the top, a free observatory.

Dai-Ichi Seimei Building

Hyatt Regency Tokyo

KOEN-DORI

TOCHO-DORI

FUREAI-DORI

Tokyo Metropolitan Government Offices
This huge complex of two blocks and a semi-circular plaza is unified by the grid-detailing on its façades (see p92), recalling both traditional architecture and electronic circuitry. An observatory gives views from Mount Fuji to Tokyo Bay on a clear day.

Shinjuku Central Park

The Washington Hotel has flowing curves (inside and out) and tiny windows in its white façade.

MINAMI-DORI

The NS Building is recognizable by its rainbow-hued elevator shafts. In the 30-story atrium is a 29-m (95-ft) high water-powered clock.

Keio Plaza Hotel

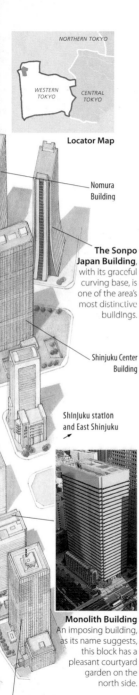

NORTHERN TOKYO

WESTERN TOKYO / CENTRAL TOKYO

Locator Map

Nomura Building

The Sonpo Japan Building, with its graceful curving base, is one of the area's most distinctive buildings.

Shinjuku Center Building

Shinjuku station and East Shinjuku

Monolith Building
An imposing building, as its name suggests, this block has a pleasant courtyard garden on the north side.

KDDI Building

0 meters 100
0 yards 100

❸ Shinjuku Station
新宿駅

Map 1 B1–2.

With over two million people passing through each day, this is the busiest train station in the world. As well as being a major stop on both the JR and metropolitan subway systems, Shinjuku station is the starting point for trains and buses into the suburbs. On the Yamanote and Chuo line platforms during the morning rush hour (from about 7:30 to 9am) staff are employed to push those last few commuters on to the train, making sure the odd body part isn't slammed in one of the closing doors.

The corridors connecting all the lines and train networks are edged with hundreds of shops and restaurants. It's easy to lose your way in this maze of seemingly identical passages, and it is often simpler to find your bearings at ground level. For a time in the 1980s and early 1990s, a substantial number of homeless (mostly men) built cardboard villages in the station's corridors. In a controversial move, the municipal government forcibly removed them; they settled in new places, including Ueno Park.

❹ Sword Museum
刀剣博物館

4-25-10 Yoyogi. **Map** 1 A3. **Tel** (03) 3379-1386. 🚉 Sangubashi stn, Odakyu line. **Open** 10am–4:30pm Tue–Sun. 📷

A little out of the way, this museum is full of fine Japanese swords dating back to the 12th century. Like many other artifacts in Japan, swords combine art and ritual in the pursuit of perfection. On the first floor is an interesting display of the process by which a sword is produced. The swords themselves are exhibited on the second floor, every detail carefully refined, even down to the pattern of burnishing on the blade's face. There is also a display of decorated hilts. English explanations trace the history of the sword, and the processes of tempering and sharpening, handling, and maintenance. Old Japanese texts, illustrated with beautiful drawings, explain the finer points of sword-making.

Ornate sword handle

Commuter Culture

Commuters packed into trains are a common sight morning and evening at Tokyo's major train stations. High urban land prices force families to look farther out of the city for affordable housing. As a consequence, a commute of at least an hour each way is practically the standard. By far the majority of commuters are men, as they are still the prime earners in many families. The commute effectively removes them from family life: they often leave before the children get up, come back after they are in bed, and collapse on weekends with fatigue. However, as two-income families become more the norm in Japan, there are also increasing numbers of women on trains. An entire industry has developed around these commuters: dozens of magazines are produced for killing time, and stand-up restaurants offer cheap meals to those with a long ride ahead.

Crowding onto a commuter train

One of the many stalls selling good-luck charms at the Meiji Shrine

⑤ Meiji Shrine

明治神宮

Map 1 B3. **Tel** (03) 3379-5511.
🚇 Harajuku stn, Yamanote line.
Treasure Museum Annex: **Open** 9am–4pm daily. 🖥 **meijijingu.or.jp/english** Treasure Museum: 9am–4pm Sat, Sun, & public hols. 🌸 Nai-en garden: **Open** daily (times vary). 🌸 Spring Festival (May 2–3), Fall Festival (Nov 1–3).

The most important shinto shrine in Tokyo, Meiji Jingu (imperial shrine) dates from 1920. Emperor Meiji (1868–1912) and his wife, Empress Shoken, are enshrined here. A focal point for right-wing militarists during Japan's colonial expansion prior to World War II, the shrine was destroyed by Allied aerial bombardment in 1945 but rebuilt with private donations in 1958. During the New Year holidays it is the most heavily visited place in Japan, with over 3 million people worshiping here and buying good-luck charms for the year ahead.

A wide graveled road under a huge torii (gate) and shaded by cedars leads into the shrine grounds. On the right is an abandoned entrance to the JR Harajuku station. Just beyond is the small entrance still used by the emperor when he visits by train for official functions. Next on the right is a complex with a café and restaurant, and the **Treasure Museum Annex.** The annex holds changing exhibitions of the royal couple's artifacts, including clothes, lacquerware, and furniture. Tickets for the Treasure Museum Annex are also valid for the main Treasure Museum. A left turn takes you under the massive **Otorii** (gate), built in

1975 of huge logs that came from a 1,500-year-old Japanese cypress on Mount Tandai in Taiwan. A short distance beyond the gate, on the left, is the entrance to the **Nai-en garden**, a favorite of the Meiji imperial couple. It is said that the Emperor Meiji designed it himself for his empress. Inside there is a teahouse overlooking a pond stocked with water lilies and carp. To the right of the pond, a path leads to the beautiful **Minami-ike Shobuda** (iris garden), at its peak in June, and containing over 150 species.

Past the entrance to Nai-en, the road turns to the right and enters the **main shrine** area, set in the middle of a grove of cedars. Another large wooden torii leads to the outer gate (Minami Shinmon) through which is a spacious outer courtyard. A second gate (Gehaiden), straight ahead, separates the public from the inner courtyard and the shrine. The simple shrine buildings are made of unadorned aging wood in deep hues of brown; the roof is copper, now oxidized bright green. Gracefully curving, the roof is in the Shinto style of architecture known as shimmei, used for imperial shrines. Around the other three sides of the outer courtyard are booths selling charms and prophecies. Through a gateway to the right is the **Kaguraden**,

a hall built in 1993 for sacred music and dance.

To reach the **Treasure Museum**, either return to the Otorii and turn left, following the signs, or walk through the woods to the left of the shrine. Lining the walls of the single high-vaulted room of the Treasure Museum are portraits of every emperor going back more than 1,000 years. The objects on display change regularly; watch for the gorgeous kimonos worn by Emperor Meiji and the empress for court functions.

Minami Shinmon gateway through a wooden torii, Meiji Shrine

⑥ Yoyogi Park

代々木公園

Map 1 A4, 1 B4. 🚇 Harajuku stn, Yamanote line.

Kenzo Tange's two **Olympic Stadiums**, the landmark structures in Yoyogi Park, were completed in 1964 for the Tokyo Olympics. They are still used for national and international sports competitions. The impressive curves of the shell-like structures are achieved with the use of steel suspension cables.

For almost three decades the park filled with a fantastic array of performers and bands every Sunday. These events were

The main Olympic Stadium in Yoyogi Park

stopped by the authorities In the mid-1990s, supposedly due to worries about the rise in criminal activities and maintaining public order. Sundays are still a good time to visit, though, for the weekly flea market. At the entrance to the park you can still see members of the *zoku* (tribes) who used to perform here, from punks and goths to hippies and break-dancers.

❼ Harajuku District

原宿地区

Map 1 B4, 1 C4. **Ⓢ** Meiji-jingumae stn, Chiyoda line. **Ⓡ** Harajuku stn, Yamanote line. Ota Memorial Museum of Art: **Tel** (03) 3403-0880. **Open** 10:30am–5:30pm Tue–Sun. **Closed** 27th–end of each month.

Harajuku station was the main station for the 1964 Tokyo Olympic village; that concentration of international culture had a great impact on the area, attracting the young and innovative of Tokyo. Today Harajuku remains a center for fashion from high-end international showcases to bargain boutiques.

Takeshita-dori, a narrow alley between Meiji-dori and Harajuku station, is the place to find what's hot in teen fashion and culture. Sundays bring the biggest crowds. Prices range from cheap to outrageous, as do the fashions. Starting from the Harajuku station end, about 200 m (220 yards) down, a left turn leads up some stairs to **Togo Shrine,** founded for Admiral Togo, the commander who defeated the Russian fleet in the Battle of Tsushima, which was part of the Russo-Japanese War. It was a huge naval victory, the first of an Asian country over a Western one. Admiral Togo remains a hero in Japan, and his shrine has a beautiful garden and pond. An **antiques market** is held in the grounds of the shrine on the first, fourth, and fifth Sundays of the month.

Large advertising screens in Harajuku

Running parallel to, and south of, Takeshita-dori is the more sophisticated **Omotesando.** With its wide, tree-shaded sidewalks and dozens of boutiques showcasing top fashion designers and brands such as Celine, Fendi, and Dior, this is one of the best strolls in Tokyo.

As you walk from Harajuku station, just before the intersection with Meiji-dori, you see a small street off to the left leading to the **Ota Memorial Museum of Art,** which houses one of the best collections of ukiyo-e prints *(see p89)* in Japan. A vivid image of a Kabuki actor portraying an *arogoto* (superhero) by Sharaku and a masterful program of a memorial Kabuki performance by Hiroshige are among many familiar works. There is a small restaurant and a shop selling prints and other ukiyo-e-related souvenirs. Just to the left down Meiji-dori is **LaForet,** a fashion mecca, with more than 150 boutiques. Leading off Omotesando, just before the pedestrian bridge, a narrow lane to the left is lined with boutiques of up-and-coming designers and gives a good idea of residential life in this upscale area. Farther up the hill from the footbridge on the left is

Street performer in Harajuku

the major landmark of Omotesando Hills. This huge complex is home to boutiques such as Jimmy Choo, and specialist luxury-goods stores, as well as dozens of brand stores such as UGG Australia and Catimini. Over the pedestrian bridge to the right is the landmark **Hanae Mori Building.** Designed by Kenzo Tange in 1974, it resembles a stack of glass blocks. Famous for incorporating butterflies in her designs, Hanae Mori built an empire that takes in everything from haute-couture clothing to place mats. Just before the Hanae Mori Building is the vermilion-and-white **Oriental Bazaar,** a collection of shops full of real and fake antiques and good handicrafts, ideal for souvenirs *(see p111).*

A group of teenagers, Harajuku

❽ Street-by-Street: Shibuya

渋谷

Shibuya is the *sakariba* (party town) for Tokyo's youth. It has been so since the 1930s, when façades featured rockets streaking across the sky. Today this is the place to see the latest in fashion, food, music, and gadgets. Shibuya really started to grow after the 1964 Tokyo Olympics, and its continuing expansion has been spurred by the affluent youth of the world's third-biggest economy. The area, which lies to the northwest of Shibuya station and south of Yoyogi Park, is a mix of trendy boutiques, fashionable department stores, and record shops, plus a couple of interesting museums, and the Bunkamura cultural center. Adjoining this area is Dogen-zaka, a jumble of sloping streets and alleyways lined with nightclubs, bars, and love hotels *(see p299)*.

VISITORS' CHECKLIST

Practical Information

S Shibuya stn, Hanzomon, Ginza, and Fukutoshin lines. Tower Records: **Tel** (03) 3496-3661. **Open** 10am–11pm daily.

Transport

🚆 Shibuya stn, Yamanote, Tokyu Toyoko, Denentoshi & Keio Inokashira lines.

Center Gai
The focus for youth entertainment in Tokyo, Center Gai is lined with shops, *pachinko* parlors, restaurants, and karaoke bars full of high-school and college-age kids.

Tokyu Hands is a huge store full of housewares and handicrafts.

Bunkamura
This cultural center is a popular site for rock and classical concerts, and has movies, an art gallery, and a theater.

BUNKAMURA-DOR

CENT

DOGEN-ZAKA

Dogen-zaka
Named after a bandit who retired here as a monk, this nighttime destination includes old houses, now art galleries.

Key

━ Suggested walk route

▭▭ Train line

This purple clock tower stands in front of the Shibuya Ward Office and is overlooked by Yoyogi Park and the NHK Studios.

The Humax Pavilion Building is one of the more fanciful buildings in the area, resembling a cartoon rocket. It also houses the Disney Store.

Yoyogi Park and Olympic stadiums

Harajuku

Locator Map
See Tokyo Street Finder Map 1

Tower Records has a good stock of Japanese and international music at prices among the best in Tokyo.

Marui Jam department store is a paradise for clothes – the place for fashionable under 25s.

Statue of Hachiko
Since 1934 this popular meeting place has had a statue of a dog who waited for his master at the station every night for more than a decade after his death. Another meeting point nearby is the Statue of Moyai.

Shibuya station

0 meters 100
0 yards 100

Pachinko

Japan's most popular form of recreation, *pachinko* is similar to pinball, but without the flippers and requiring little skill. Players buy some steel balls to feed into the *pachinko* machine, winning more steel balls; these are traded in for a prize (gambling for money is illegal). The prize in turn can be exchanged for money, usually in a small shop nearby. Shibuya and Shinjuku have hundreds of *pachinko* parlors, but they are found all over Japan.

A typical *pachinko* machine

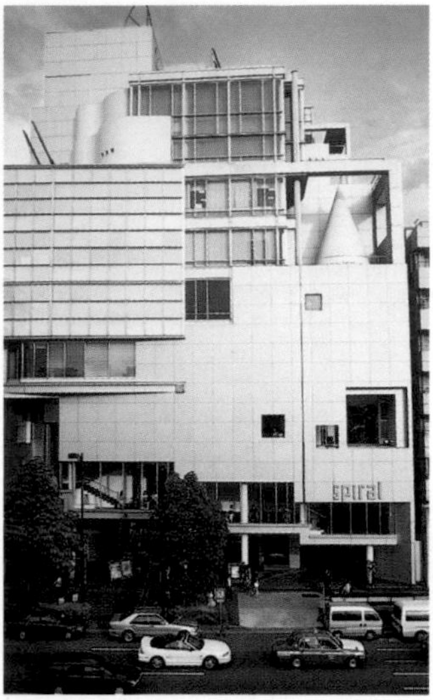

The Spiral Building, Minami-Aoyama

❾ Minami-Aoyama District

南青山地区

Map 1 C4–5, 2 D4–5. **S** Gaienmae stn, Ginza line. Museum of Contemporary Art: **Tel** (03) 5245-4111. **Open** 10am–6pm Tue–Sun. **W mot-art-museum.jp** Nezu Art Museum: **Tel** (03) 3400-2536. **Open** 10am–5pm Tue–Sun. **W nezu-muse.or.jp/en** National Children's Castle: **Tel** (03) 3797-5666. **Open** 12:30–5:30pm Tue–Fri, 10am–5:30pm Sat, Sun, public hols & school vacations. **W kodomono-shiro.or.jp**

Favored by artists, writers, and young entrepreneurs, this district lies between the large Aoyama Cemetery and Shibuya. Aoyama-dori, the wide street at its heart, is a center for boutiques and upscale life. Omotesando crosses it just about in the middle.

On Gaien-Nishi-dori, a fashionable street nicknamed "Killer-dori," is the **Museum of Contemporary Art**. Exhibits are by international and Japanese artists, and change regularly. The bookstore stocks an excellent range of art books.

Back on Aoyama-dori, turn left at the Omotesando junction for the **Nezu Art Museum**, which houses Japanese, Chinese, and Korean art and is situated in landscaped gardens containing traditional teahouses. A short walk from here is Kotto-dori, another fashionable street, which is full of antique shops selling scrolls, paintings, and porcelain, among many other items. This street is one of the hottest in Tokyo, with some notable boutiques, cafés, and shops springing up. The area is a pleasant one in which to spend an afternoon shopping or just browsing. Returning to Aoyama-dori, near the Omotesando junction toward Shibuya, the next landmark is the white, geometric **Spiral Building**, which owes its name to the large, spiral ramp inside. Designed by Fumihiko Maki in 1985, and one of the most popular places in Minami-Aoyama, this building is the figurative definition of cool. There is nothing in it that can't be described as hip and trendy (*torendi* in Japanese), and that includes most of the people. Attractions inside comprise a first-floor exhibition and performance space, the Spiral Hall (on the third floor), also used for exhibitions and performances, an Italian café, a French restaurant, a stationery and housewares boutique, and a beauty salon.

Farther along, the **National Children's Castle** is marked by a large, moon-faced sculpture by Taro Okamoto. There are many activities for kids here, open to Japanese and non-Japanese speakers alike, including areas for free play with toys, computers, music and art classes, and even a child-friendly hotel.

❿ Roppongi District

六本木地区

Map 2 E5. **S** Roppongi stn, Hibiya & Toei-Oedo lines. Mori Art Museum: **Tel** (03) 5777-8600. **Open** 10am–10pm Tue–Sun (till 5pm Tue). Suntory Museum of Art: **Tel** (03) 3479-8600. **Open** 10am–6pm Wed–Mon (to 8pm Fri & Sat).

Roppongi is the music and club center of Tokyo. You can find just about any music you want here: jazz, blues, ska, hip-hop, classic disco, country and western, soul. This is also the place for big-name international restaurant chains such as the Hard Rock Café, Spago's, and Tony Roma's.

Designed to be a "city within a city," it incorporates wide pedestrian squares, public walkways, a cinema complex, and art gallery, as well as restaurants, shops, offices, and apartments. The **Mori Art**

Nighttime scene in the district of Roppongi

Flamboyant entrance to a nightclub in Roppongi

Museum is one attraction, in which exhibitions cover contemporary art, media art, design, and fashion.

Almond (*Amando* in Japanese), at the intersection of Roppongi-dori and Gaien-Higashi-dori, is the main rendezvous spot in Roppongi. The area to the south is home to clubs that come in all shapes and sizes, most will welcome you warmly, but check the prices of drinks as they vary hugely. To the west of Almond, beyond the expressway, **Mogambo** is an intimate club that is popular with the expat community. West of Almond is the **Square Building**, full of more clubs, including Birdland jazz club (*see p117*).

To the north lies the complex known as Tokyo Midtown, which houses the **Suntory Museum of Art**. The museum has an unrivaled collection of Edo-era screens, depicting scenes from the Edo court. Traditional decorative arts are also well represented, with ceramics, lacquerware, and tea utensils.

⑪ Akasaka District

赤坂地区

Map 2 E3–4, 2 F3–4. **S** Akasaka-Mitsuke stn, Ginza & Marunouchi lines; Nagatacho stn, Yurakucho, Namboku & Hanzomon lines. 🚃 🚌 Sanno Matsuri (Jun 16, Hie Jinja).

With the Diet Building (*see p75*) and many government offices just to the east, Akasaka is a favorite place for politicians to socialize. Limousines carry dark-blue-suited men to the many exclusive establishments lining the streets here.

About 200 m (220 yards) along Aoyama-dori from Akasaka-Mitsuke station is **Toyokawa Inari Shrine** (also called Myogon-ji). With its red lanterns and flags, and dozens of statues of foxes (the traditional messengers of Inari, a Shinto rice deity), this is a pleasant place to linger for a while.

Back past the station and over the moat, you will see a large building up ahead that you may recognize from the James Bond film *You Only Live Twice* (1967), in which it featured. This is the huge, luxurious Hotel New Otani. On the 17th floor is the revolving

Ironware kettle in the Suntory Museum of Art

Blue Sky restaurant, which serves Chinese, Japanese, and Western cuisine (diners can choose the ingredients and the chefs will prepare it on the spot), and offers stunning 360-degree views across central Tokyo and the Imperial Palace. In the grounds and open to all is the 400-year-old garden of Kato Kiyomasa, lord of Kyushu's Kumamoto area.

South of Akasaka-Mitsuke station is the shrine of **Hie Jinja**, with a history dating back to 830. Shogun Ietsuna moved it here in the 17th century to buffer his castle; the present-day buildings are all modern. Each year in mid-June the Sanno Matsuri is celebrated here with a grand procession of 50 *mikoshi* (portable shrines) and people in Heian-era costumes.

A *shinowa* circle, erected for good luck, at Hie Jinja in Akasaka

Youth Culture

In Japan youth sells, although, ironically, the average age of the population is one of the highest in the world. Youth is seen by most Japanese as the time when life can be lived according to personal choice, before adult responsibilities – in the form of jobs or parenthood – take over. Products from beer and cars to the latest in technology and fashion are aimed at the youth market, and are rapidly adopted and then shed as individuals are attracted by the new and the desire to keep up with their peers. A stream of teenage *idoru* (idols) become wildly famous, mainly for singing pop songs or acting, when they are young. When they reach their twenties, the girls tend to marry and have children, while boys move into becoming talk-show hosts or game-show contestants.

A Tokyo teenager on her cell phone

Farther Afield

A short distance from Tokyo city center are a number of interesting sights. The Japan Folk Crafts Museum and Goto Art Museum are small gems in pleasant neighborhoods that give an idea of Tokyo life as well as its heritage; in contrast Ikebukuro, Daiba, and Ebisu are all modern urban centers in their own right. Ryogoku, the place for all things sumo, also has the Edo-Tokyo Museum. Rikugi-en, near Ikebukuro, is one of Edo's last great stroll gardens.

Sights at a Glance

1. Goto Art Museum
2. Japan Folk Crafts Museum
3. Tokyo Opera City
4. Arakawa Tram Line
5. Ikebukuro District
6. Rikugi-en Garden
7. Ryogoku District
8. Odaiba
9. Sengaku-ji Temple
10. Ebisu District

0 kilometers 5
0 miles 3

Key

■ Main sightseeing area
═ Expressway
▬ Main road

❶ Goto Art Museum
五島美術館

3-9-25 Kaminoge, Setagaya-ku. **Tel** (03) 5777-8600. 🚃 Tokyu Denentoshi line from Shibuya stn to Futako-Tamagawaen, then Tokyu Oimachi line to Kaminoge stn. **Open** 10am–5pm Tue–Sun. **Closed** when exhibitions change. 📷

Set in a pleasant hillside garden, this museum showcases the private collection of the late chairman of the Tokyu Corporation, Keita Goto. Avidly interested in Zen, he was originally attracted to Buddhist calligraphy, particularly that of 16th-century priests. His collection contains many examples of this work, called *bokuseki*. Also included are ceramics, calligraphy, paintings, and metalwork mirrors; items are changed several times a year. The museum's most famous works, however, are scenes from 12th-century scrolls of the *Tale of Genji*, painted by Fujiwara Takayoshi, which have been designated National Treasures. They are shown once a year, usually in "Golden Week" *(see p360).*

❷ Japan Folk Crafts Museum
日本民芸館

4-3-33 Komaba, Meguro-ku. **Tel** (03) 3467-4527. 🚃 Komaba-Todaimae stn, Keio Inokashira line. **Open** 10am–5pm Tue–Sun. 📷

Known to the Japanese as Mingeikan, this small but excellent museum was founded by art historian Muneyoshi Yanagi. The criteria for inclusion in the museum are that the object should be the work of an anonymous maker, produced for daily use, and representative of the region from which it comes. The museum building, designed by Yanagi and completed in 1931, uses black tiles and white stucco outside.

On display are items ranging from woven baskets to ax sheaths, iron kettles, pottery, and kimonos; together they present a fascinating view of rural life. There are also special themed exhibits, such as 20th-century ceramics or Japanese textiles, and a room dedicated to Korean Yi-dynasty work. A small gift shop sells fine crafts and some books.

❸ Tokyo Opera City
東京オペラシティー

3-20-2 Nishi-Shinjuku, Shinjuku-ku. **Tel** (03) 5353-0770. 🚃 Hatsudai stn, Keio line. 🌐 operacity.jp

Tokyo's impressive music and theater complex has two main halls, one primarily for Japanese classical music and theater, and a larger opera hall with a soaring vaulted roof. Performances are frequent – phone for details or pick up a leaflet from the foyer information counter.

There are 54 floors, mostly offices. On the first three are an art gallery, shops, and restaurants. The fourth has the **NTT Intercommunication Center**, with modern interactive art. The 53rd and 54th floors hold a dozen restaurants and bars with great city views.

Exhibit at the NTT Intercommunication Center, Tokyo Opera City

The aquarium at Sunshine City, Ikebukuro District

❹ Arakawa Tram Line
荒川都電

Ⓢ Edogawabashi stn, Yurakucho line. Sumida River trips: ℹ (03) 5608-8869.

In 1955, 600,000 people a day were riding the dozens of tram lines that crisscrossed the city. Now the 13 km (8 miles) Arakawa line is one of only two that remain. The others were eliminated as old-fashioned in the modernization for the 1964 Olympics.

The Arakawa tram line runs from Waseda in the west to Minowabashi in the east and costs ¥170 for each trip, short or long. Near the Waseda end of the line is the quiet stroll garden of **Shin Edogawa**. There are few outstanding sights en route, but the pleasure of this tram ride lies in seeing a quieter, residential side to Tokyo. A short walk from Arakawa Yuenchimae stop, past tightly packed, tiny houses, is a modest amusement park, **Arakawa Yuen Park**; Sumida River tourboat trips leave from here. Opposite the Arakawa Nanachome stop is **Arakawa Nature Park**.

❺ Ikebukuro District
池袋地区

Ⓢ Ikebukuro stn, Fukutoshin, Marunouchi & Yurachuko lines. 🚃 Ikebukuro stn, Yamanote & many other lines.

With the second-busiest train station in Japan (after Shinjuku), Ikebukuro is a designated *fukutoshin* (subcenter) of Tokyo.

By the station's south entrance is the flagship store of **Seibu**, perhaps the country's most innovative department store, with boutiques of up-and-coming designers and a large basement food market. To the west of the station is the large **Tobu** department store with a similar set-up.

The **Sunshine City** complex, including the **Sunshine 60** tower, is a short walk east of the station. It is built on top of what was Sugamo Prison, where seven Class-A World War II war criminals, including the prime minister, Hideki Tojo, were convicted and hanged. The **Ancient Orient Museum**, on the 7th floor of the complex, has collections from Egypt, Iran, and Pakistan. A huge Sunshine City sign points down an escalator; just before here, investigate the **Tokyu Hands** store for home furnishings and kitchen gadgets. Down the escalator is **Amlux Toyota**, five stories packed with cars, where you can sit in any model. In Sunshine 60 there is also a planetarium, an aquarium, and a rooftop outdoor viewing platform.

❻ Rikugi-en Garden
六義園

Ⓢ Komagome stn, Namboku line. 🚃 Komagome stn, Yamanote line. **Tel** (03) 3941-2222. **Open** 9am–5pm daily. 🅿

Yanagisawa Yoshiyasu, grand chamberlain of the fifth shogun, constructed this garden in seven years, starting in 1695. Yanagisawa had a well-earned reputation for debauchery, but he also managed to build this, one of the finest Edo-era stroll gardens. Iwasaki Yataro, Mitsubishi's founder, oversaw its Meiji-era renovation. The design re-creates 88 landscapes in miniature from famous *waka* (31-syllable poems), so the view changes every few steps. Near the entrance is a weeping cherry that is beautiful all year. Numerous paths and seats offer opportunities to enjoy the views. Bush warblers and turtledoves are among the birds that can be heard here.

Manicured shrubs around the lake at Rikugi-en Garden

Living in Small Spaces

Land, and therefore housing, is very expensive in Japan. The average home costs 7–8 times the family's yearly income, and space is at a premium. A traditional design has closets for storing rolled-up futons; in the morning the bedding is swapped for a low table at which the family sits cross-legged to eat meals. More and more families are opting for a semi-Western style with raised beds, table, and chairs, resulting in homes being even more cramped.

❼ Ryogoku District

両国地区

Map 4 E4–5. **S** Ryogoku stn, Toei-Oedo line. **R** Ryogoku stn, JR Sobu line. Sumo Museum: 1-3-28 Yokoami, Sumida-ku. **Tel** (03) 3622-0366. **Open** 10am–4:30pm Mon–Fri. **Closed** public hols. **W** sumo.or.jp
Edo-Tokyo Museum: 1-4-1 Yokoami, Sumida-ku. **Tel** (03) 3626-9974. **Open** 9:30am–5:30pm Tue–Sun (7:30pm Sat). 🅿
W edo-tokyo-museum.or.jp

On the east bank of the Sumida River, Ryogoku was a great entertainment and commerce center in Edo's Shitamachi. These days it is a quiet place but it still has its most famous residents: sumo wrestlers. Many *beya* (sumo stables) are here, and it is not unusual to see huge young men walking the streets in *yukata* (light cotton kimonos) and *geta* (wooden sandals).

The **National Sumo Stadium** has been here since 1945; the current building dates from 1985. During a tournament *(see p115)* many of the wrestlers simply walk from their *beya* just down the street. Inside the stadium is a **Sumo Museum** lined with portraits of all the *yokozuna* (grand champions) dating back 200 years.

Beside the stadium is the huge **Edo-Tokyo Museum**, built to resemble an old style of elevated warehouse. One of Tokyo's most imaginative and interesting museums, it has an exhibition space that is divided into two zones on two floors tracing life

Image of a Kabuki actor, Edo-Tokyo Museum

in Edo and then Tokyo, as Edo was renamed in 1868. The exhibits, some of which are interactive, appeal to both adults and children and have explanations in Japanese and English.

The route around the museum starts by crossing a traditional arched wooden bridge, a replica of Nihonbashi *(see p74)*. There are life-sized reconstructed buildings including the façade of a Kabuki theater. Marvelous scale-model dioramas, some of which are automated, show everything from the house of a daimyo (feudal lord) to a section of Shitamachi. Beside a scale model of Tokyo's first skyscraper ____ is rubble

Life in a Sumo Stable

At the age of about 15 boys are accepted into a sumo *beya*. From that day, they will probably not return home or see their parents for several years. Sumo society is supremely hierarchical, with newcomers serving senior wrestlers as well as cleaning and cooking for the entire *beya*. Their practices may start at 4am, with seniors starting about 6am. The day's single meal of *chanko-nabe*, a large stew, comes about noon with juniors getting what the seniors leave. That is followed by more work. The life is grueling – but it is a society and culture several foreigners have very successfully entered.

Sumo wrestlers training in the Ryogoku District

from the 1923 earthquake that destroyed it. There is a rickshaw and Japan's first "light" automobile: a three-seater Subaru with a 360-cc engine. In the media section is a step-by-step example of how ukiyo-e wood-block prints *(see p89)* were produced. Models of the boats that once plied the Sumida River give some idea of just how important the river was to Edo life.

❽ Odaiba

台場

R Yurikamome monorail from Shinbashi stn to Odaiba-kaihinkoen stn; Rinkai line to Tokyo Teleport. 🚢 from Hinode Pier 10:10am–7:10pm, every 20–25 mins. National Museum of Emerging Science and Innovation: **Tel** (03) 3570-9188. **Open** 10am–5pm Wed–Mon. **Closed** Dec 28–Jan 1. 🅿

When the west started to force Japan to open up in the 1850s, the shogunate constructed a series of *daiba* (obstructions) across Tokyo harbor to keep the foreigners' powerful "black ships" out. Odaiba (sometimes known as Daiba), an island almost blocking the mouth of Tokyo Bay, takes its name from these. The spectacular route to Odaiba is via the Yurikamome monorail, which climbs a loop before

Reconstruction of a Kabuki theater in Ryogoku's Edo-Tokyo Museum

joining Rainbow Bridge high over Tokyo Harbor. On Odaiba the monorail is a convenient way to travel around, although most places are within a short walk of each other.

The first station, Odaiba-Kaihin-Koen, leads to Tokyo's only beach. Nearby is the **Daisan Daiba Historic Park**, with the remains of the original obstructions. A short walk west is **Tokyo Decks** with five floors of restaurants and shops plus **Joypolis**, a huge Sega center full of the latest electronic games. In front of Decks is the station for water buses from Hinode Pier. Behind it is the headquarters of Tokyo landmark, **Fuji TV**. Nearby are a cinema complex, Mediage, and a shopping mall, Aquacity. Located in Aomi, is the **National Museum of Emerging Science and Innovation**, better known as Miraikan, with interactive robots, bio-technology, and ecological exhibits.

At Aomi station is the **Palette Town** development, where the main attraction is **Venus Fort**, a shopping mall with a stunning interior that re-creates an 18th-century Italian town at twilight. Palette Town also includes Toyota's City Showcase with a massive display area, and state-of-the-art driving simulators. In the History Garage are cleverly displayed cars from the 1950s to 1970s. Nearby is Future World with a short virtual drive into the future. Right beside all this is a large Ferris wheel.

The futuristic Fuji TV headquarters, Odaiba

Part of the Ebisu Garden Place complex, Ebisu

Wanza Ariake building has shops and restaurants and is connected to Kokusai-Tenjijo Seimon station, as is **Tokyo Big Sight** (or Tokyo International Exhibition Hall).

The gate of the famed – and much-mythologized – Sengaku-ji Temple

❾ Sengaku-ji Temple
泉岳寺

Ⓢ Sengaku-ji stn, Toei Asakusa line. Museum: **Tel** (03) 3441-5560. **Open** 9am–4:30pm (Oct–Mar: to 4pm).

This temple is the site of the climax of Japan's favorite tale of loyalty and revenge, retold in the play *Chushingura* and many movies *(see p59)*. Lord Asano was sentenced to death by *seppuku (see p58)* for drawing his sword when goaded by Lord Kira. Denied the right to seek revenge, 47 of Asano's retainers (or ronin), led by Oishi Kuranosuke, plotted in secret. In 1703, they attacked Kira's house and beheaded him, presenting the head to Asano's grave at Sengaku-ji. They in turn were sentenced to *seppuku* and are buried here. Inside the

temple gate and up the steps on the right is the well (now covered with wire) where the retainers washed Kira's head. Farther ahead on the right are the retainers' graves. Back at the base of the steps is an interesting **museum** with artifacts from the incident and statues of some of the 47.

❿ Ebisu District
恵比寿地区

Ⓢ Ebisu stn, Hibiya line. Ⓡ Ebisu stn, Yamanote line. Tokyo Metropolitan Museum of Photography: **Tel** (03) 3280-0099. **Closed** for renovation until Sep 2016. Ⓦ syabi.com Beer Museum Ebisu: **Tel** (03) 5423-7255. **Open** 11am–7pm Tue–Sun. (Last adm 30 mins before closing.)

The completion in the mid-1990s of **Ebisu Garden Place**, a commercial and residential center, brought this area to life. The **Tokyo Metropolitan Museum of Photography**, to the right of the entrance, has a permanent collection of work by Japanese and foreign photographers. In the heart of Ebisu Garden Place are a Mitsukoshi store, boutiques, two cinemas, a theater, and restaurants, including Chateau Restaurant Joël Robuchon, a French establishments that looks like a 19th-century chateau. The crowded central plaza is a great spot for people-watching. To the left of Mitsukoshi is the small **Beer Museum Ebisu** with exhibits and videos about beer worldwide and in Japan, and free samples.

SHOPPING IN TOKYO

You can buy almost anything you want in Tokyo, from a traditional *kokeshi* (cylindrical wooden doll) to a Chanel handbag or an up-to-the-minute video game. Tokyo-ites love shopping and, budget permitting, the city is a paradise for browsing and buying, with its huge department stores, informal street markets, and fascinating one-of-a-kind shops. Although half the joy of shopping here is the amazing contrasts that can be found side-by-side, some areas do specialize in certain types of shops. Ginza is the place for traditional, upscale stores, while Shinjuku mixes huge arcades with electronics shops stacked high with the latest innovations. Harajuku and Minami-Aoyama are the areas for the funkiest fashions and designs; the older quarters around Ueno and Asakusa offer more traditional Japanese crafts. For general information on shopping in Japan, see pages 340–45.

Department Stores

Department stores grew out of Edo-period mercantile houses. Customers would sit on tatami mats and describe what they wanted, then staff would bring out the goods for their perusal. After the 1923 earthquake, newly built stores allowed customers wearing shoes inside for the first time, revolutionizing shopping. Since the collapse of the "bubble" economy in about 1990, the opulence of Tokyo's department stores has been more muted and prices lower, but they continue to offer a huge variety and immaculate service. Basements are usually supermarkets, where free samples are handed out. Top floors are often filled with restaurants, both Western and Japanese, plus an art gallery and sometimes a museum, too. Ginza's **Mitsukoshi** is perhaps

Tokyo's most famous store; the main Mitsukoshi store is in Nihonbashi, with other branches in Ikebukuro, Shinjuku, and Ebisu. In Ginza **Matsuya** is aimed at a younger, yuppie crowd. Shinjuku's department stores were given a boost with the opening of **Takashimaya**, which has been hugely successful. **Tokyu Hands**, next door, is a fun cornucopia of household wares, and items for the craft enthusiast. There are other branches in Ikebukuro and Shibuya (*see pp100–01*). For a heavy dose of youth culture, try **Marui Jam** in Shibuya.

If you have time for just one department store, visit the flagship **Seibu** store in the New Yurakucho Marion Building. Filled with designer boutiques and established brand names, it elevates shopping to an art form.

Shopping Arcades

Labyrinths of corridors lined with shops occupy major subway and train stations. They are good for window-shopping and sometimes for bargains, but are notoriously disorienting. **Tokyo station** is packed with shops and kiosks. In **Shinjuku station** underground passages run for hundreds of meters to the "Subnade" (underground shopping street) below Yasukuni-dori. Tokyo's **Yaesu underground** is also huge, starting below the Daimaru department store side. Odaiba's **Tokyo Decks** (*see p107*) is five floors of shops and a promenade deck with restaurants. Nearby **Aquacity** and **Wanza Ariake** (*see p107*) are similar. The lower floors of **Tokyo Opera City** (*see p104*) also have restaurants and shops.

Crowds milling up and down Takeshita-dori in Harajuku

Markets

Street markets flourish outside many of the city's train stations. Tokyo's most famous station market is **Ameyoko** (*see p88*) under the tracks at Ueno station. **Takeshita-dori** in Harajuku (*see p99*) is full of shops for the young and fashion-conscious. The ultimate market experience is **Tsukiji Fish Market** (*see p72*); the area to the east is full of small restaurants where piles of dishes crowd the sidewalk, and shops with pungent crates of wasabi horseradish and dried fish hanging from storefronts.

Matsuya, one of Ginza's major department stores

The huge Yodobashi Camera store in Shinjuku

Electronic Goods

The best place to buy electronic goods is Akihabara *(see p77)*. Computers, video games, and software fuel the economy here, but you can usually find just about anything. Prices in Japan are high, and even with the 10 percent or so discount here, the cost is unlikely to be cheaper than elsewhere, though the selection is unmatched. Check that you are buying equipment that is compatible with voltage and systems back home *(see p363)*.

In Akihabara, **Laox** is a big favorite with tax-free shoppers, selling English-language computers and some English-language software. You will need to bring your passport for the tax-free price. **Ishimaru** and **Sofmap** are two more huge electronic department stores. **Akky** and **Takarada** are also duty free.

Camera Equipment

For the best choice of camera equipment, try **Yodobashi Camera** on the west side of Shinjuku, or **Bic Camera** in Yurakucho, Shinjuku, Shibuya, or Ikebukuro. As two of the biggest camera stores, they each have several floors of every brand and every type of equipment. Prices are high, although the margin is not as much as it once was. The language of cameras is universal, and staff can usually help find anything. Ask for the duty-free price; you can even try and bargain a little, particularly if you are willing to pay cash.

Jewelry and Accessories

Pearls are the only form of jewels native to Japan. **Mikimoto** perfected the process and marketing of cultured pearls in 1893, and sells its jewelry in opulent surroundings. For the best range of jewelry at the lowest prices, go to Okachimachi, one stop before Ueno on the Yamanote train line, where there are huge numbers of jewelry stores.

Japan's traditional jewelry for women was *kanzashi*, the hairpins worn in traditional hairstyles (with tortoise-shell combs). Nakamise-dori at Senso-ji Temple *(see pp90–91)* is the place to find these. **Matsuzakaya** sells *kanzashi*, plus other jewelry, and nearby **Ginkado** sells *kanzashi*, costume swords, and fans. Next door is **Bunsendo**, also selling fans. The last maker of handmade wooden combs is **Jusanya** in Ueno.

An *obi* sash on a kimono

Clothing

A traditional Japanese kimono can be incredibly expensive but makes a unique and beautiful souvenir; one supplier is **Kodaimaru** at the Imperial Hotel. Used kimonos are usually a much more reasonable price and are often in excellent condition: try the **Oriental Bazaar**, a complex of shops on Omotesando and **Hayashi Kimono** in Yurakucho. *Yukata* (cotton kimonos suitable for men and women) or *happi* (cotton kimono-style short jackets) are affordable alternatives.

Mainstream men's and women's clothes tend to be conservative, though immaculately designed and cut. Many international designers have their own outlets or are stocked by the major stores.

Designers, focusing on the young, are doing very inventive things with bold colors and unusual materials and cuts. **Seibu** department store in Shibuya and Ikebukuro is full of boutiques from new designers. Gaien-Nishi-dori in Minami-Aoyama *(see p102)* is packed with trendy boutiques, as is Omotesando *(see p99)* and its side streets.

Japan's internationally famous designers have outlets around the city. **Issey Miyake** has boutiques in several department stores and a shop in Minami-Aoyama. **Comme des Garçons** has three stores; go to the main store for directions to the other two. **Hanae Mori** has a shop in her own building in Harajuku.

Textiles

Silk, cotton, linen, and hemp all feature in Japan's long and rich textile history. While some traditional techniques are fading, most are alive and well. Department stores are often the best places to find a range of textiles. **Matsuzakaya** (in Ginza) grew from a Nagoya kimono merchant and stocks bolts of kimono cloth made in Kyoto, and textured *furoshiki* (square wrapping cloths). The **Tokyo National Museum shop** *(see pp84–7)* has a good selection of *furoshiki* and scarves made using traditional techniques. Also good is **Bengara** (see "Traditional Arts and Crafts"). **Miyashita Obi** on Nakamise-dori at Senso-ji Temple *(see pp90–91)* has wonderful *obi* sashes, used to wrap the kimono at the waist.

Traditional umbrellas for sale in Nakamise-dori, near Senso-ji Temple

Contemporary Art and Design

Galleries and showrooms come and go in Tokyo; check local sources of information *(see p112)* for the latest shows. The **Spiral Garden** in Minami-Aoyama's Spiral Building *(see p102)* usually has something interesting by Japanese artists. The shop on the second floor has a selection of contemporary housewares.

In Ginza you can find works by Japanese artists at **Galleria Grafica**, **Plus Minus Gallery**, and **Yoseido Gallery**. **Ginza Graphic Gallery** exhibits both Japanese and foreign works. The **Museum of Contemporary Art** (Watari-Um) near Harajuku has displays of architecture, video, and film media. In Shinjuku the **NTT Intercommunication Center** *(see p104)* features exhibits and installations using the latest technology. In the same building is the **Shinjuku Opera City Gallery**, which displays Japanese painting, watercolors, and examples of graphic art of all types.

Excellent contemporary prints can be found at the **Tolman Collection** near Tokyo Tower. For contemporary ceramics, try **Koransha** in Ginza. Good sources of modern housewares and kitchen gadgets are the department stores **Tokyu Hands** and **Matsuya**, which is also in Ginza.

Traditional Arts and Crafts

Crafts are thriving in Japan. Ceramics is by far the most active craft, and the average Japanese person has a working knowledge of the distinct styles and techniques used in different areas of the country. The larger ceramic bowls used for *matcha* (powdered green tea) are striking in their simple, natural forms; good pieces will be firmly packed in a wooden box. Lacquerware plates, trays, chopsticks, and bowls make excellent souvenirs that are light and easy to transport. The various forms of Japan's beautiful paper, *washi*, also make lightweight gifts; it can be bought as writing paper or in packs of square sheets for origami.

Ironware kettle, Japan Traditional Crafts Center

Maruzen in Nihonbashi is an excellent source of many of these craft items, including ceramics, woodcraft, and lacquerware, as is **Takumi** in Ginza. **Itoya**, also in Ginza, is packed with crafts, especially *washi*; it also has brushes, ink, and inkstones for calligraphy. **Kurodaya**, at Senso-ji Temple *(see pp90–91)*, has been selling *washi* for over 140 years and stocks everything from modern stationery to traditional kites, plus a wide selection of *chiyogami* (wrapping paper), and traditional masks and clay figurines. The **Japan Folk Crafts Museum** *(see p104)* has a small, high-quality selection.

There is a whole tradition of dolls made for viewing in glass cases; these run into hundreds, even thousands, of dollars to buy. A good supplier is **Yoshitoku** in Asakusa. **Mataro Ningyo** in Ueno specializes in Edo *kimekomi* dolls. The figurines in **Sukeroku**, at the end of Senso-ji's Nakamise-dori, are easy to carry home.

Noren, the cloth curtains that hang over the entrances to many small shops, are unique mementos. **Bengara** specializes in *noren*, with beautiful cotton and silk designs.

Wood-block prints are rarely bargains, but are available at reasonable prices. In Jinbocho two famous shops are almost next to each other: **Oya Shobo** and **Hara Shobo**. For new prints from old wood-blocks on *washi* **Isetatsu** is excellent; it also sells beautiful sheets of *chiyogami* from old designs.

Specialty Shops

There are all kinds of niche shops filled with uniquely Japanese items. The following are all in Nakamise-dori at Senso-ji: **Sanbido** sells religious statues and beautiful dolls; **Nishijima Umbrellas** has traditional umbrellas; **Tokiwado** has been selling *kaminari okoshi* crackers – famous for crackling like a clap of thunder when bitten – for 200 years; **Nakatsuka** sells candies and sweet crackers.

Kappabashi-dori *(see p88)* is Tokyo's center for kitchenware and plastic food.

A traditional candy shop in Nakamise-dori, Senso-ji Temple

DIRECTORY

Department Stores

Marui Jam
1-22-6 Jinnan, Shibuya.
Map 1 B5.
Tel (03) 3464-0101.

Matsuya
3-6-1 Ginza.
Map 5 C2.
Tel (03) 3567-1211.

Mitsukoshi
1-4-1 Nihonbashi,
Muro-machi.
Map 5 C1.
Tel (03) 3241-3311.

Seibu
New Yurakucho Marion
Building, 2-5-1 Yurakucho,
Chiyoda-ku.
Map 5 B2.
Tel (03) 6252-1381.

Takashimaya
5-24-2 Sendagaya.
Map 1 B2.
Tel (03) 5361-1111.

Tokyu Hands
5-24-2 Sendagaya.
Tel (03) 5361-3111.
1-28-10 Higashi-
Ikebukuro.
Tel (03) 3980-6111.

Electronic Goods

Akky
1-15-8 Soto-Kanda.
Map 3 C4.
Tel (03) 3253-4787.

Ishimaru
1-9-14 Soto-Kanda.
Map 3 C4.
Tel (03) 3255-1500.

Laox
1-2-9 Soto-Kanda.
Map 3 C4.
Tel (03) 3253-7111.

Sofmap
4-1-1 Soto-Kanda.
Map 3 C4.
Tel (03) 3253-1111.

Takarada
1-14-7 Soto-Kanda.
Map 3 C4.
Tel (03) 3253-0101.

Camera Equipment

Bic Camera
1-11-1 Yurakucho.
Map 5 B2.
Tel (03) 5221-1111.
1-24-12 Shibuya.
Map 1 B5.
Tel (03) 5466-1111.

Yodobashi Camera
1-11-1 Nishi-Shinjuku.
Map 1 B2.
Tel (03) 3346-1010.

Jewelry and Accessories

Jusanya
2-12-21 Ueno.
Map 3 C3.
Tel (03) 3831-3238.
Closed Sun.

Mikimoto
4-5-5 Ginza.
Map 5 B2.
Tel (03) 3535-4611.

Clothing

Comme des Garçons
5-2-1 Minami-Aoyama.
Map 1 C5.
Tel (03) 3406-3951.

Hanae Mori
3-6-1 Kita-Aoyama.
Map 1 C4.
Tel (03) 3499-1601.

Hayashi Kimono
International Arcade,
2-1-1 Yurakucho.
Map 5 B2.
Tel (03) 3501-4012.

Issey Miyake
3-18-11 Minami-Aoyama.
Map 1 C5.
Tel (03) 3423-1408.

Kodaimaru
Imperial Hotel Arcade,
1-1-1 Uchisaiwaicho.
Map 5 B2.
Tel (03) 3508-7697.

Oriental Bazaar
5-9-13 Jingumae.
Map 1 B4.
Tel (03) 3400-3933.
Closed Thu.

Textiles

Matsuzakaya
6-10-1 Ginza.
Map 5 B3.
Tel (03) 3572-1111.

Contemporary Art and Design

Galleria Grafica
1F and 2F Ginza S2 Bldg,
6-13-4 Ginza.
Map 5 B3.
Tel (03) 5550-1335.
Closed Sun & public hols.

Ginza Graphic Gallery
DNP Ginza Bldg,
7-7-2 Ginza.
Map 5 B3.
Tel (03) 3571-5206.
Closed Sun & public hols.

Koransha
6-14-20 Ginza.
Map 5 B3.
Tel (03) 3543-0951.
Closed Sun & public hols.

Museum of Contemporary Art (Watari-Um)
3-7-6 Jingumae.
Map 1 C4.
Tel (03) 3402-3001.

Plus Minus Gallery
3F TEPCO Ginza-kan,
6-11-1 Ginza.
Map 5 B3.
Tel (03) 3575-0456.
Closed Wed.

Tolman Collection
2-2-18 Shiba Daimon.
Map 5 A4.
Tel (03) 3434-1300.
Closed Tue.

Yoseido Gallery
5-5-15 Ginza.
Map 5 B3.
Tel (03) 3571-1312.
Closed Sun & public hols.

Traditional Arts and Crafts

Bengara
1-35-6 Asakusa.
Map 4 F3. **Tel** (03) 3841-6613. **Closed** 3rd Thu
of month

Hara Shobo
2-3 Kanda-Jinbocho.
Map 3 B5.
Tel (03) 3261-7444.
Closed Public hols.

Isetatsu
2-18-9 Yanaka.
Map 3 B1.
Tel (03) 3823-1453.

Itoya
2-7-15 Ginza.
Map 5 C2.
Tel (03) 3561-8311.

Kurodaya
1-2-5 Asakusa.
Map 4 F3.
Tel (03) 3844-7511.
Closed Mon.

Maruzen
2-3-10 Nihonbashi.
Map 5 B1.
Tel (03) 6214-2001.

Mataro Ningyo
5-15-13 Ueno.
Map 3 C3.
Tel (03) 3833-9662.
Closed Varies.

Oya Shobo
1-1 Kanda-Jinbocho.
Map 3 B5.
Tel (03) 3291-0062.
Closed Sun.

Takumi
8-4-2 Ginza. **Map** 5 B3.
Tel (03) 3571-2017.
Closed Sun & public hols.

Yoshitoku
1-9-14 Asakusabashi.
Map 4 D4.
Tel (03) 3863-4419.

ENTERTAINMENT IN TOKYO

Tokyo is one of the liveliest places on the planet. Contrary to the popular image, the Japanese are not simply a nation of workaholics – they play hard, too. The young in particular are demanding more "lifestyle" time. Traditionally, Japanese gather with like-minded friends at small establishments catering to their interests; as a result, thousands of entertainment venues fill the city. There's a mind-boggling range of live music from jazz and blues to pop and techno, and the classical music scene is also very active. Tokyo is the best place to see traditional drama and is well served by touring national and international theater groups. Sports fans can head for packed baseball and soccer games, or sample traditional martial arts including sumo, the national sport.

Information Sources

Local guide *Metropolis* is a free weekly magazine (and website), published every Friday, with plenty of information on entertainment in Tokyo. Saturday's *Japan Times* and Thursday's *Daily Yomiuri* also have good listings. They are often available at convenience stores and station kiosks, as well as book stores such as **Kinokuniya**, **Tower Records**, and **Maruzen**. Information on events in and around Tokyo can be accessed by visiting the **Japan National Tourist Organization (JNTO)** website.

Online sources **Where in Tokyo**, **Outdoor Japan**, **Go Tokyo**, and **Japan Visitor** (a calendar of traditional festivals happening in and around the city) are also good places to go for information.

Booking Tickets

Tickets can go very quickly, so make decisions fast, be prepared for some disappointments, and have an alternative plan. For popular Japanese entertainment (such as Kabuki, Noh, sumo, or baseball) try to book in advance via a travel agent.

In Tokyo two of the main ticket agencies are **Ticket PIA** and **CN Playguide**. They can be hard to reach by phone, so it's often easier to book in person; a convenient office is **Ticket PIA** at Ginza's Sony Building *(see p70)*. Many department stores also have their own ticket offices. Alternatively, book direct by phoning the venue; you pay when you pick up the tickets.

Staff ready to help at Daimaru department store ticket office

Most agencies speak only Japanese, so try to have a Japanese-speaker help you.

Traditional Theater

Kabuki and Noh, the two main forms of traditional theater *(see pp40–41)*, are well represented in Tokyo. Many visitors find Noh heavy-going due to the slow-paced action and dialogue in a foreign language. As a theatrical experience bordering on the mystical, however, Noh can be exceptionally powerful. The **Noh National Theater** near Sendagaya JR station usually has weekend performances. Tickets vary from ¥2,600 to ¥4,800. It is also possible to see plays at a Noh school, **Kanze Noh-gakudo**, for example. Noh can occasionally be seen as it was originally performed: on an outdoor stage in front of a temple illuminated by torchlight.

Kabuki is an all-male flamboyant spectacle with rousing stories, elaborate sets, and amazing costumes. In 1986 Super Kabuki controversially combined avant-garde ideas and high-tech special effects (such as actors flying through the air) with traditional Kabuki. The reconstructed **Kabuki-za Theater** *(see p72)* is the main venue for Kabuki, with near-daily performances starting mid-morning and lasting three or more hours. It is also possible to buy a ticket to see just one act as a taster or if short of time. Prices range from ¥2,500 to ¥17,000, or ¥900 for the one-act ticket.

The National Theater has Kabuki performances in January, March, October, November, and December. Bunraku traditional puppet theater *(see p41)* is sometimes staged in the National Theater's Small Hall.

Kyogen is Japan's oldest form of drama, and includes

Kabuki in action at the Kabuki-za Theater

Movie poster in Shinjuku, one of Tokyo's centers for cinema

acrobatics and juggling. Now played to comic effect, Kyogen is often performed as part of Noh, or as individual plays between Noh plays. Another theatrical tradition is Rakugo, a form of story-telling which literally means "falling down". Dressed in a kimono and using a minimum of props, storytellers sit on *zabuton* cushions in small theaters such as **Suzumoto** in Ueno and pass on tales old and new. Manzai, or stand-up comedy, is a Kansai tradition that can be found in Tokyo, with Shinjuku's **Lumine the Yoshimoto** a convenient venue.

International and Contemporary Theater and Dance

The theater scene encompasses everything from Shakespeare (at the **Tokyo Globe**) and Broadway musicals to comedy, classical ballet, and modern dance, with the main venues in Shinjuku, Shibuya, and Marunouchi. The level of performance is usually high.

The Tokyo Comedy Store offers non-Japanese and Japanese the chance to show off their comedy skills in English: two laughter-packed hours on the fourth Friday of the month at **Crocodile** in Harajuku.

A uniquely Japanese theater experience is Takarazuka, a company divided into five troupes and composed entirely of women. With

their own state-of-the-art **Takarazuka Theater** in Yurakucho, they perform adaptations in Japanese of Western musicals and historic love stories, and are famed for their lavish productions.

Poster advertising a Japanese theater production

Nihon Buyo Kyokai stages regular performances of traditional dance. Usually at the end of May, the Azuma Odori, an annual production of dance, drama, and music, brings Tokyo's geisha community on stage at the **Shinbashi Enbujo Theater**.

Buto – a unique and compelling art form – is contemporary dance combined with performance art. Developed in the 1960s, performances feature shaven-headed dancers, almost naked, painted with makeup. Slow, simplistic choreography seeks to create beauty out of the self-imposed grotesqueness.

Cinema

Movie-going is not cheap in Japan, costing about ¥1,800 per person. However, on Cinema Day, usually the first day of each month, ticket prices are reduced. Some American and European films may take up to three months to reach Japan. Non-Japanese films are usually shown in the original language with Japanese subtitles.

In Shibuya (*see pp100–01*), **Bunkamura** sometimes shows Japanese films with English subtitles and occasionally screens independent and European films. Also in Shibuya, the **Theater Image Forum**, designed by architect Masaharu Takahashi, uses the most advanced digital technology. The centrally located **Toho Cinemas Chanter** shows art-house and independent movies.

For mainstream movies, try **United Cinema Toyosu**, which is one of the largest in Tokyo, with 12 screens. It is possible to hire children's seats and even blankets here. **Marunouchi Piccadilly** in the Mullion Building in Ginza (*see pp70–71*) has five screens, while **Ebisu Garden Place** (*see p107*) has two. A popular choice is the nine-screen **Toho Cinema Roppongi Hills** in the Roppongi Hills complex. Fans of Japanese cinema should visit the **National Film Center**.

The annual **Tokyo International Film Festival** is held in October/November. Other worthwhile festivals include the **Tokyo International Lesbian & Gay Film Festival**.

Live performance by the Tokyo Comedy Store

Live Music

There is no shortage of venues to hear live music in Tokyo. Many big acts, Japanese and foreign, appear at Shibuya's **Club Quattro**. **O-West** and **O-East** are two other good venues in Shibuya for techno and J-pop. In Ebisu the **Liquid Room** is a trendy place to see a mix of bands. The **Akasaka Blitz** hosts J-pop groups and some foreign acts. Venues for live music and experimental performances range from the ever-exciting **SuperDeluxe** in Nishi-Azabu, to expat-hangout **The Pink Cow** in Shibuya. The **Mandala Live House** has mostly Japanese bands.

For big-name jazz performers try the **Shinjuku Pit Inn**, the **Cotton Club** in Marunouchi, and the **Blue Note Tokyo**. **Birdland**, in Roppongi's Square Building, is one of Tokyo's longest-running jazz clubs. For a cozier, more intimate setting, try the **Blues Alley Japan**, a small club featuring blues, jazz, rock, world music, and other genres. In Roppongi, **STB139** offers a very eclectic mix of music.

The domestic and international classical music and opera scene in Tokyo is flourishing. **Tokyo Opera City** (see p104), **Bunkamura** (see p100), **New National Theater**, **Suntory Hall**, **NHK Hall**, and the **Tokyo International Forum** (see p75) are all popular spots.

Roppongi, a focus for music and nightclubs in Tokyo

A popular karaoke club in downtown Tokyo

Karaoke

Karaoke, which translates from the Japanese characters as "empty orchestra", dates from the 1960s. Today it is not only a prime pastime for many Japanese, irrespective of age, but a global phenomenon. Devotees sing favorite songs to pre-recorded tapes, CDs, and DVDs in bars, pubs, and even at home. Most popular are Western standards, current pop songs, and *enka*, the Japanese equivalent of French *chanson*.

It is common for Japanese companies to build karaoke complexes consisting of small, cozy rooms for couples to much larger spaces, some with concert-style lighting, for groups of friends and large parties. Food and drinks can be ordered. It is hard to escape karaoke – it is everywhere in the city.

Big Echo is the name of one major karaoke chain that operates in Tokyo, and the well known games company Sega operates another. Family restaurant chains such as Denny's, Jonathan's, and Royal Host are also strong supporters. Sometimes venues even star in movies: Karaoke-kan in Shibuya's Center Gai (see p100) is the famed location used in the 2003 movie *Lost in Translation* – the rooms used are 601 and 602 on the sixth floor.

Gambling

Pachinko (see p101) is a form of disguised gambling; it was devised in Nagoya just after World War II and is based on the American pinball machine. A good place to go if you want to experience *pachinko* firsthand is Maruhan Pachinko Tower in Shibuya. Here, each floor has a different theme, and there are special seats for couples.

Winnings from *pachinko* are generally exchanged for goods – brand-name goods in upscale areas – or for money, but the money exchange has to be done outside the premises to remain within the law, through a hole in the wall. This is because gambling for money is illegal in Japan, except for certain approved (and unsurprisingly highly popular) activities such as horse-racing, powerboat racing, bicycle racing, and major lotteries.

More often than not, however, a blind eye is turned by the Japanese authorities to the ways in which people choose to indulge in gambling. Mahjong is played in private clubs and homes, for example. Some hostess clubs offer gambling in addition to their other services, as long as it is not for money.

Maruhan Pachinko Tower in Shibuya

Nightclubs

Tokyo's clubs are many and varied, and the club scene is very fluid; check current listings (see p112) for the latest information. There are several centers for nightclubs; Roppongi *(see pp102–3)*, the city's upscale playground, is one of the most lively. The **Square Building** (see Birdland, under "Live Music") near Roppongi station is full of clubs from top to bottom. The Ni-chome area of Shinjuku is home to some 250 gay clubs, as well as numerous pubs and bars. Many famous DJs operate at **AgeHa**, Tokyo's largest nightclub, in Shin-kiba. **Atom**, in Shibuya, attracts a mainly young clientele and has two dance floors as well as a floor just for relaxation.

Other clubs currently drawing crowds for every type of dance music from salsa to techno and house disco are **Womb**, **La Fabrique**, and **Club Asia**.

Clubs with a show tend to get going early in the evening, around 7–8pm; the last show ends in time to catch the last trains out to the suburbs, about 11–11:30pm. Smaller clubs start and end later, while dance clubs won't warm up until around 11pm and often keep going all night. Expect a cover charge at most clubs of ¥2,000–4,000, usually including one drink.

Sumo

Sumo tournaments, each lasting 15 days, are held in Tokyo in January, May (when the emperor himself attends), and September, all at the impressive 10,000-seat **National Sumo Stadium** in Ryogoku *(see p106)*.

Tournaments begin on a Sunday, with each fighter wrestling once a day. Bouts start each day at around 2:30pm with the lowest-ranking wrestlers and continue in ascending order, with the top ranks wrestling from 5–6pm, ending with a bout involving the highest-ranked wrestler, usually a *yokozuna* (grand champion). The stadium tends to fill up with spectators as the day goes on.

The best views are on the north side of the stadium. It is advisable to book tickets in advance from **Playguide**, **Ticket PIA** at the

Sumo wrestlers stand for a ceremony at the Ryogoku stadium in Tokyo

Sony Building, or any **Lawson's** convenience store. Easiest to get are midweek tickets in the first week of a tournament. If you cannot buy tickets via an agency, try asking your hotel to check for returns, or lining up at the stadium itself at about 8am on the day.

If you are not in Tokyo during a tournament, you may be able to watch the daily practice at a sumo stable, or *beya (see p106)*. Most are open to anyone who wants to watch, with a few basic rules: don't eat or use a camera flash, and be quiet. The closer a tournament is, the more likely you are to be politely turned away. The best time to view practice is 6–10am. Most of the *beya* are situated near Ryogoku station. Try **Kasugano Beya**, a tall building with a green copper gable over the entrance, **Izutsu Beya**, or **Dewanoumi Beya**. Traditional sumo has been much enlivened by an influx of

Banners outside the National Sumo Stadium, Ryogoku

foreign wrestlers from Hawaii, Mongolia, and Europe, many of whom have become very successful. Some stables with an unusually open attitude have also made special trips abroad in order to raise awareness of sumo internationally; some of their stars even appear in television and other advertisements. While eyebrows may have been raised among purists, they cannot deny that such activities have been very good for business.

Martial Arts

Martial arts *(see p39)* are practiced in many places throughout Tokyo, but different establishments vary in their openness to non-Japanese as observers and participants. Contact **Tokyo TIC** for a list of *dojo* (practice halls) that allow spectators. To find out about participating in martial arts training, contact one of the national regulatory bodies *(see pp350–53)*.

Participants in a kendo training program at a Tokyo *dojo*

Baseball and Soccer

Baseball's place as Japan's second national sport appears to be suffering in the face of soccer's rising popularity. Some young players are choosing to go abroad to escape samurai-like regimes of training but the game continues to stir fervor.

There are two professional baseball leagues in Japan: Central League and Pacific League. The winners face off at the end of the season for the final of the Japan Series. The Central League's Yomiuri Giants remain Japan's most popular pro-baseball team *(see p351)*. Their games in the **Tokyo Dome** are always sold out; book through an agent well in advance. The best place to enjoy a game in the capital is in the beautiful **Jingu Stadium**, home of the Tokyo Yakult Swallows (also

Central League). Tickets are often available at **Ticket PIA**.

The J-League, Japan's professional soccer league, started in 1993. The World Cup, staged in Japan and Korea in 2002, sent interest soaring, and this further increased when Japan reached the second round of the World Cup in 2010. But it was the women's team, Nadeshiko Japan, that really electrified the nation when they won the Women's World Cup in 2011.

Ajinomoto Stadium, with a capacity of 50,000, is home to two J-League teams – FC Tokyo and Tokyo Verdy 1969. Tourist information centers have details of games, and tickets are available at **Ticket PIA** or from the stadium on the day of the match. Gangster-linked ticket touts are much in evidence in Tokyo so always use caution.

Victory in the 2011 FIFA Women's World Cup

Uniforms on display at the Baseball Hall of Fame, Tokyo Dome

Other Sports

For details on other sports check the Sports column in *Metropolis* magazine. Entries are mostly concerned with gathering together like-minded people wanting to play, but those people will also know where to watch their favorite sports, from tennis and rugby to basketball, cycling, and cricket. For mountaineering, skiing, and watersports see pp352–3.

DIRECTORY

Information Sources

Go Tokyo
w gotokyo.org/en

Japan National Tourist Organization (JNTO)
Tel (03) 3201-3331.
w jnto.go.jp

Japan Visitor
w japanvisitor.com

Kinokuniya
3-17-7 Shinjuku.
Map 1 B2.
Tel (03) 3354-0131.
w kinokuniya.co.jp

Maruzen
1-6-4 Marunouchi.
Map 5 B1.
Tel (03) 5288-8881.
w maruzen.co.jp

Metropolis
w metropolis.co.jp

Outdoor Japan
w outdoorjapan.com

Tower Records
1-22-14 Jinnan.
Map 1 B5. Tel (03) 3496-3661. w tower.jp

Where in Tokyo
w whereintokyo.com

Booking Tickets

CN Playguide
Tel (03) 5802-9999.
w cnplayguide.com

Ticket PIA
Tel (0570) 02-9999.
w pia.co.jp

Traditional Theater

Kanze Nohgakudo
1-16-4 Shoto.
Map 1 A5.
Tel (03) 3469-5241.

Lumine the Yoshimoto
7F (South Exit from station) 3-38-2 Shinjuku.
Tel (03) 5339-1112.

Noh National Theater
4-18-1 Sendagaya.
Map 1 C3.
Tel (03) 3423-1331.

National Theater
4-1 Hayabusa-cho.
Map 2 F3.
Tel (03) 3265-7411.
w ntj.jac.go.jp/english/index.html

Suzumoto
2-7-12 Ueno.
Tel (03) 3834-5906.
w rakugo.or.jp

International and Contemporary Theater and Dance

Crocodile
6-18-8 B1 Jingumae.
Tel (03) 3499-5205.
w tokyocomedy.com

Nihon Buyo Kyokai
2-18-1 Kachidoki.
Map 6 D4.
Tel (03) 3533-6455.

Shinbashi Enbujo Theater
6-18-2 Ginza.
Map 5 C3.
Tel (03) 3541-2600.

Takarazuka Theater
1-1-3 Yurakucho. Map 5 B2. Tel (03) 5251-2001.
w kageki.hankyu.co.jp/english/index.html

Tokyo Globe
3 1 2 Hyakunin-cho, Shinjuku.
Tel (03) 3366-4020.
w tglobe.net

Cinema

Bunkamura
2-24-1 Dogen-zaka, Shibuya-ku. Map 1 A5.
Tel (03) 3477 9111.
w bunkamura.co.jp

Marunouchi Piccadilly
Mullion Building, 2-5-1 Yurakucho. Map 5 B2.
Tel (03) 3201-2881.

DIRECTORY

National Film Center
3-7-6 Kyobashi.
Map 5 C2.
Tel (03) 3561-0823.

Theater Image Forum
2-10-2 Shibuya. **Map** 1 B5.
Tel (03) 5766-0114.

Toho Cinemas Chanter
1-2-2 Yurakucho.
Map 5 B2.
Tel (03) 3591-1511.

Toho Cinema Roppongi Hills
6-10-2 Roppongi,
Minato-ku.
Map 2 E5.
Tel (03) 5775-6090
(press 9 for English).

Tokyo International Film Festival
w tiff-jp.net

Tokyo International Lesbian & Gay Film Festival
w tokyo-lgff.org

United Cinema Toyosu
3F Urban Dock LaLaport
Toyosu, 2-4-9 Toyosu,
Koto-ku.
Map 6 E4.
Tel (03) 6219-3000.

Live Music

Akasaka Blitz
TBS Square, 5-3-2
Akasaka. **Map** 2 E4.
Tel (03) 3584-8811.

Birdland
B2 Square Building, 3-10-3
Roppongi. **Map** 2 E5.
Tel (03) 3478-3456.

Blue Note Tokyo
Raika Building, 6-3-16
Minami-Aoyama.
Map 2 D5.
Tel (03) 5485-0088.

Blues Alley Japan
Hotel Wing International
Megro, 1-3-14 Meguro.
Map 1 B1.
Tel (03) 5496-4381.

Bunkamura
2-24-1 Dogen-zaka,
Shibuya-ku. **Map** 1 A5.
Tel (03) 3477 9111.
w bunkamura.co.jp

Club Quattro
4F Quattro Parco, 32-13
Udagawa-cho. **Map** 1 A5.
Tel (03) 3477-8750.

Cotton Club
7 F Tokia, Tokyo Building,
2-7-3 Marunouchi,
Chiyoda-ku. **Map** 5 B2.
Tel (03) 3215-1555.
w cottonclubjapan.
co.jp

Liquid Room
3-16-6 Higashi, Shibuya-
ku. **Tel** (03) 5464-0800.

Mandala Live House
B1 MR Building,
3-2-2 Minami-Aoyama.
Map 1 C4.
Tel (03) 5474-0411.

New National Theater
1-1-1 Honmachi,
Shibuya-ku.
Tel (03) 5351-3011.

NHK Hall
2-2-1 Jinnan. **Map** 1 B4.
Tel (03) 3465-1751.

O-East
2-14-8 Dogen-zaka.
Map 1 A5. **Tel** (03) 5458-
4681.

O-West
2-3 Maruyamacho.
Map 1 A5.
Tel (03) 5784-7088.

The Pink Cow
Villa Moderna B1
1-3-18 Shibuya.
Map 1 B5.
Tel (03) 3406-5597.
w thepinkcow.com

Shinjuku Pit Inn
B1 Accord Building, 2-12-
4 Shinjuku.
Map 1 B1.
Tel (03) 3354-2024.

STB139
6-7-11 Roppongi.
Map 2 E5.
Tel (03) 5474-0139.

Suntory Hall
1-13-1 Akasaka.
Map 2 F4.
Tel (03) 3584-9999.

SuperDeluxe
B1F 3-1-25 Nishi-Azabu.
Map 2 E5.
Tel (03) 5412-0515.
w super-deluxe.com

Karaoke

Big Echo Karaoke
Ginza 4-2-14.
Map 5 C3.
Tel (03) 3563-5100.
7-14-12 Roppongi.
Tel (03) 5770-7700.

Gambling

Japan Association for International Horse Racing
(JAIR Keiba Kokusai Koryu
Kyokai).
Tel (03) 3503-8221.
w jair.jrao.ne.jp/japan/
index.html

Maruhan Pachinko Tower
28-6 Udagawa-cho,
Shibuya.
Map 1 A5.
Tel (03) 5458 3905.

Powerboat Racing (Kyotei)
w kyotei.or.jp

Tokyo Racecourse
1-1 Hiyoshi-cho, Fuchi-shi.
Tel (042) 363-3141.
w jair.jrao.ne.jp/
courses/jra.jra001.html

Nightclubs

AgeHa
2-2-10 Shin-kiba, Koto-ku.
Tel (03) 5534-1515.

Atom
4F-6F Dr Jeekahns
2-4 Maruyama-cho,
Shibuya (along
Rambling Street).
Map 1 A5.
Tel (03) 5428-5195.

Club Asia
1-8 Maruyamacho,
Shibuya-ku.
Map 1 A5.
Tel (03) 5458-2551.

La Fabrique
Gate B1F 16-9 Udagawa-
cho, Shibuya.
Tel (03) 5428-5100.

Womb
2-16 Maruyama cho,
Shibuya-ku.
Map 1 A5.
Tel (03) 5459-0039.
w womb.co.jp

Sumo

Dewanoumi Beya
2-3-15 Ryogoku.
Map 4 E5.

Izutsu Beya
2-2-7 Ryogoku.
Map 4 E5.

Kasugano Beya
1-7-11 Ryogoku.
Map 4 E5.

National Sumo Stadium
1-3-28 Yokoami.
Map 4 E4.
Tel (03) 3623-5111.
w sumo.or.jp/eng/
index.html

Baseball and Soccer

Ajinomoto Stadium
376-3 Nishimachi,
Chofu City.
Tel (042) 440-0555.

Jingu Stadium
3-1 Kasumigaoka.
Map 2 D4.
Tel (03) 3404-8999.

Tokyo Dome
1-3-61 Koraku.
Map 3 A3.
Tel (03) 5800-9999.
w tokyo-dome. co.jp/e

TOKYO STREET FINDER

Tokyo is notoriously hard for visitors to find their way around, due to the scarcity of street names and complex numbering system for buildings *(see p377)*. The Tokyo sights covered in this guide, plus Tokyo hotels *(see p302)*, restaurants *(see pp324–6)*, and many of the city's key landmarks are plotted on the maps on the following pages. Transportation points are also marked, and indicated by the symbols listed in the key below. When map references are given, the first number tells you which Street Finder map to turn to, and the letter and number that follow refer to the grid reference. The map below shows the area of Tokyo covered by the six Street Finder maps. The Street Finder index *(see pp119–21)* lists street names, buildings, and stations. For a map of the Tokyo subway, see the inside back cover.

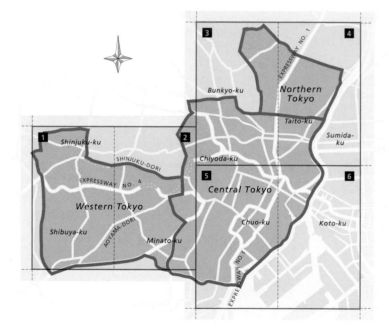

Key

▉	Major sight	🏛	Police station
▢	Other sight	🛕	Temple
▢	Other building	⛩	Shrine
S	Subway station	✝	Church
🚉	Train station	══	JR rail line
🚝	Monorail station	══	Other rail line
🚢	Riverboat boarding point	══	Expressway
i	Tourist information		Pedestrian street
➕	Hospital		

0 kilometers 2
0 miles 1

Scale of Maps 1-6

0 meters 500
0 yards 500

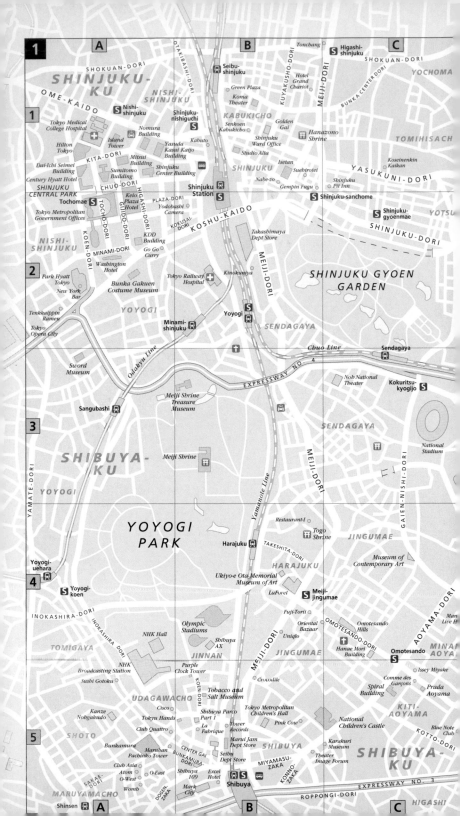

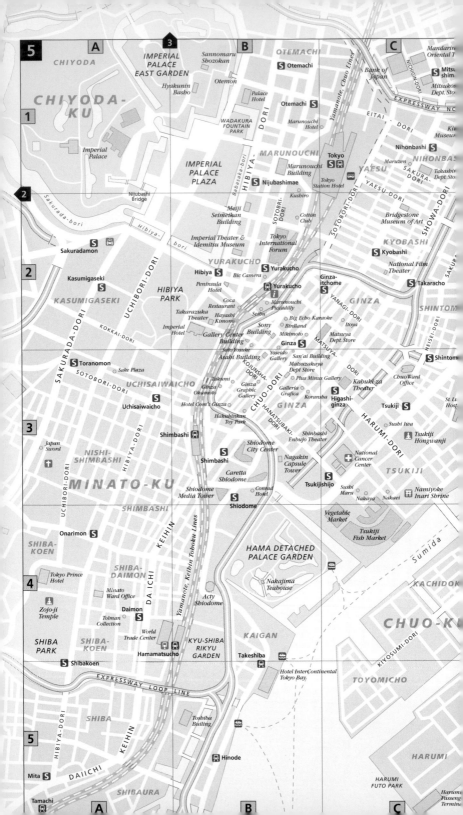

JAPAN REGION BY REGION

Japan at a Glance

Honshu, Japan's largest island, is characterized by its mountainous center and densely populated southern coastline. Most of Japan's ancient temples, shrines, and imperial cities are on Honshu, along with the capital, Tokyo. North of Honshu lies the island of Hokkaido, a largely unspoiled wilderness of national parks, snowbound for much of the year. The quiet, traditional island of Shikoku lies south of Honshu, as does Kyushu island, a varied mixture of modern cities, hot springs, and archaeological ruins. A string of subtropical islands with Okinawa at the center stretches away to the southwest.

The Inland Sea, separating Honshu and Shikoku islands

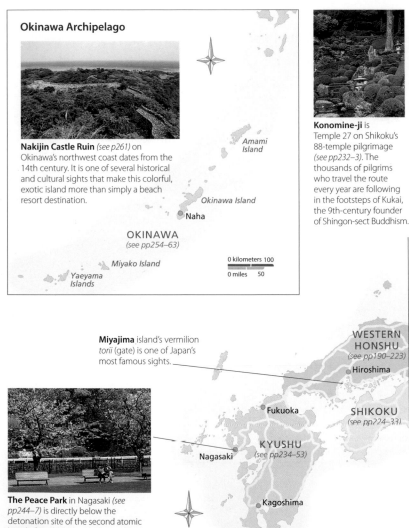

Okinawa Archipelago

Nakijin Castle Ruin *(see p261)* on Okinawa's northwest coast dates from the 14th century. It is one of several historical and cultural sights that make this colorful, exotic island more than simply a beach resort destination.

Amami Island

Okinawa Island

● Naha

OKINAWA
(see pp254–63)

Miyako Island

0 kilometers 100
0 miles 50

Yaeyama Islands

Konomine-ji is Temple 27 on Shikoku's 88-temple pilgrimage *(see pp232–3)*. The thousands of pilgrims who travel the route every year are following in the footsteps of Kukai, the 9th-century founder of Shingon-sect Buddhism.

Miyajima island's vermilion *torii* (gate) is one of Japan's most famous sights.

WESTERN HONSHU
(see pp190–223)

● Hiroshima

● Fukuoka

SHIKOKU
(see pp224–37)

KYUSHU
(see pp234–53)

Nagasaki

● Kagoshima

The Peace Park in Nagasaki *(see pp244–7)* is directly below the detonation site of the second atomic bomb, for which the city is now known worldwide. A cosmopolitan port for centuries, it has regenerated since the war to become a thriving urban center.

↓ Okinawa

0 kilometers 200
0 miles 100

Shikotsu-Toya National Park *(see pp288–9)* contains active and dormant volcanos, and hot springs. National parks are central to Hokkaido's appeal, encompassing coastal meadows, wetlands, and mountains.

The Philosopher's Walk *(see p174)* is a tranquil canalside walk famed for its cherry trees. The path links two of Kyoto's temples: Nanzen-ji and Ginkaku-ji.

HOKKAIDO
(see pp284–95)

Wakkanai

Sapporo

Hakodate

Aomori

Morioka

NORTHERN HONSHU
(see pp264–83)

Sendai

Niigata

Nagano

Takayama

CENTRAL HONSHU
(see pp132–57)

TOKYO
(see pp64–127)

Nagoya

KYOTO CITY
(see pp158–89)

ka

Nikko *(see pp268–75)* is a complex of shrines and temples in the mountains of Northern Honshu. The shrines are intricately carved with images of animals, birds, and flowers, painted in vivid colors.

Hakone *(see pp142–3)* is a hilly hot-spring area in Central Honshu on the old route between Edo (Tokyo) and Kyoto. Its many attractions include Lake Ashi, on which replicas of old ships sail; an open-air sculpture museum; and fine views of Mount Fuji, which dominates the plain to the west of Tokyo.

Nara *(see pp194–9)* was Japan's first permanent capital and a center of Buddhism. It retains beautiful buildings in a traditional layout and is home to one of Japan's most spectacular festivals, Omizu-tori *(see p46)*, each spring.

CENTRAL HONSHU

Lying between Tokyo and Kyoto, Central Honshu epitomizes the contrasts of Japan today. Its densely populated coastal belt includes the country's second- and fourth-largest cities, while the interior contains its highest, wildest mountains. Between these extremes, much of the region is relatively accessible, yet remote enough to have kept traditional rural lifestyles, architecture, and festivals.

The mountains of Central Honshu incorporate not only Mount Fuji but also the North and South Japan Alps, with many peaks over 3,000 m (10,000 ft). They dictate the area's character, and offer hiking, skiing, and hot springs. During the Edo period (1603–1868) five post roads crossed the region, two of which linked Edo (Tokyo) and Kyoto. Feudal lords were required to spend half their time in Edo, so long processions traveled the roads, and checkpoints and post towns grew up. Most heavily used were the Tokaido via Yokohama, Hakone, and Shizuoka, and the Nakasendo through the Kiso Valley. Remnants of both can be walked.

Today there is a dramatic contrast between the urban Pacific coast, including Yokohama and Nagoya, and underpopulated rural areas.

Among the latter, the post towns of Kiso and thatched villages of Shokawa have found new life in tourism thanks to unspoiled architecture, while Takayama and Chichibu attract thousands to their festivals. The former regional capitals of Kamakura and Kanazawa maintain tradition in gardens, temples, and crafts. The region produces skilled woodwork: lacquerware in Takayama, Noto, and Kiso; carving in Kamakura; *yosegi-zaiku* (Japanese parquetry) in Hakone. Until the 1970s, silkworms were raised in Shokawa and Chichibu; silk is still dyed in Kanazawa. Central Honshu cuisine focuses on seafood coastally, while mountain fare comprises river fish, *sansai* (wild vegetables), tofu, and miso. Kanazawa's refined yet down-to-earth *Kaga ryori* uses fish and duck; Nagoya is known for eel, chicken, and stronger flavors.

The waterfront at Yokohama, Japan's second-largest city

Exploring Central Honshu

The smooth cone of Mount Fuji – one of the great icons of Japan – rises from the Kanto Plain to the west of Tokyo, and is open to pilgrims and casual hikers in summer. Beyond this is the largely mountainous area known to the Japanese as Chubu. A cluster of cultural and scenic destinations, including Fuji, Hakone, Kamakura, and much of the industrialized Pacific coast, are an easy day trip from Tokyo. Other areas, especially the more rural regions such as the Kiso and Shokawa valleys and the Noto Peninsula, are harder to reach and require more time to explore.

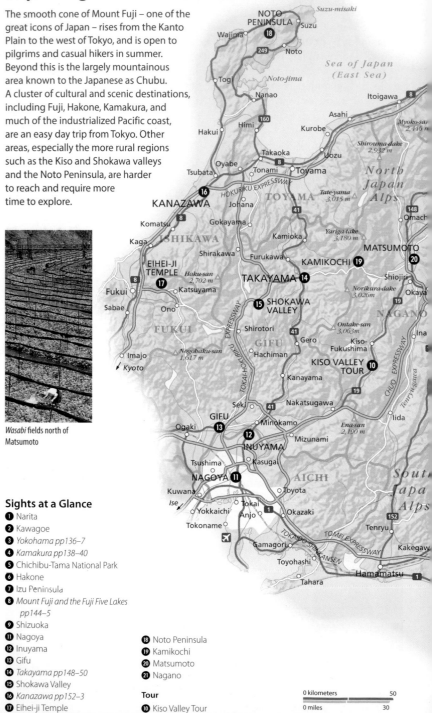

Wasabi fields north of Matsumoto

Sights at a Glance

1. Narita
2. Kawagoe
3. *Yokohama pp136–7*
4. *Kamakura pp138–40*
5. Chichibu-Tama National Park
6. Hakone
7. Izu Peninsula
8. *Mount Fuji and the Fuji Five Lakes pp144–5*
9. Shizuoka
11. Nagoya
12. Inuyama
13. Gifu
14. *Takayama pp148–50*
15. Shokawa Valley
16. *Kanazawa pp152–3*
17. Eihei-ji Temple
18. Noto Peninsula
19. Kamikochi
20. Matsumoto
21. Nagano

Tour
10. Kiso Valley Tour

0 kilometers 50
0 miles 30

For hotels and restaurants see pp302–307 and pp336

Jizo statues at Hase-dera Temple, Kamakura

SAPPORO

Sea of Japan
(East Sea)

TOKYO
KYOTO
OSAKA

Pacific Ocean

KAGOSHIMA

Locator Map

Nagaoka
Joetsu
17
Arai

Iiyama
Nagaoka

AGANO
Suzaka

GUNMA

Ueda
Asama-yama
2,560 m
Shibukawa

Komoro
18
Takasaki
Maebashi
Isesaki
Sano
Utsunomiya

JOSHINETSU EXPRESSWAY
Tomioka
Kumagaya
Koga

Koumi
Chichibu
Ageo
Ryugasaki

hino
Yatsuga-take
2,899 m
SAITAMA
Urawa
Kashiwa
356
NARITA

Nirasaki
Kotu
Enzan
**CHICHIBU-TAMA
NATIONAL PARK** 5
KAWAGOE 2
17
Kawaguchi
Funabashi
Asahi

Shirane-san
3192 m
Okutama
TOKYO
CHIBA
126

YAMANASHI
Hachioji
TOKYO
Chiba
Togane

Fujiyoshida
Otsuki
Kawasaki
Ichihara
Mobara

52
Hadano
KANAGAWA 3 **YOKOHAMA**
Kisarazu
297
128

**MOUNT FUJI
AND THE FUJI
FIVE LAKES** 8
Hiratsuka
1 Fujisawa
4 Yokosuka
Ohara

Gotenba
Odawara
KAMAKURA
*Boso
Peninsula*
128

Fujinomiya
Fuji
6 **HAKONE**
Miura
Futtsu
Katsuura

SHIZUOKA
Numazu
Atami
Kamogawa

Shimizu
Ito
128

9 **SHIZUOKA**
Toi
Shuzenji
Tateyama

Yaizu
*Amagi-san
1,406 m*

himada
7 **IZU PENINSULA**
Oshima Island

Matsuzaki
Higashi-Izu
*Mihara-yama
758 m*

Shimoda

Omae-zaki
Iro-zaki
Nii-jima

Kozu-shima

Miyake-jima

Getting Around

Much of Central Honshu is accessible by
train. The rapid Tokaido Shinkansen runs
from Tokyo to Nagoya and on to Western
Honshu. Another *shinkansen* line runs from
Tokyo to Nagano. The main Chuo line runs to
Matsumoto. Nagoya is a major transportation
hub, but Kanazawa and Eihei-ji are easier to
get to from Kyoto than Nagoya. Visitors will
need to take a bus or rent a car for some
coastal areas, including parts of the Noto
and Izu peninsulas.

Key

═══ Expressway
─── Major road
═══ Other road
─── Main railway
─── Minor railway
─── Border

❶ Narita
成田

Chiba prefecture. ⛰ 100,000. ✈
🚃 ℹ in front of JR stn (0476)
24-3198. 🎎 Setsubun-e (Feb 3).
🌐 **city.narita.chiba.jp/english**

A quiet little town, worlds
removed from nearby Narita
Airport, Narita's main attraction
is **Narita-san Shinsho-ji**, an
Esoteric-Shingon-sect temple
founded in 940 and dedicated
to Fudo Myo-o, Deity of
Immovable Wisdom. Several
times daily, the priests burn
wooden sticks to symbolize
extinguishing of earthly
passions. The streets are full of
traditional shops for the 12
million temple visitors a year.
Environs: Near Narita are over
1,000 ancient burial mounds
(*kofun*); the best are in **Boso
Historical Park**. The **National
Museum of Japanese History**
offers a good survey of Japan.

🏯 **Boso Historical Park**
15 mins by taxi from Ajiki stn.
Tel (0476) 95-3126. **Open** Tue–Sun.

🏛 **National Museum of
Japanese History**
15 mins walk from Keiseisakura stn.
Tel (043) 486-0123. **Open** Tue–Sun. ♿

❷ Kawagoe
川越

Saitama prefecture. ⛰ 335,000. 🚃
ℹ at JR stn (049) 222-5556. 🎎 Ashi-
odori (Leg-dancing, Apr 14), Kawagoe
Festival (3rd weekend in Oct).

Nicknamed "Little Edo," Kawagoe
preserves the atmosphere of
19th-century Edo (Tokyo)
because of its *kura* buildings.

A row of *kura* buildings in Kawagoe

Yokohama Bay Bridge

These clay-walled structures
have double doors, and heavy
shutters. About 30 *kura* remain
and are a 10-minute walk north
of Hon-Kawagoe station. The
Kura-Zukuri Shiryokan,
formerly a *kura* tobacconist, is a
museum. Nearby, **Toki-no-kane**
wooden bell tower was built in
1624 to tell the time and warn
of fires. East of the *kura* streets
is **Kita-in**, a Tendai-sect temple
which includes the only extant
rooms from Edo Castle.

At one time, Kawagoe
possessed its own castle, which
was the dominant structure in
the area. Part of that castle
remains in the shape of
Honmaru Goten, the former
residence of the lord, with
commodious rooms and
elegant spaces.

🏯 **Kura-Zukuri Shiryokan**
Tel (049) 225-4287. **Open** Tue–Sun.
Closed 4th Fri of month. ♿

🏛 **Honmaru Goten**
2-13-1 Kurawa-machi. **Tel** (049) 222-
5399. **Open** Tue–Sun.

❸ Yokohama
横浜

Kanagawa prefecture. ⛰ 3,690,000.
✈ 🚃 ℹ Sangyo Boeki Center Bldg.
(045) 641-4759. 🎎 Chinese New Year
(Feb), Yokohama Port Festival (May 3).
🌐 **city.yokohama.lg.jp**

Japan's second-largest city,
Yokohama has been a center for
shipping, trade, foreign contact,
and modern ideas since the
mid-19th century. Formerly a
small fishing village on the
Tokaido road, it was made a
treaty port in 1859; there
followed an influx of foreign
traders, especially Chinese and
British, making it the biggest
port in Asia by the early 1900s.
The 1923 Kanto Earthquake
wiped out 95 percent of the
city, killing 40,000 people, then
World War II bombing again
destroyed half the city. After the
war, Yokohama became a base
for US soldiers. By the 1970s, it
was once more Japan's largest
port. The heart of the city is
compact and walkable.

Minato Mirai 21, an area of
redeveloped docks, has some
creative architecture (with
hi-tech earthquake-proofing)
and on weekends comes alive
with street performers. Its focal
point is the **Landmark Tower**,
built in 1993 under US architect
Hugh Stubbins and, at 296 m
(971 ft), Japan's tallest building.
Reached by the world's fastest
elevator, at 750 m (2,500 ft) per
minute, the 69th-floor public
lounge has a spectacular
360-degree view. To the north,
Kenzo Tange's **Yokohama**

Museum of Art houses displays of modern art and photography.

In the older, more attractive part of town, the **NYK Maritime Museum** covers the history of shipping, with detailed models. Created on rubble from the 1923 Earthquake, **Yamashita Park** is a pleasant promenade overlooking ships, including the restored moored liner **Hikawa Maru**, which cruised between Yokohama and Seattle in 1930–60, and the 860-m (2,800-ft) long **Yokohama Bay Bridge** (1989).

Chinatown, the largest of Japan's three Chinatowns, has around 2,500 Chinese inhabitants, and a mass of restaurants, food shops, Chinese-medicine shops, and fortune-tellers. At its heart is the Chinese **Kantei-byo Temple** (1887), dedicated to ancient Chinese hero Kuan-yu, who was worshiped as a god of war but is now popular as a god of accountancy, business success, and prosperity.

Among the 4,500 tombs in the early 20th-century **Foreigners' Cemetery** is that of Edmund Morel, the English engineer who helped build Japan's first railroads, with a tombstone shaped like a railroad ticket. The lovely **Sankei-en Garden** belonged to silk-trader Tomitaro Hara (1868–1939). Among the ponds and flowers are 16 architectural treasures, including a three-story pagoda from Kyoto.

Landmark Tower
Tel (045) 222-5015. **Open** daily.

🏛 **Yokohama Museum of Art**
Tel (045) 221-0300.
Open Fri–Wed. 📷

🏛 **NYK Maritime Museum**
Tel (045) 221-0280.
Open Tue–Sun. 📷

Hikawa Maru
Tel (045) 641-4362.
Open Tue–Sun. 📷

🏯 **Foreigners' Cemetery**
Tel (045) 622-1311. **Open** Mar–Dec: Sat, Sun, public hols.

🌳 **Sankei-en Garden**
10 mins by bus from Negishi stn (JR) to Honmoku. **Tel** (045) 621-0634.
Open daily. 📷

Environs
Outside the center are two entertaining venues: **Kirin Beer Village**, with tasting tours of the automated Kirin brewery; and **Shin Yokohama Ramen Museum** (*see p328*). On a more serious note, the **Hodogaya Commonwealth Cemetery** (a bus ride from Yokohama, Hodogaya, or Sakuragi-cho stations) contains Allied graves from World War II (including POWs).

Kirin Beer Village
🚉 Namamugi stn, Keihin Kyuko line. **Tel** (045) 503-8250.
Open Tue–Sun.

One of the entrance gates to Yokohama's Chinatown

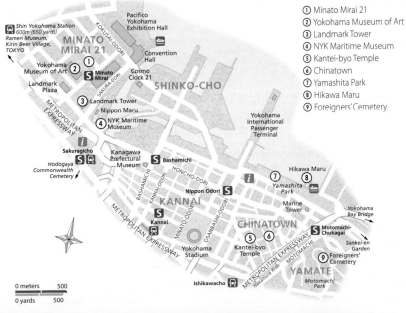

Yokohama City Center

① Minato Mirai 21
② Yokohama Museum of Art
③ Landmark Tower
④ NYK Maritime Museum
⑤ Kantei-byo Temple
⑥ Chinatown
⑦ Yamashita Park
⑧ Hikawa Maru
⑨ Foreigners' Cemetery

Shin Yokohama Station
600m (650 yards)
Ramen Museum,
Kirin Beer Village,
TOKYO

MINATO MIRAI 21

Pacifico Yokohama Exhibition Hall

KOKUSAI-ODORI

Convention Hall

Yokohama Museum of Art ②

Minato Mirai

Cosmo Clock 21

SHINKO-CHO

SAKURA-DORI

Landmark Plaza

① Landmark Tower

Nippon Maru

④ NYK Maritime Museum

Yokohama International Passenger Terminal

METROPOLITAN EXPRESSWAY

Sakuragicho

Kanagawa Prefectural Museum

Bashamichi

Hodogaya Commonwealth Cemetery

BASHAMICHI

KANNAI-ODORI

HONCHO-DORI

Nippon Odori

Hikawa Maru ⑧

⑦ Yamashita Park

KANNAI

Kannai

MINATO-ODORI

OSANBASHI-ODORI

Marine Tower

CHINATOWN

Yokohama Bay Bridge

Motomachi-Chukagai

Yokohama Stadium

⑤ ⑥ Kantei-byo Temple

METROPOLITAN EXPRESSWAY

Sankei-en Garden

⑨ Foreigners' Cemetery

YAMATE

MOTOMACHI

Motomachi Park

Ishikawacho

Nakamura River

0 meters 500
0 yards 500

❹ Kamakura

鎌倉

A seaside town of temples and wooded hills, Kamakura was Japan's administrative capital from 1185 until 1333. As a legacy, today it has 19 Shinto shrines and 65 Buddhist temples, including two of Japan's oldest Zen monasteries (in Kita Kamakura, *see p140*). Many of the temples and gardens nestle against the hills ringing the town and are linked by three hiking trails. Favored by artists and writers, Kamakura has numerous antique and crafts shops. In cherry-blossom season and on summer weekends, it can be swamped by visitors. Some parts are best explored on foot, but there are one-day bus passes and bicycles for rent at Kamakura station.

The path down the center of Wakamiya-oji, Kamakura's main street

🅗 Hase-dera Temple

🚉 Hase stn. ☎ **Tel** (0467) 22-6300. **Open** daily. 🈯 Ⓦ **hasedera.or.jp**

Simple and elegant, Hase-dera is home to a superb 11-faced Kannon, bodhisattva of mercy. The Treasure House displays characterful Muromachi-era carvings of the 33 incarnations of Kannon and a 1421 image of Daikokuten, god of wealth. Beside it is the sutra repository; rotating the sutras is said to earn as much merit as reading them. The 1264 bell is the town's oldest. Below it is a hall dedicated to Jizo, guardian of children, surrounded by countless statues to children who have died or been aborted.

🅗 Great Buddha

🚉 Hase stn. ☎ **Tel** (0467) 22-0703. **Open** daily. 🈯 Ⓦ **nkdaibutsu.com**

The Great Buddha (Daibutsu) is Kamakura's most famous sight. Cast in 1252, the bronze statue of the Amida Buddha is 13.5 m (44 ft) tall. Having survived tidal waves, fires, earthquakes, and typhoons, it now has shock absorbers in its base. Its proportions are distorted so that it seems balanced to those in front of it – this use of perspective may show Greek influence (via the Silk Road). The interior is open to visitors.

🅗 Hachiman-gu Shrine

🚉 Kamakura stn. ☎ **Tel** (0467) 22-0315. **Open** daily. Kamakura National Treasure House Museum: **Tel** (0467) 22-0753. **Open** Tue–Sun. 🈯

Hachiman shrines are dedicated to the god of war; this one is also a guardian shrine of the Minamoto (or Genji) clan. Built in 1063 beside the sea, it was moved here in 1191. The approach runs between two lotus ponds: the Genji Pond has three islands (in Japanese *san* means both three and life) while the Heike Pond, named for a rival clan, has four (*shi* means both four and death). The path leads to the Maiden stage for dances and music. The main shrine above was reconstructed in 1828 in Edo style. To the east, the **Kamakura National Treasure House Museum** contains a wealth of temple treasures.

The head of the Great Buddha, or Daibutsu

Sights at a Glance

① Engaku-ji Temple
② Tokei-ji Temple
③ Meigetsu-in Temple
④ Kencho-ji Temple
⑤ Zeni-Arai Benten Shrine
⑥ Hachiman-gu Shrine
⑦ Zuisen-ji Temple
⑧ Sugimoto-dera Temple
⑨ Hokoku-ji Temple
⑩ Myohon-ji Temple
⑪ Hase-dera Temple
⑫ Great Buddha

YOKOHAMA

🚉 Kita-Kamakura Station

Tokei-ji Temple

Zeni-Arai ⑤ Benten Shrine

🏯 Sasuke-no Inari Shrine

SHIYAKUSHO-D

Great Buddha Hiking Trail

⑫ Great Buddha (Daibutsu)

⑪ Hase-dera Temple

Yuigahama 🚉 Station

Hase 🚉 Station

HIGHWAY

NATIONAL

Yuigahama Beach

↓ ENOSHIMA

Myohon-ji Temple
Kamakura stn. **Tel** (0467) 22-0777.
Open daily.

On a hillside of soaring trees, this temple, with its unusually steep, extended roof, is Kamakura's largest of the Nichiren sect. It was established in 1260, in memory of a 1203 massacre.

Hokoku-ji Temple
Tel (0467) 22-0762. **Open** daily.
(for bamboo grove).

This Rinzai Zen temple was founded in 1334. Hokoku-ji's great attraction is its lovely bamboo grove. There is also a pleasant raked gravel and rock garden, and the temple's Sunday- morning *zazen* (meditation) sessions are open to all.

Zuisen-ji Temple
Tel (0467) 22-1191.
Open daily.

This secluded temple is known for its naturalistic garden. Created in 1327 by the monk Muso Soseki, it features a waterfall-fed lake, rocks, and sand; a Zen meditation cave is cut into the cliff. Decorative narcissi also bloom here in January, and Japanese plum trees blossom in February.

VISITORS' CHECKLIST

Practical Information
Kanagawa prefecture.
174,000. at Kamakura stn (0467) 22-3350.
New Year archery (Jan 5), Kamakura Festival (2nd–3rd Sun in Apr), Hachiman-gu Festival (Sep 14–16), Menkakegyoretsu (Sep 18), Torchlight Noh (Oct 8–9).
city.kamakura.kanagawa.jp

Transport
JR and Enoden lines.

① gaku-ji emple
③ Meigetsu-in Temple
ochi-ji emple
Hansobo Shrine
Ten-en Hiking Trail
KAMAKURA-KAIDO
Choju-ji Temple
④ Kencho-ji Temple
Kakuon-ji Temple
Zuisen-ji Temple ⑦
Enno-ji Temple
Hachiman-gu Shrine ⑥
Kamakura-gu Shrine
Prefectural Modern Art Gallery
National Treasure House Museum
KANAZAWA-KAIDO
Sugimoto-dera Temple
⑧
Jomio-ji Temple
KOMACHI-DORI
WAKAMIYA OJI
KOMACHI-DORI
Hokai-ji Temple
⑨ Hokoku-ji Temple
Kamakura Station
Gion-san Hiking Trail
⑩ Myohon-ji Temple
YUIGAHAMA-DORI
Wadazuka Station
Myoho-ji Temple
Namerin River
Ankokuron-ji Temple
Chosho-ji Temple
YOKOSUKA
1 3 4
Kuhon-ji Temple

0 meters   500
0 yards   500

Sugimoto-dera Temple
Tel (0467) 22-3463.
Open daily.

Founded in 734, this is Kamakura's oldest temple and pleasantly informal. The softly thatched hall contains three wooden statues of 11-faced Kannon, protected by ferocious guardian figures at the temple gateway.

Azalea-lined steps to the thatched hall at Sugimoto-dera temple

Exploring Kita Kamakura

Zen Buddhism came to Japan from China at the end of the 12th century. Its simplicity and accessibility appealed to the ethos of Kamakura samurai warriors as well as to ordinary people. Kita (north) Kamakura, a tranquil area of wooded gullies, includes three of Kamakura's "five great" Zen temples: Kencho-ji, Engaku-ji, and Jochi-ji (the others are Jomyo-ji and Jufuku-ji). The area is served by its own train station, from which most sights can be reached on foot. Delicate vegetarian food, which complies with Zen dietary rules, can be tried at several Kita Kamakura temples and restaurants.

🅰 Engaku-ji Temple

🚉 Kita Kamakura stn. **Tel** (0467) 22-0478. **Open** daily. 🏯

The largest of Kamakura's "five great" Zen temples, deep in trees, Engaku-ji was founded by the Hojo regent Tokimune in 1282. An influential *zazen* (meditation) center since the Meiji era, it now runs public courses.

Although much of Engaku-ji was destroyed by the 1923 Kanto Earthquake, 17 of its more than 40 subtemples remain, and careful rebuilding has ensured that it retains its characteristic Zen layout *(see opposite)*. One of its highlights, in Shozoku-in subtemple, is the Shariden. Japan's finest example of Chinese Sung-style Zen architecture, it is open only at New Year but can be seen through a gate at other times. Farther on, the Butsunichian, mausoleum of Engaku-ji's founder, serves *matcha* tea *(see p173)*. It was the setting for Kawabata Yasunari's 1949 novel *Senbazuru* (Thousand Cranes).

Stone monuments in the peaceful cemetery at Tokei-ji temple

Bosatsu statue at Kencho-ji

🅰 Tokei-ji Temple

🚉 Kita Kamakura stn. **Tel** (0467) 22-1663. **Open** daily. 🏯

This quiet little temple was set up as a convent in 1285, at a time when only men were allowed to petition for divorce. However, if a woman spent three years here she could divorce her husband. Thus Tokei-ji was nicknamed the "divorce temple." In 1873 the law was changed to allow women to initiate divorce; in 1902 Tokei-ji became a monastery. It is still refuge-like, with gardens stretching back to the wooded hillside.

🅰 Meigetsu-in Temple

🚉 Kita Kamakura stn. **Tel** (0467) 24-3437. **Open** daily. 🏯

Known as the "hydrangea temple," Meigetsu-in is a small Zen temple with attractive gardens. As well as hydrangeas (at their peak in June), there are irises; these bloom in late May, when the rear garden, usually only tantalizingly glimpsed through a round window, is opened to the public.

🅰 Kencho-ji Temple

🚉 Kita Kamakura stn. **Tel** (0467) 22-0981. **Open** daily. 🏯

Kencho-ji is the foremost of Kamkura's "five great" Zen temples and the oldest Zen training monastery in Japan. Founded in 1253, the temple originally had seven main buildings and 49 subtemples; many were destroyed in fires, but 10 subtemples remain. Beside the impressive Sanmon gate is the bell, cast in 1255, which has a Zen inscription by the temple's founder. The Buddha Hall contains a Jizo bodhisattva, savior of souls of the dead. Behind the hall is the Hatto, where public ceremonies are performed. The Karamon (Chinese gate) leads to the Hojo, used for services. Its rear garden is constructed around a pond supposedly in the shape of the kanji character for heart or mind. To the side of the temple a tree-lined lane leads to subtemples and up steps to Hanso-bo, the temple's shrine.

🈂 Zeni-Arai Benten Shrine

🚉 Kamakura stn. **Tel** (0467) 25-1081. **Open** daily.

This popular shrine is dedicated to Benten, goddess of music, eloquence, and the arts, and one of the "seven lucky gods" of folk religion. Hidden in a niche in the cliffs, it is approached through a small tunnel and a row of torii (gates). These lead to a pocket of wafting incense, lucky charms, and a cave spring where visitors wash coins in the hope of doubling their value.

Washing coins at Zeni-Arai Benten shrine

The Layout of a Zen Buddhist Temple

Japanese Zen temple layout is typically based on Chinese Sung-dynasty temples. Essentially rectilinear and symmetrical (in contrast to native Japanese asymmetry), Zen temples have the main buildings in a straight line one behind another, on a roughly north–south axis. The main buildings comprise the Sanmon (main gate), Butsuden (Buddha Hall), Hatto lecture hall, sometimes a meditation or study hall, and the abbot's and monks' quarters. In practice, subtemples often crowd around the main buildings and may obscure the basic layout. The temple compound is entered by a bridge over a pond or stream, symbolically crossing from the earthly world to that of Buddha. Buildings are beautiful but natural looking, often of unpainted wood; they are intended to be conducive to emptying the mind of worldly illusions, facilitating enlightenment. The example below is based on Engaku-ji.

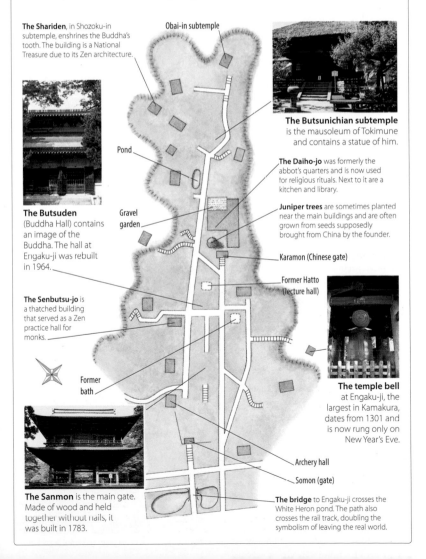

The Shariden, in Shozoku-in subtemple, enshrines the Buddha's tooth. The building is a National Treasure due to its Zen architecture.

Obai-in subtemple

The Butsunichian subtemple is the mausoleum of Tokimune and contains a statue of him.

The Daiho-jo was formerly the abbot's quarters and is now used for religious rituals. Next to it are a kitchen and library.

Juniper trees are sometimes planted near the main buildings and are often grown from seeds supposedly brought from China by the founder.

Karamon (Chinese gate)

Former Hatto (lecture hall)

Pond

Gravel garden

The Butsuden (Buddha Hall) contains an image of the Buddha. The hall at Engaku-ji was rebuilt in 1964.

The Senbutsu-jo is a thatched building that served as a Zen practice hall for monks.

Former bath

The temple bell at Engaku-ji, the largest in Kamakura, dates from 1301 and is now rung only on New Year's Eve.

Archery hall

Somon (gate)

The Sanmon is the main gate. Made of wood and held together without nails, it was built in 1783.

The bridge to Engaku-ji crosses the White Heron pond. The path also crosses the rail track, doubling the symbolism of leaving the real world.

❺ Chichibu-Tama National Park
秩父多摩国立公園

Tokyo, Saitama, Nagano, and Yamanashi prefectures. 🏔 71,000 (Chichibu city). 🚃 Seibu-Chichibu stn, Seibu-Chichibu line; Chichibu stn, Chichibu line; Okutama or Mitake stns, JR line. 🛈 Chichibu stn (0494) 25-3192. 🎎 Yo Matsuri (Dec 2–3, Chichibu city).

Chichibu-Tama National Park is a remote region of low mountains, rich in traditions and wildlife, stretching from the narrow valleys of Okutama in the south to the basin around Chichibu city in the north. The two parts of the park are separated by mountains, crossed only by a few hiking trails, and are reached by two separate rail networks. Within the park, railroads penetrate to a few spots, but travel is mostly by bus.

Chichibu was a prime silk-producing region until the early 20th century. Today it is known for its vibrant festivals and its pilgrim route linking 33 Kannon temples. To the north, at **Nagatoro**, the Arakawa River runs past rare crystalline schist rock formations.

In the Okutama area, **Mount Mitake** has good hiking, and an attractive mountaintop shrine village, easily reached by a funicular. Stalactite caves at **Nippara** are worth visiting.

🦇 Nippara Caves
NW of Okutama. **Tel** (0428) 83-8491. **Open** daily. 🚫

Yosegi-Zaiku Marquetry

Originating in the 9th century, this type of marquetry looks like inlaid mosaic but in fact employs a very different technique. It has been a Hakone specialty for over 200 years, and today there are

about 100 *yosegi-zaiku* practitioners in the area. Strips are cut from planks of up to 40 varieties of undyed woods and glued together to form patterned blocks, which are in turn glued into larger blocks. These are then either shaped with a lathe into bowls and boxes, or shaved into cross-sectional sheets, used to coat items such as boxes and purses. The paper-thin sheets are flexible and can be laminated. Some of the most popular creations are "magic" boxes, opened in a sequence of moves to reveal a hidden drawer.

Craftsman making a *yosegi-zaiku* box

Environs
South of Chichibu-Tama lies **Mount Takao**, (on the Keio train line to Takaosan-guchi.) Its slopes have pleasant walks with sweeping views of Tokyo and Mount Fuji.

❻ Hakone
箱根

Kanagawa prefecture. 🏔 14,000. 🚃 🛈 706-35 Yumoto, Hakone (0460) 85-8911. 🎎 Toriiyaki (Aug 5, Lake Ashi), Daimyo Gyoretsu (Nov 3, Hakone-Yumoto). 🌐 hakone. or.jp/ english/index.html

Hakone is a hilly hot-spring town whose scattered attractions are both cultural and natural. Popular as a resort since the 9th century, it can be very crowded. The Hakone area extends across the collapsed remains of a huge volcano, which was active until 3,000–4,000 years ago, leaving a legacy today of hot springs and steam vents.

Although Hakone can be visited as a long day trip from Tokyo, it is worth an overnight stay. Two- or three-day public-transportation passes are available on the Odakyu line from Shinjuku, Tokyo. A convenient circuit of the main sights starts from the *onsen* town of **Hakone-Yumoto**, taking the Tozan switchback train up the hillside to **Hakone Open-Air Museum**, with its modern sculptures. Continue via funicular to **Hakone Art Museum**, which has an

Crossing the rocky scree and steaming vents of Owaku-dani valley in Hakone

A statue of *The Izu Dancer* by a waterfall near Kawazu, Izu Peninsula

excellent Japanese ceramic collection and garden. Via the funicular and then a ropeway over the crest of the hill is the fascinating **Owaku-dani** ("valley of great boiling"), an area of sulfurous steam vents.

The ropeway continues to **Lake Ashi**, where replicas of historical Western-style boats run to **Hakone-machi** and **Moto-Hakone**. In clear weather there are stunning views of Mount Fuji. At Hakone-machi is an interesting reconstruction of the **Seki-sho Barrier Gate**, a checkpoint that used to control the passage of people and guns on the Edo-period Tokaido road between Edo (Tokyo) and Kyoto.

From Hakone-machi it is a short walk to Moto-Hakone. In a prominent position on a hilltop overlooking Lake Ashi, **Narukawa Art Museum** exhibits 1,500 artworks by modern Japanese masters, and has spectacular views of the surrounding mountains. Over a pass beyond Moto-Hakone is the **Amazake-chaya** tea-house, and **Hatajuku** village, known for *yosegi-zaiku*, a form of decorative marquetry.

🏛 **Open-Air Museum**
Tel (0460) 82-1161. **Open** daily. 🖼

🏛 **Hakone Art Museum**
Tel (0460) 82-2623. **Open** Fri–Wed. 🖼

🏯 **Seki-sho Barrier Gate**
Tel (0460) 83-6635. **Open** daily. 🖼

🏛 **Narukawa Art Museum**
Tel (0460) 83-6828. **Open** daily. 🖼

❼ Izu Peninsula
伊豆半島

Shizuoka prefecture. 🚃 ℹ️ Atami, Ito, and Shuzenji stns. 🎏 Daimonji Burning (Jul 22–23, Atagawa), Anjin Festival (Aug 8–10, Ito).

A picturesque, hilly peninsula with a benign climate, Izu is popular for its numerous hot springs. It was a place of exile during the Middle Ages, and in the early 1600s was home to the shipwrecked Englishman William Adams, whose story was the basis of the James Clavell novel *Shogun*. **Shimoda**, on the southern tip, became a coaling station for foreign ships in 1854, then opened to US traders. Today Shimoda has little of interest besides pretty gray-and-white walls, reinforced against typhoons with crisscross plasterwork.

Izu's east coast is quite developed, but the west has charming coves and fishing villages, such as **Toi** and **Heda**, offering delicious long-legged crabs and other seafood. The center is also relatively unspoiled, with wooded mountains and rustic hot springs, including **Shuzenji** *onsen* and a chain of villages from **Amagi Yugashima** to **Kawazu**. These latter were the setting for Yasunari Kawabata's short story *The Izu Dancer*, commemorated across Izu. Two-day transportation passes cover parts of the peninsula.

❽ Mount Fuji and the Fuji Five Lakes
See pp144–5.

❾ Shizuoka
静岡

Shizuoka & Yamanashi prefecture. 🚃 720,000. 🚉 ℹ️ in JR stn (054) 252-4247. 🎏 Shizuoka Festival (1st weekend Apr). 🌐 **pref.shizuoka.jp**

Settlement in this area stretches back to AD 200–300. Later a stop on the old Tokaido road, and the retirement home of Tokugawa Ieyasu (*see p60*), Shizuoka is today a sprawling urban center, the city in Japan at greatest risk of a major earthquake. As a result it is probably the only place that is fully prepared.

The **Toro ruins** near the port have well-explained reconstructions of ancient buildings and an excellent interactive **museum**. The view from **Nihondaira** plateau, in the east of the city, to Mount Fuji and Izu is superb. Nearby is **Kunozan Tosho-gu**, one of the three top Tosho-gu shrines.

🏛 **Toro Ruins**
Museum: **Tel** (054) 285-0476. **Open** Tue–Sun. 🖼

Environs
West of Shizuoka, **Kanaya** has one of Japan's largest tea plantations. Fields and processing plants can be visited, and the elegant **Ocha no Sato** museum portrays tea lore. Nearby, the **Oigawa steam railroad** takes you right into the untamed South Alps.

🏛 **Ocha no Sato**
Tel (0547) 46-5588. **Closed** Tue. 🖼

A reconstructed dwelling at the Toro site, Shizuoka

❻ Mount Fuji and the Fuji Five Lakes

富士山と富士五湖

At 3,776 m (12,390 ft), Mount Fuji (or Fuji-san) is Japan's highest peak by far, its near-perfect cone floating lilacgray or snow-capped above hilltops and low cloud. Dormant since 1707, the volcano first erupted 8–10,000 years ago. Its upper slopes are loose volcanic ash, devoid of greenery or streams. Until 100 years ago, Mount Fuji was considered so sacred that it was climbed only by priests and pilgrims; women were not allowed until 1872. Today it is a UNESCO World Heritage Site, and pilgrims are greatly outnumbered by recreational climbers. The Fuji Five Lakes area, at the foot of the mountain, offers sports facilities and amusement parks.

Lake Sai
This is the least spoiled of the Fuji Five Lakes and offers beautiful views of Mount Fuji.

Approaching the Crater Rim
At the top, climbers and pilgrims can visit Sengen shrine, 24-hour noodle stalls, a post office, an office for souvenir stamps, and a weather station.

KEY

① **The Fujinomiya trail** is 5 hours up from the 5th stage, and 3 hours 30 minutes down.

② **The top** is not a single summit, but a crater rim. A circuit of the rim takes about an hour.

③ **Kawaguchi-ko trail** is 5–6 hours up from the 5th stage, and 3 hours down. Another trail, the Yoshida, shares most of its route with this one.

④ **The Sea of Trees** (Aokigahara Jukai) is a primeval forest famed for being easy to get lost in.

⑤ **Lake Motosu**, the deepest lake, was once depicted on the 5,000-yen note.

⑥ **Lake Shojin** is the smallest lake and good for fishing.

⑦ **Lake Kawaguchi** is the most accessible and commercialized lake.

⑧ **Fuji-Yoshida**, the traditional pilgrim base, has old inns, and waterfalls for ritual cleansing and praying before the climb.

⑨ **Lake Yamanaka** is popular for waterskiing and swimming.

⑩ **Subashiri trail** is 4 hours 30 minutes up from the 5th stage, and 3 hours down.

⑪ **Gotenba trail** is 8 hours up from the 5th stage, and 3 hours down.

Kawaguchi-ko

139

• Fugaku Wind Cave

• Narusawa Ice Cave

⑥

⑤

④

139

5th stage

③

②

①

5th stage

Fujinomiya ↓

Key

▬▬ Expressway

══ Other road

▬ ▬ Trail

Mount Fuji in Art

Mount Fuji's graceful, almost symmetrical form, its changing appearance at different seasons and times of day, and its dominance over the landscape have made it both a symbol of Japan and a popular subject for artists. The mountain features in various series of 19th-century wood-block prints: Katsushika Hokusai (1760–1849) and Ando Hiroshige (1797–1858) both published series called *Thirty-Six Views of Mount Fuji*, and Hiroshige also depicted Fuji in his *Fifty-Three Stages of the Tokaido* published in 1833–4. It often appears in the background of prints of Edo (Tokyo), from where, at times it is still visible among Tokyo's high-rises even today. In other arts, Mount Fuji is echoed in decorative motifs, for instance on kimonos, in wood carvings, and even in the shape of window frames.

One of Hiroshige's *Thirty-Six Views of Mount Fuji*

Beneath the Wave off Kanagawa from Hokusai's *Thirty-Six Views of Mount Fuji*

VISITORS' CHECKLIST

Practical Information
Shizuoka & Yamanashi prefecture. 🛈 Fuji-Yoshida (0555) 22- 1111. 🎏 Fuji-Yoshida Fire Festival (Aug 26 & 27). 🅦 city.fujiyoshida. yamanashi.jp

Transport
🚉 Fuji-Yoshida, Kawaguchi-ko, Gotenba, Mishima (Tokaido Shinkansen), or Fujinomiya. 🚌 summer only, from all stns to the nearest 5th stage, also direct from Tokyo (Shinjuku stn W side or Hamamatsu-cho) to Kawaguchi-ko, Gotenba, and Lake Yamanaka.

Otsuki and Tokyo

· Oshino

⑨

· **Oshino**

• 5th stage

Tokyo

5th stage

138

Gotenba

Tomei Expressway

↓ *Mishima*

| 0 kilometers | 5 |
| 0 miles | 3 |

Sengen Jinja
Many Sengen shrines, including this main one at Fuji-Yoshida, can be found around Fuji. The inner sanctum of Sengen shrines is on the crater rim at the summit. They are dedicated to the deity of the mountain.

Tips for Walkers

Planning: The mountain is open for climbing only in July and August. Trails and huts can be very crowded on weekends.
Stages: The trails are divided into 10 stages. Climbers usually start at the 5th stage. To see the sunrise and avoid midday sun, it is usual to climb by night or start in the afternoon, sleep in a hut at the 7th or 8th stage, and rise very early to finish the climb.
Conditions: The climb is hard work as the steep volcanic cinder shifts underfoot like sand. Above the 8th stage, altitude sickness occasionally strikes: if you have a serious headache or nausea, descend at once. The summit is much colder than the base.
What to take: Sun-protection cream, hat, sweater, raincoat, hiking shoes, flashlight, and emergency drink supplies; a walking stick is useful.

⑩ Kiso Valley Tour

木曽谷

The Kiso River runs through a picturesque mountain valley that was the route of the Nakasendo, one of the Edo-period post roads. The Kiso Valley's 11 post towns, particularly Tsumago, Narai, and Magome, still retain much of that atmosphere, their narrow streets lined with wooden inns and stores. Parts of the old Nakasendo trail, especially between Tsumago and Magome, are as they were in the Edo days and can be followed past woods, farms, and milestones. More challenging hiking is found on nearby mountains such as Ontake.

Tips for Travelers

Tour length: 60 km (37 miles).
Travel: Car is the most flexible. Many express trains stop at Kiso-Fukushima and Nakatsugawa. Local trains run hourly.
Information: Tsumago (0264) 57-3123; Magome (0264) 59-2336; Narai (0263) 54-2001.
W town.nagiso.nagano.jp/foreign/en/index.html

① Kiso-Hirasawa
Lacquerware is a specialty here, perfected over the years to sell to travelers passing through.

② Narai
This well-preserved post town has streets lined with wooden buildings, plus a couple of interesting museums, giving an insight into how life was for travelers on the Nakasendo.

③ Torii Pass
This pass has one of the main remaining sections of genuine, stone-paved Nakasendo road, with no modern road nearby to spoil it. It takes about 2 hours to walk over the pass.

④ Kiso-Fukushima
This was the location of a major barrier gate on the Nakasendo road. Today it is the gateway to the sacred mountain of Ontake.

Shiojiri and Matsumoto

Yabuhara

Harano • Miyanokoshi

Mt Ontake

Mt Kiso-Komagatake

Agematsu

• Kuramoto

• Suhara

• Okuwa

Nojiri •

Junikane •

Nagiso

0 kilometers 10
0 miles 5

⑤ Nezame-no-toko
This pretty gorge, about half-an-hour's walk from Agematsu, holds turquoise waters strewn with boulders.

⑥ Tsumago
All signs of modernity have been hidden here – cables are buried and cars banned. A former high-class inn, the Okuya, is now an excellent museum of local and Nakasendo history.

⑦ Magome
In the hills above the Kiso Valley, Magome is a good starting point for the 8.5-km (5-mile) Nakasendo walking trail to Tsumago.

Nakatsugawa

Key

▬▬▬ Tour route
═══ Other roads
--- Walk route
△ Peak

Part of the *Tale of Genji* handscroll in Tokugawa Art Museum, Nagoya

⓫ Nagoya
名古屋

Aichi prefecture. 🏔 2,240,000. ✈ 🚉
ℹ at Nagoya JR stn (052) 541-4301.
🎎 Atsuta Shrine Festival (Jun 5),
Nagoya Festival (mid-Oct).
🌐 city.nagoya.jp/en

A major transportation hub for
the region, Nagoya is a pleasant
and convenient, if unexciting,
base. It rose to prominence in
the 17th century as a Tokaido
castle town, birthplace of Oda
Nobunaga and Toyotomi
Hideyoshi *(see pp58 and 60)*.
Japan's fourth-largest city and
an industrial center, it was
heavily bombed in World War II.

The city's one-day bus or bus-
and-subway passes are good for
exploring. **Nagoya Castle**, built
in 1610–12 and one of the
largest, most sophisticated of
the Edo period, was destroyed
in a bombing raid in 1945;
today's concrete reconstruction
has a top-floor observatory, and
the modern interior contains
exhibits about the castle.

A short bus ride east is the
Tokugawa Art Museum, with
superb Edo-period treasures, as
well as a 12th-century illustrated
handscroll of the *Tale of Genji*,
part of which is exhibited each
November. Photos and
reproductions of the scrolls
are on permanent display.

🏛 **Nagoya Castle**
🚇 Shiyakusho stn. 🚌 Nagoya-jo
Seimon-mae stop. **Tel** (052) 231-1700.
Open daily. 🎫

🚌 **Tokugawa Art Museum**
🚌 Shindeki stop. **Tel** (052) 935-6262.
Open Tue–Sun. 🎫

Environs
Trips from Nagoya, all on the
Meitetsu rail line, include
Arimatsu, a Tokaido post town,
known for *shibori* (tie-dyeing).
Tours of the **Toyota Car Factory**
nearby may be arranged.

🏛 **Toyota Car Factory**
Tel (0565) 29-3355. **Open** Mon–Fri.

Meiji-era post office at Meiji Mura
near Inuyama

⓬ Inuyama
犬山

Aichi prefecture. 🏔 76,000. ✈ 🚉
ℹ 5 mins E of station (0568) 61-2512.
🎎 Tagata Honen-sai (Mar 15),
Inuyama Festival (1st weekend Apr).

Inuyama is a quiet, friendly
castle town on the Kiso River.
Its **castle**, built in 1537, is
the oldest in Japan. It places
more emphasis on defense
than show, but is still small,
simple, and graceful, with
panoramic views across the
river far below. In nearby
Uraku-en Park is Jo-an teahouse, a classic example of
rustic simplicity.

🏛 **Inuyama Castle**
Tel (0568) 61-6000. **Open** daily. 🎫

Environs
Outside Inuyama is **Meiji Mura**,
a theme park with over 60 Meiji-
era (1868–1912) buildings,
including the lobby of Frank
Lloyd Wright's Imperial Hotel
from Tokyo. **Yaotsu**, where
Chiune Siguhara was born is a
train ride away. Japan's consul
in Lithuania in World War II,
Sugihara saved around 6,000
Jews using transit visas via
Japan. He is commemorated by
a monument and museum at
Yaotsu's **Hill of Humanity Park**.

🏛 **Meiji Mura**
15 min by bus from Inuyama.
Tel (0568) 67-0314. **Open** daily.
Closed Mon (Dec–Feb). 🎫

⓭ Gifu
岐阜

Gifu prefecture. 🏔 420,000. ✈ 🚉
ℹ at Gifu JR stn (058) 262-4415.
🎎 All-Japan Fireworks Contest (last
Sat in Jul). 🌐 city.gifu.lg.jp

A rather garish spa town, Gifu's
main attraction is *ukai* cormorant
fishing *(see p48)*. This tradition
involves using trained
cormorants to catch fish. Nightly
from mid-May to mid-October,
except at full moon or when
stormy, fishermen and their
cormorants go out on torchlit
boats; the birds dive for *ayu*
(sweetfish) and trout, which they
are prevented from swallowing
by a ring around their necks.

The town is also known for its
paper parasols and lanterns and
for the largest lacquer Buddha
in Japan, at **Shoho-ji temple**.
Dating from 1832, it comprises a
woven bamboo frame covered
with sutra-inscribed paper, then
coated in clay and lacquered.
Gifu Castle is a modern
reconstruction.

The small, reconstructed castle at Gifu,
perched on a hilltop

⑭ Street-by-Street: Takayama

高山

Takayama is a town of character surrounded by mountains. Agriculturally poor but rich in timber, it produced skilled carpenters; in the 8th century, when the region was unable to produce enough rice for its taxes (usually paid in the form of rice), it sent craftsmen instead. From 1692 to 1868 the area was under direct shogunate control as a source of timber. Its isolated mountain location has meant the survival of unspoiled Edo-period streets lined with tiny shops, museums, and eating places, while the pure water is ideal for sake brewing. The town also stages one of Japan's best-known festivals.

One of the floats at the Takayama Matsuri

Lion Dance Ceremony Exhibition Hall and Takayama Festival Floats Exhibition Hall *(see p150)*

Higashiyama Temple District

SHIMO NINOMACHI

SHIMO SANNOMACHI

YAYOI-BASHI BRIDGE

MIYA RIVER

Morning market

Yoshijima Heritage House
This beautifully maintained sake merchant's house retains its wooden beamed interior, lit by high windows.

| 0 meters | 50 |
| 0 yards | 50 |

★ Kusakabe Folk Museum
Rebuilt of Japanese cypress in 1879 after a fire, this house is a well-preserved money-lender's dwelling and includes folkcraft items and a small garden.

★ Sannomachi Quarter
An unusually large, intact area of Edo-period merchants' shops and houses, this quarter includes specialty shops and sake brewers.

Key

— Suggested route

Hirata Memorial Hall
In a former candle and pomade shop, the Hirata family's collection includes Edo-period clothing and toys.

Takayama City Museum chronicles the town's history.

Shoren-ji temple

KAMI ICHINOMACHI

YASUGAWA-DORI

KAMI NINOMACHI

KAMI SANNOMACHI

SAN-MACHI-DORI

BASHI BRIDGE

YANAGI-BASHI BRIDGE

IKEDA BASHI BRIDGE

↑ Station, tourist information

Archaeological Museum displays local finds and crafts.

Takayama Jinya, Hida Folklore Village *(see p150)*

Miya River
Some of the old houses of the Sannomachi Quarter overlook the fast-flowing Miya River.

Exploring Takayama

Takayama is best explored slowly on foot or by bicycle. Old merchant houses reveal high, skylighted ceilings, soot-covered beams, and fireproof storage rooms; the dirt-floor area at the front was the shop. The town's eight sake breweries can also be visited during the peak brewing week in January or February. To the east, the tranquil Higashiyama temple district has a 3.5-km (2-mile) walking course taking in 13 temples, five shrines, and a hilltop park.

🏛 Lion Dance Ceremony Exhibition Hall
Tel (0577) 32-0881. **Open** daily. 🎦
Lion dances, to drive away wild animals and evil spirits, are integral to festivals such as Takayama's. This exhibit contains over 800 lion masks from all over Japan plus armor, screens, pottery, and coins. There is also a performance by *karakuri* marionettes, invented in Edo (Tokyo) in 1617.

🏛 Takayama Festival Floats Exhibition Hall
Tel (0577) 32-5100. **Open** daily. 🎦
Takayama Festival dates from about 1690 and takes place twice a year, in spring, coinciding with planting, and in fall at harvest time. Both festivals involve processions of 11 tall, lavishly decorated floats, guided by townspeople in traditional costume. Four floats also feature *karakuri* marionettes. Between festivals, four of the floats are displayed in this hall along with photographs of the others. There is also a gallery of exquisite scale models of Nikko Tosho-gu Shrine (*see pp270–71*).

🏛 Takayama Jinya
Tel (0577) 32-0643.
Open daily. 🎦

The government office was built in 1615 for Takayama's lord, but in 1692 the shogunate made it their own provincial office – the only one still in existence. The front of the building comprises rooms where people of various ranks waited or met officials; behind are the kitchens and living quarters of the governor's family. To one side is a jail, with a small array of torture instruments. The storehouses contain items relating to the rice-tax system.

Environs
Just outside Takayama is **Hida Folk Village**, over 30 houses from surrounding rural areas, including a *gassho-zukuri* house from the Sho-kawa Valley. There are also storehouses, a festival stage, and traditional crafts. The buildings, on a hillside with views of the Japan Alps, are interesting both architecturally and for what they reveal – such as the demands of a snowy climate or the life of a village headman.

🏛 Hida Folk Village
40 mins walk or 8 mins by bus from Takayama stn. **Tel** (0577) 34-4711. **Open** daily. 🎦

Gassho-zukuri houses in Shirakawa-go

⓯ Shokawa Valley
庄川渓谷

Gifu and Toyama prefectures. 🚌 from Nagoya (summer only), Takayama, Gifu & Takaoka. 🛈 (0576) 96-1013. 📅 Doburoku Matsuri (Shirakawa-go, Oct 14–19). 🕸 http://shirakawa-go.org/english/index.html

A remote mountain region with unique thatched houses, the Shokawa valley comprises two areas: **Shirakawa-go** (including Ogimachi) to the south and the five hamlets of **Gokayama** to the north. Under deep snow from December to March, the region was historically a refuge for the defeated and persecuted. Until the 1970s most families here produced silk, raising silkworms in *gassho-zukuri* thatched houses.

Of the original 1,800, less than 150 *gassho* houses remain. Three settlements – **Ogimachi**, **Suganuma**, and **Ainokura** – are World Heritage sites. Every April– May, a few houses are re-thatched, one roof taking 200 villagers and volunteers two days. Ogimachi is the largest village, with 59 *gassho* houses and an **Open-Air Museum**. Suganuma has nine *gassho* buildings. Ainokura is a hillside hamlet of 20 *gassho* houses (two open to visitors).

🏛 Open-Air Museum
Across the river from Ogimachi. **Tel** (05769) 6-1231. **Open** Apr–Nov: daily; Dec–Mar: Fri–Tue. 🎦

Inside the Takayama Festival Floats Exhibition Hall

Gassho-zukuri Houses

These houses are named for their steep thatched roofs, shaped like *gassho* ("praying hands"). The climate demands strong, steep roofs able to withstand heavy snow and shed rain quickly so that the straw does not rot. *Gassho* structures meet those requirements with a series of triangular frames on a rectangular base, creating a large interior space. Generally three or four stories, they traditionally accommodated extended families of 20–30 people on the ground floor, all involved in silkworm cultivation; the upper floors housed the silkworms, permitting variations in light, heat, and air at different stages. To maximize ventilation and light, *gassho-zukuri* houses have no hipped gables, and windows at both ends are opened to allow the wind through – in Shirakawa-go, where winds always blow north–south along the valley floor, all houses are aligned on the same axis. Architectural details vary from village to village.

The straw used for thatching is miscanthus, a type of pampas grass. The thatch can be up to 1 m (3 ft) thick.

Horizontal poles near the top of the roof help to hold the thatch in place and are used for securing ropes when doing repairs.

No nails are used in constructing the houses – the timbers and braces are all bound together with straw rope. The lower part of the building is held together by wooden pins.

Gassho **roofs** slope at about 60 degrees (most roofs in Japan are up to 45 degrees).

Slats in the ceiling allow smoke from the hearth to penetrate the roof area, helping to protect the thatch against dampness and insects. If sufficient smoke reaches the thatch, it can last about 50 years.

A notched pole acts as a ladder.

Horizontal beams are often taken from trees that have been bent by snow; being slightly curved, they absorb stress better than straight beams.

The hearth is a common feature of Japanese rural houses and was used for heating, cooking, and drying. The exact style of hearth and way of hanging objects over it varies between villages.

⑯ Kanazawa

金沢

A city with a strong cultural identity, Kanazawa was historically shielded from outside influence by its location between the mountains and the sea, and supported by an ample rice yield. In 1583 the area, known as Kaga, passed from egalitarian government under the Ikko Buddhist sect to the firm rule of the Maeda lords; while much of Japan was still unstable, Kaga had three centuries of peace and became the richest domain in the land. Wealth encouraged cultural development, and artists from Kyoto came and developed new, more vibrant styles with less restraint. When Japan modernized, Kanazawa focused on culture; lack of industry meant it escaped bombing in World War II and retains its heritage today.

Walled street in the Nagamachi Samurai quarter

Exploring Central Kanazawa

Most of Kanazawa's sights are located centrally. One-day bus passes are available, and bicycles can be rented at the station. **Kenroku-en Garden** is one of Japan's "great three" gardens, and is best seen uncrowded early or late in the day. Established in the mid-17th century, it was opened to the public in 1871. Kenroku-en means "garden of six qualities" (desirable in Chinese gardens): spaciousness, seclusion, air of antiquity, ingenuity, flowing water, and views.

At the edge of the lake is a two-legged stone lantern (see p35), known as Kotoji because it is shaped like the bridge of a koto (stringed instrument). The exquisite two-story **Seisonkaku Villa** adjoining Kenroku-en was built in 1863 by Maeda Nariyasu, 13th lord, for his mother. Its lower floor has formal receiving rooms: walls are coated in gold dust, and shoji paper doors have rare Dutch stained-glass insets. Upstairs is more informal and colorful. The superb curved roof is made from sawara cypress shingles.

Kanazawa Castle, one of the largest in feudal Japan, was almost entirely destroyed by fire in 1881; only the armory and rear gate, Ishikawa-mon, survived. A section of the castle has been rebuilt and a park created. The nearby **Oyama Shrine** is dedicated to Maeda Toshiie. The **Nagamachi Samurai Quarter** retains its earthenwalled streets. With its quality woodwork, costly windowpanes, and serene garden, **Nomura House** gives an idea of samurai life. In the **Nagamachi Kaga Yuzen Silk Center**, a former samurai house, an 18-step resist-dyeing process

The unusual gate to the Oyama Shrine

is used to produce Kaga yuzen silk, popular for formal kimonos.

Most of the city's museums are in the central area. The **21st Century Museum of Contemporary Art** opened in 2004 to explore emerging new work in visual arts, design, craft, fashion, architecture, and film, particularly in the areas of multiculturalism and transportation, technology, gender issues, and the nature of identity. **Ishikawa Prefectural Museum of Traditional Arts and Crafts** has sections on more than 30 Kanazawa crafts, such as silk, ceramics, gold leaf, and folk toys. Two-day "passport" tickets give access to this museum, the **Ishikawa Prefectural Museum of Art** (the Maedas' collection), and the **Honda Museum** (Honda family possessions).

🏯 **Kenroku-en Garden**
Tel (076) 234-3800. Open daily.

🏛 **Seisonkaku Villa**
Tel (076) 221-0580. Open Thu–Tue.

🏛 **Nomura House**
Tel (076) 221-3553. Open daily.

🏛 **Nagamachi Kaga Yuzen Silk Center**
Tel (076) 264-2811. Open daily.

🏢 **21st Century Museum of Contemporary Art**
Tel (076) 220-2800. Open daily.

🏛 **Museum of Traditional Arts and Crafts**
Tel (076) 262-2020. Open daily. Closed Apr–Nov: 3rd Thu in month; Dec–Mar: Thu.

🏢 **Museum of Art**
Tel (076) 231-7580. Open daily.

🏢 **Honda Museum**
Tel (076) 261-0500. Open daily. Closed Nov–Feb: Thu.

Spring in Kenroku-en Garden

For hotels and restaurants see pp302–307 and pp334–339

Exploring the Higashi (Eastern) Pleasure District

Established in 1820, this was the grandest pleasure district outside Kyoto and Edo (Tokyo). Full of atmosphere, the area has old-fashioned street lamps and wooden-lattice windows hiding elegant restaurants and crafts galleries. The evocative **Shima Geisha House** is still much the same as it was in the 19th century. On the upper floor are guest rooms with small stages where the geisha sang and danced. Downstairs are living quarters. Nearby, at **Fukushima Shamisen**, the Fukushima family have been hand-crafting musical instruments for over 130 years. *Shamisen* are made from *karin* wood (a type of quince) and cat or dog skin; the three strings are silk. Visitors may play a finished instrument. The **Sakuda Gold-leaf Store** sells gold-leaf items and demonstrates production – it even has toilets tiled in gold. Kanazawa has produced gold leaf since 1593 and supplies over 98 percent of Japan's needs.

Wall hanging of a geisha in the Shima Geisha House

🏛 **Shima Geisha House**
Tel (076) 252-5675. **Open** daily. 🖼

🏛 **Fukushima Shamisen**
Tel (076) 252-3703. **Open** Mon–Fri.

🏛 **Sakuda Gold-leaf Store**
Tel (076) 251-6777. **Open** daily.

Exploring Southern Kanazawa

Widely known as the "ninja temple," **Myoryu-ji** is a Nichiren temple full of secret doors and passages. It was established in 1643 as a place of worship for the Maedas and a watchtower. The architecture is complex, with 23 rooms linked by 29 staircases and a maze of corridors.

Nearby, **Kutani Kosen Pottery Kiln** is the only kiln in Kanazawa. Kutani porcelain originated in the village of Kutani, south of Kanazawa, in the mid-17th century. Old Kutani-ware uses deep, over-glazed blues, greens, reds, and ochers; modern work has more delicate and varied designs. All pieces are handmade and fired two or three times.

🏯 **Myoryu-ji Temple**
Tel (076) 241-0888. **Open** daily. 🖼 🕐 (every 30 mins, reservation compulsory.)

🏛 **Kutani Kosen Pottery Kiln**
Tel (076) 241-0902. **Open** daily.

Kanazawa City Center

① Higashi Pleasure District
② Kanazawa Castle
③ Oyama Shrine
④ Nagamachi Samurai Quarter
⑤ Kenroku-en Garden
⑥ Seisonkaku Villa
⑦ Ishikawa Prefecture Traditional Products and Crafts Museum
⑧ Ishikawa Prefecture Art Museum
⑨ Honda Museum
⑩ 21st Century Museum of Contemporary Art
⑪ Myoryu-ji Temple
⑫ Kutani Kosen Pottery Kiln

Chujakumon gate at the Zen temple of Eihei-ji

⑰ Eihei-ji Temple

永平寺

Fukui prefecture. 🚃 **Tel** (0776) 63-3102 (bookings and Zen training). 🎴 Lantern offering on the river (late Aug).

Established in 1244, Eihei-ji is one of the Soto Zen sect's two head temples and has been Japan's most active Zen meditation monastery since the late 16th century. In a classic rectilinear plan (see p141), its halls and covered corridors climb up the wooded mountainside. Soto Zen pursues gradual enlightenment by practicing meditation away from the real world; the monastery has about 50 elders and 250 trainees. The atmosphere is cheerful, yet life is austere, with no heating and a simple diet. In the Sodo Hall (to the left), each trainee has just one tatami mat for eating, sleeping, and *zazen* (meditation). Silence is observed, as in the bath building and toilet. Laypeople wishing to experience the rigorous Soto Zen regime must book well ahead.

⑱ Noto Peninsula

能登半島

Ishikawa prefecture. 🚃 🚌 ℹ️ at Wajima stn (0768) 22-1503. 🎴 Seihakusai (May 3–5, Nanao); Abare Festival (1st Fri & Sat in Jul, Ushitsu); Toroyama Festival (Jul 20–21, Iida); Gojinjo Daiko (Jul 31–Aug 1, Nabune).

Projecting 70 km (45 miles) into the Japan Sea, Noto is a quiet region of fishing villages known for seafood and untouched traditions. The east coast and the sandy west near Kanazawa are quite developed, but the north and northwest are rocky and picturesque. Public transportation around Noto is limited; bus and train are similar in time and cost, but the bus network is wider.

Wajima, a weathered fishing town, produces top-quality, durable lacquerware with at least 70 layers of lacquer. Nearby **Hegura** island is a stopping-off point for migratory birds. Just east of Wajima, **Senmaida** is so famed for its "1,000" narrow rice terraces by the sea that it has been awarded heritage status by the Food & Agriculture Organization of the UN, while **Sosogi**'s coast has unusual rock formations. Many summer festivals feature demon-masked drummers and *kiriko* lanterns up to 15 m (50 ft) tall. Between events, drums are played at Wajima and Sosogi.

To the west, **Monzen** has the major **Soji-ji** Zen temple. In **Hakui** are the important shrine of **Keta Taisha** and a 2,000-year-old **sumo ring** – Japan's oldest, still used each September. Senmaida, Sosogi, and Monzen can be reached by bus from Wajima, Hakui by bus or train from Kanazawa.

⑲ Kamikochi

上高地

Nagano prefecture. 🚃 to Shin-Shima-shima, then bus. 🚌 from Hirayu Onsen. ℹ️ 3-min walk from Onota bus stop (0263) 94-2221. 🎴 Mountain Opening Festival (Apr 27).

An alpine valley with a handful of hotels and campsites, Kamikochi lies in the southern part of the Chubu Sangaku (North Japan Alps) National Park, at an altitude of 1,500 m (4,900 ft) and is a good hiking and climbing base. The valley is reached by a tunnel, open from late April to early November; in July, August, Golden Week (see p48), and on some weekends, private cars are banned. Although Japan's highest (after Fuji) and wildest mountains are in the South Alps, the North Alps have more snow and more impressive scenery. Plentiful mountain refuges allow hikes of several days from hut to hut, often via a hot spring. Most huts open from early May to late October (no reservations needed); the main mountaineering season is July to September. Tents and climbing gear can be rented in Kamikochi.

The most spectacular climb is a three-day route from Kamikochi taking in angular **Mount Yari** and **Mount Hotaka** – at 3,190 m (10,470 ft), the highest peak in the North Alps – while short hikes include the rocky scree of **Mount Yake**, the only active volcano in the North Alps. In bad weather, walks are restricted to the valley floor by the rushing river and through a half-submerged landscape shaped by eruptions from Mount Yake.

Dosojin Stones

These pairs of jaunty stone figures, a male and a female, are guardian deities of travelers. They are found at many roadsides in northern Nagano prefecture, as well as at village boundaries. Typically rounded in shape, the pair are often depicted holding hands or with the female offering sake to the male.

A man and woman, each holding a bowl of sake, on a Dosojin stone

⑳ Matsumoto
松本城

Nagano prefecture. 🏔 240,000. ✈️
🚉 ℹ️ at Matsumoto JR stn (0263)
32-2814. 🥁 Taiko Drum Festival (last
weekend in Jul, firelit Noh at castle
(Aug). 🆆 city.matsumoto.nagano.
jp/multilingual/english/guide

Gateway to the Japan Alps,
Matsumoto's main attraction is
its **castle**, a 20-minute walk
northeast of the station. It has the
oldest five-tiered keep in Japan
(1593) and walls and moat from
1504. Functional yet beautiful, it
is well preserved. Devices for
defense include niches for
archers, guns, and dropping
stones. The sixth floor, with
superb mountain views, was the
headquarters when under attack,
and its top floor contains a shrine
to the goddess of the 26th night
who was thought to protect
against fire and invasion.

Beside the keep, reached by
a covered passage, stands the
Moon-viewing Turret, added
in the 1630s for aesthetic purposes. The castle admission
includes the **Japan Folklore
Museum** in the grounds, featuring local geography, wildlife,
history, dolls, and tools.

Also in Matsumoto are the
Japan Ukiyo-e Museum, an
excellent collection of wood-
block prints, and **Matsumoto
Folkcraft Museum**, with folk
art from Japan and across
Asia; on the edge of the city,
a 20-minute bus ride away,
Asama and **Utsukushigahara**
have pleasant hot springs.

🏯 Matsumoto Castle
Tel (0263) 32-2902. **Open** daily. 🎫

🏛️ Japan Ukiyo-e Museum
7 mins drive W of stn. **Tel** (0263)
47-4440. **Open** Tue–Sun. 🎫

🏛️ Folkcraft Museum
15 mins by bus from stn,
Mingeikan-mae stop. **Tel** (0263)
33-1569. **Open** Tue–Sun. 🎫

Environs
North of Matsumoto,
Hotaka has views over the
fields of Japan's largest
wasabi (horseradish) farm,
as well as wasabi tasting.
The fields are a 40-minute
walk from Hotaka station.

An image of the physician Binzuru, follower of
Buddha, in Zenko-ji, Nagano

㉑ Nagano
長野

Nagano prefecture. 🏔 380,000. 🚉
ℹ️ at Nagano JR stn (026) 226-5626.
🥁 Gokaicho (showing of statue, mid-
Apr–mid-May, every 6 years – next
showings 2015, 2021).
🆆 city.nagano.nagano.jp

Surrounded by orchards
and low mountains, Nagano is
a skiing center and was the
main venue for the 1998
Winter Olympics. In the town,
the prime attraction is **Zenko-
ji**, a non-sect temple that
draws up to one million
pilgrims a year. It has,
unusually, always been open
to women as well as men, and
has male and female chief
priests. Established in 670, it
enshrines what is thought to
be Japan's oldest Buddhist
image, an Amida triad brought
from Korea in the 6th century.
This is kept hidden, and a copy
shown every 6 years. The
temple also has a pitch-dark
underground passage
containing a "key to paradise":
touching the key, positioned
on the right-hand wall, is
said to bring happiness in
the afterlife.

Environs
In nearby **Obuse**, the **Hokusai
Museum** is a gallery devoted
to artist Katsushika Hokusai
(1760–1849), who stayed in the
town as an old man. Farther
into the mountains **Jigokudani
Onsen**, reached by bus from
Yudan-aka, is famous for the
270 or so wild macaques living
around its hot pools.

🏛️ Hokusai Museum
10-min walk from Obuse stn.
Tel (026) 247-5206. **Open** daily. 🎫

Bridge leading to the immaculately preserved Matsumoto castle

KYOTO CITY

To truly understand Japan, the visitor must spend time in the backstreets and environs of its old imperial capital, where scores of the country's famous monuments are preserved within a lively modern city. Kyoto's citizens may grudgingly envy the economic vitality of Tokyo and nearby Osaka, but they take great pride in their refined cuisine, lilting dialect, and sensitivity to the seasons.

Founded in 794 as Heian-kyo (capital of peace and tranquility), the city was modeled on the Tang Chinese city of Chang-an. Bounded on three sides by mountains and bisected by a river flowing north to south, the site was considered ideal by Emperor Kanmu's geomancers. As the population grew, however, hygiene was a problem, especially when the Kamo River flooded. A series of rituals and festivals came into being to placate the spirits responsible for plagues and other catastrophes, resulting in a tightly knit fabric of ritual and custom, mostly still observed.

Kyoto culture became an amalgam of several influences, of which the imperial court and nobility were the first and most important. Later came the samurai, patrons of Zen Buddhism, and the tea ceremony. Merchants were also influential, especially the silk weavers of Nishijin. The city was reduced to ashes at various times by earthquakes, fires, and the ten-year period of civil strife known as the Onin War (1467–77). During the Edo period (1603–1868), the balance of power shifted from Kyoto to Edo (Tokyo), and Kyoto eventually lost its status as capital in 1869. At first glance, modern Kyoto may seem little different from other Japanese cities, but the pleasures of this repository of Japanese culture will soon reveal themselves. Life here is still largely tied to nature's rhythms, as can be gauged by visiting at different times of the year. *Kyo-ryori*, Kyoto's celebrated cuisine, for example, makes much of seasonality, and the city's exquisite gardens go through striking seasonal transitions.

Bridge on the northern edge of the Gion district, a remnant of old Kyoto

Exploring Kyoto City

Kyoto is bounded by mountains to the west, north, and east. Many of the best monuments and gardens are found in the foothills, such as the Higashiyama (Eastern Mountains) district east of the Kamo River. Kyoto's treasures have to be sought out. Only by investigating side streets with their old shops and townhouses, exploring temples, and wandering through outlying districts will you begin to get a sense of the city's cultural riches.

Sights at a Glance

Temples and Shrines

1 Toji Temple
3 Sanjusangen-do Temple
5 Nishi and Higashi Hongan-ji Temples
10 Kiyomizu-dera Temple
11 Chion-in Temple
12 Shoren-in Temple
15 Nanzen-ji Temple
16 Ginkaku-ji: the Silver Pavilion
19 Kamo Shrines
20 Daitoku-ji Temple
21 Kitano Tenman-gu Shrine
22 Kinkaku-ji: the Golden Pavilion
24 Ryoan-ji Temple
25 Ninna-ji Temple
26 Myoshin-ji Temple
27 Koryu-ji Temple

Museums and Notable Buildings

2 Kyoto Station
4 Kyoto National Museum
6 Nijo Castle pp164–5
18 Kongu Noh Theater
23 Insho Domoto Museum

Districts

7 Pontocho Alley
8 Gion District
9 Eastern Gion and the Higashiyama pp170–71
13 Okazaki Area
17 Imperial Park

Walk

14 The Philosopher's Walk

Kyoto Addresses

Despite its gridlike layout, Kyoto has no more logical pattern to its address system than anywhere else in Japan. Residences and shops are organized into *cho*, or neighborhoods, many formed from the boundaries of medieval guilds. Locations are often given in relation to an intersection or well-known landmark. Because the city is built on an incline rising from south to north, south is indicated in an address by the word *sagaru* (go down) and north by *agaru* (go up).

↑ Kamigamo Shrine

Ⓢ Kita-Oji

KITAOJI-BASHI

Shugaku-in, Manshu-in ↗

🏯 Ichijo-ji

MEI-DORI

KAMOKAIDO

Kamo River

Ⓢ Kuramaguchi

SHIMOGAMO-HON-DORI

⑲

🏯 Chayama

SAKYO-KU

Takano River

Eizan Railway

🏯 Mototanaka

MIKAGE-DORI

Ⓢ Imadegawa

KARASUMA-DORI

Kamo River

🏯 Demachiyanagi

IMADEGAWA-DORI

HIGASHI-OJI-DORI

SHIRAKAWA-DORI

⑯

Imperial Household Agency

⑱

Imperial Palace

Ⓢ Sento Imperial Palace and Omiya Palace

⑰

IMPERIAL PARK

TERAMACHI-DORI

KAWARAMACHI-DORI

Kamo River

🏯 Jingo-Marutamachi

ARUTAMACHI-DORI

⑭

ⓈMarutamachi

National Museum of Modern Art

⑬ 🏯 Heian-jingu Shrine

KEIHAN SANJO

See map below

Ⓢ Kyoto Shiyakusho-mae

⑮

Higashiyama

Ⓢ Karasuma Oike

Ⓢ Sanjo Keihan

Sanjo

⑦

Ⓢ Keage

Ⓢ Karasuma

Gion Shijo

Yasaka Shrine ⑪

⑧

Kawaramachi

Ⓢ Shijo

⑫

MARUYAMA PARK

KARASUMA-DORI

KAWARAMACHI-DORI

Keihan Railway

HIGASHIYAMA-KU

Yamashina →

⑨

⑤

Ⓢ Gojo

Kiyomizu-Gojo

⑩

GOJO-DORI

Sbosei-en Garden

Shichijo

④

③

oto

Ⓢ②Ⓢ

VISITORS' CHECKLIST

Practical Information
Kyoto prefecture. 🚹 1,475,000.
ℹ️ (075) 344-3300. 🎎 Aoi
Matsuri (Hollyhock Festival, May
15); Gion Matsuri (Jul); Jidai
Matsuri (Festival of the Ages,
Oct 22).
🌐 city.kyoto.jp/koho/eng

Transport
🚄 JR Tokaido Shinkansen and
other lines.

Getting Around

Kyoto has a subway system with
two lines: the Karasuma line runs
south to north; the Tozai line west
to east. There are several train
lines, including the private lines
of Keifuku and Eizan. Several bus
companies cover the city: City
Bus, Kyoto Bus, Keihan Bus, JR Bus,
and Hankyu Bus.

Key

═══ JR train line

═══ Private train line

--- Walk route

0 kilometers _____ 1

0 miles _____ 1

Kujo

Ⓢ

↓ Daigo, Uji

Central Shopping District and Gion

Oe Nob Stage

City Office

Kyoto Hotel Okura

OIKE-DORI

OIKE-OHASHI

KAWABATA-DORI

0 meters _____ 400

0 yards _____ 400

Ⓢ Karasuma-Oike

ANEYAKOJI-DORI

Kyoto Shiyakusho-mae

Kyoto Royal Hotel

SANJO-DORI

The Museum of Kyoto

SANJO-DORI

Ⓢ Sanjo Keihan

WAKAMATSU-DORI

SANJO-DORI

HIGASHINOTOIN-DORI

KARASUMA-DORI

TAKAKURA-DORI

SAKAIMACHI

YANAGI-NO-BANBA

TOMI-NO-KOJI

FUYACHO

GOKOMACHI

SHIN-KYOGOKU-DORI

TERAMACHI-DORI

KAWARAMACHI-DORI

Sanjo

Pontocho Kaburenjo

KIYAMACHI

Takase River

PONTOCHO

NAWATE-DORI

HANAMIKOJI-DORI

FURU-MONZEN

ROKKAKU-DORI

TAKOYAKUSHI-DORI

⑦

SHIN-MONZEN

GION

MUROMACHI

NISHIKI-KOJI

Daimaru Department Store

Kyoto Craft Center

Ⓢ Karasuma

Ⓢ Shijo

Fujii-Daimaru Department Store

SHIJO-DORI

Hankyu Kawaramachi

⑧

Minami-za Theater

Ichiriki Teahouse

SHIJO-DORI

Takashimaya Department Store

Hankyu Department Store

Gion Shijo

Gion Kobu Kaburenjo

AYANO-KOJI-DORI

Gion Corner

HIGASHI-OJI-DORI

TAKAKURA-DORI

KARASUMA-DORI

❶ Toji Temple

東寺

🚌 42 to Toji Higashimon-mae. **Open** 8:30am–5:30pm daily (4:30pm fall/winter). 🏛 Museum: **Tel** (075) 691-3325. **Open** phone for times. 🏛

Although it lacks the mossy beauty of many Kyoto temples, dusty, hoary Toji (actual name Kyo-o-gokoku-ji) impresses by the sheer weight of its history. Its Buddhas have been watching over the city ever since Kukai *(see p233)* founded the temple in 794. The city's religious foundations were laid here, and echoes of bygone rituals seem to linger in Toji's hallowed halls.

Kukai turned Toji into the main headquarters of Shingon Buddhism. The sect's esoteric rituals relied heavily on mandalas, and in the Kodo (lecture hall), 21 statues form a three-dimensional mandala, at the center of which is Dainichi Nyorai, the cosmic Buddha who first expounded the esoteric teachings. About 1,200 years old, these and other major images were carved from single blocks of wood.

Yakushi Nyorai, the Buddha of healing, and his attendants Gakko and Nikko, are enshrined in the two-story Kondo (main hall). First built in 796, the present structure dates from 1603 and is considered a masterpiece.

Rebuilt in 1644, Toji's magnificent five-story pagoda – at 55 m (180 ft) the tallest pagoda in Japan – has become

Soaring, light-filled main hall of Kyoto Station

a symbol of Kyoto. Inside are images of four Buddhas and their followers.

Northwest of the Kodo is the Miei-do or Taishi-do (great teacher's hall) where Kukai lived. It houses a Secret Buddha, a Fudo Myo-o image, shown on rare occasions, as well as an image of Kukai. A National Treasure, the graceful structure dates from 1380.

Kukai's death is commemorated on the 21st of each month, when a flea market, called *Kobo-san* by the locals, is held in the temple precincts. Many shoppers take time out for a brief pilgrimage to the Miei-do, where they offer money and incense, some rubbing the incense smoke onto whatever body part is troubling them.

❷ Kyoto Station

京都駅

Complex: ℹ️ 2nd flr main concourse, left from escalator, **Tel** (075) 361-4401. **Open** 8:30am–7pm daily. Kyoto Tourist Information: ℹ️ Kyoto station building, 2F. **Tel** (075) 343-0548. **Open** 8:30am–7pm daily.

A sleek complex of soaring spaces, glass surfaces, and bleacher-like staircases, Kyoto's JR train station provides a futuristic entry to Japan's old imperial capital. Completed in

Toji temple's five-story pagoda, the tallest in Japan

1997, the structure is the work of architect Hiroshi Hara, a former Tokyo University professor whose design triumphed in an international competition. Although it has been criticized for its refusal to incorporate traditional Japanese motifs in its design, the station is undeniably eye-catching. Thanks to its open-air spaces it also ironically resembles a traditional wooden Kyoto house: pleasant in summer, but drafty and cold in winter.

Within the station is a shopping area called **The Cube**, which includes shops specializing in Kyoto craft items and food products.

Long hall and landscaped grounds of Sanjusangen-do

❸ Sanjusangen-do Temple

三十三間堂

Tel (075) 561-0467. 🚊 Keihan Nanajo stn. 🚌 100, 206, 208 to Hakubutsukan Sanjusangen-do-mae. **Open** Apr–mid-Nov: 8am–5pm daily; mid-Nov–Mar: 9am–4pm daily. 🏛

Sanjusangen-do (popular name of Rengeo-in) induces an almost hallucinatory effect on its visitors who, once inside its elongated main hall, find themselves face to face with ranks of nearly identical Kannon (goddess of mercy) images – 1,001 of them, to be precise – all glimmering in the dark. Sanjusangen-do dates from 1164 and is the longest wooden structure in the world. Its name derives from the 33 *(sanjusan)* spaces between the building's pillars. The main, magnificent image of a 1,000-armed Kannon was carved in 1254 by Tankei at the age of 82. Upon its head are ten other heads, including a miniature image of the Amida Buddha. Stretching out on either side are 1,000 smaller images. Kannon was believed to have 33 manifestations, so the faithful would have invoked the mercy of 33,033 Kannons.

On the Sunday before Coming-of-Age Day *(see p51)* the temple hosts an archery contest for young women, who shoot arrows from one end of the veranda of the main hall to the other.

❹ Kyoto National Museum

京都国立博物館

Tel (075) 541-1151. 206 & 208 to Hakubutsukan Sanjusangendo-mae. **Open** 9:30am–6pm Tue–Sun (to 8pm Fri). **kyohaku.go.jp/eng/indextop.html**

The city's National Museum was established in 1895 and is noted for its pictorial works, including Buddhist and ink paintings, textiles and Heian-period sculptures. Special exhibitions are held in the Meiji-era brick building to the right of the entrance.

❺ Nishi and Higashi Hongan-ji Temples

西本願寺と東本願寺

Nishi Hongan-ji: **Tel** (075) 371-5181. 9, 28,75 to Nishi Honganji-mae. **Open** May–Aug: 5:30am–6pm daily; Sep, Oct, Mar, Apr: 5:30am–5:30pm daily; Nov–Feb 5:30am–5pm. **hongwanji.or.jp/english**. Higashi Hongan-ji: **Tel** (075) 371-9181. JR Kyoto Stn, then 5-min walk. **Open** Mar–Oct: 5:50am–5:30pm daily; Nov–Feb: 6:20am–4:30pm daily. **higashihonganji.or.jp**

With their massive flower-decked altars, ornately carved transoms, and shimmering expanses of tatami matting, the cavernous Hongan-ji temples testify to the power and popularity of the Jodo-Shinshu sect.

The two temples are almost identical in their layout, reflecting their common origin. Each has a huge Goei-do (founder's hall) and a smaller Amida-do housing an Amida Buddha image. **Nishi Hongan-ji** is rich in National Treasures, but not all are always on view. They include the Shoin (study hall), with its lavishly decorated Shiroshoin and Kuroshoin compartments; Kokei no Niwa, a garden featuring cycad palms; two Noh stages, one of which is thought to be the oldest Noh stage in existence; Hiunkaku, a large tea pavilion; and the Karamon, or Chinese gate. The Shoin is open twice a month, but dates vary. (The Kuroshoin, however, is never shown.) Hiunkaku is open only once a year, on May 20 or 21. Entrance requires a large donation, which includes a bowl of tea and a Noh performance.

Mythical beast detail from Nishi Hongan-ji's gate

Higashi Hongan-ji's immense and lavish Goei-do gate is one of the first traditional structures visitors to Kyoto see as they head north out of Kyoto Station. The temple's Goei-do (founder's hall) dates from 1895 and claims to be the largest wooden structure in the world. The striking white plaster and gray-tile walls on the temple's northern side belong to the temple kura, or storehouse.

Environs

Two blocks east of Higashi Hongan-ji proper is **Shosei-en** (nicknamed Kikoku-tei), a spacious garden owned by the temple. Poet-scholar Ishikawa Jozan (1583–1672) and landscape architect Kobori Enshu (1579–1647) are said to have had a hand in its design. Herons, ducks, and other wildlife find refuge here.

Detail of the main gate fronting the street at Nishi Hongan-ji

❻ Nijo Castle

二条城

With few of the grand fortifications of other castles in Japan, Nijo is instead best known for its unusually ornate interiors and so-called nightingale floors. The latter were designed to make bird-like squeaking sounds when walked upon, a warning of possible intruders. The complex was created by Shogun Tokugawa Ieyasu (1543–1616), and symbolized the power and riches of the newly established Edo-based shogunate. Ieyasu's grandson Iemitsu commissioned the best Kano School painters for the reception halls, in preparation for an imperial visit. Ironically, in 1867 the last Tokugawa shogun resigned at Nijo Castle, in the presence of Emperor Meiji.

Cherry Trees Painting
The painting of flowering cherry trees on the sliding door panels is attributed to Kano Naonobu (1607–50).

Garden
Nijo's garden is famous for the wealth and variety of its rocks.

Ninomaru Complex
The focus of Nijo Castle is the Ninomaru reception rooms, a staggered group of buildings interconnected by covered wooden walkways.

KEY

① **Kuroshoin** (inner audience chamber).

② **Shiroshoin** (shogun's living chambers).

③ **Shikidai** (reception chamber).

④ **The nightingale floors** were carefully laid so that the cramps and nails below the floorboards would rub together and squeak gently when disturbed.

★ **Ohiroma Ichi-no-ma (first grand chamber)**
Dummies representing daimyo (feudal lords) are shown paying respects to the shogun on his dais.

Large Cats Painting
This dynamic animal scene was painted at a time when Japanese artists mistook leopards for female tigers.

VISITORS' CHECKLIST

Practical Information
Entrance on Horikawa-dori.
Tel (075) 841-0096.
Open 8:45am–5pm daily.
Last admission 4pm.
Closed Dec 26–Jan 4 & Tue in Jan, Jul, Aug, Dec.

Transport
S Nijojo-mae stn. 9, 50, 101.

★ **Karamon Gate**
This Momoyama-period gate has a Chinese-style gable and gold plated fixtures.

Entrance to
Ninomaru compound

The Kano School Painters

The Kano painters, originally from a low-ranking samurai family, grew to prominence in the 15th century for their Chinese-style landscapes, figures-in-landscape, and bird and flower scenes. The paintings at Nijo Castle are the largest Kano pieces executed. Among the motifs are life-size tigers and panthers crouching among bamboo groves, wild geese and herons in a winter landscape, pine trees, flitting swallows, and frolicking peacocks.

Huge pine trees in the Shikidai, by Kano Tanyu (1602–74)

Entrance to Palace
Above the carriage porch is an unusually ornate wood carving of flying birds, peacocks, and delicately twining flowers.

❼ Pontocho Alley

先斗町通り

🚉 Kawaramachi stn, Hankyu Kyoto line. 🚌 5, 17, 205 to Shijo-Kawaramachi.

This charming alleyway is best appreciated after dusk, when it is reminiscent of an *ukiyo-e* print *(see p89)*. Formerly a sandbar, the stretch of land began to be developed in 1670. The area flourished as an entertainment district and was licensed as a gay quarter, a role it continues to play. Although neon and concrete are encroaching, the street largely remains the preserve of the traditional wooden *ochaya* – the type of teahouse where geisha entertain clients.

Pontocho is also home to the tiny **Tanuki (Badger) Shrine**. In 1978 a fire broke out in Pontocho, taking the life of a geisha. Where it stopped, a ceramic *tanuki* *(see p311)* was found shattered by the heat. Believing that Mr. Tanuki had sacrificed himself on their behalf, the residents built this little shrine to house his remains. Throw in a coin and a recorded message imparts such pearls of wisdom as "beware of fire."

From the beginning of June to mid-September, many of Pontocho's riverside restaurants erect platforms, called *yuka*, over the canal running parallel to the Kamo River.

The colorful Tanuki Shrine, dedicated to a sacrificed ceramic tanuki (badger)

Two-story gateway to Yasaka Shrine, Gion district

❽ Gion District

祇園地区

Several blocks north and south of Shijo-dori, bounded by the Kamo River to the west and the Higashiyama to the east. 🚉 Gion-shijo stn, Keihan line. 🚌 46, 201, 203, 207 to Gion.

By turns tawdry and sublime, the Gion is Kyoto's best-known geisha quarter where Japanese men come to revel in the company of professional geishas at private inns and teahouses.

The Gion's history started in feudal times, with stalls catering to the needs of pilgrims and other visitors. These evolved into teahouses fulfilling a variety of appetites. In the late 16th century, Kabuki moved from the Kamo riverbank, where it had started, into several theaters just east of the river, furthering the Gion's reputation as a playboy's paradise. One of these, **Minamiza** *(see p188)*, still exists.

The **Yasaka Shrine**, whose striking two-story vermilion gate rises above the eastern end of Shijo-dori, was established around 656 and originally called Gion Shrine. Its deities protect from illness and, in 869, were paraded through the streets to stop an epidemic – the beginning of the famous Gion Matsuri *(see p188)*. On New Year's Day, thousands flock here to pray for health and prosperity, while in early April crowds stream through its gates on their way to **Maruyama Park**, a cherry-blossom viewing site.

Gion's main shopping area is the stretch of Shijo between Yasaka Shrine and Shijo Bridge, which includes shops with expensive kimono accessories. On the southeast corner of Shijo and Hanamikoji is the Gion's most famous *ochaya*, **Ichiriki**. Easily identified by its distinctive red walls, this teahouse is the setting of a scene in the Kabuki play *Chushingura*. **Hanamikoji** itself, a historically preserved zone, shows the Gion at its classic, and classy, best. The restaurants and *ochaya* here are the haunts of politicians and company presidents, and are likely to turn a cold shoulder to people without a proper introduction. More accessible to tourists are the nearby **Gion Corner** and the **Gion Kobu Kaburenjo** venues *(see p188)*.

Running east from Hanamikoji, north of Shijo, is **Shinbashi**, a street lined with *ochaya*, and nary a neon sign to be seen. At the eastern end of this beautifully preserved area is the tiny shrine of **Tatsumi Daimyo-jin**, its red surfaces plastered with name cards of Gion geisha, hostesses, and restaurant owners who have visited to pray for prosperity.

The average Gion-goer, however, is more likely to partake of drink and karaoke than engage in geisha play at a prestigious *ochaya*. His territory is the northeastern Gion, where the cluttered streets of neon and concrete are as gaudy as Shinbashi is refined.

Geisha, Geiko, and Maiko

Geisha are female professional entertainers whose knowledge of traditional arts, skill at verbal repartee, and ability to keep a secret win them the respect, and sometimes love, of their well-heeled and often influential male clients. The profession, dating from the 17th century, is in decline and blurred by the activities of so-called *onsen geisha* and others who offer more sexual than classical arts, or who are more glorified waitress than geisha. Kyoto's proud geisha prefer the term *geiko* (child of the arts). Less polished than their *geiko* "sisters," *maiko*, apprentice geisha, are a Kyoto-only phenomenon. The city has four geisha enclaves: Gion-kobu, Pontocho, Miyagawa-cho, and Kamishichi-ken. Public dances are staged in each district in spring and fall. At other times, the only way to see geisha perform is at private functions, often held at *ryotei*, *ochaya*, and *ryokan* (upscale restaurants, teahouses, and inns).

Pontocho, one of Kyoto's historic geisha districts, has many *ochaya*, where geisha are booked to entertain prestigious clients.

The white face and delicately shaped red lips are classic ideals of beauty in Japan.

Under-kimono

Ornamental hairpins vary with the seasons.

A *maiko*'s hair is her own, not a wig.

The nape of the neck, accentuated by the unpainted part, is considered sensuous.

The *obi* (sash) of a *maiko* hangs down at the back.

Embroidered collar

The Maiko Costume

Only in Kyoto do young women training to be geiko *wear their hair in a distinctive style and sport a unique costume featuring a long, hanging obi, tall koppori clogs, and an under-kimono with an embroidered collar. When becoming a fully-fledged geiko, they exchange the embroidered collar for a white one, a transition known as* eri-kae, *or collar change.*

Tabi socks

The geisha world moves to the rhythm of the *shamisen*, a three-stringed instrument that originated in Okinawa. Geisha who choose not to specialize in dance will instead master the *shamisen* or another instrument. The skills of older geisha are held in high regard.

Poised and posture-perfect, Umegiku, of the Kamishichi-ken district, performs classical dance with a fan as prop. For more formal occasions she will paint her face and wear a different kimono.

⑨ Street-by-Street: Eastern Gion and the Higashiyama

For most of Kyoto's history, the area comprising the Higashiyama (Eastern Mountains) district lay outside the official boundaries of the capital. As a result, it was always more rustic and secluded. Furthermore, being separated from the main city by the Kamo River, it was spared the fires that often ravaged Kyoto. Consequently, Higashiyama remains one of the city's most charming and unspoiled districts. The small area shown here includes the eastern side of the Gion, leading through some delightful stone-paved roads up to Kiyomizu Temple.

Maruyama Park
Kyoto's most famous cherry-blossom viewing site is mobbed until the petals fall.

Kodai-ji was built in 1605 by the widow of Toyotomi Hideyoshi in his memory.

★ Yasaka Shrine
On the edge of Kyoto's central shopping district, the Yasaka Shrine *(see p166)* oversees the religious rites of the city's main festival, the Gion Matsuri, in July.

SHIJO-DORI

↓ Central Kyoto

HIGASHI-OJI-DORI

SHIJO

The southern exit of the Yasaka Shrine, marked by concrete and vermilion *torii* gates, leads to the eastern part of the Gion district.

★ Ishibe-Koji Lane
This charming lane with discreet inns and teahouses is an extension of the Gion entertainment district *(see p166)*. The exquisite wooden buildings with tiny gardens reflect the peaceful atmosphere of old Kyoto.

Ne-ne no Michi
Named after Hideyoshi's widow, "Ne-ne's road" is a wide flagstone-paved avenue, home to small, upscale shops and private galleries. Long, stone staircases lead up from the road to the temple of Kodai-ji and the Ryozen Kannon.

For hotels and restaurants see pp302–307 and pp324–339

Yasaka Pagoda
Not to be confused with the Shinto shrine of the same name to its north, the elegant, five-story Yasaka Pagoda is all that remains of a Buddhist temple that once stood here.

Locator Map
See Kyoto map *page 161*

Ryozen Kannon The 24-m (80-ft) high concrete figure near Kodai-ji Temple is dedicated to the Japanese soldiers who died in World War II.

Kiyomizu-yaki, a refined, brightly colored porcelain, is sold in numerous pottery shops lining the roads leading up to Kiyomizu.

★ **Kiyomizu-dera Temple**
This famous temple *(see p172)* is over a thousand years old and could almost be called an institution of Kyoto life.

NINENZAKA

SANNENZAKA

KIYOMIZUZAKA

CHAWANZAKA

E-NE NO MICHI

0 meters 200

0 yards 200

Key

— Suggested route

★ **Stone-Paved Roads**
Two flagstone-paved streets called Sannen-zaka ("three-year slope") and Ninenzaka ("two-year slope") are a preservation district. Take care on the steps – local lore maintains that a slip here will bring two or three years' bad luck.

View from the veranda of the main hall at Kiyomizu-dera Temple

⑩ Kiyomizu-dera Temple
清水寺

Tel (075) 551-1234. 🚌 100, 206, 207 to Gojyozaka. **Open** 6am–5:30pm, 6pm, or 6:30pm daily. 📷 🌐 **kiyomizu dera.or.jp/lang/01.html**

While many other famous temples are the preserves of certain sects, Kiyomizu-dera seems to belong to everyone. For over 1,000 years, pilgrims have climbed the slope to pray to the temple's 11-headed Kannon image and drink from its sacred spring. The main hall's veranda, a nail-less miracle of Japanese joinery, offers wonderful views of Kyoto. To view the temple itself, walk to the pagoda across the ravine, and you'll see why the expression "to jump off Kiyomizu's stage" is the Japanese equivalent of "to take the plunge."

Statue of Kannon at Kiyomizu-dera

On the temple's north side is a small shrine where love charms can be purchased.

⑪ Chion-in Temple
知恩院

Tel (075) 531-2111. 🚇 Higashiyama stn, Tozai line. 🚌 206 to Chion-in-mae. **Open** 9am–4:30pm daily. 📷 🌐 **chion-in.or.jp/e**

Chion-in's colossal Sanmon, the largest such gate in Japan, was built to proclaim the supremacy of Jodo-sect Buddhism, of which Chion-in is the headquarters. It was also an emphatic statement of the authority of the Tokugawa shogunate, which funded the temple's restoration.

The well-endowed complex occupies the site where Honen, the founder of the Jodo sect, started to preach in 1175. It boasts a lavish founder's hall, a smaller hall enshrining an image of Amida Buddha, and elegant reception halls decorated with Kano School *(see p165)* paintings. The Gongen-do mausoleum enshrines the spirits of Tokugawa Ieyasu, his son Hidetada, and grandson Iemitsu. The temple also possesses a huge bell that is solemnly rung 108 times (once for each sin Man is prone to commit) on New Year's Eve, an event broadcast on TV.

⑫ Shoren-in Temple
青蓮院

Tel (075) 561-2345. 🚇 Higashiyama stn, Tozai line. 🚌 5, 46, 100 to Jingu-michi. **Open** 9am–5pm daily. 📷 🌐 **shorenin.com/english/index. html**

Aristocratic Shoren-in's symbol is its ancient camphor trees whose 700-year-old gnarled limbs spread majestically on either side of the front gate. The grounds are beautifully landscaped, with a bright pond garden on one side and a mysterious, camphor-tree-shaded expanse of moss on the other. The teahouse in the garden has been rebuilt, the original having been burned in April 1993 by left-wing radicals protesting the Emperor's visit to Okinawa.

⑬ Okazaki Area
岡崎公園一帯

🚌 5 or 100 to Kyoto Kaikan Bijutsukan-mae. 🎐 Jidai Matsuri (Festival of the Ages, Oct 22, Heian Shrine).

Okazaki is home to museums, galleries, sports grounds, the municipal zoo, and **Heian-Jingu**, one of Kyoto's largest and newest shrines. Built in 1895, the shrine was intended to help boost the city's morale and economy – both at a low ebb after Tokyo was made capital in 1868. With its vermilion pillars and green tiles, the shrine harks back to Tang Dynasty China. Its pond garden is famous for irises and a Chinese-style covered bridge.

The **National Museum of Modern Art** houses a superb collection of paintings by a school of Kyoto artists active in the Meiji and Taisho eras. Across the street is the venerable **Kyoto Municipal Museum of Art**, which hosts exhibitions of European and American works. The **Kyoto International Exhibition Hall** (Miyako Messe), hosts a variety of shows, while its basement museum presents scores of Kyoto crafts, including Kiyomizu-*yaki* porcelain.

🏛 **National Museum of Modern Art**
Tel (075) 761-4111. **Open** 9:30am–6pm Tue–Sun (to 8pm Fri). 📷

🏛 **Kyoto Municipal Museum of Art**
Tel (075) 771-4107. **Open** Tue–Sun. 📷

🏛 **International Exhibition Hall**
Tel (075) 762-2630. **Open** daily.

Heian-jingu, the shrine built in 1895 in Okazaki

The Tea Ceremony

Valued for its medicinal qualities, tea was imported from China in the 8th century. The nobility took to drinking it at lavish parties, and Murato Shuko (1422–1502) later developed the custom's spiritual aspects, which appealed to the samurai. The point of the ritual *(chaji)*, in which a light meal and whisked powdered tea *(matcha)* are served by a host to a few invited guests, is summed up by the samurai notion "one lifetime, one meeting" *(ichigo, ichie)*. In other words, this is a unique moment to be treasured. In Kyoto, where the tea ceremony was developed, special rituals are put on for tourists *(see p189)*, with commentary about the complex etiquette and Zen ideals. Visitors can also enjoy *matcha* and a sweet *(wagashi)* without the ritual at many temples and specialty teashops.

Sen no Rikyu (1522–91), a student of Shuko and adviser to warlord Hideyoshi, formalized the ritual, replacing Chinese utensils with native ones. His descendants continued the legacy, resulting in two main schools of tea: Omote Senke and Ura Senke.

The ceremonial teahouse is a small, hut-like building with a garden *(see pp34–5)*, not to be confused with other types of teahouses, such as the geisha's *ochaya*, or those for wayfarers. The one shown here is at Daitoku-ji *(see pp176–7)*, the spiritual home of the tea ceremony.

The tea utensils reflect Zen values of simplicity, refinement, and restraint.

Whisk *(chasen)*

Tea jar *(natsume)*

Water jug *(mizusashi)*

Tea bowl *(chawan)*

Bamboo ladle *(hishaku)*

Charcoal burner *(furo)*

Kettle *(kama)*

To drink matcha, even informally, hold the bowl with your right hand and place it in the palm of your left. Turn it clockwise about 90 degrees, raise it with both hands, then empty it in three gulps.

The Way of Tea

The tea ceremony is a well-orchestrated series of events. The ritual involves meeting your fellow guests, walking through the grounds of the teahouse, performing ablutions, entering a cell-like room, meeting your host, admiring the features of the room and tea utensils, watching the tea being prepared, bowing, and consuming the food and tea. Each part of the ritual is symbolic; ultimately it is your appreciation of the moment that counts.

The decorative alcove *(tokonoma)* has a hanging scroll *(kakemono)* and sometimes a flower arrangement or art object to be admired.

Guests sit *seiza*, kneeling on the *tatami* matting, an uncomfortable position for the uninitiated.

Guests bow when attendants offer individual bowls of the freshly prepared tea.

⑭ The Philosopher's Walk

哲学の道

One of Kyoto's best-loved spots, the Philosopher's Walk follows a cherry-tree-lined canal meandering along the base of the scenic Higashiyama (Eastern Mountains) between Ginkaku-ji south to Nyakuoji-jinja, and connects with roads leading to the precincts of Nanzen-ji. The route is so-named because a Kyoto University philosophy professor, Nishida Kitaro (1870–1945), used it for his daily constitutional. Coffee and craft shops, restaurants, and boutiques are scattered along the route. The path becomes a veritable promenade during the cherry and maple seasons, as couples from all over the Kansai region flock to enjoy its unspoiled natural beauty.

Cherry blossoms along the canal

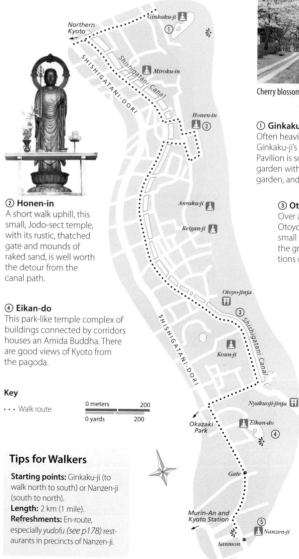

① Ginkaku-ji

Often heaving with tour groups, Ginkaku-ji's so-called Silver Pavilion is set within a remarkable garden with ponds, raked gravel garden, and pine trees.

② Honen-in

A short walk uphill, this small, Jodo-sect temple, with its rustic, thatched gate and mounds of raked sand, is well worth the detour from the canal path.

③ Otoyo-jinja

Over a bridge to the east, Otoyo-jinja is one of a few small Shinto shrines among the great Buddhist foundations of the Higashiyama.

④ Eikan-do

This park-like temple complex of buildings connected by corridors houses an Amida Buddha. There are good views of Kyoto from the pagoda.

⑤ Nanzen-ji

Rebuilt after the disastrous Onin War (1467–77), most of Zen temple Nanzen-ji's structures date from the 17th century, apart from this celebrated, Western-style Meiji-period aqueduct.

Key

- - - Walk route

0 meters   200
0 yards   200

Tips for Walkers

Starting points: Ginkaku-ji (to walk north to south) or Nanzen-ji (south to north).
Length: 2 km (1 mile).
Refreshments: En-route, especially *yudofu (see p178)* restaurants in precincts of Nanzen-ji.

Colossal, free-standing Sanmon (gateway) at Nanzen-ji

⓯ Nanzen-ji Temple

南禅寺

Tel (075) 771-0365. **S** Keage stn, Tozai line. 🚌 5 to Nanzen-ji-Eikando-michi. **Open** 8:40am–5pm daily (Dec–Feb: to 4:30pm). 🏛
W nanzenji.com

From its pine-studded outer precincts to the inner recesses of its subtemples, this quintessential Zen temple exudes an air of serenity. Nanzen-ji has been at the center of Japanese Zen history since 1386, when it was placed in control of Kyoto's Gozan, or "five great Zen temples."

The **Hojo** (abbot's quarters) includes a small but exquisite dry garden attributed to Kobori Enshu (1579–1647), and Momoyama-period paintings, including the Kano Tanyu masterpiece *Tiger Drinking Water*. Nearby is a room overlooking a waterfall and garden, where a bowl of *matcha* (ceremonial tea) and a sweet can be enjoyed for a small fee.

The temple's colossal **Sanmon**, a two-story gate built in 1626 to console the souls of those killed in the Summer Siege of Osaka Castle, is said to have been the hideout of Ishikawa Goemon, a legendary outlaw hero who was later boiled alive in an iron cauldron.

Subtemples

Three of Nanzen-ji's 12 subtemples are open to the public year-round. The most impressive, **Konchi-in**, boasts work by Kobori Enshu,

featuring pines and boulders arranged in a tortoise-and-crane motif. **Tenju-an** has a dry garden and a small, lush stroll garden. **Nanzen-in** occupies the original site of Emperor Kameyama's villa. Restored in 1703, it faces a pond-centered garden backed by a wooded mountainside.

The red-brick **aqueduct** in front of Nanzen-ji may seem incongruous, but for Japanese tourists this "exotic" Western structure is one of Nanzen-ji's greatest attractions. Built in 1890, it formed part of an ambitious canal project to bring water and goods from neighboring Shiga prefecture into the city. It was one of Meiji Japan's first feats of engineering.

Nanzen-ji is synonymous with *yudofu*, boiled tofu, a delicacy best enjoyed during cold months. Specialty restaurants are located within the temple precincts.

Environs
Gem-like **Murin-an** to the west of Nanzen-ji is the former villa of Meiji-era statesman Yamagata Aritomo. The garden's design makes good use of water from the aqueduct. North of Nanzen-ji, **Eikan-do** houses an image of Amida Buddha in the act of looking back over his shoulder, a very unusual pose.

⓰ Ginkaku-ji: the Silver Pavilion

銀閣寺

Tel (075) 771-5725. 🚌 100 to Ginkaku-ji-mae. **Open** 8am–5pm daily (Dec–Feb: 9am–4:30pm). 🏛

Ginkaku-ji – actual name, Jisho-ji; English nickname, Silver Pavilion – is considered by some to be an unequaled masterpiece of garden design; others find it overrated. Not in dispute is the importance of Ginkaku-ji to Japanese culture, for within its walls the tea ceremony, Noh, flower arrangement, and ink painting found new levels of refinement.

The temple was originally the mountain retreat of shogun Yoshimasa (1358–1408), who is remembered for an artistic renaissance now referred to as Higashiyama culture. In tribute to his grandfather, who covered Kinkaku-ji in gold leaf *(see p178)*, Yoshimasa intended to finish his pavilion in silver. However, the ruinous Onin War thwarted that ambition. Minus its final coating, the graceful Silver Pavilion now shines with the patina of age.

The Silver Pavilion, which never received its intended covering

For hotels and restaurants see pp302–307 and pp324–339

The towering entrance to the Imperial Palace (*Kyoto Gosho*)

⓱ Imperial Park
京都御苑

S Imadegawa stn, Karasuma line. Imperial Household Agency: **Tel** (075) 211-1215. **Open** 8:45am–noon, 1–5pm Mon–Fri. Apply here for tickets to the imperial palaces and gardens. (Passport required.) Imperial Palace: 🎫 tours in English: 10am, 2pm Mon–Fri. Retired Emperor's Palace: 🎫 tours in Japanese: (1 hr) 9am, 11am, 1pm, 3pm; (30 mins): 11am, 3pm. Both palaces: **Open** Mon–Fri & 3rd Sat of month (each Sat in Apr, May, Oct, Nov). **Closed** Dec 28–Jan 4, public hols.

With its stately pines and vistas of the Higashiyama, the Imperial Park (Kyoto Gyoen) is a spacious oasis in the heart of the city. On its grounds are the **Imperial Palace** (Kyoto Gosho) and **Sento Imperial Palace** (Sento Gosho), whose impressive stroll garden was built by the Tokugawa for retired emperor Go-Mizuno'o in 1630. The **Imperial Household Agency** (Kunaicho), where tickets are issued for the imperial structures as well as to Shugaku-in and Katsura villas *(see pp180 and 182)*, is in the northwest corner.

At the southern end of the park is a delightful pond with an arched bridge, all that remains of one of several noble families' estates that occupied much of what is now parkland. From the bridge is an unobstructed view all the way north to the **Kenreimon**, the majestic gate in the middle of the south wall, which may be used only by the emperor.

⓲ Kongo Noh Theater
金剛能楽堂

S Imadegawa stn, Karasuma line. **Tel** (075) 441-7222. **Open** Tue–Sun. 🎭 for performances.

The Kongo Noh Theater across from the Imperial Palace grounds opened in June 2003, following its relocation from a site in Shijo Muromachi. During the Edo period (1603–1868) Noh was adopted as the official art of the warrior class, and the Kongo Theater has the longest history of regular use as a Noh stage in Japan; its players are particularly known for their agility and acrobatic feats. The theater incorporates several features from the earlier design, including the outdoor stage, pillars, and large acoustic earthenware jars. Regular performances are held at the theater, usually on the last Sunday of the month. Look out for exhibitions of Noh costumes and masks in the lobby.

Mannequin at the Imperial Palace

Torii gates at Shimogamo, one of the Kamo shrines

⓳ Kamo Shrines
上賀茂・下賀茂神社

🚌 46, 47 to Kamigamo-jinja-mae; 4, 205 to Shimogamo-jinja-mae. Kamigamo Shrine: **Tel** (075) 781-0011. **Open** 6am–5pm. Shimogamo Shrine: **Tel** (075) 781-0010. **Open** summer: 5:30am–6pm; winter: 6:30am–5pm. Nishimura House: **Tel** (075) 781-0666. **Open** Mar 15–Dec 8: 9:30am–4:30pm. 🎭 🎏 Aoi Matsuri (Hollyhock Festival, May 15).

At the northern reaches of the Kamo River, **Kamigamo Shrine** has probably existed since the 7th century, while **Shimogamo**, its southern counterpart, is a century older. Both are dedicated to the thunder deity. Set in sylvan Tadasu no Mori, Shimogamo has long played a role in ensuring the success of the rice harvest. The Aoi Festival features a procession between the shrines, horse races, and archery. Kamigamo Shrine is noted for its Haiden hall, rebuilt in 1628. In the vicinity are several *shake*, priests' residences. Of these, **Nishimura House** is open to the public.

⓴ Daitoku-ji Temple
大徳寺

Tel (075) 491-0019. **S** Kita-Oji stn, Karasuma line. 🚌 12, 204, 205, 206 to Daitoku-ji-mae. **Open** 9am–4:30pm daily 🎭 for most subtemples.

An air of eloquent restraint pervades the grounds of Daitoku-ji, as befits a temple intimately connected with the world of the tea ceremony. Founded in 1325, the temple prospered in the latter half of the 16th century, when it came under the patronage of warlords (and tea ceremony aficionados) Oda Nobunaga and Hideyoshi. Today, a host of subtemples, many with famous tearooms and jewel-like gardens, continue to promote the ways of Zen and Tea.

Daisen-in is famous for its Muromachi-period dry garden. Ink landscape paintings by Soami and Kano Motonobu grace its interior. The south garden of **Koto-in** features a grove of slender maples rising above an expanse of moss and a *roji*, or tea garden, to the west. **Zuiho-in**, built in 1535 as the memorial temple of a Christian *daimyo*, has a modern garden by Shigemori Mirei with rocks placed in the shape of a crucifix. **Ryogen-in**, founded 1502, has four gardens in different styles.

Interior at Ryogen-in, a subtemple of Daitoku-ji

㉑ Kitano Tenman-gu Shrine

北野天満宮

Tel (075) 461-0005. 🚌 50, 101, 203 to Kitano Tenman-gu-mae.
Open 9am–5pm daily (7am–9pm on 25th of every month).
Ⓦ kitanotenmangu.or.jp

Always thronged with students praying for success in exams, Kitano Tenman-gu enshrines Heian statesman Sugawara Michizane, or Tenjin-san, the deity of learning. Michizane's favorite tree, the plum *(ume)*, is found throughout the grounds. On the 25th of each month, the shrine is the site of a bustling flea-market, where everything from blue-and-white Imari porcelains to nylon stockings are for sale.

Kamishichi-ken, an *ochaya* (teahouse) and bar-lined street running from Kitano Tenman-gu to Imadegawa-dori, is Kyoto's smallest, but oldest *geiko* (geisha) district. On February 25 the *geiko* conduct a tea ceremony in the shrine's orchard, and perform dances for the public every spring and fall at the local theater.

The Symbolism of Daisen-in Zen Garden at Daitoku-ji

Daisen-in's garden is a three-dimensional version of the Chinese Sung monochrome landscape paintings that inspired its creation. Mankind's fate, relationship with nature, and place in the universe are all expressed in this masterpiece of dry-landscape garden design.

A "waterfall" of white gravel flows from a rock representing mythical Mount Horai. Other rock groupings symbolize Earth and Heaven.

Japan's Inland Sea *(see p228)* is represented in this section.

The wall represents the point at which we are assailed by doubts.

Hojo (abbot's quarters) with *tatami* mats

"The Great Ocean," a white expanse of raked gravel, serves as an aid to meditation. The cone-shaped mounds are design accents, while the tree in the corner is said to be the same kind as that under which the Buddha achieved Enlightenment.

The river of life reemerges wider and deeper after being temporarily dammed. Takarabune ("treasure ship") Stone glides serenely down, but the nearby "turtle" tries vainly to swim upstream.

The fabulous pavilion at Kinkaku-ji, its gold-leaf outer layer shining in the sun

㉒ Kinkaku-ji: the Golden Pavilion

金閣寺

Tel (075) 461-0013. 🚌 12 or 59 to Kinkaku-ji-mae; 101, 204, 205 to Kinkaku-ji-michi. **Open** 9am–5pm daily. 📷

A glimmering legacy of medieval Japan, Kinkaku-ji (formal name Rokuon-ji) is more familiar to foreign tourists as the Golden Pavilion. It was built by the third Ashikaga shogun, Yoshimitsu (1358–1408), who, relinquishing his official duties (but not his hold on power), entered the priesthood at the age of 37. The temple originally served as his retirement villa. A fervent follower of the Zen priest Soseki, Yoshimitsu directed that the finished complex become a temple after his death, with Soseki as its superior.

The visitor approaches the temple along a tree-shaded path, then emerges into a bright garden, on the other side of which stands the fabled pavilion. An exact replica of the original, destroyed by arson in 1950 (an event dramatized in Mishima Yukio's novel *The Golden Pavilion*), the graceful three-story structure is totally covered in gold leaf and topped by a bronze phoenix.

Mount Kinugasa serves as a backdrop to the garden, a stroll-type, laid out around a central pond. The harmonious interplay of its various components makes it a superb example of Muromachi-period garden design. Both pavilion and garden are especially exquisite after a snowfall.

㉓ Insho Domoto Museum

堂本印象美術館

Tel (075) 463-0007. 🚌 12, 15, 50, 59 to Ritsumeikan Univ.-mae. **Open** 9:30am–5pm Tue–Sun. **Closed** Dec 28–Jan 4. 📷 (free to disabled visitors and over 65s.)

West of Kinkaku-ji, along the Kinukake-no-Michi, a stretch of road skirting the base of the Kitayama (Northern Mountains), lies the Insho Domoto Museum. It houses the impressive works of 20th-century *nihonga* master, Insho Domoto (1891–1975). Often translated as "Japanese-style painting," *nihonga* is a fresco-like painting technique that utilizes mineral pigments.

㉔ Ryoan-ji Temple

竜安寺

Tel (075) 463-2216. 🚋 Ryoan-ji michi, Keifuku Kitano line (10-min walk). 🚌 59 to Ryoan-ji-mae. **Open** 8am–5pm daily (Dec–Feb: 8:30am–4:30pm). 📷

Founded in 1450, Ryoan-ji's claim to fame is grounded in its rock garden, a composition of white gravel and 15 stones that many consider to be the ultimate expression of Zen Buddhism.

Although various interpretations of the rocks' symbolism have been put forth, the significance of the garden, like that of Zen itself, defies definitions. Its riddles can be unraveled only by silent contemplation, something that the hordes of high-school students, not to mention the temple's recorded explanations, do little to facilitate. To avoid both, try to arrive just as the gates open.

Though overshadowed by the famous rock garden, the temple's lower pond-garden should not be overlooked. Created at a time when Zen had not yet arrived in Japan, its soft contours serve as an interesting foil to the spiritual rigors of the rock garden.

Ryoan-ji's Zen garden, the interpretation of which is up to the viewer

For hotels and restaurants see pp302–307 and pp324–339

㉕ Ninna-ji Temple

仁和寺

Tel (075) 461-1155. 🚃 Omuro stn, Keifuku Kitano line. 🚌 10, 26, 59 to Omuro Ninna-ji. Treasure House: **Open** 9am–5pm daily (Dec–Feb: to 4:30pm). 🈲

Ninna-ji's colossal front gate, with formidable Nio (Deva King) guardians, serves as a reminder that this Shingon-sect temple used to be, until fires reduced it to its present size, a huge complex numbering up to 60 subtemples.

Completed by Emperor Uda in 888, Ninna-ji was formerly known as the Omuro Palace. Until the Meiji Restoration (1868), it was always headed by an imperial prince. The Kondo (main hall) and its wooden Amida image are National Treasures. Other sights include a soaring five-story pagoda and a stand of dwarf cherry trees – the last of Kyoto's many *sakura* (cherry trees) to bloom.

Situated in the southwest of the precincts is the Omuro Gosho, a compound with a lovely Edo period garden. On the mountain behind is the Omuro 88-Temple Pilgrimage, which reproduces in miniature the temples on Shikoku's 88-Temple Pilgrimage *(see pp232–3)*. It takes about 2 hours to complete the full circuit.

Nio guardian figure at the gate of Ninna-ji

㉖ Myoshin-ji Temple

妙心寺

Tel (075) 463-3121. 🚃 Myoshin-ji stn, Keifuku Kitano line; Hanazono stn, JR Sagano line. 🚌 26 to Myoshin-ji Kitamon-mae. **Open** 9:10am–3:40pm daily. 🈲

Founded at the behest of retired Emperor Hanazono in 1337, destroyed during the Onin War, and rebuilt on a grand scale, the spacious Rinzai-sect Zen temple

Ninna-ji's soaring five-story pagoda, dating from the 1630s

complex of Myoshin-ji boasts some 47 subtemples rich in Kano School paintings and other art objects. The main structures, aligned in a row in typically Zen fashion *(see p141)*, include the Hatto (lecture hall), famous for a huge dragon painted by Kano Tanyu on its ceiling, and its bell, the oldest in Japan.

Subtemples normally open to the public include **Keishun-in**, noted for its four gardens and famous tea arbor, **Taizo-in**, which has both a dry garden by Kano Motonobu (1476–1559) and a modern garden by

Nakane Kinsaku (1917–95). Taizo-in's prize possession is one of the most famous examples of Zen ink painting, Josetsu's *Catching a Catfish with a Gourd* (1413). A copy is on display.

Daishin-in has three gardens. Subtemples **Reiun-in**, nicknamed the Motonobu Temple because of its many Kano Motonobu works, and **Tenkyu-in**, noted for paintings by Kano Sanraku, are open on special days in spring and fall.

Ajiro, a restaurant specializing in *shojin ryori* (Zen vegetarian cuisine) is near the temple's south gate.

㉗ Koryu-ji Temple

広隆寺

Tel (075) 861-1461. 🚃 Uzumasa stn, Keifuku Arashiyama line. 🚌 11, 61, 62, 63, 71, 72, 73 to Ukyoku-Sogochosha-mae. **Open** 9am–5pm daily (Dec–Feb: to 4:30pm). 🈲

A must-see for lovers of Buddhist art, Koryu-ji was founded in 622, by a clan of Korean immigrants who contributed greatly to the development of Kyoto. Among the impressive images in its Reihoden (treasure hall), is a Miroku Bosatsu (Buddha of the future) believed to have been brought to Japan from Korea in the 7th century. Kyoto's oldest image, the seated figure is known throughout the nation for its beatific Mona Lisa-like smile. The temple's oldest structure, the Kodo, houses a 9th-century statue of the Amida Buddha.

Garden of subtemple Taizo-in, at the Myoshin-ji complex

Kyoto City: Farther Afield

Poets' hermitages, noblemen's villas, esoteric mountain temples, and unspoiled natural scenery are among the many attractions to be found in the outskirts of the old capital. Once remote regions boasting unique characteristics and customs, they are now easily accessible, and any itinerary of Kyoto should include at least two or three of these rewarding destinations.

Sights at a Glance

1. Katsura Imperial Villa
2. Arashiyama District
3. Sagano District
4. Takao District
5. Kurama District
6. Shisen-do Temple
7. Manshu-in Temple
8. Shugaku-in Villa
9. Hieizan Enryaku-ji
10. Ohara District
11. Fushimi Inari Shrine
12. Daigo District
13. Uji City

0 kilometers 5
0 miles 3

Key

Central Kyoto (see pp160–61)

Expressway

Main road

Railway

❶ Katsura Imperial Villa

桂離宮

1-1 Misono, Katsura, Nishikyo-ku. **Tel** (075) 211-1215. Katsura stn, Hankyu line. 33 to Katsura Rikyu-mae. **Open** by appt only Mon–Fri: apply at Imperial Household Agency (see p176).

With its flawless attention to detail, Katsura Imperial Villa is often cited as one of the finest examples of Japanese landscape design. Built in 1620 by Hachijo no Miya Toshihito, an imperial prince, it was later added to by his son, Toshitada. A sumptuous stroll garden (see pp34–5), Katsura is famous for the manner in which its paths and stepping stones control the visitor's line of sight, resulting in a series of ingeniously planned vistas. The view from the **Shokin-tei** (pine zither) tea arbor, replicates the scenery

of Amanohashidate (see p216). Many of the garden's scenic allusions are to places mentioned in the Chinese and Japanese classics. The somewhat hurried tour includes the **Shoka-tei** (flower-viewing teahouse) in the highest part of the garden, then down past the **Shoi-ken** (sense-of-humor teahouse), and on to the main villa, a set of halls poetically described as resembling a flock of geese in flight.

❷ Arashiyama District

嵐山地区

Arashiyama stn, Hankyu line; Hankyu Arashiyama stn. 11, 28 or 93 to Arashiyama Tenryu-ji-mae.

With something to please the eye in any season, Arashiyama has long held a special place in the hearts of the Japanese. Even today, despite omnipresent shops specializing in items emblazoned with the likenesses of TV and movie celebrities, the area still offers a lot of unspoiled natural beauty. At its center is timeless **Togetsu-kyo**, the graceful "moon-crossing" bridge. North of the bridge, mountainsides thickly forested with cherries and pines drop steeply to the river, which in summer becomes the stage for *ukai*, fishing done by firelight with trained cormorants. *Hozugawa-kudari*, running the Hozu River rapids from Kameoka to Arashiyama, is another popular activity. The narrow-gauge **Torokko Train** provides a different way of viewing the same scenery.

Rinzai-sect temple **Tenryu-ji** was founded by the first Ashikaga shogun, Takauji, in 1339. The serene garden has survived intact and features a pond in the shape of the Chinese character, *kokoro*, or "enlightened heart."

Another Arashiyama treasure is **Okochi Sanso**, the private villa of silent-screen star Okochi Denjiro. The meticulously laid-out grounds offer wonderful vistas of Mount Hiei and the Hozu River gorge.

Togetsu-kyo, the wooden "moon-crossing" bridge in Arashiyama

❸ Sagano District
嵯峨野地区

🚉 JR Saga-Arashiyama stn, Sagano line. 🚌 28 or 91 to Daikaku-ji.

The home of rice fields, bamboo groves, temples, and cemeteries, Sagano's varied sights are by turn pastoral and poignant. The best point from which to launch an exploration is **Torii Moto**, where a vermilion shrine gateway (*torii*) marks the beginning of an ancient trail leading up to sacred Mount Atago, abode of the fire divinity. Two thatched teahouses near the *torii* have been offering refreshment to pilgrims for centuries.

From the *torii*, head south past traditional farmhouses to **Adashino Nenbutsu-ji**. From the Heian to Edo periods, Adashino was a remote place where corpses were often disposed of. Established to offer solace for the souls of these forgotten dead, the temple gathered together their grave markers – rocks on which a likeness of the Buddha had been carved. The sight of row after row of these silent stone figures is strangely moving. On the evenings of August 23 and 24, more than 1,000 candles are offered to them.

Rickshaw in the pastoral Sagano district

To the south is **Gio-ji**, a tiny thatched nunnery where Gio, a cast-off mistress of warlord Taira no Kiyomori (1118–81), took the tonsure. Known for the beauty of its fall foliage, the temple is bounded on one side by a magnificent stand of bamboo, while, to the front, slender maples rise from an emerald carpet of moss.

Located in central Sagano, Jodo-sect temple **Seiryo-ji** houses an image of the Shakamuni Buddha reportedly brought to Japan in 987. **Nison-in** has standing images of Amida and Shakamuni. The many maple trees on the temple's grounds attract large numbers of visitors in the fall. Charming **Rakushi-sha** (hut of the fallen persimmons) was the

humble home of haiku poet Mukai Kyorai (1651–1704). Basho (*see p283*) composed his *Saga Diary* here in 1691.

Secluded Nichiren-sect temple **Jojakko-ji** is situated on Ogura-yama, a mountain whose beauty has been celebrated by poets since ancient times. A steep flight of stone steps leads to the temple from where there are great views of Kyoto and Mount Hiei. Halfway up the steps, a thatched gate houses two fierce-eyed Nio guards said to be the work of 13th-century sculptor Unkei. The temple's beautiful two-story pagoda is a symbol of the Lotus Sutra.

The aristocratic temple complex of **Daikaku-ji**, in the northeast of Sagano, is the headquarters of one of Japan's most popular schools of *ikebana* (flower arranging). Next to it is **Osawa-no-Ike**, a pond built in imitation of Lake Tungting in China.

❹ Takao District
高雄地区

🚌 Takao bus or 8 to Takao.

Esoteric mountain temples and refreshingly pristine mountain scenery are Takao's main attractions. **Jingo-ji**, founded in the 8th century, houses a wealth of National Treasures including the Yakushi Nyorai (Buddha of healing). Set in an ancient cryptomeria forest, **Kozan-ji**, founded in 774, has the look of an elegant estate.

Bibbed stone carvings along the wayside, Kurama

Traditional restaurant in the mountainous district of Takao

Copies of the handscroll *Choju-Jinbutsu-giga* (frolicking birds and animals) are displayed in the **Sekisui-in**, a brilliant example of Kamakura residential architecture. Japan's first tea was cultivated nearby.

❺ Kurama District
鞍馬地区

🚉 Kurama stn, Eizan line. 🚌 95 from Ohara. 🎐 Kurama no Hi-matsuri (Oct 22).

Famous as the abode of gods, demons, and superheroes, Kurama was once an isolated village of foresters. Now a Kyoto suburb, it still retains an untamed feeling, a quality fully in evidence on the night of October 22, when the town celebrates its Fire Festival.

Kurama-dera, a Buddhist temple, was built in 770 to provide refuge in the wilderness for meditation. A gate marks the beginning of a mountain trail to the main temple buildings; the main hall offers splendid views of the Kitayama mountains. From the Reihokan (treasure hall) a path winds beneath towering cryptomeria trees to the village of **Kibune**, a collection of inns and teahouses alongside a stream. Several Kurama shops sell pickled mountain herbs and vegetables. Watch for masks of *tengu*, a folkloric creature with a phallic-shaped nose.

The upper garden at Shisen-do, as viewed from the veranda

❻ Shisen-do Temple
詩仙堂

27 Kadoguchi-cho, Ichijo-ji, Sakyo-ku. **Tel** (075) 781-2954. 5 or 8 to Ichijo-ji Sagarimatsu-cho. **Open** 9am–5pm daily.

A samurai who had fallen out of favor with the shogunate, Ishikawa Jozan, constructed this retirement villa in 1641. On a small plot below the Higashiyama mountains, this Confucian scholar and poet succeeded in creating a nearly perfect blend of building and garden. Although now a Soto-sect Zen temple, the hermitage retains the feel of a home.

The famous garden is divided into two levels: the upper, best viewed from the main building's veranda, features a broad expanse of packed sand bordered by clipped azalea bushes. The lower level, which also makes use of areas of sand to add light and space, offers a fine view of the villa's tile-and-thatch roof and moon-viewing chamber.

❼ Manshu-in Temple
曼殊院

42 Takenouchi-cho, Ichijo-ji, Sakyo-ku. **Tel** (075) 781-5010. 5 to Shugaku-in Michi. **Open** 9am–4:30pm daily.

Even in spring and fall when its cherries and maples draw the crowds, Manshu-in maintains an atmosphere of dignified repose. This Tendai-sect temple was restored in 1656 by the son of the prince who designed Katsura Villa (see p180). Its elegant buildings, with their cleverly crafted door pulls and other carefully planned details, call to mind those of the imperial villa. The beautiful garden is composed of islands of rock and vegetation amid swaths of raked gravel, with the Higashiyama mountains forming a harmonious backdrop.

❽ Shugaku-in Imperial Villa
修学院離宮

Yabuzoe, Shugaku-in. Shugaku-in stn, Eizan line. 5 to Shugaku-in Michi. **Open** by appt only Mon–Fri: apply at Imperial Household Agency, (075) 211-1215 (see p176).

If Katsura Villa (see p180) could be said to be yin, then its counterpart imperial villa, Shugaku-in, could only be described as yang. While the former's garden, layered with literary and poetic allusions, is characterized by an inward-looking sensibility, spacious Shugaku-in might strike the viewer as extroverted.

Created by retired emperor Go-Mizuno'o (1596–1680), the garden was a lifetime labor of love. Divided into three levels, each with a teahouse, the complex is imbued with a spirit of understated simplicity. Yet, a surprise awaits: the approach to the uppermost teahouse is designed so that the visitor is kept unaware until the last minute of the panorama from the top of the Kitayama mountains, spread out as if an extension of the garden.

❾ Hieizan Enryaku-ji
比叡山

4220 Sakamoto Honmachi, Otsu, Shiga prefecture. **Tel** (077) 578-0001. Yase stn, Eizan line, then cable car; or Hieizan Sakamoto stn, Kosei line, then cable car. Enryaku-ji bus from Kyoto or Keihan Sanjo stns. **Open** Mar–Nov: 8:30am–4:30pm daily; Dec–Feb: 9am–4pm daily.

A once mighty monastery fortress with 3,000 subtemples and thousands of sohei, or warrior monks, Hieizan today is but a shadow of its former self. Still, the solemnity of its isolated mountain-top setting and grandeur of its remaining buildings make the trek to Mount Hiei worthwhile. Founded by the monk Saicho in 792, Hieizan became the main monastery of the Tendai sect (see p279). Although initially entrusted to protect the city from evil forces, the area itself became the bane of the capital. Emperor Go-Shirakawa (1127–92) once lamented that there were only three things beyond his control: the flooding of the Kamo River, the roll of the dice, and the warrior monks of Hieizan. In 1571,

Konpon Chu-do, the inner sanctum of Enryaku-ji

however, warlord Oda Nobunaga, angered by the temple's resistance to his authority, sent his army to attack the mountain. The complex was burned to the ground, and every man, woman, and child massacred.

The temple is divided into three precincts, connected by shuttle bus. The **Kokuho-den**, a museum of treasures, is in the east precinct. Here, too, is the famous **Konpon Chu-do**, the inner sanctum, which enshrines a Healing Buddha image said to have been carved by Saicho. Nearby **Jodo-in** (Pure Land Hall) is the site of Saicho's tomb.

In the **Jogyo-do** hall in the west precinct monks chant an invocation called the *nembutsu*, in the **Hokke-do** hall they meditate upon the Lotus Sutra, a central tenet of Tendai belief. Beyond these two buildings is the **Shaka-do**, the main hall of the west precinct.

⑩ Ohara District
大原地区

🚌 17 from Kyoto stn.

Known for thatched farm-houses, delicious pickles, and other rustic charms, Ohara is also home to two famous temples. Set in an incomparably beautiful setting, **Sanzen-in's** Amida Hall dates from 1148 and houses a meditating Amida Buddha. *Fusuma* (sliding door) paintings by Takeuchi Seiho (1864–1942) decorate the temple's Shinden. The approach to Sanzen-in is lined with shops selling such local products as *shiba-zuke*, a pickle dyed purple with the leaf of the beefsteak plant. Across the valley is tiny **Jakko-in**, a nunnery where Kenreimon-in (1155–1213) lived. The sole survivor of the Taira clan, she prayed here for the souls of her son and kin killed by the Genji.

⑪ Fushimi Inari Shrine
伏見稲荷神社

68 Yabunouchi, Fukakusa, Fushimi-ku. 🚃 Fushimi Inari stn, Keihan & Nara lines. 🚌 Minami 5 to Fushimi Inari Taisha mae. **Tel** (075) 641-7331. **Open** 24 hours.

This most famous of the many thousands of shrines dedicated to Inari, the popular deity of rice and sake (*see p30*), is located near the sake-making district of Fushimi. An avenue formed out of several hundred *torii* (gates) and leading up to the shrine has been donated by businessmen.

Daigo-ji's Heian-era pagoda

⑫ Daigo-ji Temple
醍醐寺

22 Higashioji-cho, Daigo, Fushimi-ku. 🚇 Daigo stn, Tozai line. Sanpo-in: **Tel** (075) 571-0002. **Open** 9am–4pm daily (to 5pm Mar–Dec). 🚶

Daigo-ji's main draw is subtemple **Sanpo-in**. Because Toyotomi Hideyoshi took a personal interest in restoring this after a visit in 1598, it contains some of the Momoyama period's most representative works of art. The lavish garden is noted for its many magnificent rocks,

which were gifts to Hideyoshi from his *daimyo* (feudal lords). The rest of Daigo-ji is more ancient. The graceful five-story pagoda, built in 951, is one of only two Heian-era pagodas in existence. Those venturing to upper Daigo are mainly pilgrims. The white-clad ones are headed for **Juntei-do**, a hall housing a Kannon image – No. 11 of the 33 Kannon Temples pilgrimage route.

⑬ Uji City
宇治市

🚃 Uji stn, Keihan-Uji or Nare lines. Temples: **Open** 9am–4:30pm daily. 🚶 Miho Museum: 300 Tashiro Momodani, Shigaraki-cho, Shiga. **Tel** (074) 882-3411. **Open** 10am–5pm Tue–Sun. 🚶 🌐 miho.or.jp

In addition to some of the best green tea grown in Japan, the small city of Uji boasts **Byodo-in**, which is featured on the 10-yen coin. Built in 1053, the temple's Phoenix Hall (*see p34*) and Amida Nyorai image inside are marvelous remnants of one of Japan's greatest epochs.

While Byodo-in sought to imitate palaces depicted in Tang-dynasty mandalas, **Manpuku-ji** invoked the architectural traditions of Ming China. This most Chinese of Kyoto temples was estab-lished in 1661 by Ingen, a priest who fled China after the fall of the Ming dynasty. Ingen introduced the *sencha*, or leaf tea, ceremony.

Close by, in Shigaraki, the **Miho Museum** has some fine examples of Japanese treasures such as Buddha statues and handscrolls, as well as Roman mosaics and treasures from Egypt and Persia.

Mampuku-ji, a Chinese-style temple in Uji city

SHOPPING IN KYOTO

Kyoto is famous throughout Japan for the quality of its crafts and food products, the result of many centuries of catering to the demanding tastes of its resident aristocrats, temple abbots, tea masters, and merchants. Venerable shops coexist with stores stocked with the latest fads, making shopping here a bizarre, but never boring, experience. As in other major Japanese cities, Kyoto has large branches of Japanese department store chains. Typically these offer a vast selection of goods, including foodstuffs in the basement. Specialty craft outlets are all over the city. ATM machines can be found in the basement of the Kyoto Tower building opposite Kyoto Station, as well as at the central post office. A map of the central shopping district is on *page 161*; details of opening hours are on *page 340*.

Modern storefronts along Kawaramachi

Shopping Districts

The intersection of Shijo and Kawaramachi forms the heart of the downtown shopping district. During the day, the sidewalks of Kawaramachi, which serves as Kyoto's main street, are busy with shoppers, while at night *boso-zoku* (hot-rodders) cruise noisily along its store-lined length.

Smaller shopping districts include the area around JR Kyoto station and Kitayama-dori, where Kyoto's most upscale shops can be found.

Department Stores and Arcades

The **Kyoto Marui** and **Takashimaya** department stores are located at the intersection of Kawaramachi and Shijo. Takashimaya is the place to head for men's and women's fashions; inside are boutiques stocking Issey Miyake and other brand-name clothing. The city's other main department store, **Daimaru**, is six blocks further west on Shijo's north side. Many of Kyoto's famous old shops, such as the Ippodo tea store, have outlets in department store basements.

Just west of Takashimaya is **Fujii Daimaru**, a local department store which is unrelated to the larger Daimaru department store. **Mina** is a glittering shopping mall in Shijo with a comprehensive collection of youthful fashion stores.

Shin-Kyogoku, a street situated within the network of arcades and roads between Shijo and Sanjo, caters to Japanese youngsters on school outings. Its varied offerings run the gamut from legitimate craft items to outrageous kitsch.

On the west end of Kyoto Station is **JR Kyoto Isetan**, which adds to Kyoto's department store line-up. **Porta**, an underground shopping arcade, is located beneath the station's north side, while to its south is **Avanti**, a building housing a variety of shops.

Within the station itself is a shopping area called **The Cube**, which contains a sizable number of souvenir shops specializing in Kyoto craft items. Slightly farther away, close to Shiyakusho-mae Station is **Zest Oike**, another underground mall.

Nishiki Market

Nicknamed "Kyoto's Kitchen," Nishiki is a fascinating market alley north of, and running parallel to, Shijo, from Teramachi west to Takakura. This is where most of Kyoto's *kaiseki* chefs buy their ingredients. Many of the items sold, such as *fu* (wheat gluten) and *yuba* (soy milk skin), are unique to Kyoto cuisine. In particular, a wide selection of pickles, another local specialty, is available. **Aritsugu**, at Nishiki's eastern end, is known for Japanese knives and other kitchen utensils.

Nishiki Market, the best place to shop for food items in Kyoto

Electronic Goods

The city's main outlet for cheap electronic goods and appliances is the stretch of Teramachi running south of Shijo, although the number of shops selling electronic items in the area is declining. Visitors can browse through **Midori**, a large electronic appliances store in this district; however, nearby Osaka may be a better place to find a wide range of inexpensive products.

Antiques

Having escaped the bombs of World War II, Kyoto's *kura* (family storehouses) continue to emit a small but steady stream of fascinating objects. The city's antiques fall into three main categories: Buddhist art, tea ceremony utensils, and everyday items. Some stores specialize in just one category, but most carry a range. Kyoto's most venerable antique shops are located between Nawate and Higashio-ji along Shinmonzen and Furumonzen streets. Especially reputable are **Kawasaki Bijutsu** (specializing in screens and chests), **Renkodo** (Imari-ware), and **Nakajima** (which sells a bit of everything). **Seikado** sells antique ceramics, tableware, and large items of furniture dating from the Edo and Meiji periods.

The city's up-and-coming antique district is the section of Teramachi from Oike to Marutamachi, where a host of traditional and modern shops run by young but knowledgeable owners have sprouted. The **Kyoto Antiques Center** houses many shops under one roof. **Teramachi Club**, farther up Teramachi on the same side of the street, deals mainly in Meiji and Taisho period items. Across from it is

Handmade combs

Nagata, which buys not at auction but directly from family *kura*. Fans of old lacquerware should not miss **Uruwashi-ya**, on Marutamachi, one and a half blocks west of Teramachi. Antique lovers will also want to visit **Hirooka Antique**, which is just two minutes' walk east from Exit 2 of Kitayama station. The shop is a bit out of the way but worth the trip out of the city center – Hirooka's goods are first-rate and reasonably priced.

Flea Markets

Antiques, household items, plants, food, and much more are on sale at Kobo-san, the market held on the 21st of every month at Toji Temple *(see p162)*. Tenjin-san, a similar flea market, is held on the 25th at the shrine of Kitano Tenman-gu *(see p177)*.

DIRECTORY

Department Stores & Arcades

Avanti
Opp Hachijo-guchi (south) exit of JR Kyoto stn.

The Cube
JR Kyoto stn bldg, B2F, B1F, 1F, 11F.
Tel (075) 371-2134.

Daimaru
N side of Shijo, at Takakura, Shimogyo-ku.
Tel (075) 211-8111.

Fujii Daimaru
Corner of Teramachi and Shijo, Shimogyo-ku.
Tel (075) 221-8181.

JR Kyoto Isetan
Karasuma, S of Shiokoji, Shimogyo-ku.
Tel (075) 352-1111.

Kyoto Marui
Corner of Kawaramachi and Shijo, Shimogyo-ku.
Tel (075) 223-2288.

Mina
Corner of Kawaramachi and Rokkaku, Shijo.
Tel (075) 222-8470.

Porta
N side of JR Kyoto stn.
Tel (075) 365-7528.

Takashimaya
Corner of Kawaramachi and Shijo, Shimogyo-ku.
Tel (075) 221-8811.

Zest Oike
Kawaramachi-Oike, Nakagyo-ku.

Nishiki Market

Aritsugu
On Nishiki-koji, W of Gokomachi, Nakagyo-ku.
Tel (075) 221-1091.

Electronic Goods

Midori
Taniyama Musen, W side of Teramachi, S of Shijo.

Antiques

Hirooka Antique
34-3 Minami Shibacho, Shimogamo, Sakyo-ku.
Tel (075) 721-4438.
Closed Tue.

Kawasaki Bijutsu
Shinmonzen, W of Higashi-oji, Higashiyama-ku. **Tel** (075) 541-8785.

Kyoto Antiques Center
E side of Teramachi, N of Nijo, Nakagyo-ku.
Tel (075) 222-0793.
Closed Tue.

Nagata
W side of Teramachi, N of Nijo, Nakagyo-ku.
Tel (075) 211-9511.
Closed Sun.

Nakajima
Shinmonzen, E of Hanami-koji, Higashiyama-ku.
Tel (075) 561-7771.

Renkodo
Shinmonzen, E of Nawate, Nishi-no-cho, Higashiyama-ku.
Tel (075) 525-2121.
Closed Tue.

Seikado
Opp Gojozaka bus stop, Higashiyama-ku.
Tel (075) 531-9780.

Teramachi Club
E side of Teramachi, N of Nijo, Nakagyo-ku.
Tel (075) 211-6445.
Closed Tue.

Uruwashi-ya
Marutamachi, E of Fuyacho, Nakagyo-ku.
Tel (075) 212-0043.
Closed Tue.

Specialty Souvenirs

Kyoto is one of the best places in Japan to buy crafts and souvenirs, many of them local specialties. Some outlets are actually outside the central shopping district. Among the best places to look are the roads leading up to major temples such as Kiyomizu-dera.

Craft shop on the canalside Philosopher's Walk

General Crafts

The Gion, or eastern, end of Shijo has a number of interesting craft shops, including the **Kyoto Craft Center**, which carries many contemporary craft items. The **Kyoto Handicraft Center**, north of Heian Shrine, gives regular handicraft demonstrations.

Ceramics and Tableware

Kiyomizu-yaki is the city's refined porcelain ware. A fine selection of this and other porcelains can be found at **Tachikichi**. **Asahi-do** offers a comprehensive range, as does **Tojiki Kaikan**. **Asobe**, east of Shijo, has been in business since 1807 and is well known for lacquerware. **Ichihara**, south of Shijo, offers a good selection of chopsticks and bamboo utensils.

Tea

Tea in Kyoto means Uji-cha, for neighboring Uji is, with Shizuoka, one of Japan's most famous tea-producing regions. There are many fine tea shops in town, but **Ippodo Chaho** is the granddaddy of them all.

Dolls

Kyoto dolls have been famous throughout Japan for centuries. **Oshido**, on the front approach to Kiyomizu Temple, has a fine selection of dolls, and all kinds of accessories such as *netsuke* and *kanzashi* (hair ornaments). They also stock a wide range of wooden sandals, Japanese swords, and textile goods. **Gallery K1** has an impressive collection of lifelike *Ichimatsu-ningyo*, which were once considered standard trousseau items. **Tanaka-ya** is known both for its dolls and its Noh masks.

Incense

Incense has been a Kyoto specialty since Heian times. **Kungyoku-do**, a shop with a 400-year-old history, has an aromatic selection in stick, chip, and pellet form. **Toyoda Aisan-do**, in the Gion, has a wide selection of incense and incense burners. **Lisn** is an intriguing boutique with some novel forms of incense.

Pickles and Sweets

Kyoto's many vegetables are delicious; pickled (*tsukemono*), they become sublime. In addition to Nishiki Market (*see p184*), two stores are notable. **Narita**, east of Kamigamo Shrine, has preservative-free delicacies, including its famous *suguki-zuke* (turnip pickle). **Murakami-ju**, in the city center, has more than 20 types of pickles. Works of art, *wagashi* (sweets) come in a variety of styles. The exquisite *namagashi* are meant to be eaten the same day they are made, preferably accompanied by *matcha* (powdered tea). Those at **Tsukimochi-ya Naomasa** are traditional favorites.

Footwear

On Nawate, **Minochu** has a stunning collection of traditional Japanese footwear, some in larger than standard sizes. The tall *koppori-geta* worn by Kyoto's apprentice geisha can be bought here.

Bamboo Products

An abundance of bamboo in neighboring Shiga prefecture and the development of the utensils used in the tea ceremony have helped make Kyoto a prime center for the production of this flexible natural material. **Kagoshin**, east of the Sanjo Bridge, makes wonderful bamboo craft items, including baskets for *ikebana* arrangements. **Tsujikura**, on Kawaramachi, north of Shijo, stocks a good selection of handsome and sturdy bamboo umbrellas, as well as various types of paper lanterns.

One of Kyoto's famous dolls

Umbrella with a bamboo frame, a popular shade at restaurants

Washi

Paper has been made in Japan since the 7th century. *Washi* (handmade paper) is made of tree and other plant fibers. Exquisite *washi* from all over Japan is available at **Morita Washi Wagami-no-mise**, on Higashi-no-Toin, a couple of blocks south of Shijo. **Kakimoto** also stocks an outstanding variety. **Kyukyo-do**, a shop famous for calligraphy supplies, paper, and incense, is located between Sanjo and Oike.

Other Crafts

Across from Takashimaya department store is **Terauchi**, a jewelry shop that carries a fine selection of pearls. At the corner of Rokkaku and Tomi-no-Koji is **Miyawaki Baisen-an**, an old shop that is famous for its elegant fans. **Kazurasei**, in the Gion, specializes in hair ornaments and makeup for apprentice geisha. For Japanese woodblock prints, probably the best gallery is **Nishiharu** in Teramachi.

Craftswoman making *washi*, Japanese handmade paper

DIRECTORY

General Crafts

Kyoto Craft Center
Gion, N side of Shijo.
Tel (075) 561-9660.
Closed Wed.

Kyoto Handicraft Center
Kumanojinja higashi, Marutamachi-dori.
Tel (075) 761-5080.

Ceramics and Tableware

Asahi-do
Kiyomizu, Higashiyama-ku. **Tel** (075) 531-2181.

Asobe
Higashino-toin-dori, Shimogyo-ku.
Tel (075) 344-5333.
Closed Wed.

Ichihara
E side of Sakaimachi, S of Shijo, Shimogyo-ku.
Tel (075) 341-3831.
Closed phone to check.

Tachikichi
Corner of Shijo and Tomino-koji.
Tel (075) 255-3507.
Closed Wed.

Tojiki Kaikan
Gojo-zaka, 100 m E of Higashi-oji intersection, Higashiyama-ku.
Tel (075) 541-1102.

Tea

Ippodo Chaho
E side of Teramachi, N of Nijo, Nakagyo-ku.
Tel (075) 211-3421.

Dolls

Gallery K1
Muromachi-dori, S of Kita-oji. **Tel** (075) 415-1477.
Closed Thu.

Oshido
1-276 Kiyomizu, Higashima-ku.
Tel (075) 561-3361.

Tanaka-ya
N side of Shijo, E of Yanagi-no-Banba, Shimogyo-ku. **Tel** (075) 221-1959. **Closed** Wed.

Incense

Kungyoku-do
E side of Horikawa, across from Nishi Hongan-ji, Shimogyo-ku.
Tel (075) 371-0162.
Closed 1st and 3rd Sun.

Lisn
2F Spiral Space 103 Bldg, Shimogamo-naka, N of Kitayama, Kita-ku.
Tel (075) 721-6006.
Closed Wed.

Toyoda Aisan-do
Gion, N side of Shijo-dori.
Tel (075) 551-2221.
Closed Wed.

Pickles and Sweets

Murakami-ju
Nishi-Kiyamachi, S of Shijo, behind Hankyu dept store, Shimogyo-ku.
Tel 075-351-1737.

Narita
35 Yamamoto-cho, Kamigamo, Kita-ku (E of Kamigamo Shrine).
Tel (075) 721-1567.

Tsukimochi-ya Naomasa
E side Kiyamachi, N of Sanjo, Kiyamachi Sanjo-agaru, Nakagyo-ku.
Tel (075) 231-0175.
Closed Thu.

Footwear

Minochu
Yamato-oji (Nawate) at Shinmonzen, Higashiyama-ku.
Tel (075) 561-5189.
Closed Wed.

Bamboo Products

Kagoshin
N side Sanjo, E of Sanjo Bridge, Higashiyama-ku.
Tel (075) 771-0209.
Closed Mon.

Tsujikura
E side of Kawaramachi, N of Shijo, Nakagyo-ku.
Tel (075) 221-4396.
Closed Wed.

Washi

Kakimoto
E side of Teramachi, N of Nijo, Nakagyo-ku.
Tel (075) 211-3481.
Closed Sun.

Kyukyo-do
W side of Teramachi, at Anekoji, Nakagyo-ku.
Tel (075) 231-0510.
Closed Sun.

Morita Washi Wagami-no-mise
E side of Higashi-no-Toin, N of Bukkoji, Shimogyo-ku. **Tel** (075) 341-0123.
Closed Sun & public hols.

Other Crafts

Kazurasei
Gion, N side of Shijo, nr Gion bus stop.
Tel (075) 561-0672.
Closed Wed.

Miyawaki Baisen-an
N side Rokkaku, W of Tomi-no-Koji, Nakagyo-ku. **Tel** (075) 221-0181.

Nishiharu
Corner of Sanjo and Teramachi, Nakagyo-ku.
Tel (075) 211-2849.
Closed 2–7pm daily.

Terauchi
Next to Takashimaya dept store, Kawaramachi, Shimogyo-ku.
Tel (075) 211-3511.
Closed Wed.

ENTERTAINMENT IN KYOTO

Kyoto's entertainment scene is small but varied, catering to tastes both ancient and contemporary. In addition to performances of Kabuki and buyo (classical Japanese dance), the city offers bars and clubs where you can hear guest musicians playing anything from blues guitar to Latin rhythms. Thanks to its more than 1,200 years of history, a traditional event takes place almost every day at one of Kyoto's hundreds of shrines and temples. While the majority of these are little more than arcane rituals, some are on a huge scale and attract visitors from all over the country. Of these, the month-long Gion Matsuri, put on by the silk merchants of the city, is probably the best-known festival. It culminates on July 14–17.

Buying Tickets

For help in obtaining tickets to events, check with the **Tourist Information Office** inside Kyoto Station. Tickets for most major events can be bought at the **Ticket PIA** counter – also at Kyoto Station and in Kawaramachi-Oike and Takoyakushi. Some tickets can also be purchased at branches of the convenience stores **Lawson** and **Seven Eleven** although tickets can only be bought in Japanese.

Information Sources

For an overview of what's on, consult the *Kyoto Visitor's Guide*, a free monthly publication available at tourist information centers and major hotels, and online. *Kansai Scene* lists events, news, and current affairs in the Kansai region and can be found online and at bookstores. The **Kyoto Prefecture** website has details of current events, and the website of **Japan National Tourist Organization** (JNTO) has a section on Kyoto. The *Japan Times*, and other newspapers in English also carry weekly listings of Kansai events.

Festivals

Of Kyoto's many festivals, the big three are the Aoi Matsuri (Hollyhock Festival, May 15); Gion Matsuri (all of July, especially 14–17); and Jidai Matsuri (Festival of the Ages, October 22). The Aoi and Gion festivals both started as purification rites in the Heian period. The former involves a parade of costumed nobles, courtiers, horses, and ox-carts between the two Kamo shrines *(see p176)*. The latter centers around elaborately decorated floats belonging to various neighborhoods, which are pulled through the streets on the morning of July 17, then disassembled. The Jidai Matsuri was begun in 1895 to boost morale after the emperor abandoned Kyoto for Tokyo. Characters in costumes from every epoch of Kyoto's imperial past parade from the Imperial Palace to Heian Shrine.

An old teahouse in Gion, a long-established entertainment district

Traditional Arts

For the tourist wanting a quick look at traditional arts, **Gion Corner** has a program from March to November that includes snippets of *kyomai* (classical Kyoto dance), *koto* music, Kyogen comic drama, and even *ikebana* (flower arranging). Performances are from 6pm to 7pm.

The geisha of Gion put on *Miyako Odori*, their gala dance spectacle, during April at the **Gion Kobu Kaburenjo** theater, while at Kamishichi-ken, the geisha district near Kitano Shrine, public dances, *Kitano Odori*, are staged from April 15 to 25 at the **Kamishichi-ken Kaburenjo**. Ponto-cho's geisha perform their *Kamogawa Odori* in May at the **Pontocho Kaburenjo**. Tickets for all can be bought at the theaters or at Takashimaya and Daimaru Playguide counters.

The **Minami-za** is the venue for *Kaomise Kabuki*, Kyoto's December Kabuki extravaganza. Performances of Noh and Kyogen are held at **Kyoto Kanze Kaikan** and **Kongo Nogakudo** on certain Sundays of every month. Check the *Visitor's Guide* for details.

Apprentice geisha performing at the Gion Kobu Kaburenjo theater

Anyone interested in experiencing the tea ceremony can do so at **Tondaya**. Located in Kyoto's famous Nishijin textile area, this architecturally exquisite town house is elegantly decorated with classical treasures.

Nightlife

Kyoto may not have as lively a nightlife as Osaka and Tokyo, but it still has plenty of bars, clubs, and live music spots, especially in the entertainment districts of Pontocho and Gion.

Taku Taku, one of the most popular venues for rock and folk music, is in a former sake brewery near Shijo-Kawaramachi. Live music takes place most nights. Near Kyoto University, **Ringo** is a music café devoted to The Beatles. **Cafe David**, a sumptuous art-filled coffee house on the south side of Sanjo, between Takakura

Pontocho district restaurants, with *yuka* platforms erected in summer

and Higashi-no-Toin, also has live music. **Kyoto Muse**, located 1 minute away from Hankyu Karasuma Station (take exit No. 13) hosts a varied schedule of live performances in a relaxed atmosphere. The **Pig & Whistle**, a British-style pub popular with the foreign community, offers reasonably priced food and drink in a comfortable atmosphere. Occasionally bands perform. **Café Indépendants**, in the basement of the old Mainichi Newspaper Building at

the corner of Sanjo Street and Gokomachi Street, is a relaxed eating and drinking spot that also occasionally features live music. **Metro** hosts monthly events, including a drag show ("Diamond Night"), and a Latin music night.

Hello Dolly is a jazz bar in the Ponto-cho district that offers live music most weekends. The whiskey-based drinks on sale are cheap until 8pm, when the music starts. After that, an additional fee applies..

DIRECTORY

Tickets and Information

JNTO
[w] jnto.go.jp

Kansai Scene
[w] kansaiscene.com

Kyoto Prefecture
[w] pref.kyoto.jp/en/index.html
Kyoto Theater
Kyoto Station Bldg.
Tel (075) 341-2360.

Kyoto Visitor's Guide
[w] kyotoguide.com
Lawson Ticket
Reservations:
Tel (0570) 000-777.
General inquiries:
Tel (0120) 07-3963.

Ticket PIA
Reservations:
Tel (0570) 02-9111.

Tourist Information Office
2nd Fl Kyoto Station Bldg.
Tel (075) 343-0548.

Traditional Arts

Gion Corner
Next to Gion Kobu Kaburenjo, E of Hanamikoji and S of Shijo, Higashiyama-ku.
Tel (075) 561-1119.
Closed Aug 16, Dec 29–Jan 4.

Gion Kobu Kaburenjo
Next to Gion Corner, Higashiyama-ku.
Tel (075) 541-3391.

Kamishichi-ken Kaburenjo
Kamishichi-ken, E of Kitano Tenman-gu Shrine, Kamigyo-ku.
Tel (075) 461-0148.

Kongo Nogakudo
S of Ichijo, Karasuma-dori, Kamigyo-ku.
Tel (075) 441-7222.

Kyoto Kanze Kaikan
Nio-mon, W of Jingu-michi, Sakyo-ku.
Tel (075) 771-6114.

Minami-za Theater
Corner of Kawabata and Shijo, Higashiyama-ku.
Reservations:
Tel (0570) 000-489.
General inquiries:
Tel (075) 561-1155.

Pontocho Kaburenjo
On E side of Pontocho, S of Sanjo, Nakagyo-ku.
Tel (075) 221-2025.

Tondaya
W side of Omiya, N of Ichijo.
Open 10am–5pm (reservations only)
Tel (075) 432-6701.
[w] tondaya.co.jp

Nightlife

Cafe David
Sanjo, W of Takakura, Nakagyo-ku.
Tel (075) 212-8580.
Closed Wed.

Café Indépendants
1928 Bldg B1, corner of Sanjo and Gokomachi, Nakagyo-ku.
Tel (075) 255-4312.

Hello Dolly
Off Kiya-machi Dori, near Gion-Sijio stn and Kawaramachi stn.
Tel (075) 241-1728.

Kyoto Muse
Near Hankyu Karasuma Station (exit 13), Shimogyo-ku.
Tel (075) 223-0389.

Metro
Corner of Kawabata and Marutamachi (Keihan Marutamachi stn exit 2).
Tel (075) 752-4765.

Pig & Whistle
2F Shobi Bldg, N side of Sanjo, E of Sanjo Bridge.
Tel (075) 761-6022.

Ringo
23 Tanaka Monzen-cho, nr Kyoto University.
Tel (075) 721-3195.

Taku Taku
Tomikoji, Shijo-Kawaramchi.
Tel (075) 351-1321.

WESTERN HONSHU

The cultural heartland of the country, Western Honshu is where Japan's first imperial courts held sway, in an area called Yamato. A rich fusion of literature, imagination, and religious mysticism permeates many tourist attractions, while Osaka and other teeming cities are vibrant places constantly reinventing themselves. Little wonder that this part of Japan sits high on the list of places to visit for travelers.

The name Yamato refers to where heaven and earth divide, and also to the land founded by the mythical son of the gods, emperor Jimmu. In the Japanese mind, Yamato is a holy place, a homeland "whose trees and rocks, streams and mountains," as legendary emperor Keiko expressed it in verse form almost two millennia ago, "house the gods."

Legend solidified into fact in the 4th century AD when a clan called Yamato expanded its kingdom in the region. Japan's first emperors, the Yamato rulers set up court on the Yamato Plain, the site of present-day Nara prefecture.

Nature, religion, and architecture converge in the city of Nara, its antiquity evident in its aging wooden temples. Here, the rich pantheons of India and China, reinterpreted, are set against a city characterized by quiet stroll gardens, the smell of lingering incense, and the reflections of winged pagodas in green ponds.

Hiroshima, now a surprisingly pleasant city, the international port of Kobe, and Osaka are Western Honshu's great metropolitan centers. Osaka, an industrial dynamo best known for its business deals and copious appetite for good food, is being transformed by its restless inhabitants into a forum for the arts.

Elsewhere, a strong sense of regional character is apparent at such destinations as the exquisite ceramic town of Hagi, the sacred island of Miyajima, the willow-lined canals and storehouses of Kurashiki, and Ise Grand Shrine, whose inner precincts are solemnly dedicated to the Sun Goddess.

Meoto Iwa ("wedded rocks"), representing the gods Izanami and Izanagi, Ise Peninsula

◀ The *torii* gateway to Itsukushima Shrine, Miyajima Island

Exploring Western Honshu

Western Honshu includes the region called Kansai (or
sometimes Kinki), centered on the major city of Osaka. Kyoto
is also part of Kansai but has a separate chapter in this book
(see pp158–89). The area west of Osaka is called Chugoku,
"Middle Country," and, despite being the historic heartland
of Japan, it is now less densely
populated than Kansai and Tokyo
to the east. A spine of mountains
runs through the middle of
Western Honshu, and the two
coasts are quite different in
character, with the San-in coast
rugged and more remote.

Hikone Castle garden, Lake Biwa

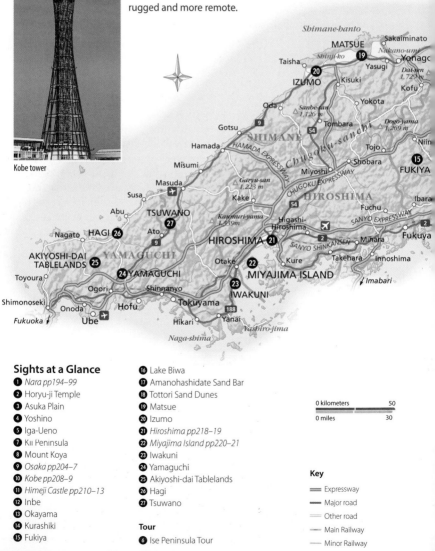

Kobe tower

Sights at a Glance

1 Nara pp194–99
2 Horyu-ji Temple
3 Asuka Plain
4 Yoshino
5 Iga-Ueno
7 Kii Peninsula
8 Mount Koya
9 Osaka pp204–7
10 Kobe pp208–9
11 Himeji Castle pp210–13
12 Inbe
13 Okayama
14 Kurashiki
15 Fukiya

16 Lake Biwa
17 Amanohashidate Sand Bar
18 Tottori Sand Dunes
19 Matsue
20 Izumo
21 Hiroshima pp218–19
22 Miyajima Island pp220–21
23 Iwakuni
24 Yamaguchi
25 Akiyoshi-dai Tablelands
26 Hagi
27 Tsuwano

Tour
6 Ise Peninsula Tour

0 kilometers 50
0 miles 30

Key

▬▬▬ Expressway
▬▬▬ Major road
▭▭▭ Other road
▬▬▬ Main Railway
▬▬▬ Minor Railway

Itsukushima shrine, Miyajima Island

Locator Map

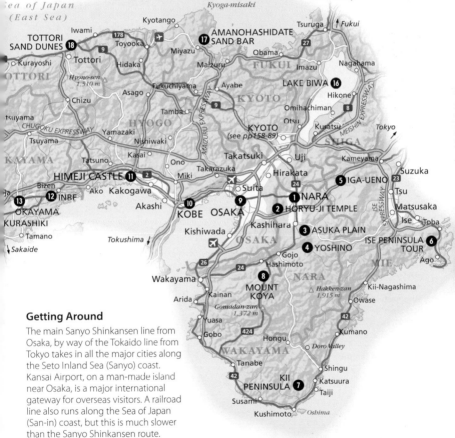

Getting Around

The main Sanyo Shinkansen line from Osaka, by way of the Tokaido line from Tokyo takes in all the major cities along the Seto Inland Sea (Sanyo) coast. Kansai Airport, on a man-made island near Osaka, is a major international gateway for overseas visitors. A railroad line also runs along the Sea of Japan (San-in) coast, but this is much slower than the Sanyo Shinkansen route.

Sanyo coast near Okayama

For keys to symbols *see back flap*

❶Nara

奈良

Founded in 710 on the Yamato Plain, Nara, then known as Heijo-kyo (citadel of peace), became one of Asia's most splendid cities. Avidly absorbing ideas from mainland Asia, the city became the grand diocese of Buddhism and the far eastern destination of the Silk Road. Miraculously, many buildings have survived. With its wooded hills, temple parks, and some of the world's oldest wooden buildings, this ancient city remains a symbol of tranquility.

Deer – "messengers of the gods" – in Nara Park

The tree ensconced temple of Todai-ji, as seen from hills to the east

Japan's foremost collections of Buddhist art, including an 8th-century statue of Ashura.

🚌 Nara National Museum

Tel (050) 5542-8600. Open 9:30am–5pm Tue–Sun. 🈲

This two-part museum consists of the original Beaux-arts building, the Buddhist Sculpture Hall and Ritual Bronzes Gallery, created in the 1870s, now

Exploring Nara

Nara's rectangular design, a checkerboard of streets based on the ancient Chinese city of Ch'ang-an, is straightforward and clearly divided into zones. The downtown area around the two stations, JR Nara and Kintetsu Nara, is within walking distance of **Nara Park**, a 1,300-acre (1,300 ha) area where most of the temples are located. Over 1,200 tame deer, regarded as messengers of the gods, roam the park. South of the center is **Naramachi**, the old city. Other notable areas like **Nishino-kyo** and **Horyu-ji** (see p200) are to the west and southwest of Nara.

🏯 Kofuku-ji Temple

Tel (0742) 22-7755. Open 9am–5pm daily. 🈲 for Treasure House and Eastern Golden Hall.

Kofuku-ji, approached up a wide staircase from Sarusawa Pond, was founded in 669. Of the 175 buildings in the original complex

only a precious few remain. In Nara, however, even reconstructions can lay claim to antiquity. The current five-story pagoda, burned to the ground no less than five times, dates from 1426. The temple's Eastern Golden Hall, containing several priceless statues, is of similar vintage. In the Treasure House is one of

The temple of Kofuku-ji, with its five-story pagoda

Map labels:
Nara Koen Chuo Byoin
Oike Pond
Todai-
①
Daibutsden
Kaidan-in
Kagami Pond
Nandai-mon Gate
②
Isui-en Garden
OMIYA-DORI
OSAKA, KYOTO
Kintetsu-Nara Station
Kofuku-ji Temple
③
Five-Storey Pagoda
Ichino-Torii Gate
Nara National Museum
⑤
SANJO-DORI
JR Nara Station 500 m (550 yards)
Toshodai-ji, Yakushi-ji, Horyu-ji temples
④
NARAMACHI
Ara Pond
Sagi Pond
Wariishi Bus Stop

0 meters 250
0 yards 250

housing the permanent collection, and a modern annex serving as a site for special exhibitions.

Most of the exhibits, including Buddhist sculptures, paintings, and calligraphy, date from the Nara and Heian periods. The museum holds an annual exhibition in October and early November of rarely seen treasures from the Shoso-in Treasure Repository, a storehouse in the Todai-ji complex that was built to preserve Emperor Shomu's private collection. The Shoso-in itself houses over 9,000 precious objects, some of which are of Central Asian and Persian extraction, evidence of Nara's interaction with these regions through its position at the end of the Silk Road. The Nara Butsuzo-kan section is closed until 2016 for renovation.

Some of the 3,000 lanterns at Kasuga Shrine

🔹 Isui-en Garden

Tel (0742) 25-0781. **Open** 9:30am–4:30pm Wed–Mon (daily in Apr, May, Oct & Nov). 🔹

The powerful shapes of Wakakusa Hill and Mt Kasuga, and the megalithic roof of Todai-ji form a backdrop to this essentially Meiji-era garden, which is popular in spring for its plum, cherry, and azalea blooms, and in autumn for red maples. Stone lanterns, a stream, and teahouses complete the picture. In the teahouses, visitors can eat *mugitoro*, a sweet potato, wheat, and rice mixture esteemed by health-food advocates.

🔺 Todai-ji Temple

See pp196–7.

🔹 Kasuga Taisha Shrine

Tel (0742) 22-7788. **Open** 9am–5pm daily. 🔹 for museum.

Originally built as the tutelary shrine of the Fujiwaras, one of the families who helped to establish Nara, Kasuga Taisha is one of the best known and most photographed Shinto sites. The original building was completed in 768 but, according to the strictures of purity and renewal governing Shinto beliefs, the structure, like the Great Shrine at Ise *(see p202)*, was demolished and rebuilt in identical fashion every 20 years. This has been repeated around 60 times over the centuries.

The approach road and walkways around this

vermilion-colored shrine boast an astonishing 3,000 or so stone and bronze lanterns. Donated by ordinary people as tokens of faith and thankfulness, the lanterns are an impressive spectacle when they are lit during festivals in early February and mid-August.

🔺 Shin-Yakushi-ji Temple

Tel (0742) 22-3736. **Open** 9am–5pm daily. 🔹

This temple was built by Empress Komyo (701–60) as an offering to the gods whose intercession she sought in the recovery of her husband from an eye disease. Some structures were rebuilt in the 13th century, but the main hall, the clay figures of the Healing Buddha (Yakushi Nyorai Buddha), and the Twelve Heavenly Generals are originals.

House in the residential and crafts quarter of Naramachi

🏛 Naramachi District

The old quarter of Naramachi includes traditional *machiya* (merchant homes), mostly from the mid-18th–19th centuries, converted into galleries and craft shops. The buildings are distinguished by narrow frontages and surprising depth, a design that developed due to taxes that were assessed by the width of a building's frontage. Red monkeys (migawari-zaru) hang in front of houses for good luck.

Nara Park

Deer Enclosure

Nigatsu-do
Sangatsu-do
Kasuga Taisha Shrine ⑦
Shin-Yakushi-ji Temple ⑥

Sights at a Glance

Exploring Nara: Todai-ji Temple

A World Heritage Site, the Todai-ji complex consists of the Great Buddha hall (Daibutsuden), subtemples, halls, pagodas, and gates of exceptional historical and architectural interest. It is also the largest wooden structure in the world. The construction of Todai-ji, completed in 752, was ordered by Emperor Shomu, ostensibly to house Nara's Great Buddha image but also to consolidate the position of the city as the capital and a powerful center of Buddhism. Todai-ji Temple is the headquarters of the Kegon school of Buddhism. Natural disasters have not diminished the scale of the 16-m (53-ft) high statue.

The 21-m (68-ft) high Nandaimon Great Southern Gate of Todai-ji

Kokuzo Bosatsu
This *bosatsu*, or bodhisattva – meaning an Enlightened Being – was completed in 1709.

Entrance

★ Great Buddha Vairocana
The casting of this vast statue in 752 deployed hundreds of tons of molten bronze, mercury, and vegetable wax. Fires and earthquakes dislodged the head several times; the current head dates from 1692.

Great Buddha Hall

The main hall of Todai-ji was rebuilt twice. The current structure, completed in 1709, is only two-thirds of the original size but is reputedly the largest wooden building in the world. The seated figure inside is the world's largest bronze image of the Buddha.

VISITORS' CHECKLIST

Practical Information
Nara Park. **Tel** (0742) 22-0375.
Open Mar: 8am–5pm daily;
Apr–Sep: 7:30am–5:30pm daily;
Oct: 7:30am–5pm daily; Nov–Feb:
8am–4:30pm daily.

Transport
 Daibutsuden Kasuga-Taisha-
mae stop.

★ Wooden Hall
This vast wooden hall, completed in
1709, has unusual bracketing and a
beam-frame construction.

Roofline
The striking roofline,
with its golden "horns"
and curved lintel,
was an 18th-century
embellishment.

KEY

① **Komokuten**, a heavenly
guardian, dates from the
mid-Edo period.

② **Behind the Buddha** is a small
hole bored into a large wooden
pillar. A popular belief holds that if
you can squeeze through the hole
you will attain Nirvana.

③ **Nyoirin Kannon Bosatsu**, like
the Kokuzo Bosatsu to the left of the
Great Buddha, is an Enlightened
Being and dates from 1709.

④ **Tamonten**, another heavenly
guardian, dates from the same
period as Komokuten on the other
side of the hall.

⑤ **Covered walkway in compound**

The beguiling "three-story" pagoda
at Yakushi-ji

Beyond Nara Park:
Nishinokyo District
Time permitting, two more
temples in the Nara vicinity
should not be missed.

Founded in 759 by the blind
Chinese sage and priest Ganjin,
Toshodai-ji's original main hall
and lecture hall, designated
National Treasures, are still
standing. Be sure to visit the
temple's stunning 5.5-m (18-ft)
high Senju Kannon statue.

A little south of Toshodai-ji,
more Buddhist statuary can be
found at **Yakushi-ji**. Emperor
Tenmu had the temple built in
the hope of effecting a recovery
for his wife, a gesture that
seems to have worked as she
outlived him by several years.
Dedicated to the Buddha of
healing, the temple's masterpiece is its famous three-
story east pagoda, the only
original structure remaining.

The pagoda, built in 730,
appears to have six levels, but
three are intermediary roofs
placed between the main floors,
creating an appealing optical
effect. The 19th-century
American scholar Ernest
Fenollosa, on a visit to Yakushi-ji,
compared the striking geometry
of the pagoda to "frozen music."

Toshodai-ji, where its founder, Ganjin,
is entombed

The majestic Osaka Castle, surrounded by towering modern buildings ▶

❷ Horyu-ji Temple

法隆寺

Regarded as the cradle of Japanese Buddhism, the Horyu-ji complex is also thought to contain some of the world's oldest surviving wooden structures, dating from the early 7th century. The temple was erected by Prince Shotoku (573–621) in his effort to entrench Buddhism alongside Shinto as a pillar of the Japanese belief system. Some exceptional works of art, including ancient images of the Buddha, are housed here.

VISITORS' CHECKLIST

Practical Information
10 km (6 miles) SW of Nara.
Open daily: 22 Feb–3 Nov 8am–5pm; 4 Nov–21 Feb 8am–4:30pm.

Transport
🚉 JR Yamatoji line from Nara, then 20-min walk. 🚌 from Kintetsu Nara stn to Horyu-ji-mae stop.

Gate at the Horyu-ji compound

Four scythes, a feature unique to Horyu-ji's pagoda, are said to stop it from being destroyed by lightning.

The nine rings *(kurin)* of the finial are made of bronze.

Wind chime

Yakushi Nyorai images dating from the 10th century are among the treasures of Horyu-ji.

Five-Story Pagoda

The pagoda is one of Horyu-ji's oldest buildings and the oldest one of its kind in Japan. The pagoda style was brought from China, which in turn had been developed from the Buddhist stupa in ancient India. The symbolism of such buildings is subject to debate. Some say that a five-story pagoda represents the elements, as shown; others disagree.

Ornamental roof crays are made of bronze.

The central column is fashioned from a single cypress tree. The entasis columns at Horyu-ji are reminiscent of classical Greek style, a legacy of the Silk Route.

Level 5: Sky

Level 4: Air/Wind

Level 3: Wood

Level 2: Water

Four sculpted scenes from the life of the Buddha face north, south, east, and west. Here, on the north side, the Buddha passes into Nirvana.

A fragment of the Buddha's bone is enshrined at the base of the central pillar.

Level 1: Earth

❸ Asuka Plain
飛鳥地方

Nara prefecture. 🚉 Asuka. 🛈 (0744) 54-3624.

The Asuka Plain is scattered with excavation sites from the proto-capital Asukakyo, which flourished in the 5th to 7th centuries. The best way to explore the burial tombs, temples, and early Buddhist statuary is by bicycle.

One of the best-known sites, **Takamatsuzuka Kofun**, is similar in design to Korean tombs of the same period and contains vivid murals of stars and mythological animals. Notable images elsewhere include **Sakabune Ishi**, a concentric stone that may have been used to make sake, **Kame and Saru Ishi**, turtle and monkey-shaped statues, and **Nimen Seki**, a stone with faces carved on each side.

Asuka-dera was Japan's first Buddhist temple. The Asuka-Daibutsu statues are influenced by various East Asian cultures.

Takamatsuzuka Kofun, a tomb site on the Asuka Plain

❹ Yoshino
吉野

Nara prefecture. 🚉 🛈 (07463) 2-3081. 🎎 Setsubun-e (Feb 3); Sakura Festival (Apr 11–12).

The attractive, elevated village of Yoshino, its multistoried houses built on graduated levels on the side of a remote mountain, is one of Japan's most popular cherry-blossom-viewing spots. The Yoshinoyama area boasts 100,000 trees planted in four

Cherry trees blossoming at altitude in Yoshino

groves at different altitudes. Each level blooms in succession, extending the viewing period to almost three weeks.

Environs

The Yoshinoyama area stretches from the south banks of the Kii River to the north end of the Omine mountain range. A UNESCO World Heritage site, the region is dotted with many temples, including **Kinpu-Senji Temple**, **Kinpu Shrine**, **Yoshimizu Shrine**, and **Yoshino Mikumari Shrine**. There is also a pilgrimage route across the mountains. **Chikurin-in** is a temple that is renowned for its stroll garden designed by the tea master Sen no Rikyu (see p173). Visitors can take advantage of the perfect vistas afforded by **Mt Yoshino-yama**

to view cherry blossom trees, as well as hot springs that are present in the area.

❺ Iga-Ueno
伊賀上野

Mie prefecture. 🚉 🚌 Ueno Tenjin Matsuri (October 23–25). 🛈 1st Floor, Haito-Pia bldg, in front of Ueno-shi stn; (0595) 24-0270.

A provincial castle town, Iga-Ueno was home to the Iga ninja, the most inventive and feared spies of Japan's feudal era, and the birthplace of Japan's most revered haiku poet, Matsuo Basho (see p283). Several sites in town, including Basho's house, a museum, and the odd **Haeseiden**, an octagonal building said to replicate Basho's standing figure, are dedicated to the poet.

The main attraction for most people, though, is the extraordinary **Iga Ninja Museum**, a clan farmhouse that served as the secret headquarters of the Iga sect of professional spies and assassins. The well-restored building retains hidden panels, spy holes, secret escape routes, and trapdoors intended to repel night attacks from enemy warlords and rival ninja groups. Ninja methods are enthusiastically demonstrated by guides dressed in pink day-glo ninja outfits.

🏛 **Iga Ninja Museum**
Tel (0595) 23-0311. **Open** daily. 🎌
🖥 iganinja.jp/en

The Ninja

Ninjutsu, the "art of stealth," was developed during the bloody clan warfare of Japan's feudal era. The ninja elevated their profession of spying and assassination into a sophisticated discipline by practicing mountain asceticism and studying such subjects as astronomy, herbalism, medicine, and nutrition. They developed ingenious devices to outwit enemies, including lock picks, collapsible floats for crossing water, clothing designed to conceal swords and knives, and over 30 different kinds of *shuriken*, which are deadly throwing stars made of metal.

Ninja sword exhibit at Iga Ninja Museum

Local guide demonstrating ninja methods

❻ Ise Peninsula Tour
伊勢志摩国立公園

The city of Ise, its Grand Shrine – the most sacred in Japan – and the Ise-Shima National Park are the main tourist attractions of this peninsula. Its jagged, indented coast, the center of cultured oyster pearl production in Japan, is in striking contrast to the undulating evergreen-clad hills inland, which are the habitat of monkeys, wild boars, and flying squirrels.

③ Mikimoto Pearl Island
Just offshore from the tourist town of Toba, this island has a memorial hall to Mikimoto Kokichi who created the original cultured pearl in 1893. Women divers can be seen collecting seaweed and sea urchins.

② Futamigaura Beach
Two rocks called the Meoto Iwa (wedded rocks), representing the parent gods of Japan, Izanami and Izanagi, are connected by a sacred rope *(see p191).*

① Ise Shrines
Reconstructed every 20 years in accordance with Shinto principles of purity and renewal, Ise's shrines are in two main groups: the Ge-ku (outer shrine) and Nai-ku (inner shrine, *see pp30–31.*)

⑥ Ise-Shima Skyline
A good route back on a clear day, this road goes over the summit of Mount Asama, with views of the peninsula and, occasionally, even to Mount Fuji in Central Honshu.

⑤ Goza Beach
The most popular stretch of sand on the peninsula, Goza Beach can be reached by road or by boat from Kashikojima.

Key

▬ Tour route
▤ Expressway
= Other road

Ise Bay
Toshi Island
Toba
Suga Island
Toba Bay
Hisai
42
167
Pearl Road
Matoya Bay
Isobe
Kumano
Ago
260
Ago Bay
Shima

0 kilometers 5
0 miles 3

Tips for Travelers

Tour length: 110 km (70 miles).
Alternative transportation: The area has excellent bus and train services. Trains run to Ise, Futamigaura, Toba, and Kashikojima, while buses run to many destinations from Toba, and between the Ise shrines.

④ Kashikojima This is one of the peninsula's best resort areas, with fine views of Ago Bay. You can take a boat trip past scenic islets, fishing boats, and hundreds of oyster rafts.

⑦ Kii Peninsula
紀伊半島

Wakayama, Mie, and Nara prefectures.
✈ Nanki-Shirahama. 🚉 JR Kinokuni
line. 🎐 Nachi Fire Matsuri (Jul 14).

The Kii Peninsula, with densely
forested mountains at its center
and craggy headlands, pine-
covered islands, and coves
along its shoreline, has largely
avoided the industrial
development that scars much
of Japan's Pacific coastline.

A good starting point is the
small port town of **Shingu**, on
the east coast. From here you
can take a bus to Shiko, then a
50-minute boat trip takes you
along the Kumano River to **Doro
Valley**, one of Japan's most
spectacular gorges. From May to
June rhododendrons and azaleas
bloom on the river's banks.

A 20-minute bus ride inland
from Shingu lies **Nachi-no-taki**,
Japan's highest waterfall. A
stone path ascending parallel to
the falls leads to **Nachi Taisha**
shrine, its origins reaching back
over 1,400 years. The next port
south of Shingu is **Katsuura**,
a pleasant pine studded bay
with several picturesque islets.
Visitors interested in the
Japanese perspective on
whaling should go to nearby
Taiji, a whaling community
since the 17th century. For
insight into a complex subject,
visit the **Taiji Whale Museum.**

Farther south, the resort of
Kushimoto is known for a chain
of 30 rocks, **Hashi-gui-iwa**, that
seem to march out to sea,
connecting the town to the
island of Oshima. The

Forested hillsides typical of the
Kii Peninsula

Kano-school screens inside Kongobu-ji, Mount Koya

peninsula's southernmost point
is marked by **Shio-no-misaki**,
a headland with a white lighthouse dating from 1863. One
of the three oldest hot springs
in Japan, **Shirahama Onsen**,
on the west coast, also has one
of the area's finest beaches.

🏛 **Taiji Whale Museum**
Tel (0735) 59-2400. Open daily. 🅿

⑧ Mount Koya
高野山

Wakayama prefecture. 🏔 4,000.
🚉 Nankai line from Osaka, then cable
car from Gokurakubashi stn. ℹ nr
Senjuinbashi bus stop (0736) 56-2616.
Open daily. 🅿 some buildings.
🎐 Aoba Matsuri (Jun 15), Rosoku
Matsuri (Candlelight Festival, Aug 13).
Ⓦ **shukubo.jp/eng/index.html**

Set amid clumps of black
cedar at an altitude of 900
m (3,000 ft) in the heart of
the Kii Peninsula, Mount
Koya, or Koya-san, is
Japan's most venerated
Shingon-Buddhist site.
It is host to over one
million pilgrims a year.
Saint Kukai (774–835),
also known by his
posthumous name,
Kobo Daishi, estab-
lished a monastic retreat here
in 816. There were almost 1,000
temples on the mountain by
the Edo period, but typhoons
and fire have since reduced the
number to 117. The mountain's
unique atmosphere is best
experienced with an overnight
stay. Traditional vegetarian
cuisine is served in Koya-san's
53 temple lodgings.

The western part of Koya-san
contains the grandest and most
revered structures. **Kongobu-ji**,

A burial stone at
Okuno-In, Mount Koya

built in 1593 by Toyotomi
Hideyoshi (see p60), is Koya-san's
chief temple. Its rhododendrons
and the sliding doors of its inner
chambers, painted in the 16th
century by artists of the Kano
school, are among its special
attractions. The magnificent
Danjogaran complex, is one
of the two most sacred sites
on the mountain, the **Fudo-
do** (Fudo Hall), built in 1189,
and the **Konpon Dai-to**, an
impressive two-story vermilion-
and-white pagoda. Rebuilt in
1937, the pagoda is regarded
as the symbol of Koya-san.

The aptly named **Reihokan**
(Treasure House) stands
opposite the complex, a cornucopia of over 5,000 paintings,
statues, and mandalas displayed
in two separate buildings. The
gigantic **Daimon** (great
gate), the traditional main
entrance to Koya-san, lies
a little west of here on the
edge of the plateau. It
affords a matchless
view of mountains,
valleys and, on clear
days, distant Shikoku
and Awaji islands.

In the eastern half of
Koya-san is a necropolis
of over 200,000 tombs,
and the **Okuno-in**
(inner sanctum), Kukai's
mausoleum. Great status is
attached to burial on Koya-san.
The stone-paved approach to
Okuno-in is flanked with statues,
monuments, and tombs housing
the remains of Japan's most
powerful and illustrious families.
In front of Kukai's mausoleum is
the **Toro-do** (Lantern Hall). Day
and night 11,000 lanterns burn
here, including two that are said
to have remained lit since the
11th century.

For hotels and restaurants see pp302–307 and pp324–339

⑨ Osaka
大阪

Osaka's prominence as a merchant city dates from Toyotomi Hideyoshi's building of Osaka Castle in 1586. He also encouraged traders from other parts of Japan to settle in the city. In the 1920s and 1930s it became an industrial powerhouse. Nowadays, though, the nondescript skyline is being replaced with galleries, international hotels, futuristic living spaces, and exciting postmodernist architecture. The city's extravagant nightlife and culinary predilections are famous. A Japanese saying, *"Kyoto kidaore; Osaka kuidaore,"* suggests that Kyoto-ites are apt to go bankrupt from buying kimonos, Osakans from eating out too much.

Exploring Osaka

Central Osaka is split into two main districts, which meet at Chuo-odori. **Kita-ku**, the northern ward around the main Osaka and Umeda stations, is where many of the city's big hotels, restaurants, and underground shopping precincts are found. It also includes the small island of Nakanoshima, between the Dojima and Tosabori rivers. **Minami**, the southern district, includes the lively downtown area called **Namba**, the core of the old merchant city where you will find Osaka's best eating and drinking options, including **Dotonbori**. This lane, running alongside the canal of the same name and crammed with karaoke bars, brothels, and *pachinko* parlors *(see p101)*, is also a mecca of cheap restaurants and bars. Namba's many pedestrian shopping zones include **America Mura** and **Europe-dori**, with their imported goods, both north of, and parallel to, Dotonbori, and **Den Den Town**, Osaka's premier electronics district which is south of Sennichimae-dori. **Chuo-ku**, the old central ward and historic center of the city is to the east; this is where Osaka Castle stands. **Osaka Port** is west of the city center.

Plenty of information and signs in English make Osaka a relatively easy place to negotiate

Young Osakans at leisure in the Dotonbori canal district

in comparison with other major Japanese cities. The city center is served by a user-friendly loop system called the JR Kanjo Line. Its color-coded subway system is also easy to ride. Visitors who intend to cover a lot of sightseeing in a limited period will benefit from buying a one-day pass *(ichi nichi joshaken)* that offers a day's unlimited travel on subways, trams, and local train lines.

🏛 Osaka Museum of History

1-32 Otemae 4-Chome, Chuo-ku. **Tel** (06) 6946-5728. **S** Tanimachi-Yon-Chome stn, Chuo or Tanimachi lines. **Open** 9:30am–5pm Wed–Mon, 9:30am–8pm Fri (last adm: 4:30pm Wed–Mon, 7:30pm Fri). 🌐 **W** mus-his.city.osaka.jp

This modern museum uses life-size reconstructions, miniature models, and video presentations to bring alive the history of Osaka from ancient times to the modern day. Its most notable exhibits are objects excavated from the 7th-century Naniwa Palace. On the 10th floor there is a model of the Daikokuden, the main building of the palace, including replicas of the vermillion-painted pillars.

The present-day museum is built partly on the site of the Naniwa Palace. Excavations in the museum basement and on the adjacent archaeological site reveal the remains of warehouses and palace walls.

Other floors explore the "Water City" of the Edo Period and a panorama of Osaka in modern times. There are good views of Osaka Castle from various points in the museum. Of special interest to children is the Resource Center on the eighth floor. Kids can complete a jigsaw puzzle using ancient pottery pieces or play with Banraku puppets.

🏯 Osaka Castle

1-1 Osakajo Chuo-ku. **Tel** (06) 6941-3044. 🚇 Osakajo-koen stn, JR Kanjo line. **S** Tanimachi-Yonchome stn, Chuo or Tanimachi lines. **Open** 9am–5pm daily (last adm: 4:30pm). 🌐 **W** osakacastle.net/english

The present reconstruction of the main donjon, dating from 1931, is smaller than the

Sweeping view of downtown Osaka

For hotels and restaurants see pp302–307 and pp324–339

The imposing keep of Osaka Castle

Tokugawa period. The modernized lower floors of the main keep display a collection of armor and memorabilia connected with Hideyoshi. An elevator travels to the eighth floor for great views of the city.

castle completed by Hideyoshi in 1586 but still gives some idea of the power and majesty of the original. The largest castle in the country at the time, Osaka-jo's turbulent history began when it was besieged and destroyed by the Tokugawa shogunate in 1615. The castle was rebuilt but struck by lightning a few years later. The remains were burned down in a fire in 1868, just before the Meiji Restoration.

Some ancillary buildings, including the Tamon tower and the impressive Otemon gate, have survived from the

🏛 National Museum of Art

4-2-55 Nakanoshima, Kita-ku.
Tel (06) 6447-4680. 🚆 Watanabe stn,
Keihan Nakanoshima line.
Open 10am–5pm Tue–Sun (last
adm: 4:30pm). 🅿 🌐 **nmao.go.jp**

The entrance of the National Museum of Art, made from curved steel and extending high above the building itself, was designed to invoke both the strength and the flexibility of bamboo. The collection inside is impressive, with works by Picasso, Cézanne, Miró, and Warhol, as well as ancient Chinese treasures and modern Japanese art.

🏛 Museum of Oriental Ceramics

Nakanoshima Island 1-1-26 Nakano-shima, Kita-ku. **Tel** (06) 6223-0055. 🚆 Naniwabashi stn, Keihan Nakanoshima line. 🚇 Yodoyabashi stn, Midosuji line. **Open** 9:30am–5pm Tue–Sun (last adm: 4:30pm). 🌐 **moco.or.jp/en**

With over 1,000 items of mostly Chinese and Korean origin, this museum houses one of the world's finest collections of Oriental ceramics. The display comes from the Ataka Collection. Computer-regulated, light-sensitive rooms highlight the surfaces of the items. A few of the Japanese pieces are National Treasures.

Osaka City Center

① Floating Garden Observatory
② National Museum of Art
③ Museum of Oriental Ceramics
④ Osaka Museum of History
⑤ Osaka Castle
⑥ National Bunraku Theater
⑦ Japan Folk Art Museum
⑧ Shitenno-ji Temple
⑨ Spa World

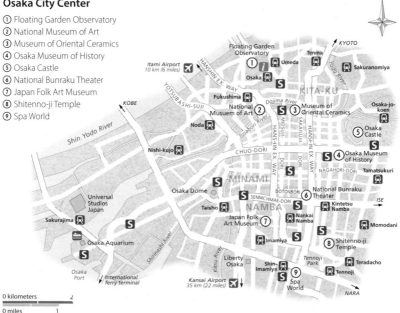

0 kilometers 2
0 miles 1

For keys to symbols *see back flap*

Exploring Osaka

Today, Osaka is Japan's third largest city after Tokyo and Yokohama. It also joins Tokyo and Kyoto as the top three culinary centers of Japan, with a local cuisine known for its practicality rather than finesse – instant noodles were invented here in 1958. Working Osakans eat out about six times a week. Favorite local dishes include *oshizushi*, in which sushi is placed in wooden molds and sliced; *udon suki*, buckwheat noodles and meat in a rich broth served in a ceramic stew pot; and *okonimiyaki*, a batter and cabbage pancake-type dish in which you choose ingredients such as seafood or pork.

Crab restaurant and motif in downtown Osaka

📺 National Bunraku Theater
1-12-10 Nippon-bashi Chuo-ku. 🚉 Nipponbashi stn, Kintetsu line. Ⓢ Nipponbashi stn, Sennichi-mae & Sakaisuji lines. **Tel** (06) 6212-2531. 🌐 ntj.jac.go.jp

Japan's main venue for Bunraku puppet dramas *(see p41)* can be spotted from the colorful banners hanging outside the theater. Bunraku shows take place every January, April, June, July, August, and November, programs normally running for about 20 days at a time. The acoustics in this specially designed theater are excellent; headsets are available for foreign tourists, with English translations for some performances.

Osaka's Umeda Sky Building, topped by the Floating Garden Observatory

✳️ Floating Garden Observatory
1-1-88 Oyodonake Kita-ku, Umeda Sky Bldg. 🚉 JR Osaka stn, JR Kanjo line. Ⓢ Umeda stn, Midosuji line. **Open** 10am–10:30pm daily (last adm: 10pm). 🌐 kuchu-teien.com

This futuristic structure, reached by taking an exposed glass escalator to the 39th floor, is not for those who suffer from vertigo or fear of being caught in high places in earthquake-prone regions.

The observatory, 173 m (576 ft) above ground, straddles the twin towers of Hara Hiroshi's Umeda Sky Building. Views of Osaka from the top are incredible. High-tech displays and a virtual-reality game center also occupy the observatory, but neither can really compete with the panoramas.

🎬 Universal Studios Japan
2-1-33 Sakurajima Konohana-ku. 🚉 Universal Studio City stn, JR Yumesaki line. **Tel** (06) 6465-3000. **Open** daily. 🎟️ (for individual rides and activities). 🌐 usj.co.jp/e_top.html

This theme park aims to attract people of all ages and is fast becoming a major landmark of Osaka. There are nine themed areas, as well as live entertainment throughout the site. Among the attractions are the Hollywood Premiere Parade, Hollywood Magic, and, in the "New York" area, a St. Patrick's Day Celebration. Children will especially love the Animal Actors Stage and Snoopy's Playland.

💧 Spa World
3-4-24 Ebisuhigashi Naniwa-ku. 🚉 Shin-imamiya stn, JR Kanjo and Nankai lines. Ⓢ Dobutsuenmae stn, Midosuji line. **Tel** (06) 6631-0001. **Open** 10am–8:45pm. 🌐 spaworld.co.jp/english

Built to cater for up to 5,000 people at any time, Spa World offers an amazing bathing experience. Piping hot water comes from springs almost 900 m (3,000 ft) underground. The main part of the complex is divided into zones representing bathing customs of various countries around the world. The Chinese section focuses on traditional Chinese medicine, while the Turkish section has mosaic-tile flooring.

🏛️ Japan Folk Art Museum
3-7-6 Nambanaka Naniwa-ku. 🚉 Namba stn, Nankai and Kintetsu lines. Ⓢ Namba stn, Midosuji line. 🚃 Nihon-teien-mae. **Tel** (06) 6641-6309. **Open** 10am–5pm Tue–Sun (last adm: 4:30pm). 🎟️

This museum has an outstanding collection of traditional folk arts and crafts, one of the best of its type in Japan. It offers a superb intro-duction to regional handicrafts centering on textiles and fabrics, ceramic ware, bamboo, toys, and more.

Ceramic bowl, Folk Art Museum

🏯 Shitenno-ji Temple
1-11-18 Shitennoji Tennoji-ku. Ⓢ Shitenno-ji stn, Tanimachi line. **Tel** (06) 6771-0066. **Open** daily. 🎟️

Prince Shotoku ordered the construction of the original temple here in 593. The com-plex is considered the birth-place of Japanese Buddhism. Destroyed many times by fire, the current concrete buildings date from 1965. As exact copies of the originals, however, they are of interest to visitors wishing to know more about early Buddhist architecture. An excellent flea market is held on the 21st of every month.

🏯 Tempozan Harbor Village

S Osaka-ko stn, Chuo line. **Open** Tue–Sun. 🐬 Aquarium: **Open** daily. 🐬 **w** kaiyukan.com

Begun as a reclamation program in the 1830s, this waterfront project in Osaka Port is the new face of an older, Edo-period landfill. The enormous Tempozan Ferris Wheel, once the world's tallest at 113 m (371 ft), offers passengers panoramic views of the entire city of Osaka, the ocean, and mountains. The ferris wheel can hold up to 480 passengers in its 60 cars. At night the grandly illuminated wheel is a popular date venue for the locals.

Nearby **Osaka Aquarium Kaiyukan** is set apart by its innovative and challenging design. Built around the concept of the Pacific "Ring of Fire," the aquarium holds almost 13.5 million liters (3 million gallons) of water. Visitors descend through 14 levels representing 35,000 fish and mammal habitats found within the Pacific Ocean belt, including manta rays and whale sharks.

Tempozan Marketplace is a large center for restaurants and shopping. Across the bay, and

Aerial view of the Aqua Metropolis area, Osaka

linked by an underwater tunnel, is **Cosmo Square**, with an observatory, and the Nanko Bird Sanctuary.

🏛 Liberty Osaka (Osaka Human Rights Museum)

3-6-36 Naniwanishi Naniwaku-ku. 🚉 Ashiharabashi or Imamiya stns, JR Kanjo line. **Tel** (06) 6561-5891. **Open** 10am–4pm Tue–Fri, 1–5pm Sat. **Closed** 4th Fri of month. 🐬

The Liberty, also known as the Osaka Human Rights Museum, provides a sobering insight into the dark side of Japan. Exhibits take a critical look at subjects rarely discussed by Japanese. Topics include the Burakumin section of society – descendants of leather-workers, who disposed of the dead and did other jobs considered polluted. Discrimination against ethnic minorities and foreigners, and environmental issues are also covered.

Environs

Situated 35 km (22 miles) south of Osaka, **Kansai International**

Airport (KIX) sits on a man-made island 2 km (1 mile) offshore in Osaka Bay. Connected to the mainland by a bridge, the airport is a long, thin, futuristic compression of glass and steel.

Osaka is also at the cutting edge of research into high-speed train technology in the form of magnetic-levitated trains (Maglevs). A prototype runs between Kadoma-minami and Taisho stations. Experiments with more advanced Maglevs have reached speeds of 580 kph (360 mph).

Takarazuka lies northwest of Osaka, in Hyogo prefecture. The town is closely associated with the enormously popular all-female Takarazuka Troupe, which was founded in 1914. Their revues can be classified as adaptations of heroic romances. Performances at the **Takarazuka Grand Theater** are held once or twice a day except Wednesday.

🎭 Takarazuka Grand Theater

🚉 Hankyu & JR lines. **Tel** (0570) 00-5100.

💧 Aqua Metropolis

🚉 Ashiharabashi or Imamiya stns, JR Kanjo line.

This area of Osaka city, known as the Aqua Metropolis, was once Japan's most important economic center. During the Edo period (1603–1868), the canals flowing through the city were filled with boats carrying products from all over the country. Today, the Aqua Metropolis is still thriving, with various attractions and cafés lining the riverfront of this "Water Corridor." River cruises are available all year.

The Yakuza

A large tattoo, often the sign of a yakuza member

The word *yakuza* was originally used to describe the classless groups of thieves, gamblers, and outlaws who floated around large cities and ports during the Edo period. Osaka is the center of the modern *yakuza* and many of the country's largest and most influential crime syndicates. *Yakuza* are involved in a wide range of illegal activities that run from prostitution, drug- and light-arms-smuggling to loan-sharking. Gangs are also adept at corporate extortion, preventing, for a suitable fee, embarrassing questions being asked at stockholder meetings. Irezumi (tattoos), though traditionally an art form, are considered anti-social in Japan and are strongly associated with the *yakuza*.

⑩ Kobe
神戸

Kobe enjoyed a brisk trade with China and Korea from the 8th century on and was one of the first ports to benefit when Japan reopened to Western trade in 1868. Today, there is a large expatriate community, notably Chinese and Koreans, but also Europeans, Americans, and Indians. The city became famous overnight in 1995 when a huge earthquake struck. However, there is little evidence of the disaster now, so effectively has this cosmopolitan city been rebuilt. The downtown area is famous for its nightlife. Kobe beef, meanwhile, is one of the world's most well-known meats.

One of the elegant European residences in Kitano-cho

Exploring Kobe

Kobe's central business, shopping, and nightlife districts, Kitano-cho, nearby Chinatown, and the narrow north-south axis of Flower Road are easily negotiated on foot. With little room left to expand beyond these urban parameters, Kobe has turned to the sea for extra space. Reclamation projects include Rokko and Port Islands.

The excellent subway system has lines running east-west. An unmanned monorail, the Port Liner, runs from Sannomiya station in a circle around Port Island. The City Loop bus offers a day pass that includes most of the city's key sights.

🏛 Kitano-cho

12-min walk from Sannomiya stn along Kitano-zaka.
🏠 some houses.

Wealthy foreign traders and diplomats built homes in this area after Kobe was chosen to serve as one of Japan's major international ports at the start of the Meiji period. Over 20 of these beautifully preserved homes are open to the public. The stone and clapboard buildings, many in the Gothic Victorian style, are called *ijinkan*. The area, which suggests fin de siècle European elegance to many Japanese people, enjoys a reputation as one of Kobe's more fashionable districts.

🏛 Chinatown

5-min walk S of Motomachi stn.

The city's 14,000 or more Chinese residents have turned this quarter (Nankin-machi) into a lively and colorful slice of Kobe life. Approached through four large gateways, the central plaza, Nankin Park, is surrounded by Chinese restaurants and trinket shops, and it is filled with street vendors. The park has statues representing the 12 animals of the Chinese astrological calendar.

🏛 Kobe City Museum

10-min walk S of Motomachi stn.
Open 9:30am–5:30pm Tue–Sun, but check website for temporary closures.
🏠 🌐 city.kobe.lg.jp/culture/
culture/institution/museum

This museum covers the history of the city from the earliest times until its reconstruction after the 1995 earthquake. There is an intriguing display of objects retrieved from the Old Foreign Settlement and a scale model of the area. The museum also has the world's premier collection of 16th-century Nanban art. The word Nanban ("Southern Barbarian") was at first applied to all foreigners who arrived from the south, mainly the Portuguese. Later it was applied to Europeans in general.

🚢 Meriken Park

🚉 10-min walk south of Motomachi stn. Museum and Port Tower:
Open daily. 🏠

West of the monorail bridge that takes you across to Port

The Great Hanshin Earthquake

Shoehorned into a narrow strip of land between hills to the north and the Inland Sea to the south, Kobe paid a high price for its location on the morning of January 17, 1995. At 5:46am the Great

The center of Kobe in ruins following the January 1995 earthquake

Hanshin Earthquake struck, its epicenter 10 miles beneath the Akashi Strait near Kobe. The tremor lasted almost a minute and measured 6.9 on the Moment Magnitude scale. The initial quake, hundreds of aftershocks, and ensuing fires together destroyed over 100,000 buildings and killed over 6,000 inhabitants.

Sake brewery in Kobe, open to visitors

Island lies Meriken Park. Meriken was the Meijiera rendition of "American." From the park you will see the distinctive outline of the **Kobe Maritime Museum**, which has a roof designed like the sails of a ship. The displays inside it focus on the city's role as a port. For a good overview of the area climb the **Kobe Port Tower** on Naka Pier.

Nada Sake Breweries

Although most of the best breweries were razed during the earthquake, reconstruction and preservation of the few that were left has been going on at a furious pace, and it is now possible once again to visit some of the best-known brand-name producers.

Kikumasamune Shuzo Kinenkan, a sake museum located within 3 minutes' walk of Rokko Liner Minami Uozaki station. Although its storehouses perished in the quake, the watermill cottage survived and now houses a small but interesting display of brewing utensils. At **Hamafuku Ginjo Brewery and Shop**, a 5-minute stroll from Hanshin Uozaki station, visitors can watch the fermenting process. Sake-tasting takes place at both breweries.

Environs

Behind Shin-Kobe station, the **Nunobiki Falls**, with four cascades, have been celebrated in Japanese literature since the 10th century. **Mount Rokko**, the highest peak of the chain of the same name, can be reached by cable car or ropeway. The view of the Inland Sea and city below is sensational. On the north slope is **Arima Onsen**, a spa that has been operating since the 7th century. The waters were a favorite of the 16th-century

shogun Toyotomi Hideyoshi and his wife, who sometimes came with the tea ceremony master, Sen no Rikyu.

The cable-car ride up Mount Rokko

VISITORS' CHECKLIST

Practical Information
Hyogo prefecture. 1,545,000. in front of JR Sannomiya stn (078) 322-0220. http://feel-kobe.jp

Transport
Kobe airport, 18 mins by Port Liner to Sannomiya stn; Kansai airport, 25 mins by high-speed boat, The Bay Shuttle; Port Island. JR Shin-Kobe stn, Sanyo Shinkansen line; Sannomiya stn, JR Tokkaido, Hankyu, & Hanshin lines.

Kobe City Center

① Kitano-cho
② Chinatown
③ Kobe City Museum
④ Kobe Port Tower
⑤ Kobe Maritime Museum
⑥ Meriken Park

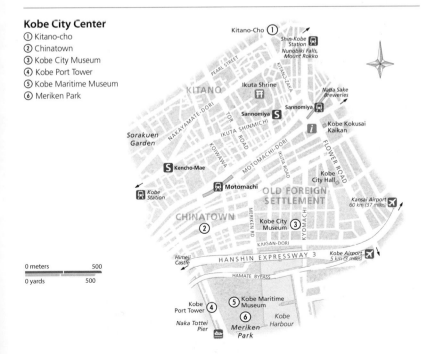

⑪ Himeji Castle

姫路城

Built on a high bluff, Himeji-jo, the grandest of Japan's 12 remaining feudal castles, dominates the city of Himeji. The building is better known among the Japanese as Shirasagi-jo, the "white egret castle," because of the supposed resemblance of its plastered walls, stretched either side of the main donjon, to the image of a bird taking flight. For many people its military architecture, ameliorated by graceful aesthetic lines, qualifies Himeji-jo as the ultimate samurai castle. Its cinematic potential was exploited by Akira Kurosawa in his 1985 film *Ran*. The castle is now designated a UNESCO World Heritage Site.

View from lower floor of the donjon to the modern city of Himeji

Vanity Tower
The abode of Princess Sen (1597–1667) and other women was locked each night under guard.

Gates and Passageways
Though never put to the test, the castle's labyrinth of passageways and gateways in the outer zones were designed to confuse enemies.

Entrance

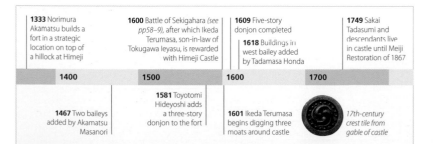

1333 Norimura Akamatsu builds a fort in a strategic location on top of a hillock at Himeji	**1600** Battle of Sekigahara *(see pp58–9)*, after which Ikeda Terumasa, son-in-law of Tokugawa Ieyasu, is rewarded with Himeji Castle	**1609** Five-story donjon completed **1618** Buildings in west bailey added by Tadamasa Honda	**1749** Sakai Tadasumi and descendants live in castle until Meiji Restoration of 1867
1400	**1500**	**1600**	**1700**
1467 Two baileys added by Akamatsu Masanori	**1581** Toyotomi Hideyoshi adds a three-story donjon to the fort	**1601** Ikeda Terumasa begins digging three moats around castle	*17th-century crest tile from gable of castle*

★ Main Tower
The current five-story donjon was developed by Ikeda Terumasa in 1609, transforming a modest military stronghold into a symbol of the Tokugawa shogunate's newly consolidated power. For more details about the main tower see pages 212–13.

VISITORS' CHECKLIST

Practical Information
1 km N of Himeji stn, Himeji city, Hyogo prefecture. **Tel** (079) 285-1146. **Open** 9am–4pm daily (to 5pm Jun–Aug). 🎫 Matsubara Festival (Oct 14–15). **city.himeji.hyogo.jp/english/himeji/index.html**

Transport
🚉 Himeji stn, Shinkansen line.

| 0 meters | 50 |
| 0 yards | 50 |

KEY

① **West bailey** (*nishi-nomaru*)

② **Sangoku moat**

③ **Second bailey** (*ninomaru*)

④ **The waist quarter** (*koshi-kurawa*), behind the main tower, is the weakest point of the stronghold.

⑤ **Main bailey** (*honmaru*)

⑥ **The suicide quarter** may have been intended as a place for ritual suicide when it was built. However, it was probably used only for its water supply.

★ Fan Walls
Samurai castles are notable for their graceful fan-shaped stone walls, which were very difficult for enemies to scale.

Exploring Himeji Castle: the Main Tower

The stronghold of Himeji Castle, the main tower was used by the feudal lords in the event of a siege or during drills. From the exterior, the tower appears to have five floors. In fact, it has six floors and a basement – the second and third floors from the top appear to be one floor from the outside. The tower benefitted from a restoration project that was completed in 2015.

Fish Motifs
Dolphin-like *shachi-gawara* motifs on the roof are of a mythical beast believed to protect the main tower from fire.

Interior of Keep
Originally an armaments store, the interior remains largely unadorned and houses exhibits relating to castle life.

Rock Chutes
Angled chutes set at numerous points in the walls enabled stones, boiling oil, and water to be dropped on the heads of any invaders.

Entrance through basement

KEY

① **Basement level**

② **Portholes** in the shape of circles, triangles, and rectangles were for musketeers and archers.

③ **The uppermost chamber** offers panoramas on four sides.

④ **The division** between these two floors is not obvious from the exterior.

⑤ **Slippery wooden stairs** ascend through rooms of diminishing size.

⑥ **Storehouses for grain**

Museum of Weaponry
Displays of samurai arms and armor are complemented by guns and pouches of gun powder, introduced to Japan by the Portuguese in the 16th century.

For hotels and restaurants see pp302–307 and pp324–339

Himeji Castle in springtime, with cherry blossoms in the foreground

Modern facade of Hyogo Prefectural Museum of History

Castle Environs

The grounds at Himeji are particularly attractive during April, when the cherry trees are in bloom. **Koko-en**, an elegant composite of nine separate Edo-style gardens, was built in 1992 on the site of former samurai homes. The **Hyogo Prefectural Museum of History** provides excellent exhibits, including models of Japanese castles and a section on Bunraku puppet drama, with models that can be operated by the public.

Just beyond the castle grounds, the **Himeji City Museum of Literature** pays tribute to nine influential local writers, but it is more notable for its architecture, designed by one of Japan's most respected contemporary architects, Ando Tadao (see p29).

On the nearby hill called Shoshazan, **Shoshazan Enkyo-ji** is a well-known Buddhist training center and pilgrimage sight. Priceless sculptures include the Kongo Satta, a Buddha image carved in 1395. The Yakushido is the oldest building here, dating from the 14th-century Kamakura period. At the foot of the hill is **Shosha Art and Craft Museum**, with traditional crafts and toys from all over Japan, and craft demonstrations by artisans on Sundays and public holidays.

Gables
Dormer gables combined with Chinese arched gables create an undulating effect.

Latticed Windows
Latticed bay windows, called *degoshimado*, are on the first level above the basement.

🟢 **Koko-en Garden**
Castle grounds, W of main entrance. **Tel** (079) 289-4120. **Open** daily.

▦ **Hyogo Prefectural Museum of History**
Just behind castle. **Tel** (079) 288-9011.

▦ **Himeji Museum of Literature**
84 Yamanoi-cho, NW of castle. **Tel** (079) 293-8228. **Open** Tue–Sun.

▦ **Shosha Art and Craft Museum**
Tel (079) 267-0301. **Open** Tue–Sun.

Koraku-en Garden in Okayama, with carefully landscaped mounds and an artificial lake

⑫ Inbe
伊部

Okayama prefecture. 🚶 38,000.
🚉 ℹ in Inbe JR stn (0869) 64-1100.
🎎 Bizen-yaki Matsuri (Pottery Festival, 3rd weekend in Oct).

The home of Bizen pottery, Inbe has a huge range of shops, galleries, and kilns. Originating in the Kamakura period, Bizen-ware is earthy, unglazed, and prized by tea-ceremony enthusiasts. The **Bizen Pottery Traditional and Contemporary Art Museum**, near the station, has modern pieces and superb examples from the Muromachi, Momoyama, and Edo periods.

🏛 **Bizen Pottery Museum**
Tel (0869) 64-1400. **Open** daily.
Closed Mon. 🎫

⑬ Okayama
岡山

Okayama prefecture. 🚶 693,000.
✈ 🚉 ℹ outside JR stn (086) 222-2912. 🎎 Saidai-ji Eyo (3rd weekend in Feb). 🌐 city.okayama.jp

The former center of a domain ruled by the feudal Ikeda family, Okayama today is a vibrant modern city, much visited by Japanese tourists who come to marvel at the **Seto Ohashi Bridge** (see 193), connecting Okayama with Shikoku, which is over 13 km (8 miles) long. Trains now reduce the crossing time, which used to take an hour by ferry, to 30 minutes. The

main sights are just over 1 km (half a mile) east of the station.

A highlight is the **Koraku-en Garden**, one of Japan's "famous three" gardens. Commissioned by Lord Ikeda, it was completed in 1700. Though a classic stroll garden, it was the first in Japan to use large expanses of lawn in the overall design. The garden is divided into three sections and features bamboo, pine, plum, and cherry trees, along with tea bushes. The nearby castle is incorporated into the composition as "borrowed scenery," a classic device in Japanese gardens. Also included are streams and a pond crossed by an elegant red bridge.

Okayama Castle is nicknamed the "Crow's Castle" due to its black walls. Destroyed in World War II, the exterior of the 16th-century castle was faithfully reconstructed in 1966. The interior has an authentic period collection of palanquins, samurai helmets, swords, and the like. Visitor facilities include an elevator to the top of the four-story keep, and in the river below the castle,

The reconstructed keep of Okayama castle, with its striking black walls

rental paddleboats shaped like swans and teacups. More items owned by the Ikeda clan, notably armor, swords, pottery, lacquerware, and a collection of Noh costumes, are on view at the **Hayashibara Museum of Art**, just south of the castle.

To the northeast is the **Orient Museum**, tracing how Near-Eastern art reached and influenced Japan via the Silk Route. The nearby **Okayama Prefectural Museum of Art** has an interesting collection of mostly 20th-century Japanese paintings and a few works by older artists including the 15th-century master Sesshu.

🌳 **Koraku-en Garden**
🚋 Koraku-en-mae stop.
Open daily. 🎫

🏯 **Okayama Castle**
Open daily. 🎫

🏛 **Hayashibara Museum of Art**
Open Tue–Sun. 🎫

🏛 **Orient Museum**
Tel (086) 232-3636. **Open** Tue–Sun. 🎫

🏛 **Okayama Prefectural Museum of Art**
Tel (086) 225-4800. **Open** Tue–Sun. 🎫

⑭ Kurashiki
倉敷

Okayama prefecture. 🚶 478,000.
🚉 ℹ North building, 2nd Floor (1-7-2 Achi) (086) 424-1220.
🌐 city.kurashiki.okayama.jp

Civic pride and a strong preservation ethic have saved the Edo-period mercantile town of Kurashiki from the development that has swept away so much of Japan's architectural heritage. Kurashiki means "storehouse village," a reference to the dozens of granaries (kura), characterized by mortar and black-tiled walls, that are the main feature of the town.

In the heart of the old city, the **Bikan Historical Area** just south of the station, 200-year-old kura flank a tranquil canal lined with willows. Many of the kura have been converted into galleries, restaurants, Japanese inns, and tasteful shops and boutiques. The largest commercial conversion, a short walk from the canal, is **Kurashiki Ivy Square**, a complex of shops, restaurants, hotels, museums, and an orchid center housed in the former Kurabo Textile Mill.

In the old district the finest museum is the **Ohara Museum of Art**. The collection was commissioned by industrialist Ohara Magosaburo in 1930 on the premise that great art should be accessible – even to the people of a relative backwater such as Kurashiki. It includes some rare works by the likes of Matisse, Renoir, Picasso, Degas, and Gauguin. Some genuine masterpieces, like El Greco's The Annunciation, are here. The annex, converted from a traditional storehouse, houses an outstanding collection of works from Japan's mingei (or folk-craft) movement, among them ceramic objects crafted by Hamada Shoji, Kawai Kanjiro, and Bernard Leach, founders

Asian exhibits at the Japan Rural Toy Museum, Kurashiki

of the movement in the early 20th century.

The **Kurashiki Archaeological Museum** occupies an old kura by the canal and includes items excavated in the region along with comparative objects from elsewhere in the world. In the **Kurashiki Folk Art Museum** are folk crafts housed in connecting kura. The **Japan Rural Toy Museum** has a delightful and extensive display of traditional old toys, both international and Japanese. Several of the latter are painted red, a defense, it was believed, against smallpox. A charming shop near the entrance sells traditional toys. **Kurashiki Tivoli Park**, by the north exit of the station, is an immensely popular Danish theme park.

Woven rush shoes from Kurashiki

🏛 **Ohara Museum of Art**
Tel (086) 422-0005.
Open Tue–Sun. 🖼

🏛 **Archaeological Museum**
Tel (086) 422-1542.
Open Tue–Sun. 🖼

🏛 **Folk Art Museum**
Open Tue–Sun. 🖼

🏛 **Japan Rural Toy Museum**
Open daily. 🖼

🎡 **Kurashiki Tivoli Park**
Tel (086) 434-1111. **Open** variable. 🖼

⑮ Fukiya
吹屋

Okayama prefecture, Takahashi city.
🚌 from Bitchu Takahashi.

A prosperous boom town at the center of a local copper and red-ochre mining industry in the 19th century, Fukiya is now a rustic hamlet tucked into some of the area's most beautiful mountain countryside. Well-to-do mine owners and merchants put much of their wealth into build-ing grand houses. Characterized by white plaster walls and red-ocher colored lattice-work windows and doors, these distinctive buildings, the work of master carpenters, are the village's main cultural asset.

Several are open to the public, including the former house of the ocher-rich Katayama family, now Fukiya's **Local History Museum**, several renovated stores, and an old plaster-and-tile schoolhouse. One of the prefecture's six International Villas, an inn based on the design of a traditional soy sauce ware-house, is in Fukiya.

Just outside the village is a copper and ocher mine, which can be visited. An unusual Edo-period home called the **Hirokane-tei**, about 4 km (2 miles) outside, resembles a fortified chateau.

🏛 **Local History Museum**
Open daily. 🖼

🏛 **Hirokane-tei**
Open daily. 🖼

One of Kurashiki's storehouses, now a shop

View across Lake Biwa toward hotels on the shore

⓰ Lake Biwa
琵琶湖

Shiga prefecture. 🚉 ℹ️ outside Otsu stn (077) 522-3830. 🎏 Sanno Matsuri (Apr 12–15, Otsu).

With a total mass of 674 sq km (263 sq miles), and a depth at some points of 105 m (340 ft) Biwa-ko, Japan's largest lake, covers an area greater than any Japanese city, including Tokyo. A calm expanse of water dotted with islets, the lake is named after the *biwa*, a Japanese musical instrument whose outline it is said to resemble. In the 15th century the highlights of Lake Biwa were named Omi Hakkei, "the eight views of Omi." Although development has changed some of these views radically, Lake Biwa is still one of Western Honshu's most beautiful places, its shore fringed with shrines, temples, hotels, and modest pensions. **Lake Biwa**

Windsurfing on Lake Biwa

Museum gives visitors a chance to learn more about this ancient lake.

  Otsu, on the southwest edge, is the lake shore's largest city with a population of nearly 336,000. Visitors come here to see **Onjo** Temple with its huge gates. Also in Otsu is **Ishiyama-dera** Temple, which has some 8th-century buildings. Murasaki Shikibu, author of the *Tale of Genji*, is believed to have used one of the chambers of the Main Hall in which to write her early 11th-century masterpiece.

  Hikone, on the lake's eastern shore, has the 17th-century **Hikone Castle**, remarkable for retaining its original structure

virtually intact. From the top floor of the keep is a superb view of Lake Biwa.

🏛 **Hikone Castle**
Open daily. 🎏

🏛 **Lake Biwa Museum**
Open 9:30am–5pm Tue–Sun. 🎏

⓱ Amanohashidate Sand Bar
天橋立

Kyoto prefecture. 🚉 Amanohashidate. ℹ️ at Amanohashidate stn (0772) 22-8030.

One of the highlights of Miyatsu Bay, along the San-in coast, is Amanohashidate, the "bridge of heaven." The 4-km (2-mile) pine-studded sand bar separates the bay from Asoumi lagoon. According to Japanese mythology, Amanohashidate is the spot where the gods conceived the Japanese islands. Many writers have used the setting for novels and poetry. Visitors usually take the boat across the lagoon from the pier near the station, then the cable car from the base of

Kasamatsu Park to its hilltop summit, which is the best viewing point of the sand bar. It is said that if you look at Amanohashidate upside down through your legs it seems to be floating in mid-air.

⓲ Tottori Sand Dunes
鳥取砂丘

Tottori prefecture. 🚉 Tottori. 🚌 from stn to entrance to dunes. ℹ️ at Tottori stn (0857) 22-3318.

A huge expanse of wavy, sahara-brown and yellow undulations, the Tottori sand dunes stretch for 16 km (10 miles) along the San-in coast. To the Japanese, the towering dunes, some rising to 90 m (300 ft), and the shifting patterns and shadows formed across the sand, are lyrical reminders of the human condition. Abe Kobo's powerful existential novel, *The Woman in the Dunes* (1962), made into a classic Japanese film, is set here. Commercialization has inevitably hit the area – head east acrosss the dunes or rent a bike for a quieter experience.

⓳ Matsue
松江

Shimane prefecture. 🚹 193,000. ✈️ Yonago and Izumo. 🚉 ℹ️ at Matsue JR stn (0852) 21-4034. 🎏 Matsue Castle Festival (Mar–Apr), Doh Drum Festival (Nov 3). 🌐 **city.matsue.shimane.jp/**

Situated at the intersection of Lake Shinji with Miho bay and Nakaumi

The towering keep of Matsue Castle

Lafcadio Hearn's residence with its well-tended garden, in Matsue

Matsue Castle
Kencho-mae stop. **Tel** (0852) 21-4030. **Open** daily.

Buke Yashiki
Tel (0852) 22-2243.

Meimei-an Teahouse
Tel (0852) 21-9863. **Open** daily.

Tanabe Art Museum
Tel (0852) 26-2211. **Open** Tue–Sun.

Lafcadio Hearn Residence
Tel (0852) 23-0714. **Open** daily.

Lafcadio Hearn Memorial Hall
Tel (0852) 21-2147. **Open** daily.

lagoon, Matsue is, not surprisingly, also known as the "water city." Rarely included in the itineraries of foreign visitors, the area has several worthwhile cultural features. Matsue is referred to at length in *Glimpses of Unfamiliar Japan* (1894), by Lafcadio Hearn, a journalist of Irish-Greek descent who spent 15 months in the town.

Hearn described **Matsue Castle** in the colorful superlatives that mark his style as "a veritable architectural dragon, made up of magnificent monstrosities." One of the few in Japan to remain intact, the castle was built in 1611 of pine and stone, then partially reconstructed 31 years later. Its five-story keep is Japan's tallest.

Within 5 minutes' walk of the castle are two more modest architectural gems. The **Buke Yashiki** is an interesting mansion built in 1730 by the Shiomi family, who were chief retainers at the castle. Furniture and household items provide an insight into their life. Above Shiome Nawate street is the **Meimei-an Teahouse** (1779), one of Japan's oldest and best preserved. Along the same street is the **Tanabe Art Museum**, with a refined collection of tea bowls and other tea-related objects.

Just north of the castle, the **Lafcadio Hearn Residence** is beautifully preserved. Its immaculate garden inspired one of Hearn's most engaging essays, *In A Japanese Garden*. Beside the house, the **Lafcadio Hearn Memorial Hall** has a good collection of his memorabilia, including such items as manuscripts, photos, and his desk and smoking pipes.

⑳ Izumo
出雲

Shimane prefecture. 148,000. at Taisha-mae stn; (0853) 53-2298. Daisairei (May 14–16), Kamiari Festival (11–17th days of 10th lunar month).

Alive with myths, legends, and tales of the supernatural, Izumo, known until the 3rd century as the "eightfold-towering-thunderhead land," has an enthralling heritage. The town is well known throughout Japan for the **Izumo Taisha Grand Shrine**, one of the most revered and oldest Shinto shrines in the country. It is dedicated to Okuninushi-no-Mikoto, a deity who is closely associated with agriculture and medicine, as well as

marriage – the latter explaining the popularity of the shrine for wedding ceremonies. The entrance to the shrine, through 11 torii (gates), is impressive. Unusually tall, the **Honden** (Main Hall) is not open to the public, although the **Treasure House** can be visited. The shrine's environs are sacred and therefore ecologically pristine, with towering cryptomeria trees surrounding the main compound. Just east of the shrine are a number of old houses occupied by priests who serve here. Note the traditional clay and stone walls.

Just past the shrine, on Route 431 to Okuni, there is a **monument** to a nun who is said to have danced on the banks of the Kamo River in Kyoto to raise money for the shrine. The dance was developed into the Kabuki theatrical form (*see pp40–41*).

Izumo Taisha Grand Shrine
Tel (0853) 53-3100. **Open** daily. (Treasure Hall).

Izumo shrine, dominated by the distinctive rafters of the Honden

Lafcadio Hearn

Lafcadio Hearn (1850–1904) arrived in Japan in 1890. He published several books, many of which are still in print and widely read, such as *In Ghostly Japan*, *Japan: An Interpretation*, and *Glimpses of Unfamiliar Japan*. The Japanese continue to be fascinated by Hearn, whose books allowed them for the first time to view their culture through the eyes of a foreigner. He was also one of the foremost interpreters of Japan for the West. A bold and unconventional thinker in his time, he was interested in the folklore and superstitions of Japan. Hearn's first Japanese home was Matsue, where he took up a teaching post, but quickly fell ill. The woman who nursed him back to health – the daughter of a local samurai family – eventually became Hearn's wife. He later acquired Japanese citizenship, changing his name to Koizumi Yakumo.

Writer and journalist Lafcadio Hearn

㉑ Hiroshima

広島

For the worst of reasons, Hiroshima needs no introduction. Each year millions of visitors are drawn to the city where so many people were wiped out in one instant of apocalyptic destruction. An unusual tourist attraction, the sober monuments of Hiroshima can induce an unexpected sense of listlessness and enervation in many visitors. However, there is more to the reconstructed city than its sorrowful atomic legacy.

Hiroshima's Peace Memorial Park and the A-Bomb Dome

The Peace Memorial Museum, with exhibits on the bomb's effects

Exploring Hiroshima

Rather than resurrect the tortuous pre-war streets, the modern city was rebuilt on a grid system, making it easy to negotiate. Trams are the most convenient form of transportation. Downtown Hiroshima lies to the east of the Peace Park. The lively nightlife area of Nagarekawa is not far away.

The A-Bomb Dome, all that remains of the old bombed city

🅒 Peace Memorial Park

🚉 Genbaku-Domu-mae. Museum: **Tel** (082) 241-4004. **Open** 8:30am–6pm daily (Aug: to 7pm; Dec–Feb: to 5pm). 🈂

Located at the confluence of the Honkawa and Motoyasu rivers, just outside the park proper, the **A-Bomb Dome** is a haunting reminder of the destructive forces that were unleashed on the city. The former Industrial Promotion Hall stood close to the hypocenter, or ground zero, the point at which the bomb exploded. The occupants of the building were killed instantly. Its twisted girders, gaping holes, and piles of rubble have been preserved as a UNESCO World Heritage Site.

By the northern entrance to the park is the **Peace Bell**, which visitors can ring themselves. Nearby is the **Memorial Mound** containing the ashes of tens of thousands of people cremated on this spot. Farther into the park is the **Children's Peace Monument**, depicting a girl with outstretched hands. A crane, the Japanese symbol of longevity and happiness, passes above her. The work refers to the story of a child victim of the bomb who believed that if she could make 1,000 paper cranes she would recover from her illness. The girl did not survive, but her story is known throughout Japan, and fresh paper cranes sent by school children adorn the memorial.

Across the road is the **Flame of Peace**, which will be extinguished only when all nuclear weapons have been eliminated from the earth. Adjacent to it is the **Cenotaph**, designed by Kenzo Tange, for the victims of the bomb. It contains the names of all those who died, together with an inscription that reads "Rest in peace. We will never repeat the error."

The centerpiece of the park is the **Peace Memorial Museum**. This graphically explains the consequences of the bomb on the city by means of photos, videos, and the victims' personal

The Bombing of Hiroshima

As World War II dragged on into the summer of 1945, the US decided to deploy an entirely new weapon to force Japan to surrender. On August 6 a B29 bomber dropped the first atomic bomb on Hiroshima, a city that had seen little conventional bombing. It exploded at 8:15am, 580 m (1,900 ft) above the city center. Tens of thousands of people were killed instantly by the blast, and the death toll rose to 180–200,000 over the following years as after-effects took hold. Nagasaki (see pp244–5) suffered a similar fate three days later.

The ruins of Hiroshima in 1945, all but flattened by the atomic blast

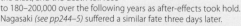

effects. Poignant exhibits include a half-melted bronze Buddha, a mangled tricycle, and the imprint of a dark shadow on the granite steps of the Sumitomo Bank building – the sole remains of someone who was sitting there at the time.

Outside the museum are the so-called **Phoenix trees** which were growing 1.5 km (1 mile) from the hypocenter. Transplanted here since, they still show scorch marks on one side of their crowns.

Other Sights in Hiroshima

A look at the city's other attractions helps to dispel the gloom that descends on some visitors to the Peace Memorial Park. A relaxing spot is the **Shukkei-en** stroll garden. Its pond, islets, streams, miniature bridges, and pine-studded banks carefully replicate scenes from a legendary lake in China.

The Flame of Peace, fringed by sculpted bushes

Hiroshima Castle was destroyed in the bomb, but a faithful reconstruction was completed in 1958. The **Museum of Contemporary Art** was designed by world-renowned Japanese architect Kurokawa Kisho and houses a collection of modern, post-war art. An outdoor sculpture garden is attached to the museum. The fascinating **Hiroshima Children's Museum** has lots of hands-on equipment and displays.

VISITORS' CHECKLIST

Practical Information
Hiroshima prefecture.
🗺 1,172,000. 🛈 at Memorial Park.(082) 247-6738.
🎭 Flower Festival (May 3, 4, 5); Peace Memorial Ceremony (Aug 6). 🖥 hiroshima-navi.or.jp

Transport
✈ Hiroshima airport 40 km (25 miles) E. 🚉 Shinkansen line. 🚢

🌼 **Shukkei-en Garden**
Nr Shukkei-en-mae stop.
Open daily. 🖼

🏯 **Hiroshima Castle**
🚋 Kamiya-cho. **Open** daily. 🖼

🏛 **Museum of Contemporary Art**
🚋 Hijiyama-shita. **Open** Tue–Sun. 🖼

🏛 **Hiroshima Children's Museum**
10-min walk from Genbaku-dome mae. **Open** Tue–Sun.

Peace Memorial Park

The park was built in the 1950s, covering an area close to the hypocenter of the blast. The half-melted wreckage of the Industrial Promotion Hall (A-Bomb Dome) is the only remnant from the destruction. Scores of monuments have been erected on behalf of different groups of victims. The main memorials of interest to foreign visitors are shown here.

The Cenotaph, erected in memory of the victims of the bombing

Sights at a Glance

① A-Bomb Dome
② Peace Bell
③ Memorial Mound
④ Children's Peace Monument
⑤ Flame of Peace
⑥ Cenotaph
⑦ Phoenix Trees
⑧ Peace Memorial Museum

0 meters	250
0 yards	250

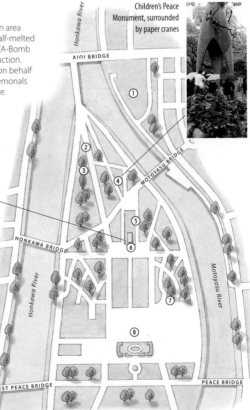

Children's Peace Monument, surrounded by paper cranes

Honkawa River

AIOI BRIDGE

MOTOYASU BRIDGE

HONKAWA BRIDGE

Honkawa River

Motoyasu River

WEST PEACE BRIDGE

PEACE BRIDGE

㉒ Miyajima Island

Miyajima, as this sacred island is commonly known, means shrine island, although its official name is Itsukushima. A UNESCO World Heritage Site, it is symbolized by Itsukushima Shrine's prominent vermilion *Otorii* (Grand Gate) rising from the sea during low tide. Felling trees is forbidden so the island has maintained its virgin forest and provides a home to a variety of flora and fauna, while tame deer roam freely.

★ Itsukushima Shrine
This famous shrine, founded in 593, is built on stilts over a cove. It is best viewed at high tide when the buildings are reflected in the sea. Part of the deck facing the bay includes an old Noh stage.

★ Five-Story Pagoda
On a bluff overlooking the shrine is the Goju-no-to, a five-story pagoda built in 1407. Next to it is the Senjokaku, or "pavilion of the thousand tatami mats," built in 1587.

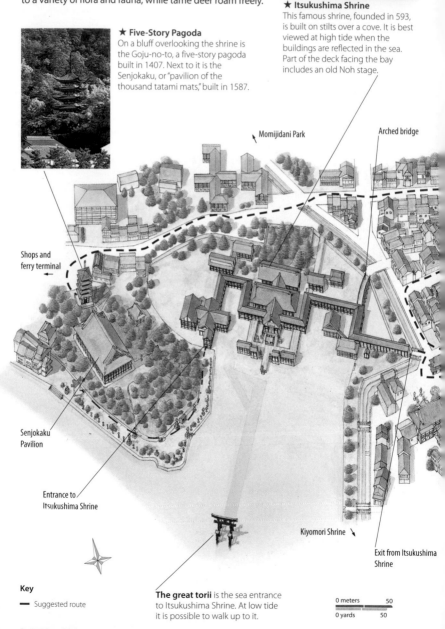

↖ Momijidani Park

Arched bridge

Shops and ferry terminal ←

Senjokaku Pavilion

Entrance to Itsukushima Shrine

Kiyomori Shrine ↘

Exit from Itsukushima Shrine

Key

— Suggested route

The great torii is the sea entrance to Itsukushima Shrine. At low tide it is possible to walk up to it.

| 0 meters | 50 |
| 0 yards | 50 |

Mount Misen
On the slopes behind the shrine is Momijidani ("maple leaf valley")
Park. A cable-car station in the park goes to the summit of Mount
Misen, where there are superb views of the Seto Inland Sea *(see p228)*.
There are also several nature trails on the mountainside.

VISITORS' CHECKLIST

Practical Information
Hiroshima prefecture. 🛈 at
ferry terminal (0829) 44-2011.
🎴 Kangensai Music Festival
(Jul, or Aug – varies). All sights:
Open daily. 🎴
🅦 visit-miyajima-japan.com

Transport
🚆 from Hiroshima to Miyajima-
guchi, then ferry. 🛳 from
Hiroshima port or Miyajima-
guchi stn.

Mount Misen
nature trails

Daisho-in Temple is a delightful complex
with an eclectic mix of Buddhist statuary.
It is blissfully peaceful, away from the crowds
of the waterfront and Itsukushima Shrine.

Treasure House
This building, completed in
1934, houses a valuable
collection of gifts presented
to the shrine by the Taira
clan and other patrons
over the centuries.

Two-story Tahoto Pagoda

Miyajima Aquarium

**Municipal History and
Folklore Museum**
Housed in a beautiful mid-
19th century mansion is a
collection of artworks, household utensils, and furniture.

The Famous Floating Torii

Acclaimed by the Japanese as one of the country's
three most scenic views (Nihon Sankei), the *torii* of
Itsuku-shima Shrine appears to float in the water. (The
sand bar Amanohashidate, *see p216*, and Matsushima
Bay, *see p280*, are the two other famous sights.) The

The *torii* at dusk

warlord Taira no Kiyomori,
who provided funds for
the shrine, built the first
torii in the bay in the
12th century. The present
structure dates from
1875 and is about 16 m
(50 ft) high. Its four-
legged (*yo-tsuashi*)
style provides stability.

23 Iwakuni

岩国

Yamaguchi prefecture. 150,100. Sanyo Shinkansen line to Shin-Iwakuni, JR Sanyo line to Iwakuni. at 2F bus terminal near Iwakuni stn, (082) 721-6050.

The town of Iwakuni's main draw is the elegant **Kintai-kyo**, or "brocade sash" bridge. It earns its name from the rippling effect created by its five linked arches. The original structure, built in 1673, was destroyed by a typhoon in 1953. Rebuilt in an almost exact replica of the original, the bridge depends on first-rate joinery and an invisible quantity of reinforced steel.

Beyond the bridge in **Kikko Park** are a number of samurai houses, including the beautiful **Mekata House**. A short stroll west of the park lies **Iwakuni Art Museum**, housing an impressive display of armor and weapons. A cable car takes visitors to **Iwakuni Castle**, a faithful 1962 reconstruction of the original 1608 donjon. There is a good view from here of the town and surrounding countryside and, on fine days, the islands of the Inland Sea.

Mekata House
Open Tue–Sun.

Iwakuni Art Museum
Tel (0827) 41-0506.
Open Fri–Wed.

24 Yamaguchi

山口

Yamaguchi prefecture. 190,000. Yamaguchi stn, 2nd Floor, (083) 933-0090. Gion Matsuri (Jul 20–27). **yamaguchi-city.jp/w/en/index.html**

Laid out in the 14th century, Yamaguchi was modeled on Kyoto. When the Jesuit Francis Xavier visited here in 1550 he found a city of incredible wealth and sophistication. The **Xavier Memorial Chapel**, built in 1952, marks the 400th anniversary of the priest's two-month stay. The painter Sesshu (1420–1506) designed a garden for the temple of **Joei-ji** on the outskirts of town. To the north of Yamaguchi, the temple of **Ruriko-ji** has a Japanese cypress-wood, five-story pagoda. Nearby is a set of tombs belonging to the Mori family, another influential clan.

25 Akiyoshi-dai Tablelands

秋吉台

Yamaguchi prefecture. from Yamaguchi. at bus stn (0837) 62-0304.

Akiyoshi-dai is a massive limestone plateau of grassland and rocky outcrops, which tour buses pass on their way to **Akiyoshido Cave**, one of the largest limestone grottos in Asia. The cave is 10 km (6 miles) deep, only 1 km (half a mile) is

In the limestone Akiyoshido Cave in the Akiyoshi-dai Tablelands

open to the public. Passageways are well lit, and a clear map is provided.

Akiyoshido Cave
Tel (0837) 62-0304. **Open** daily.

26 Hagi

萩

Yamaguchi prefecture. 53,000 (0838) 25-1750. Hagi-yaki Festival (May 1–5).

An intensely cultural city, Hagi was a minor fishing port until Mori Terumoto fortified it in 1604. Mori samurai helped spark off the anti-Tokugawa revolt in the mid-19th century, and many of Meiji Japan's

Five-arched "brocade sash" bridge at Iwakuni

For hotels and restaurants see pp302–307 and pp324–339

founding fathers came from Hagi. Today it is best known for its over 400-year-old pottery-making tradition. Hagi's charm is in the details: its teahouses, mossy cemeteries, and the tiny, purple bloom of bush clover (*hagi*), the town's namesake.

The central **Teramachi** district contains old temples and shrines, each with its own special features. **Jonen-ji** is noted for its finely carved gate, **Hofuku-ji** its bibbed Jizo statues, **Kyotoku-ji** for its immaculate garden, and **Choju-ji** for an atmospheric cemetery. Camellias and *natsu mikan* (summer oranges) hanging over long, whitewashed mud walls typify the **samurai quarters** to the west of Teramachi. Several residences are located here, including the homes of the Kido and Takasugi families, and **Kikuya House**, a merchant villa with a small museum and beautiful garden attached. The **Ishii Tea Bowl Museum** has a superb ceramics collection.

Wealthy merchants appointed by the Mori clan once owned the fine collection in the **Kumaya Art Museum** to the north of here. It includes teaceremony utensils, literati paintings, and screens.

Little remains of the original **Hagi Castle** – about 4 km (2 miles) west of Higashi-Hagi station – except its stone walls and broad moat. The picnic grounds include **Hagijo Kiln**, a good place to watch potters at work. Beside the castle walls **Hananoe Tea House** is a lovely thatched-roof building, where green tea is served in local ware.

Cemetery of Toko-ji temple near Hagi

🏛 **Kikuya House**
Open daily.

🏛 **Ishii Tea Bowl Museum**
Open Thu–Tue.

🏛 **Kumaya Art Museum**
Open Tue–Sun.

Environs
East of the river is the house of Yoshida Shoin, an influential late-Edo educator, philosopher, and revolutionary. **Shoin shrine** and **memorial** are dedicated to him. The nearby temple of **Toko-ji**, with its impressive three-story gate, was founded in 1691 by the third Mori lord. The Mori tombs are at the end of a path flanked by almost 500 stone lanterns.

The natural salt-water **Myojin Lagoon** is 5 km (3 miles) from town. A volcano, **Mount Kasayama**, stands beside the far end of the lake.

Yoshida Shoin monument, outside Hagi

㉗ Tsuwano
津和野

Shimane prefecture. 🚗 9,200. 🚉 i next to Tsuwano stn (0856) 72-1771. 🎭 Sagimai (Heron Dance Festival, Jul 20, 24, 27).

This tiny 700-year old former castle town, tucked into a river valley deep in the mountains,

has a large number of well-preserved samurai houses. Thousands of carp inhabit the town's brooks, outnumbering the residents, it is said, by ten to one. Tsuwano's **Catholic Church** (1931) commemorates 36 Japanese Christians who were martyred here in 1868.

On the other side of town, the hillside **Taikodani Inari Shrine** is one of the most important Inari (fox) shrines in Japan. It is reached through a tunnel of vermilion torii (gates), 1,174 in all. A cable car goes up the other side of the slope to the scant remains of **Tsuwano Castle** with a stunning view from the top.

Nishi Amane (1829–97), a Meiji-period statesman and philosopher, was born here. **Nishi House**, now a museum, is on a quiet street in the south of town. Opposite is **Mori Ougai House**, a museum to the army surgeon, writer, and translator Mori Ogai (1862–1922), known for novels such as *The Wild Geese* and *Vita Sexualis*, and also a Tsuwano native.

🏛 **Nishi House**
Open Mon. **Closed** Dec–mid-Mar.

🏛 **Mori Ougai House**
Tel (0856) 72-3210. **Open** daily.

Taikodani Inari Shrine in the town of Tsuwano

Hagi's Ceramic Arts

Hagi's first kilns date from the Heian period, but the town's reputation for refined tea vessels and other wares began in the 16th century with the introduction of apprentice potters from Korea. A distinguishing mark of *hagi-yaki* (Hagi-ware) is its translucent glaze. *Hagi-yaki* improves with age, the muted pinks and pastels of the stoneware softening to beiges and umbers as tannin from the tea soaks through the porous glaze. Members of some of Hagi's oldest families, like the Sakas and Miwas, have been designated Living National Treasures.

Hagi's pink stoneware

SHIKOKU

For centuries, the Seto Inland Sea formed a natural barrier isolating Japan's fourth largest island from much of the forces of population growth and Westernization. Still relatively off the tourist track, despite the construction of bridges across the water, Shikoku offers a nostalgic glimpse of fishing and farming villages, and of rice paddies set against a backdrop of forested hills, castles, and temples.

Late Paleolithic sites and *kofun* (tumuli) dating from the 3rd century AD are evidence of early human activity on Shikoku. The Dogo Onsen (spa) in Matsuyama is referred to in the *Kojiki*, Japan's oldest chronicle, written in 712. Despite such ancient sites, however, Shikoku has mainly been on the margin of Japanese history. The island's most famous figure is Kukai, who was born into a poor aristrocratic Shikoku family in 774. This Buddhist priest, who has been called the Father of Japanese Culture, visited 88 of the island's temples in a pilgrimage that has been imitated by others for more than a thousand years.

In 1183, as chronicled in the *Tale of the Heike*, the war between the Taira and Minamoto clans for dominance of Japan spilled over into the Inland Sea and Shikoku. Some of the defeated Taira went into hiding in a gorge in central Shikoku, where many of their descendants still live. Farmland and mountains continue to dominate Shikoku's landscape, although agriculture employs only three percent of the island's four million residents. Assembly of autos and manufacture of electronic goods, particularly in the ports along the Seto Inland Sea, are the most important industries. Other industries include fruit farming (mandarin oranges in particular), seaweed and pearl cultivation, and food and chemical processing.

Shikoku's coastline remains relatively unspoiled, despite construction altering most of Japan's coastal areas. The capes that jut into the Pacific, Muroto to the east and Ashizuri to the west, offer panoramic vistas rarely seen in Japan.

Shikoku is connected to Honshu by the Great Seto Bridge and two other bridges.

Matsuyama Castle, first built in 1603 and reconstructed in 1835 after a lightning strike

◀ The vibrant shades of green rice paddies in Shikoku

Exploring Shikoku

Shikoku's north coast facing the Inland Sea is much more industrialized than its south coast, though not as much as Western Honshu's Sanyo coast. The interior of the island is mountainous and rugged and not conducive to rice cultivation. Shikoku's main cities and historical sights, including most temples on the pilgrimage circuit, are thus on or near the Seto Inland Sea coast. Takamatsu is a popular entry point. Kochi is the main city on the Pacific coast.

Vine suspension bridge at Shikoku Mura village, near Takamatsu

Reclining image of the Buddha at Uchiko

Key

- ≈ Expressway
- ▬ Major road
- ▬ Other road
- ═ Main railway
- ── Minor railway
- ▬ Border

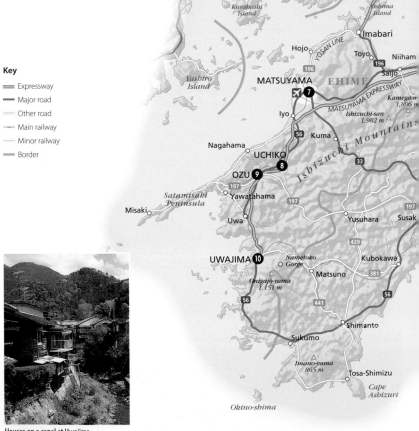

Houses on a canal at Uwajima, western Shikoku

Getting Around

Taking a direct train from Okayama to Takamatsu, via the Seto-Ohashi Bridge, is the most popular gateway for tourists traveling from Honshu to Shikoku. Matsuyama, the island's main city, has an airport with good links to other parts of Japan. There is no *shinkansen* line, but the other types of train lines are efficient and connect all the main towns. However, unless you plan to emulate walkers on the 88-Temple Pilgrimage, it is best to rent a car to explore the mountainous interior and visit the rugged southern capes.

Locator Map

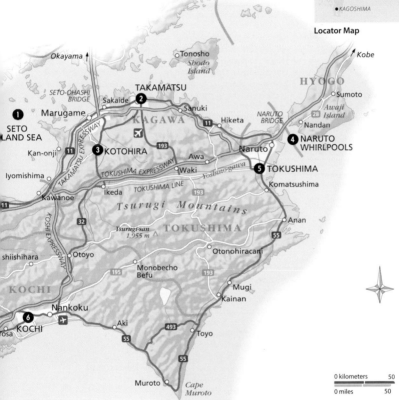

Seto-Ohashi Bridge near Takamatsu, joining Shikoku to Honshu

Sights at a Glance

1. Seto Inland Sea
2. Takamatsu
3. Kotohira
4. Naruto Whirlpools
5. Tokushima
6. Kochi
7. Matsuyama
8. Uchiko
9. Ozu
10. Uwajima

Pilgrimage Route

The 88-Temple Pilgrimage
pp232–3

For keys to symbols *see back flap*

Typical view of islands in the so-called Seto Inland Sea, which separates Shikoku from Honshu and Kyushu

❶ Seto Inland Sea
瀬戸内海

Setonaikai-kisen (Inland Sea cruises): (082) 253-1212.

The Seto Inland Sea, Japan's most beautiful body of water, is not landlocked, as its name suggests, but seems almost one with its serene waters and over 3,000 pine-studded islands. Donald Richie, in his classic travelogue *The Inland Sea* (1971), sets the scene of a boat journey westward through the narrow defiles of water: "On the left are first the sharp and Chinese-looking mountains of the island of Shikoku, so different that it appears another land, and then the flat coasts of Kyushu. This shallow sea is a valley among these mountainous islands."

You can cycle along a path that stretches from Onomichi to Imabari. Bridges, local ferries, and cruise boats provide access to the 750 or so inhabited islands. The remote fishing villages on these islands, with their salt-weathered wooden houses and black ceramic-tiled

roofs, seem to hail from a different era. Among the most visited are **Awaji**, the largest island, **Setoda**, **Omi**, and **Shodo**, a beautiful island that, with its olive and orange groves, seems to belong more to the Mediterranean than the Orient.

❷ Takamatsu
高松

Kagawa prefecture. ⚑ 427,000. ✈ ⚑ ⓘ at JR stn (087) 851-2009. ⚑ Sanuki Takamatsu Matsuri (Aug 12–14).

The capital of Kagawa prefecture on the Inland Sea, Takamatsu is the main hub between Shikoku and the outside world. Nonetheless, it maintains a local charm with its neighborhood shops and historic landmarks. The town expanded after Ikoma Chikamasa erected **Takamatsu Castle** in 1588, the remains of which can still be seen. When the Tokugawa shoguns assumed power in 1600, they granted the town, castle, and surrounding fiefdom to their relatives, the

Matsudaira clan. The family devoted nearly a century to landscaping the six ponds and 13 artificial hillocks that make **Ritsurin Garden** the city's most famous landmark.

Takamatsu's location as an entry port for Shikoku made it the setting for such historic battles as the one between the Minamoto and the Taira clans in 1185. The **Wax Museum of the Tale of the Heike** offers a surprisingly effective recreation of the story's high points, which are also the subject matter of the classic Noh play *Yashima*.

Wax Museum
Tel (087) 823-8400. **Open** daily. ⚑

Environs
At Yashima volcanic plateau, **Shikoku Mura** is a village where immaculately preserved buildings and other artifacts of rural life display Shikoku craftsmanship.

Shikoku Mura
Tel (087) 843-3111. ⚑ Kotoden Yashima stn. **Open** daily. ⚑

❸ Kotohira
琴平

Kagawa prefecture. ⚑ 9,800. ⚑ Kotohira stn . ⚑ Kotohira-gu Reitaisai (Grand Festival, Oct 9–11). ⓦ **town.kotohira.kagawa.jp/ pages/language**

Kotohira, which can be reached by train via either the old-fashioned Kotoden or the JR line from Takamatsu, is the home of famous shrine complex **Kotohira-gu**, also affectionately known as

Bridge within the landscaped grounds of Ritsurin Park, Takamatsu

Palanquin on the steps leading up to Kompira-san

Konpira-san, the spiritual guardian of seafarers. The target of pilgrimages for centuries, the shrine now attracts four million visitors per year and is believed to bestow good luck upon fishermen and sailors.

A 785-stair climb (or ride in one of the palanquins available) takes visitors up the rugged mountainside to the shrine, set in beautiful grounds. Within the complex, the Asahi shrine is built of zelkova, a rock-hard wood that forms an excellent medium for carved relief work. The nearby Omote Shoin and Oku Shoin have celebrated screen paintings by Maruyama Okyo. The first presents burly tigers bristling with Zen energy, the second includes a waterfall flowing across a corner of the room.

The oldest Kabuki theater in Japan, the **Kanamaru-za**, can also be found in the town.

Votive hall at Konpira-san, near Kotohira

Awa-Odori Dancing

Tokushima's celebrations for O-Bon, the festival of the dead on August 12–15, are the liveliest in Japan. Special dances, called Awa-Odori, are meant to welcome ancestral spirits on their yearly visit to the land of the living. Nicknamed "the fool's dance" because the refrain "you're a fool whether you dance or not, so you might as well dance" is sung, the Awa-Odori allegedly originated when rice wine was passed out to the townspeople of Tokushima to celebrate completion of a castle.

Awa-Odori dancers, Tokushima

❹ Naruto Whirlpools
鳴門の渦潮

Tokushima prefecture. 🚉 Naruto stn, then bus to Naruto Park 🚢 Uzushio line ferry (088) 687-0613; Aqua Eddy (088) 687-0101.

Where the tip of Awaji Island nearly touches Shikoku – a wedge between Osaka Bay, Seto Inland Sea, Honshu, Shikoku, and the Pacific Ocean – the tidal pull on these distinct bodies of water creates large disparities spawning powerful currents and whirlpools. Navigating the churning waters of this 1.6 km (1-mile) strait has been a part of Shikoku lore for over a millennium.

Sightseeing boats now ply the 20-kmph (13-mph) currents and whirlpools, and provide startling views of the Naruto suspension bridge, part of a bridge system linking Shikoku and Honshu via Awaji Island. When the northern end of the system was completed in 1998, it had stretched 1 m (3 ft) as a result of ground shifts caused by the Kobe earthquake.

At the Awaji end of the bridge, the **Onarutokyo Memorial Hall** includes exhibits of *Awaji ningyo joruri*, a variant of Bunraku puppet theater.

🏛 **Memorial Hall**
Tel (079) 952-2888. **Open** daily. 🎭

❺ Tokushima
徳島

Tokushima prefecture. 🏙 265,000. ✈ 🚉 ℹ 6F Clement Plaza (088) 656-3303. 🎭 Awa-Odori (Awa dancing festival, Aug 12–15). 🌐 city.tokushima.tokushima.jp

Tokushima forms the gateway into Shikoku from the Kansai region of Honshu and is the traditional point of entry for those who set out to duplicate Kukai's pilgrimage (see pp232–3). The old name of the province, Awa, gives its name to the town's Awa-Odori celebration in August, which is broadcast nationwide.

Environs
South of Tokushima, the **Anan Coast** is known for fishing villages, beaches, and the sea turtles that lay and hatch eggs from June to August.

The impressive suspension bridge at Naruto, completed in 1985

Flooded rice fields in the shadow of gentle forested hills, near Kochi

⑥ Kochi

高地

Kochi prefecture. 🏔 345,000. ✈
🚉 ℹ at JR stn (088) 882-7777.
🎎 Yosakoi Matsuri (Aug 9–12).

Kochi city offers a rare blend of sandy beaches, mountain views, and well-preserved historic sites.

The Kochi region, formerly called Tosa, is known for its forging of cutlery, and shops selling knives line the street in front of **Kochi Castle**, built in 1603. A startlingly long sword, over 1.5 m (5 ft) in length, is among the weapons on display in the castle. Breathtaking views can be seen from the top floors.

At Katsurahama, a white-sand beach area in the southern part of the city, the **Sakamoto Ryoma Museum** is devoted to the Tosa patriot admired for his part in the overthrow of the shogunate and restoration of the emperor in the 1860s. He was assassinated in 1867. Most Japanese visitors make a point of paying homage at a bronze statue of the man looming over the beach. Also at Katsurahama is the **Tosa Dog Museum**, the venue for the Tosa Fighting Dogs. Dogfights are staged here in a caged enclosure rather like a miniature Sumo wrestling ring. The animals are also paraded in Sumo-like garments. To create the Tosa fighting dog of today, breeders matched its local ancestors with mastiffs and other powerful Western dogs. A photo exhibition documents major events in the history of this sport, including visits by the emperor. The gambling that helped make the fights popular is now illegal, and increasing numbers of people are repulsed by the dogfights.

Statue of patriotic figure Sakamoto Ryoma, Kochi

🏯 **Kochi Castle**
Open 9am–5pm daily. **Closed** Dec 26–Jan 1. 🎫

🏛 **Sakamoto Ryoma Museum**
Open 9am–5pm daily. 🎫

🏛 **Tosa Dog Museum**
Open daily. 🎫 🌐 tosa.or.jp/index.html

Environs

From Kochi, take a day trip to **Cape Muroto** at the southeast tip of Shikoku or **Cape Ashizuri** to the southwest. Both have views of the Pacific Ocean and some unusual rock formations.

⑦ Matsuyama

松山

Ehime prefecture. 🏔 515,000. ✈ 🚉 ℹ at JR stn (089) 917-5678. 🌐 **city. matsuyama.ehime.jp/lang/en**

The capital of Ehime prefecture and a castle town since 1603, Matsuyama has many powerful associations for the Japanese.

The **Dogo Onsen**, a famous hot-spring spa, has been in use for over a millennium, and has a fine 19th-century bathhouse. Deeper into the mountains behind the historic bathhouse, **Oku-Dogo Onsen** is a much newer hotel resort area. Natsume Soseki, an author whose portrait appears on the ¥1,000 bill, moved to Matsuyama in 1895 and later wrote about the town in his autobiographical novel *Botchan* (1906).

The **Shiki Masaoka Museum** is devoted to Soseki's friend Shiki (1867–1902), a Matsuyama native held by many to be Japan's finest modern haiku poet. Shiki was also a fine painter, and the museum's highly visual presentation includes manuscripts, paintings, and photographs of Shiki and Soseki in the city.

Matsuyama Castle is an extensive complex on a bluff overlooking the city and Inland Sea. Plaques offer intelligent commentary on the castle's strategic features.

♨ **Dogo Onsen**
🚋 Dogo stn. **Tel** (089) 921-5141.
Open daily. 🎫

🏛 **Shiki Masaoka Museum**
3-min walk from Dogo Onsen.
Open daily. 🎫

🏯 **Matsuyama Castle**
🚋 Kencho-mae stop, then steep walk, or Shinonome-guchi stop, then cable car or lift. **Tel** (089) 921-4873.
Open daily. 🎫

Exterior of the bathhouse of Dogo Onsen, Matsuyama

Stage of the historic Kabuki Theater in Uchiko

❽ Uchiko

内子

Ehime prefecture. 🏔 20,000. 🚉
ℹ️ Uchiko (0893) 44 3790.
🌐 we-love-uchiko.jp

Located in a small valley where the Oda River splits into three branches, the town of Uchiko is famous for its historic Kabuki theater, the **Uchiko-za**, and its sloping street of two-story wooden buildings with whitewashed walls, tiled roofs, and broad fronts. In 1982 the government moved to ensure the preservation of these structures, which date from the mid-19th century. Several are open to the public, and others function as craft shops and restaurants. The area is often used for location shooting of historical dramas for film and television. A quaint touch is the steam locomotive preserved in front of the station.

Handmade umbrellas, Uchiko

🎭 **Uchiko-za**
Open daily. 📷

❾ Ozu

大洲

Ehime prefecture. 🏔 50,000. 🚉
ℹ️ at JR stn (0893) 24-2111.
🎎 Kawa Matsuri Hanabi Taikai (River Festival Fireworks, Aug 3–4).

A castle town built where the Hiji River snakes in an S-curve through a valley rimmed by picturesque bluffs, Ozu is known to insiders as the "little Kyoto" of Ehime prefecture.

However, whereas it could be argued that Kyoto offers well-preserved relics of Japan's past, Ozu offers a past that is still alive. The riverfront is lined by quaint, narrow streets of tile-roofed bars and restaurants with sliding wood shutters. A riverside villa called **Garyu Sanso**, built in 1907, is one of the most spectacular buildings. On the river itself, shallow-bottomed skiffs shunt cormorant fishermen back and forth through the river breezes. Traditional culture is still the norm in Ozu, where raw silk, dairy products, and vegetables form the basis for the local economy. The town's restaurants serve fish and eel caught in nearby rivers.

The panorama of seasonal change is especially vivid in the wooded hillsides of Ozu. August is marked with a festival

of fireworks launched from an islet in the river.

🏛 **Garyu Sanso**
Open daily. 📷

❿ Uwajima

宇和島

Ehime prefecture. 🏔 89,000. 🚉
ℹ️ 1 min from stn (0895) 22-3934.

Uwajima, a harbor town with a castle, old temple district, and mountain setting, is probably best known for its bullfighting, conducted on a system with ranks modeled on Sumo wrestling. The bullfights are held on six days each year, but a video presentation is available year-round at the **Shiei Togyu-jo**.

The **Taga-Jinja** shrine has famously sexually explicit statues and other objects associated with fertility.

🏟 **Shiei Togyu-jo**
Open Mon–Fri for video; bullfights Jan 2, 1st Sun of Apr, Jul 24, Aug 14, 4th Sun of Oct. 📷

Environs

Uwajima is best appreciated as a hopping-off spot for trips by car, bus, or boat to the nearby islands and coastal areas. In the mountains northwest of Uwajima, just off Route 320, the **Nametoko Gorge** is noted for its waterfall and fine views.

🏞 **Nametoko Gorge**
ℹ️ Uwajima bus from JR Uwajima Stn to Nijinomori Koen bus stop, then taxi to Nametoko.

Grave markers in the old temple district of Uwajima

The 88-Temple Pilgrimage

四国八十八箇所巡礼

When pilgrims retrace the route of Kukai, the founder of Shingon Buddhism *(see p279)* who made a pilgrimage of 88 of the island's minor temples in the 9th century, they are honoring a cultural icon and hoping some of the magic rubs off. Those who hope to atone for a grave error complete the pilgrimage in reverse order; it is believed they will encounter the saint as they walk or in their dreams. In Shingon, 88 represents the number of evils that can beset us. About 100,000 pilgrims complete the circuit each year; countless others follow part of it.

The birthplace of Kukai is marked by Temple 75: Zentsu-ji, one stop from Kotohira.

Popular with tour groups, Temple 51: Ishite-ji, in Matsuyama, is associated with the legend of a rich man breaking Kukai's begging bowl.

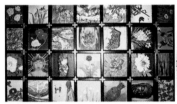

These unusually colorful ceiling paintings are found at Temple 37: Iwamoto-ji. The 90-km (55-mile) stretch between this temple and number 38 is the longest on the circuit.

Tips for Pilgrims

Length: About 1,400 km (700 miles).

Walking time: average 6 to 8 weeks for the whole circuit.

Alternative transportation: bus tours organized by numerous operators take about a week.

Accommodations: many temples offer lodgings and meals to pilgrims for around ¥6,500 and there are numerous inns and restaurants all along the route.

Official stamps: pilgrims can collect a series of rubber stamps as they visit each temple in turn.

Waymarkers: signs on rocks and posts are mostly in Japanese.

Information: (0877) 56-5688.

Guides for foreign visitors: Oliver Statler's book *Japanese Pilgrimage* (Tuttle, 1984) has extensive background information. Personal accounts in English, French, and other languages can be found on the Internet.

Matsuyama

Yawatahama

Uwajima

Sukumo

Nakamura

White-robed pilgrims are called *henro*, seen here at Temple 31, Chikurin-ji.

Temple 1: Ryozen-ji, near Naruto, is the start and end of the pilgrimage on Shikoku, though devout pilgrims will extend the start and end to Koya-san *(see p203)* on Honshu, the headquarters of the Shingon sect. Temple stalls sell the traditional garments for pilgrims: straw hats, white cotton coats, colored sashes, and staves. Visitors sign the book of completion here.

The Gokuraku in the name of Temple 2: Gokuraku-ji, refers to the Pure Land, or Western Paradise, of the Amida Buddha, a fundamental concept in Shingon Buddhism.

To Kurashiki Okayama

Takamatsu

78 81 82
77 74 76 79 80 84 85
71 73 75 83 86
72 87
69 70 67
68 66 88
65 10 8 **Naruto**
2 1
9 7 6 5 4 3
11 15 16 17 **Toku-**
13 14 **-shima**
12 18 19
20
21
Kochi 30 22
31 29 28 23
33 32
27

Between temples 11 and 12 is an uphill trek notorious as the "pilgrim crusher."

Incense urn at Temple 24, Hotsumisaki-ji

26
25 **Muroto**
24

Key

▨ Expressway
— Other roads

0 kilometers 25
0 miles 15

Shingon deities come in both benign and, as this Fudo figure at Temple 27, Kounomine-ji, demonstrates, fierce guises.

Kukai (774–835)

Kukai, who was also known as Kobo Daishi (Great Saint) after his death, helped to integrate Buddhism into Japanese life. Sailing to China as a student monk, he returned to found Japan's esoteric Shingon sect. Spending most of his time in the Kansai region of Honshu, he later returned to his native Shikoku to visit some of its temples. His accomplishments were legion: he invented the *kana* syllabary, wrote influential religious treatises, achieved lasting distinction as a poet, calligrapher, and sculptor, wrote Japan's oldest extant dictionary, and founded a school.

Statue of Kukai

KYUSHU

Long regarded as a backwater by the rest of Japan, the island of Kyushu's history of interaction with China, Southeast Asia, and Europe has, in fact, made it one of Japan's most cosmopolitan and culturally progressive regions. Such diversity creates the sensation, as you journey from prehistoric sites to urban centers such as the main city of Fukuoka, of traveling through a microcosm of Japan.

Organized communities settled in Kyushu in the Jomon period (14,500–300 BC). According to legend, it was from Kyushu that the first emperor of Japan, Jimmu, set out on his campaign to unify the country in the 6th century BC. And it was through Kyushu in the 4th century AD that Chinese and Korean culture, including Buddhism and the Chinese writing system, first infiltrated Japan. Not all foreign incursions were welcomed, however. The natives of the island repelled several Mongolian invasions, the last and most formidable in 1274 only by the intervention of a powerful storm, the *kamikaze* (divine wind), which scuttled the Mongolian fleet.

In the 16th century, Christianity, firearms, and medicine were introduced through the port cities of Nagasaki and Kumamoto by the merchants and emissaries of Portugal, Spain, and Holland. Later, during the two centuries of Japan's self-imposed isolation, the tiny island of Dejima off the coast of Nagasaki was the country's sole entrepôt for Western trade and learning.

The island landscape is characterized by volcanic activity. Kagoshima lies in the shadow of Sakurajima, which daily belches ash; Mount Aso is the world's largest caldera; and steaming fissures and fumeroles are found at Beppu, Unzen, and other spa towns.

Kyushu is one of the world's foremost ceramic centers. Pottery and porcelain techniques, learned from craftsmen brought from Korea, were perfected at the workshops and kilns of Arita, Imari, and Karatsu.

The island offers the visitor a rich concentration of sights, ranging from feudal castle towns and Shinto mountain shrines to hi-tech museums.

Buddhist figures carved into the cliffs at Usuki

◀ Exquisitely decorated room in Honmaru Goten Palace, Kumamoto Castle

Exploring Kyushu

The northern tip of Kyushu is separated from Honshu only by the narrow Kanmon Straits, less than one kilometer (half a mile) wide in parts. The island's mild climate and geothermal character has created a land of undulating green countryside, ancient volcanic cones, lava spills, hot-spring resorts, and lush, subtropical vegetation.

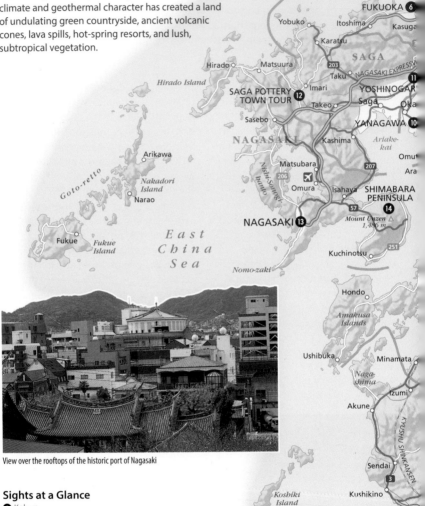

O-shima

Katsumoto
Iki Island
Gonoura

FUKUOKA **6**
Yobuko   Itoshima   Kasuga
Karatsu
SAGA
Matsuura   Taku   *NAGASAKI EXPRESSW*
Hirado   203
Hirado Island   Imari   **YOSHINOGARI 11**
SAGA POTTERY **12**   Takeo   Saga   Oka
TOWN TOUR   **YANAGAWA 10**
Sasebo   Kashima   *Ariake-*
NAGASAKI   *kai*
Arikawa   Omu
Nakadori   207   Ara
Island   206   Matsubara
Goto-retto   Narao   Omura   Isahaya   **SHIMABARA**
Nagao   **PENINSULA**
Omura   57   **14**
NAGASAKI 13   *Mount Unzen*
1,486 m
Fukue   Kuchinotsu   251
Fukue   Nomo-zaki
Island   *East*
China
Sea
Hondo
Amakusa
Islands
Ushibuka   Minamata
Naga-
shima   Izumi
Akune
KYUSHU SHINKANSEN
Sendai   **3**
Koshiki   Kushikino
Island   Hioki
270
Kaseda   **CHIKAN 6**
Satsum
hantc
Makurazaki

View over the rooftops of the historic port of Nagasaki

Key

═══ Expressway
──── Major road
──── Other road
──── Main railway
──── Minor railway
═══ Border

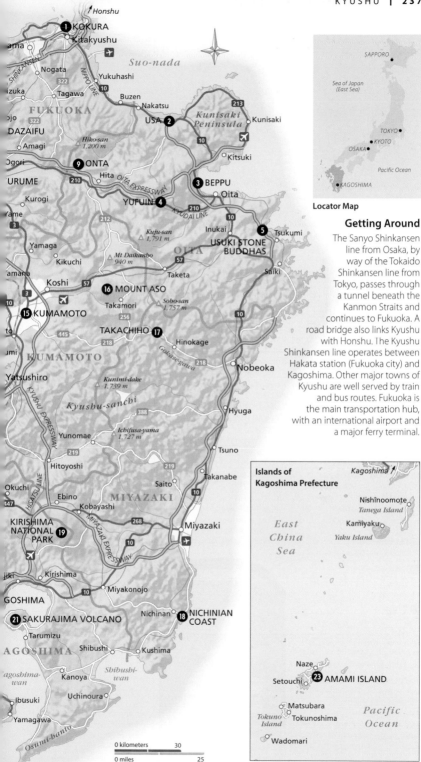

Locator Map

Getting Around

The Sanyo Shinkansen line from Osaka, by way of the Tokaido Shinkansen line from Tokyo, passes through a tunnel beneath the Kanmon Straits and continues to Fukuoka. A road bridge also links Kyushu with Honshu. The Kyushu Shinkansen line operates between Hakata station (Fukuoka city) and Kagoshima. Other major towns of Kyushu are well served by train and bus routes. Fukuoka is the main transportation hub, with an international airport and a major ferry terminal.

Islands of Kagoshima Prefecture

Gardens surrounding Umi Jigoku, or Ocean Hell, in Beppu

❶ Kokura

小倉

Fukuoka prefecture. 🏔 395,000. 🚊
ⓘ Kitakyushu Tourist Information
(093) 541-4151. 🎎 Mekari Shinji
(Shinto ceremony, early Feb); Kokura
Gion Daiko (3rd weekend in Jul).
Ⓦ kcta.or.jp/english

The gateway to northern Kyushu,
Kokura is a town in Kita Kyushu.
Its image as a modern city is
embodied in the designs of
architect Arata Isozaki, especially
Chuo Toshokan (Central Library,
1974). The city and its environs –
including **Dan no Ura** battlefield,
where the Taira clan were
defeated, and the straits of
Shimonoseki – can be seen in
one sweep from **Kokura Castle**.
Next to the castle, the beautifully
laid out **Kokura Garden**
surrounds a samurai house.

🏛 **Chuo Toshokan**
Nr Kokura Castle. **Open** Tue–Sun.

🏯 **Kokura Garden**
Tel (093) 582-2747. **Open** daily. 🎟

❷ Usa

宇佐

Oita prefecture. 🏔 60,000. 🚊 🚌
Sightseeing bus tour recommended.
🎎 Usa Furusato Matsuri (mid Nov).

The center of Tendai-sect
sanctuaries and shrines
dedicated to Hachiman,
the god of war, the area
including Usa and the Kunisaki
Peninsula is believed to have
been the nucleus of ancient
Buddhist sites of Korean

inspiration and origin. The
most famous site, **Usa Jingu**,
a shrine to the ancient
Japanese deities, is also
identified with the influential
figure of Hachiman.

On the peninsula, to the
east of Usa, are stone tombs,
Heian-period statues, and, at
Kumano Magaibutsu, the
largest carved rock-face reliefs
in Japan. The ancient
ambience of the peninsula
can be sensed near the
summit of Mount Futago,
where stone guardians mark
the approach to **Futago-ji**.
Twin avatars of the mountain
are enshrined at the temple
hall here, built into the side
of a cliff. The oldest religious
structure on Kyushu, the main
hall of the **Fuki-ji**, dating from
the Heian period, has faint,
eerily beautiful frescoes of
the Buddhist paradise.

Doorway at the vermilion hall of
Usa Jingu

❸ Beppu

別府

Oita prefecture. 🏔 122,000. ✈ Oita.
🚊 🛳 from Osaka, Kobe, and
Hiroshima. ⓘ Beppu stn (0977)
24-2838; also Foreign Tourist
Information Service at stn (0977)
23-1119. Ⓦ city.beppu.oita.jp

If you can accept its brazen
commercialism, Beppu, a glitzy,
neon-strung hot-spring resort,
situated in a wide bay and visited
by over 12 million tourists a year,
constitutes an amazing thermal
and entertainment roller coaster.
The city's porous skin is
punctured by an infinite number
of vents from which steam
continuously rises, making it
feel at times like a huge,
malfunctioning boiler room.

Scalding water not only surfaces at the 3,750 hot springs
and 168 public baths but is also
piped into private homes to
heat rooms and fuel ovens.

Beppu offers some interesting
variations on the theme of a hot
bath. Visitors can soak in a series
of tubs of graded temperatures,
plunge into thermal whirlpools,
be buried in hot black sand, or sit
up to the neck in steaming mud.

The most famous sights are
the **Boiling Hells** (Jigoku) –
pools of mineral-colored water
and bubbling mud. A circuit of
the Nine Hells is recommended;
seven of them are within
walking distance of each other
in the Kannawa district in the
north of Beppu. Each has a
different function, color, and
mineral property. For example,

the waters of Ocean Hell (Umi Jigoku) are the color of a tropical sea, while Blood Pond Hell (Chi-no-Ike Jigoku) takes its color from dissolved red clay. Visitors are shown and sold baskets of eggs that have been lowered into pools for hard-boiling.

Many of the baths are attached to hotels but also open to the public. For high kitsch and hilarity, the hugely popular **Suginoi Palace**, a hotel on the western fringes of town, is an irresistible hot-spring fantasy. Built in 1879 just inland from Beppu Bay, **Takegawara Bathhouse** is one of Beppu's oldest public baths, in which visitors are buried in black-sand baths before plunging into adjacent hot pools. Up in the hills north of Kannawa, **Myoban Hot Spring** is a quieter place to which Japanese have been coming for well over a thousand years for curative baths. For an overview of Beppu, climb the 125-m (410-ft) **Global Tower**, between the station and Suginoi Palace.

🔥 **Boiling Hells**
Tel (0977) 66-1577. Open daily. 📷

🔥 **Suginoi Palace**
Tel (0977) 24-1141. Open daily. 📷

🔥 **Takegawara Bathhouse**
Tel (0977) 23-1585. Open daily. 📷

🔥 **Myoban Hot Spring**
Tel (0977) 24-2828. Open daily. 📷

Eggs cooking at one of Beppu's Boiling Hells

Waterwheel at Yufuin Folk Art Village

❹ Yufuin
由布院

Oita prefecture. 🚹 12,000. 🚇 ℹ️ at JR stn (0977) 84-2446. 🎬 Film Festival (late Aug); Music Festival (late Jul).

Yufuin spa town, known throughout Japan for picturesque wisps of morning mist rising from its thermally warm lake, is located at the foot of Mount Yufudake. In contrast to Beppu, it aspires to be a more refined hot spring, priding itself on elegant country inns, boutiques, summer concerts, and a host of museums and galleries.

Yufuin's more highbrow pretensions are evident from the moment you arrive at **JR Yufuin Station**, a cedarwood construction with a sooty, black exterior intended to suggest the boiler of a locomotive. The station, which was built in 1990 by Arata Isozaki, has art displays in its exhibition hall, and the floors are heated from an underground hot spring.

Serene **Lake Kinrin** is the centerpiece of Yufuin. A walking and cycling path follows the shore, passing through lakeside woods. **Shitan-yu** is an old outdoor bath with a thatched roof beside the lake. The bathing here is mixed, as baths often were before the arrival, during the Meiji period, of Americans and Europeans who shamed the Japanese into segregating their baths.

The **Sueda Art Museum** and the **Yufuin Museum** are both worth visiting for their original postmodernist architecture. A cluster of traditional samurai and thatched-roofed houses, located beside a warm stream, have been carefully converted into a collection of folk-craft galleries at the **Kyushu Yufuin Folk Art Village**. It contains a museum of crafts, and local artisans can be seen at work making ceramics, toys, and glassware, among other items. There is also an indigo dyeing house and a miso factory.

🏛️ **Sueda Art Museum**
Open daily. 📷

🏛️ **Yufuin Museum**
Open Wed–Mon. 📷

🏛️ **Yufuin Folk Art Village**
Open daily. 📷

❺ Usuki Stone Buddhas
臼杵石仏

Oita prefecture. 🚇 Usuki stn, then JR bus to Usuki-Sekibutsu.

Despite the wide dissemination of images of Oita's Seki Butsu (stone Buddhas) throughout Japan, the site itself is, fortunately, only a minor tourist area. Although some realignment and fissuring has been caused by centuries of earth tremors in the area, the 60 or more consummately carved Buddhas at Usuki remain remarkably intact.

Though it is probable that the work was begun during the late Heian period and completed in the early Kamakura era, there appears to be no consensus regarding the origin of the site, who commissioned or executed the carvings, or why such a large, relatively remote area was dedicated for the images.

All of this adds a great deal of mystery and charm to the place. Late afternoon is very atmospheric, when sculptured sunlight draws out the earth hues from the faces and torsos of these mysterious and peaceful stone Buddhas.

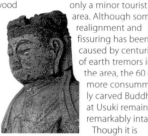
One of the Usuki stone Buddhas

Riverside view of the Nakasu district, Fukuoka

❻ Fukuoka

福岡

Fukuoka prefecture. 🏔 1,480,000.
✈ 🚉 ℹ Hakata stn (092) 431-3003;
Rainbow Plaza, IMZ Bldg, Tenjin (092)
733-2220. 🌐 **city.fukuoka.lg.jp/
english/index.html** 🎏 Hakata
Dontaku Matsuri (May 3–4); Yamakasa
Matsuri (Jul 1–15).

Strikingly modern, Fukuoka
bills itself as the gateway to
southern Japan. Divided in two
by the Naka River, the east side
of the city is also known as
Hakata, a name deriving from
its first mercantile district.
Eschewing the heavy manu-
facturing industries of nearby
Kokura in favor of administra-
tion, wholesaling, and distribu-
tion, Japan's closest city to
mainland Asia has, for at least a
millennium, been the country's
main port of entry for Chinese
and Korean culture. This has lent
it an attractive foreign Asian
flavor that the local government
is eager to exploit. **Tenjin**, to the
west of the river is the city's
commercial and shopping
district, while **Nakasu**, to the
east of the river, is an
entertainment district
with over 3,000 night-
clubs, restaurants, and
bars. **Fukuoka Yahoo
Dome** is a large baseball
stadium with a 12,000-
ton retractable roof.
The stadium is also
used for rock concerts.

The waterfront
development of
Momochi is dominated
by the **Fukuoka Tower**
and the massive resort
of **Hawks Town**. The nearby
Fukuoka City Museum has
exhibits tracing the relationship
between the city and its Asian
neighbors, including a gold
3rd century Chinese seal.

Despite its modernity,
Fukuoka also has religious
sights of impressive antiquity.
Shofuku-ji, northwest of Hakata
station, is said to be the oldest
Zen Buddhist temple in Japan.
It was founded in the late 12th
century by the priest Yosai, who
introduced both Zen and tea to
Japan. The **Kushida Shrine**, just

Fukuoka City Center

① Shofuku-ji Temple
② Hakata Machiya
   Folklore Museum
③ Fukuoka Asian Art Museum
④ Kushida Shrine
⑤ Canal City
⑥ Sumiyoshi Shrine
⑦ Ohori Park
⑧ Hawks Town
⑨ Fukuoka Tower
⑩ Fukuoka City Museum

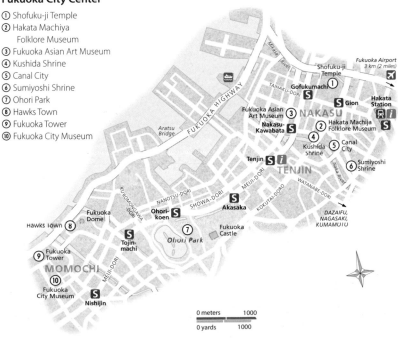

For keys to symbols *see back flap*

to the west, dates from the 8th century and displays one of the Yamakasa festival floats. Almost opposite is the **Hakata Machiya Folk Museum**, its exhibits and dioramas within this traditional building celebrating the heritage of the area. It is also possible to watch local artisans at work here, including demonstrations of Hakata silk weaving.

A huge and vibrant shopping mall in the center of town, **Canal City**, features sleek shops in a setting of hanging gardens and exploding fountains, a variety theater, and a 13-screen cinema complex. The **Asian Art Museum** holds an interesting collection of contemporary Asian art.

Southwest of Hakata station, **Sumiyoshi Shrine**, dotted with cedar and camphor trees, contains a working Noh theater. The city hosts a sumo tournament at the **Fukuoka Kokusai Center** in November. In the southwest, **Ohori Park** is the city's most popular green space, with delightful pathways, lake, pavilions, and islets connected by traditional bridges.

Fukuoka is regarded as one of the best places to eat in Japan and is celebrated for its *yatai*. These sit-down food stalls are legendary, with their colorful, lamp-lit stalls serving steaming bowls of buckwheat noodles and open-pot stews.

A Shinto priest inside the shrine of Dazaifu Tenman-gu

🏛 **Fukuoka City Museum**
Tel (092) 845-5011. **Open** Tue–Sun.

🏛 **Hakata Machiya Folk Museum**
Tel (092) 281-7761. Ⓢ Gion stn.
Open daily.

🏛 **Asian Art Museum**
Tel (092) 263-1100. Ⓢ Nakasu-Kawabata stn. **Open** Thu–Tue.

⑦ Dazaifu
太宰府

Fukuoka prefecture. 🚹 68,000. 🚉
🛈 at Nishitetsu-Dazaifu stn (092) 925-1880. 🎭 Usokae (Bullfinch Exchange, Jan 7); Sentomyo Festival (Jul 25 and Sep 25).

Dazaifu was of military importance under the Yamato government *(see p191)* and an administrative center in the later Nara period. Most visitors come here today to visit the shrine of **Dazaifu Tenman-gu**. Located in a tranquil district close to the station, the shrine is dedicated to the calligrapher, scholar, and poet Sugawara Michizane. The guardian of learning, Michizane, who died in AD 903, is also known by his divine name of Tenjin.

The shrine is a site of pilgrimage for students who pray for success in their exams, writing their wishes on small, votive wooden boards *(ema)*. The Treasure House can be visited, and just behind it a hall displays curious tableaux of Hakata clay dolls representing scenes in Michizane's life. The nearby

A detail from the festival float at Kushida Shrine, Fukuoka

Kyushu National Museum opened in 2005 and focuses on the interaction of Japan with other Asian countries. Exhibits include 75 hand-drawn Edo period *Um sum* cards depicting Japanese and Chinese customs.

Visitors can also enjoy a stroll around the stone, sand, and moss garden of the nearby temple, **Komyo Zen-ji**. Ten minute's walk away, **Kyushu History Museum** has some good displays of Jomon-, Yayoi-, and Kofun-period items excavated at Dazaifu.

Kanzeon-ji, a temple to the southwest of the station, contains a great bell and a number of highly prized statues, including an unusual horse-headed Kannon.

🏛 **Dazaifu Tenman-gu Shrine**
Tel (092) 922-8225. **Open** daily.
(for Treasure House).

🏛 **Kyushu National Museum**
Tel (092) 918-2807. **Open** Tue–Sun.

🏛 **Kyushu History Museum**
Tel (092) 918-2807. **Open** Tue–Sun.

Statue of a bull near the shrine of Dazaifu Tenman-gu

❽ Kurume

久留米

Fukuoka prefecture. 🏯 305,000. 🚉
ℹ (0942) 30-9137. 🎎 Suiten-gu
Spring Festival (May 3–7); Mizu-no-
Saiten (water festival, Aug 3–5).

The unattractive, sprawling city of Kurume is the center of *kasuri* textiles. These employ a distinctive ikat weaving style, in which the threads have been tie-dyed before weaving; unlike Southeast Asian forms of ikat, both the warp and weft are patterned. The **Kurume Regional Industry Promotion Center** has a superb display and sells *kasuri* textiles. *Rantai-shikki* is a local basket-

Kasuri cloth
from Kurume

weaving style whereby layers of lacquer are applied to bamboo to produce attractive, durable basketware. Examples can be bought at **Inoue Rantai-Shikki**, opposite the Honmachi-yon-chome bus stop. The **Ishibashi Bunka Center**, a

five-minute bus ride from the station, has an art museum and Japanese garden. By the river is the **Suiten-gu**, the head shrine of a popular sect.

🏛 **Kurume Regional Industry Promotion Center**
2nd flr, Jibasan Kurume Center.
Tel (0942) 44-3700. **Open** daily.

🏛 **Ishibashi Bunka Center**
Tel (0942) 33-2271. **Open** Tue–Sun.

Environs

Many artisans work in the villages of **Hirokawa** and **Yame**, a 40-minute bus ride from Kurume. In Hirokawa, the **Workshop of Moriyama Torao** is well worth a visit. Paper-making, using mulberry-tree fibers, dates from the 16th century. Traditional cauldrons can still be seen in use at **Yamaguchi Seishijo** paper workshop in Yame.

🏛 **Workshop of Moriyama Torao**
Tel (0943) 32-0023 (reservation required). **Open** Mon–Sat.

A boatman plying one of Yanagawa's canals

❾ Onta

小鹿田

Oita prefecture. 🏯 60. 🚉 Hita, then bus. ℹ (0973) 23-3111. 🎎 Onta Pottery Festival (2nd weekend in Oct).

Tucked into a wooded mountain valley, this tiny village has been producing Onta-ware since a group of Korean potters set up their kilns here in 1705. Later luminaries of the *mingei* (folk craft) movement, such as Yanagi Soetsu and Bernard Leach, praised Onta-ware for its unpretentious rustic quality. The kilns, dug into the hillside and water-powered, are still used. Ten families have converted their homes into open galleries. The simple, functional objects are characterized by marked, dribbled glazes in earth colors.

Potter crafting distinctive Onta-ware in an artisanal studio

❿ Yanagawa

柳川

Fukuoka prefecture. 🏯 72,000.
🚉 ℹ Inari-machi (0944) 73-2145.
🎎 Dorotsukudon Matsuri (early Oct).

The Stone Quays of Yanagawa are not as busy as they used to be, but the canals and old moats that run through this former castle town are still vital to its economy. Visitors can

board gondolas to glide past old samurai villas and storehouses. The canals are at their best in spring.

Other Yanagawa sights include **Suiten-gu**, a pretty shrine used by the same sect as the shrine in Kurume; **Toshi-mashi-tei**, an Edo-period tea garden; and a house-museum, **Hakushu Kinenkan**, the birthplace of Kitahara Hakushu (1885–1942), a prolific writer best known for children's poems.

🏛 **Hakushu Kinenkan**
Tel (0944) 72-6773. **Open** daily. 🎎

⓫ Yoshinogari Ruins

吉野ヶ里遺跡

Saga prefecture. 🚉 Yoshinogari-koen, then 15-min walk or take taxi.
ℹ (0952) 55-9333. **Open** daily.
🌐 **yoshinogari.jp/en**

Pit dwellings and hundreds of burial urns excavated at Yoshinogari point to the existence of a sophisticated Yayoi-period society (300 BC–AD 300) in the region. Irrigation systems and rice cultivation were begun in this period, laying the pattern for later Japanese society. The area is believed by some to be the home of Queen Himiko, mentioned in 3rd-century Chinese annals. Watchtowers and Yayoi-period homes have been reconstructed.

Urn in the museum
at Yoshinogari

⑫ Saga Pottery Towns Tour

佐賀県陶器生産地

Ceramics enthusiasts will thoroughly enjoy Saga prefecture, where pottery towns have been producing high-quality wares for at least 500 years. Korean potters were brought to Kyushu in the 1590s and given sovereign control over the kilns they set up. The three main pottery towns – Arita, Imari, and Karatsu – are all within convenient distances of each other, and provide access to other interesting destinations nearby.

④ Imari porcelain was exported in the 17th century via the Dutch East India Company to Europe where it was highly prized. Today much Imari-ware is produced in the kilns of Okawachiyama, a nearby village.

⑥ Yobuko
In this fishing town, the daily produce market includes stalls devoted to good-quality ceramics that are reasonably priced.

⑤ Karatsu Karatsu-ware resembles Korean pottery and is much sought after by tea ceremony practitioners. The Nakazato Taroemon Kiln is run by descendants of the first Korean potters who lived here.

③ Arita This small town has ceramic-decorated bridges, a shrine to potters, and dozens of kilns. The Kyushu Ceramic Museum gives an overview of the range of the region's pottery.

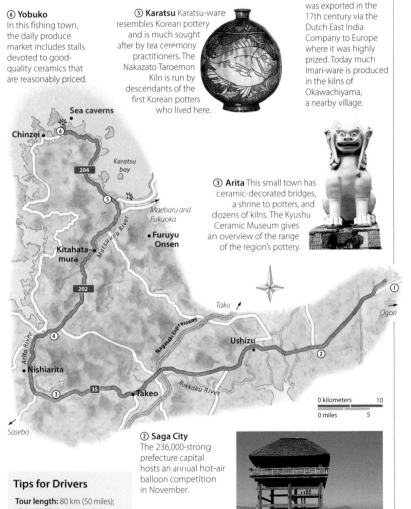

Sea caverns
Chinzei
⑥
204
Karatsu bay
⑤
Maebaru and Fukuoka
Matsuura River
Furuyu Onsen
Kitahata-mura
202
Taku
Nagasaki Expressway
④
Arita River
Ushizu
②
Nishiarita
Rokkaku River
③
35
Takeo
Sasebo
①
Ogori

0 kilometers 10
0 miles 5

② Saga City
The 236,000-strong prefecture capital hosts an annual hot-air balloon competition in November.

Tips for Drivers

Tour length: 80 km (50 miles); allow 7–8 hours by car.
Alternative transportation: Some Japanese-language tour buses cover the sights. There are also some train links from Fukuoka – allow more time for these.

Key

▬▬ Tour route by car
▬▬ Expressway
═══ Other roads

① Yoshinogari Ruins
This site, with its 2,500-year-old ceramics and reconstructed buildings, is a good starting point for the tour.

⓭ Nagasaki

長崎

A history of contact and interaction with Europe, its tragic fate as victim of the second atomic bomb, and miraculous resurgence since the war have made Nagasaki one of the most cosmopolitan and eclectic cities in Japan. After the Portuguese were expelled from the country in 1638, the Dutch, confined to the tiny island of Dejima, were the only foreign power permitted to remain throughout Japan's long period of self-imposed isolation. When Japan opened its doors to foreigners in 1854, Nagasaki thrived once more as a center of Western trade and culture.

Figures carved on the facade of the shrine to the 26 Martyrs

Ornate red gateway leading into Nagasaki's Chinatown

Getting Around Nagasaki

Despite the encroachments of modern industry, Nagasaki – with its magnificent harbor setting, meandering streets, and beautiful terraced slopes – is a city of which its inhabitants are roundly proud. Although the main sights are fairly scattered, signs in English and well-marked walking routes make Nagasaki an easily navigable city. Surprisingly inexpensive streetcars are the easiest means of transportation with four main lines running through the center of the city. Organized bus tours provide another perspective on the city. The main concentration of shops, restaurants, and nightspots is to the southeast of Nagasaki Station in the Hamanmachi arcade district, while the Peace Park, an essential place of pilgrimage for any visitor to Nagasaki, lies to the north of the station. Chinatown, once an artificial island but now attached to the mainland, is located in the district of Shinchi. Shrines, temples, and churches are scattered between.

🛂 Shrine to the 26 Martyrs

5-min walk N of stn.

Christianity was officially banned in 1597 by the shogun Toyotomi Hideyoshi who feared that conversions would lead to political intrigues and the undermining of the state by foreign powers. In that year, to emphasize the point, 26 defiant Christians were crucified on Nishizaka Hill, the first of over 600 documented martyrdoms in the Nagasaki area alone.

A short walk from the station leads to the shrine built on the site of the martyrdom. A stone relief, a small chapel, and a museum honor the martyrs who, in 1862, were declared saints by the pope. The museum's treasures include letters by Saint Francis Xavier. Without a clergy or a single chapel to worship in, Christianity, astonishingly, managed to survive covertly for 200 years after the martyrdoms until the end of Japan's isolationism.

🏛 Dejima

🚋 Dejima. Dejima Museum & Dutch Factory Historic Site: **Tel** (0958) 21-7200. **Open** daily. 🏯

The old Dutch enclave of Dejima was once surrounded by mud walls, and the only people allowed to enter were traders, prostitutes, and monks collecting alms. **Dejima Museum**, housed in Japan's first Protestant seminary, and **Dejima Dutch Factory Historic Site** next door contain historical artifacts from excavations

| 0 meters | 250 |
| 0 yards | 250 |

Shrine to the 26 Martyrs ⑤

Peace Park, Atomic Bomb Museum, Huis ten Bosch

Ken-ei Bus Terminal

Nagasaki-eki-mae

Nagasaki Station

Fukusai-ji

NISI

City

Oura River

Dejima ⑥

Dejima Museum

DEJIMA

Tsuki-machi

Nagasaki Prefectural Art Museum ⑪

CHINATOWN

Shimin Byoin

Hollander Slope ⑦

Ouratenshudoshita

Confucian Shrine ⑧

Ishibashi

Glover Garden ⑨

Oura Catholic Church

⑩

Nagasaki City Center

1. Suwa Shrine
2. Kofuku-ji Temple
3. Sofuku-ji Temple
4. Spectacles Bridge
5. Shrine to the 26 Martyrs
6. Dejima
7. Hollander Slope
8. Confucian Shrine
9. Oura Catholic Church
10. Glover Garden
11. Nagasaki Prefectural Art Museum
12. Nagasaki Museum of History and Culture

Inner gate detail at the temple of Sofuku-ji

on the site. Nearby is the **Nagasaki Prefectural Art Museum**, featuring the Suma collection of Spanish art.

🏛 Spectacles Bridge

🔲 Nigiwaibashi, Kokaidomae.

One of the most photographed sights of Nagasaki is the modest but curious Spectacles Bridge (Megane-bashi), a Chinese bequest to the city. Built by the Chinese Zen priest Mozi in 1634, it remains the oldest stone bridge in Japan. The curve of the bridge reflected in the Nakashima River resembles a pair of spectacles.

About 10 minutes' walk north from here is the **Nagasaki Museum of History and Culture**, featuring exhibits such as crime notebooks from the city's magistrate's office and "trample tablets" used in Christian persecution.

🏯 Sofuku-ji Temple

Sofuku-ji-dori. 🚋 Shokakuji-shita. 🖼

The Chinese provenance of this temple is proclaimed in the entrance gate. This depicts the gateway that, according to legend, is to be seen in the Chinese undersea paradise. A second, more illustrious gate known as First Peak Gate farther into the temple precinct has been designated a National Treasure of the late Ming period. Also worth seeing is the Treasure Hall.

Sofuku-ji is one of the three largest Chinese places of worship in Nagasaki. The temple was founded, with the help of local Chinese residents, by a monk from Fukien province in 1629. The gigantic cooking pot that stands enigmatically in the temple grounds was used to make gruel to feed over 3,000 people each day during one of Nagasaki's worst famines in 1682. A fascinating 20-minute walk north from here along narrow streets leads to Kofuku-ji temple.

🏯 Kofuku-ji Temple

Teramachi-dori. 🚋 Kokaidomae. 🖼

Kofuku-ji, located at the heart of the Teramachi district, was Japan's first Obaku Zen Buddhist temple. Founded by a Chinese priest in 1623, the building is also known as the Nanking Temple and is often visited by residents from that city. The main buildings, including the Buddha hall, are constructed in Chinese style.

🏯 Suwa Shrine

Kaminishiyama-dori. 🚋 Suwa Jinjamae.

Located in a wooded hilltop precinct at the top of 227 stone steps, Suwa Shrine affords fine harbor views. The original buildings were destroyed by fire in 1857 but later beautifully restored. The purpose of this popular shrine, home to the city's pantheon of Shinto gods, was to promote Shintoism and eradicate the last vestiges of Christianity from the area. The autumn festival, Kunchi Matsuri, is celebrated here, with blazing floats and dragon dances.

The Chinese-style Buddha hall in the temple of Kofuku-ji

For keys to symbols *see back flap*

Exploring Nagasaki

To the north and south of the city center there are many sights of interest, most of them reflecting the diverse foreign influences that have shaped Nagasaki. For a view of the city take a boat trip from Ohato Pier, or, better still, cross the harbor and take the ropeway to the lookout tower on the summit of Mount Isa.

View across Nagasaki's temple rooftops with the city skyline in the distance

🈁 Confucian Shrine

🈁 Oura Tenshudo. 🈁

Vibrant yellow roof tiles and vermilion walls instantly announce this building as a shrine dedicated to the scholar Confucius. Built by the Chinese community in 1893, the repairs and extensions accorded the shrine after it was damaged in the atomic bombing included the addition in 1982 of a National Museum of Chinese History. The antiquities on display are on loan from the Chinese National Museum and the prestigious Palace Museum in Beijing.

🈁 Glover Garden

🈁 Oura Tenshudo Shita.
Open daily. 🈁

With the reopening of the port to Westerners in the latter half of the 19th century, Nagasaki flowered as a prosperous and sophisticated international city. Suitable housing was required for the sudden influx of foreigners who made their homes here. Many of the comfortable stone and clapboard residencies that

were built during this period survive today, preserved in Glover Garden, overlooking Nagasaki harbor. The best-known European-style residence here is **Glover House**. Built in 1863, it was the setting for Puccini's opera *Madame Butterfly*.

Thomas Glover, who was responsible for bringing the first steam locomotive to Japan, was an extraordinary British entrepreneur whose ventures included coal mining, a tea import house, ship repair yards, and the founding of a beer company, the forerunner of today's Kirin Beer.

Statue of Petitjean, Oura church

Other notable buildings in the park include **Ringer House**, standing on foundation stones brought from Vladivostok, and **Walker House**, with a private garden and hall displaying the colorful floats used in the annual Kunchi festival. The **Old Hong Kong and Shanghai Bank Building** is a restored stone structure that now houses displays tracing Nagasaki's contact with Western ideas.

🈁 Oura Catholic Church

🈁 Oura Tenshudo Shita. 🈁

This white church was built in 1864 under the direction of Bernard Petitjean, a French priest who became the first Bishop of Nagasaki.

The church, which boasts some impressive stained-glass windows, was erected in order to serve the foreign community that settled in Nagasaki after the new trade treaties were signed. It was also intended to honor the city's 26 martyred saints. Shortly after its foundation, Father Petitjean was approached by members of a group of Japanese Christians who had practiced their faith in secret and at risk for over 200 years.

Classed as a National Treasure, Oura is one of the oldest churches in Japan and the country's earliest Gothic wooden structure. A wooden building beside the church contains items connected with the persecution of Nagasaki's early Christians.

🈁 Hollander Slope

🈁 Shimin-Byoin-mae.

A pleasant cobblestone street built by the Dutch, the Slope was once the center for the city's expatriate community. For a time, all Westerners, irrespective of nationality, were called "Hollanders" by the Japanese. Some of the wooden houses along the Slope are open to the public. One of the most imposing, the 1868 **Junibankan**, was once the Prussian Legation building.

Interior of the compelling and poignant Atomic Bomb Museum

Tulips by the canal in Huis Ten Bosch

🔲 Peace Park

🏯 Matsuyama-machi.

A black stone pillar marks the spot where the US detonated its second atom bomb at 11:02 on August 9, 1945, three days after Hiroshima. The intended target was the nearby shipyards. The blast killed an estimated 75,000, while 75,000 more were injured in its wake. Small wonder that the citizens of Nagasaki have become staunch advocates of world peace, erecting several monuments in the park, including a 9-m (30-ft) tall Peace Statue. A 1959 reconstruction of the **Urakami Catholic Church**, which stood at the epicenter, stands near the park.

🔲 Atomic Bomb Museum

Tel (095) 844-1231. **Open** daily. 🔲

This museum is a must for anybody visiting the city. Displays depict Nagasaki before and after the explosion and also the reconstruction. It traces with great objectivity and fairness the events leading up

to the bombing, the history of nuclear weapons, and the evolution of the peace movement. Photographs, artifacts, videos, and dioramas vividly re-create the event. A clock, frozen at the moment the bomb exploded, is one of the most poignant items.

🔲 Huis ten Bosch

Near Sasebo. 🔲 Huis ten Bosch. **Tel** (0570) 064-110. **Open** daily. 🔲

Built in 1992 at the staggering cost of US$1.75 billion, Huis ten Bosch is a reproduction of a traditional Dutch village. Replete with churches, houses, shops, windmills, a farmhouse, and canals, it is one of the largest theme parks in Japan. Replicas of Queen Beatrix's palace and of Holland's tallest church tower are highlights. Horse-drawn carriages, old-fashioned taxis, and canal boats complete the picture.

🔲 Penguin Aquarium

🔲 From Nagasaki stn to Suizokukanmae. **Tel** (095) 838-3131. **Open** daily. 🔲

Children and adults will enjoy this aquarium, which has a huge 4-m (13-ft) deep pool for the penguins to frolic in. There are seven different types of penguin here.

Foreigners in Nagasaki

The Portuguese and Dutch were the first to arrive when the harbor opened to international trade in 1571, followed by Chinese merchants who established their own community. Portuguese cargos of guns and Catholicism, however, foreshadowed Kyushu's troubled history of rebellion and persecution. Only the Dutch were allowed to trade between 1638 and 1854. After the port reopened, British, American, French, German, and Prussian trade missions came to the city. The legacy of this extraordinary foreign contact survives in some of the local festivals and cuisine, like the Portuguese *castella*, an egg and flour mixture, and the Chinese *champon* noodles, invented in 1899.

Replica of the 17th-century Dutch cargo ship *Prince Willem*

The scenic Nita Pass in the Shimabara peninsula

🔲 Shimabara Peninsula
島原半島

Nagasaki prefecture. 🔲 Shimabara city. 🔲 from Kumamoto. 🔲 Unzen Spa (0957) 73-3434; Shimabara City Hall (0957) 63-1111.

Ruled until 1616 by the Christian Lord Arima, Shimabara peninsula is known as the site of anti-Christian pogroms ordered by the Tokugawa shogunate. However, in the 1880s, **Unzen Spa** became a resort for Westerners. At an altitude of 700 m (2,300 ft) and surrounded by pine forests, it was an ideal retreat from the summer heat. Thousands of azaleas bloom in the peninsula in spring, and in autumn the maple leaves turn brilliant shades of red. In 1934 the **Unzen-Amakusa National Park**, Japan's first such protected area, was created.

Most hotels in Unzen Spa have their own hot-spring baths. Visitors in a more somber mood can see the notorious **Hells** (Jigoku): scalding sulfurous cauldrons in which 30 Christians were boiled alive after the outlawing of Christianity in Japan. As a demonstration of the ferocity of the waters in the Hells, elderly ladies in bonnets and smocks lower eggs placed in baskets into the pools and sell them hard-boiled to tourists.

Mount Unzen, thought to be dormant until one of its peaks erupted in 1990, can be climbed from the Nita Pass, reached by bus from Unzen.

The eaves and roofs of Kumamoto Castle, one of the great fortresses of Japan

⓯ Kumamoto

熊本

Kumamoto prefecture. 🏔 670,000.
✈ 🚃 🛈 (096) 352-3743.
🎏 Hinokuni Matsuri (Fire Festival, mid-Aug); The Great Festival of Fujisaki Hachimangu Shrine (Sep 13–19); Kumamoto Oshiro Matsuri (Kumamoto Castle Festival, Oct).
🌐 manyou-kumamoto.jp

A city with a small-town atmosphere, a mild climate, and semitropical flora, Kumamoto was an important seat of power during the Tokugawa shogunate (1603–1868). Its star attraction, one of the largest castles in Japan, dates from this period. The city's main shopping precinct and sights are compressed into an area south of Kumamoto castle, the original location of merchants' and artisans' quarters attached to the castle.

The longevity of Kumamoto's feisty residents (the city has numerous centenarians) is ascribed to a passion for living and a healthy diet. The latter includes *karashi renkon* (deep-fried lotus root stuffed with mustard miso) and various brands of sake made from water supposedly purified by the area's rich volcanic soil.

Dominating the center of the city from an imposing hill, **Kumamoto Castle** was constructed on the orders of Kato Kiyomasa, a warrior who fought alongside Tokugawa Ieyasu at the decisive Battle of Sekigahara in 1600. He was rewarded for his loyalty with lands encompassing most of present-day Kumamoto. The castle was completed in 1607 – a hard 7-year undertaking. Unlike more decorative castles such as Himeji *(see pp210–13)*, Kumamoto's citadel is stridently martial in appearance with steep, almost impregnable walls. The original structure had 49 towers and 29 gates, but it was almost completely destroyed during the Seinan War in 1877. Although the main keep was reconstructed on a smaller scale using ferroconcrete in 1960, it is a highly effective replica, successfully evoking the fearsome magnificence of the original.

Gyobu-tei, an over 300-year-old residence once owned by the powerful Hosokawa clan, is located a little northwest of the castle grounds. It presents insights into the way the feudal elite lived during the Edo period.

The family possessions of the powerful Kato and Hosokawa clans can be found near the castle in the **Kumamoto Prefectural Art Museum**, a distinctive modern building with a pleasant tea room. The museum also has interesting replicas of ancient burial mounds and archaeological finds from the region.

Suizen-ji Garden, Kumamoto's other main attraction, was laid out by the Hosokawa family in 1632 as the grounds for a detached villa. With a central spring-fed lake, it is a classic stroll garden *(see pp34–5)*. Its representational designs are not labeled and not always apparent. They include scenes in miniature from the 53 stages of the old Tokaido Highway and outlines of Lake Biwa and Mount Fuji. Kumamoto is renowned for its crafts, especially damascene inlay designs, Amakusa pearls, and Yamage lanterns. These lanterns, made from gold paper, are a feature of the city's festival in August. The **Kumamoto Traditional Crafts Center** has a good selection of these local crafts.

🏯 **Kumamoto Castle**
Tel (096) 352-5900.
Open daily. 🏠

🏯 **Gyobu-tei**
Tel (096) 352-6522.
Open daily. 🏠

🏛 **Kumamoto Prefectural Art Museum**
Tel (096) 352-2111.
Open Tue–Sun. 🏠

🌿 **Suizen-ji Garden**
Open daily. 🏠

🏯 **Kumamoto Traditional Crafts Center**
Tel (096) 324-4930.
Open Tue–Sun. 🏠 for 2nd flr.

⓰ Mount Aso

阿蘇山

Kumamoto prefecture. 🚃 Aso, then bus. 🚌 Kyushu Kokusai Kanko sightseeing bus from Beppu or Kumamoto. 🎏 Aso-no-hi Matsuri (Aso Fire Festival), Kuginomura (mid-Mar).

Actually a series of five volcanic cones, Mount Aso is one of the world's largest caldera, with a circumference of 130 km (80 miles). Of the five peaks, **Mount Takadake**, at about 1,590 m (5,220 ft), is the highest. **Mount Nakadake** is still active, emitting sulfurous fumes and hot gases, earning

Blocks of sulfuric rock on sale at the top of the Nakadake cable car

The fuming crater of Nakadake, one of the five volcanic cones in the Mount Aso caldera

Kumamoto the epithet *hi-no-kuni* ("the land of fire").

Below these peaks, the caldera is dotted with towns set among forests, grasslands, bamboo groves, and hot springs. Arriving tour buses pass a curious, grass-covered mountain resembling an inverted rice bowl, aptly named **Komezuka** (Rice Mound), and often stop at the pretty **Kusasenri Meadow**.

A cable car runs to the top of Nakadake, providing, on clear days, awesome views into the depths of the crater and its malodorous green lake. Hikers can follow a path to the summit for a closer look. A popular hiking route starts at the top of the ropeway, proceeds to **Mount Takadake** around the crater rim, and descends to **Sensui Gorge**.

Mount Aso Volcanic Museum, at the base of Nakadake, offers a fascinating preview of the mountain even when the crater is closed due to a high level of dangerous, sulfuric fumes. Two cameras on the crater wall relay continuous images of the cone's volcanic activity.

Mount Aso Volcanic Museum
Open 9am–5pm daily.

⑰ Takachiho
高千穂

Miyazaki prefecture. 15,000. Amano Iwato Shrine Festival (May 2–3, Sep 22–23); Yo-Kagura Kokai Festival (Nov 22–23).

The Takachiho mountain region, a place of homage for those with an affection for Japan's ancient pantheon of gods and goddesses, is alive with the resonances of legend. Most of the sights are connected with Japan's rich mythology. Kagura, a mime-dance said to have been first performed by the Sun Goddess Amaterasu Omikami, is thought to have originated here. The cave into which Amaterasu vanished, casting the world into a contemporary gloom until she could be lured out, faces **Ama no Iwato Shrine**, a pavilion-style shrine noted for a sacred tree that stands in its grounds. A short walk from here, **Ama no Yasugawara** is the grotto where the gods are supposed to have convened in order to devise a way to entice the Sun Goddess from her lair. The entrance to the cavern is next to a clear, pebble-strewn river. Many visitors have placed miniature cairns there in the

Shrine in the Mount Aso caldera

hope that, by association, some of the wisdom and power of the gods will rub off on them.

The area's main shrine, **Takachiho Jinja** is famous for its ancient cryptomeria trees, a common feature of Japanese shrines and temple grounds. It was founded by the 11th Emperor of Japan around 1900 years ago. The shrine stages nightly extracts of Kagura lasting half an hour and giving a rare opportunity to witness a performance in such atmospheric surroundings. Visitors usually try to factor into their itinerary a rowboat trip along **Takachiho Gorge**, with its scenic rock formations and waterfalls.

Waterfall in the picturesque Takachiho Gorge

The volcanic cone of Komezuka, Mount Aso ▶

Udo Jingu, a cave shrine on the Nichinan Coast dedicated to fertility

⑱ Nichinan Coast
日南海岸

Miyazaki prefecture. 🚃 Nichinan line from Miyazaki.

The Nichinan coastal landscape is known in Japanese as Onino Sentakuita, the "devil's washboard," an apt description for the eroded, rippled effect presented by the rock shelves.

The gateway to the coast is **Aoshima Island**, barely a mile in circumference and connected to the mainland by a walkway. An attractive vermilion shrine stands at the center of this densely forested islet, which can get crowded in summertime. **Miyazaki** city, to the north, is known for its year-round flowers.

Udo Jingu, another vermilion-colored shrine about 30 km (20 miles) south of Aoshima, stands in a cave beside the ocean. The shrine is dedicated to Emperor Jimmu's father, who is believed to have been washed there at birth, and serves as a catalyst for propitious marriages and fertility. The water dripping from breast-shaped rocks is compared to mother's milk, and milk candies are sold at the shrine shop. North of Udo Jingu is **Sun-Messe Nichinan**, where perfectly reproduced statues of Moai, officially approved by Easter Island, are displayed. One stop farther on the Nichinan line lies **Obi**, an old castle town, where the ruins of the castle and samurai houses may be visited. Farther south, **Ishinami Beach** is a stretch of fine white sand.

⑲ Kirishima National Park
霧島国立公園

Miyazaki and Kagoshima prefectures. 🚃 Kobayashi or Ebino Iino stn (JR Nippo line), then Miyazaki Kotsu bus.

This region, identified with Japanese foundation myths, centers on the volcanic plateau of **Ebino-Kogen** (Shrimp Meadow), which is surrounded by volcanoes, crater lakes, and hot springs. The Ebino-Kogen Nature Trail is the best of several hiking routes, going past three ponds, two of which are cobalt blue. The climb up to the peak of Mount Karakunidake is popular in summer. There are many hot springs in the area, including Iodani onsen, Arayu onsen, Hayashida onsen, and Sakura onsen.

Roof detail from Iso Garden, Kagoshima

⑳ Kagoshima
鹿児島

Kagoshima prefecture. 🔼 610,000. ✈🚃⛴ from Osaka and Nagasaki. ℹ at stn (099) 253-2500. 🎏 Sogadon no Kasayaki (4th Sat in Jul).

With one of the most stunning settings of any city in Japan, Kagoshima looks out across the broad sweep of a bay to the brooding silhouette of Sakurajima, an active volcano that sometimes showers the city in a gray blanket of volcanic ash.

Historically, this semitropical city, far from the old capital of Edo, enjoyed an unusual degree

of independence. Center of the feudal domain of Satsuma, Kagoshima's Shimazu clan ruled Okinawa for eight centuries, absorbing much of the culture of China and Southeast Asia transmitted through the islands. The legacy of that contact is evident today in a cuisine that relies on sweet potatoes rather than rice, and in its typically Okinawan preference for pork dishes.

Shochu, Kagoshima's favorite liquor made from sweet potatoes, is believed to have passed through Okinawa from China or Korea. There are over 120 *shochu* distilleries in Kagoshima alone. Local craft traditions, particularly Satsuma ceramics and fine silk brocades, reflect an aesthetic of Asian provenance. Kagoshima's sultry climate is apparent at **Sengan-en**, where semitropical plants grow alongside plum trees and bamboo groves. The garden's centerpiece is a pond and small waterfall.

On an artificial island in the harbor is the **Kagoshima Aquarium**, with species from local waters and the coral reefs around the Nansei islands, southwest of Kyushu. Also worth seeing is the **City Museum of Art**, with its displays of Satsuma ceramics.

Japan first came into contact with Christianity at Kagoshima, in 1549, in the person of the Spanish missionary Francis Xavier. The 20th-century **St. Xavier's Church** commemorates this event. The city is also associated with Saigo Takamori (1827–77), who led the ill-fated Seinan Rebellion.

Fish in one of the tanks of Kagoshima's City Aquarium

Sakurajima volcano across the strait from Kagoshima

Japanese visitors pay their respects to him in a cave on Shiroyama Hill where he committed ritual suicide.

🏯 **Sengan-en**
Tel (099) 247-1551. **Open** daily 🈺

🐟 **Kagoshima Aquarium**
Open daily. 🈺

🏛 **City Museum of Art**
Open Tue–Sun. 🈺 🌐 **kagoshima. digital-museum.jp/artmuseum**

㉑ Sakurajima Volcano
桜島

🚢 every 15 mins from the pier near Kagoshima stn.

A dramatic eruption of Sakurajima in 1914 deposited three billion tons of lava in the narrow strait separating the mountain from the peninsula, thus joining the island to the mainland. The rich volcanic soil produces the world's largest white radishes, giant specimens growing to a diameter of 1.5 m (5 ft). Such is the fascination of the cone that one of Japan's foremost writers, Endo Shusaku, is said to have had himself lowered by helicopter into the smoking crater of Sakurajima, the model for his 1959 novel

Kazan (Volcano). One peculiar sight is the **Kurokami Buried Torii Gate**, the protruding lintel of a stone Shinto gate, a casualty of the 1914 eruption.

㉒ Chiran
知覧

Kagoshima prefecture. 🏔 13,000. 🚌 from Kagoshima. ℹ️ (0993) 83-2511.

Tucked into the green folds of neatly manicured tea plantations and wooded hills, exquisite Chiran was one of 113 castle-towns built to protect the feudal lords of Satsuma. Seven preserved samurai houses and gardens on **Samurai Lane** can be visited with a single entrance ticket. **Sata** combines a dry-landscape

garden, an expanse of white raked sand, and mountains used as "borrowed scenery." **Morishige** is a stroll garden with a pond representing the sea with islands. **Hirayama** is composed almost entirely of hedges, clipped with precision into the illusion of undulating hills blending seamlessly with a backdrop of mountains. A hill above the village was the site of a World War II training ground for kamikaze pilots. Cherry trees are dedicated to 1,026 young men who flew their fatal missions from Chiran.

㉓ Amami Island
奄美大島

Kagoshima prefecture. 🏔 76,000. ✈️ 🚢 from Kagoshima to Naze. 🌐 city.amami.lg.jp

Subtropical Amami is home to a wealth of flora and fauna. The coral reefs and offshore islets of **Setouchi**, in the south, are part of a protected marine park offering excellent diving, snorkeling, fishing, and boat trips.

The **Amami Oshima Tsumugi Mura** is an artisan village set aside for the production of *tsumugi* (also known as Oshima pongee), a delicate handwoven silk fabric used to make kimonos. It can take up to one year to produce sufficient silk to make a single kimono. Halfway down the east coast, two rivers form a saltwater delta, which supports the world's most northerly mangrove forest.

One of the six perfectly maintained samurai gardens in Chiran

OKINAWA

An exotic coral bar slicing through the Pacific Ocean and East China Sea, the Okinawa archipelago was a vassal of China from the 14th century; its masters named it Liu-chiu (Ryukyu in Japanese). Under the Chinese, then later suzerainty of the Satsuma domain, the islands assimilated diverse influences, creating a unique, exotic culture that still sets them apart from mainland Japan.

Present day Okinawans, a people with a reputation for warmth and native good manners, are the heirs of a diverse racial intermingling, the result of maritime migrations from Southeast Asia, the Philippines, Mongolia, China, and the peninsula of Korea. The geography of the islands matches this rich ethnographic map. Encircled by stunning coral reefs and transparent waters, Okinawa has a richly varied topography and subtropical flora and fauna. This is one source of inspiration for the exquisite handiwork of the islanders, particularly their textiles. Created using light, natural fabrics and innovative dyeing methods, they vary from island to island.

Okinawa, the largest and busiest island in the group, gives its name to the prefecture, which was established in 1879. In the closing stages of World War II, this was the scene of fierce fighting, in the Battle of Okinawa, and the mass suicide of thousands of civilians. Naha, the main city, was damaged in the battle but has since become a heady mix of refined civilization and neon glitz. Art galleries and teahouses stand alongside red-light bars, snake restaurants, and karaoke cabins. Ceramic *shisa* lions, topping the red-tiled roofs of traditional Okinawan houses, add to the eclectic mix of war memorials, sacred groves, flower-covered coral walls, craft shops, luxury hotels, and discos.

Those who venture to the more remote islands southwest of Okinawa itself will encounter idyllic beaches, tropical rainforests, and superb diving – the nearest thing to terra incognita it is possible to find in the Japanese archipelago.

Part of the Nakamura House on Okinawa, a fine example of traditional architecture

◀ Okinawa's subtropical Pacific shoreline

Exploring Okinawa

The archipelago, also known as the Ryukyu islands, consists of 160 subtropical islands stretching for 1,000 km (620 miles) from the southwest coast of Kyushu to within television-reception distance of Taiwan. About 48 islands are inhabited. Just 107 km (66 miles) long, narrow Okinawa island is the most accessible part for tourists, with its vibrant capital Naha, beach resorts, and historical monuments. The more remote islands to the southwest are part of Okinawa prefecture; the ones to the northeast are actually part of Kyushu's Kagoshima prefecture.

Battle of Okinawa war memorial at Cape Kyan

The massive remaining wall at Nakijin Castle, Okinawa

Key

═══ Expressway
▬▬▬ Major road
═══ Minor road
- - - Ferry route

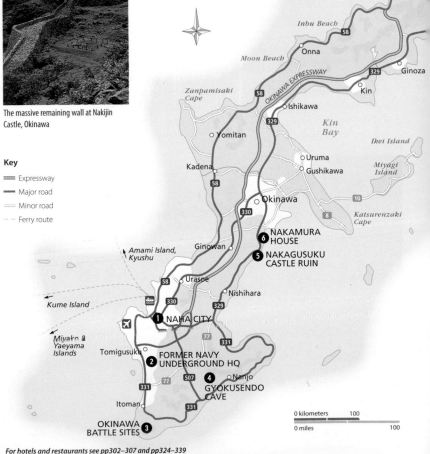

East China Sea

Nago Bay

Kin Bay

8 IE ISLAND

NAKIJIN CASTLE RUIN 9

OCEAN EXPO PARK 7
Motobu
Nakijin

Nago

Inbu Beach

Moon Beach

Onna

Ginoza

Kin

Ishikawa

Zanpamisaki Cape

Yomitan

Uruma
Gushikawa

Ikei Island

Miyagi Island

Kadena

Katsurenzaki Cape

Okinawa

NAKAMURA HOUSE 6

NAKAGUSUKU CASTLE RUIN 5

Ginowan

Amami Island, Kyushu

Urasoe

Nishihara

Kume Island

NAHA CITY 1

Miyako & Yaeyama Islands

Tomigusuku

FORMER NAVY UNDERGROUND HQ 2

GYOKUSENDO CAVE 4

Nanjo

Itoman

OKINAWA BATTLE SITES 3

0 kilometers 100
0 miles 100

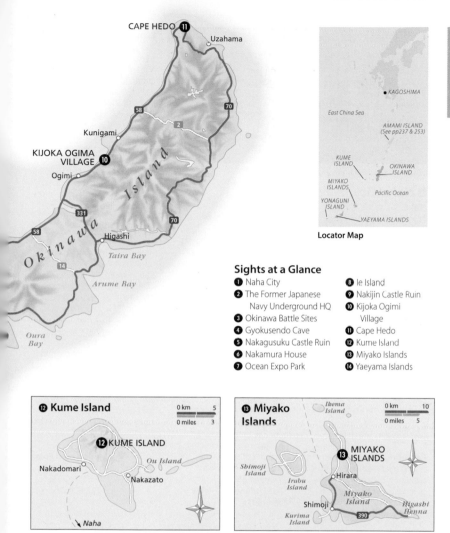

CAPE HEDO ⑪
Uzahama
KIJOKA OGIMA
VILLAGE ⑩
Ogimi
Kunigami
Higashi
Taira Bay
Arume Bay
Oura Bay

Locator Map

KAGOSHIMA
East China Sea
AMAMI ISLAND
(See pp237 & 253)
KUME
ISLAND
MIYAKO
ISLANDS
YONAGUNI
ISLAND
OKINAWA
ISLAND
Pacific Ocean
YAEYAMA ISLANDS

Sights at a Glance

1. Naha City
2. The Former Japanese Navy Underground HQ
3. Okinawa Battle Sites
4. Gyokusendo Cave
5. Nakagusuku Castle Ruin
6. Nakamura House
7. Ocean Expo Park
8. Ie Island
9. Nakijin Castle Ruin
10. Kijoka Ogimi Village
11. Cape Hedo
12. Kume Island
13. Miyako Islands
14. Yaeyama Islands

⑫ Kume Island

0 km   5
0 miles   3

⑫ KUME ISLAND
Ou Island
Nakadomari
Nakazato
Naha

⑬ Miyako Islands

0 km   10
0 miles   5

Ihoma Island
⑬ MIYAKO ISLANDS
Shimoji Island
Irabu Island
Hirara
Miyako Island
Shimoji
Kurima Island
Higashi Henna
390

⑭ Yaeyama Islands

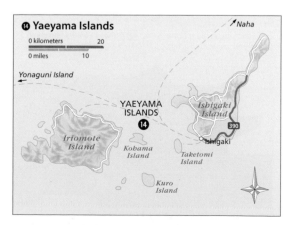

0 kilometers   20
0 miles   10
Naha
Yonaguni Island
YAEYAMA ISLANDS ⑭
Ishigaki Island
Iriomote Island
Kobama Island
Taketomi Island
Ishigaki
390
Kuro Island

Getting Around

Flying is by far the easiest way to reach Okinawa and to travel between the islands. The flight time from Tokyo is approximately 3 hours. Naha airport also has direct flights to other parts of Asia. A monorail connects Naha airport with Naha city. Ferries serve many islands in the archipelago, but journey times are long. It is also possible to take a ferry from Taiwan. Local buses can be slow, so the best way to get around may be to rent a car or scooter.

For keys to symbols see back flap

Kokusai-dori, Naha's vibrant main shopping street

❶ Naha City
那覇市

Okinawa Island. 🏔 322,000. ✈ 🚢 Naha. 🚏 ℹ Airport 1F (098) 857-6884. 🎎 Naha Matsuri (around Oct 10).

Shuri, the most historical settlement in Okinawa, was its capital until the islands became part of Japan in 1879, after which Naha was declared the capital. The two cities have since expanded and merged. Naha prospered through its seaborne trade with other parts of Asia and, eventually, the West. The city that emerged from the ruins of World War II is a bustling center, with the archipelago's best restaurants, nightlife, and shopping.

Exploring Central Naha
A long shopping and entertainment thoroughfare in the heart of Naha, **Kokusai-dori** (International Street) typifies the new city, with its boutiques and craft shops selling Okinawan crafts. The atmosphere along **Heiwa-dori** market street (to the south, off Kokusai-dori) harks back to an older Naha. Started by widows who had lost their husbands in the Battle of Okinawa, the market is full of Asian aromas, crowded alleys, and stalls selling Okinawan art, crafts, bric-a-brac, and exotic foods.

To the east, along Himeyuri-dori, the pottery quarter of **Tsuboya** dates from the late 17th century. Over 20 workshops still produce wine flasks, tea bowls, and *shisa* (statues of a legendary lion, used all around the island as propitious roof ornaments). The **Tsuboya Pottery Museum** has displays.

Also of interest in central Naha are the **Sogen-ji Ishimon Gates**. The temple itself, originally a 16th-century memorial to the Ryukyu kings, was destroyed in the war, three of the original arched stone gates have been restored.

The **Commodore Perry Memorial** by Tomari port marks the point where the commander of the American "black ships" landed on June 6, 1853.

🏛 Tsuboya Pottery Museum
Tel (098) 862-3761.
Open Tue–Sun. 🎫

Tsuboya pottery from Naha

Exploring Shuri
The 16th-century former capital, 6 km (4 miles) east of central Naha, contains various shrines, temples, ceremonial gates, and fortifications – a reminder of the sophistication of the Ryukyu kingdom. *Ryusen* and *bingata* (see p261) fabrics are made, exhibited, and sold at the **Shuri Ryusen**, where the materials are dyed. With over 4,000 exhibits, the **Okinawa Prefectural Museum** is a good introduction to the area's culture, and has the original bells from Shuri Castle and the temple Engaku-ji.

Shuri Castle was the headquarters of the Japanese High command during the war, resulting in its total destruction. **Shurei-mon**, the castle's ceremonial entrance gate, was rebuilt in 1958; as the symbol of Okinawa, it is popular with tour groups. The grand **Seiden** (hall) has also been well restored.

Natural disasters and war have led to the constant rebuilding of the 16th-century **Benzaiten-do** temple, north of the castle park. Now it is surrounded by a lotus pond spanned by stone bridges.

The **Kinjo Stone-Paved Road**, from the reign of King Shin in the 16th century, is a vestige of old Naha, meandering past old red-roofed homes with small tropical gardens enclosed by sturdy coral walls.

🏛 Okinawa Prefectural Museum
Tel (098) 941-8200.
Open Tue–Sun. 🎫

🏛 Shuri Ryusen
Tel (098) 886-1131. **Open** daily.

The splendid restored Seiden state hall at Shuri Castle

For hotels and restaurants see pp302–307 and pp324–339

Cliffs at Cape Kyan, also called Cape of Tragedy

❷ The Former Japanese Navy Underground HQ
旧海軍司令部壕

5 km (3 miles) S of Naha. 🚌 from Naha bus terminal to Tomigusuku Koen-mae. **Tel** (098) 850-4055. **Open** 8:30am–5pm daily. 🚹

Parts of the subterranean rooms and tunnels where the Japanese Navy conducted the closing stages of World War II have been restored and opened to the public. The Imperial Navy Admiral was one of over 4,000 men who committed suicide here on June 13, 1945. Many of the officers dispatched themselves by *seppuku* (ritual disembowelment); others used hand grenades – scorch marks can still be seen on tunnel walls.

❸ Okinawa Battle Sites
沖縄戦跡国定公園

15 km (9 miles) S of Naha. 🚌 bus tour from Naha recommended.

At the southern end of Okinawa, the scene of the heaviest fighting at the close of World War II, are various battle sites and memorials to victims and those who committed suicide rather than surrender to advancing American forces.

Cape Kyan saw some of the fiercest exchanges. Many locals jumped to their deaths here. To the northeast, **Himeyuri Peace Museum** is a much-visited memorial to a group of schoolgirls and teachers who died while working as volunteer nurses during the Battle of Okinawa. A total of 136 people died inside a cave while trying to escape from the carnage. Most perished from the effects of a gas bomb fired into the cavern, others committed suicide. **Konpaku no To**, 2 km (1 mile) south, is a cliffside memorial where 35,000 unknown soldiers and civilians were interred.

One of the heaviest losses of life was on **Mabuni Hill**. Now a memorial park, it is dotted with monuments dedicated to both military and civilian dead. A comprehensive display, with photos, memorabilia, and personal accounts of the battle can be seen at the nearby **Peace Memorial Museum**.

🏛 **Peace Memorial Museum**
Tel (098) 997-3844. **Open** 9am–5pm daily. **Closed** Dec 29–Jan 3. 🚹

❹ Gyokusendo Cave
玉泉洞

30 km (19 miles) SW of Naha.

Japan's largest stalactite grottoes were discovered in 1967 by students from Ehime University. With over 460,000 stalactites, this natural fantasia is negotiated with the help of rather slippery pathways and wooden walkways. The stalactites have been likened to giant bamboo, wine glasses, organ pipes, and statues by Rodin. At the center is a pond known as Golden Cup.

The cave lies near the **Gyokusendo Okokumura**, a park and museum with a large snake collection, including the *hubu*, Okinawa's most poisonous reptile.

🏛 **Gyokusendo Okokumura**
Tel (098) 949-7421.
Open 9am–6pm daily. 🚹

Densely packed stalactites in Gyokusendo Cave

The Battle of Okinawa

Kamakazi attack on an American battle ship

Few conflicts in modern history have been fought with such ferocity on both sides as the Battle of Okinawa. The final phase in the Pacific War began when five American divisions, supported by a massive aerial and naval bombardment, landed on Easter Sunday, April 1, 1945. Although logistically outnumbered, the Japanese were well prepared for the attack with a maze of tunnels and shelters. The horrors of these engagements, utilizing flame-throwers, grenades, bayonets, and kamikaze pilots (Japanese suicide bombers), almost defies imagination. By the end of the battle, which lasted 82 days, 13,000 American soldiers and 250,000 Japanese soldiers and civilians had died.

Guest room in the Nakamura House

❺ Nakagusuku Castle Ruin

中城城跡

13 km (9 miles) NE of Naha City, 5-min walk E of Nakamura House. **Tel** (098) 935-5719. **Open** 8:30am–5pm daily (6pm Jun–Sep).

Built by Lord Gosamaru, Nakagusuku was one of the first stone castles to be built in Japan. Construction began in 1450 and continued for many years, encompassing a range of masonry styles. The views along the east coast of central Okinawa are excellent. Lord Gosamaru was betrayed by the northern noble Amawari, who convinced the Shuri king that Gosamaru was raising troops against him. The king sent forces to attack, and Gosamaru committed suicide rather than oppose a ruler he loyally supported. The walls are the only structures to survive the ravages of time and the 1458 Amawari Rebellion. Passages link three main compounds, each enclosed by high, fortified walls.

❻ Nakamura House

中村家

13 km (9 miles) NE of Naha City. **Tel** (098) 935-3500. **Open** 9am–5:30pm daily.

A visit to this well-to-do 18th-century farmhouse, now a museum with exhibits about Okinawan daily life, offers rare insights into a more refined

Shisa ornament, Nakamura House

style of rural architecture. It consists of five buildings around a stone courtyard. Okinawan masons were renowned, and even the pig pens here, with their finely cut stones, are remarkably well made. A stone enclosure, with a barrier to repel evil spirits – a typical Okinawan feature – faces the entrance. Descendants of the Nakamura family continue to live in the private inner quarters of the house.

❼ Ocean Expo Park

海洋博記念公園

20 km (12 miles) NW of Nago. Kinenkoen-mae. **Open** 8am–7:30pm (8pm in summer); last adm 1 hour before closing. for some attractions. **w** oki-park.jp/kaiyohaku/

The Okinawa International Ocean Exposition was held here in 1975; since then several new attractions have been added to this coastal park, which is also known as the Ocean EXPO Park and the Commemorative National Government Park. The **Dolphin Theater** is popular with families who come to see the regular shows. The adjacent **Okinawa Churaumi Aquarium** houses more than 700 species of fish in three sections: tropical, ocean, and deep sea. The **Oceanic Culture Museum** relates the

development of the Okinawan people to the maritime culture of Oceania through fishing and navigation exhibits.

The **Native Okinawan Village** is a faithful reconstruction of traditional 17th- and 18th-century dwellings, incorporating sacred springs and forest, places of worship, store houses, and an arboretum with native plants. On the coast close by is the **Tropical Dream Center**, a complex of high-tech greenhouses and botanical gardens.

Environs

There are beaches about 30 km (19 miles) to the south of the park, along the coast of **Nago Bay**. Between Cape Busena and Inbu Beach is one of the world's finest underwater observatories, at **Busena Marine Park**. Don't miss the excellent undersea aquarium.

Busena Marine Park
Tel (0980) 52-3379. **Open** daily.
w busena-marinepark.com

❽ Ie Island

伊江島

5,200. from Motobu port.

Ie is a picturesque little island ideal for bicycling. Bike rentals are plentiful, and the whole island can be explored in under 8 hours. The north terminates in steep cliffs, while the interior is an expanse of sugarcane, tobacco, and pineapple fields, and old houses with kitchen gardens. **Gusukuyama**, Ie's only hill, provides a first-rate view.

Sea turtle at Ocean Expo Park

View of Ie Island from the entrance to Ocean Expo Park

Okinawan Arts and Crafts

Okinawan artists and craftsmen are honored as masters or, in a few rare cases, Living National Treasures. The island's textiles are among the finest in Japan, particularly the linen-dyed *bingata* and *ryusen* fabrics, *bashofu*, and *kasuri*, a high-quality cloth made from the finest natural fibers. Equally, the glossy, black Okinawan lacquerware has been made for

Dyeing fabric in a *ryusen* workshop

over 500 years, using the wood of the indigenous *deigo* tree as a base. New crafts have appeared since the war, most notably Okinawan glassware, its vibrant colors reflecting the island's sparkling coral seas.

The island saw considerable action in World War II. **Nyateiyagama**, a cave in the southwest, was used as a shelter by locals during the fighting. The **Ernie Pyle Monument** is dedicated to the US war correspondent who died when his jeep was blown up on the island only a few weeks before the end of the conflict.

Visitors are welcome at the friendly cooperative where locals process the day's catch of fish and seaweed.

⓿ Nakijin Castle Ruin

今帰仁城跡

🚌 66 from Nago to Nakijin Jo Ato
Tel (0980) 56-4400. **Open** 8am–6pm daily. 🚶 🔳 nakijinjo.jp/guide.html

The foundations, gate, and 1,500-m (4,900-ft) stretch of remaining wall give some indication of the original size of Nakijin Castle. It was built in the 14th century by King Hokuzan, founder of the North Mountain Kingdom, an esoteric and short-lived domain.

The entrance, with its flat stone ceiling, is still intact. Because the castle faced the sacred island of **Iheya**, three wooden shrines were built here to allow the local priestesses to conduct rituals, but none has survived. There are stunning views across the East China Sea toward several other offshore islands including the Amami and Yoron groups.

⓾ Kijoka Ogimi Village

喜如嘉村

🚹 25 km (16 miles) N of Nago. 🚶 350.
🚌 67 from Nago to Daiichi Kijoka.

The main reason for a visit to Kijoka Ogimi Village is to watch the making of *bashofu*, a rare textile made of plantain fiber. The village is famous for the cloth, which is exported to mainland Japan and sold at prices far above those here. Unlike traditional Japanese kimonos, Okinawan apparel was made from plain woven cotton, ramie, and lightweight fabrics such as *bashofu*. The stages involved in producing this increasingly scarce linen can be seen at the **Bashofu Hall**, a well-known workshop.

Stone lion from Kijoka village

🏛 Bashofu Hall

Tel (0980) 44-3033. **Open** 10am–5pm Mon–Sat. **Closed** Dec 29–Jan 3.

⓫ Cape Hedo

辺戸岬

🚹 50 km (31 miles) N of Nago.
🚌 67 from Nago to Hentona.

The remote, northernmost point of Okinawa Island is a wild and breathtaking area of outstanding natural beauty and, mercifully, few tour buses. A grassy plateau runs to the edge of a steep, 100-m (330-ft) high cliff, beyond which are coral reefs. The views of distant Yoron, Iheya, and Izena Islands are magnificent. The road to Hedo Point passes through a number of traditional villages. One of the most interesting is **Ogimi Village**, renowned for pale yellow *bashofu* cloth. A short distance east of Hedo Point is the village of **Uzahama** and the remains of a prehistoric settlement.

Cape Hedo, the northernmost cape of Okinawa

Tatami-ishi pentagonal stones on Ou Island, just off Kume

⑫ Kume Island

久米島

90 km (56 miles) W of Okinawa Island. ✈ from Naha. 🚌 9,300. ⛴ from Naha Tomari port. 🛈 (098) 985-7115.

Regarded by many as the most beautiful island in the prefecture, volcanic Kume is famous for its sugarcane and pineapple plantations, and Kumejima-*tsumugi*, an exquisite silk pongee. Buses serve many of the island's sights.

The village of **Nakadomari**, in the southwest, boasts one of the oldest houses in Okinawa. **Uezu-ke** was built in the 1700s in the Okinawan samurai style. An extraordinary tree, the **Goe Pine Site**, which has five separate trunks spanning out, is just a short walk from the house. Rice-planting rituals and prayers for rain are still conducted at **Chinbei-donchi**, the island's foremost shrine, north of Nakadomari. Nearby, the sacred **Yajiya-gama Cave** was used for burials 2,000 years ago.

To the north, the 200-m (650-ft) high **Hiyajo Banta** cliff affords good views toward the Aguni and Tonaki islands and the barrier reef below, one of Kume's outstanding natural sights. The Teida-ishi (sun stone), in a beautiful grove not far from the cliff, was used as a sundial.

Nakazato village, in the east of the island, is one of its most traditional settlements, with several well-preserved buildings. You can see women weaving and dyeing Kumejima-*tsumugi* here. Nearby **Eef Beach** is Kume's largest resort.

Tiny **Ou Island** is well worth the 20-minute walk across a connecting bridge from Naka-zato's Tomari port. In the southwest is a mosaic of over 1,000 pentagonal stones, called Tatami-ishi, which resemble flattened tortoise shells.

⑬ Miyako Islands

宮古諸島

330 km (200 miles) SW of Okinawa Island.

Set amid coral reefs in a transparent emerald sea, Miyako consists of eight almost perfectly flat islands. Unique customs and a distinct dialect set the inhabitants of Miyako apart from Okinawan mainlanders. Spared the devastation of World War II, traditional houses are squat, one-story buildings with red-tiled roofs and surrounding coral walls that serve as shelters against typhoons.

Miyako Island

🚌 55,000. ✈ from Naha and Ishigaki Island. ⛴ from Naha. 🛈 at airport (0980) 72-1212.

Hirara town, a former city now merged to make up the city **Miyakojima**, is the island's main area. North of the port is **Harimizu Utaki** shrine, dedicated to the two gods who created the island. The fascinating **mausoleum** of the 15th-century chieftain Nakasone Toimiya has graves and tombs that combine local styles with the more elaborate Okinawan style. Northeast of Hirara, the **Hirara Tropical Botanical Gardens** contain over 40,000 tree and almost 2,000 plant species from around the world.

In the backstreets of Hirara you can see women drying strips of Miyako-*jofu* indigo cloth, used as a tributary payment when the islands were under nominal Chinese rule. Just north of Hirara is the 1.4-m (55-in) stone, called the **Nintozeiseki**, used to assess tax eligibility when the islands fell under the suzerainty of the

Sweep of sand at Yonaha Maehama Beach, Miyako Island

Satsuma domain in the 17th century. When someone grew to the height of the stone they were deemed old enough to start paying taxes.

At the tip of **Higashi Henna** cape on the east coast you can look out over the Pacific Ocean to the left and the East China Sea to the right.

On the southwest coast, facing Kurima island, **Yonaha Maehama Beach**, a 4-km (2-mile) stretch of pristine white sand, offers the island's best swimming, fishing, and diving.

🔲 **Hirara Tropical Botanical Gardens**
Open daily.

Other Islands
🚌 from Miyako Island; or by road bridge to Kurima and Ikema. Mostly set aside for sugarcane plantations, **Kurima** is of interest to ornithologists as sea hawks rest here for a few days in October on their way to the Philippines. The main sight on **Ikema**, off the far north of Miyako, is the Yaebishi reef, which emerges in all its splendor during low spring tides.

Off the west coast is **Irabu**, linked by six bridges to neighboring Shimoji. On **Shimoji**, two deep green lakes called Tori-ike are connected to the sea by an underground river and tunnel. Locals believe that the lakes are haunted; for those brave enough, the area is a superb diving locale.

⑭ Yaeyama Islands
八重山諸島

430 km (270 miles) SW of Okinawa Island.

The Yaeyamas are Japan's most southerly islands, its last frontier of tourism. Some of the finest scuba diving in Asia is found here.

Ishigaki Island
🏝 48,000. ✈ from Naha and Miyako. 🚢 from Naha and Hirara port, Miyako Island. 🛈 (0980) 82-2809. 🎎 Angama Festival (late Aug).
Ishigaki's airport and harbor serve the outlying islands in the group. Glimpses of the unique Yaeyama culture can be seen at the

Shiritsu Yaeyama History Museum, Ishigaki Island

Shiritsu Yaeyama Museum, near the harbor, which contains ancient ceramics, Yaeyama-*jofu* textiles, and Polynesian-style canoes. Not far away is **Miyara Donchi**, a 19th-century nobleman's home. **Shiraho Reef**, off the southeastern tip of the island, is the world's largest expanse of blue coral. **Kabira Bay** on the north shore, is full of small islets and supports a cultured black pearl industry.

🏛 **Shiritsu Yaeyama Museum**
Open Tue–Sun. 🖼

🏛 **Miyara Donchi**
Open Wed–Mon. 🖼

A dancer in traditional costume, Ishigaki Island

Taketomi Island
🏝 330. 🚢 from Ishigaki. 🛈 (0980) 82-5445.
Meaning "prosperous bamboo," Taketomi is a quiet, unspoiled island. Its neatness stems from an old custom by which it was, and still is, the responsibility of all householders to sweep the street in front of their own

The orderly, sandy lanes of Taketomi Island village

property. The island can easily be explored on foot or by bike. Taketomi is famous as the source of *minsa*, an indigo fabric used for kimono belts, which can be seen in the main village. It also has some of Okinawa's best-preserved houses.

To the west, is **Kondoi Beach**, the island's finest beach and Kaiji Beach, which has star-shaped sand – the fossilized skeletons of tiny sea animals. The stunning aquamarine waters here support bountiful tropical sealife, and brilliantly colored butterflies swarm around the beach.

Iriomote Island
🏝 2,300. 🚢 from Ishigaki.
Possibly the wildest landmass in Japan, 90 percent of Iriomote is forest and jungle. Visitors can take cruises along its two main rivers, the **Nakama** and **Urauchi**, where black oyster beds, mangroves, and tropical trees, including the rare Yaeyama coconut palm, can be seen. The three-stage **Mariyudo Falls** end the Urauchi River trip. The island is famous as the last habitat of the Iriomote wild cat.

Yonaguni Island
🏝 1,700. 🚢 from Naha and Ishigaki. ✈ from Naha. 🛈 (0980) 87-2402.
Yonaguni is the ultimate retreat – the last island in the archipelago. Excellent swordfish and bonito fishing provide interest along with Japan's strongest sake – *hanazake*.

NORTHERN HONSHU

When haiku poet Matsuo Basho set out in 1689 on his five-month trek to northern Japan, he likened it to going to the back of beyond. Three centuries later, shinkansen lines and expressways provide easy access, and the north is as much a part of the information age as the rest of Japan. The region nevertheless retains its quiet, rural image, a place where life is lived at a more congenial pace.

The backcountry reputation of Northern Honshu belies its rich history. Long ago, it was home to indigenous people, who may have been Ainu *(see p291)*. In the 11th century, Hiraizumi was the capital of the Northern Fujiwara clan, rivaling Kyoto in splendor. During feudal times, Morioka, Tsuruoka, Hirosaki, and Aizu-Wakamatsu were thriving castle towns. Foremost, though, was Sendai, ruled by the north's most powerful clan and now the region's largest city. These and other north-country wonders, such as the shrines and temples of Nikko and Dewa Sanzan, are now tourist attractions.

Known for its excellent rice and fine sake, northern Japan is the country's main rice-producer. Agriculture is now mechanized, but farmers still work hard for a living. Mushrooms in autumn, wild vegetables in spring, oysters in winter, and seafood all year are other reasons to visit the north, while its cool summers provide relief from the heat and humidity farther south. The wealth of crafts and folk arts, such as Nanbu *testsubin* (iron kettles) in Morioka, wooden *kokeshi* dolls, Aizu and Tsugaru lacquerware, *kabazaiku* (cherry-bark craft), and Mashiko pottery, are renowned in Japan and internationally.

On March 11, 2011, a 9-magnitude earthquake and subsequent tsunami hit this northern part of Japan. Much of the area was damaged with some coastal areas completely destroyed. The Fukushima Daiichi nuclear plant was also badly damaged by the tsunami, resulting in the evacuation of people living near the plant.

One of the extravagant carvings by the Yomeimon gate at Nikko's Tosho-gu Shrine

◀ A red *torii* shrine gate on an island in Matsushima Bay

Exploring Northern Honshu

Northern Honshu is much more rural than Central and Western Honshu. Snow-covered mountains, thick forests, and rice paddies characterize most of the region, with towns and ski resorts fairly evenly scattered. North of the major city of Sendai, tiny pine-covered islands lie in calm bays facing the Pacific Ocean, forming some of the most beautiful coastal scenery in Japan. The six northeastern prefectures of Aomori, Akita, Iwate, Yamagata, Miyagi, and Fukushima make up the area known as Tohoku. This chapter also includes parts of Niigata, Tochigi, Gunma, and Ibaraki prefectures.

A *kabuto-zukuri*-style farmhouse in the grounds of Chido Museum, Tsuruoka

Sights at a Glance

1. Nikko pp268–75
2. Nikko National Park
3. Mashiko
4. Aizu Wakamatsu
5. Kitakata
6. Bandai-Asahi National Park
7. Sado Island
8. Tsuruoka
9. Dewa Sanzan
10. Sendai
11. Matsushima
12. Hiraizumi
13. Hanamaki
14. Tono
15. Morioka
16. Kakunodate
17. Oga Peninsula
18. Towada-Hachimantai National Park
19. Hirosaki
20. Aomori
21. Shimokita Peninsula

For hotels and restaurants see pp302–307 and pp324–339

Hokkaido

Minmaya

Goshogawara

Fukaura
Iwaki-san
1,625 m

HIROSAKI

Hachimori
101
Oda
Takanosu

Noshiro
7

OGA PENINSULA
17
Gojome

Oga
Moriyoshi-zan
1,45

Akita

KAKUNODATE

Omagari

Honjo
Yokot

Kisakata

Tobi-shima
Chokai-san
2,237 m
Ogachi

Sakata
Kaneyama
13

TSURUOKA
8
9
DEWA SANZAN
Shin

Atsumi
Obanazawa

Sanpoku
YAMAGATA

Awa-shima
112
Te

Hajiki-zaki

Murakami
Yamagata

Aikawa
Ryotsu
Arakawa
6
Nanyo

Shibata
113

SADO ISLAND
Niigata
Yonezawa

Ogi
7
Niitsu
121
13

Shirone
Ide-san
2105 m
KITAKATA
Fukushima

BANETSU EXPRESSWAY
5
Nihonmatsu

Nagaoka
NIIGATA
AIZU WAKAMATSU
4
Koriyama

Kashiwazaki
Ojiya
Koide
Sukagawa

Itoigawa
8
FUKUSHIMA
Tajima
Ishika

Joetsu
Muika
Shirakaw

Hiuchiga-take
2346 m
NIKKO NATIONAL PARK
2
Kuroiso

Mikuni-toge
1244 m
Shirane-san
2578 m
120
Yaita
4
349

Maebashi
1
NIKKO
Dai

TOCHIGI

Utsunomiya
MASHIKO
3

Tokyo
Kasama

Oyama
Shimodate
Mi

IBARAKI

0 kilometers 50
0 miles 30

Clear waters and the rugged coastline of
Sado Island

Locator Map

Getting Around

Two main shinkansen lines penetrate this region:
one from Tokyo to Niigata, the other from Tokyo to
Hachinohe via Sendai. Branch shinkansen lines run
to Yamagata and Akita. From Hachinohe, a main line
continues north and on to Hokkaido via the Seikan
Tunnel. Much slower branch lines – some private –
serve towns along both coasts and in the interior.
Nikko is an easy day trip from Tokyo; elsewhere allow
plenty of time for travel. A rental car is a good option
for getting off the beaten track.

Key

Expressway
Major road
Other road
Main Railway
Minor Railway
Border

Weeping cherry trees in Hirosaki

❶ Nikko

日光

Over 1,200 years ago, the formidable Buddhist priest Shodo Shonin, on his way to Mount Nantai, crossed the Daiya River and founded the first temple at Nikko. Centuries later, Nikko was a renowned Buddhist-Shinto religious center, and the warlord Tokugawa Ieyasu (see p271) chose it for the site of his mausoleum. When his grandson Iemitsu had Ieyasu's shrine-mausoleum – Tosho-gu – built in 1634, he wanted to impress upon any rivals the wealth and might of the Tokugawa clan. Since then, Nikko, written with characters that mean sunlight, has become a Japanese byword for splendor.

Bato Kannon, with a horse on the headdress, at Rinno-ji Temple

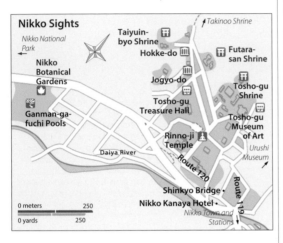

Nikko Sights

- Takinoo Shrine
- Nikko National Park
- Nikko Botanical Gardens
- Taiyuin-byo Shrine
- Hokke-do
- Futara-san Shrine
- Jogyo-do
- Ganman-ga-fuchi Pools
- Tosho-gu Treasure Hall
- Tosho-gu Shrine
- Rinno-ji Temple
- Tosho-gu Museum of Art
- Daiya River
- Urushi Museum
- Route 120
- Route 119
- Shinkyo Bridge
- Nikko Kanaya Hotel
- Nikko Town and Stations

0 meters 250
0 yards 250

Exploring Nikko Town

Of the two stations in Nikko, the JR station, the oldest in eastern Japan, is a classic. It was built in 1915 (contrary to popular misconception, it was not designed by Frank Lloyd Wright). Buses to many of Nikko's sights run from here. The 1-km (about half-a-mile) long avenue from the train stations to the Tosho-gu precincts is lined with shops, restaurants, and inns. A good shop for Nikko wood carvings and geta (wooden sandals) is Tezuka, on the left halfway up the street. An architectural treat is the venerable 19th-century Nikko Kanaya Hotel (see p307), situated on a rise to the left, just before the Daiya River.

Shinkyo Bridge

Open daily.
This red-lacquered wooden bridge, just to the left of the road bridge, arches over the Daiya River where, legend has it, Shodo Shonin crossed the river on the backs of two huge serpents. The original, built in 1636 for the exclusive use of the shogun and imperial messengers, was destroyed by flood. The current bridge dates from 1907.

🏯 Rinno-ji Temple

Open daily; the garden and museum may be closed for special events or renovation. 🅿
The first temple founded at Nikko, by Shodo Shonin in 766, this was originally called Shihonryu-ji. When it became a Tendai-sect temple in the 17th century, it was renamed Rinno-ji. Its **Sanbutsu-do** (Three Buddha Hall) is the largest hall at Nikko. The three gilt images, of Amida Buddha, Senju (thousand-armed) Kannon, and Bato (horse-headed) Kannon, enshrined in the hall correspond to the three mountain deities enshrined at Futara-san Shrine. Beyond the hall, the nine-ringed bronze pillar, **Sorinto**, contains 1,000 volumes of sutras (Buddhist scriptures) and is a symbol of world peace. The **Treasure Hall** (Homotsuden) has a large and fascinating array of temple

The Shinkyo Bridge spanning the Daiya River

For keys to symbols see back flap

The Sanbutsu-do hall at Rinno-ji

treasures, mainly dating from the Edo period. Behind it is the **Shoyoen**, a lovely Edo-style 19th-century stroll garden carefully landscaped for interest in all seasons. Its path meanders around a large pond, over stone bridges, and past mossy stone lanterns.

🔧 Tosho-gu Shrine
See pp270–71.

🖥 Tosho-gu Treasure Hall and Museum of Art
Tel (0288) 54-2558 (Treasure Hall); (0288) 54-0560 (Museum of Art). **Open** daily; some sections may be closed for special events or renovation. 🖼

In the Treasure Hall are shrine treasures along with armor and swords used by the Tokugawa shoguns. In the Museum of Art is an outstanding collection of early 20th-century painted doors and panels by Taikan Yokoyama and others.

🏛 Hokke-do and Jogyo-do
These two halls belong to Rinno-ji and house Buddhist relics. Linked by a corridor, they are often referred to as the twin halls.

🔧 Futara-san Shrine
Open daily. 🖼 🔲 futarasan.jp
Founded by Shodo Shonin in 782, this shrine is dedicated to the gods of the mountains Nantai (male), Nyotai (female), and Taro, their child. It is actually the main shrine of three; the other two are at Lake Chuzenji and on Mount Nantai. The bronze torii (gate) here is an Important Cultural Property. More interesting is the tall bronze lantern, which was said to take the shape of a monster at night. The gashes in the lantern are from the sword of a terrified samurai.

🔧 Takinoo Shrine
Tel (0288) 21-0765. **Open** daily.
A quiet 30-minute uphill walk through the woods via a stone path to the left of Futara-san Shrine, this peaceful, rustic shrine, thought to be dedicated to a female deity, draws women and those looking for love. Toss a stone through the hole in the top of the torii (gate) and into the shrine grounds and your wish, they say, will come true.

VISITORS' CHECKLIST

Practical Information
Tochigi prefecture. 🚶 1,980,000. 🛈 at Tobu Nikko stn (0288) 54-2496. 🎎 Tosho-gu Grand Festival May 17–18); Tosho-gu Fall Festival (Oct 17).
🔲 nikko-jp.org/english

Transport
🚃 JR and Tobu-Nikko lines.

🔧 Taiyuin-byo Shrine
See pp274–5.

🏞 Ganman-ga-fuchi Pools
🚌 to Nishisando bus stop.
Lava flows from an old eruption of Mount Nantai combine with the limpid waters of the Daiya River to make these unusual scenic pools, which are a spot sacred to Buddhism. About 70 stone statues of Jizo, the bodhisattva of children, line the path by the river. They are known as phantom statues because their numbers always appear to change.

🌿 Nikko Botanical Gardens
🚌 to Rengeishi bus stop.
Tel (0288) 54-0206. **Open** Tue–Sun. **Closed** Dec 1–Apr 14. 🖼
Some 3,000 varieties of plants and flowers from Japan and around the world are at these gardens, a branch of the Koishikawa Botanical Gardens of the University of Tokyo. Flora from Nikko National Park are showcased. April to July, when skunk cabbages and irises bloom, is a lovely time to visit.

🖥 Urushi Museum
🚌 to Marumi bus stop.
Tel (0288) 53-6807. **Open** Mar 20–Nov 20: Sat, Sun, Mon. 🖼
This small museum, which opened in 1998 in wooded Ogurayama Park, showcases the lacquerware arts of Nikko and Japan – *urushi* is Japanese for lacquer. Used in Japan for over 5,000 years, lacquer has reached the height of refinement only in the past 1,000 years. The museum collection also includes examples of lacquerware from China, India, and Egypt.

Painted sliding doors at the Tosho-gu Museum of Art

Nikko: Tosho-gu Shrine

Tokugawa Iemitsu set out to dazzle with this mausoleum-shrine for his grandfather Ieyasu. For two years some 15,000 artisans from all over Japan worked, building, carving, gilting, painting, and lacquering, to create this flowery, gorgeous Momoyama-style complex. Almost anything that can be decorated is. Although designated a shrine in the Meiji period, it retains many of its Buddhist elements, including its unusual pagoda, sutra library, and Niomon gate. The famed *sugi-namiki* (Japanese cedar avenue) leading to the shrine was planted by a 17th-century lord, in lieu of a more opulent offering.

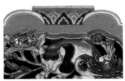

Sleeping Cat Carving
Over an entrance in the east corridor, this tiny, exquisite carving of a sleeping cat is attributed to Hidari Jingoro (Left-handed Jingoro).

KEY

① **The Rinzo** contains a sutra library of Buddhist scriptures in a revolving structure.

② **Drum tower**

③ **The Honji-do**'s ceiling is painted with the "crying dragon," which echoes resoundingly if you clap your hands beneath it.

④ **The Karamon** gate is the smallest at Tosho-gu.

⑤ **Haiden (sanctuary)**

⑥ **Honden (inner sanctuary)**

⑦ **Bell tower**

⑧ **The three sacred store-houses** are built according to a traditional design.

⑨ **The Niomon** (or Omotemon) gate is guarded by two fearsome Nio figures, one with an open mouth to pronounce the first letter of the Sanskrit alphabet (ah), the other with a closed mouth for the last letter (un).

⑩ **Ticket office**

⑪ **Granite Torri (gate)**

★ **Yomeimon Gate**
Lavishly decorated with beasts and flowers, this gate has one of its 12 columns carved upside-down, a deliberate imperfection to avoid angering jealous spirits. Statues of imperial ministers occupy the niches.

Sacred Fountain The granite basin (1618), for ritual purification, is covered with an ornate Chinese-style roof.

★ **Pagoda**
Donated by a daimyo (feudal lord) in 1650, this five-story pagoda was rebuilt in 1818 after a fire. Each story represents an element – earth, water, fire, wind, and heaven in ascending order.

↘ To Ieyasu's Tomb and Treasure Tower

Tokugawa Ieyasu

Ieyasu (1543–1616) was a wily strategist and master politician who founded the dynasty that would rule Japan for over 250 years. Born the son of a minor lord, he spent his life accumulating power, not becoming shogun until 1603, when he was 60. He built his capital at the swampy village of Edo (now Tokyo), and his rule saw the start of the flowering of Edo culture. He ensured that after his death, he would be enshrined as a god and *gongen* (incarnation of the Buddha). His posthumous name was Tosho-Daigongen (the great incar-nation illuminating the East).

Ieyasu's treasure tower, containing his ashes

Entrance

★ **Sacred Stable**
A carving of the three wise monkeys decorates this unpainted wooden building. A horse given by the New Zealand government is stabled here for several hours a day.

A Shinto priestess sweeping under the Yomeimon gate ▶

Nikko: Taiyuin-byo Shrine

Finished in 1653, Taiyuin-byo is the mausoleum of Tokugawa Iemitsu (1604–51), the grandson of Ieyasu and powerful third shogun, who closed Japan to foreign commerce and isolated it from the world for over 200 years. Tayuin is his posthumous Buddhist name. If Tosho-gu is splendid, Taiyuin-byo is sublime. Set in a grove of Japanese cedars, it has a number of ornate gates ascending to the Haiden (sanctuary) and Honden (inner sanctuary). The shogun's ashes are entombed beyond the sixth and final gate.

Kokamon Gate
This unusual Ming-dynasty Chinese-style gate is beside the path to Iemitsu's tomb.

★ **Haiden**
Decorated with carvings of dragons, the Haiden also has some famous 17th-century lion paintings by Kano School painters. Its exterior is decorated with black and gold lacquer.

Yashamon Gate
The third gate is beautifully gilded and contains four statues of Yasha, a fierce guardian spirit. It is also known as Botanmon, or peony gate, after its detailed peony carvings.

Niomon Gate
This marks the main entrance to the shrine. One Nio warrior god stands guard on each side.

Entrance

VISITORS' CHECKLIST

Practical Information
Tel (0288) 53-1567.
Open 8am–5pm daily (to 4pm Nov–Mar).

Bell Tower This structure forms a pair with the drum tower. They are no longer used, but the drum signifies positive/birth, while the bell is negative/death.

★ **Nitenmon Gate** Four guardian statues occupy the niches here. At the front are the gods Komoku and Jikoku, while at the back are the green god of wind and the red god of thunder.

Granite Fountain
On the ceiling above the basin is a dragon painting by Kano Yasunobu, which is sometimes reflected in the water below.

KEY

① **The Honden** (usually closed to the public) holds a gilded Buddhist altar with a wooden statue of Iemitsu.

② **The Ai No Ma** is a richly decorated connecting chamber.

③ **The Karamon** gate is adorned with delicate carvings, such as a pair of cranes.

④ **Drum Tower**

⑤ **Stone lanterns** were donated over the years by *daimyo* (feudal lords).

A monkey by the roadside, Nikko National Park

❷ Nikko National Park

日光国立公

Tochigi, Fukushima, and Gunma prefectures. 🚌 from Nikko stations.
ℹ 3-4 Namiki-cho, Nikko-shi (0288) 22-1525. 🌐 nikko-kankou.org

The magnificent national park that includes Tosho-gu and its environs is largely a mountainous volcanic plateau, studded with lakes, waterfalls, hot springs, and swamplands. For a taste of Oku-Nikko, the mountainous interior, take the bus west from Nikko to **Lake Chuzen-ji**. The hairpin curves of Irohazaka, along the old ascent to the sacred **Mount Nantai**, start at Umagaeshi (horse return), where pilgrims had to give up their horses and walk. Halfway up, at Akechidaira, there is an excellent view of Mount Nantai, which dominates the lake. At the east end of the lake, the **Kegon Falls**, named for the Buddhist principle of universal unity, cascade 96 m (315 ft) to the Daiya River below. An elevator through the cliff runs to an observation deck at the base of the falls.

At the nearby temple of **Chuzen-ji**, the main image is the Tachiki Kannon, a 1,000-armed Kannon said to have been carved from a live tree by Shodo Shoin, Nikko's founder. On July 31 hundreds of pilgrims make an overnight climb of Mount Nantai, reaching the top by sunrise. **Yumoto**, a lakeside *onsen* town, linked by bus to Nikko station and Lake Chuzen-ji, is one of several spas in the park.

❸ Mashiko
益子

Tochigi prefecture. 🚶 23,600.
🚃 (local trains only). 🚌 from Tobu-
Utsunomiya stn. 🛈 next to Mashiko
stn (0285-70-1120). 🎎 Pottery
Festivals (end Apr to early May;
end Oct to early Nov).

Known for its folk pottery,
Mashiko was home to the
world-famous potter Shoji
Hamada (1894–1978), a founder
of the *mingei* (folk art) movement. A long stretch of a town,
Mashiko has hundreds of
pottery shops and workshops.
Bicycles are easy to rent and
are the best way to explore.

The excellent **Mashiko Reference Collection Museum**
contains Hamada's studio and
kiln, and his eclectic collection
of ceramics and other crafts,
housed in beautifully restored
local buildings. Moegi and Toko
galleries, on the main street,
showcase local potters. On the
corner, by Toko, is the eighth-
generation **Higeta Dyeworks**
and its indigo dye vats, sunk in
the floor of a thatched workshop.

🏛 **Mashiko Museum**
Tel (0285) 72-7555.
Open Thu–Tue. 🎫

🏛 **Higeta Dyeworks**
Tel (0285) 72-3162. **Open** Tue–Sun.

❹ Aizu Wakamatsu
会津若松

Fukushima prefecture. 🚶 120,000.
🚃 🛈 in View Plaza at JR stn. 🎎 Aizu
Aki Matsuri (Fall Festival, Sep 22–24).
🌐 city.aizuwakamatsu.fukushima.
jp/e/index.htm

Once home to the north's
second most powerful clan,
Aizu Wakamatsu takes pride in
its samurai past. With ties to the
Tokugawas, the Matsudaira clan
bitterly resisted the
19th-century
movement to
reinstate the
emperor. In the
1868 Boshin War,
the Byakkotai
(White Tigers), a
band of teenage
samurai fighters
against imperial

Lacquerware bowl from
Aizu Wakamatsu

Shimenawa (straw rope) at the entrance to Kumano Jinja near Kitakata

forces, mistakenly thought the
castle had fallen and committed
mass suicide on **Iimoriyama**,
the hill (east of the station)
where they are now buried. On
the hill is a Pompeian marble
column topped by a bronze
eagle, sent by Rome in 1928 as
a salute from the Fascist party
to the Byakkotai.

The main sights are fairly
spread out: all-day bus passes
are available at the station bus
office. **Tsuruga Castle** has been
the heart of the city for over
600 years. It was last rebuilt in
1965 as a museum. To the east,
the **Samurai Residence** (Bukeyashiki), a good reproduction
of a 38-room samurai manor,
shows feudal life, down to a
160-year-old rice mill. Nearby,
the **Oyakuen**
(medicinal herb
garden) of a
17th-century villa
contains over 200
herbs. For shopping,
Nanukamachi-dori is
lined with old shops
selling traditional
crafts, including

painted candles, kites, striped
Aizu cotton, and the famed
Aizu lacquerware.

🏛 **Tsuruga Castle**
🚌 to Tsurugajo. **Tel** (0242) 27-4005.
Open daily. 🎫

🏛 **Samurai Residence**
🚌 Aizu bus to Bukeyashiki-mae.
Tel (0242) 28-2525. **Open** daily. 🎫

🌼 **Oyakuen**
🚌 Haikarasan bus to Oyakuen.
Tel (0242) 27-2472. **Open** daily. 🎫

❺ Kitakata
喜多方

Fukushima prefecture. 🚶 50,000. 🚃
🛈 next to JR stn (0241-24-2633).
🎎 Suwa Jinja Matsuri (Aug 2–3).
🌐 city.kitakata.fukushima.jp

Mud-walled *kura* (storehouses)
were long used to keep sake,
miso, rice, and other provisions
from fire, theft, and vermin.
Kitakata has more than 2,600,
including a *kura*-style temple.
Most are tucked away on back
streets. South of the **Kai Honke**,
a handsome sake-merchant's
house with a coffee-shop inside,

is a *kura*-lined walking lane. Along the way, the **Sake-Brewing Museum** offers informative tours, with tastings of Yamatogawa sake. Kitakata is also known for its ramen noodles and *oki-agari* dolls, which roll upright when knocked over.

Kai Honke
Tel (0241) 22-0001. **Open** variable. **Closed** New Year's holiday.

Sake-Brewing Museum
Tel (0241) 22-2233. **Open** variable.

Environs
Seven km (5 miles) south of the station is the unusual **Kumano Jinja**, an 11th-century shrine restored in the 1970s without walls, just wooden columns supporting a thatched roof.

❻ Bandai-Asahi National Park
磐梯朝日国立公園

Yamagata, Niigata, and Fukushima prefectures. to Fukushima, Koriyama, or Inawashiro. at Yamagata and Aizu-Wakamatsu stns. Bandai Matsuri (last weekend in Jul, Inawashiro).

On July 15, 1888, Mount Bandai erupted, killing 477 people. Dammed streams formed hundreds of lakes and marshes, creating the lush natural beauty of the Bandai-Asahi National Park. Crisscrossed by five scenic toll roads, including the Bandai-Azuma Skyline (open April 22–November 5), the park is studded with hot springs and camping grounds. The best way to explore is by car or bus.

Goshikinuma (five-colored marshes) is a popular 4-km (2-mile) trail starting at the Bandai-kogen or Goshikinuma bus stops. In Inawashiro the **Aizu Minzokukan** folk museum has over 24,000 items, and a garden of phallic rocks associated with fertility.

Aizu Minzokukan
from JR Inawashiro stn. **Tel** (0242) 65-2600. **Open** Apr 1–Nov 15: daily; Nov 16–Mar 31: Fri–Wed.

Lake on the Bandai-Asahi plateau

❼ Sado Island
佐渡島

Niigata prefecture. 63,000. ferry or hydrofoil from Niigata (city) to Ryotsu. Niigata port (025) 245-1234. frequently, spring to fall.

Though it receives more than a million visitors a year, Sado Island still feels remote. This mellow little island, 60 km (37 miles) off Honshu's northwest coast, offers a chance to enjoy fresh seafood and meet friendly people. For centuries, Sado was home to political exiles, including the emperor Juntoku in 1221, the priest Nichiren in 1271, and Zeami, the Noh actor and playwright, in 1433. Of the 88 Noh theaters once here, about 35 are left. In 1601 the discovery of gold in Aikawa brought an influx of convicts who were forced to work in the mines.

Buses connect the island's small towns, and tour buses stop at major attractions. In the main port of **Ryotsu** in the east, outdoor Noh performances are held at the **Honma Noh Stage**. In **Aikawa**, on the west coast, the touristy **Gold Mine** has mechanical dolls recreating the harsh mining conditions. **Aikawa Museum** has exhibits

on gold mining, ragweaving, and the local red-clay pottery.

The **Kodo** drummers have put Sado on the international map. The group, based in **Ogi**, in the southwest, should be contacted directly for further information. Nearby **Shukunegi**, with outlying rice paddies, is one of the island's loveliest villages.

Gold Mine
to Aikawa Eigayosho. **Tel** (0259) 74-2389. **Open** daily.

Aikawa Museum
to Aikawa Hakubutsukan-Mae. **Tel** (0259) 74-4312. **Open** daily. **Closed** Dec 29–Jan 3; Dec–Feb: Sat, Sun & public hols.

Kodo
Kodo Village, 148-1 Kaneta Shinden, Sado, Niigata 952-0611. **Tel** (0259) 86-3630. **W** kodo.or.jp

Clear seas and jagged rocks off the coast of Sado Island

The Kodo Drumming Group

A Kodo drummer beating a huge *o-daiko* drum

Kodo, one of the most famous and dynamic *taiko* drumming groups, formed in 1981, is known for performances of drum, flute, song, and dance. Kodo means both "children of the drum" and "heartbeat". The throbbing heart of Kodo is the *o-daiko*, a convex wooden drum used in Japanese folk festivals. Kodo spends much of the year performing in Japan and worldwide, and hosts an annual three-day Earth Celebration, when international musicians come to Sado to perform.

⑧ Tsuruoka

鶴岡

Yamagata prefecture. 🏔 132,000.
🚉 ℹ️ City Office, 9-25 Baba-cho
(0235) 25-2111. 🎎 Tenjin Matsuri
(May 25), Shonai Taisai (Feudal Lord's
Procession Aug 15).

Gateway to Dewa Sanzan,
Tsuruoka was the Sakai
clan's castle seat. Best
of this friendly
town's attractions is
the **Chido Museum**,
west of the former
castle grounds. It
includes a *kabuto-
zukuri* (helmet-style)
farmhouse, and
marvelous folk objects
such as lacquered sake
caskets, bamboo
fishing poles, and
decorative straw
bandori (backpacks).
Southeast of the castle
is the 1806 **Chidokan**, a
school for young samurai.
For the famous local painted
candles, visit the over 300-year-
old Togashi Candle Shop.

*Bandori backpack,
Chido Museum*

🎏 **Chido Museum**
Tel (0235) 22-1199. **Open** daily. 📷

🏛 **Chidokan**
Tel (0235) 23-4672. **Open** Mon–Fri.

⑨ Dewa Sanzan

出羽三山

Yamagata prefecture. 🚌 from Shoko
Mall near JR Tsuruoka stn. ℹ️ at
Tsuruoka stn (0235) 25-7678. Mt
Haguro: **Open** daily. 🎎 Hassaku
Matsuri (Aug 31), Shoreisai Matsuri
(Dec 31). Mt Gassan: **Open** Jul 1–fall.
Mt Yudono: **Open** late Apr–early Nov.

Dewa is the old name for this
region and Sanzan are its three
mountains – Haguro-san
(Mount Black Wing), Gassan
(Mount Moon), and Yudono-san
(Mount Bath) – opened for
religious purposes 1,400 years
ago by Hachiko, an Imperial
prince turned wandering
priest. The three are sacred to
yamabushi, mountain ascetics
of the Shugendo sect.
    Millions of pilgrims and sight-
seers visit Dewa Sanzan on foot
or by toll road. The route to the
peak of **Mount Haguro** is a climb

up the 2,446 stone steps of the
Japanese cedar-lined path. Take
the bus to Haguro Center to start
the climb. At the second stage
is a teahouse with a view of the
Mogami River valley. A side path
goes to the ruins of a temple
where Basho stayed. At the top
is the **Dewa Sanzan Shrine**, an
impressive lacquered
building with the largest
thatched roof in
Japan, and Prince
Hachiko's tomb.
After the 1868 Meiji
Restoration, all
Shugendo temples
were turned into
Shinto shrines. The
only true Buddhist struc-
ture left is the graceful
five-story **pagoda**
at the foot of the
stone steps.
    Mount Gassan, also
topped by a shrine,
offers alpine flowers
and summer skiing. It is a two-
hour trek to the top from the
Hachigome bus stop. The shrine
on **Mount Yudono**, a 2.5-km
(2- mile) hike from the Yudonosan
Hotel bus stop, has a sacred
hot-water spring in which pilgrims bathe their feet. Mummified priests, examples of *soku-
shin jobutsu* (living Buddhas),
can be seen at the temples of
Dainichi-bo and **Churen-ji**, on
the way to Mount Yudono.

*Equestrian statue of Masamune, founder of
the city of Sendai*

⑩ Sendai

仙台

Miyagi prefecture. 🏔 1,067,000.
✈️ 🚉 ℹ️ at Tohoku Shinkansen stn.
🎏 Sendai Aoba Matsuri (3rd
weekend in May), Sendai Tanabata
(Weavers' Festival, Aug 6–8).
🌐 city.sendai.jp/index-e.html

Laid out in a grid pattern in the
1600s by the dynamic lord Date
Masamune, Sendai is the north's
largest city. **Osaki Hachiman
Shrine** is a black lacquer
architectural beauty in the
northwest of the city. Overlooking the ruins of **Aoba Castle**
from 1602 is a statue of the
warrior Masamune, nicknamed
the "one-eyed dragon." The ruins
are set in a park a bus ride to the
west of the station. Nearby, the
ornately carved Date
mausoleums at **Zuihoden**,
rebuilt after the war, are
remarkable replicas of
Momoyama-period architecture.
    In March 2011,
Sendai became the
epicenter of the worst
earthquake and
tsunami in recorded
Japanese history.
Sendai airport was
engulfed by the 7-m
(24-ft) high tsunami
wave resulting in its
complete closure,
and significant
damage was done
to the road, rail and
subway networks. The
city is slowly starting
to recover, and with
the help of the US
army the airport
has since reopened.
However, it is best
to contact the
tourist office before
visiting the area.

Cedar-lined stone steps up to Mount Haguro

For hotels and restaurants see pp302–307 and pp324–339

Buddhist Sects

In the course of 1,500 years or so, since the time that priests from mainland Asia first brought Buddhism *(see pp32–3)* to Japan, hundreds of separate Buddhist movements, sects, and subsects developed in the country. Contrasting beliefs appealed to different groups of nobility, samurai, and commoners, who each adapted practices to their own ends. In the eyes of many foreigners today, Zen, one-time favorite of the samurai, is the quintessential religion of Japan, but it is just one of several major movements originating in China, and is itself subdivided into various sects. Of other movements flowering in Japan, the Tendai and Shingon sects of esoteric Buddhism still have millions of devotees.

Zen Buddhism

The Taoist-inspired Chan school from China first gained popularity in Japan during the Kamakura period (1185–1333). There are three main Zen sects: Soto, Rinzai, and Obaku. All place emphasis on *zazen* (sitting meditation) and self-help. As developed in the great Zen temples of Kyoto during the feudal era, the rigorous mindset and uncluttered aesthetics of Zen have had a profound influence on Japanese culture at large.

Zen gardens express a sublime harmony between humanity and nature.

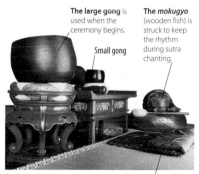

The large gong is used when the ceremony begins.

The *mokugyo* (wooden fish) is struck to keep the rhythm during sutra chanting.

Small gong

At Zuiho-in, a subtemple of the great Zen temple Daitoku-ji *(see p177)* in Kyoto, priests use percussion instruments while chanting the sutras as part of their daily training.

The cushion is used to sit on while listening to lectures.

Shingon

This branch of esoteric Mahayana Buddhism was founded in Japan in the 9th century by Kukai *(see p233)*. It incorporates such Hindu elements as mandalas and multi-armed deities, and places emphasis on hand gestures *(mudra)* and the chanting of mantras. The headquarters are at Mount Koya *(see p203)*, and there are 50 or so subsects today.

Shingon deity from Mount Koya displaying the *yogan semui-in* mudra with the hands.

Shingon sect follower

Tendai

Brought to Japan in the 9th century by Saicho, Tendai is another branch of esoteric Buddhism and places emphasis on selfless devotion. From its base at Mount Hiei, Tendai helped spawn the Jodo (Pure Land), Jodo Shin, and Nichiren sects.

The Amida Buddha (Amida Nyorai) of the Tendai sect leads the way to the Pure Land.

Shugendo

Dewa Sanzan in Northern Honshu is the most sacred site for the Shugendo sect. This offshoot of Shingon combines Buddhism and Shinto, and promotes ascetic practices on mountain retreats.

Yamabushi (ascetic) at Shugendo-sect Dewa Sanzan

Irregularly shaped pine-covered islands in Matsushima bay

⓫ Matsushima
松島

Miyagi prefecture. 🚇 16,000. 🚃 to Matsumisha and Matsushima-Kaigan. 🚢 from Shiogama. 🛈 outside JR Matsushima-Kaigan stn (022) 354-2263. 🎊 Toronagashi Hanabi Taikai (floating lanterns, Aug 15), Osegakie (Consolation Festival, Aug 16, Zuigan-ji).

Take a hint from Matsuo Basho's 1689 visit to the bay of Matsushima and make Shiogama your starting point. The busy **Shiogama Wholesale Fish Market**, active from early morning until about 1pm, is known for its huge tuna auctions. Dedicated to both mariners and mothers-to-be is the beautiful hilltop **Shiogama Shrine**. Make time to lunch at one of Shiogama's superb sushi restaurants before taking the ferry to Matsushima.

Although the tsunami of March 2011 caused widespread destruction along Japan's northeast coast, Matsushima was greatly spared thanks to

the numerous islands in its bay. These pine-covered islets are the reason Matsushima became renowned as one of Japan's "three famous views." Post-tsunami reconstruction is under way, but sites such as **Zuigan-ji**, a handsome Zen training temple, have long been open to the public.

⓬ Hiraizumi
平泉

Iwate prefecture. 🚇 8,800. 🚃 🛈 next to JR stn (0191) 46-2110. 🎊 Fujiwara Matsuri (May 1–5 & Nov 1–3).

Nine hundred years ago, the Northern Fujiwara clan, under Fujiwara Kiyohira, made this small town into a cultural and economic capital, second only to Kyoto. Three generations later, Hiraizumi was in ruins. Yoshitsune, Japan's archetypal tragic hero, sought refuge here from Yoritomo, his jealous brother and Japan's first shogun, but was betrayed by Yasuhira,

the last Fujiwara leader, and killed. Yoritomo then turned against Yasuhira and had the clan wiped out.

At its peak, Hiraizumi had a population of 100,000. Wishing to create a Buddhist paradise on earth, Kiyohira enriched the 9th-century temples Chuson-ji and Motsu-ji. **Chuson-ji** is 5 minutes by bus from the station, followed by a long climb lined with towering Japanese cedars. Only two of its many original buildings remain: the small **Golden Hall**, splendid with gold leaf, lacquer, and mother of pearl, where the first three Fujiwara leaders are buried; and the **Sutra Hall**. In the **Treasure Hall** are remarkable precious artefacts from the Fujiwara coffins and the temple.

All that remains of the original **Motsu-ji** (a 10-minute walk from the station) are its foundations and beautiful Heian-period paradise garden, the best in Japan.

⓭ Hanamaki
花巻

Iwate prefecture. 🚇 105,000. ✈ 🚃 🛈 at JR Shin-Hanamaki and JR Hanamaki stns. 🎊 Hanamaki Matsuri (Fri–Sun, 2nd weekend in Sep); Kenji Sai (Kenji Festival, Sep 21). 🌐 **city.hanamaki.iwate.jp**

Kenji Miyazawa (1896–1933), one of Japan's best-loved writers, was born in Hanamaki, a thriving hot-spring town. He wrote more than 1,200 poems and 90 children's stories, and worked to improve conditions

Steps up to Hiraizumi's Golden Hall at Chuson-ji, Hiraizumi

For hotels and restaurants see pp302–307 and pp324–339

for poor farmers in Iwate. The **Miyazawa Memorial Museum** has exhibits that reflect Miyazawa's lifelong interests in minerology, astronomy, wildlife, agriculture, Esperanto, and Buddhism. There is also the Ihatov, a free arts and research center. Ihatov was Miyazawa's Esperanto name for Iwate.

🏛 **Miyazawa Memorial Museum**
Tel (0198) 31-2319. **Open** daily. 🖼

A wooden *torii* (gate) to Mount Hayachine

⓮ Tono
遠野

Iwate prefecture. 🏔 31,000. 🚉
ℹ by JR stn (0198) 62-1333.
🎏 Tono Matsuri (mid-Sep).

In Tono people still live in rhythm with nature, and observe old ways and traditions. Much has changed, though, since folklorist Kunio Yanagita compiled the *Legends of Tono* in 1910. Few of the *magariya* (L-shaped houses,

shared by people and horses) are left, but the mountains ringing the Tono basin are still beautiful.

Tono's attractions are best reached by car or bicycle, both of which can be rented at the station. At the private **Naka-yama House**, in Kamigo district, you can see wonderful 350-year-old *oshirasama* dolls. The **Municipal Museum** in the town center introduces local culture. At **Denshoen**, a mellow tourist venue in Tsuchibuchi district, local experts teach traditional crafts. A short walk away are **Kappabuchi** stream and the temple of **Joken-ji**, both traditionally the home of *kappa* (water imps). Northwest of the railroad station **Tono Furusato Village** has six *magariya*, where you can see traditional craftwork being made. **Hayachine Shrine**, a 30-minute drive from the station, is known for its Kagura (sacred dances), and **Mount Hayachine** is popular with climbers.

🏛 **Nakayama House**
Tel (0198) 65-2609. **Open** by appt only.

🏛 **Municipal Museum**
Tel (0198) 62-2340. **Open** Apr–Oct: daily; Nov–Mar: Tue–Sun. **Closed** last day of month in May–Oct, Mar 1–4, Nov 24–30, public hols. 🖼

Morioka's "stone-splitting" tree

⓯ Morioka
盛岡

Iwate prefecture. 🏔 295,000. 🚉
ℹ 2nd flr, JR stn (019) 625-2090.
🎏 Chagu chagu Umakko (Horse Festival, 2nd Sat in Jun).
🌐 city.morioka.iwate.jp

An old castle town, once the center of the Nanbu domain, Morioka is now Iwate's capital and a transportation hub for the north, known for its Nanbu *tetsubin* (iron kettles) and Mount Iwate, the majestic volcano overlooking it. In October salmon run up the Nakatsu River, one of three rivers that bisect the city.

All that remains of **Morioka Castle**, in Iwate Park, are its stone walls and moats. Nearby is the over 350-year-old "stone-splitting" cherry tree, which has grown from a crevice in a bowlder.

Over Nakatsu River is the **Mor-ihisa Iron Studio**, which has superb iron pieces on display. If you want to buy folk crafts, head for **Konya-cho** (dyers' street), to the north, and **Zaimoku-cho** (lumber street), to the left across Asahi bridge.

Morioka is home to the noodle-eating tradition of *wanko-soba*. At **Azumaya Soba Shop**, small bowls of soba buckwheat are placed in front of customers who are then encouraged to finish as many as possible. At the end, they get official certificates indicating the total number of bowls consumed.

Nanbu iron kettle

🏛 **Morihisa Iron Studio**
Tel (019) 622-3809. **Open** daily.

🍜 **Azumaya Soba Shop**
Tel (019) 622-2252.

Japanese Dolls

More than a thousand years ago, simple cloth dolls called *sarukko* were attached to babies' clothing as charms against harm. The thousands of clay dolls unearthed at Jomon-period sites are also believed to have had symbolic functions. These dolls remind some scholars of *oshirasama* dolls – stick figures, usually of a horse and a girl, made of mulberry or bamboo and draped in layers of cloth – still found, and venerated, in parts of northern Japan. Other favorites include: the limbless painted *kokeshi* dolls, made by woodturners at hot-spring towns around northern Japan; *ohinasama*, the elaborate tiered arrays of silk court dolls displayed each Girls' Day (March 3); and *anesan ningyo* (big sister dolls), ingenious figures folded from paper.

Oshirasama dolls in Tono's Nakayama House

⑯ Kakunodate
角館

Akita prefecture. 14,000.
JR stn (0187) 54-2700.
Aki Matsuri (Fall Festival, Sep 7–9).

Famed for its samurai quarter and weeping cherry trees, Kakunodate does not have a large number of its original samurai houses remaining. But the overall atmosphere of the place, centered on its broad avenue, faced with the gated houses, is beautifully evocative of the past. More than 150 of the weeping cherries in the Uchimachi district, brought from Kyoto almost 300 years ago, have been designated National Natural Treasures.

Among the samurai houses that are open to the public, the large **Aoyagi-ke** has three small museums in its grounds. Look for the ceilings painted with waves as protection from fire. At the classic **Ishiguro-ke**, known for its beautiful garden, note the transoms between rooms, carved to project shadows by candlelight. Also on Uchimachi, the red-brick **Denshokan Museum** has exhibits of historical and craft items and demonstrations of outstanding local crafts, including *kabazaiku* (objects of polished cherry bark) and *itayazaiku* (baskets and folk objects woven of split maple).

Aoyagi-ke
Tel (0187) 54-3257. **Open** daily.

Ishiguro-ke
Tel (0187) 55-1496. **Open** daily.

Denshokan Museum
Tel (0187) 54-1700. **Open** daily.

Looking into the garden from Ishiguro-ke samurai house, Kakunodate

⑰ Oga Peninsula
男鹿半島

Akita prefecture. JR Oga stn.
next to JR Oga stn (0185) 23-2111.
Namahage Sedo Matsuri (2nd Fri–Sun in Feb); Namahage (Dec 31).

Kicking 20 km (12 miles) into the Sea of Japan (East Sea), this foot-shaped peninsula has a scenic rocky coastline, pleasant little fishing villages, good seafood, and hills covered with Akita cedar. The lookout on **Mount Kanpu**, at the neck of the peninsula, offers a panoramic view of mountains, sea, and spreading rice fields. The peninsula is best known for its Namahage Festival, held on New Year's Eve, when men dressed in horned demon masks and bulky straw coats go from house to house, scaring children into being good and idlers into working. A tourist version of the festival, the Namahage Sedo Matsuri, is held at **Shinzan Shrine**, in the city of Oga.

⑱ Towada-Hachimantai National Park
十和田八幡平国立公園

Akita, Aomori, and Iwate prefectures.
JR Morioka & JR Aomori stns.
from stns to Lake Towada.
at Lake Towada (0176) 75-2425.

Touching three prefectures, the Towada-Hachimantai National Park is in two sections with the mountainous Hachimantai section 60 km (37 miles) south of the Towada section. Car is the best way to get around: trains are limited and buses not available in winter. **Hachimantai** offers hiking and ski trails, frozen lava flows, alpine flora, and mountain views. A favorite with Japanese tourists, it has scenic toll roads, hot-spring and ski resorts, and a variety of tourist facilities. Good stopping places include **Goshogake** *onsen*, **Hachimantai Resort** ski complex, and the tourist village of **Putaro**.

In the **Towada** section highlights include **Lake Towada**, a lovely caldera lake. Its symbol, a statue of two maidens (1953) by Kotaro Takamura, is on the southern shore. More dramatic is the 9 km (6-mile) **Oirase Gorge** to the east of the lake. While it is possible to travel the gorge by bus, car, or bike, it is best to get off the busy highway and walk. Also impressive are Towada's virgin beech forests, rightly dubbed an ocean of trees. North of the lake are some atmospheric spa inns, such as the excellent Tsuta Onsen.

Beech forest in the Towada section of Towada-Hachimantai National Park

For hotels and restaurants see pp302–307 and pp324–339

⑲ Hirosaki
弘前

Aomori prefecture. 🚋 175,000. 🚉
ℹ️ Hirosaki stn (0172) 26-3600.
🎎 Neputa Matsuri (Aug 1–7).
🌐 city.hirosaki.aomori.jp

Long the cultural and educational center of Aomori, Hirosaki is a delight to explore, its main attraction being its castle, a pocket of feudal history in a thriving modern city. Most streets lead, more or less, to **Hirosaki Park**, the old castle grounds of the Tsugaru lords. The castle was destroyed by lightning but its picturesque 1810 keep, some smaller towers, several gates, and three moats remain. **Kamenokomon**, the imposing main gate, is on the north, where historic samurai houses still stand. Nearby is the **Tsugaruhan Neputa Mura**, displaying the Neputa floats used in Hirosaki's more refined version of Aomori's Nebuta festival.

The wooded castle park is famous for its cherry blossoms, at their best in late April. The **Municipal Museum**, inside the park, has exhibitions of local history, including old photographs of the Neputa Festival.

One of the temples en route to Chosho-ji, Hirosaki

Twenty-two temples line the approach to **Chosho-ji**, the family temple of the Tsugaru, about a 15-minute walk southwest of the park, built on a bluff overlooking the Hirosaki plain and Mount Iwaki. Its handsome two-story gate has extra-deep eaves because of the heavy snows common in the area. A side hall contains interesting polychrome statues of the Buddha's 500 disciples. The naturally mummified body of the 12th Tsugaru lord is displayed in the main hall.

Like most feudal towns, the streets around the castle were designed to twist and turn to confuse enemy forces. The large **Kankokan** (municipal information center) just south of the park is a good place to get oriented. It also has displays of local crafts. Other good craft outlets include Tanakaya, on the corner of Ichiban-cho, which has a fine selection of traditional and contemporary Tsugaru lacquerware. Miyamoto Kogei, on Minami Sakura-cho, handles baskets of *akebi*, a vine that grows wild in the mountains. Not to be missed is the lively restaurant Kenta *(see p337)*.

🎎 **Tsugaruhan Neputa Mura**
NE corner outside castle park.
Tel (0172) 39-1511. **Open** daily. 🎎

🏛️ **Municipal Museum**
Tel (0172) 35-0700. **Open** Tue–Sun.

🏯 **Chosho-ji**
Tel (0172) 32-0813. Main hall: **Open** Mar–Nov: daily (appt other times). 🎎

Reconstructed dwellings at Sannai-Maruyama

⑳ Aomori
青森

Aomori prefecture. 🚋 300,000. 🚉
ℹ️ JR Bus stn bldg (017) 723-4670.
🎎 Nebuta Matsuri (Aug 2–7).
🌐 city.aomori.aomori.jp

Rebuilt after World War II, Aomori is a nondescript city with two outstanding attractions. One is the Nebuta Matsuri *(see p50)*; the other **Sannai-Maruyama**, a Jomon-period (10,000–300 BC) site. Since its discovery in 1993, the site has yielded relics and ruins from 4,000–5,500 years ago, including a woven pouch, red lacquerware, and clay figures. Most impressive are the reconstructed pit dwellings and a standing-pillar building.

🚌 **Sannai-Maruyama**
🚌 from JR stn to Sannai-Maruyama Iseki. **Tel** (017) 734-9924. **Open** daily.

㉑ Shimokita Peninsula
下北半島

Aomori prefecture. 🚉 JR Ominato stn. ℹ️ at JR Ominato stn.

This ax-shaped peninsula offers unspoiled beauty. In the interior is the desolate **Osorezan** (Mount Dread), one of three Japanese mountains sacred to spirits of the dead, with a crater lake and sulfur hot springs. It is open from May to October. Blind mediums communicate with the spirits from July 20–24. Take the ferry from Sai along the west coast to **Hotoke-ga-ura** (Buddha Coast) with sea-worn cliffs and rock formations. In the southwest the port of **Wakinosawa** is home to sassy snow monkeys. A ferry runs from here to Aomori.

Basho and Haiku

Matsuo Basho (1644–94), a master of style and a thinker to whom life and art were one, perfected the form that came to be known as haiku. It is now practiced internationally. A classical haiku is 17 syllables (written 5-7-5), includes a seasonal word, and refers to an objective image in the present. Basho spent most of his life traveling and writing haiku. His most famous travel journal, a superb guide to northern Japan, is *The Narrow Road to the Deep North*, about his five-month pilgrimage in 1689; the northernmost point of his journey was Akita prefecture.

Statue of Basho

HOKKAIDO

Japan's northernmost island is on the Pacific "ring of fire" at the southern edge of the Sea of Okhotsk. Russia lies to the north, west, and east, while the Tsugaru Strait to the south separates Hokkaido from Honshu. With both sea-ice and active volcanoes, it is truly a land of fire and ice. Dramatic peaks, gorges, and lakes all contribute to making Hokkaido the part of Japan where nature is at its most vivid.

First settled 20,000 years ago, this remote northern island became the homeland of the indigenous Ainu people after the 12th century. The Japanese made early forays to Yezo, as the island was called, in ancient times, but it was perceived as remote, inhospitable, and cold. For centuries only the persecuted Ainu, refugee warriors, and banished criminals lived there. In the late 1860s, however, the new Meiji government decided officially to develop the island. Thereafter it became known as Hokkaido, or "north sea road."

Since then, the population has risen to just under 6 million. The few Ainu left number somewhere between 24,000 and 60,000. Fishing, farming, forestry, and mining are the main industries, but tourism draws several million people north each year.

Sapporo, the capital, is a lively, growing city, home to spectacular festivals. Outside Sapporo, the lifestyle of the Ainu is one of the few points of cultural and historical interest for the visitor. By contrast, many national parks offer boundless opportunities for outdoor enthusiasts, including camping, hiking, and hot-spring bathing. Extensive forests, broad mountain ranges, numerous lakes and wetlands, and a long coastline support a wealth of plant, animal, and birdlife.

The prevailing winter winds blow in from Siberia, resulting in an almost arctic winter climate, with temperatures sometimes dropping to -30°C (-22°F). This results in perfect powder snow for skiers. Between May and September temperatures rise well into the 20°s C (70°s F).

Nighttime scene in Susukino, the entertainment district of Hokkaido's modern capital, Sapporo

◀ The picturesque gorge at the *onsen* resort town of Sounkyo, Daisetsu-zan National Park

Exploring Hokkaido

Just five percent of the Japanese population has settled on Japan's second-largest island, mainly in the capital, Sapporo, and the port of Hakodate. Volcanic mountains, caldera lakes, and rocks stained by yellow sulfur characterize the wild interior, while forests and wetlands provide breeding grounds for wildlife. Wildflowers are bountiful on coasts and mountains in spring and summer. Information in English is not readily available outside Sapporo and Hakodate, and distances between sights are great, so planning ahead is essential if time is limited. Allow at least a week to explore the island.

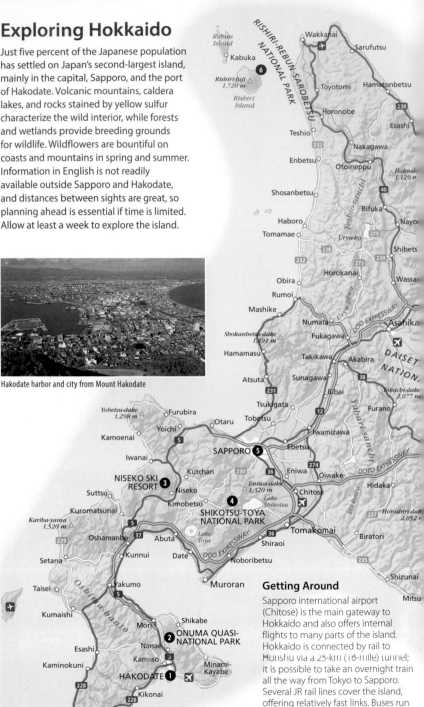

Hakodate harbor and city from Mount Hakodate

Getting Around

Sapporo international airport (Chitose) is the main gateway to Hokkaido and also offers internal flights to many parts of the island. Hokkaido is connected by rail to Honshu via a 25-km (16-mile) tunnel; it is possible to take an overnight train all the way from Tokyo to Sapporo. Several JR rail lines cover the island, offering relatively fast links. Buses run to many destinations, although a car or bicycle provides more flexibility. Numerous hiking routes crisscross the national parks.

For hotels and restaurants see pp302–307 and pp324–339

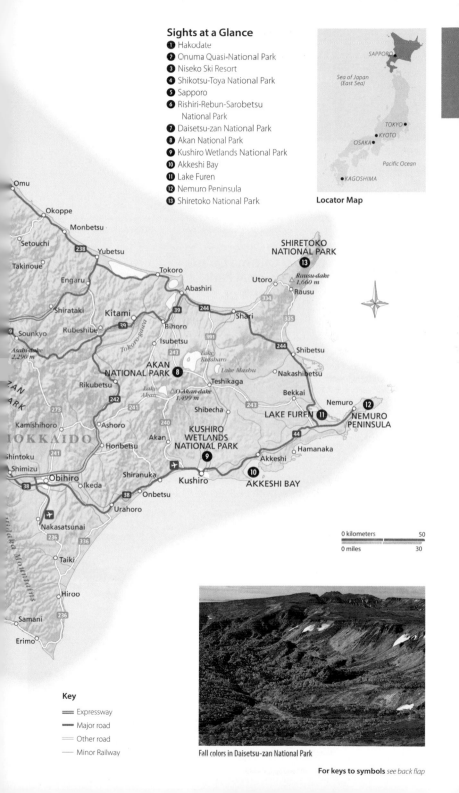

Sights at a Glance

1. Hakodate
2. Onuma Quasi-National Park
3. Niseko Ski Resort
4. Shikotsu-Toya National Park
5. Sapporo
6. Rishiri-Rebun-Sarobetsu National Park
7. Daisetsu-zan National Park
8. Akan National Park
9. Kushiro Wetlands National Park
10. Akkeshi Bay
11. Lake Furen
12. Nemuro Peninsula
13. Shiretoko National Park

Locator Map

SAPPORO

Sea of Japan
(East Sea)

TOKYO
KYOTO
OSAKA

Pacific Ocean

KAGOSHIMA

Omu
Okoppe
Monbetsu
Setouchi
238
Takinoue
Yubetsu
Engaru

SHIRETOKO
NATIONAL PARK
13

Utoro
Rausu-dake
1,660 m
Rausu

Shirataki
Kitami
Rubeshibe
39
Bihoro
Isubetsu

Sounkyo
*Asahi-dake
2,290 m*

Tokoro-gawa

334
Abashiri
244
Shari
335

243
Lake
Kussharo
Lake Mashu
**AKAN
NATIONAL PARK** 8

244
Shibetsu
Nakashibetsu

Rikubetsu
242
241
Lake
Akan
O-Akan-dake
1,499 m
Teshikaga
Shibecha

Bekkai
LAKE FUREN 11
Nemuro 12
**NEMURO
PENINSULA**

Kamishihoro
273
HOKKAIDO
Ashoro
Honbetsu
240
Akan

**KUSHIRO
WETLANDS
NATIONAL PARK** 9

243

44
Hamanaka

Shintoku
241
Shimizu
38
Obihiro
Ikeda
Shiranuka
Onbetsu
38
Urahoro

Kushiro
Akkeshi
AKKESHI BAY 10

236
Nakasatsunai
336
Taiki

Hidaka Mountains

Hiroo
236
Samani
Erimo

0 kilometers   50
0 miles   30

Key

═══ Expressway
─── Major road
─── Other road
─── Minor Railway

Fall colors in Daisetsu-zan National Park

For keys to symbols *see back flap*

Blossom-viewing in Hakodate's Goryokaku Park

❶ Hakodate
函館

🏙 273,000. ✈ Hakodate. 🚉 from Sapporo. 🚢 from Aomori. ℹ JR stn (0138) 23-5440. 🎌 Hakodate Port Festival (Aug 1–5). 🌐 **city.hakodate.hokkaido.jp**

Once an island, the fan-shaped city of Hakodate now straddles a low sandbar that links it to the mainland. In 1854, Hakodate was designated one of the first treaty ports in Japan. Fifteen years later the city was the scene of the last battle in Japan before World War II.

Within easy reach of the center is **Mount Hakodate**, the peak of which can be reached by cable car, road, or on foot. The spectacular view of the shimmering city lights fanning out between the two dark arms of the sea is considered one of the finest night views in all of Japan.

The quiet **Motomachi** district, nestling beneath Mount Hakodate in the south of the city, is the most attractive area. Western-style buildings are a feature here, a legacy of the treaty-port status. They include the **Old Public Hall**, with its stately blue-and-yellow clapboarding; the **Russian Orthodox Church** with its spire and onion domes; and, nearby, the **Old British Consulate**.

In the north, **Goryokaku Park** provides a peaceful haven for strolling, and its more than 1,500 cherry trees create a popular springtime spectacle. The pentagon-shaped **Goryokaku Fort** was built in 1865 to defend against the Russians, but it fell to imperial forces in 1869.

Environs
Hot-spring enthusiasts will want to stay at the *onsen* resort of **Yunokawa** 15 minutes from the center. An hour's drive to the east of the city is the active **Mount Esan** volcano with nearby azalea gardens and forested slopes.

❷ Onuma Quasi-National Park
大沼国定公園

🚉 Onuma-Koen stn. 🚌 from Hakodate. ℹ next to stn (0138) 67-2170.

Three large, islet-studded lakes – Onuma, Konuma, and Junsainuma – are surrounded by forest and form the Onuma Quasi-National Park. Deer and foxes inhabit the forests, and the lakes support many kinds of waterfowl, particularly during the spring and fall migrations. Wildflowers are abundant in summer and among the rare birds that come to Onuma are the ruddy kingfisher, white-tailed eagle, and Steller's sea eagle. The graceful form of **Mount Komagatake** provides a stunning backdrop to the north. An easily followed hiking trail from the north side of Lake Onuma to the upper mountain provides a fabulous view of southwestern Hokkaido.

❸ Niseko Ski Resort
ニセコスキーリゾート

🚉 Niseko stn. 🚌 from Sapporo.

Some of Japan's best skiing can be found in the Niseko mountains. Snowboarders and skiers alike favor this area for its long, cold winter season, numerous slopes, and quality off-piste powder. In summer it offers adventure-sports vacations. Three major resorts are connected at the top of the same mountain and shuttle buses link them at the base. A single pass can be used for all the resorts. **Hirafu** is very popular among foreigners, and during the skiing season it takes on the character of a lively alpine village.

❹ Shikotsu-Toya National Park
支笏洞爺国立公園

🚉 Toya stn. 🚌 from Sapporo. ℹ 142-5 Toyakoonsen-cho, Toyako-cho, Abuta District (0142) 75-2555. 🌐 **toyako-vc.jp/en**

The disjointed Shikotsu-Toya National Park is like an open-air museum to vulcanology. It contains the 1,900-m- (6,230-ft-) high **Mount Yotei** (also known as Ezo-Fuji, due to its conical

Mount Komagatake across Lake Onuma

shape), two large crater lakes, and the spa towns of **Jozankei** in the north and **Noboribetsu** in the south. Summer weekends and fall tend to be busy with visitors from nearby Sapporo.

By **Lake Shikotsu** is the popular hot-spring resort of **Shikotsu Kohan**, as well as the remarkable moss-covered **Kokenodomon** gorge. The lake is dominated to the north by the rugged peak of **Mount Eniwa**, and to the south by the recumbent forms of **Mount Fuppushi** and **Mount Tarumae**, with its cinder cone.

Lake Toya, 40 km (25 miles) farther southwest, contains the picturesque central island of Oshima and three smaller satellite islands. Nearby stands Japan's youngest volcano, the bare-sloped **Showa Shinzan** (formed 1943–5), beside the extremely active **Mount Usu**.

The mountains in the park make for rewarding day hiking; trails are well defined, and the views from the tops of Eniwa and Tarumae are superb.

⑤ Sapporo

札幌

🏙 1,930,000. ✈ Shin-Chitose, Okadama. 🚊 ℹ️ Sapporo International Communication Plaza, opposite Sapporo Clock Tower (011) 211-3678. 🎿 Snow Festival (1st week in Feb); Hokkaido Shrine Festival (Jun 14–16); Summer Festival (Jul 21–Aug 20); Bon Odori (mid-Aug). 🌐 plaza-sapporo.or.jp/english/access_e.html

Capital of Hokkaido, the modern city of Sapporo lies on the Ishikari plain, straddling the Toyohira River. Four subway lines, street cars, and a well laid-out grid structure make getting around fairly straightforward. At Sapporo's heart lies the long **Odori Park**, dominated at the east end by the metal television tower and at the west by a view to the mountains. One block north, opposite the historic wooden **Tokei-dai** clocktower, is the **Sapporo International Communication Plaza**, an essential stop for information on travel all over Hokkaido,

Neon lights in Sapporo's busy Susukino district

with friendly staff to help with planning and booking. The city gives its name to the famous local beer; its brewing is shown at the **Sapporo Beer Garden and Museum** northeast of the station. Nightlife is focused on the **Susukino** area, two stops south of the station on the Nanboku subway line, with thousands of restaurants and bars. Local specialties include "Genghis Khan" – mutton and vegetables grilled at the table on a charcoal-fired griddle.

A large collection of Ainu artifacts is displayed at the **Exhibition Room of Northern Peoples** in the **Botanical Gardens**. The gardens themselves are a refreshingly quiet spot, with a representative collection of Hokkaido's flora. The large-scale outdoor sculptures at the **Sapporo Art Park** make for an interesting hands-on excursion.

🏛 **Sapporo Beer Museum**
Tel (011) 748-1876. **Open** Tue–Sun.

🏛 **Botanical Gardens and Exhibition Room of Northern Peoples**
10-min walk SW of stn. **Tel** (011) 591-0090. **Open** end Apr–early Nov: Tue–Sun. 🎫

🏛 **Sapporo Art Park**
Open daily. **Closed** Nov 4–Apr 28: Mon.

Environs
Lying 14 km (9 miles) east of the city, the **Historical Village of Hokkaido** commemorates the official settlement of the island in the 1860s. This cluster of late 19th- and early 20th-century buildings has been gathered from around Hokkaido. Some have displays of traditional life inside.

🏛 **Historical Village of Hokkaido**
Tel (011) 898-2692. **Open** Tue–Sun. 🎫 🌐 **kaitaku.or.jp**

Sapporo Snow Festival

The annual Snow Festival (Yuki Matsuri) transforms Sapporo's Odori Park and the nearby Susukino area and Makomanai Park into a fairy-tale land of snow sculptures and ice carvings, drawing up to two million visitors. Watching the making of these imaginative and complex forms (from about a week before the start of the festival) can be even more interesting than seeing the finished objects. The festival overlaps with the Sapporo White Illumination: (mid-November to mid-February) when strings of white lights adorn Odori Park and Ekimae-dori. A night visit is magical.

One of the elaborate snow carvings at Sapporo's Snow Festival

❻ Rishiri-Rebun-Sarobetsu National Park

利尻礼文サロベツ国立公園

✈ Wakkanai. 🚉 Wakkanai stn.
🚌 from Wakkanai to both islands.

Consisting of the Sarobetsu coast of north Hokkaido and the two islands of Rishiri and Rebun, this park is within sight of the Russian island of Sakhalin. Although remote – at least a 6-hour drive north of Sapporo – the park is easily accessible by plane or train. The coastal meadows in the **Sarobetsu** area and the shores of the shallow lagoons in the coastal plain, are carpeted with flowers in summer, including yellow-orange lilies, white cotton grass, white rhododendrons, and purple irises.

About 20 km (12 miles) offshore on the island of Rishiri, the startling 1,720-m (5,650-ft) high conical peak of **Mount Rishiri** (Rishiri-Fuji) appears to rise straight from the sea. A road runs around its coastline, making for scenic cycling and linking the various settlements including **Oshidomari**, the main port, and **Kutsugata**, the second port on the west side. Trails to the top of Mount Rishiri thread through a host of alpine summer flowers. Those less inclined to hike may choose to fish or simply relax and enjoy the excellent fresh fish at local restaurants.

Rebun, Rishiri's partner and Japan's northernmost island, is lowly in comparison but is renowned as the "isle of flowers."

Kabuka is its main port; the fishing village of **Funadomari** is at the opposite, north end of the island. There's great hiking (sometimes hard-going), especially on the west coast; the island's youth hostel organizes guided walking groups.

Women cutting dried kelp at Kutsugata on Rishiri Island

❼ Daisetsu-zan National Park

大雪山国立公園

✈ Okadama and Asahikawa.
🚉 Asahikawa and Obihiro stns.
ℹ Sounkyo, Kamikawa-cho (01658) 9-4400.

At 2,310 sq km (890 sq miles), Daisetsu-zan is Japan's largest national park. A huge raised plateau ringed with peaks, right in the center of Hokkaido, the park was established in 1934. **Asahikawa** to the northwest or **Obihiro** to the south make the best starting points for visiting the park, with easy car access by routes 39 and 273. Buses connect the major *onsen* resorts of **Sounkyo**, **Asahi-dake**, and

Tenninkyo. The plunging **Sounkyo Gorge**, with the cascading Ryusei and Ginga waterfalls, is best explored by bicycle or on foot. The ropeway at Sounkyo and the cable car at Asahi-dake tend to be packed but offer quick access; away from the top stations people become scarcer and the views more spectacular.

In Ainu legend the peaks of the Daisetsu mountains are the dwelling places of benevolent but powerful god-spirits who, in human form, helped in times of need. To hike among these mountains is certainly to feel among the gods. A network of trails provides everything from day hikes to week-long tramps, and it is worth taking the time to hike or go by cable car up from the low access roads to the higher levels for the breathtaking views. The dramatic, conical, steam-venting peak of **Mount Asahi** (or Asahi-dake), Hokkaido's highest at 2,290 m (7,500 ft), offers an uplifting panorama across the high plateau. June and July bring alpine flowers, while fall colors are at their best in late August and September. En route, you may see bears and pika, as well as rubythroats and nutcrackers among other species.

An excellent route for the fit day-hiker starts from Sounkyo *onsen*. From there take the ropeway and cable car, then hike southwest over Mount Kuro-dake, continuing along well-marked trails to Mount Asahi. From the top, descend via the cable car to Asahi-dake *onsen*. It should take around 7 hours.

Snow-capped peaks in Daisetsu-zan National Park

Lake Mashu, one of Hokkaido's most beautiful sights, in Akan National Park

❽ Akan National Park

阿寒国立公園

🚉 Memanbetsu (Abashiri), Nakashi-betsu, and Kushiro. 🚉 Teshikaga and Kawayu stns. 🚌 from Kushiro stn. ℹ️ near Akan Kohan bus terminal (0154) 67-3200. 🎭 Marimo Festival (3 days in early Oct).

This enormous national park of 905 sq km (350 sq miles) in east-central Hokkaido is possibly the most beautiful in Japan. Travel around the park is limited; there are tour buses, but cycling, hitching, or rental car are all better options.

The western portion, around **Lake Akan** (famed for its bizarre green spherical algae known as *marimo*) is dominated by a pair of volcanic peaks: in the southeast is the 1,370-m (4,500-ft) **Mount O-Akan** while in the southwest is the still-active **Mount Me-Akan**, at 1,500 m (4,920 ft). The day hike up Me-Akan from **Akan Kohan** *onsen* and down the other side on a well-trodden trail to attractive **Lake Onetto** affords marvelous views in any season, but especially in fall. O-Akan is a more serious hike but also possible in a day.

East of Akan, over the pass toward **Teshikaga** (a spectacular drive in itself), are splendid views back to the two volcanoes. Farther east lies **Lake Kussharo**, in a huge caldera with a 57-km (35-mile) perimeter. Beautiful all year,

this enormous lake freezes over almost entirely in winter when the harmonics created by pressure in the ice make the lake sound as if it is singing. Thermal vents keep tiny portions ice-free; here flocks of whooper swans remain throughout the winter.

Farther east again lies **Lake Mashu**, prized as one of the greatest scenic spots in all Hokkaido, especially when the weather is kind. The crater's steep internal cliffs rise 200 m (650 ft), the water of the lake is astonishingly clear, and

the lake has no inlets or outlets. The panoramic view from the crater rim takes in Mount Shari to the north, the Shiretoko Peninsula to the northeast, and Lake Kussharo and beyond to the Akan volcanoes in the west.

The park's forests are home to many woodpeckers, including the black woodpecker, other forest birds, red foxes, sika deer, red squirrels, and Siberian chipmunks.

For those interested in geothermal activity, in addition to active Me-Akan, there are simple outdoor hot-spring pools at **Akan Kohan** and **Wakoto**, both on Lake Kussharo's south shore, steaming sulfuroles on **Mount Iou** (between Kussharo and Mashu lakes), and "bokke" (small areas of bubbling mud) beside Lake Akan. The larger and more tourist-oriented spa resorts of **Kawayu** and **Akan** are crowded with souvenir shops selling Ainu carvings.

Ainu Culture

Ainu culture in Japan is believed to have developed its distinctive characteristics between the 8th and 14th centuries. Physically large, typically bearded, and often with wavy hair, the Ainu more closely resemble Caucasians than Japanese. Their relationship with nature was a powerful one, linked to their direct dependence on it for food, clothing, and building materials. Animals they hunted or encountered were often revered as *kamui* (gods), and killing for food was a necessity that invoked rituals to thank the god-spirits. The lives of many animal and bird species were intimately known. Ainu dances, including a crane dance, mimic nature, and their crafts include implements and clothing made from locally available materials such as salmon skin and deer antlers.

After the Japanese settled Hokkaido in the 1860s, Ainu land was confiscated and hunting and fishing rights suppressed. Much of the tra-ditional orally transferred wisdom disappeared as the Ainu were encouraged to "assimilate." Only recently have many of the old oral epics or *yukars* been transcribed. Few people now use the language, even though there has been something of a revival since 1990.

A traditionally dressed Ainu man and woman

The Strait of Nemuro, with the mountains of the Shiretoko Peninsula in the background ▶

❾ Kushiro Wetlands National Park
釧路湿原

✈ Kushiro. 🚉 Kushiro stn. 🚌 from Kushiro. ℹ JR Kushiro stn (0154) 22-8294.

If any creature represents Japan, it is the beautiful *tancho*, or red-crowned crane, regarded as a symbol of happiness and long life (myth has it that it lives a thousand years). To the Ainu, the crane is a god of the marshes – *sarurun kamui*. The Kushiro Wetlands National Park is typical of its natural environment. This enormous peat swamp, an expanse of undulating reed beds bisected by streams, north of the coastal port city of Kushiro is one of the main homes of these enormous, graceful birds that stand 1.4 m (4 ft 6 in) high. The cranes are also found in other wetlands of southeast Hokkaido, albeit in smaller numbers.

In the early 20th century, the cranes were pushed to the verge of extinction in Japan by a combination of hunting and loss of habitat, but now protection and provision of food for them during the winter months has helped the young cranes survive, boosting the population to around 700 birds.

During the winter nights (December to March) the cranes roost in the safety of flowing rivers. By day, they forage along streams and marsh edges, or fly to one of three major feeding sites north of Kushiro: two in **Tsurui** village and one in **Akan** village. These sites offer the best opportunities for viewing the cranes year round. On late winter days, the birds display, calling and dancing to one another in the snow as they prepare for the breeding season ahead.

In summer (May to September), the cranes are territorial, occupying large, traditional nesting grounds where they usually raise just one chick, or occasionally two. In the lush green summer reed beds, even these tall birds are well hidden, but may be spotted at the marsh fringes.

A red-crowned crane

❿ Akkeshi Bay
厚岸湾

✈ Kushiro. 🚉 Akkeshi stn. ℹ 1st Floor, Akkeshi Gourmet Park, 2-2 Suminoe, Akkeshi-cho, Akkeshi-gun (0153) 52-4139.

Akkeshi's sheltered tidal lagoon is renowned for the quality of its oysters. The bay is extensively farmed, and there is a shrine to the oysters on a rocky islet. Throughout the winter, and especially during spring and fall migration, hundreds of whooper swans gather in the inner bay, while in summer red-crowned

Whooper swans congregating at Akkeshi Bay

cranes breed upriver and at the nearby **Kiritappu wetland**. The coastal road from Akkeshi around to Kiritappu is well worth driving – both for the scenery and for an insight into the fishing and seaweed-harvesting lifestyles of some of the people in this region. Walking at the cape beyond Kiritappu is exhilarating, but early summer mornings are best avoided because this is when a sea mist is most likely to conceal the view.

⓫ Lake Furen
風蓮湖

✈ Kushiro. 🚉 Nemuro stn.

A far cry from Japan's crowded cityscapes, the huge 52 sq-km (20 sq-mile) lagoon of Lake Furen is surrounded by expansive, eye-relaxing landscape. Situated on Hokkaido's east coast, this lake is the seasonal haunt of hordes of birds: migrating waterfowl in spring and fall, swans in late fall, sea eagles in winter, and breeding red-crowned cranes during summer.

Nearly 20 km (12 miles) long and up to 4 km (2 miles) wide, the lagoon is only 2 m (6 ft) deep or less in places. It is fringed by forests of fir and spruce, with alder and birch scrub in wetter areas. Some easy forest walks start from the south end of the lake, at **Hakkuchodai** and **Shunkunitai**, offering a wealth of birdwatching opportunities and plenty of wildflowers en route. In winter, the frozen lagoon and adjacent areas are good for cross-country skiing.

Kushiro Wetlands, Japan's largest peat swamp

⑫ Nemuro Peninsula
根室半島

🛫 Nemuro-Nakashibetsu.
🚉 Nemuro stn. ℹ️ in front of
Nemuro stn (0153) 24-3104.

In contrast to the rugged,
mountainous Shiretoko Peninsula of northeast Hokkaido, the
Nemuro Peninsula in the southeast is low-lying, essentially a
coastal plateau carved by streams
into steep-sided gullies, and well
loved by naturalists. The best
way to explore the area is by car.

The red fox is common here
and, in forests around the base
of the peninsula, particularly in
the Onetto area, there are also
many sika deer. In summer, lilies,
fritillaries, and other wildflowers
are abundant, while in winter,
although the cape appears
bleak and inhospitable, both
white-tailed and Steller's sea
eagles can be seen. Offshore
and in the many sheltered
harbors and bays, there are
flocks of sea ducks, particularly
scoters and harlequins, and
many other seabirds can be
spotted in the coastal waters.

At the base of the peninsula,
the quiet town of **Nemuro** has
little to offer the visitor, apart
from being a practical base.
At **Cape Nosappu** the viewing
tower overlooks the Russian-
occupied islands across the
narrow Nemuro Channel.

⑬ Shiretoko National Park
知床国立公園

🛫 Memanbetsu (Abashiri) or
Nakashibetsu. 🚉 Shiretoko-Shari stn.
ℹ️ Shiretoko Shizen center (01522)
4-2114.

This rugged finger of land,
jutting 65 km (40 miles)
northeast into the Okhotsk Sea,
was named Shiretoko ("the end
of the earth") by the Ainu. Now
a World Heritage Site, Shiretoko
National Park is the wildest such
park in Japan. Its 386 sq km
(150 sq miles) consist of a well-
forested mountainous ridge of
volcanic peaks dominated by
the 1,660-m (5,450-ft) **Mount**

A red fox, often seen on the
Nemuro Peninsula

Rausu. The peninsula supports
one of the healthiest remaining
populations of brown bears
left in Hokkaido. Sightings are
few and far between, although
the boat ride from **Utoro** (on
the northwest coast) north to
the cape during the summer
is one possible way of seeing
them as they forage along
the coastal strip.

Minke whales, dolphins,
and porpoises may be
seen in summer, too,
along with seabirds
such as spectacled
guillemots, Japanese
cormorants, and
migratory short-
tailed shearwaters.
Several pairs of white-tailed
sea eagles nest along the peninsula. In winter their numbers
are swollen by hundreds more
arriving from Russia, but then

Steller's sea eagle

they are overshadowed by the
world's largest eagle: Steller's
sea eagle. Both types of eagles
are best seen in winter north of
Rausu on the southeast coast.

North of Utoro lie the pretty
Shiretoko Five Lakes, reflecting
Mount Rausu. There is an easy
2-km (1-mile) trail starting
beyond the Visitor Center, and
onsen-enthusiasts will not want
to miss the hot waterfall known
as **Kamuiwakka**, northeast of
here. From June to October the
high pass from Utoro to Rausu
(Route 334) is open, and the view
east from here to Kunashiri island
is dramatic. This road passes
through the subalpine zone,
which is dominated by dwarf
stone pine trees. From near
the pass, a hiking trail strikes
off south for Lake
Rausu and Mount
Onnebetsu, while
another heads north
for Mounts Rausu,
Io, and Shiretoko
and the cape beyond.
For most levels of
fitness, Mount Rausu
is a manageable day
hike along a good trail. The
journey to the cape, however,
requires several days and
careful planning. The long, cold
winters and short summers
here make hiking possible
only from June to September.

Utoro lighthouse on the northwest coast of Shiretoko National Park

TRAVELERS' NEEDS

WHERE TO STAY

The tradition of hosting travelers is so deep-rooted in Japan that every town is well endowed with welcoming places to stay. There are two basic classifications of accommodations: Western-style and traditional. No visit to Japan is complete without staying at least one night in a Japanese inn, called a *ryokan (see pp300– 301)*. These tend to be multi-generational enterprises, offering a glimpse into a more traditional way of life. The range of hospitality is diverse in every sense – style, price, the size and quality of rooms, and facilities provided. There is also a certain amount of cultural crossover. Only the quality of service is a non-variable: friendly and eager to please. Indeed, staff who lack communication skills in foreign languages, willing to provide nothing but the best, have been known to turn foreigners away rather than compromise their renowned quality of service.

Helpful Organizations

The **Japan National Tourism Organization** (JNTO) website contains useful information about the various types of accommodation available in Japan. There is also a hotels and *ryokan* search function that scans an extensive list of all types of accommodation provided by the two main English-language booking sites in Japan: **Rakuten Travel** and **Japanican**.

You can also find *ryokan* geared to foreign visitors via the **Japanese Inn Group**, while the **Japan Hotel Association** has online information about member hotels and advance bookings. The **Japan Economy Hotel** (JEH) group offers clean rooms at reasonable rates in good locations.

Booking and Paying

Booking accommodation in advance is strongly advised, especially at times of major public holidays *(see p51)*. Reservations made directly

Lofty views from the east lobby of the Mandarin Oriental, Tokyo *(see p302)*

need to be confirmed by letter, fax, or e-mail. Rates quoted are often per person, not per room. In more remote and rural areas of Japan staff may speak little or no English.

Most hotels accept the best-known international credit cards. The bill is usually payable on departure, but business hotels and some others request advance payment. A 10–20 percent service charge (on top of the 8 percent consumption tax) is often added, depending on the style and quality of the hotel. A small hotel tax is also added in Tokyo hotels for rooms priced above 10,000 yen per person.

Deluxe Hotels

Top American chains such as the Hilton, Sheraton, Hyatt, Westin, and Four Seasons are well established in Japan.

Among Japanese-owned hotels, there is a vast range:

staid conservatism; over-the-top opulence; discreet exclusivity; chic minimalism; quaint eccentricity. Increasingly common are "intelligent" hotels, which monitor temperature, have electronic cards in place of room keys, computerized toilets, a voice-mail message system, and broadband telecommunication networks.

Business Hotels

As the name suggests, business hotels (*bijinesu hoteru*) cater to budget-conscious business travelers. Anyone can stay, and being generally located in city centers around train stations, they are very convenient. Do not expect English to be spoken.

Rooms are Western-style, small, and clean. Slippers and a cotton robe are generally supplied. There is no room service, but vending machines offer the ubiquitous "health

The homely Nishi-Itoya Mountain lodge set in the beautiful alps, Kamikochi *(see p303)*

drinks," beer, and sake. There is often at least one restaurant with a choice of Japanese or Western-style breakfasts.

Capsule Hotels

Unique to Japan, these custom-built hotels feature encapsulated beds in and out of which guests must slide, since there is little room to sit up, let alone stand. Rattan blinds or curtains can be pulled across for a degree of privacy. Usually constructed in two tiers, they cater mainly to *"salarymen"* who are too tired or inebriated to make the last train home. Most are clustered around major train stations or nightlife areas. Facilities include a personal TV, radio, alarm call system, and air-conditioning. Smoking is not allowed. Vending machines may be nearby. Baths and sometimes saunas are included in the price.

The size of such hotels varies widely, ranging from 50 capsules to over 600. Some still cater only to men, but women are increasingly being accepted and encouraged to stay.

Love Hotels

Love hotels are designed especially for dating couples and married partners living in extended families who may feel that they need some privacy, but they can also be a common location for affairs and where prostitutes take clients. They are mainly found in entertainment

Benesse House on Naoshima island, designed by revered architect Tadao Ando *(see p306)*

areas and along expressways and highways, much like motels. Prices are twofold: "rest" (for a quickie) and "stay" (up to an overnight stay). The most entertaining offer thematic decor as an additional turn-on.

Budget Options

Some 360 youth hostels are scattered across Japan, most are located in regional areas or on the edges of towns and cities. The quality is variable, and hosts range from the welcoming to dictatorial. Some lodgings run by hostel associations require membership to their organization to obtain the cheapest rates, but anyone can stay for an additional charge, and there is no upper age limit.

There are also approximately 2,800 official campsites, where tents, lodges, and cabins can be rented. Beware that overcrowding is common in holiday seasons. The JNTO leaflet *Camping in Japan* gives further details.

Recommended Hotels

The hotels in this section have been chosen to cater to a range of budgets and needs, including everything from expensive once-in-a-lifetime *ryokan* to simple and cheap, but conveniently located business hotels. In each region, one or two have been designated as DK Choice hotels. These have been chosen because they offer something very special – be that atmospheric temple accommodation that allows guests to observe or take part in morning rituals, a modern hotel that offers unparalleled levels of design, service, cuisine, and facilities, or a *ryokan* steeped in history. With *ryokan*, unlike the other types of accommodation covered here, the price listed is inclusive of dinner and breakfast unless otherwise specified, as many such traditional places don't offer room-only deals.

Typical capsule hotel, with two tiers of beds

Traditional Accommodations

A *ryokan* is a unique fusion of private and communal styles of living. Such Japanese traditions as removing shoes at the right point are important, no matter what the cost of the room, and the most expensive of these traditional inns may demand a high level of etiquette. A family-run *minshuku* – a type of guesthouse – is an even more intimate way to experience the Japanese lifestyle. There are also options that are *ryokan* at heart, but with Western-style touches such as private bathrooms.

of waiting house slippers *(see p364)*. Then, before entering the guestroom, remove the house slippers and leave them outside the door. Other *ryokan* allow shoes in the building, but these are always taken off in the entranceway to your room.

Traditional exterior of a guesthouse on Miyajima Island

What is a Ryokan?

A *ryokan* is a traditional inn, as likely to be found in a city area as a mountain hamlet. Some are set in Edo-period buildings – confections of wood, glass, bamboo, paper screens, and tatami matting. Others have a more contemporary setting. Of the 80,000 *ryokan* scattered nationwide, most cater only to Japanese-speaking tourists, but they will usually welcome foreigners with limited language skills. About 1,500 *ryokan* are registered as well-suited to providing for foreign visitors.

Certain important Japanese customs apply: the biggest difference and surprise for many foreigners is that bathing facilities are traditionally communal, not private. In many cases these baths are natural hot-spring baths, or *onsen* *(see pp346–7)*, and elaborate bathing procedures apply.

Most *ryokan* place emphasis on the quality of their meals, and the room price typically includes breakfast and dinner. This can be ideal in quiet towns

where few restaurants are open in the evening, but a constraint elsewhere. Another possible problem, mainly for elderly tourists, is the Japanese tradition of living at floor level, using legless chairs and beds.

Note that many *ryokan* impose a curfew around 11pm, so make special arrangements about keys in advance if you plan to stay out late.

Arriving at a Ryokan

Guests generally check in to a *ryokan* in the mid- to late afternoon, to allow plenty of time for bathing and dinner. At larger *ryokan*, there may be a doorman to smooth the way, but in smaller establishments, guests should slide open the front door and politely call *"gomen kudasai"* to announce arrival.

Do not step up into the lobby proper until the *okamisan* (female owner or manager) appears. In more traditional *ryokan* this is the signal to remove outdoor shoes and step up into a pair

Typical Rooms

Guestrooms are floored in tatami mats *(see p33)*. In one corner of the room is an alcove, called *tokonoma*, which may contain a hanging scroll, flowers, or other artifacts. The *tokonoma* is to be respected: no suitcases, ashtrays, or drinks should be placed in it. There will also be a low table surrounded by cushions *(zabuton)*, or folding chairs. On the table top will be a tray, bearing a tea set and possibly traditional sweets *(wagashi)*.

Your futon mattress and bedding will be stowed in cupboards when you first enter the room. These will usually be laid out discreetly for you in the evening while you are out of the room.

Ordinarily a room will be further supplied with a TV and air conditioner and/or heater. There is usually a telephone, although it may not have an international connection. You should also find a small towel in a box or basket, which you can take to the communal bathroom to use as a washcloth A personal outdoor bath *(rotenburo)* counts as luxury. A screened-off veranda, with Western-style table and armchairs, is more commonplace. There may be other Western-style touches.

Room with *tatami* mats, low table, and *zabuton* (floor cushion)

Small communal bath and separate low shower for cleansing

Handle everything in the room with care, and walk only in bare feet or socks on the tatami.

Wearing Yukata

Somewhere in the room will be traditional robes for you to wear, called *yukata*. Most people change into *yukata* for the duration of their stay, since the loose cotton kimonos symbolize relaxation and leisure time. In resort towns and hot springs, they are even worn outside on the streets, together with the high wooden sandals called *geta*. A loose jacket may also be provided. It is best to follow the example of others as to exactly where and when to wear the robes.

Fold *yukata* left-side over right. Right-side over left symbolizes death in Buddhism and, although most people either will not notice nor care, it could cause upset. Use the *obi* sash provided to secure the gown.

Bathing Arrangements

Within the *ryokan* will be at least one communal bath and a toilet block with either Western-style cubicles or Japanese squat toilets or a choice of the two styles.

In smaller *ryokan* with only one bath, bathing times may differ for men and women. In larger establishments bathing is segregated, with one entrance for men, another for women. Mixed-sex bathing *(konyoku)* used to be the norm but is very rare these days. The size of the bath and bathroom naturally dictate how many people can bathe at any one time. Check with the *okamisan* if you are unsure about the house rules, which vary between establishments.

In the bathroom, there will be an area for undressing; a low shower or tap area; and the large bath itself. The golden rule to observe is that you must wash with the shower first and not enter the hot bath until you are clean and fully rinsed. The bath itself is intended only for therapeutic relaxation. The same bathwater is used by other guests; thus it is considered extremely bad manners to contaminate

People wearing *yukata*, the design of which is often specific to each *ryokan*

the water either with an unwashed body or soap and shampoo.

Eating Arrangements

Meals are sometimes served in a dining room, but more often in the room by a maid or the *okamisan*. The more exclusive the establishment, the more likely meals will be served in private.

Meal times are usually set quite early in the evening. Depending on the situation, the *okamisan* may stay for a while, explaining the dishes, demonstrating how they should be eaten, and to chat. Or she may leave discreetly, returning only to clear the table.

Staying in a Minshuku

These family-run enterprises open the family home to travelers as and when demand requires. With rates from ¥4,000–¥10,000, this is an economical option as well as a good opportunity to see how regular working people live. The atmosphere is more homey than professional; guests are treated as part of the family at mealtimes and bathtime, and should fold up and stow away their own bedding.

Staying in Lodgings

People's lodges, or Kokumin-Shukusha, are moderate-rated accommodations within the national parks. Rooms, baths, and toilets are Japanese style. Meals are often very good. Mountain lodges, *Yamagoya*, are aimed at hikers and range from the relatively comfortable to spartan.

DIRECTORY

Japan Ryokan & Hotel Association
Tel (03) 5298-2270
w ryokan.or.jp

Minshuku Network Japan
Tel (0120) 07-6556.
w minshuku.jp

Where to Stay

Tokyo

BUNKYO-KU: Homeikan Honkan ¥¥
Ryokan
5-10-5 Hongo
Tel *(03) 3811-1181* **Map** 3 A3
W homeikan.com
One of the highlights of this stylish, wooden *ryokan* is a pretty manicured Japanese garden.

CHIYODA-KU: Capsule Value Kanda ¥
Capsules and Love Hotels
1-4-5 Kajicho
Tel *(03) 6206-0724* **Map** 5 B1
This no-frills capsule hotel has English-speaking staff and offers a small range of free business facilities, including computer access and photocopy services.

**CHIYODA-KU:
Imperial Hotel** ¥¥¥
Deluxe
1-1-1 Uchisaiwaicho
Tel *(03) 3504-1111* **Map** 5 B2
W imperialhotel.co.jp/e
First opened in 1890, the Imperial is one of the oldest hotels in Tokyo – and one of the most prestigious.

**CHUO-KU:
Hotel Com's Ginza** ¥¥
Business
8-16-15 Ginza
Tel *(03) 3572-4131* **Map** 5 B3
W hotelcoms.jp
Perfect for the business traveler staying in Ginza, this hotel offers stylish "urban rooms" designed for functionality and relaxation.

CHUO-KU: Mandarin Oriental, Tokyo ¥¥¥
Deluxe
2-1-1 Nihonbashi-Muromachi
Tel *(03) 3270-8800* **Map** 5 C1
W mandarinoriental.com/tokyo
Housed in a sleek high-rise, the Mandarin Oriental is arguably Tokyo's most luxurious hotel, featuring a Presidential Suite that truly is fit for a president.

MEGURO-KU: Meguro Gajoen ¥¥¥
Ryokan
1-8-1 Shimo-Meguro
Tel *(03) 3491-4111*
W megurogajoen.co.jp
At this luxurious *ryokan* in one of Tokyo's more upmarket neighborhoods, guests can opt to stay in the Western-style rooms, which have a tatami seating area.

MINATO-KU: Hotel Arca Torre Roppongi ¥¥
Business
Roppongi
Tel *(03) 3404-5111* **Map** 2 E5
W arktower.co.jp
Rooms have basic facilities at this hotel near Roppongi.

MINATO-KU: Hotel Roppongi ¥¥
Capsules and Love Hotels
7-19-4 Roppongi
Tel *(03) 3403-1571* **Map** 2 E5
This attractive love hotel has a range of differently themed rooms, including Edwardian chic and traditional Japanese style.

SHIBUYA-KU: Hotel Villa Giulia ¥¥
Capsules and Love Hotels
2-27-8 Dogenzaka
Tel *(03) 3770-7781* **Map** 1 A5
W hotenavi.com
A love hotel with good-sized rooms. Push a button, take a slip, then follow the spoken (Japanese) instructions for payment.

SHIBUYA-KU: Shibuya Excel Hotel Tokyu ¥¥¥
Deluxe
Shibuya Mark City Building, 1-12-2, Dogenzaka
Tel *(03) 5457-0109* **Map** 1 B5
W tokyuhotelsjapan.com
Overlooking Shibuya's famous crossing, this high-end hotel is comfortable and modern.

SHINJUKU-KU: Wakana ¥¥
Ryokan
4-7 Kagurazaka, Shinjuku-ku
Tel *(03) 3260-3769*
This small *ryokan* in the old geisha quarter is known as the "writers' inn," since many Japanese authors have stayed here.

The high-rise building housing the Mandarin Oriental Toyko hotel at dusk

DK Choice

SHINJUKU-KU: Park Hyatt Tokyo ¥¥¥
Deluxe
3-7-1-2 Nishi-Shinjuku
Tel *(03) 5322-1234* **Map** 1 A2
W tokyo.park.hyatt.com
This legendary hotel, the setting for the well-known film *Lost in Translation*, is one of the most luxurious and best-located hotels in Tokyo. As well as fine views of Shinjuku's Chuo-koen Park and excellent pool and spa facilities, it also boasts the New York Bar and Grill, a popular spot.

TAITO-KU: Sauna and Capsule Hotel Dandy ¥
Capsules and Love Hotels
Egg Bldg, 6F, 2-6-11 Ueno
Tel *(03) 3839-8100* **Map** 3 C3
Guests here enjoy excellent bathing facilities, including an open-air bath and natural wood sauna, plus a good restaurant.

TAITO-KU: Hotel Marutani ¥¥
Business
6-7-6 Ueno
Tel *(03) 3831-4308* **Map** 3 C3
W hotel-marutani.com
The Marutani offers its guests the option of staying in either Japanese-style tatami rooms or Western-style rooms. With communal baths.

TAITO-KU: Asakusa View Hotel ¥¥¥
Deluxe
3-17-1 Nishi-Asakusa
Tel *(03) 3847-1111* **Map** 4 E2
W viewhotels.co.jp
Comfortable rooms here have views of both old and new Tokyo – from the Senso-ji temple to the SkyTree.

TOSHIMA-KU: The b Ikebukuro ¥¥
Business
1-39-4 Higashi-Ikebukuro
Tel *(03) 3980-1911*
W theb-hotels.com
This smart business hotel is located in lively Ikebukuro. Rooms have comfortable furnishings and bright decor.

Central Honshu

FUJI FIVE LAKES:
Fuji View Hotel ¥¥
Resort
511 Katsuyama, Fujikawaguchiko-
machi, Minamitsuru-gun,
Yamanashi 401-0310
Tel *(0555) 83-2211*
W fujiview.jp
Located beside Lake Kawaguchi,
this hotel has many rooms
with unforgettable views of
Mount Fuji. It also has an *onsen*
and a short golf course.

FUJI FIVE LAKES:
Hotel Konanso ¥¥¥
Ryokan
4020-2 Funatsu, Fujikawaguchiko-
machi, Minamitsuru-gun,
Yamanashi 401-0301
Tel *(0555) 72-2166*
W konansou.com
Guests enjoy exceptional service
and facilities that include an
onsen, a spa, and even karaoke
booths. Near Lake Kawaguchi.

DK Choice

HAKONE: Fujiya Hotel ¥¥
Western-style
359 Miyanoshita,
Hakone-machi,
Kanagawa 250-0404
Tel *(0460) 82-2211*
W fujiyahotel.jp
Established in 1878, Fujiya is
famed for playing host to the
rich and famous, with a guest-
book that includes Charlie
Chaplin and the current
emperor. A night in this hot-
spring retreat is like staying in
a museum – albeit one where
fine French cuisine is served
and cocktails can be sipped in
a bar where John Lennon is said
to have played the piano.

HAKONE: Ichinoyou Honkan ¥¥
Ryokan
90 Tounosawa, Hakone-machi,
Ashigara-shimogun,
Kanagawa 250-0315
Tel *(0460) 85-5331*
W english.ichinoyu.co.jp/honkan
Stay in pleasant tatami-mat rooms,
some with private outdoor hot-
spring baths. English is spoken.

IZU: Shimoda Prince Hotel ¥¥¥
Western-style
1547-1 Shirahama, Shimoda-shi,
Shizuoka 415-8525
Tel *(0558) 22-2111*
W princehotels.co.jp/shimoda
A modern beachfront resort
at the tip of the Izu Peninsula.
Simple rooms in a great setting.

Private outdoor hot-spring baths – a major draw at Ichinoyou Honkan, Hakone

KAMIKOCHI: Nishi-Itoya
Mountain lodge ¥¥
Lodge
Kamikochi, Matsumoto-shi, Nagano
390-1516
Tel *(0263) 95-2206*
W nishiitoya.com
Clean and simple rooms and
dorms, plus mountain views
from the hot-spring baths. The
rates also include two meals.

KANAZAWA: Yogetsu ¥¥
Minshuku
13-22-1 Higashiyama, Kanazawa-
shi, Ishikawa 920-0831
Tel *(076) 252-0497*
Run by the same family for over
40 years, this friendly, well located
inn is popular with foreign visitors.

KISO VALLEY:
Ryokan Fujioto ¥¥¥
Ryokan
Tsumago, Minami-kiso-cho, Kiso,
Nagano 399-5302
Tel *(0264) 57-3009*
W tsumago-fujioto.jp
The warm hospitality and multi-
course dinners here have earned
this place consistently rave
reviews from overseas guests.

MATSUMOTO: Buena Vista ¥¥
Western-style
1-2-1 Honjo, Matsumoto-shi,
Nagano 390-0814
Tel *(0263) 37-0111*
W buena-vista.co.jp
This contemporary hotel has
smart rooms and benefits from
an excellent central location.
Helpful English-speaking staff.

NAGOYA: Nagoya B's Hotel ¥¥
Business
1-16-2 Nishiki, Naka-ku, Nagoya-shi,
Aichi 460-0003
Tel *(052) 220-3131*
W bs-hotel.co.jp
A business hotel with a few
extra touches, including a spa.
Decent rates on single rooms.

NAGOYA: Nagoya
Kanko Hotel ¥¥¥
Deluxe
19-30-1 Nishiki, Naka-ku, Nagoya-
shi, Aichi 460-8608
Tel *(052) 231-7711*
W nagoyakankohotel.co.jp/en
Defined by conservative
elegance and unstinting service,
this is the grand old lady of
Nagoya's hotel scene. Amenities
include a gym and free Wi-Fi.

SHIRAKAWA: Koemon ¥¥
Minshuku
456 Ogimachi, Shirakawa-mura,
Gifu 501-5627
Tel *(0576) 96-1446*
W shirakawago-kataribe.com
Family-run and very welcoming,
this renovated farmhouse oozes
character. Room rates include
two meals.

TAKAYAMA:
Sumiyoshi Ryokan ¥¥
Ryokan
4-21 Honmachi, Takayama-shi,
Gifu 506-0011
Tel *(0577) 32-0228*
W sumiyoshi-ryokan.com
This over 100-year-old former
merchant's house enjoys a
peaceful riverside location and
has a pleasant Old World feel.

Kyoto

CITY CENTER: First Cabin ¥
Capsules and Love Hotels
Karasuma Higashi-iru 331,
Shimogyo-ku, Kyoto, 600-8099
Tel *(075) 361-1113*
W first-cabin.jp/locationlist/
kyoto.html
In a stylish interpretation of
the capsule theme, this hotel
boasts a decor inspired by
airplane cabins. First Cabin
has a women-only floor and
boasts a good central location.

For more information on types of hotels *see pages 298–301*

DK Choice
CITY CENTER: Hiragaya ¥¥¥
Ryokan
*Nakahakusancho, Fuyacho
Anekoji-agaru, Nakagyo-ku,
Kyoto 604-8094*
Tel *(075) 221-1136*
Ⓦ hiiragiya.co.jp
Enjoy traditional Japanese-style
accommodation at its most
refined and sophisticated in this
19th-century building that is
full of character. The *kaiseki-ryori*
(haute cuisine) dinners, the
finely honed levels of service
and hospitality, and the garden
views from the individually
designed tatami-mat
guestrooms combine to make
the Hiiragaya one of Japan's
most unforgettable *ryokan*.

CITY CENTER: The Screen ¥¥¥
Boutique
*640-1 Shimogoryomae-cho,
Teramachi Marutamachi-sagaru,
Nakagyo-ku 604-0995*
Tel *(075) 252-1113*
Ⓦ screen-hotel.jp
Asian design meets Scandinavian
style at The Screen. Rooms feature
iPod docks and Bose DVD players.
The champagne lounge and
candlelit rooftop lounge are
standout features.

EASTERN KYOTO:
Hyatt Regency, Kyoto ¥¥¥
Deluxe
*644-2 Sanjusangendo-mawari,
Higashiyama-ku, Kyoto-shi,
Kyoto 605-0941*
Tel *(075) 541-1234*
Ⓦ kyoto.regency.hyatt.com/en/
hotel/home.html
A stylish design hotel with a
renowned spa, good restaurants,
and exceptional levels of service.

EASTERN KYOTO: Kinmata ¥¥¥
Ryokan
*Shijo-agaru Gokomachi, Nakagyo-
ku, Kyoto-shi, Kyoto 604-8044*
Tel *(075) 221-1039*
Ⓦ kinmata.com
Intimate setting in a charming
old wooden townhouse. A
kaiseki-ryori (haute cuisine) dinner
is included in the room rate.

KYOTO STATION AREA:
Tour Club ¥
Budget
*362 Momijicho, Higashi-nakasuji,
Shomen-sagaru, Shimogyo-ku,
Kyoto-shi, Kyoto 600-8345*
Tel *(075) 353-6968*
Ⓦ kyotojp.com
Popular *ryokan*-style hostel near
Kyoto station. Both dorms and
private rooms are available.

Key to Price Guide *see page 302*

KYOTO STATION AREA:
Matsubaya ¥¥
Ryokan
*Nishi-iru, Higashitouin,
Kamijuzuyamachi-dori, Shimogyo-ku,
Kyoto-shi, Kyoto 600-8150*
Tel *(075) 351-3727*
Ⓦ matsubayainn.com
A simplified *ryokan* experience,
without *onsen* or evening meals,
but with great hospitality and a
traditional atmosphere.

WESTERN KYOTO:
Shunkoin Temple ¥
Budget
*42 Myoshinji-cho, Hanazono,
Ukyo-ku, Kyoto-shi, Kyoto 616-8036*
Tel *(075) 462-5488*
Ⓦ shunkoin.com
Simple *shukubo* (temple
accommodation) run by the
friendly, bilingual vice abbot,
who also offers meditation
classes. Rooms are fitted with
traditional tatami mats.

Western Honshu

DK Choice
AMANOHASHIDATE:
Genmyoan ¥¥¥
Ryokan
*32-1 Monju, Miyazu-shi, Kyoto
626-0001*
Tel *(0772) 22-2171*
Ⓦ genmyoan.com
From its mountainside perch,
this hotel offers sweeping views
across the Amanohashidate
land bridge and Miyazu Bay.
Along with English-speaking
staff, it also provides refined
hospitality, elegant tatami
rooms, hot-spring baths, and
highy rated *kaiseki-ryori* (haute
cuisine) at night.

HIMEJI: Grand Vrio Hotel ¥¥
Business
*210 Nishino-machi, Sanzaemonbori,
Himeji-shi, Hyogo 670-0940*
Tel *(0792) 84-3311*
Ⓦ himejicastlehotel.co.jp
Modern no-frills hotel with
simple rooms and a handy
location near Himeji castle.

HIROSHIMA: World
Friendship Center ¥
Budget
*8-10 Higashi Kanon, Nishi-ku,
Hiroshima-shi, Hiroshima 733-0032*
Tel *(082) 503-3191*
Ⓦ homepage2.nifty.com/
wfchiroshima
Friendly Japanese-style hostel
with an international vibe.
Singles and twins available.

HIROSHIMA: Hotel Sunroute ¥¥
Business
*3-3-1 Ote-machi, Naka-ku,
Hiroshima-shi, Hiroshima 730-0051*
Tel *(082) 249-3600*
Ⓦ sunroutehotel.jp/hiroshima
Located near Hiroshima's main
attractions, rooms have stylish
decor compared to the average
business hotel.

ISE: Hoshidekan ¥¥
Ryokan
2-15-2 Kawasaki, Ise-shi, Mie 516-0009
Tel *(0596) 28-2377*
Ⓦ hoshidekan.jp/
In a charming wooden building
with antique furnishings, this
ryokan serves macrobiotic fare
using local seasonal produce.

KOBE: ANA Crowne Plaza ¥¥
Western-style
*1 Kitano-cho, Chuo-ku, Kobe-shi,
Hyogo 650-0002*
Tel *(078) 291-1121*
Ⓦ anacrowneplaza-kobe.jp
Modern rooms with soft tones
in a tower that offers superb city
views. Numerous dining options.

Ryokan Kurashiki is an indulgent retreat in a converted Edo-era warehouse, Kurashiki

KOBE: The b Kobe ¥¥
Western-style
2-11-5 Yamate-dori, Chuo-ku,
Kobe-shi, Hyogo 650-0011
Tel *(078) 333-4880*
W http://theb-hotels.com/the-b-kobe/jp
Within walking distance of the station, this design hotel has chic and well-equipped rooms.

KURASHIKI:
Ryokan Kurashiki ¥¥¥
Ryokan
4-1 Honmachi, Kurashiki-shi,
Okayama 710-0054
Tel *(086) 422-0730*
W ryokan-kurashiki.jp
Immaculate tatami-mat or wood-floored rooms in a converted Edo-era warehouse. No children.

MATSUE: Minamikan ¥¥¥
Ryokan
Tamatsukuri, Tamayu-cho,
Matsue-shi, Shimane 699-0201
Tel *(0852) 62 0331*
W kasuien-minami.jp
High-end *ryokan* with fine dining, a sumptuous garden, outdoor baths, and spa treatments.

MIYAJIMA: Iwaso Ryokan ¥¥¥
Ryokan
Momijidani, Miyajima, Hatsukaishi-shi, Hiroshima 739-0522
Tel *(0829) 44-2233*
W iwaso.com
Dating from the 1850s, this historic, hospitable, and refined inn is aging gracefully.

DK Choice

MOUNT KOYA:
Ekoin Temple ¥¥¥
Minshuku
497 Koya-san, Koya-cho, Ito-gun,
Wakayama 648-0211
Tel *(0736) 56-2514*
W ekoin.jp
One of about 40 temple lodgings in Koya-san, this one is special because guests can take part in the early-morning temple rituals, including a spectacular fire ceremony. Rooms are fairly spartan, but the monks – who offer free meditation and sutra writing classes – are friendly, and some speak English. Vegetarian meals.

NARA: Ryokan Seikanso ¥¥
Ryokan
29 Higashikitsuji-cho, Nara-shi,
Nara 630-8327
Tel *(0742) 22-2670*
W nara-ryokanseikanso.com
The *ryokan* experience on a budget: nice tatami rooms, but communal baths and no dinners.

NARA: Nara Hotel ¥¥¥
Western-style
1096 Takabatake-cho, Nara-shi,
Nara 630-8301
Tel *(0742) 26-3300*
W narahotel.co.jp
Built in 1909, the older of the two buildings here has Meiji-era Western-influenced interiors.

OSAKA: First Cabin ¥
Capsules and Love Hotels
4-2-1 Namba, Chuo-ku, Osaka-shi,
Osaka 542-0076
Tel *(06) 6631-8090*
W first-cabin.jp/locationlist/osaka.html
Capsule hotel meets boutique design at First Cabin. There are large communal baths and English-speaking staff.

OSAKA: Dotonbori Hotel ¥¥
Business
2-3-25 Dotonbori, Chuo-ku,
Osaka-shi, Osaka 542-0071
Tel *(06) 6213 9040*
W dotonbori-h.co.jp
Easily recognized by the Easter Island-like heads outside, the Dotonbori has basic but spotless rooms. Amenities include Wi-Fi, free bike rental, and a library.

OSAKA: Granvia Osaka ¥¥¥
Western-style
3-1-1 Umeda, Kita-ku, Osaka-shi,
Osaka 530-0001
Tel *(06) 6344 1235*
W granvia-osaka.jp
This contemporary hotel above Osaka station offers smart single, twin, and double rooms. The Granvia Suites, on the top floor, feature breathtaking views of the city. There are also several good restaurants and bars.

TSUWANO: Meigetsu ¥¥
Ryokan
Uomachi, Tsuwano-cho, Kanoashi-gun, Tottori 699-5600
Tel *(0856) 72-0685*
This *ryokan* is housed in an over 100-year-old building, providing the perfect setting for very traditional service and well-prepared local cuisine.

Shikoku

CAPE ASHIZURI: Ashizuri
Kokusai Hotel ¥¥¥
Resort
662 Ashizurimisaki, Tosa-Shimizu-shi,
Kochi 787-0315
Tel *(0880) 88-0201*
W ashizuri.co.jp
This well-run *onsen* resort has both Japanese- and Western-style rooms. Excellent seafood served.

A simple, comfortable room at Ekoin Temple, Mount Koya

KOCHI: Hotel No.1 ¥
Business
16-8 Nijudai-machi, Kochi-shi,
Kochi 780-0843
Tel *(088) 873-3333*
W hotelno1.jp/kochi
A budget option with basic but clean singles and doubles, plus a women-only floor.

KOTOHIRA: Sakuranosho
Kotohira Grand Hotel ¥¥¥
Ryokan
977-1 Kotohira-cho, Nakatado-gun,
Kagawa 766-0001
Tel *(0877) 75-3218*
W sakuranosho.jp
Elegant rooms, attentive service, and a prime location at the foot of Mt. Zozu and Konpira Shrine.

MATSUYAMA: Hotel Check-in ¥
Business
2-7-3 Sanban-cho, Matsuyama-shi,
Ehime 790-0003
Tel *(089) 998-7000*
W checkin.co.jp/matsuyama
Standard single, double, and family rooms in an excellent location, near Matsuyama castle.

DK Choice

MATSUYAMA: Dogo Kan ¥¥¥
Ryokan
7-26 Dogo, Takou-cho,
Matsuyama-shi, Ehime 790-0841
Tel *(089) 941-7777*
W dogokan.co.jp
Dogo Kan offers a modern take on the classic *ryokan*. The Japanese decor incorporates greenery throughout to create a calm atmosphere. Rooms are either Western or Japanese in style, and the *kaiseki* (haute cuisine) dinners are centered around the daily catch from the Seto Inland Sea. Facilities include a beauty salon, lounge bar, and a footbath in the lobby.

For more information on types of hotels *see pages 298–301*

The chic Benesse House, which is beautifully situated right on the ocean, Naoshima

DK Choice

NAOSHIMA:
Benesse House ¥¥¥
Deluxe
Gotanji, Naoshima,
Kagawa 761-3110
Tel *(087) 892-3223*
Ⓦ benesse-artsite.jp
Part of the Art Site project that
saw the island of Naoshima
transformed from small
industrial community to
contemporary art haven, this
ocean-front hotel features chic
designs throughout, as well as a
truly indulgent spa. In addition,
guests have unlimited access to
the own on-site international
art gallery, the picturesque
grounds are dotted with art
installations by famous artists
such as Yayoi Kusama.

TAKAMATSU: Dormy Inn ¥
Business
1-10-10 Kawaramachi, Takamatsu-
shi, Kagawa 760-0052
Tel *(087) 832-5489*
Ⓦ hotespa.net/hotels/takamatsu
Part of a nationwide chain with
basic but smart singles and
doubles, plus *onsen* and saunas.

Kyushu

BEPPU: Yukemuri no Sato
Azumaya ¥¥¥
Ryokan
1029-1 Kannawa-kami, Beppu-shi,
Oita 974-0046
Tel *(0977) 27-7547*
Ⓦ gloria-g.com/azumaya
Everything you would expect
from a top-class *ryokan*, plus
magical night views over Beppu.

FUKUOKA: Kashima Honkan ¥
Ryokan
3-11 Reisen-cho, Kakata-ku,
Fukuoka-shi, Fukuoka 812-0039
Tel *(092) 291-0746*

Ryokan by name, but *minshuku*
by nature, with elegant tatami
rooms, friendly hosts, and a
beautiful courtyard garden.
Room-only rates available.

KAGOSHIMA:
Shiroyama Kanko ¥¥¥
Western-style
41-1 Shinsoin-cho, Kagoshima-shi,
Kagoshima 890-8586
Tel *(099) 224-2200*
Ⓦ shiroyama-g.co.jp
Conservative luxury, with elegant
rooms and decor. There is also an
excellent spa.

KUMAMOTO: Kumamoto Castle
Hotel ¥¥
Western-style
4-2 Jyoto-machi,
Chuo-ku, Kumamoto-shi,
Kumamoto 860-8565
Tel *(096) 326-3311*
Ⓦ hotel-castle.co.jp
Standard interiors are accented
with dark or light wooden
furnishings and the occasional
floral print. Great location.

NAGASAKI: Minshuku Tanpopo ¥
Minshuku
21-7 Houeimachi, Nagasaki-shi,
Nagasaki 852-8016
Tel *(095) 861-6230*
Ⓦ tanpopo-group.biz/tanpopo
Simple tatami rooms in a
minshuku just a short walk from
Nagasaki's main sights. Meals
cost extra but are good value.

NAGASAKI: Garden Terrace
Nagasaki ¥¥¥
Boutique
2-3 Akizuki-cho, Nagasaki-shi,
Nagasaki 850-0064
Tel *(095) 864-7777*
Ⓦ gt-nagasaki.jp
Surrounded by mountains, this
hilltop hotel has won many architectural awards for designer Kengo
Kuma for its combination wood
tones, bold patterns, and open
spaces. The service, facilities, and
ocean views are sublime.

YUFUIN: Sansou Murata ¥¥¥
Ryokan
1264-2 Kawakami, Yufuin, Yufu-shi,
Oita 879-5102
Tel *(0977) 84-5000*
Ⓦ sansou-murata.com
Sprawling and exclusive,
this mountainside retreat is
comprised of several private
farmhouse-style villas. Plush
bars and restaurants on site.

Okinawa

IRIOMOTE-JIMA: Iriomote
Eco Village ¥¥¥
Resort
80-36 Takana, Taketomi-cho,
Yaeyama-gun, Okinawa 907-1431
Tel *(0980) 85-5115*
Ⓦ eco-village.jp
Affordable by Japanese resort
standards, Iriomote offers bright
and airy beachside villas, plus a
range of activities such as diving,
kayaking, and trekking.

ISHIGAKI-JIMA: Kohamato ¥
Minshuku
441-1 Tonoshiro, Ishigaki-shi,
Okinawa 907-0004
Tel *(0980) 82-2369*
Ⓦ kohamoto.com
Guests enjoy free bicycle rental
at this friendly, well-located, and
well-maintained budget option.

MIYAKO-JIMA: Miyako-jima
Tokyu Resort ¥¥¥
Resort
914 Shimojiaza-yonaha,
Miyakojima-shi, Okinawa 906-0305
Tel *(0980) 76-2109*
Ⓦ miyakojima-r.tokyuhotels.co.jp
Located on one of Okinawa's
nicest beaches, this plush hotel
offers facilities such as a golf
course, a spa, and a diving pool.

DK Choice

NAGO: Busena Terrace ¥¥¥
Resort
1808 Kise, Nago,
Okinawa 905-0026
Tel *(0980) 51-1333*
Ⓦ terrace.co.jp/busena
The sprawling Busena Terrace,
on a private white-sand beach
on picturesque Cape Busena,
offers ample opportunities for
five-star play and pampering –
from sailing, snorkeling,
and diving, to indulgent
spa treatments and yoga.
Design-wise, the feeling is
fresh and natural, yet very
opulent. It is no coincidence
that this is considered Japan's
premier beach resort.

**NAHA: Nikko Naha
Grand Castle** ¥¥
Western-style
*1-132-1 Yamakawa-cho, Shuri,
Naha-shi, Okinawa 903-8601*
Tel *(098) 886-5454*
W hotelnikkonaha.co.jp
With an almost resort-like feel
and a light, airy, contemporary
room design, this hotel is well
geared to both business and
leisure travelers.

Northern Honshu

**AIZU-WAKAMATSU:
Shibukawa Donya** ¥¥¥
Western-style
*3-28 Nanoka-machi, Aizu-
Wakamatsu, Fukushima 965-0044*
Tel *(0242) 28-4000*
W shibukawadonya.com
Housed in a lovely European-
style Taisho-era building, this
hotel offers period interiors
combined with all modern
conveniences and amenities.

AKITA: Dormy Inn ¥
Business
*2-3-1 Naka-dori, Akita-shi,
Akita 010-0001*
Tel *(018) 835-6777*
W hotespa.net/hotels/akita
The Dormy Inn offers a central
location, pleasant and well-
equipped rooms, a sauna,
and a rooftop *onsen*.

**KAKUNODATE: Tamachi
Bukeyashiki** ¥¥¥
Boutique
*23 Tamachi-shimocho, Kakunodate,
Akita 014-0312*
Tel *(0187) 52-1700*
W bukeyashiki.jp
Gleaming dark-wood floors and
paper screen doors give this
boutique hotel in Kakunodate's
historic heart an Edo-period feel.

DK Choice

**MORIOKA:
Kumagai Ryokan** ¥¥
Ryokan
*3-2-6 Osawakawara, Morioka-shi,
Iwate 020-0025*
Tel *(019) 651-3020*
W kumagairyokan.com
A combination of factors –
great value for accommodation
and dinning combination,
fantastic regional cuisine,
elegant tatami rooms, laid-back
bar serving local sake and beer,
and extremely friendly English-
speaking owners – makes this
traditional *ryokan* a very
welcoming place to stay.

The highly regarded Miyako-jima Tokyu Resort, with its white-sand beach

DK Choice

**NIKKO: Nikko
Kanaya Hotel** ¥¥
Western-style
*1300 Kamihatsuichi, Nikko-shi,
Tochigi 321-1401*
Tel *(0288) 54-0001*
W kanayahotel.co.jp
In business since 1873 and
having welcomed people such
as Charles Lindbergh and Indira
Gandhi, the Nikko Kanaya is
regarded as one of Japan's
"classic" Western-style hotels.
The rooms themselves are fairly
unspectacular, but the public
areas, from the rustic bar to the
French restaurant, are full of old
charm. Great location, too.

SADO: Yado Hananoki ¥¥
Minshuku
*78-1 Jukeneki, Sadogashima,
Niigata 952-0612*
Tel *(0259) 86-2331*
W sado-hananoki.com
This family-run inn is situated
in pretty countryside near Ogi
village. Rooms have splendid
views across the rice fields. Rates
vary depending on meal choices.

SENDAI: Dormy Inn ¥¥
Business
*2-10-17 Chuo, Aoba-ku, Sendai-shi,
Miyagi 980-0021*
Tel *(022) 715-7077*
W hotespa.net/hotels/sendai
Centrally located, this branch of a
reputable nationwide hotel chain
features modern rooms, a sauna,
and an *onsen*.

TONO: Minshuku Tono ¥¥
Minshuku
*2-17 Zaimoku-cho, Tono-shi,
Iwate 028-0521*
Tel *(0198) 62-4395*
W minshuku-tono.com
Beautiful tatami rooms with shared
bathrooms. The highlight is the
dinner around the *irori* (hearth)
served with home-brewed sake.

YAMAGATA: Hotel Castle ¥¥
Western-style
*4-2-7 Tokamachi, Yamagata-shi,
Yamagata 990-0031*
Tel *(023) 631-3311*
W hotelcastle.co.jp
The Hotel Castle offers western-
style singles, twins, and doubles.

Hokkaido

**FURANO: Furano
Prince Hotel** ¥¥¥
Resort
*18-6 Kitanomine-machi, Furano,
Hokkaido 076-0034*
Tel *(0167) 23-4111*
W princehotels.co.jp/furano
A winter ski resort, at other times
this hotel shares activities with
neighboring New Furano Prince.

**HAKODATE: Wakamatsu
Ryokan** ¥¥¥
Ryokan
*1-2-27 Yunokawa-cho, Hakodate-shi,
Hokkaido 042-0932*
Tel *(0138) 59-2171*
W wakamatsuryokan.com
The Wakamatsu motto –
"An ocean view with warm
hospitality" – says it all.

**RISHIRI AND REBUN:
Kitaguni Grand Hotel** ¥¥
Western-style
*93 Oshidomari, Rishirifuji-cho,
Rishiri-gun, Hokkaido 097-0101*
Tel *(0163) 82-1362*
W kitaguni-gp.com
A good base for exploring the
island. Hot-spring baths on site.

**SAPPORO: Sapporo
Grand Hotel** ¥¥
Western-style
*Nishi 4, Kita 1, Chuo-ku, Sapporo-shi,
Hokkaido 060-0001*
Tel *(011) 261-3311*
W grand1934.com
Rooms at this long-standing
hotel range from elegant to
simple. English-speaking staff.

For more information on types of hotels *see pages 298–301*

WHERE TO EAT AND DRINK

Considering the country's present profusion of restaurants (about 90,000 in Tokyo alone) and its wealth of regional and foreign cuisines, it is hard to believe that for centuries the average Japanese diet consisted of little more than rice or millet, miso soup, and pickles. In a land of limited resources austerity was the rule, but it taught the Japanese to make the most of seasonal foods, and to serve them artfully so that a little looked

appetizing. Tokyo, Osaka, and Kyoto are the celebrated culinary centers, but each town takes pride in its specialties. Budget and mid-range restaurants can often be found clustered around train stations, in malls, and taking up whole floors of department stores. Many eateries can be identified by the half-curtains (*noren*) above the door, with the name of the restaurant written on them in Japanese.

Savoring a sushi meal at a restaurant in Jingumae, Tokyo

Meals and Meal Times

Most *ryokan (see pp300–301)* and some hotels serve traditional breakfasts *(see p318)* from 7 to 9am. When Japanese eat breakfast out, they usually do so in coffee shops that serve sets called *mo-ningu* (morning), consisting of coffee, toast, a hard-boiled egg, and a small salad.

Lunch runs from about 11:30am to 1:30 or 2pm. Many eateries then re-open for dinner around 6pm. Upscale restaurants generally stop serving around 9 or 10pm, while establishments catering to the after-hours office crowd stay open to around 11pm or midnight.

Soba (noodle) shops generally open around 11am or earlier and continue to serve until early evening. In major cities, street stalls selling ramen (Chinesestyle noodles) and other snacks might open for business late in the evening and serve beyond midnight. In smaller towns and

rural areas, few restaurants may be open after 7pm, because most visitors will be dining at their *ryokan*.

Reservations and Dress Code

Reservations are essential at many *kaiseki* restaurants *(see p310)* – occasionally months in advance – but it is quite normal to turn up at others, even good places, without a reservation. Hotel concierges are usually willing to help with bookings, and to draw a map of a restaurant's location *(see p383) for you*.

Jeans and casual shirts are acceptable in most places, provided they are not torn or dirty. Women may find long, loose clothing advantageous when dining at a place with *zashiki* seating *(see p312)*. Also be sure to wear clean socks or stockings without holes if traditional seating on tatami mats is involved, as you will have to take off your shoes. Avoid wearing strong

Realistic-looking plastic "food" display in restaurant window

perfumes or colognes if dining at a *kaiseki* restaurant or participating in a tea ceremony.

Set Menus and Teishoku

Budget restaurants often have wonderfully realistic-looking plastic "dishes" in their windows, or photographs on the menu or wall. Simply point to the item you want if you don't know its name. At some canteens, you may need to use a ticket machine with buttons corresponding to certain dishes, before you eat.

Many restaurants offer *teishoku* (set menus), especially at lunch, allowing you to choose *teishoku* A or B. You may be met with bewilderment if you request any variations within a set menu. In upscale restaurants, you will probably need to choose among various elaborate set menus ("courses") for each diner. For advice about ordering à la carte see page 312.

Prices and Paying

The price range among restaurants in Japan is vast. While you can eat a satisfying bowl of noodles for just ¥500, a single dish with the famous Kobe steak – with beer-fed, hand-massaged beef – may cost up to ¥20,000.

Many upscale restaurants, whose dinner courses may start at ¥10,000 or ¥20,000, might offer excellent value at lunchtime in the ¥3,000–5,000 range.

The consumption tax of 8 percent is included in the quoted price (if not, this should be clearly stated on the menu). At coffee shops and lunch places,

WHERE TO EAT AND DRINK | **309**

the bill is usually automatically placed on your table, and you should take it to the cashier to pay. Even if you have exact change, do not leave it on the table and walk out.

At bars and certain restaurants you have to ask for the bill. The amount, written on a slip of paper, will generally be presented to you on a small tray. You place the money or your credit card on this tray, and your receipt or any change will be returned on the same tray. Tipping is not expected, even when the tray is used, and may even be refused.

The Japanese usually divide the bill equally among diners, or one person pays for all. Asking for an itemized breakdown for groups of three or more is rarely done and is most unpopular.

Vegetarian Food

Japanese cuisine is rich in vegetables and non-animal high-protein foods such as tofu, *natto* (fermented soybeans), and other soy products. Unfortunately, it is not quite a vegetarian's paradise, because almost every dish relies to some degree for its flavoring on the fish stock called *dashi*. The exception to this rule is *shojin ryori (see p316)*, which uses kelp- and mushroom-based stocks.

Fast Food and Convenience Stores

Western chains such as McDonald's are everywhere. Japan has its own fast-food chains, too, including one called Mosburger, which has come up

A typical set lunch in traditional surroundings at Harishin, Nara *(see p332)*

with some innovative twists on the hamburger theme.

Convenience stores offer a good selection of *bento* boxes and snack foods such as *onigiri (see p319)*.

Food Halls and Market Stalls

Cavernous food halls are found in the basements of many department stores. The colorful delicatessen-type stalls might include uncut sushi rolls, *bento* boxes, and imported foodstuffs. About an hour before closing time, stores lower the prices of many food items by ¥100–300. You may also be offered free samples, with no obligation to buy.

Food markets have artful displays and stalls offering snacks and presentation boxes of sweets, tea, rice crackers, and fruit.

Bakeries

Bakeries abound but much of what is sold tends to be of the

sweet-bun variety; bread for the Japanese is often more snack than staple. However, the quality of items such as baguettes and croissants is excellent.

In large cities almost every kind of bread, including international varieties such as bagels, can be found. In rural areas the plain white loaf bread called *shokupan* (meal bread) is still predominant.

Recommended Restaurants

The restaurants selected in this section cover a wide range of budgets and the full breadth of Japanese cuisine, from exquisite *kaiseki-ryori* to stand-up noodle bars. The one thing they have in common is that the food they serve is of a high-quality. Some restaurants have been included because of they have a particularly special setting or ambiance, while others have been chosen due to a specialization in a regional cuisine or an interesting local variation of a dish. However, not all restaurants listed serve Japanese food. For variation there are also a number of good eateries that offer food from other parts of Asia, as well as Europe and North America. Finally, navigating can be hard work in Japan. For restaurants outside of Tokyo (the city's restaurants are marked on the Tokyo street finder maps; *see pp 118–27*), which don't have a map on their website, simple directions are included in the listings.

Vending Machines

Japan has the highest number of vending machines per capita in the world, and they are literally present everywhere (even at the summit of Mt Fuji). They dispense an astounding range of items, including soft drinks, hot and cold teas, coffees, snacks, cigarettes, and beer.

Some have unusual products such as potted plants, fresh eggs, hot meals, underwear, pornography, and live rhinoceros beetles.

Types of Restaurants and Bars

Japan has a restaurant to suit every taste and budget, from hole-in-the-wall noodle stands to havens of haute cuisine called *ryotei*. If you have difficulty distinguishing between different types, stick to restaurants with a menu and prices posted outside near the door. Lanterns mark out restaurants by name or description, though in some places they may bear the name of a district or event.

Re-created traditional warehouse restaurant *(kura)*, Tokyo

Ryotei and Kaiseki Restaurants

Sanctums of manicured courtyard gardens and spare but elegant private rooms, *ryotei* are the ultimate in Japanese dining. These are where the politicians and business elite entertain their customers with *kaiseki (see p308)*, the haute end of Japanese cuisine, and also maybe *geisha (see p167)* hired for the evening. Used to catering to an established clientele, many *ryotei* will not accept new customers without introductions.

More accessible to tourists are what are termed *kaiseki* restaurants, which serve the same food as *ryotei*, but in a less exclusive setting.

Kyo-Ryoriya

A *kyo-ryoriya* (Kyoto-style restaurant) is usually another name for a *kaiseki* restaurant, Kyoto being the place where *kaiseki* achieved its apotheosis. Outside Kyoto, the name will emphasize that flavors conform to Kyoto standards, being delicate and light, and that typical Kyoto ingredients (*fu*, wheat gluten,

and *yuba* (tofu skin), soy-milk skin, for example) will be featured.

Shojin Ryoriya

Shojin ryori was developed in Kyoto, in the kitchens of the city's Zen monasteries. The vegetarian cuisine is served on lacquered utensils in private rooms. Most *shojin ryoriya* are located near large monastery complexes.

Kappo, Ippin-Ryoriya, Koryoriya, and Izakaya

Akin to French bistros or Spanish tapas restaurants, these are places where one goes to drink and eat, rather than eat and drink. Most dishes are à la carte. *Kappo* tend to be pricey; the quality and seasonality of food is closer to that of *kaiseki* restaurants. *Ippin ryoriya* and *izakaya* (the two are almost synonymous) feature fancier versions of Japanese home-cooking. Many will have large platters of pre-cooked items on their counter tops. *Koryoriya* means a "small dish" restaurant. Without reading Japanese, visitors may find such places hard to distinguish from one another.

Nomiya and Aka-Chochin

Tavern-like *nomiya* (literally "drink shop") and *aka-chochin* are proletariat versions of the restaurants described above. The *aka-chochin*, or "red-lantern restaurant," is named after the bright lantern often hanging over the door (but note that not all red lanterns denote a "red-lantern restaurant"). They rarely have menus, the shop's offerings being written on strips of wood attached to the wall or handwritten on a blackboard. They tend to be frequented almost entirely by locals and, to confuse matters, are very often still called *izakaya*. To complicate matters further, *nomiya* can also be used to describe expensive drinking places like hostess bars, although in this guide the term refers only to the tavern-like incarnation.

Sushi Restaurants

Restaurants specializing in sushi *(see pp320–21)* vary in style from low-priced *kaiten-zushi* shops, where the sushi comes to you on a conveyor belt, to astronomically expensive places where everything, from the fish to the ginger, is of optimum freshness and quality. As a general rule, if there are no prices listed anywhere, you are in for an expensive dinner.

If you sit at the counter, it is customary to order *nigiri-zushi* (hand-pressed sushi) a serving at a time. A serving consists of two "fingers," which are placed on the counter in front of you.

Restaurants in Kyoto decorated with lanterns naming a local festival

Diners watching the chef at work in a sushi restaurant in Ginza, Tokyo

If you sit at a table or on a *zashiki* (see p312) then it is customary to order a combo of *nigiri-zushi*. It will be brought all at once on a platter or slab of polished wood.

Noodle Shops

Noodles in Japan come in two main forms: the domestic variety and the Chinese-style version known as ramen (see p314). The former is found at *sobaya*, which in spite of the name, sell not only *soba* (brown buckwheat) noodles, a staple of Edo cuisine (see p316-7) but also white wheat *udon* noodles. Ramen are served in cheap Chinese restaurants called *chuka-ryoriya*, in specialty shops called *ramenya*, and at night street stalls called *yatai*. Regional variations of ramen, *soba* and *udon* abound, with some of the best variations including Sapporo ramen (made with a miso-based soup) and *soki-soba* in Okinawa

(where the noodles are topped with delicious pork spare rib).

Speciality Restaurants

Many restaurants in Japan specialize in one dish, such as tempura or *tonkatsu* (see p315). *Oden-ya* serve *oden*, a simmered dish with a variety of ingredients. *Unagi-ya* specialize in eel, grilled to perfection over charcoal. *Yakitori-ya* accomplish the same thing with skewered chicken. *Fugu* restaurants prepare poisonous blowfish, raw and cooked. *Okonomiyaki-ya* serve *okonomiyaki*, a thick pancake-shaped mix of cabbage, egg and meat or seafood cooked on a griddle. The Kantō region specializes in a variant of *okonomiyaki* known as *Monjayaki*.

Foreign Asian Restaurants

Yakiniku-ya are Korean-style barbecue restaurants with plenty of red meat, as well as the more esoteric parts of the cow, plus the standard spicy *kimchi* pickles. *Chuka-ryori-ya* are cheap Chinese restaurants. Found mainly in urban areas, there are also many Indian, Indonesian, Vietnamese, Thai, and other Asian restaurants. So-called *esunikku* (ethnic) restaurants, generally found only in urban centers, serve a mix of South- and Southeast Asian-inspired dishes.

Western Restaurants

Youshoku (Western meal) restaurants are modest places

that serve such things as *ebi-furai* (fried shrimp) and *korokke* (croquettes). These items became very popular among Japanese during the Meiji and Taisho periods. The Japanese still think of these dishes as Western although outside of Japan they would hardly be recognized as such. Rice is served on a plate, not in a bowl, and eaten with a fork.

Famiri resutoran (family restaurants) are American-style chains (Royal Host is a typical example), whose extensive picture menus, late hours, and parking lots have won them a devoted following in Japan. In the major cities, French and Italian restaurants are abundant. Servings, especially of wine, however, tend to be skimpy, and bread comes by the piece, not the basket.

Kissaten, Coffee Shops, and Bars

For decades the Japanese have taken their breaks at tea rooms called *kissaten*, where, over an unrefillable cup of painstakingly brewed *kohi* (coffee), served either *hotto* (hot) or *aisu* (iced), they can spend hours leafing through magazines and chain-smoking. *Kissaten* also offer such standbys as *kare raisu* (see p320), *pirafu* (rice pilaf), and *sando* (sandwiches, of the pale English variety).

The neighborhood *kissaten* still exists but is increasingly challenged by well-known international coffee shop chains such as Starbucks and Tully's, which offer a range of coffees. Local chains such as Excelssior and Doutor also offer a similar variety, albeit at a lower cost.

Any fair-sized Japanese town will have a bar quarter, a warren of hole-in-the-wall places each presided over by a *"mastaa"* (master) or *"mama."* In large cities, entire buildings will be filled with such places, each its own little universe. Customers come as much for the atmosphere as the drinks.

Karaoke is the main form of entertainment in "hostess bars." Note that some are little more than rip-off joints.

The Tanuki

In Japanese folklore *tanuki* raccoon dogs are celebrated as lovable buffoons or drunken rascals. This is why the ceramic likeness of the *tanuki* is often found at the entrance of drinking places.

Food Customs and Etiquette

Eating food in Japan is markedly different from eating in Western countries. Seating arrangements, tableware, and much of the etiquette regarding the social eating of food differ even from those in nearby countries such as Korea and China. The main point of etiquette is to take your shoes off for traditional seating. Many Japanese assume that you will not be able to use chopsticks properly and will be impressed if you show any finesse at all.

Sitting *seiza*-style on *zabuton*

Seating Arrangements

Many Japanese restaurants have a few Western-style tables and chairs, and/or a counter, as well as traditional *zashiki* seating.

The *zashiki* is a low wooden platform covered with tatami mats and low tables. Diners sit here on cushions (*zabuton*), feet tucked behind. Remove your shoes before you step up onto the *zashiki*.

Women wearing skirts sit *seiza* (on their knees with their buttocks on their heels) or mermaid-style. Men usually sit cross-legged, although if there is a formal toast they will adopt the more uncomfortable *seiza* pose until it is over.

Some *zashiki* actually have sunken areas for the diners' legs, a definite plus for long-legged customers and foreigners who find sitting on the floor uncomfortable. Alternatively, chairs may be used that have backs but not legs.

In restaurants with a choice of seating, the counter is by no means regarded as a second-rate option. In sushi places, particularly, it is the preferred seat of the gastronome who wants to watch the food being skillfully prepared by chefs with years of training.

How to Order

If a set menu (*see p308*) is not available, then follow these guidelines for ordering à la carte.

Specify drinks (*see pp322–3*) first, usually from a choice of sake, beer, *shochu* liquor, perhaps wine, and whiskey.

If you are in an area frequented by foreigners, the menu may have some English translations. Menus are often divided into the main categories of Japanese cuisine: grilled, simmered, and so on (*see p315*). Sashimi is ordered first. If you can't decide on one fish, ask for a *moriawase*, or combination.

The custom is to have about three or four dishes to start and more later as you deem fit. Calling *"sumimasen!"* (excuse me!) is the standard method of attracting attention.

Alternatively, tell the chef behind the counter how much you want to spend (between ¥3,000 and ¥5,000 per person is reasonable), and let him make the decisions for you.

Polite Phrases and Toasts

Japanese people say *"Itadaki-mass"* ("I humbly receive") before eating, and *"gochiso-sama desh'ta"* ("I have been treated") at the end.

Japanese drinking etiquette requires that you pour for the other person and vice versa. When on the receiving end, you should pick up your glass, supporting the bottom with the fingers of the other hand. When a toast (*kanpai*) is made, beer and whiskey glasses should be clinked, while sake cups are generally raised in a salute.

What to do with the Oshibori

Most restaurants offer customers an *oshibori* at the beginning of a meal. This small damp cotton or paper towel is used first to wipe your hands (in strict etiquette, not the face and neck). You then leave it on the table top and use it discreetly to dab fingers and spills, rather than placing it on your lap. It is fine to use your own handkerchief as a napkin on your lap. However, remember never to blow your nose into the *oshibori* or any handkerchief in public.

Using Chopsticks

Chopsticks (*hashi*) are shorter and more delicate than Chinese chopsticks, with a pointed lower end. The use of disposable wooden chopsticks in restaurants is widespread. Knives and forks are rarely seen

Sitting on stools at the counter of a *yatai* noodle stall in Fukuoka

except in staunchly Western restaurants and for certain dishes still regarded as foreign such as *kare raisu (see p314)*.

Spearing food with your chopsticks is considered bad form, as is pushing food straight from the bowl into the mouth (entirely acceptable in China). Passing food from your chopsticks to those of another and sticking them upright in a bowl of rice are both associated with funerary customs and are therefore strictly taboo at the dinner table. Gesturing and pointing with your chopsticks are also definite no-nos, as is using them as levers to pull or push things around the table.

If some morsel proves difficult to cut on the plate, you can take a chopstick in each hand and make a sawing motion to cut it. This may not be the most elegant of moves but is unavoidable in some situations.

When they are not in use, lay the chopsticks on your chopstick rest *(hashi-oki)*, or if a rest is not provided then across the lowest dish. Lay them neatly and uncrossed, and parallel with your side of the table.

Using Tableware

Japanese tableware is wonderfully eclectic and can run to over a dozen vessels per person, of wildly differing shapes and materials such as porcelain, lacquer, wood, and even leaves. When several dishes are served at once, feel free to take morsels from them in whatever order you please, including from lidded pots containing soups.

Many small bowls and plates are designed to be picked up and brought to about chest level, easing the path of each morsel to the mouth. Do this rather than bending your head down to get to the food. It is perfectly good manners to sip directly from small bowls of soup.

How to Hold Chopsticks (Hashi)

A common mistake by foreigners is to hold chopsticks too close to the ends instead of a third of the way down, thus losing leverage. They also often hold them too tightly, leading to hand cramps and dropped food.

Thumb and first finger doing most of the leverage with the top stick

Third finger acting as a rest for the lower stick

The lower stick should rest in the crook of the thumb and on the third finger, while the thumb, first, and second fingers control the movement of the top stick. Note that the *hashi* and technique are slightly different from those used in China.

However, do not eat directly from any communal serving platters and bowls. Instead, put one or two bite-sized portions first onto the *kozara*, which is a small saucer-like plate provided for each diner. Use the separate chopsticks and spoons, if provided, for communal dishes. Note that it is fine to bite off part of a piece of food and return the uneaten part to your *kozara* until ready for the next bite.

Ceramic teapot

Eating Rice

Japanese rice has a slightly glutinous, heavy texture. Japanese people treat it with respect, and do not feel they have truly eaten until they have consumed rice in some form.

In a meal with several dishes, rice is always served in a separate bowl. If alcohol is drunk, then the bowl of rice is saved till the end of the meal, when it is eaten with miso and pickles *(see p318)*. Since sake is a rice derivative, the two are often considered too similar to consume together.

No matter how tempted, do not take rice from the bowl and put it on your plate to soak up any juices or sauces or pour juices (even soy sauce) onto it. As acceptable as this is

elsewhere, it will be an unappetizing sight in Japan. The exception to this rule is one-pot rice dishes, in which vegetables and meat are placed on the rice in a deep bowl, almost hiding the rice.

Seasonal Eating Patterns

The seasons have a major influence on Japanese eating habits. The temperature of food is seen as an important way of regulating body temperature. Hence, tea and sake may be drunk hot in winter and cold in summer. Similarly, *nabemono* (hot pot) dishes are consumed during cold months, while cold noodles are welcomed in warm ones. Tempura is normally a cold weather dish, and the desire of tourists to eat it on a hot summer day may surprise some Japanese. Some restaurants famous for seasonal fish such as *fugu (see p321)* may serve an entirely different menu at other times.

Kamameshi, a one-pot rice dish

Slurping

The Japanese slurp with gusto when eating noodles or soupy rice dishes. Indeed, an audible intake of air is necessary to eat piping hot noodles without scorching the mouth. Many foreigners are loathe to make this noise, with the result that it takes them three times as long to eat *soba*.

Reading the Menu

General vocabulary likely to be useful when eating out is given in the *Phrase Book* on *pages 407–08*. Individual ingredients are also listed there. A selection of some of the most popular dishes and styles of cooking are listed in this glossary, including Japanese script to help you read menus in Japanese. Further details about some of the dishes follow on *pages 316–21*.

Donburi: Rice-bowl Dishes

Katsudon
カツどん
Rice bowl topped with a breaded, deep-fried pork cutlet and semi-cooked egg.

Nikudon
肉どん
Rice bowl with beef, tofu, and gelatinous noodles.

Oyakodon
親子どん
Rice bowl with chicken, onions, and runny, semi-cooked egg.

Tamagodon
卵どん
Rice bowl topped with a semi-cooked egg.

Tendon
天どん
Rice bowl that has one or two shrimp tempura and sauce.

Other Rice Dishes

Kamameshi
釜飯／かまめし
Steamed rice and tidbits served in a clay or metal pot with a wooden lid.

Kare raisu
カレーライス
"Curry rice". Can be *ebi-kare* (shrimp curry), *katsu-kare* (with deep-fried pork cutlet), etc.

Makunouchi bento
幕の内弁当
Classic *bento* (see p319).

Ocha-zuke
お茶漬け
Rice in a bowl with a piece of grilled salmon, pickled plum, etc., over which tea is poured.

Omu-raisu
オムライス
Thin omelet around rice mixed with tomato sauce and meat bits.

Onigiri
おにぎり
Triangular blocks of rice wrapped in strips of dried seaweed (*nori*).

Unaju
鰻重
Grilled eel served over rice in a lacquered, lidded box.

Yaki-onigiri
焼おにぎり
Variation of *onigiri*, without sea-weed, grilled over a flame.

Zosui
雑炊
Rice soup made with the leftover stock of a one-pot meal.

Noodle Dishes

Kitsune soba/udon
きつねそば／うどん
Soba or *udon* noodles in flavored *dashi* broth with bits of fried tofu.

Nabe yaki udon
鍋焼うどん
Noodles simmered with a *dashi* broth, often with shrimp tempura, shiitake mushroom, and egg.

Ramen
ラーメン
Chinese-style noodles in a broth. Usually there are thin slices of roast pork on top, sliced leeks, seaweed, and fish-paste roll.

Reimen (Hiyashi chuka)
冷麺（冷やし中華）
Chinese noodles topped with strips of ham or roast pork, cucumbers, and cabbage.

Somen
そうめん
Thin noodles, usually in ice water.

Tamago-toji soba/udon
卵とじそば／うどん
Soba or *udon* in a flavored *dashi* broth into which an egg has been stirred to cook gently.

Tempura soba/udon
天ぷらそば／うどん
Soba or *udon* in a flavored broth with pieces of shrimp tempura.

Yakisoba
焼そば
Soft Chinese noodles sautéed on a griddle with vegetables and some form of meat or fish.

Zarusoba
ざるそば
Soba noodles served cold on a bamboo rack. *Ten-zarusoba* has shrimp and vegetable tempura.

Dishes Prepared at the Table

Mizutaki/Chirinabe
水焚き／ちり鍋
Nabemono (one-pot meal) of vegetables, tofu, and chicken (*mizutaki*) or fish (*chirinabe*).

Rice Crackers and Nibbles

Crackers (*senbei* or *osenbe*) are sold in supermarkets all over Japan. Beautifully made and presented, they are also sold at station gift counters and stalls at the popular tourist attractions.

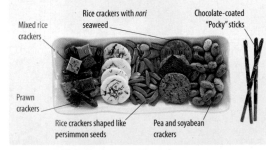

Mixed rice crackers

Rice crackers with *nori* seaweed

Chocolate-coated "Pocky" sticks

Prawn crackers

Rice crackers shaped like persimmon seeds

Pea and soyabean crackers

Okonomiyaki
お好み焼
Thick pancake-shaped mix of cabbage, egg, shrimp, squid, or pork cooked on a griddle.

Shabu-shabu
しゃぶしゃぶ
A hot pot of thinly sliced beef and vegetables.

Sukiyaki
すき焼き
Pan-cooked beef and vegetables.

Teppanyaki
鉄板焼
Grilled meat and/or shrimp or squid and vegetables.

Udon-suki
うどんすき
Udon noodles, chicken, and sometimes clams or shrimp simmered in a soup.

Sushi
Chirashi-zushi
ちらし寿司／鮨
"Scattered" sushi *(see p320)*.

Nigiri-zushi
握り寿司／鮨
"Fingers" of sushi *(see p320)*.

Maki-zushi
巻寿司／鮨
"Rolled" sushi *(see p321)*.

Set Meal
Teishoku
定食
A set meal *(see p308)*, with rice, soup, some vegetables, salad, a main meat dish, and pickles.

Menu Categories
Aemono
和え物
Dressed salad dishes.

Agemono
揚げ物
Deep-fried foods.

Nimono
煮物
Simmered foods.

Sashimi (Otsukuri)
刺身（お造り）
Raw fish *(see p321)*.

Sunomono
酢の物
Vinegared dishes.

Yakimono
焼き物
Grilled foods.

À La Carte
Agedashi-dofu
揚げだし豆腐
Deep-fried tofu (bean curd) in a stock.

Chikuzen-ni
筑前煮
Vegetables and bits of chicken simmered together.

Edamame
枝豆
Soybeans steamed in the pod.

Hiya-yakko/Yudofu
冷やっこ／湯豆腐
Cold/simmered tofu.

Kinpira
きんぴら
Sautéed burdock and carrot strips seasoned with sauces.

Natto
納豆
Fermented soybeans.

Niku-jaga
肉じゃが
Beef or pork simmered with potatoes and other ingredients.

Oden
おでん
Hot pot with fried fish cakes and various vegetables.

Ohitashi
おひたし
Boiled spinach or other green leafy vegetable with sauce.

Shio-yaki
塩焼
Fish sprinkled with salt and grilled over a flame or charcoal.

Tamago-yaki
卵焼
Rolled omelet.

Tonkatsu
豚カツ／トンカツ
Breaded, fried pork cutlet with shredded cabbage.

Grilled eel *(unagi)* basted in a sweet sauce, a *yakimono* dish

Tori no kara-age
鶏の空揚げ
Deep-fried chicken.

Tsukemono no moriawase
漬物の盛り合わせ
Combination of pickles.

Yakitori
焼鶏／やきとり
Chicken grilled on skewers.

Chinese-style Dishes
Gyoza
餃子／ギョウザ
Fried dumplings.

Harumaki
春巻
Spring roll.

Yakimeishi
焼めし／チャーハン
Fried rice.

Izakaya Snacks

Cucumber and seaweed

Dried squid

Onion and bonito

At *izakaya* and *ippin-ryoriya* establishments *(see p310)*, which are tavern-like places serving food, rather than restaurants, dishes such as dried strips of squid and pickles complement the beer, *shochu* and other drinks *(see pp322–3)*.

The Flavors of Japan

More so than in most developed countries, where the produce of the entire world is available in supermarkets all year round, Japan is a country in which local and seasonal produce is still highly valued. The Japanese often use a region's speciality as a reason for travel, going out of their way to find a restaurant famed for local cuisine. The food cultures of Tokyo and the Kansai region were in competition for hundreds of years. The eventual dominance of Tokyo's Edo cuisine mirrors the historical trend whereby Kyoto and the Kansai region have gradually lost their cultural supremacy.

Ramen noodles

Chef at work, using chopsticks to arrange exquisite dishes

Edo Cuisine

In the early 17th century Tokyo, then known as Edo, became the administrative capital of Japan after the powerful Tokugawa family had moved there. With them arrived thousands of rich landowning samurai and wealthy merchants. This led to the development of Edo cuisine, a fusion of dishes from diverse parts of the country, that is today the most commonly recognized form of Japanese food.

The story of the ascendancy of Edo cuisine is also that of the decline in dominance of typical Kansai flavors. *Soba* has been a popular food among Edo residents since the late 17th century and is renowned as one of the true tastes of Edo cuisine. As more people from the north of Japan moved to Edo, *udon* noodles, which were popular in the south, were replaced by soba noodles. *Soba* is most commonly eaten in the same simple way that it was eaten all that time ago: in a *zaru* (a small bamboo sieve). The weaker soy sauce of the

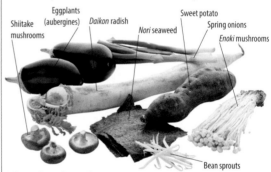

Shiitake mushrooms
Eggplants (aubergines)
Daikon radish
Nori seaweed
Sweet potato
Spring onions
Enoki mushrooms
Bean sprouts

Selection of vegetables that feature in Japanese cuisine

Traditional Japanese Specialties

A typical banquet, such as might be served at a *ryotei* (see p310), may have up to 20 courses. Much is made of seasonal ingredients, with decorative flourishes also chosen to reflect the time of year. *Kaiseki* is a traditional style of cuisine in which a dozen or more dishes are served to each person, categorized on the menu according to cooking method, not ingredients. Sake (see p323) is the usual accompaniment. Vegetarian cusine, called *shojin ryori*, uses protein-rich tofu rather than meat or fish. It was developed by Zen Buddhists and is now found in many restaurants located in or near the precincts of Zen temples. The Japanese have also elevated tea snacks to an art form – delicate and pretty *wagashi* are usually made from sweet bean paste.

Bonito tuna flakes

Unadon, featuring grilled eel over a bed of rice, is popular as it is thought to have great health benefits.

Tuna being laid out for sale at Tokyo's Tsukiji Fish Market *(see p72)*

Certain dishes from Osaka have also made their mark on the rest of Japan. One of the most popular snacks in the Kansai region is *takoyaki*, which is griddle-cooked octopus in batter. *Takoyaki* stalls have sprung up in most Japanese cities. Another famous dish from Osaka is *okonomiyaki*, which is often likened to a pancake. The name means "as you like it" and, as the phrase suggests, it is made with any ingredients the customer wants.

Kansai region also became less favored when people in Edo adopted a stronger tasting sauce. Even grilled eel, which is thought to be a typical part of Edo cuisine, was originally a dish from Kyoto, but it is the Edo method of cooking the eel and preparing the sauce that we know today. Other foods that feature strongly in Edo cuisine are sushi, tempura, and oden – a hotpot of fishcake, boiled eggs, and other ingredients.

Kansai Cuisine

Although in many respects the Kansai region has lost its position as the most important area in Japan's culinary landscape, it should not be seen as a spent force: food from the Kansai region is still one of the strongest regional cuisines in Japan. Top quality local produce can be found in the area. In this inland region, seafood has not been as central to the cooking of Kyoto as in the rest of Japan. Instead, Kyoto's superb chefs have developed a vast range of dishes using their top-quality tofu, which is famous all over Japan. In nearby Kobe, many dishes celebrate the area's internationally sought-after beef.

Omoide Yokacho, a lane of restaurants in Shinjuku, Tokyo

KOBE BEEF

One significant contribution that the Japanese have given to meat connoisseurs across the world is Kobe beef. The black *wagyu* cows of Hyogo prefecture, of which Kobe is the capital, are bred and reared using strictly guarded and time-honoured traditions to make some of the highest-quality beef in the world. Although similar cows are raised in the US and Australia, the meat is not considered to be genuine if it's not from Hyogo, which makes authentic Kobe beef an expensive delicacy. Kobe beef is an extremely tender meat, and it is identifiable by the striations of fat that run through it. It is used in a range of Japanese dishes – it can be eaten raw as *sashimi*, cooked as *teppanyaki* or, as is popular nowadays, served simply as a big hearty steak or even a luxurious burger.

Tempura, originally a Portuguese dish, is lightly battered deep-fried vegetables or fish.

Okonomiyaki is a thick, pancake-shaped mix of egg and other ingredients, cooked on a griddle.

Yakiudon are thick noodles fried with seafood, seaweed, shiitake mushrooms, tuna flakes, and beansprouts.

The Japanese Meal

Along with the indispensable rice and miso soup (made from fermented soy bean paste), a Japanese meal usually consists of a variety of smaller dishes which are designed to complement each other. Plain ingredients are often given strong flavors, such as a bowl of rice topped off with an *umeboshi* (sour plum) or pickled ginger, or tofu that has been marinated in a strong, vinegary sauce. Two liquid ingredients central to most Japanese dishes are *dashi*, a light stock made from giant kelp *(konbu)* and dried skipjack tuna shavings, and Japanese soy sauce *(shoyu)*.

Firm tofu

Japanese family enjoying breakfast together

The Japanese Breakfast

One of the many attractions of staying in the home of a Japanese family, or in a traditional Japanese hotel, is sampling the Japanese breakfast. Like most other Japanese meals, it consists of different dishes served separately. At its heart is a bowl of rice and some miso soup. It is polite for the rice to be

placed to the left and the soup to the right of the sitter. Not only is it common for there to be variations in miso soup from region to region, individual families tend to have their own idiosyncratic method of producing this most Japanese of soups.

The basic rice and soup are accompanied by a range of side dishes, of which the most common is a portion of grilled fish, often salted salmon or mackerel. Other dishes may include dried seaweed, omelet, and a small portion of pickles.

Natto is a dish made out of fermented soy beans and it is a much-loved breakfast dish among health-conscious Japanese. Usually eaten with rice, it is famous not only for being extremely healthy, but also for the noxious smell that it gives off.

Some of the ingredients for a typical Japanese breakfast

Pickled eggplant (aubergine), Miso soup, *Umeboshi* pickled plums, *Nori* seaweed, Rice, Pickled *daikon* radish, Tofu, Grilled salmon

Preparation and Portions

A fastidiousness about detail characterizes both the preparation and presentation of Japanese food. Good presentation is vital to a Japanese restaurant's success, but it is not only the highly expensive, multi-course *kaiseki* meals that display this quality; even the cheapest food has a touch of the meticulous about it. This attention to culinary aesthetics naturally favors portions that are small and served individually to maximize the impact that they have on both taste and sight. Vegetables are cooked to remain crisp and retain their colors and, even when fried, food is not allowed to become greasy – the oil is heated high enough to seal the food instantly. The serving of small portions also has health benefits, and it should come as no surprise that obesity is much less of a problem here than in Western developed countries. Nowhere else in the world is healthy eating so attractive, varied or delicious.

Small portions of a number of complementary dishes

The Bento Box

A *bento* is a take-home meal in a compartmentalized box: office workers buy them for lunch, schoolchildren eat from them at their desk, and business travelers have them with a beer on the bullet train. In its neat, individual compartments there will invariably be a large portion of rice, a main serving of meat or fish, pieces of omelet, some vegetables, and a selection of pickles. But part of the charm of the *bento* is that anything goes. It is not uncommon to open a *bento* and find a small octopus or a tiny whole fish gazing up at you, or even something that completely defies identification.

Gari (slices of pickled ginger)

Pickled *daikon* radish

Tempura

Tamagoyaki (omelet)

Sake (salmon)

Hijiki (seaweed)

Rice with black sesame

Umeboshi (pickled plums)

Nishime (simmered vegetables)

Typical selection of food to be found in a bento box

In The Bento Box

Agedofu Fried tofu.

Chikuwa Tubular steamed fishcakes.

Furikake Variety of condiments to add extra flavor, including nori (seaweed) flakes and toasted sesame seeds.

Jako Miniature whole dried fish.

Kabocha Squash, often served simmered.

Konnyaku Gelatinous paste made from Devil's Tongue (similar to sweet potato).

Korokke Croquettes filled with potato and meat.

Kurage Jellyfish.

Maguro sashimi Tuna sashimi.

Negi Salad onion, used for flavoring and garnish.

Onigiri Triangles of rice with various fillings.

Saba sashimi Mackerel sashimi.

Takenoko Bamboo shoots.

Tonkatsu Deep-fried breaded pork.

Tsukemono Pickled vegetables.

Umeboshi Pickled plum.

Unagi Grilled eel in black bean sauce.

Yakiniku Miniature meatballs.

Japanese student eating lunch from a *bento* box

Sushi and Sashimi

Newcomers to Japan are often both fascinated and intimidated by these native dishes. The term "sushi" applies to a variety of dishes (usually written with the suffix "-zushi") in which cold, lightly sweetened and vinegared sushi rice is topped or wrapped up with raw fish or other items such as pickles, cooked fish, and meat. Sliced fillets of raw fish served without rice are called sashimi. Even those visitors used to Japanese restaurants abroad may be surprised at how ubiquitous such foods are in Japan. There is no need to worry unduly about hygiene: Japan's highly trained chefs always use fresh fish, and the vinegar in sushi rice is a preservative.

Sushi bar counter and sushi chefs with years of training

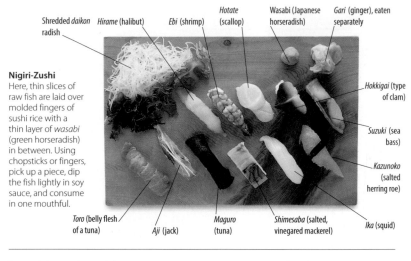

Shredded *daikon* radish

Hirame (halibut)

Ebi (shrimp)

Hotate (scallop)

Wasabi (Japanese horseradish)

Gari (ginger), eaten separately

Nigiri-Zushi
Here, thin slices of raw fish are laid over molded fingers of sushi rice with a thin layer of *wasabi* (green horseradish) in between. Using chopsticks or fingers, pick up a piece, dip the fish lightly in soy sauce, and consume in one mouthful.

Hokkigai (type of clam)

Suzuki (sea bass)

Kazunoko (salted herring roe)

Toro (belly flesh of a tuna)

Aji (jack)

Maguro (tuna)

Shimesaba (salted, vinegared mackerel)

Ika (squid)

Tamagoyaki (sweetened egg omelet), a popular non-fish item often accompanying sushi and sashimi

Denbu, flakes of shrimp and whitefish that have been boiled, then dried and seasoned

Kazunoko (prepared herring roe)

Ebi (shrimp)

Aji (jack)

Chirashi-Zushi
The "scattered" style of sushi involves a colorful combination of toppings arranged artfully with a deep bed of cold sushi rice. There are two main regional variations. In Tokyo, slices of raw fish, fish roe, chunks of omelet, and other raw or cooked vegetables are placed on top of the rice (as shown). In Osaka, the fish and vegetable toppings are cooked, then mixed with the rice and overlaid with strips of omelet.

Uni (the ovaries of a sea urchin), a highly prized delicacy in Japan

Ikura (salmon roe)

Gari (ginger)

Slice of *kamaboko*, a type of steamed fish-paste roll with pink-dyed rim

Thin slice of *ika* (squid)

Maki-Zushi

"Rolled" sushi is becoming increasingly familiar outside Japan – the California roll, for instance, is a version using avocado and other non-Japanese ingredients. For maki-zushi the sushi rice is combined with slivers of fish, pickles, or other morsels, and rolled up in a sheet of toasted seaweed (*nori*).

Umejiso-maki (pickled plum and *shiso* herb)

Negitoro-maki (scallions and tuna)

Natto-maki (fermented soy beans)

Oshinko-maki (pickled *daikon*)

Kampyo-maki (gourd)

Kappa-maki (cucumber)

Tekka-maki (tuna)

Hoso-maki, or thin-rolled sushi, has one central ingredient at its core. It is rolled into a cylindrical shape with the help of a bamboo mat.

Temaki-zushi is rolled by hand into a large cone shape.

Kappa (cucumber)

Takuan (pickled *daikon*)

Ebi (shrimp)

Kampyo (gourd)

Tamago (egg)

Futo-maki, or thick-rolled sushi, has three or more ingredients.

Ebi (shrimp) tempura

Tail end of *ebi*

Ura-maki, or reverse rolls, are made so that the sushi rice, rather than the *nori*, forms the outside of the cylinder.

Hotate (scallop) arranged in the shell

Thick slices of raw *maguro* (tuna)

Tarako, cod roe rolled up in squid and strips of seaweed

Red seaweed garnish

Hotate (scallop) arranged with thin strips of *nori* (seaweed)

Hokkigai (surf clam), out of its shell

Tako (octopus)

Aji (jack), topped with finely sliced scallions

Wasabi (green horseradish) molded into the shape of a *shiso* leaf

Sashimi

Sliced fillets of the freshest uncooked fish may be served as a single course. Sashimi is delicate and creamy, and the only accompaniments should be soy sauce, wasabi, *daikon*, and maybe a shiso leaf.

Popular Fish in Japan

Of the 3,000 or so varieties of fish eaten in Japan, the most common, available year-round, are *maguro* (tuna), *tai* (sea bream), *haze* (gobies), *buri* (yellowtail), *saba* (mackerel), crustaceans such as *ebi* (shrimp) and *kani* (crab), and fish that are usually salted such as *sake* (salmon) and *tara* (cod). Spring is the start of the season for the river fish *ayu* (sweetfish), traditionally caught by trained cormorants (*see p48*). *Katsuo* (skipjack tuna) is available in spring and summer, *unagi* (eel) in midsummer, *sanma* (saury) in the fall. Winter is the time for *dojo* (loach), *anko* (angler fish), and *fugu* (blowfish), prized for its delicate flavor but also feared for deadly toxins in its liver and ovaries.

Fish display at Kochi street market

What to Drink in Japan

Green tea and sake are the traditional drinks of Japan. Both have ancient histories, and the appreciation of each has been elevated to connoisseurship. The tea ceremony *(see p173)* is the ultimate expression of tea appreciation, a social ritual imbued with Buddhist ideals. Sake (rice wine) has long associations with Shinto – the fox god Inari presides over sake *(see p30)* – and some Shinto festivals still involve the drink as a central theme. Other Japanese drinks include *shochu* spirit and "health" drinks.

Picking green tea in May, when leaves are at their most tender

Types of Tea

Green tea leaves are divided into three main grades – *gyokuro*, which are the most tender, protected leaves that come out in May; *sencha*, which are tender leaves picked in May or June; and *bancha*, which are large leaves left until August. Leaves are sterilized with steam and then dried. *Bancha* is often roasted or mixed with other ingredients such as brown rice to form robust teas. Other teas are available; of foreign ones the Japanese especially enjoy imported fine English teas.

Basic green tea is sold loose or in tea bags.

Mugicha is a tea brewed from roasted barley.

Hojicha is roasted *bancha*, a coarse tea.

Genmaicha is brown rice (*genmai*) and *bancha*.

Sencha is a popular medium- to high-grade tea.

Gyokuro is a delicate, high grade of tea.

Powdered *matcha* is used in the tea ceremony.

Soft Drinks

With names that conjure up disturbing images for English-speaking foreigners, Calpis and Pocari Sweat are among the most popular Japanese brands of canned soft drinks. Some are marketed as quick energy and vitamin boosters. Vending machines *(see p309)* stock them alongside canned green tea and coffee, and a wide range of fruit juices in cartons.

Chawan, a wide-brimmed cup without handles

Kyusu (teapot)

Wagashi (traditional candy)

Tea leaves, usually loose, are placed in a teapot. *Bancha* is brewed with boiling water, but *sencha* and *gyokuro* should be brewed with boiled water that has been allowed to cool slightly first. The brewing tea should then stand for about a minute.

Sake (Rice Liquor)

Sake is made from rice and water, which are fermented together then pasteurized to create a superb wine-like beverage. Many connoisseurs judge sake on the five qualities of sweetness, sourness, pungency, bitterness, and astringency. Sake may be drunk warm, but the finer types should be lightly chilled to retain the subtle flavors. Unlike wine, sake is rarely expected to improve in the bottle. Store it in a cool, dry place for no more than a few months.

Everyday *hon-jozo* type by Gekkeikan

Fine *ginjo* type by Nihonsakari

Finer *dai-ginjo* by Tsukasa Botan

Taruzake (cask sake) is matured in wooden casks made of cypress. Casks are often presented to Shinto shrines as offerings. The brewer's logo is displayed prominently.

The finest grade of sake, *dai-ginjo*, is made from the hardest core of the rice – more than 50 percent of each grain is shaved away. For the *ginjo* type about 40 percent is shaved; for *hon-jozo*, the average sake, about 30 percent. Some are brewed with added alcohol; those without are called *junmai*, "pure rice."

A classic serving set consists of a ceramic bottle *(tokkuri)* and matching cups *(sakazuki)*. The bottle can be placed in hot water to warm the sake to about 50°C (122°F).

Sake breweries traditionally hang a ball of cedar leaves *(sakabayashi)* and sometimes a sacred rope *(shimenawa)* over their entrance.

Other Alcoholic Drinks

Japan has several beers that have become well known around the world. Suntory whiskey is also sold abroad, and it is popular with those who prefer a milder whiskey. Less well known abroad, *shochu* is a name for a group of Japanese spirits made from barley or other grains, or potatoes. The alcohol content of *shochu* varies from 40 to 90 proof. The distilled spirit is often mixed with hot water or used as a base for cocktails, but it is also drunk neat, either heated or on the rocks. It is used to make bottled fruit liqueurs such as *umeshu*, which is made with whole Japanese apricots.

Suntory whiskey   Sapporo beer   Asahi beer   Barley *shochu*   Rice *shochu*

Where to Eat and Drink

Tokyo

Central Tokyo

Nakaei ¥
Japanese curry **Map** 5 C3
5-2-1 Tsukiji, Chuo-ku
Tel *(03) 3541-8749* **Closed** *Sun*
This curry shop, which has been going strong for over 100 years, is where the locals go for good, cheap Japanese curry.

Birdland ¥¥
Yakitori **Map** 5 B2
Tsukamoto Sozan Building, B1F,
4-2-15 Ginza, Chuo-ku
Tel *(03) 5250-1081* **Closed** *Sun & Mon*
This is a high-end *yakitori* restaurant that serves up the top cuts of free-range chicken in an agreeable atmosphere.

DK Choice

Coca ¥¥
Thai **Map** 5 B2
Bic Camera Yurakucho, 6F,
1-11-1 Yurakucho, Chiyoda-ku
Tel *(03) 3201-5489*
A popular Thai restaurant with a difference: the specialty is "Thai-suki," a spicy Thai take on the classic Japanese hotpot dish *sukiyaki* re-imported to Japan. The Issan-style spicy BBQ chicken is also delicious, and they use high Hakata Hanamidori chickens from Japan's Kyushu region.

Kushiro ¥¥
Traditional Japanese **Map** 5 B1
JP Tower Kitte, 6F, Marunouchi 2-7-2,
Chuo-ku
Tel *(03) 6256-0817*
An attractive *izakaya* (bar) that serves charcoal-grilled seafood, vegetables, and other specialties from the Hokkaido region.

Monja Oedosakai ¥¥
Monjyayaki **Map** 6 D3
Eye Mark Tower 102, 1-8-1,
Tsukishima, Chuo-ku
Tel *(03) 3531-0521*
Located on Monja Street in Tsukishima, this place puts you right at the center of Tokyo's *monjayaki* boom.

Sato Yosuke ¥¥
Noodle **Map** 5 B2
Idei Honkan, 6-4-17 Ginza, Chuo-ku
Tel *(03) 6215-6211*
This restaurant specializes in *inaniwa udon* from Akita prefecture, one of the most loved varieties of the noodle in Japan.

Sushi Iwa ¥¥
Sushi **Map** 5 C3
2-15-10 Tsukiji, Chuo-ku
Tel *(03) 3541-5951*
Established over 50 years ago, Sushi Iwa knows how to make perfect sushi, served in classy, minimalist surroundings.

Sushi Maru ¥¥
Sushi **Map** 5 C3
Tsukiji Fishmarket Area 10,
Tsukiji 5-2-1, Chuo-ku
Tel *(03) 3541-8414* **Closed** *Sun*
Popular, counter-style sushi eatery in Tsukiji market. The *omakase* (chef's choice) set meal is huge.

Ginza Okamoto ¥¥¥
Kaiseki **Map** 5 B3
5F, 8-3-12 Ginza
Tel *(03) 3571 5110*
Before opening this excellent *kaiseki* restaurant, owner and head chef Hidetsugu Okamoto trained at legendary Wakuden in Kyoto, and he brings that experience to the table here.

Nobu Tokyo ¥¥¥
Seafood **Map** 5 A3
Toranomon Tower Office, 1F,
4-1-28 Toranomon, Minato-ku
Tel *(03) 5733-0070*
Founder Nobu Matsuhisa is one of the best-known Japanese chefs in the world. Nobu Tokyo serves Japanese-style seafood cuisine, with strong American influences.

Les Saisons ¥¥¥
European **Map** 5 B2
Imperial Hotel Tokyo (main building),
1-1-1 Uchisaiwaicho, Chiyoda-ku
Tel *(03) 3539-8087*
French dining at its best – delicious and well presented food with top-quality service.

Asakusa Imahan in Northern Tokyo – renowned for its beef

Price Guide

Prices are based on an average-size dinner for one. Lunchtime special menus are often cheaper.

¥	up to ¥1,000
¥¥	¥1,000 to ¥8,000
¥¥¥	over ¥8,000

Northern Tokyo

Asakusa Imahan ¥¥
Shabu-shabu **Map** 4 E2
3-1-12 Nishi-Asakusa Taito-ku
Tel *(03) 3841-1114*
Founded in 1895, this *shabu-shabu* and *sukiyaki* restaurant chain offers high-grade *wagyu* beef boiled in a tasty broth.

Daikokuya ¥¥
Tempura **Map** 4 E3
1-38-10 Asakusa, Taito-ku
Tel *(03) 3844-1111*
Close to Sensoji Temple, this long-running tempura restaurant is famous for its *ebi tendon* (prawn tempura laid on a bowl of rice).

Daitoryo ¥¥
Traditional Japanese **Map** 4 D2
6-10-14 Ueno, Taito-ku
Tel *(03) 3832 5622*
This popular *izakaya* in the heart of Ueno's Ameyoko Market is a great spot to dine and socialize.

Iidaya ¥¥
Seafood **Map** 4 F2
3-3-2 Asakusa, Taito-ku
Tel *(03) 3843 0881* **Closed** *Wed*
This local family restaurant has served *dojo* (cold-water fish) to the locals since the Edo period, always using the same recipe.

Otafuku ¥¥
Oden **Map** 4 E2
1-6-2 Senzoku, Taito-ku
Tel *(03) 3871-2521* **Closed** *Mon*
This place has been serving up *oden* (boiled egg, *daikon*, and processed fish cake) since the Meiji Period, and is still popular with both locals and visitors.

Sasanoyuki ¥¥
Tofu **Map** 4 D1
5-15-10 Negishi, Taito-ku
Tel *(03) 3873-1145* **Closed** *Mon*
The official suppliers of tofu to the imperial family serve a wide range of dishes made from the best tofu in Japan.

Sometaro ¥¥
Okonomiyaki **Map** 4 E3
2-2-2 Nishi-Asakusa, Taito-ku
Tel *(03) 3844-9502*
Enjoy *okinomiyaki*, Japanese pancake made with fresh seafood, in a rustic setting.

DK Choice

Vin Chou   **¥¥**
Yakitori   Map 4 E3
2-2-13 Nishi-Asakusa, Taito-ku
Tel *(03) 3845-4430*
Yakitori in Japan is usually eaten
in crowded, smoky hole-in-the-
wall places located in narrow
back alleys. Vin Chou has
retained that down-to-earth
traditional taste but added an
up-market French twist. As well
as the standard *yakitori* classics,
they also offer quail, wine, and
cheese. The presentation is
excellent, and even top-of-the-
line champagne is available, if
you have money to burn.

Yakiton   **¥¥**
Yakitori   Map 4 D4
4-10-2 Asakusabashi, Taito-ku
Tel *(03) 3864-4869*   **Closed** *public
hols*
More than just *yakitori*, this
hole-in-the-wall-style standing
bar offers pretty much any meat
you can think of on a skewer,
including pig heart and tongue.

Kanda Yabu Soba   **¥¥¥**
Noodle   Map 3 C4
*2-10 Kanda-Awajicho,
Chiyoda-ku*
Tel *(03) 3251-0287*
Enjoy handmade *soba* noodles
while sitting on tatami matting
in a traditional, wooden Edo-
style building.

Western Tokyo

Go Go Curry   **¥**
Japanese curry   Map 1 A2
*YU-WA Building, B1,
2-13-6 Yoyogi, Shibuya-ku*
Tel *(03) 3320-3855*
Gaudy pop culture meets tasty,
rich curry. The pork cutlet
topping is excellent.

A selection of dishes available at Western
Tokyo's Sushi Gotoku

Classy interior at Birdland, which specializes in top-quality free-range chicken dishes

DK Choice

Tenkkaippin Ramen   **¥**
Noodle   Map 1 B2
*Atlas Nishi-Shinjuku Building, 1F,
1-15-8 Nishi-Shinjuku,
Shinjuku-ku*
Tel *(03) 3342-2427*
This small but lively restaurant is
popular with hard-core *ramen*
fans who come flocking for the
heavy, high-fat *kotteri* broth,
which is so thick that it is almost
more of a gravy. Ask for an
ajitama, or soy-sauce-flavored
boiled egg, as a topping. The
service is good and fast.

Chinese Café Eight   **¥¥**
Chinese   Map 2 E5
*Court Annex Roppongi, 2F,
3-2-13 Nishi-Azabu, Minato-ku*
Tel *(03) 5414-5708*
Relaxed and popular Chinese
restaurant open 24 hours and
famed for its Peking duck.

Gempin Fugu   **¥¥**
Fugu   Map 1 B1
2F, 3-8-2 Shinjuku, Shinjuku-ku
Tel *(03) 3341-9529*
This is the place to try *fugu*, the
infamous poisonous blowfish,
in style, with a bottle of sake.

DK Choice

Kabuto   **¥¥**
Yakitori   Map 1 B1
1-2-11 Nishi-Shinjuku, Shinjuku-ku
Tel *(03) 3342-7671* **Closed** *Sun &
public hols*
Join businessmen for beer and
yakitori in the old black-market
quarter of Omoide Yokocho
("Memory Lane"). The origins
of this smoky alley near
Shinjuku station lie in the
drinking shacks built in the
aftermath of World War II. The
area still evokes the carefree
camaraderie of the time.

Nabe-zo   **¥¥**
Nabe   Map 1 B1
*Shinjuku Takano Building No. 2, 8F,
3-30-1 Shinjuku, Shinjuku-ku*
Tel *(03) 5363-4629*
Modern-style Japanese
restaurant specializing in a full
range of hotpot dishes, namely
nabe (hotpot), *sukiyaki* (stew),
and *shabu-shabu* (thinly sliced
beef boiled in water).

Nagi Shokudo   **¥¥**
Vegetarian   Map 1 A5
*15-10 Uguisudanicho,
Shibuya-ku*
Tel *(050) 1043-7751*
Innovative vegetarian café/
restaurant in the Shibuya area,
with a range of tasty dishes,
many of which are vegan.

Restaurant-I   **¥¥**
European   Map 1 B4
*1F Park Court Jingumae 1-4-20
Jingumae, Shibuya-ku*
Tel *(03) 5772-2091*
Michelin-starred chef Keisuke
Matsushima takes the delicate
cuisine of the south of France
and gives it a Japanese twist.

Senkoen Kabukicho   **¥¥**
Chinese   Map 1-B1
*2F, 1-16-12 Kabukicho,
Shinjuku-ku*
Tel *(03) 5272-2118*   **Closed** *Tue*
Laid-back and friendly Chinese
restaurant specializing in spicy
Sichuan-style dishes that go well
with *shaoxingjiu* rice wine.

Sushi Gotoku   **¥¥**
Sushi   Map 1-A5
*8-2 Kamiyamacho,
Shibuya-ku*
Tel *(03) 5454-5595*
High-end sushi restaurant in
Shibuya with a touch of Western
influence. The set menu is
the best option as the chef will
make the dishes according
to the best ingredients available
on the day.

For more information on types of restaurants *see pages 310–311*

Tonchang
Yakiniku   ¥¥
Map 1 B1
Lisbon Building, 1F,
2-32-3 Okubo,
Shinjuku-ku
Tel *(03) 5155-7433*
Located in the heart of Tokyo's
Korea Town, this is the place to
eat authentic Korean BBQ.

Inakaya
Robatayaki   ¥¥¥
Map 2 E5
Renu Building, 1F,
5-3-4 Roppongi, Minato-ku
Tel *(03) 3408-5040*
An up-market *robatayaki*
(Japanese BBQ) restaurant
serving a wide range of fire-
grilled fresh meat and vegetables
to be eaten at the counter.

DK Choice

Ryugin
Kaiseki   ¥¥¥
Map 2 E5
Side Roppongi Building,
7-17-24 Roppongi, Minato-ku
Tel *(03) 3423-8006*   **Closed** *Sun*
With a raft of prestigious awards
bestowed on Ryugin since its
opening in 2003 – including
Michelin stars and its inclusion
in the influential 50 Best Restaurant Awards – this 20-seater
effortlessly combines traditional
kaiseki-ryori with molecular
gastronomy. Dishes are created
using seasonal ingredients.
Reserve in advance.

Farther Afield

Ramen Jiro
Noodle   ¥
2-16-4 Mita, Minato-ku
Tel *(03) 3455 5551*   **Closed** *Sun*
Since opening in 1968, Ramen
Jiro has been a mecca for *ramen*
lovers far and wide, who come
here to taste the delicious soy-
sauce-based broth.

Chabuzen
Vegetarian   ¥¥
6-16-20 Daita, Setagaya-ku
Tel *(080) 6603-8587*   **Closed** *Mon*
This vegetarian restaurant in
trendy Shimokitazawa specializes
in *yakuzen* cuisine, believed to
have medicinal properties.

Hoto Fudo
Nabe   ¥¥
707 Kitamoto,
Fujikawaguchiko,
Minamitsuru-gun
Tel *(0558) 76-7800*
Hoto noodles, which are similar
to *udon*, are a specialty of the
Fuji Lakes Area, and you can eat
them here, piping hot and served
with lots of local vegetables.

Sanzan'uindou
Traditional Japanese   ¥¥
1F, 5-29-16, Daizawa,
Setagaya-ku
Tel *(03) 3412-8200*
One of Tokyo's best Okinawan-
cuisine restaurants, this place
offers the much sought-after
agu (Okinawan braised pork
belly) and many other treats.

DK Choice

Yoshiba
Nabe   ¥¥
2-14-5, Yokoami,
Sumida-ku
Tel *(03) 3623-4480*   **Closed** *Sun*
Located in the sumo-wrestling
district of Ryogoku, Yoshiba
specializes in hotpot dishes
such as the famed *chanko
nabe* (a vast stew made of
udon noodles, chicken meatballs, tofu, Japanese vegetables
and flavoured with miso, *dashi*
and soy sauce). This meal is
responsible for helping sumo
wrestlers put on all those
pounds. The restaurant was
formerly a sumo stable, and
there is a preserved wrestling
ring in the center of the
dining area.

Central Honshu

FUJI FIVE LAKES:
Houtou Fudou   ¥¥
Regional
3631-2 Numazu,
Kawaguchi-ko,
Yamanashi 401-0302
Tel *(0555) 72-5560*
Located opposite Kawaguchi-ko
station, this rustic place does
houtou, a hotpot with a miso
base that contains thick, flat
wheat noodles along with
chicken and vegetables, all
served in a large iron cauldron.

Former sumo stable Yoshiba, Western Tokyo
– now better known for it hotpots

FUJI FIVE LAKES:
Mama no Mori   ¥¥
Kaiseki-ryori
2470 Heiya,
Yamanaka-ko-mura,
Yamanashi 401-0502
Tel *(0555) 62-0346*   **Closed** *Thu*
Set *kaiseki* menus with a
homemade feel in an old
thatched building at Lake
Yamanaka-ko. Simple *teishoku*
set meals are also available.

GIFU: Kawaraya   ¥¥¥
Kaiseki-ryori
4-15 Inamachi, Gifu-shi,
Gifu 500-8023
Tel *(058) 262-1530*   **Closed** *Tue*
Refined multi-dish meals
centered on seafood and local
vegetables, as well as seasonal
ayu sweetfish caught in the
nearby river. Good lunch deals.

HAKONE: Kokoro   ¥
Curry
206 Hakone-Yumoto,
Ashigara Shimo-gun,
Kanagawa 250-0311
Tel *(0460) 85-8556*   **Closed** *Mon*
Near the golf driving range in
Hakone-Yumoto, this bright
and friendly shop specializes in
Japanese-style curry and rice.

Enjoy a bowl of hoto noodles in the modern surroundings of Houtou Fudou, Yamanashi

HAKONE: Yama Soba ¥
Noodle shop
*704 Hakone-Yumoto, Ashigara
Shimo-gun, Kanagawa 250-0311*
Tel *(0460) 85-7889* **Closed** *Thu*
Yama Soba on Hakone-Yumoto's
main street has wood tables and
paper screen windows, which
make for a traditional setting for
excellent handmade *soba*, as well
as tempura dishes.

HAKONE: Bella Foresta ¥¥
European
*1121 Ninotaira, Hakone,
Kanagawa 250-0493*
Tel *(0460) 82-1141*
A healthy lunch-only buffet
within the Hakone Open-Air
Museum. The mostly European
dishes provide enough variety
to suit all tastes.

HAKONE: The Fujiya ¥¥¥
European
*Fujiya Hotel, 359 Miyanoshita,
Hakone, Kanagawa 250 0404*
Tel *(0460) 82-2211*
Highly rated French cuisine is
served here, in the elegant
surroundings of one of Japan's
most historic Western-style
hotels *(see p303)*. Reservations
are required.

KAMAKURA: Nakamura-an ¥
Noodle shop
*1-7-6 Komachi,
Kamakura-shi,
Kanagawa 248-0006*
Tel *(0467) 25 3500*
Handmade *soba* in various
guises, including chilled and
topped with dried seaweed,
and in hot broth with tempura.
Two minutes northwest of
Kamakura station.

KAMAKURA: Hachinoki ¥¥
Vegetarian
*7 Yamanouchi,
Kamakura-shi,
Kanagawa 247-0062*
Tel *(0467) 22-8719* **Closed** *Mon*
Come here to try high-quality
shojin-ryori on a budget. Situated
near Kencho-ji Temple; other
branches in Kamakura offer full
shojin dinners.

KAMAKURA: T-Side ¥¥
Bangladeshi and Indian
*2-11-11 Komachi,
Kamakura-shi,
Kanagawa 248-0006*
Tel *(0467) 24-9572*
Delicious meals from Bangladesh
and India are served here, and
the lunch menu is excellent
value. It is situated just two
minutes' walk northwest from
Kamakura station along Komachi-
dori, then turn right.

Dine in historic Edo-era surroundings at Raitei, Kamakura

DK Choice

KAMAKURA: Raitei ¥¥¥
Kaiseki-ryori
*3-1-1 Kamakurayama,
Kamakura-shi,
Kanagawa 248-0031*
Tel *(0467) 32-5656*
The beautifully presented
meals here, featuring multiple
small dishes centered on
seasonal produce, exemplify
Japanese cuisine at its most
sublime. The setting, in an
Edo-era building connected
to a sprawling 50,000-sq-m
(538,000-sq-ft)garden complete
with pagodas and Buddhist
statues, is equally special.
Reservations are essential at
this ever-popular spot.

KANAZAWA: Shiguretei ¥
Teahouse
Within Kenroku-en Garden
This lovely little tatami-mat-floored
teahouse within Kanazawa's
famous garden, Kenroku-en,
serves matcha green tea along
with traditional wagashi (sweets).

KANAZAWA: Kitamaro ¥¥
Ryotei
*2-3-3 Katamachi, Kanazawa-shi,
Ishikawa 920-0981*
Tel *(076) 261-7176*
Established over 150 years ago,
this restaurant offers *kaiseki*-style
dinners as well as serving
interesting local dishes, such as
the *jibuni teishoku* set meal,
which features duck stew.

KANAZAWA: Miyoshian ¥¥
Teahouse
Within Kenroku-en Garden
Tel *(076) 221-0127*
Offers a choice of simple set teas
or excellent value *kaiseki*-style
bento boxes, which are centered
on the local *kaga-ryori (produce
sourced in Kanazawa region)*.

KANAZAWA: Kotobukiya ¥¥¥
Kaiseki-ryori
*2-4-13 Owari-cho, Kanazawa-shi,
Ishikawa 920-0902*
Tel *(076) 231-6245*
The elegantly presented set meals
here blend traditional cuisine with
occasional modern touches in a
19th-century former merchant's
house. Reservations are required.

KAWAGOE: Unton ¥
Noodle shop
*10-5 Saiwaicha, Kawagoe-shi,
Saitama 350-0063*
Tel *(049) 225-6701*
Udon is the specialty inside this
old *kura* building on Kawagoe's
main sightseeing street. Chilled,
hot, and even unconventionally
spicy variations are available.

KAWAGOE: Ichinoya ¥¥
Ryotei
*1-18-10 Matsue-cho,
Kawagoe-shi,
Saitama 350-0056*
Tel *(049) 222-0354*
Set menus catering to a range of
budgets and centered around
unagi (eel), which is said to fight
off summer fatigue.

KISO VALLEY:
Yamagiri Shokudo ¥
Regional
*2179-1 Azuma Shitamachi, Kisoji,
Nagano 399-5302*
Tel *(0264) 57-3134*
Serves a local version of *udon*
incorporating mountain
vegetables *(sansei udon)*, plus
sweet rice cakes *(gohei mochi)*.

MASHIKO: Yamani ¥
Noodle shop
*88 Jyonaizaka, Mashiko-cho,
Saitama 321-1404*
Tel *(0285) 72-7711* **Closed** *Fri*
Curry, rice, *udon*, and *soba* in
handmade ceramics. Try the
filling vegetable curry *udon (yasai
kare udon)*.

For more information on types of restaurants *see pages 310–311*

MATSUMOTO: Kisoya ¥¥
Regional
4-6-26 Ote,
Matsumoto-shi,
Nagano 390-0874
Tel *(0263) 32-0528* **Closed** *Tue*
The specialty of this rustic
place is *dengaku*, miso-covered
skewers of food grilled over
charcoal. *Udon*, *soba*, and *unagi*
(eel) are also served.

MATSUMOTO: Kura ¥¥
Koryoriya
1-10-22 Chuo,
Matsumoto-shi,
Nagano 390-0611
Tel *(0263) 33-6444* **Closed** *Wed*
This restaurant is housed
within an old warehouse with
a striking white facade, just east
of Matsumoto station. Dishes
include tempura, sashimi, and
bazashi (raw horse meat).

NAGOYA:
Craft Beer Keg Nagoya ¥¥
Bar
1-10-13 Higashisakura,
Higashi-ku, Nagoya-shi,
Aiichi
Tel *(052) 971-8211*
Brilliant craft beers from around
Japan are matched here with
homemade pizza and beer-
infused dishes in a mellow,
smoke-free environment.

NAGOYA: Ibasho ¥¥
Unagi
3-13-22 Nishiki,
Naka-ku, Nagoya-shi,
Aiichi
Tel *(052) 951-1166* **Closed** *Sun &*
2nd & 3rd Mon of each month
Come here for *hitsumabushi*
(grilled eel in miso paste, served
on rice) in an old building with
views of small, ornate gardens.

NAGOYA: Kasen ¥¥
Izakaya
1-1-4 Meieki,
Nakamura-ku,
Nagoya-shi, Aiichi
Tel *(052) 541-7888*
Lively atmosphere and good
food that includes fresh sashimi
set meals. Easy to find, sited on
the 12th floor of the Nagoya
station building.

NAGOYA:
Sekai-no-Yamachan ¥¥
Izakaya
4-9-6 Sakae, Naka-ku,
Nagoya-shi, Aiichi
Tel *(052) 242-1342*
Flagship branch of a chain
specializing in *tebasaki* (deep-
fried chicken wings), which
come coated in a sweet-and-
spicy sauce.

NAGOYA:
Yamamoto-ya Honten ¥¥
Noodle shop
3-25-9 Meieki, Nakamura-ku,
Nagoya-shi, Aiichi 450-0002
Tel *(052) 565-0278*
No-frills flagship of a chain
serving miso *nikomi – udon* in
miso soup, topped with meat
and vegetables. Find it near
exit 6 of Nagoya station.

NARITA: Kikuya ¥¥
Unagi
385 Naka-cho, Narita-shi,
Chiba 286-0027
Tel *(0476) 22-0236*
In the same family for 11
generations, this eel restaurant
opposite the tourist office
also serves *yakitori*, tempura,
and sashimi.

SHIMODA: Gorosaya ¥¥
Seafood
1-5-25 Shimoda-shi,
Shizuoka 415-0021
Tel *(0558) 23-5638* **Closed** *Thu*
Good-value set meals here, a few
minutes south of Izukyu Shimoda
station, feature sashimi, grilled
fish, and other seafood dishes.
English menu available.

DK Choice

TAKAO: Ukai Toriyama ¥¥¥
Sumibiyaki
3426 Minami, Asakawa,
Takao, Tokyo 193-0846
Tel *(0426) 61-0739*
After a hike up and down
Mount Takao, Ukai Toriyama's
collection of thatched-roof
cottages and pleasant mossy
gardens make for a relaxing
setting in which to try the
well-prepared *sumibiyaki*
(charcoal-grilled) meat, fish, and
vegetables. This restaurant is
beautifully located right at the
foot of the mountain.

Fresh vegetables and produce at
Nishiki Market, Kyoto

TAKAOKA: Takenoko ¥¥
Noodle shop
1-1-14 Nakagawa, Takaoka-shi,
Toyama 933-0056
Tel *(0766) 75-1248* **Closed** *Sun*
& Mon
Near the beautiful Kojo Park, this
bright and friendly restaurant
serves authentic handmade *soba*
and high-quality tempura.

TAKAYAMA: Agura ¥¥
Asian fusion
4-7 Shinmei-cho, Takayama-shi,
Gifu 506-0015
Tel *(0577) 37-2666* **Closed** *Mon*
All sorts are served here – from
pizza, to Southeast Asian, to
American. In an old *kura* near the
northeast end of Shiroyama Park.

TAKAYAMA: Susaki ¥¥¥
Ryotei
4-14 Shinmei-cho, Takayama-shi,
Gifu 506-0821
Tel *(0577) 32-0023*
Near Nakabashi Bridge, this
eatery serves refined multi-dish
meals in the Honzen style, a
kaiseki-like dinner heavily
influenced by the tea ceremony.

YOKOHAMA: Enokitei ¥
Café
89-6 Yamate-cho, Naka-ku,
Yokohama-shi, Kanagawa 231-0862
Tel *(045) 625-2288*
Tea, coffee, and cake in one of
Yokohama's early Western-style
buildings. There is a rose garden
ideal for people watching.

YOKOHAMA: Bashamichi
Taproom ¥¥
Bar
5-63-1 Sumiyoshi-cho,
Yokohama-shi, Kanagawa 231-0013
Tel *(045) 264-4961*
Shizuoka-based Baird Brewing
offers its innovative craft beers
alongside BBQ meats. IPA
fans shouldn't miss the Suruga
Bay IPA.

DK Choice

YOKOHAMA: Shin Yokohama
Ramen Museum ¥¥
Noodle shop
2-14-21 Shin Yokohama,
Kohoku-ku, Yokohama-shi,
Kanagawa 222-0033
Tel *(045) 471-0503*
The Ramen Museum brings
together nine *ramen* shops
from around Japan, each high-
lighting a regional style, within a
space designed to look like a
streetscape from 1958. The result
is heaven for *ramen* addicts, of
which Japan has legion. Admission to the museum is ¥300.

Enjoy an English afternoon tea on the patio at Enokitei, Yokohama

YOKOHAMA: Kaisero ¥¥¥
Chinese
*186 Yamashita-cho, Chinatown,
Naka-ku, Yokohama-shi,
Kanagawa 231-0023*
Tel *(045) 681-7777*
This Chinatown restaurant
specializes in Beijing cuisine,
including Peking duck. The decor
is a very formal red and gold.
Reservations are necessary for
this ever-popular spot.

YOKOHAMA: Manchinro ¥¥¥
Chinese
*153 Yamashita-cho, Chinatown,
Naka-ku, Yokohama-shi,
Kanagawa 231-0023*
Tel *(045) 681-4004*
Opened in 1893, Manchinro has
long been Chinatown's best-
known place for Cantonese
cuisine. Lunch set menus are
half the cost of dinners.

Kyoto

ARASHIYAMA: Sagano ¥¥
Tofu
*45 Susuki-no-bambacho,
Tenryu-ji, Ukyo-ku, Kyoto-shi,
Kyoto 616-6946*
Tel *(075) 871-6946* **Closed** *4th Wed
& Thu in Jul)*
In a quiet setting near Tenryu-ji
Temple, kimono-clad servers
bring *yudofu* (boiled tofu)-based
set menus that also feature other
tofu variations.

ARASHIYAMA: Nishiki ¥¥¥
Kyo-ryori
*Nakanoshima, Arashiyama,
Ukyo-ku, Kyoto-shi,
Kyoto 616-8383*
Tel *(075) 871-8888* **Closed** *Tue*
On an island in the Hozugawa,
the sumptuous 13-dish course
here covers every Kyoto culinary
base. Smaller set dinners are
available, too.

**CENTRAL KYOTO:
Le Bouchon** ¥¥
European
*71 Enoki-cho, Nijo-dori Tera-machi,
Nakagyo-ku, Kyoto-shi, Kyoto*
Tel *(075) 211-5220* **Closed** *Thu*
This quaint little French-styled
bistro is somewhere you can sit
down either for a substantial and
authentic meal or just to sip wine
and have a snack.

CENTRAL KYOTO: Ippudo ¥
Noodle shop
*653-1 Bantoya-cho, Higashitoin,
Nishikikoji-higashi-iru, Nakagyo-ku,
Kyoto-shi, Kyoto 604-8143*
Tel *(075) 213-8800*
Expect to stand in line a while to
get into this extremely popular
ramen eatery one block north
and one west of Karasuma station.

CENTRAL KYOTO: Bungalow ¥¥
Bar
*15 Kashiwayacho, Shimogyo-ku,
Kyoto-shi, Kyoto 600-8498*
Tel *(075) 256-8205* **Closed** *Tue*
This laid-back place attracts
expats with craft beers, organic
wines, and food such as stews,
pâtés, fries, and salads.

A traditional tea ceremony at the
En teahouse, in Central Kyoto

CENTRAL KYOTO: En ¥¥
Teahouse
*272 Matsubara-cho,
Higashiyama-ku, Kyoto-shi,
Kyoto 605-0063*
Tel *(080) 3782-2706* **Closed** *Wed*
This small tatami-mat teahouse
near Yasaka Shrine offers the
traditional tea ceremony (in
English) four times a day.
Reservations are required.

**CENTRAL KYOTO:
Manzara-tei** ¥¥
Izakaya
*321 Kawaramachi-dori,
Ebisugawa-agaru Sahimono-cho,
Nakagyo-ku, Kyoto-shi,
Kyoto 604-0903*
Tel *(075) 253-1558*
Smart dark-wood interiors give
this eatery a sophisticated setting
for trying tofu dishes, tempura,
grilled Kyoto beef, and other
traditional fare.

CENTRAL KYOTO: Matsuno ¥¥
Unagi
*Gion Minami-za, Higashi Yonkenme,
Higashiyama-ku, Kyoto-shi,
Kyoto 605-0075*
Tel *(075) 561-2786* **Closed** *Thu*
The staple dish here, prepared
for several generations, is *unagi-
don*, in which chargrilled eel is
covered in a sweet-and-savory
sauce and served on rice.

**CENTRAL KYOTO:
Sumiyaki Akari** ¥¥
Yakitori-ya
*2-1 Gyoganji Monzen-cho,
Teramachi-dori Marutamachi-
sagaru, Nakagyo-ku,
Kyoto-shi, Kyoto*
Tel *(075) 255-1390* **Closed** *Sun*
The contemporary wooden
decor at Sumiyaki Akari belies the
traditional chargrilled (*sumiyaki*)
food on offer. Much is *yakitori*,
but there is also *donburi*, steaks,
and risotto.

DK Choice

**CENTRAL KYOTO:
Giro Giro Hitoshina** ¥¥¥
Japanese fusion
*420-7 Nanba-cho, Nishi
Kiyamachi-dori, Shimogyo-ku,
Kyoto-shi, Kyoto 602-8207*
Tel *(075) 343-7070* **Closed** *last
Mon of month*
This lively and formality-free
restaurant has built a reputation
as being the place to go for
uber-modern takes on
traditional *kyo-ryori*. Opt for a
set dinner (from ¥3,600) to
make ordering easy, and try to
take a counter seat so you can
watch the chefs at work.

Kikusui in Eastern Kyoto – exquisite in both decor and culinary offerings

CENTRAL KYOTO:
Yoshikawa   ¥¥¥
Tempura
Tominokoji, Oike-sagaru, Nakagyo-ku, Kyoto-shi, Kyoto 604-8093
Tel *(075) 221-5544*   **Closed** *Sun*
Specializing in the Kyoto version of tempura, which is lighter and more subtle than that served in other parts of Japan.

EASTERN KYOTO: Omen   ¥
Noodle shop
Ginkakuji Bus pool Minami donari, Sakyo-ku, Kyoto-shi, Kyoto 606-8406
Tel *(075) 771-8994*
Great *udon* shop with a very rustic feel. Turn left, and walk 50 m (164 ft) when you are one block from the northern end of the Philosopher's Path.

EASTERN KYOTO: Yojiya Café   ¥
Café
Sanjo TC Building, Higashi Kita kado, Fuyacho, Chukyo-ku, Kyoto-shi, Kyoto 604-8082
Tel *(075) 221-4503*
A bright and airy place in Sanjo that serves tea and coffee along with green-tea-flavored sweets such as *maccha* roll cake.

EASTERN KYOTO: A Womb   ¥¥
Japanese fusion
35-2 Ichijoji Hinokuchi-cho, Sakyo-ku, Kyoto-shi, Kyoto
Tel *(075) 721-1357*   **Closed** *Wed*
Part café, part bar, part gallery, but also part restaurant, serving very good contemporary *izakaya* and sushi-based *kyo-ryori* fare.

EASTERN KYOTO: Menami   ¥¥
Kyo-ryori
96 Nakajima-cho, Sanjo-agaru, Nakagyo-ku, Kyoto-shi, Kyoto 606-8004
Tel *(075) 231-1095*   **Closed** *Sun*
Obanzai (home-style *kyo-ryori*) – lots of little precooked dishes, ideal with sake or beer – is served here, at the intersection of Sanjo-dori and Kiyamichi-dori.

EASTERN KYOTO: Takocho   ¥¥
Oden
1-237 Miyagawasuji, Higashiyama-ku, Kyoto-shi, Kyoto 605-0000
Tel *(075) 525-0170*   **Closed** *Wed*
This counter-only spot has been on the corner of Donguri-dori and Kawabata-dori for over 100 years. Point to choose your food.

EASTERN KYOTO: Hyotei   ¥¥¥
Kaiseki-ryori
35 Kusagawa-cho, Nanzen-ji, Sakyo-ku, Kyoto-shi, Kyoto 606 8437
Tel *(075) 771-4116*   **Closed** *2nd & 4th Tue*
Tatami-mat floors, garden views, and beautiful multi-dish meals are found here. Reservations and a healthy budget are essential.

EASTERN KYOTO: Kikusui   ¥¥¥
Ryotei
31 Nanzenjifukuchi-cho, Sakyo-ku, Kyoto-shi, Kyoto 606-8435
Tel *(075) 771-4101*
Exquisite set dinners with dishes such as *yudofu* (simmered tofu), sashimi, and other classic *kaiseki* components. Good lunch deals.

EASTERN KYOTO: Nontaro   ¥¥¥
Sushi
357 Shinchi Kiyomoto-cho, Higashiyama-ku, Kyoto-shi, Kyoto 605-0084
Tel *(075) 561-0770*   **Closed** *Mon*
Excellent, at times unexpectedly creative, sushi served over a gorgeous red-lacquer counter. Reservations required. Fifteen-piece courses start at ¥4,000.

WESTERN KYOTO:
Tofu Café Fujino   ¥
Café
843-7 Kamiyagawa-cho, Kamigyo-ku, Kyoto-shi, Kyoto 602-8384
Tel *(075) 463-1028*

Kitchen staff busy with food orders at A Womb, in Eastern Kyoto

Come here for healthy set lunches based around tofu. For those with a sweet tooth, desserts include tofu brownies, tofu cheesecake, and more.

WESTERN KYOTO: Urume   ¥
Noodle shop
51 Koyama Nishi Oono-cho, Kita-ku, Kyoto-shi, Kyoto 603-8167
Tel *(075) 495-9831*   **Closed** *Tue*
Family-run *soba* shop in an old *machiya* (traditional wooden townhouse) near Daitoku-ji serving homemade noodles. It is located on Kitaoji-dori, two blocks west of Horikawa-dori.

WESTERN KYOTO:
Colori Caffe   ¥¥
European
394-1-113 Juyonken-cho, Kamigyo-ku, Kyoto-shi, Kyoto 602-8164
Tel *(075) 801-5634*   **Closed** *Mon*
Organic ingredients are used in a wide range of pastas, soups, salads, and sweets at this friendly, self-proclaimed "queer-positive Italian café."

WESTERN KYOTO: Izusen   ¥¥
Vegetarian
4 Murasakino Daitokuji-cho, Kita-ku, Kyoto-shi, Kyoto 603-8231
Tel *(075) 491-6665*
Served up in attractive lacquer-ware, the excellent *shojin-ryori* here does not come with the usual hefty price tag.

WESTERN KYOTO:
Siam the Curry   ¥¥
Thai
6 Nishinogyo, Nishishikagaki-cho, Nakagyo-ku, Kyoto-shi Kyoto 604-8495
Tel *(075) 822-1119*   **Closed** *Wed*
The curries here burst with flavor, as do side dishes like the deep-fried fish cakes and spicy *tom yam kun* soup.

DK Choice

WESTERN KYOTO:
Ikkyu-an   ¥¥¥
Vegetarian
20 Daitokujimae, Murasakino, Kita-ku, Kyoto-shi, Kyoto 603-8215
Tel *(075) 493-0019*
This restaurant by the entrance to Daitoku-ji Temple can trace its roots back to the 15th century, when it been serving Chinese-style Buddhist cuisine called *fucha-ryori*. The sublimely flavored vegetable- and tofu-based meals are served on beautiful lacquerware in tatami rooms with temple-garden views. Reservations required.

Western Honshu

HIMEJI: Kidoriya ¥¥
Yakitori-ya
180-4 Shouda Asamiyashita,
Himeji-shi,
Hyogo 670-0951
Tel *(079) 224-3751*
Lively place serving all manner
of grilled chicken skewers.
Tsukune (meatballs) and
momo (thigh meat) are good
starting points.

HIMEJI:
Public House Hosanna ¥¥
Bar
9 Tatemachi, Himeji-shi,
Hyogo 670-0903
Tel *(079) 288-3299* **Closed** *Mon*
English-style pub on one floor
and wine bar on another,
serving a selection of pasta
dishes, pizzas, nibbles, and even
fish and chips.

HIROSHIMA: Kissui ¥¥
Izakaya
2-25 Naka-ku, Fukuro-machi,
Hiroshima-shi, Hiroshima 730-0036
Tel *(082) 246-8455* **Closed** *Sun*
Seafood is the focus at this
restaurant near the Peace Park,
with the excellent sashimi set
meals made according to the
day's catch.

HIROSHIMA:
Mario Espresso ¥¥
European
7-9 Fukuro-machi, Naka-ku,
Hiroshima-shi, Hiroshima 730-0036
Tel *(082) 241-4956*
This Italian eatery is known for
its great pasta dishes and pizza.
The white and blue panelled
walls and chalkboard menus
almost transport you to the
Italian seaside.

DK Choice

HIROSHIMA:
Okonomimura ¥¥
Okonomiyaki
5-13 Shintenchi, Naka-ku,
Hiroshima-shi,
Hiroshima 730-0034
Tel *(082) 241-2210*
Hiroshima is the city most
associated with *okonomiyaki*
(Osaka is also very well known
for this dish), and this bustling
multi-floored venue combines
23 different stalls specializing
in subtle variations of the
delicious, hearty pancake. Try
the local Hiroshima style,
which includes noodles in
the *okonomiyaki*. Some stores
have English menus.

DK Choice

HIROSHIMA:
Kakifune Kanawa ¥¥¥
Seafood
3 Otemachi, Naka-ku,
Hiroshima-shi,
Hiroshima 730-0051
Tel *(082) 241-7416*
This old houseboat moored
near Heiwa Ohashi bridge
specializes in one of
Hiroshima's signature foods:
oysters. They come in
elaborate *kaiseki*-like meals,
served up raw, deep fried,
grilled, and stewed, in a
traditional setting that feels
more like a Kyoto teahouse
than a boat. Reservations are
recommended, even for the
good-value set lunches.

ISE: Daiki ¥¥
Kaiseki-ryori
2-1-48 Iwabuchi, Ise-shi,
Mie 516-0037
Tel *(0596) 28-0281*
Kaiseki dinners for ¥5,000, as well
as cheaper *teishoku* set meals
and a ¥1,000 lunch *bento*. Great
value. Next to Ujiyamada station.

KOBE: Café Fish ¥¥
Café
2-8 Hatoba-cho, Chuo-ku, Kobe-shi,
Hyogo 650-0042
Tel *(078) 334-1820*
This café/bistro in the Motomachi
district is a relaxing place to
watch the world go by. Good
burgers, pasta, and other dishes.

KOBE: Kitano Club ¥¥¥
European
1-5-7 Kitano-machi, Chuo-ku,
Kobe-shi, Hyogo 650-0002
Tel *(078) 222-5123*
Sophisticated restaurant and bar
with views over Kobe. It serves
classic French courses using Kobe
beef and organic vegetables.
Reservations recommended.

KOBE: Mouriya ¥¥¥
Steakhouse
2-1-17 Shimoyamate-dori,
Chuo-ku, Kobe-shi,
Hyogo 650-0011
Tel *(078) 391-4603* **Closed** *Call*
for details
In business since 1885, Mouriya
is the most famous place in
Kobe to try the expensive and
renowned *wagyu* beef.

KOBE: Totenkaku ¥¥¥
Chinese
3-14-18 Yamate-dori, Chuo-ku,
Kobe-shi, Hyogo 650-0003
Tel *(078) 231-1351*
Come to this classic Euro-inspired
Meiji-era building to splurge on
set dinners that include lobster
and Peking duck.

KURASHIKI: El Greco ¥
Café
1-1-11 Chuo, Kurashiki-shi,
Okayama 710-0046
Tel *(086) 422-0297* **Closed** *Mon*
Opened in 1959 and now
completely covered in ivy, El
Greco has a mellow vibe and
simple menu of tea, coffee, ice
cream, and cheesecakes.

KURASHIKI: 9494 ¥¥
Izakaya
2-16-41 Achi, Kurashiki-shi,
Okayama 710-0055
Tel *(086) 421-0949* **Closed** *Tue*
This fashionable place
(pronounced *ku-shu-ku-shu*)
combines Japanese and other
Asian flavors to put a modern
twist on typical *izakaya* fare.

KURASHIKI: Tsurugata ¥¥¥
Kaiseki-ryori
1-3-15 Chuo, Kurashiki-shi,
Okayama 710-0046
Tel *(086) 424-1635*
This historic *ryokan*, dating from
1774, opens its restaurant to non-
guests. The 12-dish dinner takes
in delicate tempura, sashimi, and
seasonal vegetables.

Kakifune Kanawa, Western Honshu – for high-end food and an unusual venue

For more information on types of restaurants *see pages 310–311*

MATSUE: Yakumo-an ¥¥
Noodle shop
308 Shiominawate,
Matsue-shi,
Shimane 690-0000
Tel *(0852) 22-2400*
Set in an old samurai house,
Yakumo-an specializes in
Yakumo soba served in a bowl
of duck broth.

MATSUE: Naniwa ¥¥¥
Ryotei
21 Suetsugu Hon-machi,
Matsue-shi,
Shimane 690-0843
Tel *(0852) 21-2835*
Chopped eel on *ochazuke*
and grilled sea bass are two
of the local specialties at this
traditional riverside restaurant.

MIYAJIMA:
Tachibana Shokudo ¥¥
Seafood
566-1 Kitano-cho,
Miyajima-cho,
Hiroshima 739-0559
Tel *(0829) 44-0240*
Between Itsukushima Shrine
and the ferry terminal; come
here for local oysters and other
fresh Inland Sea catches.

NARA: Hiyori ¥¥
Kaiseki-ryori
26 Nakashinya-cho,
Nara-shi,
Nara 630-8333
Tel *(0742) 24-1470* **Closed** *Tue*
On offer here is an odd but
enjoyable combination of classic
Buddhist vegetarian dishes and
fine steaks. Very good *shojin-ryori* lunch deals, too.

NARA: Washoku Happo ¥¥
Izakaya
22 Higashimuki Naka-cho,
Nara-shi,
Nara 630-8215
Tel *(0742) 26-4834*

Sashimi, *yakitori*, tempura, and
most other *izakaya* fare is served
in a relaxed atmosphere right by
Nara station. There is also an
excellent range of sake on offer.

NARA: Yoshikawa-tei ¥¥
Youshoku
17 Hanashiba-cho,
Nara-shi,
Nara 630-8266
Tel *(0742) 23-7675* **Closed** *Mon*
French bistro-style dishes and
the *youshoku* classic hamburger
in a demi-glacé sauce; 300 m
(330 yards) north of Kintetsu
Nara station.

DK Choice

NARA: Harishin ¥¥¥
Kaiseki-ryori
15 Nakashinya-cho,
Nara-shi,
Nara 630-8333
Tel *(0742) 22-2669* **Closed** *Mon*
This very traditional restaurant
in an early 18th century
wooden building likes to keep
things simple. It serves a
single set lunch (great value
at ¥2,980) and a single set
dinner. The menu changes
seasonally but always features
multiple beautifully presented
dishes that use fresh local
vegetables along with high-quality seafood and meat.

NARA: Tsukihitei ¥¥¥
Ryotei
158 Kasugano-cho,
Nara-shi,
Nara 630-8212
Tel *(0742) 26-2021*
You'll need reservations to
sample this *ryokan's* sublime
food, presented in private
rooms like works of art and
starting at an eye-watering
amount for lunch.

Simple setting and a short but incredible menu at Harishin, Nara

OKAYAMA: Kappo Kadoya ¥¥
Kappo
1-10-21 Nodaya-cho, Kita-ku,
Okayama-shi, Okayama 700-0815
Tel *(086) 222-3338* **Closed** *Mon*
Sea bream (*tai*) with thin *soumen*
noodles is the signature dish here,
but *nabemono* (hotpots) and
kaiseki set meals are also served.

OKAYAMA: Matsunoki-tei ¥¥¥
Koryoriya
20-1 Ekimoto-cho, Kita-ku,
Okayama-shi, Okayama 700-0024
Tel *(086) 253-4111* **Closed** *Mon*
From full *kaiseki* dinners, to
hotpots and fancy lunchtime
bento – all served in elegant
tatami-mat rooms.

OSAKA: Café Absinthe ¥¥
Bar
1-2-27 Kitahorie, Nishi-ku, Osaka-shi,
Osaka 550-0014
Tel *(06) 6534-6635*
This is the place to go for late-night cocktails or a bit of *shisha*. It
also serves Arabic and Greek food.

OSAKA: Daruma ¥¥
Izakaya
2-3-9 Ebisu-higashi, Naniwa-ku,
Osaka-shi, Osaka 556-0002
Tel *(06) 6645-7056*
The focus here is *kushiage* –
deep-fried skewers of meat,
seafood, and vegetables dipped
in a sweet soy-based sauce.
Perfect with beer.

OSAKA: Mimiu Honten ¥¥
Noodle shop
4-6-18 Hirano-cho, Chuo-ku,
Osaka-shi, Osaka 541-0046
Tel *(06) 6231-5770* **Closed** *Sun*
Udon gets high-end treatment at
this over 200-year-old restaurant.
The signature dish *udon suki* sees
the noodles simmered in a beef-and-vegetable hotpot.

OSAKA: Okonomiyaki-ya
Chigusa ¥¥
Okonomiyaki
4-11-18 Tenmabashi,
Kita-ku, Osaka-shi, Osaka 530-0000
Tel *(06) 6351-4072* **Closed** *Tue*
Osaka's most famous food
(*okonomiyaki*) and fried noodles
(*yaki soba*) in a typically lively
Osakan atmosphere. Well hidden
100 m (109 yards) north of Tenma
station – ask for directions.

OSAKA: Portugalia ¥¥
European
4-12-11 Nishi-Tenma, Kita-ku,
Osaka-shi, Osaka 530-0047
Tel *(06) 6362-6668* **Closed** *Sun*
Portugalia offers an extensive
wine list, perfect with both the
light tapas dishes and hearty
Portuguese cooking on offer.

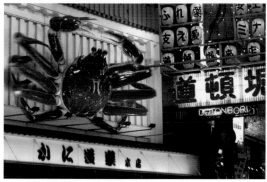

For excellent crab-based dishes head to Kani Douraku in Osaka

DK Choice

OSAKA: Kani Douraku ¥¥¥
Seafood
1-6-18 Dotonbori,
Chuo-ku, Osaka-shi,
Osaka 542-0071
Tel *(06) 6211-8975*
Crab is cooked (and sometimes not) all ways at this landmark restaurant, which is easily recognized by the giant mechanical crab hanging off the building. To make things simple, opt for a set menu such as the *kani kaiseki*, which ranges from crab tempura and sushi to grilled or steamed crab.

OSAKA: Kigawa ¥¥¥
Kappo-ryori
1-7-7 Dotonbori,
Chuo-ku, Osaka-shi,
Osaka 542-0071
Tel *(06) 6211-3030* **Closed** *Mon*
The quality and cost of *kaiseki* but à la carte and with a more down-to-earth feel. Reservations are essential here.

OSAKA: Ume no Hana ¥¥¥
Kaiseki-ryori
2-6-20 Umeda, Kita-ku,
Osaka-shi, Osaka 530-0001
Tel *(06) 6343-6320*
Traditional interiors and thoughtful presentation of meals centered on tofu and *yuba* (sheets of dried soy milk) are served here – without the usual high *kaiseki* price tags.

TSUWANO: Saranoki ¥¥
Koryoriya
Tonomachi, Tsuwano-cho,
Shimane 699-5605
Tel *(0856) 72-1661*
A variety of beautifully presented lacquerware *bento* boxes are on offer, including small vegetable and tofu side dishes alongside tempura and *udon* or *soba*.

TSUWANO: Yuki ¥¥
Regional
271-4 Ushiroda, Tsuwano-cho,
Shimane 699-5605
Tel *(0856) 72-0162*
The menu here is based on local mountain vegetables and carp, which comes as sashimi and in miso soup. Opposite the Hokusai Museum.

Shikoku

DK Choice

KOCHI: Hirome Ichiba ¥¥
Market
2-3-1 Obiya-cho,
Kochi-shi,
Kochi 780-0841
Tel *(088) 822-5287*
Nowhere else in Kochi is better for soaking up the city's nightlife or striking up a conversation than this market full of food stalls. Choose from noodles, *teishoku*, sashimi, curries, and dozens more options, then set up on one of the communal tables with a drink or two.

KOCHI: Mamma Italia ¥¥
European
4-4 Nijudai-machi,
Kochi-shi, Kochi 780-0843
Tel *(088) 873-3131* **Closed** *Mon & Tue*
Come to this smart place opposite the Kochi Annex Hotel for the delicious pizzas, which are made in a wood-fired oven by a Japanese chef who was trained in Italy.

KOCHI: Tokugetsuro ¥¥¥
Kaiseki-ryori
1-17-3 Minami Hariyama-cho,
Kochi-shi, Kochi 780-0833
Tel *(088) 882-0101*

Exquisite seafood restaurant. Some of the tatami mat rooms have views of a landscaped garden and carp-filled pond.

KOCHI: Tsukasa ¥¥¥
Regional
1-2-15 Hariyama-cho,
Kochi-shi, Kochi 780-0822
Tel *(088) 873-4351*
Serves the local *tosa-ryori*, which is heavy on sashimi and other lightly flavored fish dishes. The seared skipjack tuna (*katsu-no-tataki*) is a must try.

KOTOHIRA: Toraya Soba ¥
Noodle shop
814 Kotohira-cho,
Nakatado-gun,
Kagawa 766-0002
Tel *(0877) 75-3131*
Despite *soba* in the name here, the special is handmade *udon*. In a lovely old wooden building opposite the Maritime Musuem.

MATSUYAMA: Flankey Kobayashi's ¥¥
Bar
2-3-4 Ichiban-cho,
Matsuyama-shi,
Ehime 790-0001
This lively tachinomi-ya (standing bar) on a backstreet corner two blocks east of Mitsukoshi is a popular expat hangout. Drinks start at ¥300.

MATSUYAMA: Tipitina's ¥¥
Izakaya
2-6-18 Sanban-cho,
Matsuyama-shi,
Ehime 790-0003
Tel *(089) 921-7011*
This hip place has a menu that includes grilled meats, fried rice, and salads. One of the quirkier dishes available is 'toast pizza' –a favorite among regulars.

Well-presented plate of deep-fried pork and salad, a classic dish in Shikoku

For more information on types of restaurants *see pages 310–311*

Sumptuous food offerings, typical of Beppu regional cuisine

MATSUYAMA:
Aqualung Imura ¥¥¥
Teppanyaki
3-2-8 Niban-cho,
Matsuyama-shi, Ehime 790-0002
Tel *(089) 931-2329* **Closed** *Tue*
Wines from around the world
paired with high-quality, quickly
seared steaks. Wood and brick
interiors, with lots of semi-
private corners.

MATSUYAMA: Kawasemi ¥¥¥
Kaiseki-ryori
2-5-6 Niban-cho,
Matsuyama-shi, Ehime 790-0002
Tel *(089) 907-6010*
Artful presentation in tatami
rooms of multi-dish courses
centered on steak or blowfish
(*fugu*). Lunch deals start at
around ¥1,500.

OZU: Tonomachi Tarui ¥¥
Regional
553 Nakamura, Ozu-shi,
Ehime 795-0054
Tel *(0893) 24-3000* **Closed** *Mon*
Donburi shop where the special
is *unagi-don* (eel on rice).
Cheaper and equally good is
the *katsu-don* (deep-fried pork
cutlet on rice).

TAKAMATSU: Uchara Honten ¥
Noodle shop
1-18-8 Ritsurin-machi,
Takamatsu-shi, Kagawa 760-0073
Tel *(087) 831-6779*
Try Shikoku's version of *udon*,
sanuki udon, chilled (*hiyashi kake
udon*) or in hot broth (*kake udon*).
Near the famed Ritsurin Garden.

TAKAMATSU: Cantina ¥¥
European
3-2 Kitahama-cho,
Takamatsu-shi, Kagawa 760-0031
Tel *(087) 811-7718*
This is a casual and fashionable
restaurant in an old warehouse in
Kitahama Alley. Good paella and
tapas-like appetizers.

TAKAMATSU: Gowariyasu ¥¥
Izakaya
6-3 Fukuda-machi,
Takamatsu-shi, Kagawa 760-0048
Tel *(087) 851-5030*
Yakitori is the pick of the menu
at this bustling, good-value
place, which is decorated with
old film posters.

TAKAMATSU: Tenkatsu ¥¥
Seafood
7-8 Hyogo-machi,
Takamatsu-shi, Kagawa 760-0024
Tel *(087) 821-5380*
Grab a counter seat to watch as
chefs pluck fish from large tanks
and prepare the sushi and other
excellent seafood dishes.

TOKUSHIMA: Wada no Ya ¥
Teahouse
5-3 Otakiyama, Bizan-cho,
Tokushima-shi, Tokushima 770-0908
Tel *(088) 652-8414* **Closed** *Thu*
Take in the garden views while
you enjoy green tea and sweets
such as the local *yaki mochi*, a
grilled pounded rice cake.
Located at the foot of Mt. Bizan.

TOKUSHIMA: Tori Tori ¥¥
Yakitori-ya
2-16 Ichiban-cho, Tokushima-shi,
Tokushima 770-0833
Tel *(088) 654-3766* **Closed** *Sun*
The skewered meat at this
lively joint includes kangaroo,
ostrich, and alligator. Located
100 m (109 yards) southwest of
Tokushima station.

TOKUSHIMA:
Toraya Kochuan ¥¥¥
Kaiseki-ryori
1 Murakami, Sanogo-kawauchi,
Myodo-gun, Tokushima 711-4102
Tel *(088) 679-2305*
Walk through the lattice gateway
and follow the garden pathways
to tatami rooms for fine seasonal
dishes served on local ceramics
and lacquerware.

UWAJIMA: Gansui ¥¥
Izakaya
2-3-10 Hon-machi Ote,
Uwajima-shi,
Ehime 798-0041
Tel *(0895) 22-3636* **Closed** *Tue*
The specialty among many
well-prepared seafood dishes at
this elegant *izakaya* is *taimeshi*
(sea bream steamed on rice).

UWAJIMA: Kadoya ¥¥
Seafood
8-1 Nishiki-machi,
Uwajima-shi, Ehime
Tel *(0895) 22-1543* **Closed** *Thu*
Smart counter or tatami seating
for ultra-fresh locally caught
sashimi, as well as simmered
whole fish and *taimeshi* (sea
bream steamed over rice).

Kyushu

DK Choice

BEPPU: Fugumatsu ¥¥¥
Seafood
3-6-14 Kitahama, Beppu-shi,
Oita 874-0920
Tel *(0977) 21-1717*
The potentially deadly *fugu*
(blowfish), which contains
toxins can kill the diner if
not prepared properly, is the
sole focus of this friendly,
traditional restaurant. You'll
be in safe hands with
Fugumatsu's skilled chefs,
who serve the delicate fish
as *shabu-shabu* with citrusy
dips, as sashimi, and in
several other methods too.

BEPPU: Shin-zushi ¥¥¥
Sushi
1-2-2 Kitahama,
Beppu-shi,
Oita 874-0920
Tel *(0977) 25-0005*
Here, three blocks east of
Beppu station, high-quality
fresh fish is prepared as sushi
and sashimi, alongside an
excellent choice of local sake
and shochu.

CHIRAN: Takian ¥¥
Regional
6329 Chiran-cho,
Minami Kyushu-shi,
Kagoshima 897-0300
Tel *(0993) 83-3186*
Teishoku set meals in an Edo-era
samurai house combining
soba or *udon* noodles with local
flavors such as *tori sashimi*
(raw chicken) and *satsuma age*
(deep-fried fish cake).

Key to Price Guide *see page 324*

FUKUOKA: Isshin Furan ¥
Noodle shop
2-6 Daimyo, Chuo-ku,
Fukuoka-shi, Fukuoka 810 0041
Tel *(092) 733-3768*
Tonkotsu (pork broth) *ramen* is
Fukuoka's gift to the *ramen* world,
and few places do it better here.

FUKUOKA: Bassin ¥¥
Japanese fusion
1-9-63 Daimyo, Chuo-ku,
Fukuoka-shi, Fukuoka 810-0041
Tel *(092) 739-3210*
Fashionable interiors and a
blending of Japanese and
European cuisines.

FUKUOKA: Hakata Mizutaki Toriden ¥¥
Regional
2-3-30 Yakuin, Chuo-ku, Fukuoka-shi,
Fukuoka 810-0022
Tel *(092) 716-2202*
Minimalist concrete and dark-
wood interiors meet traditional
food. The specialty is *mizutaki*, a
chicken-and-vegetable hotpot
made with a light stock.

FUKUOKA: Ume no Hana ¥¥¥
Kaiseki-ryori
1-15-6 Tenjin-machi, Chuo-ku,
Fukuoka-shi, Fukuoka 810-0001
Tel *(0120) 27-4080*
Various set menus are available,
all beautifully presented and
based around tofu and *yuba*
(sheets of dried soy milk).

FUKUOKA: Yamanaka ¥¥¥
Sushi
2-8-8 Watanabe-dori, Chuo-ku,
Fukuoka-shi, Fukuoka 810-0004
Tel *(092) 731-7771*   **Closed** *Sun*
Fashionable natural-toned wood
interiors and exceptional sushi
and sushi-oriented *kaiseki*. Pricey
at night, but good deals at
lunchtime.

KAGOSHIMA: Kokinta ¥
Noodle shop
11-5 Tenokuchi-cho, Kagoshima-shi,
Kagoshima 892-0845
Tel *(099) 223-9455*
The lines here tell you how good
the *ramen* is – especially the miso
ramen topped with roast pork.
Situated on the southern edge of
Tenmonkan Park.

KAGOSHIMA: Gonbee ¥¥
Tofu
8-12 Higashi Sengoku-cho,
Kagoshima-shi,
Kagoshima 890-0000
Tel *(099) 222-3867*   **Closed** *Sun*
Homemade tofu is used to create
yudofu, served with a refreshing
yuzu (Japanese citrus) dipping
sauce. Three blocks north of
Tenmonkandori station.

KAGOSHIMA: Satsuma Aji ¥¥¥
Regional
6-9 Higashi Sengoku-cho,
Kagoshima-shi, Kagoshima 892-0842
Tel *(099) 226-0525*
The focus here, alongside a
selection of regional dishes, is
shabu-shabu, using the
renowned local *kurobuta* pork.
Reservations are recommended.

KUMAMOTO: Aoyagi ¥¥
Regional
1-2-10 Shimotori, Chuo-ku,
Kumamoto-shi, Kumamoto 860-0807
Tel *(096) 353-0311*
Tatami matting, *ikebana* flower
arrangements, and paper screens
create a lovely setting for sushi,
tempura, *kame-meshi*, and other
dishes using local ingredients.

KUMAMOTO: Gorohachi ¥¥¥
Regional
12-8 Hanabata-cho,
Chuo-ku, Kumamoto-shi,
Kumamoto 860-0806
Tel *(096) 321-8586*
This spectacularly plush
restaurant serves Kyushu
specialties such as *fugu* (blowfish)
and *bazushi* (raw horse meat),
as well as a range of sushi and
kaiseki set meals.

KUMAMOTO: Kikumoto ¥¥¥
Ryotei
1-1-12 Shin-machi,
Kumamoto-shi, Kumamoto 860-0004
Tel *(096) 352-2088*
The traditional set menus
here include Chinese influences
alongside Kumamoto flavors
such as *bazashi*. It is advisable to
book several days in advance.

MOUNT ASO: Nouka Restaurant Tangoyama ¥¥
Steak
285 Mikubo, Aso-shi,
Kumamoto 869-2302
Tel *(0967) 32-5070*   **Closed** *Wed*

This rustic restaurant located
on a cattle farm is known
for its fine steaks, which it
serves with refreshing citrus
dips and a selection of
organic vegetables.

NAGASAKI: Harbin ¥¥
European
4-13 Yorozuya-machi,
Nagasaki-shi,
Nagasaki 850-0852
Tel *(095) 824-6650*   **Closed** *Wed*
Simple 1950s decor gives Harbin
a certain retro charm. Russian
and French bistro dishes,
including its signature borscht,
make it worth visiting.

NAGASAKI: Kouzanrou ¥¥
Chinese
13-13 Shinchi-machi,
Nagasaki-shi,
Nagaski 850-0842
Tel *(095) 820-3735*
Nagasaki-style Chinese food is
served here, including *champon*,
a noodle dish with a thick sauce
that combines squid, prawns,
and vegetables.

DK Choice

NAGASAKI: Ichiriki ¥¥¥
Regional
8-20 Suwa-cho,
Nagasaki-shi,
Nagasaki 850-0873
Tel *(095) 824-0226*
Nagasaki's oldest restaurant,
opened in 1813, serves
shippoku, a local style of cooking
that reflects Nagasaki's overseas
influences by combining
Japanese, Chinese, Dutch, and
Portuguese cuisines with dishes
such as stewed meats, sashimi,
and soups. All this is delivered
in gracefully ageing tatami-mat
surroundings. Reservations are
recommended.

Masterfully prepared array of sashimi

For more information on types of restaurants *see pages 310–311*

Table-side music at Amuritanoniwa, in Ishigaki-jima

NAGASAKI: Kagetsu ¥¥¥
Ryotei
2-1 Maruyama-machi,
Nagasaki-shi, w 850-0902
Tel *(095) 822-0191*
The elegant meals at this
tranquil hillside restaurant
come in traditional Japanese
ryotei guise or *shippoku*, which
combines Japanese, Chinese,
and European influences.

YUFUIN: Yunotake-Ann ¥¥
Regional
2633-1 Kawakami,
Yufuin-machi, Yufu-shi, Oita
Tel *(0977) 84-2970*
This charming cottage with a
lush garden is a cozy setting
for local Bungo beef: roast,
steak, and *sukiyaki*. Great lunch
bento is available.

Okinawa

CHATAN: Hamaya ¥
Noodle shop
2-99 Miyagi, Chatan-cho,
Nakagami-gun, Okinawa 904-0113
Tel *(098) 936-5929* **Closed** *Sun*
This ocean-front eatery does the
Okinawan noodle dish *soki soba*,
topped with melt-in-the-mouth
spare ribs.

CHATAN: Transit Café ¥¥
Café
2-220 Miyagi, Chatan-cho,
Nakagami-gun, Okinawa 904-0113
Tel *(098) 936-5076*
Beach views, fresh white interiors,
cocktails, and good Italian dishes
such as *porchetta* (Italian roast
pork) and white-fish carpaccio.

ISHIGAKI-JIMA: Akebono ¥¥
Seafood
12-11 Misaki-cho, Ishigaki-shi,
Okinawa 907-0012
Tel *(0980) 82-7759*

Super-fresh catches are prepared
here mainly as sushi but are also
vinegared, as sashimi, and deep-
fried. Near Ishigaki city hall.

ISHIGAKI-JIMA: Amuritanoniwa ¥¥
Bar
282 Ookawa, Ishigaki-shi,
Okinawa 907-0022
Tel *(0980) 87-7867*
Run by a musician-and-artist
couple, this laid-back bar
serves cocktails, local *shochu*,
and herb teas. Good Thai
curries, burgers and vegan
dishes, too.

MIYAKO-JIMA: Goya ¥¥
Izakaya
570-2 Hiraranishizato,
Miyakojima-shi,
Okinawa 906-0012
Tel *(0980) 74-2358*
Fun place to try fresh sashimi,
local *shochu*, and local
Okinawan dishes such as *goya
champuru*, while catching
nightly live performances
of Okinawan music.

NAGO: Orion Brewery Yanbaru no Mori ¥¥
Izakaya
2-2-1 Agarie, Nago-shi,
Okinawa 905-0021
Tel *(0980) 52-2126*
Connected to the Orion Brewery,
and ideal after a brewery tour,
this restaurant sells Okinawa's
iconic beer alongside pizza, pasta
dishes, and beer snacks.

NAHA: Dao ¥¥
Vietnamese
2-8-28 Matsuo, Naha-shi,
Okinawa 900-0014
Tel *(098) 867-3751*
The *pho* noodles, spring rolls
(*harumaki*), and coconut-based
curry are the main highlights
here. Low prices at lunchtime.

NAHA: Helios Pub ¥¥
Pub
1-2-25 Makishi, Naha-shi,
Okinawa 900-0013
Tel *(098) 863-7227* **Closed** *Sun*
Run by the Helios Microbrewery
and serving their five craft
beers together with pizza, pasta,
and Okinawan dishes such as
goya champuru.

NAHA: Perestroika ¥¥
European
1-13-22 Izumisaki, Naha-shi,
Okinawa 900-0021
Tel *(098) 863-2206* **Closed** *Mon*
This colorful expat-run Russian
restaurant serves fare such as
borscht and beef stroganoff.

NAHA: Umi no Chinboraa ¥¥
Izakaya
2-13-15 Maeshima, Naha-shi,
Okinawa 900-0016
Tel *(098) 863-5123*
Come to this place, one minute
from Tomarin Harbor, to try
excellent sashimi and Okinawan
seafood dishes.

NAHA: Yuunangi ¥¥
Izakaya
3-3-3 Kumoji, Naha-shi,
Okinawa 900-0015
Tel *(098) 867-3765* **Closed** *Sun*
Try the excellent strong local
versions of *shochu* (*awamori*),
plus good Okinwana dishes.

> ### DK Choice
> ### NAHA: Ryukyu Ryori Mie ¥¥¥
> Regional
> *1-8-8 Kumoji, Naha-shi,*
> *Okinawa 900-0015*
> **Tel** *(098) 867-1356* **Closed** *Sun*
> The old red-tiled building that
> houses Ryukyu Ryori Mie is
> the perfect traditional setting
> for Ryukyu palace food, a
> sublimely presented *kaiseki*-
> style cuisine incorporating local
> flavors from Okinawa, which
> was once an independent
> kingdom called Ryukyu.
> Reservations are essential.

OKINAWA CITY: Mukaiya ¥
Noodle shop
96 Koja, Okinawa-shi,
Okinawa 904-2161
Tel *(098) 929-4163* **Closed** *Wed*
Cozy rustic-looking restaurant
that serves the classic Okinawan
noodle dish *soki soba*.

OKINAWA CITY: Steak House Four Season ¥¥¥
Teppanyaki
3-1-25 Sonoda, Okinawa-shi,
Okinawa 904-0022
Tel *(098) 933-5731*

Sit around the grill and watch the chefs sizzle high-quality Kobe-*gyu* steaks and local lobster. Good deals at lunchtime.

TAMAGUSUKU:
Hamabe no Chaya ¥
Café
2-1 Tamagusuku, Nanjo-shi,
Okinawa 901-0604
Tel *(098) 948-2073*
This mellow wood-decked spot with a magical view over the ocean offers snacks, light meals, teas, and coffee.

URASOE: Applemint Café ¥¥
Café
5-5-1 Makiminato,
Urasoe-shi,
Okinawa 901-2131
Tel *(098) 878-4452* **Closed** *Sun & Mon*
A homely organic café with a pleasant garden. The good-value set meals range from simple *teishoku* to Japanese curry and pasta dishes.

Northern Honshu

AIZU-WAKAMATSU:
Mitsutaya ¥¥
Dengaku
1-1-25 Oo-machi,
Aizu-Wakamatsu-shi,
Fukushima 965-0042
Tel *(0242) 27-1345* **Closed** *1st & 3rd Wed of each month*
At this over 150-year-old former miso factory they specialize in *dengaku* – skewers of tofu, fish, and vegetables dipped into a miso paste and chargrilled.

AKITA:
Hamanoya Bekkan ¥¥¥
Regional
4-2-11 Oo-machi, Akita-shi,
Akita 010-0921
Tel *(018) 862-6611*

A deadly delicacy: *fugu* (blow fish) is served in speciality restaurants throughout Osaka

Head to this lovely old wooden house for *ryotei* and Akita's signature dish *kiritampo*, a hearty stew of meat, vegetables, and grilled pounded rice cakes.

AOMORI: Nishimura ¥¥
Seafood
1-1-40 Yusukata, Aomori-shi,
Aomori 030-0803
Tel *(017) 734-5353*
One of several good restaurants in the Aspam building. Try *Jappajiru* (cod and miso stew) or *kaisendon* (sashimi on a bowl of rice).

DEWA-SAN: Sanko-in ¥¥
Vegetarian
92 Haguro-machi Touge,
Tsuruoka-shi, Yamagata 997-0211
Tel *(0235) 62-2302*
Sanko-in Temple serves subtly flavored multi-dish *shojin-ryori*, the strict vegetable-and-tofu cuisine eaten by monks.

HIROSAKI: Kenta ¥¥
Robatayaki
3 Okeya-cho, Hirosaki-shi,
Aomori 036-8004
Tel *(0172) 35-9514*
Ordering is simple here – point to the meat, seafood, or veg you want, and it will be grilled for you.

HIROSAKI: Anzu ¥¥¥
Izakaya
44-1 Oyakata-machi, Hirosaki-shi,
Aomori 036-8191
Tel *(0172) 32-6684* **Closed** *Sun*
Sashimi, *nabemono*, and good regional dishes are on the menu, but the nightly *shamisen* (a three-stringed instrument) performances are the main draw.

KAKUNODATE:
Aoyagi Samurai Manor ¥
Noodle shop
26 Katuraku-cho, Kakunodate-machi, Akita 014-0325
Tel *(0187) 54-3257*
Explore the samurai houses and gardens, then stop here for the mushroom, bamboo shoot, and onion-loaded *inaniwa udon* noodles.

KAKUNODATE: Ryotei Inaho ¥¥
Regional
4-1 Tamachi Kami-cho, Kakunodate-machi, Akita 014-0311
Tel *(0187) 54-3311* **Closed** *Thu*
Rustic *ryotei*-style cuisine featuring local flavors such as grilled pounded rice cakes. Great lunch *bento* from ¥1,500.

MATSUSHIMA: Donjiki Chaya ¥
Noodle shop
129 Matsuchima-aza-chonai,
Matsuchima-cho, Miyagi 981-0213
Tel *(022) 354-5855*
Soba and sweets in a 17th-century thatched building near Entsuin Temple. Try the skewered and grilled *dango* (pounded rice balls) in a sugary soy sauce.

MORIOKA: Pairon ¥
Noodle shop
5-15 Uchimaru, Morioka-shi,
Iwate 020-0023
Tel *(019) 624-2247*
The Morioka specialty *jajamen* served here are addictive thick wheat noodles with a meaty miso paste and cucumber slices. At northern edge of Iwate Koen.

Famed Okinawan noodle dish, *soki soba* topped with pork spare ribs

For more information on types of restaurants *see pages 310–311*

DK Choice

MORIOKA: Chokurian ¥¥
Noodle shop
1-12-13 Nakanobashi-dori,
Morioka-shi,
Iwate 020-0871
Tel *(019) 624-0441* **Closed** *Wed*
Come to Chokurian for a
simple, cheap bowl of *soba*,
or indulge in an epic Morioka
challenge: *wanko soba*, where
stomachs versus noodles. With
this all-you-can-eat option,
dinners can get bowl after
small bowl of *soba*, to which
a variety of ingredients can be
added until you can't take the
slurping any more.

NIKKO: Masudaya ¥¥
Tofu
439-2 Ishiya-machi,
Nikko-shi,
Tochigi 321-1405
Tel *(0288) 54-2151* **Closed** *Thu*
Although not all the dishes on
offer at Masudaya are vegetarian,
the carefully arranged and
delicately flavored set menus on
offer here are predominantly
tofu- and *yuba*-based.

NIKKO: Gyoshin-Tei ¥¥¥
Kaiseki-ryori
2339-1 Sannai, Nikko-shi,
Tochigi 321-1433
Tel *(0288) 53-3751* **Closed** *Thu*
Tatami-mat rooms with mossy
garden views and equally
attractive *shojin-ryori* multi-dish
meals. Neighboring sister
restaurants offer non-vegetarian
kaiseki options.

SENDAI: Aji Tasuke ¥¥
Regional
4-4-13 Ichiban-cho,
Aoba-ku, Sendai-shi,
Miyagi 980-0811
Tel *(022) 225-4641* **Closed** *Tue*

Grilled ox tongue (*gyu-tan*) with
a lemon-pepper dip is a Sendai
specialty. Try it here in a *teishoku*
set meal with oxtail soup.

SENDAI: Kakitoku ¥¥
Seafood
4-9-1 Ichiban-cho,
Aoba-ku, Sendai-shi,
Miyagi 980-0811
Tel *(022) 222-0785* **Closed** *Mon*
Locally caught oysters come
prepared in many different ways
here. Besides the classic option of
enjoying them raw, try a few
deep fried (*kaki-furai*).

SENDAI: Jiraiya ¥¥¥
Izakaya
2-1-15 Kokubun-cho,
Aoba-ku, Sendai-shi,
Miyagi 980-8671
Tel *(022) 261-2164* **Closed** *Sun*
Jiraiya calls itself a Slow Food
restaurant, although the bustling
atmosphere feels anything but.
Specializes in seafood dishes, as
well as sake.

TONO:
Maruman Jingisukan ¥¥
Regional
1-8 Chuo-dori, Tono-shi,
Iwate 028-0500
Tel *(0198) 60-1185* **Closed** *Tue*
Named after Genghis Khan,
jingisukan is a hearty barbecue
that comprises marinated slices
of lamb grilled at your table. Four
blocks south of Tono station.

TSURUOKA: Kanazawaya ¥¥
Noodle shop
163 Maeda, Mitsubashi
Haguro-machi, Tsuruoka-shi,
Yamagata 997-0166
Tel *(0235) 62-4564*
Kanazawaya have been skilfully
making *soba* and *udon* noddles
by hand for over 30 years. The
¥1,500 set meal comes with
tempura and pickles.

Hokkaido

HAKODATE: Asari ¥¥
Sukiyaki
10-11 Takaragi-cho,
Hakodate-shi,
Hokkaido 933-0343
Tel *(0138) 23-0421* **Closed** *Wed*
Meaty hotpots are served in
tatami-mat rooms at Asari, located
above the owner's butcher's
shop, near Takaragicho station.

HAKODATE: Hakodate Beer ¥¥
Bar
5-22 Ote-machi,
Hakodate-shi,
Hokkaido 040-0064
Tel *(0138) 23-8000*
Four locally brewed types of beer
are served here in spacious
natural-wood surroundings,
alongside good seafood dishes
and *youshoku* fare.

HAKODATE: Kihara Sushi ¥¥
Sushi
2-1-2 Yukawa-cho, Hakodate-shi,
Hokkaido 042-0932
Tel *(0138) 57-8825* **Closed** *Wed*
Fresh catches landed in Hakodate
are transformed at Kihara Sushi in
to top-grade yet affordable sushi
and sashimi menu items. Wash
your meal down with one of the
50 sakes on offer.

HAKODATE: Megumi at
Hakodate Bay Bishoku Club ¥¥
Regional
12-6 Toyokawa-cho,
Hakodate-shi, Hokkaido 040-0065
Tel *(0138) 24-8070*
One of seven good restaurants
in Hakodate Bay Bishoku Club,
Megumi does soup curry, a
warming Hokkaido dish that is
similar to mulligatawny.

KUSHIRO: Kushiro Robata ¥¥
Robatayaki
3-1 Sakae-maci,
Kushiro-shi,
Hokkaido 085-0013
Tel *(0154) 22-6636* **Closed** *Sun*
Grilled scallops and *hokke* (*atka*
mackerel) are two standouts at
this very rustic restaurant that
was established over 50 years
ago. Also serves sashimi, grilled
meats, and local sake.

NISEKO: Café Jo Jo's ¥¥
Café
179-53 Aza-Yamada,
Kutchan-cho, Abuta-gun,
Hokkaido 044-0081
Tel *(0136) 23-2093*
This hip Australian-run eatery
has views of Mount Yotei. Good
burgers, pizzas, and pasta dishes
are on offer, as well as cocktails.

One of the indulgent dishes on offer at the highly regarded Michel Bras, Shimizu

The cavernous Sapporo Beer Garden, offering Hokkaido specials and beer aplenty

NISEKO: Izakaya Bang Bang ¥¥
Izakaya
188-24 Aza-Yamada, Kutchan-cho,
Abuta-gun, Hokkaido 044-0081
Tel *(0136) 22-4292* **Closed** *outside*
of ski season
Lively after-ski watering hole
with a large menu centered on
yakitori and other skewered
meat and vegetables.

NISEKO: Kabuki 1 ¥¥
Izakaya
170-26 Aza-Yamada,
Kutchan-cho, Abuta-gun,
Hokkaido 044-0081
Tel *(0136) 21-2233* **Closed** *outside*
of ski season
Hotplates are set on each table
for cooking up *okonomiyaki,*
teppanyaki, and *yaki soba.* The
friendly English-speaking staff
will show you how.

DK Choice

OTARU: Kita no Ice Cream ¥
Dessert
1-2-18 Ironai, Otaru-shi,
Hokkaido 047-0031
Tel *(0134) 23-8983*
Located in one of the old brick
buildings along the picturesque
Otaru Canal, Kita no Ice Cream
specialises in one of the products
that the renowned diary region
of Hokkaido is famous for: ice
cream. The selection on offer
ranges from classic flavors to
the bizarre. Try the *ikasumi*
(squid ink) or *uni* (sea urchin)
flavors, if you dare.

OTARU: Masazushi ¥¥
Sushi
1-1-1 Hanazono, Otaru-shi,
Hokkaido 047-0024
Tel *(0134) 23-0011* **Closed** *Mon*
This multi-floored restaurant
delivers good quality at

reasonable prices. Keep it simple
with a 12-piece "sushi plate."
Children's meals are available.

SAPPORO: Ramen Kyowakoku ¥
Noodle shop
2 North 5-jo West, Chuo-ku,
Sapporo-shi 060-0005
Tel *(011) 209-5031*
Eight *ramen* shops from around
Hokkaido combine on the 10th
floor of Sapporo station. The
Sapporo miso *ramen* is great.

SAPPORO: Matsujin ¥¥
Regional
4-16-1 South 1-jo West,
Chuo-ku, Sapporo-shi,
Hokkaido 060-0061
Tel *(011) 219-2989*
Jingisukan, the Hokkaido-born
grilled mutton dish is traditionally
prepared at your table at Matsujin,
and servings are all-you-can-eat.

SAPPORO: La Piazza ¥¥
European
11-1-35 South 23-jo West,
Chuo-ku, Sapporo-shi,
Hokkaido 064-0923
Tel *(011) 563-7717* **Closed** *Mon*

Handmade pasta, excellent
pizzas, and a friendly, laid-back
vibe. A wide selection of Italian
wines and desserts, too.

SAPPORO: Sapporo Beer Garden ¥¥
Regional
9-2-10 Norh 7-jo, Higashi-ku,
Sapporo-shi, Hokkaido 065-0007
Tel *(0120) 150-550*
Sup Sapporo beer in a cavernous
red-brick hall accented by a
ceiling-high brewing cauldron.
Various Hokkaido dishes served.

SAPPORO: 21 Club ¥¥¥
Teppanyaki
6-1-21 South 10-jo West,
Chuo-ku, Sapporo-shi,
Hokkaido 064-8561
Tel *(011) 561-1000*
This plush dining experience on
the 25th floor of the Novotel
hotel offers a cityscape backdrop
as you watch the chefs at work
from your counter seat.

SAPPORO: Kani Honke ¥¥¥
Seafood
2-1-18 North 3-Jo West,
Chuo-ku, Sapporo-shi,
Hokkaido 060-0003
Tel *(011) 222-0018*
Crab sushi and sashimi, as well
as boiled and grilled crab, are
served here by kimono-clad
waitresses. Choose between
tatami rooms and table seating.

TOYA NATIONAL PARK: Michel Bras ¥¥¥
European
Windsor Hotel, Shimizu,
Toyako-cho, Abuta-gun,
Hokkaido 049-5722
Tel *(0142) 73-1111* **Closed** *Wed &*
lunch Thu
This Michelin-starred French
restaurant offers two highly
refined and sumptuous options:
the five-course "Meeting" and
the four-course "Walk".

The entrance to Ramen Kyowakoku in Sapporo

For more information on types of restaurants *see pages 310–311*

SHOPPING IN JAPAN

Shopping in Japan is an amazing experience. With as many traditional arts and crafts products as contemporary and imported items, there is the most fascinating choice imaginable. Equally interesting is the range of shops – from glitzy department stores and huge shoppings malls to roadside stalls and tiny craft workshops. Within 24 hours, the constant greetings of *"irasshaimase"* ("Welcome!") on entering a shop are either driving visitors crazy or have become part of the general background noise. Japan is no longer the most expensive country in the world, but still the price of certain commodities may shock. Some goods made in Japan, such as cameras and other electronic items, are actually cheaper to buy abroad. On the other hand, it is possible to buy original and unusual souvenirs surprisingly inexpensively. For details on shopping in Tokyo, *see pages 108–11*; for Kyoto, *see pages 184–7*.

Canal City shopping complex in Fukuoka, Kyushu

Shopping Hours

Supermarkets and department stores are usually closed for just one weekday a month or one weekday every two months – the day varies, depending on local custom. A number of specialty shops – boutiques included – may not open on Sundays and national holidays. Family-run businesses are generally open daily, including Saturdays, Sundays, and national holidays.

The opening hours of most shops are 10am to 8pm. Department stores usually close 1 hour earlier. Supermarkets are often open until 10pm or midnight. Convenience stores – chains such as **Seven-Eleven** and **Lawson's** – are open seven days a week, 24 hours a day. Vending machines *(see p309)* are widespread in hotels and at roadsides, offering practical items 24 hours a day.

Prices and Sales Tax

In department stores and boutiques, and in inner-city areas, prices are nearly always marked in Arabic numerals. In local shops and supermarkets, and in areas where non-Japanese are few and far between, prices may be written only in kanji characters. When shopkeepers are unable to make themselves understood verbally to visitors, they may type the numbers on a calculator, write them down, or sign with their fingers. If you are traveling off the beaten track, it is useful to learn the characters for the numbers one to ten, one hundred, and one thousand, and for the word "yen" *(see pp404–08)*.

All purchasable items and services are subject to a government-imposed consumption tax of 8 percent. Be aware that the price displayed might not include the tax, although this should change in March 2017.

In the booming 1980s, all prices were fixed, but in more recessive times, the emphasis is on discount shopping, with stores lowering prices to match strong competition. Flea markets and antique fairs are the only places where haggling is accepted as an integral part of the proceedings.

How to Pay

The Japanese yen continues to be regarded as a stable currency, despite various ups and downs since the late 1980s. Cash is by far the easiest method to pay for goods. There need be no anxieties about being given the right change; the Japanese are scrupulously honest – especially in handling guests from abroad. It is customary, when paying, for a small tray to be offered;

Prices displayed in Arabic numerals in a sweet shop

Inside Mikimoto Pearl shop in Ginza, Tokyo's premier shopping district

you should place money on it, and your change will be returned without hand-to-hand contact. International credit cards are still surprisingly unpopular in smaller shops. In general, the larger the emporium, the wider the range of international cards taken. VISA, American Express, Diners Club, and MasterCard are the most widely accepted.

Rights and Refunds

Refunds are not encouraged but are legal if the sales slip can be produced, and the item in question has not been tampered with. Some stores give redeemable coupons rather than money, so that they do not lose out. Without a receipt, return is impossible.

Tax-Free Shopping

Japan tax-free shops offer a good range of domestically made and imported brand items all free of the five percent sales tax added elsewhere. You will need to show your passport. Authorized outlets are mainly located in shopping districts and urban areas frequented by tourists, as well as the international airports. The best-known in the capital are the **Tokyo International Arcade** (near the Imperial Hotel) and **Laox** (see p111) for electronic goods; and in Kansai, the **Kyoto Handicraft Center** (see pp186–7). It is a good idea, however, to compare the prices of goods in these shops with those in

specialty and discount stores, as the latter may work out the same or even cheaper.

In some shops, particularly department stores, you may have to pay the full price for an item, then obtain a refund and customs document from a tax-exemption counter. This document is retained by customs as you leave Japan.

Exporting Large Items

Most specialty duty-free outlets will arrange packaging of bulky goods for export if required.

The same applies to antiques such as *tansu* (chests) and screens. There are also a large number of moving companies that specialize in handling large-size items; shop around in English-language newspapers and listings publications.

Compatibilty of Electrical Goods

Great care should be taken when buying electrical or electronic products. Make absolutely sure that circuits are either compatible with, or can be easily adjusted to, a home country's power system (see p363). Also, the FM radio band is different (from 76 to 90) from that used elsewhere in the world.

Japan uses the NTSC system for video and DVD, which is compatible with Canada, the US, and much of South and Central America. PAL video systems, used in other parts of Asia, Australia, and Europe, among other places, are available at electronic specialists such as those in the Akihabara district of Tokyo (see p77).

Clothing Sizes

Buying clothing in Japan can be a problem. Young people are growing to Western sizes now, but a lot of clothing is still cut for older-style Japanese physiques – that means smaller overall and with shorter sleeves in particular. The range of sizes available tends toward small to medium with a few large (but not as large as Western large). Remember to take your shoes off when entering a fitting room.

Men's Suits and Coats

Japanese	S	M	L	XL
US	34	36	38	42
British	34	36	38	42
Continental	44	46	48	52

Women's Clothes

Japanese	9	11	13	15	17	19	21
US	4	6	8	10	12	14	16
British	8	10	12	14	16	18	20
Continental	36	38	40	42	44	46	48

Shoes

Japanese	23.5	24	24.5	25	25.5	26	26.5
US men's	–	–	–	–	7.5	8	8.5
US women's	7	7.5	8	8.5	9	9.5	10
British	4.5	5	5.5	6	6.5	7	7.5
Continental	37.5	38	38.5	39	40	40.5	41

An elegant display of watches in the window of Tokyo's Wako store

Department Stores

Japan's mainstream department stores often fulfill a remarkable number of functions, housing ticket agencies, art galleries, and currency exchanges, alongside a huge range of consumer goods. Some stores are built over or enclose major train stations, resembling a city in microcosm. The early *depato* (department store) developed out of Edo-period kimono suppliers, with stores such as **Takashimaya** and **Mitsukoshi** leading the way. Others were rooted in the fortunes of industrialists seeking in patriarchal fashion to meet the needs of the masses.

Most major stores are laid out in a similar fashion. Food – together with rich pickings of free samples – is usually located in the basement; the first floor is often given over to candies, cosmetics, or accessories; restaurants serving a range of different cuisines tend to be on the top floor; playgrounds for small children are often on the roof. In between are fashion, furniture and furnishings, electrical goods, kitchenware, kimonos, and traditional crafts, even pets. Customers tend to ride to the top by elevator and then descend by escalator, browsing and buying en route; Japan calls this the "shower effect." Sales are held in spring, summer, fall, and winter, and there are additional special discount events.

The really top-notch department stores are more specialized. **Matsuya** is associated with upscale fashion brands. **Wako**, regarded by many as the most elite department store in Japan, sells expensive jewelry, lingerie, and accessories. At the other end of the scale, Seibu's **Parco** caters to the affluent youth market, housing new-wave fashion and the full range of contemporary arts all under one roof.

Restrooms are often luxuriously appointed with areas for feeding and changing babies.

Shopping Malls and Arcades

A Japanese city is not a city without its fair share of malls and arcades. Many date from the postwar period and, being generally located in downtown areas, are old-fashioned in style and appearance. Nevertheless they are where most people eat and play *pachinko (see p101)* in between routine shopping and bargain hunting.

Adjoining Senso-Ji Temple in Tokyo *(see pp90–91)* is an old-fashioned arcade of shops selling a mixture of tourist souvenirs and quality traditional crafts. In Osaka, Umeda Underground Arcade is famed.

Discount Stores and Supermarkets

In many respects, supermarkets are the same in Japan as elsewhere. A few sections and products may seem strange and exotic, such as the extensive displays of noodles, tofu, *kamaboko* (fish-paste products), tempura, sashimi, and *bento* (prepared lunch boxes). Under the same roof as the supermarket may be a florist, bakery, dry cleaners, and drugstore *(kusuriya)*.

Kinokuniya and **Meiji-ya** supermarkets specialize in high-quality imports. At the other end of the scale, **Jusco** offers economically priced store-brand goods with an emphasis on recycling and environmental concern. **Hundred Yen** shops sell household goods, stationery, toys, cosmetics, and batteries – all at ¥100. **Ito-Yokado**, **Seiyu**, and **Daikuma** cater to families; outlets like **Aoki** and **Konaka** specialize in men's suits. Being cheap, cheerful, in strong competition, and often near train stations, they are always packed.

Arts and Crafts Centers

Arts and crafts are held in equally high esteem in Japan. A finely lacquered comb is therefore regarded with as much respect as *nihonga*

Imaemon pottery from Arita in Kyushu

(traditional Japanese painting). Nowhere else in the world can such a wealth of techniques and genuine appreciation of this labor-intensive work be found. There are 2,000 potters in Tokyo alone, and all make a living.

Bamboo has a huge number of traditional uses, and it is still used for brushes, baskets,

Goods on display in a basketware shop in Yufuin, Kyushu

tableware, and furniture. The best place to see a full range of what is available nationwide is at a handicraft center. Both Tokyo and Kyoto have excellent craft centers *(see pp110–11 and pp186–7)*, with regular demonstrations of traditional arts and crafts as well as items on sale, often at tax-free prices.

Regional arts and crafts centers abound, displaying the work of local artists and artisans. Ask at the nearest TIC for details of local centers. Certain areas specialize in ceramics, *washi* (handmade paper), marquetry, ironware, or textiles, for example. Boutiques mixing indigo-dyed or specialty woven fabrics with other crafts, such as woodturning, glassware, and ceramics, are popular.

Stalls en route to the shrine of Tenman-gu in Dazaifu, Kyushu

Temple and Shrine Stalls

In these sacred precincts, there are usually a number of stalls selling religious charms and votive plaques. These are reasonably priced and make good souvenirs. Other types of shopping here fall into two categories: flea markets, and traditional goods associated with seasonal festivals and changes of climate. Regular flea markets, which are listed in English-language publications in Japan, provide rich pickings of everything from junk to rare treasures. Items are not as inexpensive as they used to be, but these markets are still cheaper than antique and secondhand shops for kimonos, books, and so on.

Many fairs are staged toward the end of the year. Two examples in the capital are Torii-no-ichi at Otori Shrine in mid-November *(see p50)*, and Hagoita-ichi (Toshi-no-ichi), held December 17–19 at Senso-ji Temple *(see p51)*. New Year decorations to hang above doorways and on gateposts are also very popular. In summer there are often stalls selling potted *asagao* (morning glory) plants, and metal and glass wind chimes *(furin)*, which catch the breeze.

A colorful range of food stalls in Nishiki market alley, Kyoto

Markets

Food markets provide an insight into the Japanese enthusiasm for food and cooking. The basement food floor of a major department store is a good place to start.

Small local markets, where farmers sell fresh produce, are usually operated by the agricultural cooperatives *(nokyo)*. These markets can be found all over the country and even in inner city areas, since vegetable plots nestle between homes, factories, and *pachinko* parlors.

Markets for manufactured goods flourish in urban wholesale districts, where industries are concentrated, selling everything from kitchenware to TVs.

The Japanese Art of Wrapping

Japanese culture is quintessentially wrapping based: the body is wrapped and tied into kimonos; tasty tidbits are encased in rice, and further cloaked in seaweed to make *onigiri* (rice balls); hand luggage is innovatively wrapped and tied for ease of carrying in a decorative cloth *(furoshiki)*. Shops will almost invariably wrap goods exquisitely in handmade paper *(washi)*, often in several layers. While the beauty, intrigue, and ultimate revelation of such a tradition has obvious appeal – and is ideal when the purchase is a present – the level of waste is high: now even Japanese consumers are beginning to question the custom.

Decorative paper wrapping

Ribbon adorning a packet of spice

A set of chopsticks, boxed

What to Buy in Japan

The abundance of specialty shops and craft outlets in Japan makes shopping a pleasure. Items available range from beautiful handmade crafts to useful everyday objects and kitsch toys. As a result, there should be something for every budget, and many of the most interesting souvenirs are also compact and light to carry home. Tokyo and Kyoto have the widest choice of shops that are used to dealing with foreign visitors, and many towns around the country have specialty craft centers or workshops. If time is limited, visit a large department store or a crafts emporium.

Origami paper

Ceramics

Ordinary pottery shops sell a wide selection of attractive bowls, dishes, cups, and sake bottles for everyday use. For a more unique – and expensive – souvenir, visit regions that specialize in pottery (see p42), or a large craft shop, which should stock a good selection of the main regional styles.

Leaf-shaped dish

Vase from Okinawa

Paper and Calligraphy

Traditional Japanese paper (washi) is handmade and often dyed in bright colors or embedded with petals or colored flecks. It is available as stationery, or made into boxes and various origami shapes.

Mobile made of paper

Calligraphy Set
An inkstone, water pot, brush, and ink make up a calligraphy set. The components can be bought separately or boxed.

Wood and Bamboo

A huge range of wood and bamboo souvenirs is available. Lacquerware trays, bowls, and boxes can be expensive but make original souvenirs. They need to be kept in humid conditions to last. Wooden combs, boxes, and dolls are also good buys. Large wooden chests, new and antique, are well designed but costly to ship.

Bizen-ware Vase
A form of unglazed earthenware pottery, Bizen ware has been produced in Inbe (see p214) for almost 1,000 years. Firing at a high temperature produces different surface finishes. Sake bottles, vases, and other storage vessels are popular.

Echizen-ware vase

Umbrella
Made of bamboo and paper, this umbrella is typical of those seen at onsen resorts. These traditional umbrellas are also available from craft shops.

Lacquer bowl

Woven basket

Wood-Block Prints

Known as ukiyo-e *(see p89)*, wood-block prints are uniquely Japanese mementoes. Antique and original prints are sold in specialty shops and can be very expensive; modern reproductions are widely available and often of good quality.

Print of a scene in a women's bath house by Yoshiiku

Wood-block print of Mount Fuji by Takamizawa

Ironware

The center for iron tea kettles *(tetsubin)* in Japan is Morioka in Northern Honshu *(see 281)*. These items were orignally manufactured for use in the tea ceremony. Many are now mass-produced. Nonetheless, they make useful, durable purchases but are heavy to carry home.

Iron tea kettle

Clothing and Textiles

Kimonos run into tens of thousands of yen to buy new but will last for years; second-hand ones are more affordable. Light cotton kimonos, known as *yukata*, are also less expensive to buy. Lengths of silk or hand-dyed fabrics are readily available in department stores.

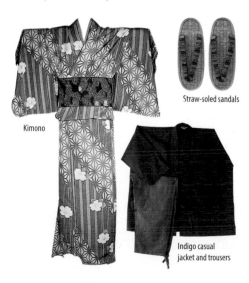

Kimono

Straw-soled sandals

Indigo casual jacket and trousers

Toys and Lucky Charms

Decorative figures and toys are enormously popular in Japan, and there are plenty to choose from. Wooden dolls may be expensive as many are handmade and have become collectors' items.

Charms
Charms, such as this classic lucky cat, are often sold at temple and shrine stalls.

Tin robot

Candy

All manner of candy, cookies, and rice crackers can be found in specialty shops and in department stores. You can usually choose from a selection and have your choice decoratively wrapped. Some tourist sites sell their own distinctively shaped candy.

Fox-printed candy from Tsuruoka

Cookie shaped like a leaf

Boxed Candy
The Japanese themselves often give boxes of candy as gifts. These are decorated as characters in a Kabuki play *(see p41)*.

ONSEN

Japan is peppered with geothermal springs, known as *onsen*. Communal bathing in these has been a custom for centuries, as a religious ritual (from the Shinto emphasis on purification), health cure, or just for pleasure. Many spa baths tap into natural volcanic activity, taming the thermal waters; some are artificially heated and enhanced with therapeutic herbal concoctions. A visit to an *onsen* is an antidote to the hectic pace of urban life, a chance to recuperate after sightseeing or business, and an insight into a soothing and companionable side of Japan. Hot springs are even used by animals: Jigokudani Onsen near Nagano, for example, is popular with wild monkeys, who sit in the pools to keep warm.

Enjoying a cup of sake in a traditional onsen

Types of Onsen

The variety of *onsen* is phenomenal. They come in every format: natural and man-made; indoors and outdoors; as small as a bath and as large as a swimming pool; lobster-hot and lukewarm; milky and clear; sulfurously foul-smelling and sweetly earthy. Certain chemical compositions in the waters are said to help different ailments, such as arthritis, hypertension, and skin problems.

Outdoor baths are generally rustic, made of wood or stone, and often by a river or the sea. Some are in caves, under jungle canopies, or behind waterfalls, or take the form of thermal mud or sand baths. Many *onsen* are in the mountains: after hiking, a dip in an outdoor pool in deep snow with a mountain view is perhaps the ultimate *onsen* experience. Exotic indoor *onsen* include baths in cable cars.

Many *onsen* operate as hotels, with meals and *onsen* facilities all included in the room price per person.

Staying overnight allows you to sample the pleasures of nighttime bathing. Entire *onsen* resorts have been developed so that between baths guests may wander around the town in their *yukata* (lightweight kimonos) or dine on local fare, often excellent. Other *onsen* hotels are in isolated hamlets in spectacular settings. At some *onsen* hotels and public bathhouses it is possible to stay for just a few hours rather than overnight. Fees can be very reasonable for these short visits – from ¥300 to ¥2,000. For details of individual *onsen*, consult a TIC or local tourist office, or *A Guide to Japanese Hot Springs* by Anne Hotta and Yoko Ishiguro. English may not be spoken at *onsen* hotels and local tourist offices; try to have a Japanese-speaker help you book accommodations.

Onsen Etiquette

Etiquette at *onsen* is similar to that for communal baths in *ryokan (see p301)*. Pools are usually single-sex; women rarely use mixed pools, except perhaps at night, when mixed bathing is more acceptable. Occasionally people in outdoor pools *(rotenburo)* wear swimsuits, but mostly everyone is naked. Nonetheless, the atmosphere is not sleazy, and visitors need have no qualms.

If you're staying overnight, change into the *yukata* provided in your room; either way, when you reach the baths, leave all clothes and possessions in the changing room. As with any Japanese bath, wash and rinse yourself thoroughly at the showers and taps provided outside the bath and take great care not to get any soap or shampoo in the bath itself.

The small towel provided can be used as a washcloth, draped across strategic parts of your body, placed on your head while in the pool (said to prevent fainting), or used to dry yourself when you emerge.

Keep all jewelry well away from steam, as the minerals can tarnish metal. Pregnant women, babies and young children, and anyone with high blood pressure should not enter the hottest baths without consulting a doctor first.

A steaming sand bath in southern Kyushu

Selected Onsen Areas in Japan

There are over 2,000 hot spring areas across the country, concentrated particularly in Kyushu, the Izu Peninsula west of Tokyo, and the mountainous backbone of Northern and Central Honshu.

Outdoor hot spring at Yufuin, Kyushu

Key to Onsen Areas Map

① **Noboribetsu** Hokkaido prefecture. Numerous hotels and huge choice of baths. *i* (0143) 84-3311.

② **Kuroyu** Akita prefecture. Remote and unspoiled, with a single thatched inn; inaccessible in winter. *i* (0187) 46-2214.

③ **Naruko** Miyagi prefecture. Medium-size *onsen* town known for fall foliage. *i* (0229) 83-3441.

④ **Zao** Yamagata prefecture. Popular but not over-commercialized ski resort and summer hiking base. *i* (023) 694-9328.

⑤ **Jigokudani** Nagano prefecture. Famed for *onsen*-loving monkeys; a single, simple inn, plus hotels in nearby villages. *i* (0269) 33-4379.

⑥ **Echigo Yuzawa** Niigata prefecture. Traditional resort (on *shinkansen* line); the setting for Kawabata's novel *Snow Country*. *i* (025) 785-5353.

⑦ **Kusatsu** Gunma prefecture. Three-minute baths in scalding water. Many public baths and inns. *i* (0279) 88-0800.

⑧ **Hoshi** Gunma prefecture. One lovely traditional *ryokan* with a large wooden bath-house, situated in woodland. **Tel** (0278) 66-0005 (ryokan).

⑨ **Takaragawa** Gunma prefecture. Perhaps the best riverside hot pools in Japan; one thatched *ryokan*. **Tel** (0278) 75-2121 (ryokan).

⑩ **Nikko Yumoto** Tochigi prefecture. Small *onsen* village in Nikko National Park; good hiking. *i* (0288) 54-2496.

⑪ **Yunishigawa** Tochigi prefecture. Atmospheric old *onsen* village in remote valley. *i* (0288) 97-1126.

⑫ **Hakone** Kanagawa prefecture. Old *onsen* town, sprawling up hillside; wide range of inns and baths. *i* (0460) 5-7410.

⑬ **Shuzenji** Shizuoka prefecture. Traditional *onsen* town, commercialized but charming; many inns. *i* (0558) 72-2501.

⑭ **Osawa** Shizuoka prefecture. A handful of picturesque *onsen* hotels in rural serenity. *i* (0558) 42-2799.

⑮ **Odaru** Shizuoka prefecture. Numerous pools, waterfalls, and caves; several inns. *i* (0558) 32-0290.

⑯ **Hokkawa** Shizuoka prefecture. Coastal *onsen* with inns and outdoor baths overlooking the sea. *i* (0557) 23-3997.

⑰ **Renge** Niigata prefecture. High in the alps, with pools around one inn (closed in winter). **Tel** (090) 2524-7237 (inn).

⑱ **Shirahone** Nagano prefecture. Relaxed mountain town near skiing and hiking areas. *i* (0263) 93-3251.

⑲ **Katsuura** Wakayama prefecture. An established resort, with jungle-theme and seaside pools, including a cave-bath. *i* (0735) 52-0555.

⑳ **Shirahama** Wakayama prefecture. Popular, coastal resort town with sandy beaches. *i* (0739) 43-5511.

㉑ **Kinosaki** Hyogo prefecture. Picturesque old-style town with traditional inns. Tasty crabs. *i* (0796) 32-3663.

㉒ **Arima** Hyogo prefecture. Commercial resort with many hotels; pleasantly secluded. *i* (078) 904-0708.

㉓ **Tamatsukuri** Shimane prefecture. Japan's oldest hot spring and largest outdoor pool. *i* (0852) 62-0634.

㉔ **Dogo** Ehime prefecture. Old-established spa town with classic bathhouse; many inns. *i* (089) 921-5141.

㉕ **Beppu** Oita prefecture. Vintage complex of hot-spring towns (*see pp238–9*). *i* (0977) 21-1111.

㉖ **Yufuin** Oita prefecture. Small craftsy spa town with horse-drawn carriages and very little nightlife. *i* (0977) 85-4464.

㉗ **Unzen** Nagasaki prefecture. Bubbling pools in Unzen-Amakusa National Park. *i* (0957) 73-3434.

㉘ **Ebino Kogen** Miyazaki prefecture. Beautiful scenery and good hiking by Mount Karakuni. Rocky outdoor pools. *i* (0984) 35-1111.

㉙ **Ibusuki** Kagoshima prefecture. Modern resort with tropical atmosphere and hot-sand baths. *i* (0993) 22-3252.

THEME PARKS

Japan has an astonishing number of theme parks, and Japanese tourists are especially drawn when the theme is new. This has created a lot of competition among managements to come up with fresh and innovative attractions. While many overseas visitors have little interest in this aspect of tourism in Japan, others – especially families and visitors from other Asian countries – travel thousands of miles to these vast playgrounds. Indeed, some foreigners find the Japanese fascination with theme parks fascinating in itself. Enthusiasts go back again and again, seeking to gain a sense of the outside world in complete security, or in search of an escape from the responsibilities of adulthood in an artificially created, idealized notion of childhood.

History Theme Parks

Even those overseas visitors who do not usually visit theme parks may be interested in those devoted to Japanese history and culture. North of Tokyo, the **Nikko Edo Village** has re-created 18th-century buildings and has guides dressed in period costume. Under the same management, **Noboribetsu Date Jidai Mura** in Hokkaido's Shikotsu-Toya National Park has assembled over 90 reconstructed 16th–19th-century buildings from all over the country.

Ise Azuchi-Momoyama Bunkamura is a 16th-century theme park with a reproduction of Azuchi Castle, which used to stand on the shores of Lake Biwa. Near Inuyama, **Meiji Mura** (see p147) is an open-air museum that preserves fine examples of Meiji-period architecture. On a smaller scale, **Nihon Minka-en**, between Kawasaki and Yokohama, has local traditional buildings, including farmhouses, a Shinto shrine, and a Kabuki theater, all in a garden setting.

Foreign Culture Theme Parks

These hugely popular theme parks give overseas visitors an insight into the way their own cultures are perceived by the Japanese. In central Honshu is **Little World**, an open air museum that explores world cultures. **Porto Europa**, south of Osaka, depicts the flavor of a typical medieval European port.

Tobu World Square near Tokyo reproduces more than 100 famous buildings from all over the world in miniature. **Nijinosato** in Shizuoka prefecture has Canadian, British, and Japanese villages and a "fairy garden." The attractive **Parque-España** in Ise-Shima offers attractions and restaurants with a Spanish atmosphere.

Best of all is **Huis ten Bosch** in Nagasaki (see p247). The whole development is ecologically designed, with faithful reproductions of Dutch architecture. On-site hotels are connected to the sea by inland waterways.

The Dutch-themed Huis ten Bosch park in Nagasaki

Amusement Parks

Since opening in 1983, **Tokyo Disney Resort°** has welcomed millions of visitors each year. In 2001 DisneySea° joined Disneyland° on the outskirts of the capital, east of Daiba, in Chiba prefecture, attracting visitors from all over Asia. A monorail system links the two parks.

In Tokyo itself, **Namco NamjaTown** offers 26 hi-tech virtual reality attractions in themed zones depicting different areas such as European cities; **Toshimaen** is probably the biggest amusement park in Tokyo; **Sanrio Puroland** made history as Japan's first completely indoor theme park. **Universal Studios Japan** is a Hollywood-inspired theme park with a range of shows, attractions, and rides that re-create blockbuster movies. Another favorite is **Green Land**, in Kumamoto in southern Japan. This large park has around

Frontage of Frank Lloyd Wright's Imperial Hotel in Meiji Mura, Inuyama

90 attractions including a 105-m (344-ft) Ferris wheel with transparent gondolas, and nine roller coasters.

South of Tokyo, **Yomiuri Land** features the White Canyon, an all-wood roller coaster. **Joypolis**, designed by Sega, has many interactive attractions, including the world's first virtual-reality motion ride.

Yokohama's dockside **Minato Mirai 21** complex *(see p136-7)* boasts a huge Ferris wheel, capable of carrying up to 480 people at a time.

Science Parks

Despite being on the cutting edge of invention, Japan is not well endowed with science parks. Tokyo Bay is now home to **Palette Town** *(see p107)*, which houses

several technically based attractions, including Toyota City Showcase, the History Garage, Future World, driving courses, and the E-Com ride. **Space World** is a huge complex in Fukuoka prefecture, with many hi-tech rides. It incorporates a Space Camp where children can experience NASA astronaut training.

Marine Theme Parks

Hokkaido's **Noboribetsu Marine Park Castle Nixe** offers marine and European themes in whimsical combination. In the Kanto region are **Kamogawa Sea World** and Yokohama's **Hakkeijima Sea Paradise** – a man-made island with one of Japan's largest aquariums. The highlight of Osaka's Tempozan Harbor Village *(see p207)* is the huge

Viewing turtles in one of Japan's many spectacular aquariums

Osaka Aquarium Kaiyukan, housing 580 marine species. **Marinpal Yobuko** In Kyushu offers a cruise in its "submarine ship" *Zeela*, from which you get a close-up view of the fish through the submerged windows of the vessel. In Okinawa, **Westmarine** offers a similar kind of cruise. The **Okinawa Churaumi Aquarium** is one of the biggest in the world, housing about 740 marine species.

DIRECTORY

SPORTS AND OUTDOOR ACTIVITIES

Japan enjoys many traditional sports activities as well as imports from abroad. Some sports that are closely identified with Japan – judo, for instance, which is a matter of extreme national pride at international competition level – have been adopted worldwide. Others, like sumo wrestling, are more exclusively Japanese. It is relatively easy to see most sports in action; participation, especially in some of the martial arts, takes more planning. As competitive and spectator sports, sumo and baseball rank uppermost along with soccer. Golf and fishing are immensely popular pastimes. With its long coastline, mountainous interior, and range in climate, Japan is also ideal for outdoor pursuits, from water sports to mountain climbing, a perfect complement to the pleasures of urban Japan.

Sumo wrestlers preparing for a bout, Tokyo

Sumo

A unique mix of sport and ritual, sumo *(see pp38–9)* has had new life breathed into it in recent years by the successes at the highest level of foreigners such as the Hawaiian ex-*yokozuna* (grand champion) Akebono, the Mongolian *yokozuna* Asashoryu and an influx of foreigners at lower ranks.

There are six major tournaments *(sumo basho)* a year, held bi-monthly in four locations: Tokyo (January, May, and September); Osaka (March); Nagoya (July); and Fukuoka (November).

Tokyo *basho (see p115)* are held in the **National Sumo Stadium** (Kokugikan) in Ryogoku *(see p106)*. The venue in Kyushu is the **Fukuoka Kokusai Center**; in the Kansai region of Western Honshu, the **Osaka Prefectural Gymnasium** (Osaka Furitsu Taikukaikan); and in Nagoya, **Aichi Prefectural Gymnasium** (Aichi-ken Taikukan). It is best to buy tickets in advance, via **Playguide** service centers and other outlets. The most expensive tickets buy a boxed off-area *(masu)* for four near the ring, with *zabuton* (cushions) for seating. While ringside vantage points have the added luster of 100 kg (220 lb) plus of naked muscle and flab landing in the lap, most spectators settle for bench-style seating, rising in tiers.

Each *basho* lasts 15 days. The wrestling starts early morning, a good time to see newcomers in action. Champions compete last, between 5 and 6pm. The Japanese crowds tend to side with winners rather than the underdogs. If you can't make it to see the action live, NHK provides expert TV commentary by native English speakers.

The stables *(beya)* most likely to accept non-Japanese who wish to train in sumo are usually run by foreign stablemasters under the auspices of the **Japan Sumo Association** (Nihon Sumo Kyokai).

Other Martial Arts

These fall into two categories, traditional *(budo)*, and the others. They can be further classified as those involving weapons, and those that are empty-handed *(see p39)*. While it is relatively easy to view most sports in action, to be accepted for training in one of the traditional martial arts usually requires personal introductions.

Kendo, under the official eye of the **All-Japan Kendo Association,** is the only form of traditional weaponry practiced widely in Japanese schools and clubs. Championships are usually held in the **Nippon Budokan**, which also has a school.

Judo is the most popular of the empty-handed sports. It is also big internationally; many students come to Japan for intensive practice. For all English-speaking services, contact the Department of International Affairs at the **Kodokan Judo Institute** in downtown Tokyo.

Karate expert breaking roof tiles with one blow of his elbow

Landscaped golf course at the Horin Country Club, Ichihara, southeast of Tokyo

The **International Aikido Federation** promotes the sport according to the ideals of founder Morihei Ueshiba. It welcomes visitors, and classes are often held in the early mornings and late afternoons.

The **Japan Karate-Do Federation** is the official karate organization, but there are many offshoots. The **International Karate Organization**, for example, is eager to promote *kyokushin* karate. The **Japan Karate Association** has weekday classes open to observers. The best time to watch is 7–8pm.

There have been moves in recent years to combine various martial arts, often to extremely violent effect. **World Pancrase Create**, which established its first amateur pancrase *dojo* (practice hall) in 1997, invites interest in this new form of "total fight."

K-1, in which contenders from various martial arts square off against each other, is now a hugely popular sport in Japan. Gloves are worn and attacks are limited to kicking and punching. Often, technique and speed overpower size and strength. The international K-1 Grand Prix is now an annual event.

Golf

Of the 50 million people who play golf worldwide, 17 million are teeing off in Japan. Visitors staying in major hotels should have little problem in finding a game; most big hotels have ties to a reputable golf club. The same applies to visiting executives; Japanese corporations consider playing a game basic to establishing relationships and will effect all the necessary introductions.

Courses are either private or public. An introduction by a member is essential to gain entry to a private club. If invited, expect to be treated; if reciprocating, expect the day to be very expensive. Public courses are less expensive but often less challenging. The attitude of staff may also be daunting; some welcome non-Japanese players, others may be cautious. JNTO *(see p363)* should be able to recommend public courses. A fun alternative might be to practice at a netted driving range in urban areas.

For the ultimate treat, book a golf-hotel package, such as offered in Hakone by the **Sengoku Golf Course** in collaboration with the Fujiya Hotel *(see p303)*.

Baseball

Japanese baseball is America's national game transplanted. It is believed to have taken root in the 1870s from American expatriates in Yokohama. Pro baseball is organized into two leagues of six teams each: the **Central League** and the **Pacific League**. The season is between April and October.

NHK, Fuji, TV Asahi, Nippon TV, TBS, and other local and cable channels broadcast games live on TV, and the seven national sports dailies become increasingly hysterical as the season progresses, especially when the Japan Series gets underway. The spring and summer Koshien high-school baseball tournaments at **Hanshin Koshien Stadium** in Hyogo Prefecture, hold the nation's attention.

Soccer

Though played for as long as baseball, soccer took longer to capture public interest in Japan. It was not until 1993 that the professional **J-League** kicked off with 10 teams. The opening match between Verdy Kawasaki and Yokohama Marinos played to a capacity crowd at Tokyo's National Stadium. There are now two divisions: J1 with 18 teams, and J2 with 22, each playing a series of round-robin matches.

The **Japan Football Association** organizes a national league in which amateur teams can also participate. Honours in recent years have been shared between the Kashima Antlers and Jubiro Iwata. In 2011, Nadeshiko Japan became the first Asian team to win the FIFA Women's World Cup.

In 2002, the FIFA World Cup was jointly hosted by Japan and Korea, which helped to increase the game's popularity nationwide.

Team members playing baseball, one of the most popular sports in Japan

Hiker resting by a marker post on Mount Fugen, Kyushu

Hiking

Japan is a hiker's heaven. Mountainous and hilly regions, including the many national parks, are crisscrossed with a comprehensive network of trails. Signboards often give precise distances and the average time to be allowed between each stage, but usually only in Japanese.

Much of north and west Japan is covered in deep snow for up to five months a year. Winter and spring hiking should be avoided unless you have an experienced guide and adequate clothing.

Summer and early autumn offer different challenges: extremes of heat and humidity, and thick vegetation that may be difficult to penetrate. But the comfort and clean green of lower slopes, and the wild beauty of many remote places make hiking Japan's most rapidly growing pastime.

Mountaineering

Chains of peaks run through all four of Japan's main islands. Among the Japan Alps of Central Honshu, for example, many mountains rise steeply to 3,000 m (10,000 ft) and can be as challenging as anywhere in the world. Others are gentler and ideal for less experienced climbers.

Japan's mountains claim fatalities every season. While there is no law forbidding climbing at any particular time, many mountainous areas and peaks have designated climbing seasons – check for dates in advance.

Volcanoes also occasionally take lives; even if an active volcano is not actually in the process of erupting, poisonous gases can be emitted without warning. Check up-to-date safety announcements with local tourist information centers.

There are usually facilities for overnight stays on the foothills and peaks of mountains, though these can be heavily overcrowded. Expect the standard and quality of hospitality in such mountain huts to be variable. Many close outside the climbing season.

Skiing

The great skiing that Japan has to offer is spoiled only by the numbers of people in the most popular resorts. Long lines for lifts are common, and

Skiers setting off for the piste at Niseko ski resort in Hokkaido

accommodations are often sold out. Snow is generally of an excellent quality, though, and in most resorts there are courses marked for beginners and intermediates.

Weekend trips, daily excursions, and skiing tours linked to domestic air, road, and rail routes are widely available inside Japan and to many agents abroad. Sometimes these include equipment rental. Large-size ski-boots are hard to find, so check on availability or bring your own.

The most popular areas are in Hokkaido, Northern Honshu (Tohoku), and Central and Western Honshu. JNTO (see p363) publishes a Top 20 ski resorts list, with full details and contact numbers.

Watersports

In a country with over 4,000 islands and innumerable inland rivers and lakes, water is naturally a favorite playground for the Japanese. Since the sea is often polluted around major conurbations, indoor and outdoor complexes of pools, wave machines, and water slides are popular. Unfortunately many outdoor pools are open for a limited time in midsummer only, coinciding with the time the sea is officially open for swimming from mid-July to the end of August.

Jet skiing, wind surfing, and yachting are all popular. Renting equipment is no problem on good beaches close to major cities; piloted yachts can be chartered from marinas. **Hayama Marina** near Kamakura is classy and expensive. To sail a cruiser in Japan, a specially issued license is necessary. Apply to the **Japan Marine Recreation Association**: a copy of a foreigner's registration card is required.

Many parts of the coastline lend themselves to scuba exploration. Around any developed area, diving can be murky to say the least;

by contrast, waters around the islands of Okinawa (see pp254–63) are a semi-tropical paradise.

Lively day at the Korakuen swimming pool in Tokyo

Eco-tourism

Though Japan lags behind many nations in ecological conservation, concern about the environment has been building since the 1970s, when pollution in many areas reached record levels.

The **Nature Conservation Society of Japan** has a list of accommodations In unspoiled areas, run by people who are concerned with putting guests in touch with nature.

Birdwatching is a very popular activity in Japan. The **Wild Bird Society of Japan**, founded in 1935, has 80 chapters nationwide, each organizing local events. In areas

where commercial whaling was once a way of life, organized whale- and dolphin-watching trips now provide an alternative source of income. The best season in the remote Ogasawara Islands (a 25-hour ferry trip south of Tokyo) is March–April; in Ogata, Kochi prefecture, off the southern tip of Shikoku, the chance of seeing whales between April and October is 80–90 percent.

For visitors looking for action-packed adventure, **Canyons Japan**, with four locations around the country, offers a range of tours and courses, including canyoning, rafting, caving, and skiing.

DIRECTORY

Sumo

Aichi Prefectural Gymnasium
1-1 Ninomaru,
Naka-ku, Nagoya.
Tel (052) 971-2516.

Fukuoka Kokusai Center
2-2 Chikko-honmachi,
Hakata-ku, Fukuoka.
Tel (092) 272-1111.

Japan Sumo Association
1-3-28 Yokoami,
Sumida-ku, Tokyo.
Tel (03) 3623-5111.
W sumo.or.jp

Osaka Prefectural Gymnasium
3-4-36 Namba Naka,
Naniwa-ku, Osaka.
Tel (06) 6631-0121.

Other Martial Arts

All-Japan Kendo Association
2F Yasukuni Kudan-minami Bldg, 2-3-14 Kudan-minami, Chiyoda-ku, Tokyo. **Tel** (03) 3234-6271.
W kendo-fik.org

International Aikido Federation
17-18 Wakamatsu-cho,
Shinjuku-ku, Tokyo.
Tel (03) 3203-9236.
W aikido-international. org

International Karate Organization
2-38-1 Nishi-Ikebukuro,
Toshima-ku, Tokyo.
Tel (03) 5992-9200.
W kyokushinkaikan. org

International Aikido Federation
W aikido-kyokai.com/ en/index.html

Japan Karate-Do Federation
1-11-2 Toranomon,
Minato-ku, Tokyo.
Tel (03) 3503-6637.
W karatedo.co.jp

Japan Karate Association
2-23-15 Koraku,
Bunkyo-ku, Tokyo.
Tel (03) 5800-3091.
W jka.or.jp

K-1 Group
3F 2 18-22 Jingumae,
Shibuya-ku, Tokyo.
Tel (03) 3796-5060.
W k-1.tv

Kodokan Judo Institute
1-16-30 Kasuga,
Bunkyo-ku, Tokyo.
Tel (03) 3818-4172.
W kodokan.org

Nippon Budokan
2–3 Kitanomaru Koen,
Chiyoda-ku, Tokyo.
Tel (03) 3216-5100.

World Pancrase Create
4-2-25 Minami-Azabu,
Minato-ku, Tokyo.
Tel (03) 5792-0815.
W pancrase.co.jp

Golf

Sengoku Golf Course
1237 Sengokuhara,
Hakone-machi, Ashigara-Shimo-gun, Kanagawa-ken. **Tel** (0460) 84-8511
W sengokugolf.jp/ english.html

Baseball

Central & Pacific Leagues
Asahi Bldg, 6-6-7 Ginza,
Chuo-ku, Tokyo.
Tel (03) 3572-1673
(Central); (03) 3573-1551
(Pacific).

Hanshin Koshien Stadium
1-82 Koshien-cho,
Nishinomiya-shi,
Hyogo-ken.
Tel (0798) 47-1041.

Soccer

Japan Football Association
W jfa.or.jp/eng
Tel (03) 3830-2004.

J-League
W j-league.or.jp

Watersports

Hayama Marina
50-2 Horiuchi,
Hayama-cho, Miura-gun,
Kanagawa-ken.
Tel (046) 875-2670.
W hayamamarina.com

Japan Marine Recreation Association
Kaiji Bldg,
1-3 Kaigan-dori,
Naka-ku, Yokohama.
Tel (045)-201-1222.
W kairekyo.gr.jp

Eco-tourism

Canyons Japan
Tel (0278) 72-2811.
W canyons.jp/ index_E.html

Nature Conservation Society of Japan
2F Mitoyo Bldg,
1-16-10 Shinkawa,
Chuo-ku, Tokyo.
Tel (03) 3553-4101.
W nacsj.or.jp

Wild Bird Society of Japan
Marawa Bldg,
3-9-23 Godanda,
Shinagawa-ku, Tokyo.
Tel (03) 5436-2620.
W wbsj.org

SPECIAL INTERESTS

Besides the more obvious tourist sights, Japan has many attractions for visitors who wish to learn more about diverse aspects of Japanese culture. Traditional medicine and Zen Buddhism, for example, are of great interest to many Western tourists, and various organizations exist in Japan to promote foreigners' understanding of these subjects. Other visitors are more interested in modern Japan and will want to take the opportunity to visit factories or design showcases. Various systems have been developed to facilitate more contact and

exchange of ideas between Japanese and overseas visitors. Goodwill Guides are locals, often housewives and retired people, who want to practice and maintain their foreign language skills, and who are willing to show foreigners around the local sights free of charge. Invariably, such individuals are enthusiastic about their own and other people's cultures. Using conversation lounges is an excellent way to establish intercultural friendships, while the Homestay and Home Visit systems offer unique insights into Japanese culture.

Nagomi Visits offer travelers a more rounded experience of life in Japan

Goodwill Guides, Home Stays, and Home Visits

Established for over 20 years, the **Goodwill Guide** system is made up of Japanese volunteers, registered with JNTO *(see p363)*, all eager to assist vistors from overseas. JNTO has 82 SGG (Systematized Goodwill Guide) groups, which offer local tours in English. JNTO and local TICs have a list of contact numbers, and visitors should contact each SGG group for information. Visitors are requested to pay their guide's expenses.

EIL Japan (the Japanese Association of Experiment in International Living) runs a Homestay Program, which enables people from abroad to stay with a Japanese family for one to four weeks in various locations. Visitors, who must bear all their own costs, are

treated as one of the family and involved in regular daily activities. Contact EIL Japan at least eight weeks before your visit, requesting an application form.

The **Home Visit System** offers the opportunity to visit a Japanese family at home, usually in the evening after dinner. Up to four or five guests are invited at a time. English is spoken by most host families, but some family members may speak other languages. About 800 families are involved, in 13 cities and towns (the scheme excludes Tokyo, Honshu, and Kyushu). JNTO overseas offices and local TICs have a list of contact numbers.

Conversation Lounges

The basic premise of conversation lounges is to bring together Japanese who want to practice their English and other foreign languages, and visitors from abroad who want to meet Japanese people in relaxed surroundings. Sometimes also described as coffee lounges, these conversation venues can vary in both intent and tone.

Mickey House in Takadanobaba is free for native English speakers; others can pay each visit. They also have an informal Japanese conversation lounge twice a week. Other such venues in Tokyo include **Leafcup**. Conversation lounges come and go fairly regularly, or may change direction to become more like language schools; listings magazines are the best source of information for finding up-to-date spots. Be aware that some lounges operate as commercial matchmaking enterprises –

Guides lead a tour group through the grounds of Myoshinji Temple in Kyoto

for Western men and Japanese women, though rarely the other way around.

Specialty Tours

Visitors interested in thematic tours rather than the usual kind of sightseeing can try **Sunrise Tours** in Tokyo, operated by the Japan Travel Bureau. A tour might focus on a visit to a calligraphy studio, participation in a tea ceremony, or exploring a downtown area. Sunrise also runs tours specializing in sumo or Tokyo nightlife, including trips to see traditional Japanese theater.

The **Hato Bus Tour Company's** has a similar range of half-day, full-day, and night-time tours for non-Japanese tourists, including a visit to a tea ceremony and a garden tour. **Greyline** runs trips around Tokyo as well as to places such as Mount Fuji and Hakone, and will also arrange private tours tailored to a customer's wishes; the more individual a tour is, the higher the cost.

The City of Tokyo's **Tokyo Walking Tours** organizes

An outdoor tea ceremony in Kyoto

free walking tours around the capital in various languages. In Kyoto, details about Hirooka Hajime's personally guided tours, **Walk in Kyoto, Talk in English**, are available from hotels and information centers; the tours take place on Mondays, Wednesdays, and Fridays.

In Kyoto you can experience a tea ceremony at **Kyoto City International Foundation** on Tuesdays at 2pm, or at **Westin Miyako Hotel** every day from 10am–7pm. You will need to make a reservation at both

Traditional Japanese ingredients

these venues, however, as the tea ceremony is very popular.

Factory Visits

Three automobile manufacturers – **Toyota** (in Aichi prefecture), **Nissan** (in Kanagawa), and **Mazda** (in Hiroshima) – welcome visitors to their various plants. Tours in English can be arranged. The electronics-oriented **Toshiba Science Insitute** in Kanagawa prefecture offers an hour-long tour.

Most tours are on weekdays only, exclusive of national holidays, and it is best to contact the relevant organization in advance.

DIRECTORY

Illustration of traditional acupuncture points on the body

Traditional Medicine

In the Meiji period, with its emphasis on all things foreign, it became fashionable in Japan to reject traditional healing methods and instead to embrace Western science and medicine. Today, as alternative medicine, including Eastern methods, is burgeoning in popularity in the West, the trend in Japan is also toward a blend of ancient and modern practices.

Natural ingredients prescribed in accordance with traditional Chinese medical custom are known as *kampo*. Ready-mixed and prepared *kampo* products are available from pharmacies, often alongside manufactured prescription drugs. Some restaurants specialize in *kampo* cuisine, designed to balance the metabolism. *Kampo* can also be made up to suit individual needs in specialty stores. In Yokohama or Kobe, Chinatown is the place to go. In Tokyo, **Kampo Museum** has a restaurant and boutique based on *kampo* principles, where customers may consult specialist *kampo* counselors.

Acupuncture and moxibustion, a form of heat therapy, are often used in combination. **Zen Nihon Shinkyu Massage Shikai** in Tokyo and **Meiji University of Integrative Medicine** in Kyoto have information. **Imoto Seitai** practices and teaches traditional manual therapy.

Other forms of alternative healing also exist, for example the **Japan Academy of**

Colorpuncture uses colored light to restore well-being. The **Japanese Homeopathic Medical Association** is the governing body for homeopathy practitioners in the country. **Lifeforces** offers a range of holistic, complementary therapies including *reiki*, a form of energy healing originally developed in Japan, and *sekhem*, an ancient Egyptian form of energy healing. They also run a free *reiki* share group, where participants can exchange energy, every second and fourth Sunday of the month. The same organizers run **Circle of Light**, which holds a discussion group on the third Sunday of each month to introduce their healing arts to a wider audience.

Pilgrimage Routes

For many centuries pilgrimages provided Japanese farmers and townspeople with a reason to leave behind work and responsibilities and take to the open road. Nowadays pilgrimages are regarded as a form of spiritual meditation, concerned with making amends and preparing for death. Some non-purists drive or ride the pilgrim routes.

Many of the oldest pilgrimages were connected with a mystical Shugendo cult of mountain worship, which combined elements of Shinto and Buddhism. Its most devout followers, laymen known as

Sticks carried by traditional pilgrims

yamabushi (mountain priests), still practice in the **Dewa Sanzan** mountains in Northern Honshu *(see p278)*. During the Edo period, **Mount Fuji** *(see pp144–5)* became a similar object of worship. Even today, among the thousands of tourists who climb every summer, aged white-clad pilgrims (*henro*) wearing conical straw hats can be seen.

The most famous and demanding route is the **88-Temple Pilgrimage** on Shikoku *(see pp232–3)*. The **Western Japan 33 Kannon Temple Circuit** involves visiting temples to Kannon, the goddess of mercy *(see p33)*, in Western Honshu. It includes temples in Kyoto, Nara, Ise, and Mount Koya. There is a shorter route for pilgrims in Kamakura *(see pp138–41)*, starting a brief bus ride away from the main station and finishing at the temple of Engaku-ji in Kita Kamakura.

Religious Studies

Based in downtown Tokyo, the **International Shinto Foundation** was formed in 1994 to disseminate understanding of Japan's native religion. The **Association of Shinto Shrines** publishes a range of free English-language pamphlets and booklets. There are displays on Shinto history and rituals at **Kokugakuin University Shinto Museum**. The **Zen Buddhist**

Resting pilgrims on the 88-Temple pilgrimage in Shikoku

Center for International Exchange provides non-Japanese visitors with access to Zen practices. Their temple, located near Mount Fuji, is remote, with no electricity or telephone. Other Buddhist foundations offering English-language instruction include the **International Buddhist Association**, which conducts a meeting in English toward the end of each month, and **Rissho Kosei-Kai**, which offers dharma seminars four times a year. **Toshoji Temple** holds free *gyoten zazen* (zen meditation) every morning except on Sundays and public holidays. At **Kyoto International Zendo**, just west of the city in rural Kameoka, *zazen* can be practised in tranquil surroundings. Foreigners are welcomed to the temple, main hall, and guest quarters

in a traditional farmhouse. A small donation is requested for lodging and meals. A number of temples around the country also offer religious instruction; contact local tourist information offices for more information.

For visitors interested in the fascinating history of Christianity in Japan the **Eastern Cross Museum** in Tokyo displays artifacts from the Keikyo (*keikyo* was the ancient name for Christianity in Japan), Kirishitan, and Kakure Kirishitan eras to the present day, including rare *keikyo* documents, Meiji-era porcelain, and *fumie* – wooden boards on which early Kirishitan were forced to renounce their faith. The same organization also provides useful

The 19th-century Oura church, Nagasaki

information on Christian-related sights, including museums and memorial sites throughout Japan, via their website.

DIRECTORY

Traditional Medicine

Imoto Seitai (Tokyo Headquarters)
1-25-4 Sendagaya,
Shibuya-ku, Tokyo.
Tel (03) 3403-0185.
W imoto-seitai.com

Japan Academy of Colorpuncture
3-7-17-102 Jiyugaoka,
Meguro-ku, Tokyo.
Tel (03) 3718-7613.
W is-inter-web.com/
color

Japanese Homeopathic Medical Association
2-30-14 Ikejiri,
Setagaya-ku, Tokyo.
W jphma.org

Kampo Museum
3-25-29 Takanawa,
Minato-ku, Tokyo.
Tel (03) 3280-2005.
W nihondo.co.jp/shop/
museum

Lifeforces and Circle of Light
1308 Forme Yotsuya
Galen Higashi,
14-61 Samoncho,
Shinjuku-ku Tokyo.
Tel (03) 3472-1714.
W lifeforces.org

Meiji University of Integrative Medicine
6-1 Honoda-hinotani,
Hiyoshi-cho,
Nantan-shi, Kyoto.
Tel (0771) 72-1181.
W meiji-u.ac.jp/
otoiawase

Zen Nihon Shinkyu Massage Shikai
3-12-17 Yotsuya,
Shinjuku-ku, Tokyo.
Tel (03) 3359 6049.
W zensin@zensin.or.jp

Religious Studies

The Association of Shinto Shrines
1-1-2 Yoyogi,
Shibuya-ku, Tokyo.
Tel (03) 3379-8011.
W jinjahoncho.or.jp

Eastern Cross Museum
Art Plaza, Tokyo, near
Kamiyacho stn (exit 2),
Hibaya line.
Tel (03) 5780-5456,
W keikyo.com

International Buddhist Association
Tsukiji Honganji temple,
3-15-1 Tsukiji,
Chuo-ku, Tokyo.
Tel (03) 3541-1131.

International Shinto Foundation
Best Yoga, 2F 2-1-15
Tamagawa Dai
Setagayaku, Tokyo.
Tel (03) 6805-7729.
W shinto.org

Kokugakuin University Shinto Museum
1F Tokiwamatsu No 3
Bldg, 4-10-28 Higashi,
Shibuya-ku, Tokyo.
Tel (03) 5466-0210.
W kokugakuin.ac.jp/
english/index.html

Kyoto International Zendo
Inukai, Sogabe-cho,
Kameoka City, Kyoto.
Tel (0771) 24-0152.
W tekishin.org;
zen@tekishin.org

Rissho Kosei-Kai
2-11-1 Wada,
Suginami-ku, Tokyo.
Tel (03) 3383-1111.
W rk-world.org

Toshoji Temple
4-5-18 Yutaka-cho,
Shinagawa-ku, Tokyo.
Tel (03) 3781-4235.
W toshoji@nifty.com

Zen Buddhist Center for International Exchange
Hatsukari-cho, Otsuki-shi,
Yamanashi-ken.
Fax (0554) 25-6282.
W oocities.org/tokyo/
towers/3169

SURVIVAL GUIDE

PRACTICAL INFORMATION

From a practical point of view, Japan is easier for foreign tourists to negotiate than is generally believed. Being unable to speak or read Japanese is not usually a serious problem, especially in large cities. Many everyday signs in major cities and at tourist attractions are displayed in Roman script along with Japanese characters. Where problems can arise for foreigners, however, is in the contrasts in Japan's East-West culture – for instance, the difference between the relative ease with which even foreigners can get around on the rail network compared with the difficulty everyone, including the Japanese, has with finding an address *(see pp377 and 383)*.

A serene park with a cherry tree in blossom

When to Go

The best times to visit Japan are spring (April and May) and fall (September–November). Temperatures within the country vary widely according to latitude *(see pp52–3)*, but July and August are mostly hot, humid, and better avoided. Expect more rain, often very heavy, in the rainy season (early June–mid-July). Typhoons do not always strike Japan during the typhoon season – peak months are August and September – but they usually bring heavy rainfall, strong winds, and can paralyze transport.

Japan has numerous festivals throughout the year *(see pp48–51)*. Cherry-blossom time (late March–early April in central Japan) brings out large blossom-viewing groups who fill the parks day and night, while late summer is a time for local festivals. Peak vacation periods for the Japanese are New Year (December 29–January 4), "Golden Week" (April 29–May 5), the period around Obon, and the Buddhist Festival of the Dead (in mid-August). At these times flights and some accommodations are sold out. However, the only big shutdown of attractions occurs at New Year.

Visas and Passports

For up-to-date information on visa conditions it is best to contact a Japanese embassy before traveling. Citizens of most Western countries may enter Japan for short visits as a Temporary Visitor with a valid passport. There is no need to obtain a visa. The period of stay for a Temporary Visitor is 90 days. On no account should you overstay your permission to be in Japan. Visitors are allowed to enter on this basis for tourism, sports, visiting friends or relatives, study, or business, but may not undertake paid employment.

Citizens of some countries, including the UK and Germany, may extend this stay by another 90 days at immigration offices in Japan (at least 10 days before the expiration date). The length of the extension is at the discretion of immigration officers.

On the plane you will be given a landing card: fill in the arrival section – the second part will be attached to your passport for when you depart. There are no immunization requirements for entering Japan, but some countries recommend getting the Japanese Encephalitis vaccine if you are traveling to rural areas or planning to stay longer than 30 days.

Anyone planning on undertaking paid work, long-term study, or voluntary work in Japan should obtain a visa from a Japanese embassy before traveling *(see also p369)*. Foreigners planning to stay in Japan for more than 90 days will need a Resident Card, which will typically be issued at the Port of Entry. This card must be carried at all times – not doing so could lead to a hefty fine or possible arrest.

Visa holders who want to leave the country and return within the duration of their visa will be allowed to leave without a re-entry permit as long as they return within one year. Contact the **Ministry of Foreign Affairs** for information.

Customs Information

Visitors aged 16 or over are fingerprinted and photographed at the point of entry. You will also be asked to complete a written declaration of your belongings.

Duty free allowances on entering the country are 400 cigarettes or 500 grams of tobacco or 100 cigars; three 0.76-liter (27 oz) bottles of alcohol; 57 g (2 oz) of perfume; and gifts and souvenirs of a total value up to ¥200,000 (this does not include items less than ¥10,000). For guidelines on tax-free shopping in Japan, *see p341*.

◄ Visitors enjoying a gentle cruise on the Kiyotaki river in Arashiyama, west of Kyoto

Certain articles are forbidden: counterfeit money; pornography; articles that infringe on patents or copyrights; and firearms and ammunition. Guns, authentic swords, and some high-quality personal computers require an export license, obtained from the **Ministry of Economy, Trade and Industry**. Art objects may be subject to restrictions.

Japan has a zero-tolerance policy toward the possession of even small amounts of narcotics, including marijuana. The punishment is a jail sentence and a heavy fine. Vicks inhalers and some over-the-counter medicines, especially for allergies and sinus problems, containing pseudoephedrine, and even mild painkillers, such as those containing codeine, are prohibited. Prescription drugs are also limited. Contact a Japanese embassy for more information. Animals and plants are subject to quarantine inspection.

There is no limit on the amount of currency that may be taken into or out of the country, but sums over ¥1 million must be declared at immigration.

Tourist Information

Outside Japan, tourist information can be obtained from branches of the **Japan National Tourism Organization** (JNTO). The JNTO has a large range of useful leaflets and brochures on locations and specialist interests.

In Tokyo, the TIC or **Tourist Information Center** has knowledgeable staff and offers suggestions on tour itineraries. It also has a counter for the Welcome Inn Reservation Center, where staff will arrange hotel reservations on your behalf throughout Japan. There is no charge for this service.

Local information can be obtained from the Tourist Information Offices found in almost every town, usually in or near the main station. Nearly 100 of these offices are designated "i" Tourist Information Offices, meaning they have multilingual staff and keep pamphlets in English. Information on local events is also available from **Information Counters** in Yokohama, Osaka, and Nagoya.

In major cities, details of attractions and events can be gleaned from local publications such as *Metropolis* (also online; *see p112*), *Fukuoka Now* in Kyushu, **Kansai Scene, Japanzine**, and free magazines – all available at hotels, bookstores, and TICs.

Hotels will usually help reserve tickets for entertainment venues. Ticket-agency booths located in most of the larger cities, inside department stores, convenience stores, and near train stations also book seats in advance and sell tickets up to the last minute. Ticket PIA and CN Playguide are the main agencies *(see p116)*.

Matsue International Tourist Information Office

Admission Prices

Admission to most Buddhist temples and Shinto shrines is free; however, famous temples and shrines in tourist spots, such as Kamakura and Kyoto, charge an admission fee, usually between ¥200 and ¥500. Entrance fees to most attractions are generally under ¥1,000, but may be more on occasion.

Several cities offer a **Welcome Card** to foreign visitors, and a number of different ones are available. Intended to reduce the cost of a visit, the card can be used to obtain discounts on accommodations, shopping, food and drink, plus various other tourist facilities and services. Many of the cards can be printed out from the Welcome Cards page of the JNTO website for a fee.

Opening Hours

Temple buildings are open from 8 or 9am to 4pm in winter, and until 5pm in summer, although times vary. Shrines are often open 24 hours. Museums, art galleries, and many other tourist attractions, such as technology centers and aquariums, are usually open from 10am until 4 or 5pm. Many of these sights are open every day except Monday; when Monday is a public holiday, they often close on Tuesday instead. Many attractions are closed for a number of days over the New Year period. Certain Kyoto sights – Katsura and Shugaku-in Imperial Villas, for example – require reservations well in advance of visiting.

For shopping hours, *see p340*; for banking hours see *p372*; and for post offices *see p376*.

Konpon Dai-to Pagoda on Mount Koya, like many attractions, is open daily

Children playing on the sidewalk

Public Conveniences

Toilets in Japan range from highly sophisticated to very basic (notably in train stations). Japanese-style toilets are simple troughs over which one squats, facing the end with the hood. Non-Japanese toilets are similar to Western-style toilets; many public facilities, including trains, have both. Toilet paper and hand towels are often not provided, so carry tissues with you.

Modern toilets may have a panel that, if pressed, plays a tune or makes a flushing sound to discreetly mask natural noises. Some hi-tech toilets have heated seats, automatic seat covers, bidets, and hot-air-drying facilities. For protocol on toilet slippers, see p364.

Travelers with Special Needs

Facilities for the disabled are of mixed quality. The visually impaired are well provided for, but the elderly and people in wheelchairs occasionally face problems with some smaller stations and pedestrian over- and underpasses, which can have endless steps and often no escalator or elevator. Barrier-free access and universal design are only starting to become implemented around Japan. Most modern buildings have toilet facilities for the disabled.

The **Accessible Tokyo** website provides information about disabled access and facilities at individual tourist attractions, parks, and hotels in Tokyo. This website also covers sites in Kyoto, and Kamakura.

Traveling with Children

Children are welcomed in Japan and taking them to restaurants and pubs poses no problems. Discreet breast-feeding in public is accepted, and baby formula, milk, and disposable diapers are easily obtainable. Hotels tend to be geared toward adults, but top ones sometimes offer baby-sitting services and nurseries. Most attractions, including some of the many theme parks (see pp348–9), offer reduced rates for children, which are typically half the adult price. Children under 6 can ride free on buses and trains; those aged 6 to 11 pay half fare. It is best to avoid traveling on rush-hour trains in the big cities with small children.

Student and Senior Travelers

The **International Student Identity Card (ISIC)**, gives reductions of 10–50 percent for students at locations throughout Japan, including museums, hotels, ferries, and eateries. At locations that do not formally recognize the ISIC, students may be able to receive a discount just with their regular student identity cards – or even simply with a verbal claim to being a student. For information and tips on traveling in Japan on a budget visit the **Japan Guide** website.

The general safety of the country makes Japan a popular choice among senior travelers. Despite the fact that Japan has one of the most rapidly aging populations in the world, many facilities are not as well adapted as might be presumed to support the needs of those with mobility problems. With Japan's low retirement age, people aged 60 and above often receive admission discounts.

Gay and Lesbian Travelers

There is a good deal of tolerance for same-sex couples traveling around Japan, and they are unlikely to encounter many problems. However, open displays of affection may not go down too well with some Japanese. Attitudes are broader in Tokyo, which has an active gay scene and a small, lively gay quarter.

Gay and lesbian bars and clubs can be found throughout Japan; many are listed in **Utopia Asia**. **Magnet Tours** is a tour operator that focuses specifically on lesbian, gay, bisexual, and transgender (LGBT) travelers and offers various tour packages.

What to Take

An umbrella is a must and cheap plastic ones can be bought in convenience stores. Casual clothing is acceptable everywhere – even in smart restaurants. Since footwear occasionally has to be removed when entering some traditional tourist attractions (see p364), it may be helpful to wear shoes that can be easily slipped on and off. Keep luggage to a minimum and choose items that are easy to carry since stations often have many steps and no porters.

A colorful display of practical and souvenir fans for sale

As with any destination, travel insurance is advisable *(see p371)*. If you plan to travel extensively around Japan, consider obtaining a Japan Rail Pass before you go *(see p381)*.

Time and the Calendar

Japan is 9 hours ahead of Greenwich Mean Time and 14 hours ahead of Eastern Standard Time. There is no daylight-saving time. When countries that use daylight-saving time switch to summer time, the time difference is one hour less.

The Japanese calendar combines the Western system with the Chinese system: years are designated Year of the Tiger, Rabbit, and so on, but they begin on January 1 and not, as in China, in mid-February. Years are numbered both by the Western system and by the reign of the current emperor. The present era, Heisei, began when Emperor Akihito came to the throne in 1989, which became Heisei 1.

The Japanese system is used within the country, especially on official documents, while Western years are mostly used in international contexts.

Misunderstandings about timings and dates are common, so clearly confirm arrangements and, when booking accommodations, state the number of nights and,the dates of your stay.

Electricity

Japan runs on 100 volts, AC – a system similar to that of the US. The country has two different cycles: 50 Hz in eastern Japan (including Tokyo) and 60 Hz in western Japan. Plugs with two flat pins are standard. Most British and other European appliances can be used only with transformers suitable for US voltage (which are large and expensive). If in doubt consult, the appliance's instructions. Some hotels have two outlets – 110 and 220 volts – although these only accept two-pin

plugs. Adapters are available from some electronics stores.

Responsible Tourism

Environmental consciousness is relatively strong in Japan, however, the country is not as conscientious as other first-world nations. Containers for recycling Styrofoam food trays, PET bottles, and used paper drink cartons stand outside most supermarkets and convenience stores. However, not so eco-friendly is the disposal of wooden chopsticks *(waribashi)*, the commonest implements in Japanese eateries. Tourists can avoid this waste of wood by taking along their own chopsticks to restaurants.

Farmers' markets are quite common, but they may be difficult to find without understanding Japanese. The best way to find out if there is one in a neighborhood would be to ask at a *koban* (manned police box): "Faamaaz maaketo wa doko dess ka?"

DIRECTORY

Customs Information

Ministry of Economy, Trade and Industry
W meti.go.jp/english

Tourist Information

Information Counters
Nagoya
Tel (052) 581-0100.
Osaka
Tel (06) 6773-6533.
Yokohama
Tel (045) 222-1209.

Japan National Tourism Organization (JNTO)
W jnto.go.jp

In Australia
Suite 1, Level 4,
56 Clarence St,
Sydney, NSW 2000.
W jnto.org.au

In Canada
481 University Ave,
Suite 306, Toronto,
Ontario M5G 2E9.
W ilovejapan.ca/en

In Singapore
16 Raffles Quay,
15-09 Hong Leong Building,
Singapore 048581.
W jnto.org.sg

In UK
5th Floor,
12–13 Nicholas Lane,
London EC4N 7BN.
W seejapan.co.uk

In USA
11 West 42nd St,
19th Floor,
New York, NY 10036.
340 East 2nd St,
Little Tokyo Plaza,
Suite 302, Los Angeles,
CA 90012.
W japantravelinfo.com

Japanzine
W seekjapan.jp

Kansai Scene
W kansaiscene.com

Tourist Information Center (Tokyo TIC)
Marunouchi Trust Tower
Nth 1F, 1-8-1 Marunouchi,
Chiyoda-ku, Tokyo.
Tel (03) 5220-7055.
W tictokyo.jp/en

Admission Prices

Welcome Cards
W jnto.go.jp/eng/
arrange/essential/
welcome.html

Travelers with Special Needs

Accessible Tokyo
W http://accessible.
jp.org/tokyo/en

Student and Senior Travelers

International Student Identity Card (ISIC)
W http://isic.univ
coop.or.jp/e

Japan Guide
W japan-guide.com

Gay and Lesbian Travelers

Magnet Tours
4F Mitsuya Building,
1-12-12 Shintomi,
Chuo-ku,
Tokyo, 104-0041.
Tel (03) 5542-0356.
W magnettours.jp

Utopia Asia
W utopia-asia.com/
tipsjapn.htm

Etiquette and Language

Etiquette is important in Japan – the social lubricant for a crowded community. Over time attitudes have relaxed, yet even the most apparently rebellious Japanese won't break certain rules. What constitutes correct behavior often varies according to the situation and status of individuals. Foreigners will be forgiven most gaffes, but good manners will earn you respect. The best approach is to be as sensitive as possible to situations, avoid loud or dogmatic behavior, and follow the lead of those around you.

Gauze mask, worn to stop the spread of colds

Taboos

Few allowances are made even for foreigners on certain points, mainly relating to Japanese standards of hygiene. Surprisingly for many visitors, it is considered unforgivable to get soap or shampoo in a bathtub; washing belongs to the shower area *(see p301)*.

When it comes to table manners, serious errors include touching food in a communal dish with your chopsticks but then not taking it, and shoveling food direct from bowl to mouth (though the latter may be practiced by the Japanese at home). For more information about eating etiquette, *see pp312–13*.

At one time, eating while walking was seldom seen, though customs have changed over time: many older people would still never engage in such a practice. Eating on longer train trips is fine. Bodily emissions are considered very rude, though anything drawn inward is acceptable; sniffing is fine, but blowing your nose in public is reviled. Gauze face masks are worn in public to stop infecting others and to avoid catching colds, and as a preventive measure during hay fever season.

Shoes

Shoes are an important element of etiquette, and it is a serious mistake to wear shoes indoors in all private and some public buildings. When you enter a Japanese house or traditional restaurant, take off your shoes and put on slippers before stepping onto the raised floor. If no slippers are provided, or if they are too small, go in socks or tights. The principle is not to contaminate the clean interiors with dirt from outside.

If the area immediately beyond the entranceway to a room or building is at a higher level than the entrance itself, shoes should normally be removed. Other people's shoes will usually be evident or there will be some kind of rack in which shoes are to be placed. In a Western-style hotel, the main part of the room is not raised above the entranceway, and so

Traditional footwear neatly lined up on racks outside a temple

shoes can be worn by both guests and staff. Ordinarily, to walk on *tatami* matting, slippers should be removed and socks or tights worn instead.

Most restrooms, public and private, have special toilet slippers waiting outside: be sure to change into them as you go in (this is one way people know the restroom is occupied!) and to change back again when you emerge.

Smoking

Restrictions on smoking have increased around Japan. In many Tokyo wards, smoking on the street is banned (sometimes punishable by on-the-spot fines) except in specially designated areas, but this is not strictly enforced. Smoking zones are usually well marked and can often be found near major stations. Smoking is banned on buses and trains (except for some long-distance trains, such as the shinkansen, which have smoking cars) as well as in most stations, but smoking is usually permitted in bars and restaurants. However, the number of non-smoking bars and restaurants is on the increase.

Taxes and Tipping

A consumption tax of 8 percent is paid by consumers for goods and services. Shops and service providers are required to include the tax in their prices.

Other than with really exceptional service, there is no tipping in Japan, and an attempt at tipping might even cause offense.

Body Language

This is not as sensitive an issue as in many other Asian countries, although it is considered rude to point your feet at people, and it is preferable to avoid wild gesticulations or talking loudly. The Japanese appreciate that sitting on the floor can be a strain for those not used to it, but try not to stretch out your legs. Men may sit cross-legged, while women should tuck their feet to one side.

The Japanese practice good posture from childhood: a straight back is respected.

Attitudes to Physical Contact and Sex

Members of the same sex are physically at ease with each other. The atmosphere in single-sex public baths is relaxed. Between the sexes, however (outside immediate family, who often bathe together), a public display of contact is not as common as in the West. Kissing is viewed as purely sexual. A "hello" kiss on the cheek might cause embarrassment, and hugging is not so common.

Skimpy clothing, is worn by most girls and will not cause offense, but a shapely or hirsute Westerner in revealing clothes might invite stares and giggles.

In general, sex is seen as free from shame, though something to be indulged discreetly. Shinto emphasizes fertility, and some objects in shrines can be quite explicit (see p31).

Homosexual activity, though widely practiced by samurai in the feudal era, is less openly accepted today than in many Western nations (see p362).

Sadly, the sleazier side of sex trade includes schoolgirl prostitution. Cartoon pornography is widely sold in convenience stores. Nonetheless, everyday life is relatively sanitized, and it is important to remember that geisha (see p167) and the majority of bar hostesses are not prostitutes.

Etiquette at Temples and Shrines

The atmosphere in Buddhist temples and Shinto shrines is casual, and there are no general restrictions on clothing. Visitors should show respect, and not be noisy, but there are few of the taboos found in some other

Paying respects at a family tomb in a Tokyo cemetery

Buddhist nations. Japan is a superstitious society rather than a religious one, with its religion mixing together and priests leading down-to-earth lives.

Fertility statue at Uwajima's Taga Shrine museum

If you enter buildings in a shrine or temple, except those with stone floors, leave your shoes at the entrance or carry them with you. Plastic bags are often provided for this, especially if there are several exits. Some temples allow photography, some only without flash, others not at all. For advice about paying respects in Shinto and Buddhism, see pp30–33.

Lining Up and Jaywalking

Social behavior in Japan is full of contradictions. When waiting for a train, people line up neatly but may resort to pushing and shoving in order to get on. To get off a crowded train, simply push your way through. If you are stuck and cannot reach the door in time, call out "orimasu" ("I'm getting off") as you try to push your way toward the exit.

Pedestrians should be careful about jaywalking. It is not so common among Japanese. If you do it, others may assume you are crossing correctly and follow you unthinkingly, or you may be reprimanded by the police.

The Hierarchy

Respect for seniors is fundamental to Japanese

society even today. The emphasis on seniority has its roots in Confucianism (a set of social rules imported from China that places great emphasis on loyalty and filial piety).

All older people are treated with respect: not only parents, grandparents, company bosses, and teachers but even those a year or two senior in school or employment. The term sensei ("teacher") is used as a term of respect for elders, experts, and those with high professional status, such as doctors. Social attitudes are reflected in the Japanese language, which has a special form of honorific speech.

Many Japanese regard the imperial family as the ultimate parent in such a social system. Until the end of World War II, emperors were worshiped as having descended from the deities that created the country. Today, some liberals reject the imperial system and the national anthem as symbols of the country, though right-wing groups fiercely protect the imperial family and may exercise extreme violence against those who speak out against it. Most people show a lot of respect for the emperor, but stop short of veneration.

Commuters line up for a train at the station

Group posing for a photograph while on a religious pilgrimage

Group Mentality

One key to understanding Japanese society is that of the emphasis on the group, which may be a family, village, school, company, or the Japanese nation as a whole. Foreigners are likely to see Japanese group mentality in operation at major tourist sights, where large tour groups are much in evidence.

Within a group, peer pressure leads everyone to conform to accepted ways of doing things. A popular saying is "the nail that stands out will be hammered down." Even artists and those on the fringes of society only occasionally show genuine individualism. Foreigners, however, are expected to be more individualistic. The group mentality in Japan has always permeated attitudes and behavior, but the concept is becoming less strong.

Bowing

The traditional greeting in Japan is a bow, its depth reflecting the relative status of participants. Foreigners, however, rarely need to bow; a handshake is fine. In many situations, bows are part of the service, for instance, in elevators, department stores, restaurants, and hotels. They can be ignored or met with a brief smile. If you feel the need to bow, hold your arms and back straight, bend from the waist, and pause for a moment at the low point.

How the Japanese React to Foreigners

Thanks to a fundamentally courteous culture, visitors meet with warm hospitality. But you will also encounter curiosity and occasional rudeness. Do not be surprised by apparently naive and insular attitudes: Western culture may flood the country, but it is filtered and Japanized. Foreigners may still be a curiosity away from the larger urban centers (especially blondes and black people) and are expected to be different. This can lead to comments that are unintentionally racist. Young Japanese and those who travel abroad are helping to change the nation's perception of foreigners.

Because of the "them-and-us" group mentality, foreigners (gaijin) inevitably remain outsiders however much they are welcomed with warmth and open arms. Foreigners who show sensitivity to Japanese culture, especially those who speak the language well, are usually accepted to a greater extent (and expected to conform to Japanese ways), but even they can never fully belong.

Meeting Japanese People

The Japanese have a reputation for their reserve and politeness, but in fact their social behavior is more complex, dictated by the situation, the place, the people involved, as well as the social expectations. The contrast between, say, the formal etiquette required at a tea ceremony (see p173) and the casual abandon often encountered in such places as bars, is extreme.

You will find classic manners in hotels, restaurants, and shops, where courteous, efficient service is seen as simply the correct way of doing a job and not demeaning. The response to waiters and sales assistants is up to you: some Japanese treat them as invisible, but a token inclination of the head or quiet "domo" ("thank you") does no harm.

Sometimes, officials such as tour guides seem autocratic, but this is largely due to imperfect English intonation and the expectation of Japanese travelers. If you somehow clash with authority, such as a traffic policeman, use a quiet conciliatory demeanor, not the loud assertiveness that might get results in your own country. The same applies to poor service: being articulate about your complaint is fine,

Bow between business colleagues close in status to each other

but do so quietly and politely. In conversations generally, avoid confrontation and causing loss of face (although this is not as vital as in some other parts of Asia). The main purpose of conversation for many Japanese people is not the interchange of ideas but building a relationship. Therefore, small talk is considered important.

Away from the big cities, you may well be asked to pose for photographs or find yourself engaged in practicing English with strangers.

Japanese and English signboard at the JR train station, Tokyo

Traditionally designed boxes used to store tea make lovely souvenirs

Gift-Giving

Gift-giving is big business in Japan, one of the most important aspects of etiquette, though it is not likely to be a concern for most visitors. Any trip means bringing home souvenirs, called *omivage*, for colleagues and friends, usually something edible. Small gifts may be exchanged at a first business meeting, and if you visit someone's home, never go empty-handed: buy a luxury food item or take a small gift from your home country.

Keep gifts small, to avoid placing an obligation on the recipient. Gifts are generally not opened in front of the giver. It is regarded as unlucky to give four of anything. Be aware that white is often regarded as the color of mourning (though it is also worn by brides) and red signifies celebration.

Language

Despite the profusion of brand names written in Roman script and often using Western-sounding words, Western visitors may face some language problems outside the main tourist areas. Signs for transportation systems are transliterated in many areas, though often inconsistently *(see pp380–83)*. Linguistically and culturally, the scope for misunderstanding is vast. The American English taught in schools is heavily weighted to grammar rather than conversation, so few Japanese are comfortable with everyday spoken English. When English is spoken, it is generally pronounced as if it were Japanese.

In Japanese, many words are abbreviated and all syllables are evenly stressed. All consonants are followed by a vowel except *n*. The letters *r* and *l* merge into an intermediate sound. Thus, for instance, taxi becomes *takushi*, hotel is *hoteru*, McDonalds becomes *Makudonarudo* or *Makku*, convenience store becomes *konbini*, and personal computer becomes *pasokon*; London is *Rondon*, New York is *Nyu Youku*, Sydney is *Shidoni*, and Los Angeles often simply *Ros*. For guidelines about pronunciation, see the Phrase Book on *pp404–8*.

Further confusion comes from words imported from English that have undergone a change in meaning, for example

manshon is not a palatial house but a large apartment building; *roman*, a romance novel. Resulting product names, such as the isotonic drinks Pocari Sweat and Calpis *(see p322)*, and "Japlish" text on t-shirts can be entertaining for visitors.

Even with good English speakers, subtleties may be lost. If a Japanese person says "yes," it often means "I understand," not "I agree"; if they say "it's difficult," this usually means no. For clarity, avoid negative and either/or questions.

Japanese Names

The traditional order of Japanese names is that of the family name followed by the given name. However, many Japanese automatically reverse this order when giving names to Westerners, so you may need to check which are the given names and surnames. Japanese generally call each other by the family name, even if they are quite close friends, but they will happily call you by your first name if you prefer.

When speaking to or about an adult other than yourself, add "-san" to their name, which stands for Mr., Mrs., Ms., etc – for instance, Smith-san or John-san. For babies and young girls add "-chan," for young boys "-kun." One should never refer to oneself as "-san."

Helpful sign written in both Japanese and transliteration for English-speaking visitors

Doing Business and Working in Japan

In business, as in other areas, Japan is a complex blend of hi-tech and old-fashioned. Practicalities are fairly easy in a land that is technologically up to date, but doing business in Japan can be a challenge. The structure and culture of business are so different from the West that misunderstandings often arise. With a little luck and planning, it is possible to find work in Japan, although living expenses, especially for accommodations, can be high.

Employees doing communal exercise before starting work

Business Attitudes and Structures

Japanese business attitudes are dominated by the long term. This shows in corporate planning and the slow pace of decision-making as well as individual attitudes. Lifetime employment at a single firm, although still the norm, is becoming less common. However, the company is still a community around which the *salaryman* (male office worker) builds his life. If you ask someone what they do, the answer may often not be their trade, but the company for which they work.

The system can be hard for foreigners to break into. Major companies tend to be bound together, officially or unofficially, in huge industrial groups *(keiretsu)*, comprising networks of subsidiaries and subcontractors. Exporting is not so difficult, but dealing with the bureaucracy and paperwork for import and export can be time-consuming. Nonetheless, effort invested in groundwork and building contacts and relationships can pay dividends.

Business Facilities

Most major hotels in Japan have excellent business facilities and can provide email and Internet access, arrange rooms for meetings and conferences, and recommend interpreters. Business services also advertise in Yellow Pages, English-language magazines, and newspapers. Outgoing telephone calls from hotels are charged at near-normal rates, without exorbitant surcharges. For details on cell phones, fax, email, and Wi-Fi and Internet facilities, *see pages 374–5.* The majority of convenience stores offer inexpensive photocopying and faxing.

SoftBank's widely recognized Wi-Fi logo in Japan

Business Cards

Known as *meishi*, business cards are an essential part of business and social transactions in Japan. They are vital for learning a person's status as well as their name; bear in mind that job titles may not correspond to Western equivalents, and people may have varied experience within a company. Have a large stock of business cards printed, preferably in English on one side and Japanese on the other. Major hotels and department stores often provide this service overnight.

The card's design is not important, but avoid rounded corners, as these were traditionally used by geisha and other women in the entertainment world, and the implication of frivolity lives on.

Business cards should be treated with respect: when meeting someone for the first time, proffer your card with both hands, and say your name clearly; then hand over the card with your right hand, taking the other person's card with your left. Keep their card in front of you during the meeting. Forgetting their card or putting it in a pocket where it may be crumpled would be seen as signs of disrespect to the other person.

Negotiating

Patience and good manners are the keys to successful negotiation in Japan. Japanese who are used to dealing with foreigners will make allowances for Western ways, but to stand the best chance of success it is worth being open to Japanese expectations. The basics of etiquette are outlined on pages 364–7. Avoid dressing too informally; arrive for meetings on time or early; speak respectfully; and initially decline the seat of honor (farthest from the door or offering the best view over the room).

Improving personal connections through small gifts or business entertaining

Computerized bidding at the Tokyo Stock Exchange

is very much part of the system, but overt bribery is not. Japanese companies reach decisions by consensus, so elements of face-saving vagueness or flexibility can be useful. On the other hand, to minimize linguistic confusion, it is essential to speak simply and unambiguously. In some situations, an interpreter may help. Be aware, however, that you will not be given a clear no, even if that is what is meant. Discussion of money is usually left until last and should not be approached too bluntly.

Business Entertaining

Socializing with business contacts is essential: there is little chance of establishing a good working relationship if you have not built a rapport over a few drinks or perhaps a game of golf (see p351). Expect the Japanese to extend the first invitation, and allow them to pay – usually the person who does the inviting picks up the tab. If you would like to return the compliment but are not sure where to take people, ask their advice, or choose a hotel bar (where prices are clearly marked).

Conversation can include business matters, but should not be intense. Drunken behavior is normal and rarely taken seriously. Although the world of business entertaining is basically male, exceptions are made for foreign business-women and, despite under-lying sexist attitudes, women should encounter few prob-lems. For eating and drinking etiquette, see pages 312–13.

Finding Work

Finding work in Japan is not as easy as it was during the economic boom of the 1980s. Most common are English-teaching jobs, which usually require a university degree and at times a TEFL (Teaching English as a Foreign Language) qualifica-tion. The **Japan English Teacher** website is a good resource.

The **JET (Japan Exchange and Teaching) Programme** sends college graduates under the age of 35 to work in Japan, initially for a year, sometimes extendable to two or three. Details are available on the JET website. After checking this, contact the Japanese embassy in your country. Other common English-teaching opportunities include *eikaiwa* or conversation schools.

There are also limited opportunities in Japan for other kinds of work. Some job offers appear in Japan's English-language newspapers, such as **Metropolis,** and in a few magazines, including **Japanzine** and **Kansai Scene**. There are also a number of websites that are helpful for those looking for work in Japan (see directory).

Working Visas

Long-term stays in Japan require a working visa (with a commitment for two or three years working for one firm) or a student visa (which allows part-time work). Citizens aged 18 to 30 of the following countries can obtain a working-holiday visa, allowing part-time work, for up to a year: Australia, Canada, Denmark, France, Germany, Ireland, Korea,

New Zealand, UK, and residents of Hong Kong and Taiwan. Although officially discouraged, it is sometimes possible to enter Japan as a Temporary Visitor (see p360) and then find a job or study course.

Long-Term Accommodations

Some apartments in major cities can be found at rental rates similar to those in Western cities, but the initial start-up costs are extremely high. Cheaper options include "gaijin houses," accommodations for foreigners ranging from shared apartments for three or four to disheveled hostels with 20 sharing a kitchen. The next step up is a weekly or monthly apartment, at the cost of a budget hotel or less, which is like a regular apartment but requires little or no deposit. In descriptions, room size is measured by the number of tatami mats (although the size does vary, a 6-mat room can be taken to be 9.18 sq m/99 sq ft), and apartments may be said to have, for instance, "2DK" – two bedrooms, a dining room, and kitchen.

DIRECTORY

Finding Work

Dai Job
ⓦ daijob.com/en

Gaijin Pot
ⓦ gaijinpot.com

Japan English Teacher
ⓦ japanenglishteacher.com

JET Programme
ⓦ jetprogramme.org

Jobs in Japan
ⓦ jobsinjapan.com

Kansai Scene
ⓦ kansaiscene.com

Metropolis
ⓦ http://metropolis.co.jp

Tokyo Employment Service Center for Foreigners
ⓦ http://tokyo-foreigner.jsite.mhlw.go.jp/english.html

Personal Security and Health

Hygiene standards in Japan are as high as in Western countries, and crime rates are low. Pickpockets occasionally operate in crowds, but bags can generally be put down freely in a store or at a station, and there is little risk in carrying large amounts of cash. *Koban* (manned police boxes) are found in every neighborhood; their presence helps to keep crime down. Japan lies at the juncture of several tectonic plates, making it very prone to earthquakes, tsunamis, and volcanic eruptions, some of which cause extreme devastation. It also lies in the path of typhoons, which can wreak enormous damage.

A traffic policeman wearing a protective mask

Police

Police are generally helpful, and at the *koban* (manned police boxes), usually located close to train stations, they are accustomed to dispensing directions, but their ability to speak English may be limited. Being arrested in Japan, even for a minor offence, can result in police detention for 23 days while the case is being investigated. Police interviews can last many hours, will not be recorded, and under questioning detainees will not have access to a lawyer. The **Police English Help Line** can provide more information.

What to be Aware of

Thefts and muggings do occur at times in Japan. There are also sporadic incidents of bag snatching and pickpocketing in crowded areas. It is generally safe to walk around at night, but be careful in Tokyo's Roppongi entertainment district. There have been reports of drinks being spiked with drugs leaving victims unconscious for several hours, allowing fraudulent billings to be made to credit

cards. It is advisable to avoid the *yakuza* (mafia; *see p207*), extremist political groups, and questionable religious sects.

Women Travelers

Official statistics for sexual assault in Japan are very low, and any unwanted propositions from men can usually be shaken off with a simple no. However, groping hands on crowded trains are an acknowledged problem, and increasing evidence suggests that sex crimes tend to go unreported or unprosecuted. Women should avoid mountain paths after dark and be wary of men outside stations trying to initiate a conversation.

In an Emergency

Emergency calls are free. The Tokyo Police operates a Police English Help Line for foreign visitors. The **Tokyo Metropolitan Health and Medical Information Center** provides health information in English, Spanish, Korean, Chinese, and Thai. In case

of translation difficulties regarding medical treatment, contact the **Emergency Medical Translation Services**. **Japan Helpline** offers 24-hour assistance in English for all kinds of problems. Visitors who need counseling can contact the **Tokyo English Life Line**, which offers an excellent free service.

Lost and Stolen Property

The loss of most items should be reported at the nearest *koban*. The Japanese are generally very honest and items such as lost wallets are often handed in intact to the authorities by responsible citizens. If your passport is lost or stolen, report it at the local police station, not the *koban*. The station will provide an official police report, which can be presented at your embassy to obtain a replacement or emergency passport.

Hospitals and Pharmacies

Facilities are generally as good as in the US or Europe, but the cost of treatment is high. If you are sick, consult a doctor at a local clinic; for minor problems, see a pharmacist.

To find a hospital or get other information about medical institutions such as dentists, contact the Tokyo Metropolitan Health and Medical Information Center. Other options include the **AMDA International Medical Information Center** and **Japan Healthcare Info**. The former offers free medical consultation over the telephone

An ambulance driving down a street in Tokyo

in eight languages and also provides a free telephone interpreter service for use in consultations. The latter can locate English-speaking doctors anywhere in Japan for free, and can also provide interpretation services for a small fee. The **US Embassy** website has a list of medical resources around Japan with English-speaking staff.

Medicines are dispensed at pharmacies. Western brands are available, if expensive, at pharmacies such as **American Pharmacy**. Contact lenses can be obtained with relative ease, and Western-brand lens solutions are very reasonably priced. Insect repellents and soothing lotions for mosquito bites (Mu-hi is a popular brand) are sold in pharmacies. Chinese herbal medicine is widely available (see p356).

Minor Hazards

Despite the nuclear accident in Fukushima in 2011 (see p265), the water is considered safe to drink, but buy bottled water if you prefer. Radiation levels in food are closely monitored, so there should be no danger in consuming food that has been distributed.

Food poisoning is rare and tap water is drinkable throughout Japan. Avoid drinking water from streams. Raw seafood in sushi and sashimi is not a risk. Fugu (blowfish) is safe since all

School children practicing an earthquake drill

the fish served in restaurants and on sale in supermarkets is prepared by experts. Eat raw meat only in a good restaurant. Fruit and vegetables are clean, but it is wise to wash or peel, as appropriate, before eating.

If you are staying in Japan for over a month or visiting rural areas, it is advisable to get an encephalitis vaccine.

Natural Disasters

Each year, Japan experiences more than 1,000 earthquakes strong enough to be felt, but not cause any destruction. In major cities, tall buildings have mechanisms to absorb motion. During a strong earthquake, especially in an old building, open doors (to prevent them from buckling and jamming) and turn off any gas. Do not go outside, where debris may fall, but take shelter under a reinforced doorway or sturdy table. Avoid sleeping close to heavy objects that may fall or

heavy furniture not securely fixed to a wall. The Tokyo Government has issued a useful bilingual **Earthquake Survival Manual**, and the **Japan Meteorological Agency** provides early warnings.

Typhoons may bring strong winds and cause flooding or landslides so it is best to stay indoors. Active volcanoes are usually fenced off so no one goes dangerously close. Poisonous fumes occasionally seep from the crater or its vicinity so keep a lookout for warning notices.

Travel and Health Insurance

All visitors should take out comprehensive travel insurance before traveling. It is important to confirm that it covers medical costs since these can be extremely high in Japan. Without insurance, an emergency can be very expensive. Insurance should also cover areas loss of belongings, theft, and cancellation of journey.

DIRECTORY

Police

Police English Help Line
Tel (03) 3501-0110.
W japantravelinfo.com

In an Emergency

Police/Fire/ Ambulance
Tel 110.
Tel 119.

Emergency Medical Translation Services
Tel (03) 5285-8185. **Open** 5–8pm Mon–Fri, 9am– 8pm Sat, Sun, & pub hols.

Japan Helpline
Tel 0570-000-911.
W jhelp.com/en/jhlp. html

Tokyo English Life Line
Tel (03) 5774-0992.
Open 9am–11pm daily.
W telljp.com

Tokyo Metropolitan Health and Medical Information Center
Tel (03) 5285-8181.
Open 9am–8pm daily.
W himawari.metro. tokyo.jp

Hospitals and Pharmacies

AMDA International Medical Information Center
Tel (03) 5285-8088.

American Pharmacy
B1 Marunouchi Bldg,
2-4-1 Marunouchi
Chiyoda-ku, Tokyo.
Tel (03) 5220-7716.

Japanese Healthcare Info
Tel (080) 4421-7477.
W japanhealth info.com

US Embassy

W japan.usembassy. gov/e/acs/tacs-7119. html

Natural Disasters

Earthquake Survival Manual
W metro.tokyo.jp/ ENGLISH/POLICY/ security.htm

Japan Meteorological Agency
W jma.go.jp/jma/en/ Activities/eew.html

Banking and Local Currency

Visitors used to easy and instant access to cash 24 hours a day in their home country, may find Japan's banking system a little antiquated. Japan is largely a cash economy and so it is important to always carry some cash. However, credit cards are accepted at a growing number of shops, convenience stores, restaurants, hotels, and JR stations. Payments can be made using debit cards at select places, but cash withdrawals using foreign debit cards are only possible at a limited number of ATMs.

Banks and Bureaux de Change

The nation's central bank, the Bank of Japan (Nippon Ginko), issues the yen currency. However, this and the prefectural, and local city banks are not geared to tourists. Buying yen, exchanging travelers' checks, and any other regular banking transactions may be more easily conducted via major Japanese banks that are authorized money exchangers. **Sumitomo Mitsui** and **Mizuho Bank** are two banks that offer these services. Some foreign banks, notably **Citibank**, also offer useful services and have English-speaking staff. Note that local banks in rural areas may charge large fees. Even leading city banks may be unfamiliar with foreign currency apart from dollars, so be prepared for bank tellers to check with their superiors.

Banks are typically open 9am–3pm on weekdays and remain closed on weekends and national holidays. They post the exchange rate for US dollars at about 10am, and later for other

People lining up at an ATM to withdraw money

currencies. Some city banks offer exchange facilities from 9am.

It is also possible to change cash and travelers' checks at major hotels (which generally offer the same exchange rates as banks), some *ryokan* (inns), all central post offices, and a number of city department stores, although staff may not be familiar with the procedure at these locations.

Bureaux de change can often be found in the vicinity of major stations. Banks and post offices may also offer money-transfer facilities. In city centers, staff

Sign for an automatic teller machine (ATM)

may speak English, and forms are often supplied in English – if not, staff will indicate where to write. Transactions are relatively simple, but usually time-consuming. Always carry your passport for identification.

At international airports, currency-exchange counters may be open for longer than regular banking hours; at Narita International Airport, the counter is open from 6:30am to 11pm. However, the rates at airports are not very competitive, and travelers would be better advised to change their money elsewhere. It is illegal for public transport, stores, and restaurants to accept payment in foreign currencies, so some Japanese yen will be required on arrival to cover immediate needs. It is always wise to obtain cash before traveling anywhere outside the major cities.

ATMs

Although automatic teller machines are commonly available in large urban areas throughout Japan, many do not accept foreign credit or debit cards. However, most Japanese post offices and 7-Eleven convenience stores (around 13,000 in Japan) have ATMs that will accept **VISA**, Plus, **MasterCard**, Maestro, Cirrus, **American Express**, and **JCB** cards, through an English menu. ATMs in

---

DIRECTORY

Banks

Citibank
1F Ote Center Building,
1-1-3 Otemachi, Tokyo.
Tel (03) 3215-0051.
1-4F Citibank Shinjuku
Building, 3-19-4 Shinjuku,
Tokyo.
Tel (03) 3226-4395.
1F & 2F Midosuji
Diamond Building, 2-1-2
Nishi-Shinsaibashi, Osaka.
Tel (06) 6213-2731.
W citibank.co.jp/en/

Mizuho Bank
1-1-5 Uchisaiwaicho,
Chiyoda-ku, Tokyo.
Tel (03) 3596-1111.

Sumitomo Mitsui Bank
1F Yurakucho Marion,
Yurakucho, Chiyoda-ku,
Tokyo.
Tel (03) 3211-0711.
4-6-5 Kitahama,
Chuo-ku, Osaka.
Tel (06) 6227-2111.
W smbc.co.jp/global

Credit and Debit Cards

American Express
Tel (0120) 020-120 (toll-free; English explanation follows the Japanese) for lost cards.
W americanexpress.com

Diners Club
Tel (0120) 074-024 (toll-free nationwide) for lost cards. W dinersclub.com

MasterCard
Tel (00531) 11-3886 (free international assistance number) for lost cards.
W mastercard.com

JCB
W jcbusa.com

VISA
Tel 00531-44-0022 (24-hour).
W visa.com
W visaatm.infonow.net

other convenience stores have stickers on the display indicating which cards are accepted. Contact your bank or credit card company, before traveling, for locations of suitable ATMs.

Operating hours of ATMs vary. For post office opening hours see *p376*. ATMs at 7-Eleven stores and many other convenience stores are open 24 hours. A number of Citibank ATMs are also open 24 hours, though even in Tokyo the network of Citibank branches is not extensive.

Credit and Debit Cards

International credit cards, such as American Express, Master-Card, VISA, and **Diners Club** are

generally accepted by leading banks, hotels, restaurants, and stores in cities. In addition, credit cards are accepted at popular tourist areas for a charge. These cards can also be used at major stations to buy JR train tickets and are accepted by some taxis. Obtaining cash with credit cards is not always possible or easy from an ATM as the machine (e.g. at gas stations) may have a problem reading it. Many places accept only Japanese-issued cards such as JCB.

In order to ensure your card works overseas, it is worth contacting your bank or credit card provider in advance of traveling. If your credit or debit card is lost or stolen,

contact your card company immediately.

Although travelers' checks provide a convenient way to carry money around Japan, they are usually accepted only in major city banks and large hotels. Travelex, VISA, and American Express are the most widely recognized.

Currency

The Japanese currency, yen (¥), is available as bank notes in denominations of ¥1, ¥5, ¥10, ¥50, ¥100, and ¥500, ¥1,000, ¥2,000 (very rare), ¥5,000, and ¥10,000. Bank notes, in limited amounts, can be reconverted at the point of departure.

Bank Notes

Each of the banknote denominations carries a portrait of an historical figure, such as the novelist Higuchi Ichiyo, on the ¥5,000 note.

10,000 yen

5,000 yen

2,000 yen

1,000 yen

Coins

500 yen

The denominations of Japan's coins are all marked in Arabic numerals, except for the ¥5. On the reverse side of most of the coins is a flower or plant design; on the ¥10 is a temple.

| 100 yen | 50 yen | 10 yen | 5 yen | 1 yen |

Communications and Media

As befits a country that has long been on the cutting edge of technology, the range of communication tools is extensive and state-of-the-art. Just about everyone has a mobile phone, but although Internet cafés are widely available, free Wi-Fi hotspots are rare. Due to the prevalence of cell phones, public phones are not as common as they used to be; they can usually be found in shopping areas, outside convenience stores, and around stations, though not all are suitable for making international calls. Newspapers and magazines are printed in abundance, and English-language versions are readily available in major cities. The postal system is fast and efficient.

Making International and Local Calls

Some public phones take international credit cards as well as phone cards. As with domestic calls, the call will be routed via **NTT Communications** unless you purchase a calling card issued by one of the other major telecom companies offering international calls, such as **KDDI** and **SoftBank**. The following phone cards are available from the three main operators: **Comica Card**, **KDDI Super World Card**, and **World Prepaid Card**. Phone cards may be purchased from a wide variety of outlets, including station kiosks, vending machines, and convenience stores. Various foreign companies, for example callingcards.com and speedypin.com, offer useful information on the best calling cards to purchase for international calls.

Use the gray public phones to make international calls. Dial the appropriate company's access code *(see p376)*, then the country code, area code (minus any initial zero), followed by the desired number. The major companies are in competition, so charges and services are constantly changing; each has a toll-free number for information.

All major hotels offer international direct-dialing. You may be surcharged for calls from your room. KDDI and NTT offer international collect calls; dial the appropriate access code and then ask the operator to

Gray public phone, suitable for international calls

place a collect call. The cheapest times for international calls are between 11pm and 8am daily; the second-cheapest is from 7pm to 11pm.

The charge for a local call is ¥10 per minute. Use small coins

International Dialing Codes

Use these codes after the international access codes to dial the following countries: Australia **61**, Brazil **55**, Canada **1**, China **86**, France **33**, Germany **49**, Hong Kong **852**, India **91**, Indonesia **62**, Ireland **353**, Israel **972**, Italy **39**, Republic of Korea **82**, Malaysia **60**, Netherlands **31**, New Zealand **64**, Peru **51**, Philippines **63**, Russia **7**, Singapore **65**, Spain **34**, Sweden **46**, Switzerland **41**, Taiwan **886**, Thailand **66**, United Kingdom **44**, and US **1**.

or phone cards in a public phone; unused coins will be returned to you. In this guide, area codes are given in brackets; omit the code if calling from within the area.

Cell Phones

Foreign cell phones may not work in Japan; GSM, for example, is not deployed. However, some may work if the operator is an inbound roaming partner of such Japanese operators as SoftBank and Docomo. Check with your cell operator before traveling.

A good option for the visitor is renting a cell phone from companies such as **Rentafone Japan**. Payment is typically made by credit card. Prepaid phones (though not prepaid SIM cards) are also a possibility from operators including KDDI and SoftBank. The operator's conditions may differ, but a passport as ID and a hotel address should be sufficient. Even though cell phones are cheap, buying one is not really an option unless you are planning a long stay, since operators ordinarily demand a one- or two-year contract and require a Resident Card.

Some public places, have areas set aside for cell phone use. For example, on bullet trains it is encouraged that talking on cell phones should take place in the deck areas between cars.

Public Telephones

Although their numbers have declined, the most common public phones are green and are situated everywhere from stations to inside trains, outside convenience stores, and on the street in busier areas. Older versions of the green phones accept ¥10 and ¥100 coins only; newer models take a wider range of coins as well as telephone cards. These phones are for local calls only. Gray public phones have an LCD display, a button for converting information into English, volume control (handy in noisy public places), and an emergency button for dialing police, fire, and ambulance (see p371). These phones also offer international direct dialing.

The old-fashioned pink phones occasionally found in restaurants are for local calls and only accept ¥10 coins.

Calls from public phones are automatically connected via NTT unless you use a phone card issued by another operator (see opposite).

Internet

Internet cafés, also known as manga cafés, are widely available. You usually pay for a private booth with a reclining chair. **Kinko's** provides Internet access; it has many branches in Tokyo and also in other major cities. Some computer stores, including Apple, provide free Internet access. A number of coffee shops such as Tully's or Starbucks offer free or inexpensive Wi-Fi. For a list of Wi-Fi hotspots, check **JiWire Global Wi-Fi Finder** or **Freespot**. Another option for finding free Internet access is to search for unsecured spots on crowded shopping streets, or try the lobbies of large hotels, which sometimes have free Wi-Fi zones. Some shops and restaurants display the SoftBank Wi-Fi logo (see p368) to indicate that free Wi-Fi service is available for SoftBank users.

Cover of a magazine printed by *Japanzine*

Newspapers and Magazines

The range of newspapers in Japanese is extensive. The most demanding of the reader is *Asahi Shimbun*; the least, *Gendai*, a tabloid containing a fair amount of pornographic material. Somewhere in between, selling around ten million copies daily, is the *Yomiuri Shimbun*. Japanese magazines come and go, seeking to follow news, business, and leisure trends. As for *manga* comic books (see p29), they cover every subject imaginable; the regular bestseller is *Shonen Jump*, aimed at young men.

Three English-language newspapers are printed in Japan – **The Japan Times**, **The Japan News**, and **The Asahi Shimbun**. They are sold at kiosks in train stations, major hotels, foreign-language bookstores (see p116), and

sometimes in convenience stores. These newspapers and the *Mainichi Daily News* are also accessible online. For news about business and technology, the best publication is the *Nikkei Weekly*.

There are several easily available English-language magazines, in particular *Metropolis*, *Japanzine*, and *Kansai Scene* (see p363), with extensive listings and classified advertisements. Foreign-language bookstores often stock imported magazines. The three magazines mentioned above, along with many others, are also available online. Another good source of information that is only accessible online is **Japan Today**. As the names indicate **Outdoor Japan Online** and *Outdoor Japan Traveler Magazine* are great resources for visitors who aim to travel out of the cities.

Television and Radio

NHK is the state broadcaster, and it runs two terrestrial and two satellite channels. The nightly 7pm and 8pm (only at 7pm on weekends) news bulletins on NHK can be heard in English on bilingual TVs, which are often found in hotels. Other nationwide networks include Nippon TV, TBS, Fuji TV, and TV Asahi. Cable and satellite are also widely available, as is digital broadcasting on NHK and the other networks. Check *Metropolis* for English-language TV program listings.

The state radio station NHKFM broadcasts news and mainly classical music. There are also several commercial radio stations, among which some, such as **J-Wave** and **Inter FM** in Tokyo and Cocolo in Central Honshu, offer a number of programs in English. Check up-to-date listings pages for frequencies and for times of programs. It is possible to listen to J-Wave and Inter FM online and check listings on the websites given in the directory.

Bright posters and signs at an Internet cafe

Logo identifying post offices and also found on mailboxes

Postal Services

Post offices (yubin-kyoku) and mailboxes in Japan are identified by the character looking like a "T" with an extra horizontal bar across the top. Main post offices are usually open 7am–11pm on weekdays with shorter hours on weekends. Some large central post offices are open 24 hours. Smaller post offices may open 9am–4pm on weekdays but are often closed on weekends. Stamps are also sold at smaller stores, including convenience stores, and larger hotels. Make sure any mail is addressed correctly and legibly; the postal code is the most important.

Large post offices in major cities may have a counter (indicated by a sign) where English is spoken. The clerk will weigh the letter and sell the correct stamp. An express service is available for more urgent mail inside Japan. **EMS** (Express Mail Service) operates like an international courier service run by the post office, and it is a speedy way to send documents and goods up to 66 lb (30 kg) overseas. It can even be cheaper than regular airmail. Post office staff can advise as to which is the cheaper option. In major cities, the central post office often has a late or overnight counter.

Many mailboxes have two slots, which separate the mail according to destination and type. The slots are labeled in English. Parcels have to be mailed from a post office: a form will be supplied to fill in, which staff will attach

Japanese mailbox

to the package. For deliveries within Japan, takuhaibin (see the next section) is often a faster option.

Couriers and Other Mail Services

Japan is well served with efficient door-to-door delivery services (takuhaibin): for fast delivery, they are a better alternative to regular post. The best known of these domestic companies are **Yamato Transport Co.** and **Sagawa Express**. Small packages can be sent via these courier services from convenience stores and other shops; larger items will be picked up at the source. There are also a number of courier services for sending printed materials and packages abroad. **FedEx** and **DHL** are among the best known. **Nippon Courier Services** is also reliable.

DIRECTORY

International and Local Telephone Calls

Comica Card
w tm.softbank.jp/english/consumer/comica

KDDI
Tel 001-010 (access code), or 0057 (toll-free information), or 0120-977-097 (toll-free).

KDDI Super World Card
w kddi.com

NTT Communications
Tel 0033-010 (access code). Tel 0120-50-6506 (toll-free information).

SoftBank Telecom
Tel 0061-010 (international call service access code). Tel 0088-41 (toll-free information).
w tm.softbank.jp/english

World Prepaid Card
w 506506.ntt.com/english/service/p_card

Cell Phones

Rentafone Japan
w rentafonejapan.com

Internet

Freespot
w freespot.com/users/map_e.html

JiWire Global Wi-Fi Finder
w v4.jiwire.com/hotspot-directory-browse-by-state.htm?country_id=109&provider_id=0

Kinko's
w kinkos.co.jp/store/top.html

Newspapapers and Magazines

The Asahi Shimbun
w asahi.com/english

The Japan News
w the-japan-news.com

The Japan Times
w japantimes.co.jp

Japan Today
w japantoday.com

Outdoor Japan Online
w outdoorjapan.com

Television and Radio

Inter FM
w interfm.co.jp

J-Wave
w interfm.co.jp

Postal Services

EMS
w post.japanpost.jp/int/ems/index_en.html

Tokyo Central Post Office
2-7-2 Marunouchi, Chiyoda-ku, Tokyo.
Tel (03) 3217-5246.

Tokyo International Post Office
3-5-14 Shinsuna, Koto-ku, Tokyo. Tel 0120-59-3158. (international mail service).

Couriers

DHL
Tel 0120-39-2580, then press 0.
w dhl.co.jp/en.html

FedEx
Tel 0120-00-3200 (toll-free). w fedex.com/jp

Nippon Courier Services
Tel (03) 5461-3550.
w nippon-courier.co.jp

Sagawa Express
Tel 0120-18-9595.
w sagawa-exp.co.jp

Yamato Transport Co.
Tel 03-3541-3411.
w kurone koyamato.co.jp/english

Addresses

In Japan, only the main thoroughfares have names, and there is no consistent numbering system for addresses. The numbering of buildings in a block is often dictated by the order in which they were built, so locating an address can be a puzzle, even for the Japanese. It is slightly easier in a few cities, such as Nara, Kyoto, and Sapporo, which were built on a grid pattern, since at least the blocks are numbered sequentially. There is, however, no such order in most cities, such as Tokyo and Osaka. (All Tokyo sights, hotels, and restaurants listed in this guide are marked on the Street Finder.) To reach a particular destination, it is best to ask at the hotel, where staff should be able to provide maps and directions.

Japan's Prefectures

Japan's main islands, Honshu, Hokkaido, Shikoku, Kyushu, and Okinawa are divided into 47 administrative units called prefectures, 43 of which are referred to as *ken*. The other four are different types of prefectures. Tokyo, for example, is called Tokyo-to, "to" meaning metropolis. Each prefecture is governed independently under the overall control of the central government. The prefectural office is usually located in the largest urban center, which also has its own city or town office. Tokyo has its own metropolitan government; each of the capital's wards has its own administrative office.

Key to the Prefectures

Hokkaido
1 Hokkaido

Tohoku
2 Aomori
3 Akita
4 Iwate
5 Yamagata
6 Miyagi
7 Fukushima

Kanto
8 Tochigi
9 Ibaraki
10 Saitama
11 Tokyo
12 Chiba
13 Kanagawa
14 Gunma

Chubu
15 Niigata
16 Toyama
17 Ishikawa
18 Fukui
19 Nagano

20 Yamanashi
21 Shizuoka
22 Aichi
23 Gifu

Kansai/Kinki
24 Hyogo
25 Kyoto
26 Shiga
27 Osaka
28 Nara
29 Mie
30 Wakayama

Chugoku
31 Tottori
32 Okayama
33 Shimane
34 Hiroshima
35 Yamaguchi

Shikoku
36 Kagawa
37 Tokushima
38 Ehime
39 Kochi

Kyushu
40 Fukuoka
41 Saga
42 Nagasaki
43 Oita
44 Kumamoto
45 Miyazaki
46 Kagoshima

Okinawa
47 Okinawa

Okinawa Archipelago

0 kilometers 300
0 miles 300

KAGOSHIMA
OKINAWA 47
46

TRAVEL INFORMATION

Most visitors fly to Japan and then use the excellent railroad system to get around the country. Many famous sightseeing areas lie on or near the bullet train lines between Tokyo, Osaka, and Fukuoka – visiting places such as Kyoto, Himeji Castle, and Hiroshima is easy, despite the distances involved. For travel to destinations in Shikoku, Kyushu, and Hokkaido, flying may be a better option. Slower local trains connect to popular sights such as Nara and Nikko. Local public transportation systems such as streetcars, subways, and buses are often very efficient, but you may need to rent a car to explore remote regions. The Japan National Tourist Organization (JNTO) website (see p363) provides useful travel information for tourists, including lists of travel agents who can make reservations and sell travel tickets and Rail Pass vouchers (see p381). In Tokyo, the JNTO also has a Tourist Information Center (TIC), which provides travel information in English.

Aeroplanes parked at Kansai International Airport

Arriving by Air

The usual gateways for foreigners entering Japan are **Narita International Airport**, located at some distance from Tokyo, and Osaka's **Kansai International Airport**. Other major airports handling international flights, mainly from Asia, include Naha in Okinawa; Fukuoka and Nagasaki in Kyushu; Hiroshima, Nagoya, Niigata, and Sendai in Honshu; and Sapporo in Hokkaido.

Japan Airlines (JAL) and **All Nippon Airways (ANA)** are the main airlines of Japan and offer nonstop flights between London and Tokyo. **Virgin** and **British Airways** also have direct flights between London and Tokyo. The flying time is around 12 hours. **Qantas**, Air New Zealand, and JAL operate nonstop flights between Tokyo and Australia and New Zealand. with a flying time of about 10 hours for Australia and 12 hours for New Zealand. **Delta** and **United** are the main carriers between Tokyo and North America, but American Airlines, and ANA also link Tokyo with some American cities.

Getting to and from Narita Airport

Located 35 miles (57 km) from Tokyo Station, Narita International Airport has two terminals connected by a free shuttle bus, which takes about 10 minutes. Tourist Information Offices (TIC) are located in the arrival lobby of each terminal and have a multilingual staff.

Visitors who have bought a Japan Rail Pass Exchange Order (see p381) before arriving in Japan should visit the Japan Railways (JR) ticket counter. If validated from the day of arrival in Japan, the pass can be used to make the trip from the airport into central Tokyo by JR train. The journey by taxi will cost at least ¥22,000.

Airport limousine buses are convenient but often slow, depending on traffic. Buses run non-stop to various points within Tokyo, Yokohama, and other nearby airports. A good fast link between Narita and Tokyo is the Narita Express (N'EX) train, which departs from beneath the terminal building. It travels non-stop to Tokyo station in 53 minutes and then on to Shinjuku or Shinagawa, Shibuya, and Ikebukuro stations in the capital or to Yokohama and Ofuna, near Kamakura. The Japan Rail Pass can be used on this train. All signs and announcements for the N'EX are in Japanese and English, and English-language information is available via an onboard telephone service. Remember to reserve a seat when returning to the airport on the N'EX.

Another fast option for travelers is the Keisei Skyliner, which takes just 36 minutes from Narita to Nippori station and 41 minutes to Ueno station. However, the JR Pass cannot be used on this service. Skyliner trains can be boarded at Narita Airport station.

Getting to and from Kansai Airport

Situated on a man-made island 3 miles (5 km) off the coast in

Cars at the entrance of Narita International Airport, Tokyo

Interior of the check-in lobby at Kansai International Airport

Osaka Bay, Kansai International Airport has direct connections with Europe, North America, and other regions. Taxis, limousine buses, and trains are all efficient ways to reach Osaka. There is also a high-speed boat service to Kobe. The TIC is in the arrivals lobby. For onward journeys by rail, Rail Pass Exchange Orders *(see p381)* may be exchanged at the JR Information Counter, TiS Travel Service Center, or Ticket Office *(see p381)*.

Air Fares and Tickets

Ticket prices are comparable. A return trip costs about £500 from London and $800 to $1,000 from the US. Prices are highest around New Year, Golden Week, and summer (July and August).

Domestic Flights

JAL and ANA maintain an extensive network of flights covering the four main islands and many of the smaller ones. Often there is very little difference in price between flying and going by *shinkansen* (bullet train), so flying can be better unless using a JR Rail Pass. On domestic flights, JAL and ANA offer economy seats and a "Super Seat" service, which is a combination of first and business class. You can make reservations through a travel agent or directly with the airlines. The domestic low-cost airline **Skymark** operates flights between Tokyo, Nagoya, Ibaraki, Fukuoka and various other cities in Japan, including Sapporo in Hokkaido and Naha in Okinawa.

Airport Tax

Visitors traveling from Kansai, Narita, Nagoya, or Fukuoka airports are subject to a Passenger Service Facilities Charge (PSFC). At Kansai this is about ¥2,650 per person, at Nagoya it is ¥2,500, and at Narita and Fukuoka the charge is around ¥2,040 and ¥945 respectively. This tax is included in the cost of the ticket. Other airports do not make this charge.

Luggage Delivery

This is a service whereby luggage can be delivered from airports to either a hotel or a private address the following day. It is also possible to have luggage picked up for delivery to an airport, although this has to be ordered two days in advance. Companies offering this service operate counters at Narita and Kansai airports. Among the service providers are **JAL ABC**, **Yamato**, and **ANA Sky Porter**. The basic cost for one large bag is about ¥2,000–3,000 depending on the size, weight, and destination.

Arriving by Ferry

It is possible to travel to Japan by ferry from some parts of mainland Asia, including Pusan in South Korea and Shanghai in China, from where boats run to Kobe and Osaka. The Far Eastern Shipping Line connects Niigata/Takaoka with the port of Vladivostock in Russia.

Traveling around by Train

Japan's rail system is one of the best in the world in terms of safety, efficiency, and comfort. Trains linking major cities tend to have announcements and digital displays in both Japanese and English. In rural areas, the names of train stations may not be given in translation, but railway staff and members of the public generally try to be helpful to foreigners. The Japan Rail Pass is recommended for those planning to travel extensively around Japan.

Travelers buying tickets at Tokyo JR station

The Railway Network

The Japan Railways Group, known as **JR**, is the main operator. It includes all the *shinkansen* super express trains (bullet trains) and a nationwide network of over 12,400 miles (20,000 km) of tracks. There are also many private railroads linking smaller communities in more remote regions. Often travelers have a choice of lines to the same destination.

Other train types include Tokkyu ("limited express," usually the fastest), Kyuko ("express"), Kaisoku (misleadingly called "rapid"), and Futsu local trains.

The main train stations in the Tokyo metropolitan area are on the JR Yamanote line.

The Shinkansen: Bullet Trains

The first "bullet train" drew out of Tokyo Station in 1964, the year of the Tokyo Olympics. Although they are no longer the world's fastest trains, their efficiency, as proved by long-distance journeys timed to the minute, is legendary. Each *shinkansen* line runs different types of trains. Most familiar is the Tokaido *shinkansen* line running from Tokyo to Osaka. It

has the *Kodama* train service that stops at every *shinkansen* station along the way; the *Hikari*, which stops only at larger stations, and the *Nozomi*, which runs directly from Tokyo to Shin-Osaka, stopping only at Nagoya and Kyoto.

Announcements in English and clear signs make the *shinkansen* an appealing form of transportation for foreigners, often more convenient than flying, although there is little space for luggage larger than a carry-on suitcase or backpack. It is best to reserve a seat (see p381), as the non-reserved

Aerodynamic nose of the fabled *shinkansen*, or "bullet train"

carriages can be very crowded. Reserve a seat well in advance if traveling over a holiday period. *Shinkansen* also have designated smoking cars on some routes.

Getting Around Stations

Tokyo's Shinjuku station (see p97) is the world's busiest, and several others in Tokyo and major cities are on a vast scale. Finding a particular line or exit during rush hour can be intimidating and exhausting for newcomers with heavy baggage. Though not always possible, it is a good idea to find out which named or numbered exit is best for you before arriving at one of the major stations.

The level of signs in English varies greatly. Tokyo's Shibuya station, for example, is a major hub but notoriously difficult to navigate. By contrast, Kyoto's station is geared to tourists, Japanese and foreign.

Even at large stations, *shinkansen* lines are clearly marked, and other lines are color-coded. The yellow bobbles on the floor are intended to help visually impaired people navigate. Escalators, and more often elevators, are readily available at larger stations for commuters.

Many trains, especially the *shinkansen*, stop only briefly in order to keep on schedule. Thus, travelers are encouraged to line up prior to boarding on platforms. Floor markings, typically lines or numbers, on the platform indicate where the train doors will open. There may also be numbers correlating to car numbers for trains with reserved seats. Tokyo trains, especially the Yamanote loop line, get overcrowded at rush hour, and station staff have to help push passengers inside.

Stations in major tourist areas have baggage lockers (often full during busy hours) and information booths; staff here may speak English and occasionally other languages.

Tickets and Fares

Basic fare tickets for short distances are normally bought from ticket machines. Most machines accept ¥1,000 and ¥5,000, while some take ¥10,000 notes and all supply change. Many stations have maps in English, indicating the fares to destinations. If in doubt about the cost of a trip, simply buy a cheap ticket and pay any excess at the destination using the Fare Adjustment machine near the exit barrier. Several have an English-translation button. The machine supplies you with a new ticket. If there is no such machine, station staff will work out the excess for payment. You will not be penalized for having the wrong-value ticket.

Tickets and seat reservations for longer trips can be bought at the Ticket Offices at JR train stations. You can also buy tickets at Travel Service Centers in the larger stations and from authorized travel agents. Credit cards are usually accepted. *Shinkansen* tickets can also be purchased at ticket machines at train stations and many machines have an English function to do so.

Seat reservations are recommended for long-distance trips; a small extra fee is charged unless you have a **Japan Rail Pass**. The reservation ticket will bear the date and time of the train, and also the car and seat number. If in doubt about these numbers, ask the vendor to point out what they refer to. On the platform, try to find the number that corresponds with the car number and line up.

There are also other less expensive regional rail passes. The **JR East Rail Pass** covers Honshu northeast of Tokyo, and can be purchased both in Japan and overseas. There are two types of **JR West Rail Pass**: the Sanyo Area Pass covers the *shinkansen*, including Nozomi and Mizuho, as well as regular bullet trains from Osaka to Okayama, Hiroshima, and Hakata; the Kansai Area Pass includes Osaka, Kobe, Kyoto, Himeji, and Nara. Both can be bought within or outside Japan.

Many cities have their own special tickets: ask at local TICs or "i" centers. The Tokyo Free Kippu covers most of the subway, bus, and streetcar lines in central Tokyo.

Signboard listing the arrival of trains, Keihin Tohoku Line

Passenger holding the popular Japan Rail Pass

The Japan Rail Pass

Specially devised for people visiting Japan on tourist visas, the Japan Rail Pass is an excellent, relatively cheap option for those planning on traveling around the country. However, it must be purchased before the trip from an agent abroad, as it is not on sale within Japan.

The pass gives unlimited travel on all JR lines and affiliated buses and ferries, including the Narita Express (*see p378*), city-center JR trains, and *shinkansen*, except Nozomi. Subways and private railroads are not included. You can choose a 7-day, 14-day, or 21-day Pass, first or standard class. Standard prices are ¥29,110, ¥46,390, and ¥59,350 respectively. Showing it to staff at station ticket barriers also saves having to buy tickets and negotiate ticket gates with luggage. If you want to explore Japan by train for more than 21 days, or prefer to break up your travels by staying in one place for more than a few days, consider buying more than one pass.

JNTO offices (*see p363*) have a list of Rail Pass agents overseas. The agent issues a Japan Rail Pass Exchange Order, the price is usually based on the day's exchange rate with the yen. This voucher is exchanged for the actual Japan Rail Pass at designated JR Travel Service Centers in Japan, including Narita and Kansai airports and major train stations. You need to show your passport in order to obtain the pass and also specify the date on which you wish to start using it, which must be within three months of issue of the exchange order. After the start date of the pass, its cost cannot be refunded; the exchange order and pass cannot be replaced if lost or stolen.

Traveling within Cities

There are numerous systems of local transportation in the major cities, all of which are efficient, safe, and clean. The only complication for foreigners is in the purchase of tickets: systems vary from city to city; ticket machines tend to be only in Japanese, except for train stations in cities; and few staff speak English.

Green Travel

In one sense, travel in Japan's larger cities is already quite green in that the superb public transportation means people do not have such a great need to use cars. Velotaxis (cycle rickshaw) are eco-friendly, and they have started appearing in the more touristy areas. Also in major cities, a small number of regular taxis now use hybrid cars, and these are usually marked as such.

Subway

The Tokyo subway system (see inside back cover) is extensive and color-coded on maps to match the color of the cars. Other cities, including Osaka, Nagoya, Kobe, Sendai, Yokohama, Fukuoka, Kyoto, and Sapporo, also have subway systems. Modes of operation differ slightly.

The JR Rail Pass (see p381) cannot be used on any subway system. Buy a ticket from either a vending machine or a ticket window. Subway ticket vending machines, are often only in Japanese. However, with a color-coded transliterated map, such as the Tokyo subway system, you can match the Japanese characters of your destination with those on the fare chart by the machine. The chart will show in Arabic numerals how much to pay. Press the corresponding

fare key on the machine and insert the money. Change will be dispensed with the ticket.

If you are in any doubt about how much to pay, then simply buy the cheapest ticket and pay the excess at the end.

In Tokyo, the Pasmo and Suica electronic card can be purchased from vending machines at many stations. Hold your card against the barriers at the station entrance to access the platform. These cards are valid on most forms of city transport.

Station names are often displayed on platform signboards in romanized (romaji) form as well as Japanese.

All mass-transit systems close at around midnight until about 5am.

Streetcars

Streetcars still run in quite a few Japanese cities, including Hiroshima, Nagasaki, and Sapporo. Tokyo has two streetcar lines, and the Enoden Railway in Kamakura is also classed as a streetcar. Fares and systems for paying on streetcars differ from city to city; some charge a flat fare irrespective of the distance traveled. The fare machine is sometimes manned separately. Follow the example of other passengers as to when to pay, and whether to pay the fare collector or put money into the box.

Monorail

Many cities operate monorail systems that are easy to negotiate. Hiroshima has one such line, which was installed for the Asian Games of 1994. In Tokyo, the monorail links Hamatsucho (Yamanote Line) with Haneda Airport, and the monorail-like Yurikamome runs from

Shinbashi to Tokyo Teleport Town in Odaiba (see pp106–7).

Buses

Bus depots (basu noriba) are often located outside of train stations in cities. The method of paying fares varies. Some buses are boarded at the front, and the fare – often a flat rate – is deposited into a slot beside the driver. If in doubt, state your destination and offer the driver a selection of small coins to select the correct amount. Exit from the door in the middle of the bus.

A second system invites passengers to step aboard toward the center or back of the bus; a machine distributes numbered tickets. The number on this ticket appears on a screen at the front of the bus, which shows fares to be paid. If the ticket reads "2," look along the line at the top of the screen and check the sum in yen below the corresponding figure. Before you disembark, drop the indicated amount and your ticket into the box beside the driver.

Kagoshima sightseeing bus, a convenient way of touring the city

Walking

Walking is a great way of exploring Japan's cities. The city of Tokyo organizes free walking tours for foreigners in various languages. There are also a dozen paid walking tours covering various areas of the city that each last around 3 hours; they cost ¥650 to ¥3,540 and focus on themes such as sumo, the tea ceremony, architecture, traditional gardens, and nature. Other cities, such as Nagoya, Kyoto, and Hiroshima, also have English-language walking tours.

Sign to subway and JR trains

Signage indicating stations on the wall of a subway platform

Tourists aboard a Shiretoko sightseeing boat

Addresses

Addresses in Japanese start with the name of the prefecture and work backward through various districts to the number of a small block in which the particular building is located. When Japanese addresses are written in Roman letters, the order is reversed, so that the block number comes first, following Western convention. In an address, the first number of, for example, 2-3-4 Otemachi refers to the *chome* (main block). The second number points to a smaller block of buildings within the original *chome*. The last is the number of a yet smaller block of buildings. On city streets, the block address numbers are sometimes given on utility poles and lampposts.

Local *koban* (manned police boxes) are often used to help people reach their destinations. Telephone operators will not supply an address, even if a number is known. **Diddlefinger** is an easy way to look up Japanese addresses exclusively in English.

Taxis

Taxis come in various colours, but all have a "taxi" sign on the roof. A red sign to the left of the driver indicates that the taxi is free. You can flag a taxi on the street or look for a stand: they are invariably located near main stations. The cost to hire one is expensive with rates starting around ¥600–¥700 for the first mile. Fares increase per mile, and are higher at night and on weekends. Fares also increase in standing traffic.

Drivers operate taxi doors electrically from inside so you do not need to bother opening and closing them. Few taxi drivers speak much English, so it is best to carry a map marked with instructions in Japanese and the phone number of your destination.

Ferries and Tourist Boats

Tickets for some ferries can be bought at the ferry terminal on the day of departure. Usually, there is a form to fill in, which enables the ferry company to compile a list of passengers. JNTO's travel manual details the main services. There are many long-distance ferry routes, including ones to mainland Asia *(see p379)*.

Bicycles

As indicated by the often large bicycle parks outside big stations and the huge numbers of bikes parked on the streets of Japan's cities, the bicycle is an extremely popular way of getting around – even though there are few cycle paths to speak of. Rickshaws *(jin-riki-sha)* are also back in fashion in predominantly tourist areas for those who prefer a more leisurely and traditional way of getting around.

Rickshaw, an old-fashioned, but popular, mode of transportation

There are often bicycle-rental companies in tourist areas. A good option in the capital is **Rent a Bike.jp**. Sidewalks are frequently used by cyclists, despite the fact that it is illegal to do so. However, this is not strictly enforced and some towns prefer cyclists to use sidewalks rather than roads.

Long-Distance Buses

The efficiency and extent of the rail network in Japan is such that few foreign tourists tend to use long-distance buses. However, the bus network is comprehensive, and for those without a JR Rail Pass, a bus is a much cheaper option. While styles and services vary, buses are uniformly comfortable, and often have toilets. Local information centers have timetable details or see **JR Bus Kanto**.

DIRECTORY

Walking

City of Tokyo Walking Tours
W tourism.metro.tokyo.jp/english/tourists/guideservice/guideservice/index.html

Hiroshima Walking Tour
W hiroshimatours.info

Kyoto Walking Tour
W web.kyoto-inet.or.jp/people/h-s-love

Nagoya Walking Tour
W geocities.jp/aichiguide/walk-e.html

Addresses

Diddlefinger
W diddlefinger.com

Bicycles

Rent a Bike.jp
W rentabike.jp

Long-Distance Buses

JR Bus Kanto
W jrbuskanto.co.jp

Traveling around by Car

Japan is an enjoyable and relatively safe country in which to take to the road. In the countryside, renting a car is usually the best and most flexible way to get around, though car-rental companies tend not to be used to dealing with customers in English. It is surprisingly inexpensive to rent a vehicle; however, the cost of road tolls and parking charges can quickly mount up. Road surfaces are usually good, and rental cars are very well maintained. Driving is on the left. The main problem foreign drivers in Japan will face is navigation. It can be difficult trying to find one's way around Japan's towns and cities, which often have networks of one-way streets. Only main thoroughfares have names, and although rented cars are usually equipped with sat-nav systems, these are in Japanese. Very heavy traffic is a common feature of Japan's major cities. Other problems include hazards such as roads blocked by snow in winter, flooding during the rainy season, and occasional landslides.

Road sign at a crossing in Kyoto, with some *romaji* transliteration

Quiet road in the Shiretoko Peninsula, Hokkaido

Drivers' Licenses

Vehicles are available for rental at ports of entry, major train stations, and local dealers. Visitors must produce an international driver's license (International Driving Permit) at the car-rental agency. Unfortunately, Japan does not recognize international driving permits from Switzerland, Germany, and Taiwan. However, drivers are instead allowed to drive in Japan for up to one year with an official Japanese translation of their license; available from the **Japan Automobile Federation** or their country's embassy or consulate in Japan. A valid passport must be carried at all times.

Driving in Japan

Japanese drive on the left-hand side of the road. On local roads, the maximum speed allowed on unmarked roads is usually 37 mph (60 kph), although it may be less, from 18–31 mph (30–50 kph). On expressways, maximum speeds vary between 50–62 mph (80–100 kph). Drivers may not turn left on a red light in Japan, as is allowed in some other countries.

Drivers don't always drive sensibly, and although there are some drivers who adhere to the laws, most tailgate, speed, and have a habit of driving over intersections after a light has turned red. It is not a good idea to follow suit. Vehicles to the front and rear should be observed carefully when approaching traffic lights.

Street signs are easier to decipher in cities, but the pressure of traffic and the network of roads, which may include several one on top of another, can be daunting for even the most experienced driver from abroad. A wide berth should be given to dump trucks, whose drivers are paid by the load and are therefore under pressure to drive fast. Although they are less of a problem now than they used to be, watch out for large gangs of notorious *boso-zoku* ("crazy drivers"), who often gather on weekends in convoys of customized cars and motorcycles, with the sole intention of waking up neighborhoods and causing trouble.

For visitors who wish to acquaint themselves with driving conditions in Japan, the Japan Automobile Federation publishes "Rules of the Road" in five languages. This can be purchased for ¥1,000 from its regional offices, which are listed on its website. It is unlikely that English speakers will be available at most JAF offices.

Roads and Tolls

Japan has an extensive system of expressways, but they invariably charge tolls. The rate for a standard size car is typically about ¥24.6/kilometer, so the 202-miles (325-km) journey from Tokyo to Nagoya on the expressway would cost ¥7,100 in tolls for a standard size car.

"Beware of bears" road sign in forested mountain region

Road Maps

Most foreign drivers rely on *Japan: A Bilingual Atlas*, published by Kodansha International, which gives route maps but does not indicate toll roads or charges. For longer-term visitors who are seriously interested in driving around Japan, Shobunsha's thick *Road Atlas Japan* is the best investment. The atlas can be purchased at specialist travel bookstores abroad or any bookstore in Japan with a good foreign book section.

Parking

Public parking is available, but it tends to be expensive, and the parking fee becomes more expensive as you move closer to the city center. There are cheaper car parks in most city neighborhoods, but these may be hidden away on backstreets and difficult to find. On-street parking is not permitted in Japan, and parking meters are a rarity. To overcome the problem of lack of sufficient space, the Japanese have developed various innovative parking solutions, such as lifts and roll-over systems.

Gas Stations

Gasoline is readily available in Japan. It is cheaper than in the UK, but it is almost double the cost of gas in the US. The international chain ESSO is familiar to drivers in Japan. JOMO is a popular Japanese chain, the name being derived from the phrase "Joy of Motoring."

Breakdown Services

Rental cars are invariably well maintained and mechanical problems are extremely rare. In the event of a breakdown, the driver should call the car-rental company at the number provided when hiring the vehicle.

Car Hire

Since very few short-term visitors to Japan hire cars, car-rental companies are generally not used to dealing with customers in English. Two companies more likely to have English-speaking staff are **Toyota Rent a Car** and **Nippon Rent-A-Car**. Costs are on par with the US and Western Europe, in some cases cheaper. There is also a greater chance of finding English-speaking staff with international car rental companies such as **Avis**, **Budget**, and **Hertz**, though their rates are much higher than those of Japanese companies.

In the capital, **Japan Bike Rentals** specializes in renting motorcycles to foreigners. To combat the problems of navigation, it also offers GPS self-guided tours. For renting a motorbike outside Tokyo, check for local motorbike dealers through the nearest Tourist Information Office. A 50cc scooter can usually be ridden on an international driver's license (check your license); anything above this capacity requires an international motorcycle license.

DIRECTORY

Drivers' Licenses

Japan Automobile Federation (JAF)
2-2-17 Shiba, Minato-ku, Tokyo 105-8562. **Tel** (03) 6833-9100.
w jaf.or.jp/e

Car Hire

Avis
Tel (0120) 31-1911.
w avis-japan.com/jpn/reservation/reservation_e.shtml

Budget
Tel (0120) 054-317.
w budgetrentacar.co.jp/english.htm

Hertz
Tel (0120) 489 882
(toll-free in Japan).
w hertz.com

Japan Bike Rentals
7-7-3-101 Akasaka, Minato-ku, Tokyo 107-0052.
Tel (03) 3584-5185.
w japanbikerentals.com

Nippon Rent-A-Car
Tel (03) 3485-7196.
w nipponrentacar.co.jp/english

Toyota Rent a Car
Tel (0800) 7000-815
(toll-free in Japan);
Tel (03) 5954-8020.
w rent.toyota.co.jp/en/index.html

A busy street outside Shinjuku Station in Tokyo

General Index

Page numbers in **bold** type refer to main entries

Acknowledgments

Blue Island Publishing would like to thank the following people at Dorling Kindersley:

Managing Editor Anna Streiffert

Managing Art Editor Kate Poole

Editorial Directors Vivien Crump, Louise Bostock Lang

Art Director Gillian Allan

Publisher Douglas Amrine

Production
Marie Ingledew, Michelle Thomas.
The Publishers would also like to thank the following people whose contributions and assistance have made the preparation of this book possible:

Main Contributors
John Benson lives in Kyoto and has written and edited many travel articles and website guides about Kyoto, Osaka, and other parts of Kansai.
Mark Brazil, a biologist, natural history and travel writer, and also film consultant, has lived for extended periods in Hokkaido and is a specialist in the natural history of the island.
Jon Burbank is a travel writer and photographer who lives in Chiba prefecture, to the east of Tokyo, with his family.
Angela Jeffs, a writer and editor, moved to Japan in 1986. She lives in Kanagawa prefecture, southwest of Tokyo.
Emi Kazuko is a writer and broadcaster who moved to London from Japan in the 1980s. She is the author of several books about the cuisine of her home country.
Stephen Mansfield is a travel writer and photographer based in Chiba prefecture, whose works about Japan and Asia have appeared in over 80 publications worldwide.
William F. Marsh, a versatile writer, editor, and filmmaker, sadly died in Tokyo while this book was in preparation.
Catherine Rubinstein is a London-based editor and writer who has lived and traveled for extended periods in Japan.
Jacqueline Ruyak is a travel writer who spends half of the year in the United States and the other half in a thatched farmhouse in the mountains of Northern Honshu.

Additional Contributors
Jane Anson, Harry Cook, Brian Burke-Gaffney, Chie Furutani, Ronan Hand, Saradia Hunnisett, Daniel Inman, Yumiko Isa, David Webb.

Design and Editorial Assistance
Amaia Allende, Emma Anacootee, Ikuko Burnett, Imogen Corke, Karen D'Souza, Caroline Elliker, Annette Foo, Stephen Forster, Fay Franklin, Anna Freiberger, Emer FitzGerald, Robert Goss, Emily Grigg-Saito, Katharina Hahn, Mohammad Hassan, Kaberi Hazarika, Victoria Heyworth-Dunne, Nicholas Inman, Rupanki Kaushik, Juliet Kenny, Sumita Khatwani, Shika Kulkarni, Anthony Limerick, Carly Madden, Hayley Maher, Nicola Malone, Alison McGill, Kate Molan, Scarlett O'Hara, Helen Partington, Sangita Patel, Susie Peachey, Marianne Petrou, Samuel Richardson, Simon Richmond, Ellen Root, Lupus Sabene, Sands Publishing Solutions, Yumi Shigematsu, Jaynan Spengler, Ashley Thompson, Julie Thompson, Conrad van Dyk.

Indexer Hilary Bird

Special Assistance David Hodgson at the Japan National Tourist Organization, the owners and chefs at Kiku Restaurant in London.

Artwork Reference Photonica/Amana Images.

Additional Photography Stephen Bere, Demetrio Carrasco, Martin Hladik, Ian O'Leary, Martin Plomer, Yumi Shigematsu, Chris Stowes.

Photography Permissions
The Publishers thank all the temples, castles, museums, hotels, restaurants, shops, and other sights for their assistance and kind permission to photograph their establishments.

Picture Credits
a-above; b-below/bottom; c-centre; f-far; l-left; r-right; t-top.
The Publishers thank the following individuals, companies, and picture libraries for permission to reproduce their photographs:
123RF.COM: gjee 15bc; Tagstock Japan 14br. 4CORNERS: Tim Draper 16bc. AFP: Hwang Kwang 25tc; Kauhiro-Nogi-STF 39cb; A WOMB: 330bc. ALAMY IMAGES: AEP 103bc; Aflo Co., Ltd 17bl; Terry Donnelly 292-3; Stéphane Groleau 326br. Hemis 168-9; ImageState/Pictor International 369tl; imageBROKER/Klaus-Werner Friedrich 355tr; age fotostock Spain, S.L. 101cra; JTB Media Creation, Inc. 216tl; Frank Kletschkus 264; John Lander 329tl; Luo-Foto 337tr; yannick luthy 158; Tony McNicol 15tr; Mixa 250-1, 333br; Pacific Press Service/Ben Simmons 317tl; Photo Japan 318br, 354br; Prisma Bildagentur AG 78-9; Darby Sawchuk 115tr; Mark Scheuern 28tr; Jeremy Sutton-Hibbert 317c, 318cl; VisualJapan 339tl; Chris Willson 132, 319br, 333tl. AMURITANONIWA: 336tl. ARCAID: Richard Bryant 1988/ Tadao Ando 29crb; THE ASAHI SHIMBUN: 70cla; ASKAEN CO LTD: 200bl; AWL IMAGES: Aurora Photos 384cl; Gavin Hellier 284; Christian Kober 2-3, 156-7, 190, 358-9; Travel Pix Collection 198-9, 234. AXIOM: Michael Coster 38br, 38–39, 173bc; Jim Holmes 27tr, 42cra, 45tl/crb, 112br, 364bc; Paul Quayle 33tl, 39bl, 39cr, 347tr. DAVE BARTRUFF: 38tr, 39crb, 41bc, 45bc, 263tr/c/bc, 350br; BENESSE HOUSE: Suzuki Shin 306tl; Tadasu Yamamoto 299tr. BEPPU TOURISM ASSOCIATION CORP: 334tl. BRIDGEMAN ART LIBRARY, London, New York, and Paris: British Museum, London, Katsushika Hokusai (1760–1849) *Fuji in Clear Weather* from the series *36 Views of Mount Fuji* pub by Nishimura Eijudo in 1831, 61br; Fitzwilliam Museum, Cambridge, UK, Katsushika Hokusai (1760–1849) *Block Cutting and Printing Surimono*, 1825, 89bc; Katsushika Hokusai (1760-1849) / Private Collection/ Photo © Christie's Images *Autumn leaves on the Tsutaya River, from the series 'One Hundred Poems as Told by the*

Nurse,' c. 1839 (colour woodblock print) 8-9; Hermitage, St. Petersburg, Russia. Private Collection Ando or Utagawa Hiroshige (1797–1858) *Mountains and Coastline*, two views from *36 Views of Mount Fuji* pub by Kosheihi in 1853, 145tc; Private Collection/Bonhams *Satsuma Oviform Vase Decorated with Woman Playing the Samisen*, 19th century, 42br; Victoria and Albert Museum, London, Utagawa Kuniyoshi (1798–1861) *Mitsukini Defying the Skeleton Spectre* c.1845, 89crb; BRITISH AIKIDO FEDERATION 39bc; BRITISH LIBRARY: Maps Collection Maps 63140 (2) *Map of Yedo Japan*, 1704, 61clb. CHRISTIE'S IMAGES: 42cla/cb, 43cl, 57t, 59cb; 61tc, 89clb; CORBIS: 63tl, 218br, 259b, 356tl; Aflo 224; Asian Art and Archaeology Inc 40tr, 58cla, 89cla; Morton Beebe S.F. 318tr; Bettmann 32tr; Horace Bristol 33bl; Burstein Collection 56tl; Ric Ergenbright 144tr; Eye Ubiquitous/John Dakers 46–7; Natalie Forbes 291br; Historical Picture Archive 145ca; Robbie Jack 40br; Catherine Karnow 13tr; Rolf Kosecki 116c; Ludovic Maisant/Hemis 92; Will and Deni McIntyre 385bl; Kevin R. Morris 351br; Sol Neelman 106cra; Richard T. Nowitz 43bl; Philadelphia Museum of Art 62tl; Sakamoto Photo Research Lab 197tl; Liba Taylor 364cla; Steven Vidler 381c; Michael Yamashita 34tr, 39ca, 41/clb/crb, 47tr/47bl, 144b, 301bc, 352bc. DREAMSTIME.COM: 000zzz 367tr, 380cla; Aaleksander 370cla; Anthony Brown 16tr; Cowardllon 12cra; Dorregaray 144cla; Chun Kit Ho 229br; Sean Pavone 14tr, 20, 64-5, 246cla, 272-3; Runinex 337bl; Pichung 128-9; Srlee2 213tl; Torsakarin 12tr, Tupungato 176tc. EKOIN TEMPLE: 305tr. EN TEAHOUSE: 329bc. MICHAEL FREEMAN: 27br; STEPHEN FORSTER: 113tl, 368 bc, 374c, 375bl; FURUHATA BIJUTSU PRINTING COMPANY: Possesion of Rinno-ji Taiyuin-byo, Nikko, National Treasure, World Heritage 274ca; ZAIDANHOJIN FUSHIN-AN: 173cla. GETTY IMAGES: Bloomberg 370br; Tom Bonaventure 68; Stone/Thierry Cazabon 38clb; Stone/Paul Chesley 29tl, 371tr; Danita Delimont 13bl; Stone/Charles Gupton 312t, 316cl, 366br; Ultra.F 144tr. ROBERT HARDING PICTURE LIBRARY: Elly Beintema 365tr; Nigel Blythe 23tl, 37tl; Robert Francis 22br; Christopher Rennie 32–33c, 200cra; Michael Runkel 80. HARISHIN: 309tr, 332bl. NIGEL HICKS: 28cla, 31tr, 34br, 35tr/cra, 47crb, 173crb, 290tc; HIKONE CASTLE MUSEUM: 58–9; HIMEJI CITY OFFICE: 211bl; GEOFF HOWARD: 28bc. ICHINOYU HONKAN: 303tr. JAPAN NATIONAL TOURISM ORGANIZATION: Hokkaido Tourism Organization: 339br; Japan Convention Services, Inc 109tl, 309bc; Nagomi Visits 354cla; Yasufumi Nishi 361tr, 383tl; Y. Shimizu 328bc; Showado co.ltd/Iki City/Iki City Tourism Federation 335br. JAPANESE MAGAZINES: 375tc; KAKIFUNE KANAWA: 331br. KIKUSUI: 330tl. KOBE CITY MUSEUM: 58clb; RYOKAN KURASHIKI: 304br. KYORYOKUKAI CORP IN AID OF THE TOKYO NATIONAL MUSEUM: 4cr, 54, 56t, 56cb, 57c, 67cr, 84–85 all, 86–7 all; Important Cultural Properties 54, 56cb, 84bl/br, 85cb/b, 86cl/bl, 87br. LONELY PLANET IMAGES: Phil Weymouth 114tc. MAISON BRAS, Toya: Windsor Hotels 338bl. MANDARIN ORIENTAL HOTEL GROUP: 298cra, 302bc. MARUHAM CORPORATION: 114crb. MIYAKOJIMA TOKYU RESORTL 307tr. NARITA INTERNATIONAL AIRPORT CORPORATION: 378br; NIJO CASTLE: 164tr/br, 165tl/bl; NISHI-ITOYA MOUNTAIN LODGE: 298bl. MOH NISHIKAWA: 30–31c. ORION PRESS 49br, 52tr; Angle Photo Library 294tl, 295c; Tori Endo 291tl; Asao Fujita 294tr; Masami Goto 295br; Hirohito Hara 34cla; Masaaki Horimachi 50t, 287br, 290b, 295tc; Daimei Kato 45tr; Shoji Kato 47tl; Kitakanto Colour Agency 268b; Mitsutoshi Kimura 45tc; Fuji Kogei 44cla; Morita Collection 44tr; Nigata Photo Library 44cr; Yoshiharu Nuga 44clb; Minoru Okuda 53cra; Akinari Okuyama 27tl/bl, 294bl; Jiichi Omichi 173cra; Yoshikazu Onishi 262br; Sai 26cla; Motonobu Sato 28–9; Shikoku Photo Service 229tr; Koichi Sudo 35tl; Hideaki Tanaka 44bl, 47cra, 208bc; Nobuo Tanaka 36cb; Kosuke Takeuchi 46cla; Yoshio Tomii 51bl; Tohoku Colour Agency 36tr; Eizo Toyoshima 45cr; Yoshimitsu Yagi 40c; Yuzo Yamada 50bl; Hiroyuki Yamaguchi 262t; Kenzo Yamamoto 35clb; Noriyuki Yoshida 34bl, 36tr, 44bc, 45cl. OSAKA CONVENTION AND TOURISM BUREAU: 207tr; PHOTONICA: Amana Images/Seigo Matsuno 252tl; /Ikuo Nonka 51ca; / Hiroyoshi Terao 36bl; PICTOR: 46tr, 63br. RAITEI: 327tr. REIMEIKAN COLLECTION, Kagoshima City: 58cb; SIMON RICHMOND: 36br; BOARD OF TRUSTEES OF THE ROYAL ARMOURIES: Accession Number XXVIS.162–3 59tl; Accession Number XXVIA.24 59cr; CATHERINE RUBENSTEIN: 141cr, 143tl, 154tl. SHOGAKUKAN INC: publishers of *Big Comic Superior* illustration by Koyama Yuu, Ishikawa Yuugo, Hayakawa Shigei, layout by Norma Takashi & Kachidokii 29bl; STOCKHOUSE HONG KONG: 62cb. SUPERSTOCK: JTB Photo 17tr; JTB Photo Communicati/JTB Photo 11bl, 12bl; Bryan Mullennix/age fotostock 296-7. SUSHI GOTOKU: 325bl. TELE-GRAPH COLOUR LIBRARY: Tim Graham 25clb; /Bavaria-Bidagentur 368cla; Colorific/Jean Paul Nacivet 353tl; Michael Yamashita 25cl/br, 26br, 38cla, 173clb, 346cla; 351tl; Black Star/Fiji Miyazawa 207bl; Matrix/Karen Kusmauski 322tr; /Japack Photolibrary/FPG © Travelpix 289br; TOKYO COMEDY STORE: Jun Imai 113br; TREASURES FROM THE TOKUGAWA ART MUSEUM: 58–9b, 60tl, 147tl. WERNER FORMAN ARCHIVE: 40bl/clb/br, 41tr, 165cra, / Victoria and Albert Museum, London, 89cra.

Front Endpaper: ALAMY IMAGES: Frank Kletschkus Rtl; yannick luthy Rbl; Chris Willson Rcr. AWL IMAGES: Gavin Hellier Rtr; Kristian Kober Ltr; Travel Pix Collection Lclb. CORBIS: Aflo Ltl, Lcr, Ludovic Maisant/Hemis Rfbr. GETTY IMAGES: Tom Bonaventure Rbc. ROBERT HARDING PICTURE LIBRARY: Michael Runkel Rbr.

JACKET Front and spine - AWL IMAGES: Gavin Hellier

All other images © Dorling Kindersley. For further information see: www.dkimages.com

Special Editions of DK Travel Guides

DK Travel Guides can be purchased in bulk quantities at discounted prices for use in promotions or as premiums. We are also able to offer special editions and personalized jackets, corporate imprints, and excerpts from all of our books, tailored specifically to meet your own needs.

To find out more, please contact:
in the United States **SpecialSales@dk.com**
in the UK **travelspecialsales@uk.dk.com**
in Canada DK Special Sales at **general@tourmaline.ca**
in Australia **business.development@pearson.com.au**

Phrase Book

The Japanese language is related to Okinawan and is similar to Altaic languages such as Mongolian and Turkish. Written Japanese uses a combination of three scripts: Chinese ideograms, known as *kanji*, and two syllable-based alphabet systems known as *hiragana* and *katakana*. These two latter are similar, *katakana* functioning as italics are used in English. Traditionally, Japanese is written in vertical columns from top right to bottom left, though the Western system is increasingly used. There are several romanization systems; the Hepburn system is used in this guide. To simplify romanization, macrons (long marks over vowels to indicate longer pronunciation) have not been used. Japanese pronunciation is fairly straightforward, and many words are "Japanized" versions of Western words. This Phrase Book gives the English word or phrase, followed by the Japanese script, then the romanization, adapted to aid pronunciation.

Guidelines for Pronunciation

When reading the romanization, give the same emphasis to all syllables. The practice in English of giving one syllable greater stress may render a Japanese word incomprehensible.

Pronounce vowels as in these English words:

a	as the "u" in "cup"
e	as in "red"
i	as in "chief"
o	as in "solid"
u	as the "oo" in "cuckoo"

When two vowels are used together, give each letter an individual sound:

ai	as in "pine"
ae	as if written "ah-eh"
ei	as in "pay"

Consonants are pronounced as in English. The letter *g* is always hard as in "gate," and *j* is always soft as in "joke." *R* is pronounced something between *r* and *l*. *F* is sometimes pronounced as *h*. "*Si*" always becomes "*shi*," but some people pronounce "*shi*" as "*hi*." *V* in Western words (e.g., "video") becomes *b*. If followed by a consonant, *n* may be pronounced as either *n* or *m*.

All consonants except *n* are always either followed by a vowel or doubled; however, sometimes an *i* or *u* is barely pronounced. In this Phrase Book, to aid pronunciation, apostrophes are used where an *i* or *u* is barely pronounced within a word, and double consonants where this occurs at the end of a word.

Dialects

Standard Japanese is used and understood throughout Japan by people of all backgrounds. But on a colloquial level, there are significant differences in both pronunciation and vocabulary, even between the Tokyo and Osaka Kyoto areas, and rural accents are very strong.

Polite Words and Phrases

There are several different levels of politeness in the Japanese language, according to status, age, and situation. In everyday conversation, politeness levels are simply a question of the length of verb endings (longer is more polite), but in formal conversation entirely different words (*keigo*) are used. As a visitor, you may find that people try to speak to you in formal language, but there is no need to use it yourself; the level given in this Phrase Book is neutral yet polite.

In an Emergency

Help!	たすけて！	Tas'kete!
Stop!	とめて！	Tomete!
Call a doctor!	医者をよんで ください！	Isha o yonde kudasai!
Call an ambulance!	救急車を よんでください！	Kyukyusha o yonde kudasai!
Call the police!	警察を よんでください！	Keisatsu o yonde kudasai!
Fire!	火事！	Kaji!
Where is the hospital?	病院はどこに ありますか？	Byoin wa doko ni arimass-ka?
police box	交番	koban

Communication Essentials

Yes/no.	はい／いいえ	Hai/ie.
… not …	･･･ない／ちがい ます。	… nai/ chigaimass.
I don't know.	しりません。	Shirimasen.
Thank you.	ありがとう。	Arigato.
Thank you very much.	ありがとう ございます。	Arigato gozaimass.
Thank you very much indeed.	どうもありがとう ございます。	Domo arigato gozaimass.
Thanks (casual).	どうも。	Domo.
No, thank you.	結構です。	Kekko dess,
	ありがとう。	arigato.
Please (offering).	どうぞ。	Dozo.
Please (asking).	おねがいします。	Onegai shimass.
Please (give me or do for me).	･･･ください。	… kudasai.
I don't understand.	わかりません。	Wakarimasen.
Do you speak English?	英語を 話せますか？	Eigo o hanasemass-ka?
I can't speak Japanese.	日本語は 話せません。	Nihongo wa hanasemasen.
Please speak more slowly.	もう少し ゆっくり 話して ください。	Mo s'kkoshi yukkuri hanash'te kudasai.
Sorry/Excuse me!	すみません。	Sumimasen!
Could you help. me please? (not emergency)	ちょっと手伝って いただけません か？	Chotto tets'datte itadakemasen- ka?

Useful Phrases

My name is ….	わたしの 名前は･･･ です。	Watashi no namae wa … dess.
How do you do, pleased to meet you.	はじめまして、 どうぞ よろしく。	Hajime-mash'te, dozo yorosh'ku.
How are you?	お元気ですか？	Ogenki dess-ka?
Good morning.	おはよう ございます。	Ohayo gozaimass.
Good afternoon/ good day.	こんにちは。	Konnichiwa.
Good evening.	こんばんは。	Konbanwa.

Good night.	おやすみなさい。	Oyasumi nasai.
Good-bye.	さよなら。	Sayonara.
Take care.	気をつけて。	Ki o ts'kete.
Keep well (casual)	お元気で。	Ogenki de.
The same to you.	そちらも。	Sochira mo.
What is (this)?	（これは）何ですか？	(Kore wa) nan dess-ka?
How do you use this?	これをどうやって使いますか？	Kore o doyatte ts'kaimass-ka?
Could I possibly have …? (very polite)	・・・をいただけますか？	… o itadake-mass-ka?
Is there … here?	ここに・・・がありますか？	Koko ni … ga arimass-ka?
Where can I get …?	・・・はどこにありますか？	… wa doko ni arimass-ka?
How much is it?	いくらですか？	Ikura dess-ka?
What time is …?	・・・何時ですか？	… nan-ji dess-ka?
Cheers! (toast)	乾杯！	Kampai!
Where is the restroom/toilet?	お手洗い／トイレはどこですか？	Otearai/otoire wa doko dess-ka?
Here's my business card.	名刺をどうぞ。	Meishi o dozo.

Useful Words

I	わたし	watashi
woman	女性	josei
man	男性	dansei
wife	奥さん	ok'san
husband	主人	shujin
daughter	むすめ	musume
son	むすこ	mus'ko
child	こども	kodomo
children	こどもたち	kodomo-tachi
businessman/ woman	ビジネスマン／ウーマン	bijinessuman/ wuman
student	学生	gakusei
Mr./Mrs./Ms. …	・・・さん	…-san
big/small	大きい／小さい	okii/chiisai
hot/cold	暑い／寒い	atsui/samui
cold (to touch)	冷たい	tsumetai
warm	温かい	atatakai
good/ not good/bad	いい／よくない／悪い	ii/yokunai/warui
enough	じゅうぶん／結構	jubun/kekko
free (no charge)	ただ／無料	tada/muryo
here	ここ	koko
there	あそこ	asoko
this	これ	kore
that (nearby)	それ	sore
that (far away)	あれ	are
what?	何？	nani?
when?	いつ？	itsu?
why?	なぜ？／どうして？	naze?/dosh'te?
where?	どこ？	doko?
who?	誰？	dare?
which way?	どちら？	dochira?

Signs

Open	営業中	eigyo-chu
closed	休日	kyujitsu
entrance	入口	iriguchi
exit	出口	deguchi
danger	危険	kiken
emergency exit	非常口	hijo-guchi
information	案内	annai
restroom, toilet	お手洗い／手洗い／おトイレ／トイレ	otearai/tearai/ otoire/toire
free (vacant)	空き	aki
men	男	otoko
women	女	onna

Money

Could you change this into yen please.	これを円に替えてください。	Kore o en ni kaete kudasai.
I'd like to cash these travelers' checks.	このトラベラーズチェックを現金にしたいです。	Kono toraberazu chekku o genkin ni shitai dess.
Do you take credit cards/ travelers' checks?	クレジットカード／トラベラーズチェックで払えますか？	Kurejitto kado/ toraberazu chekku de haraemass-ka?
bank	銀行	ginko
cash	現金	genkin
credit card	クレジットカード	kurejitto kado
currency exchange office	両替所	ryogaejo
dollars	ドル	doru
pounds	ポンド	pondo
yen	円	en

Keeping in Touch

Where is a telephone?	電話はどこにありますか？	Denwa wa doko ni arimass-ka?
May I use your phone?	電話を使ってもいいですか？	Denwa o ts'katte mo ii dess-ka?
Hello, this is ….	もしもし、・・・です。	Moshi-moshi, …dess.
I'd like to make an international call.	国際電話、お願いします。	Kokusai denwa, onegai shimass.
airmail	航空便	kokubin
e-mail	イーメール	i meru
fax	ファクス	fak'su
postcard	ハガキ	hagaki
post office	郵便局	yubin-kyoku
stamp	切手	kitte
telephone booth	公衆電話	koshu denwa
telephone card	テレフォンカード	terefon kado

Shopping

Where can I buy …?	・・・はどこで買えますか？	… wa doko de kaemass-ka?
How much does this cost?	いくらですか？	Ikura dess-ka?
I'm just looking.	見ているだけです。	Mite iru dake dess.
Do you have …?	・・・ありますか？	… arimass-ka?
May I try this on?	着てみてもいいですか？	Kite mite mo ii dess-ka?
Please show me that.	それを見せてください。	Sore o misete kudasai.
Does it come in other colors?	他の色もありますか？	Hoka no iro mo arimass-ka?
black	黒	kuro
blue	青	ao
green	緑	midori
red	赤	aka
white	白色	shiro
yellow	黄色	kiiro
cheap/expensive	安い／高い	yasui/takai
audio equipment	オーディオ製品	odio seihin
bookstore	本屋	hon-ya
boutique	ブティック	butik
clothes	洋服	yofuku
department store	デパート	depato
electrical store	電気屋	denki-ya
fish market	魚屋	sakana-ya
folk crafts	民芸品	mingei-hin
ladies' wear	婦人服	fujin fuku
local specialty	名物	meibutsu
market	市場	ichiba
menswear	紳士服	shinshi fuku
newsstand	新聞屋	shimbun-ya

pharmacist	薬屋	kusuri-ya
picture postcard	絵葉書	e-hagaki
sale	セール	seru
souvenir shop	お土産屋	omiyage-ya
supermarket	スーパー	supa
travel agent	旅行会社	ryoko-gaisha

Sightseeing

Where is …?	･･･はどこ ですか？	… wa doko dess-ka?
How do I get to …?	･･･へは、どうやって いったらいいですか？	… e wa doyatte ittara ii dess-ka?
Is it far?	遠いですか？	Toi dess-ka?
art gallery	美術館	bijutsukan
reservations desk	予約 窓口	yoyaku madoguchi
bridge	橋	hashi/bashi
castle	城	shiro/jo
city	市	shi
city center	街の 中心	machi no chushin
gardens	庭園／庭	tei-en/niwa
hot spring	温泉	onsen
information office	案内所	annaijo
island	島	shima/jima
monastery	修道院	shudo-in
mountain	山	yama/san
museum	博物館	hakubutsukan
palace	宮殿	kyuden
park	公園	koen
port	港	minato/ko
prefecture	県	ken
river	川	kawa/gawa
ruins	遺跡	iseki
shopping area	ショッピング街	shoppingu gai
shrine	神社／神宮／宮	jinja/jingu/gu
street	通り	tori/dori
temple	お寺／寺	otera/tera/dera/ji
tour, travel	旅行	ryoko
town	町	machi/cho
village	村	mura
ward	区	ku
zoo	動物園	dobutsu-en
north	北	kita/hoku
south	南	minami/nan
east	東	higashi/to
west	西	nishi/sei
left/right	左／右	hidari/migi
straight ahead	真っ直ぐ	mass-sugu
between	間に	aida ni
near/far	近い／遠い	chikai/toi
up/down	上／下	ue/sh'ta
new	新しい／新	atarashii/shin
old/former	古い／元	furui/moto
upper/lower	上／下	kami/shimo
middle/inner	中	naka
in	に／中に	ni/naka ni
in front of	前	mae

Getting Around

bicycle	自転車	jitensha
bus	バス	basu
car	車	kuruma
ferry	フェリー	feri
baggage room	手荷物一時 預かり所	tenimotsu ichiji azukarijo
motorcycle	オートバイ	otobai
one-way ticket	片道切符	katamichi kippu
return ticket	往復切符	ofuku kippu
taxi	タクシー	takushi
ticket	切符	kippu
ticket office	切符売場	kippu uriba

Trains

What is the fare to …?	･･･までいくら ですか？	… made ikura dess-ka?
When does the train for… leave?	･･･行きの電車 は、何時に 出ますか？	… iki no densha wa nan-ji ni demass-ka?
How long does it take to get to …?	･･･まで時間は、 どのぐらい かかりますか？	… made jikan wa dono gurai kakarimass-ka?
A ticket to …, please.	･･･行きの切符 をください。	… yuki no kippu o kudasai.
Do I have to change?	乗り換えが 必要ですか？	Norikae ga hitsuyo dess-ka?
I'd like to reserve a seat, please.	席を予約 したいです。	Seki o yoyaku shitai dess.
Which platform for the train to …?	･･･行きの 電車は、 何番ホーム から出ますか？	… yuki no densha wa nanban homu kara demass-ka?
Which station is this?	この駅は、 どこですか？	Kono eki wa doko dess-ka?
Is this the right train for …?	･･･へは、この 電車でいい ですか？	… e wa kono densha de ii dess-ka?
bullet train	新幹線	shinkansen
express trains:		
"limited express" (fastest)	特急	tokkyu
"express" (second)	急行	kyuko
"rapid" (third)	快速	kaisoku
first-class	一等	itto
line	線	sen
local train	普通／各駅 電車	futsu/kaku-eki-densha
platform	ホーム	homu
train station	駅	eki
reserved seat	指定席	shitei-seki
second-class	二等	nito
subway	地下鉄	chikatetsu
train	電車	densha
unreserved seat	自由席	jiyu-seki

Accommodations

Do you have any vacancies?	部屋があります か？	Heya ga arimass-ka?
I have a reservation.	予約をして あります。	Yoyaku o sh'te arimass.
I'd like a room with a bathroom.	お風呂つきの 部屋、お願い します。	Ofuro-ts'ki no heya, onegai shimass.
What is the charge per night?	一泊いくら ですか？	Ippaku ikura dess-ka?
Is tax included in the price?	税込ですか？	Zeikomi dess-ka?
Can I leave my luggage here for a little while?	荷物を ちょっとここに 預けてもいい ですか？	Nimotsu o chotto koko ni azukete mo ii dess-ka?
air-conditioning	冷房／エアコン	reibo/eakon
bath	お風呂	ofuro
check-out	チェックアウト	chekku-auto
hair drier	ドライヤー	doraiya
hot (boiled) water	お湯	oyu
Japanese-style inn	旅館	ryokan
Japanese-style room	和室	wa-shitsu
key	鍵	kagi
front desk	フロント	furonto
single/twin room	シングル／ツイン	shinguru/tsuin